SOLDIERS

The One That Got Away
Chris Ryan, MM

War Dogs
Keith Cory-Jones

LEOPARD

The One That Got Away

In the Beginning

I believed,
But found the time for doubting.
He made no sound,
I heard the Devil shouting.

I wanted peace,
I did not want the glory.
I walked in Hell,
And now I tell my story.

I sing sad song,
I did not write the music.
I find sad words
Waiting – just inside my mind.

I played my part,
But seldom did I choose it.
I held a gun,
I did not want to use it.

Call it fate or destiny –
By either name, it troubles me.

And now,

If you should look into my eyes,
By chance you might just see
A sad, sad soul that sheds its tears,
Yet lets the heart go free.

And in between the two of them
If you should read my mind,
You'll know the soul still sheds its tears,
For deeds left far behind.

But if you see the eagle there,
Then don't ignore the dove,
For now that all the killing's done
There's nothing left but love.

J. Miles

for Sarah

Acknowledgements

I wish to thank the following:

Duff Hart-Davis for all his encouragement, patience and
  valuable time that he spent on this project.
All my family and friends for the patience and understanding
  they showed me throughout this whole adventure.
My editor Mark Booth and his team at Random House for their
  help and hard work.
Jeff Pope and Paul Greengrass at LWT for the initial debrief.
Last but not least Barbara Levy my agent for pointing me in the
  right direction.

Chapter One

Stand By . . . Stand By . . . Go!

Our target was a disused mental hospital – a large, red-brick, Victorian building, once handsome but now derelict, standing in spacious grounds that had gone to seed. According to the exercise scenario, the five Middle Eastern terrorists who had gone to ground inside were holding nine hostages captive, and after a three-day siege matters were moving swiftly to a head.

As commander of the Sniper Team, I was in charge of eight men, pre-positioned with their rifles at observation points in outhouses, trees and on the ground. Two men were watching each face of the hospital and sending back running commentaries over their throat-mike radios to the Command Centre, which had been established in a separate building some two hundred metres from the front door. Each face of the hospital had been accorded a special code for instant recognition.

From the Command Centre the police negotiator was talking to the chief terrorist, but the man's patience appeared to be running out. He was demanding safe conduct to Heathrow for himself and his colleagues, threatening that if transport were not provided immediately he would shoot one of the hostages. Meanwhile, the officer commanding the SP (Special Projects, or counter-terrorist) team was continuously refining his plan for a deliberate assault on the building.

One sniper had just reported, 'There's a terrorist moving in a particular window,' when a shot cracked out from within the hospital. The negotiator established that a hostage had been executed. The terrorists called for a stretcher party to take the body away. The front door opened briefly, and a limp figure was bundled out. A four-man team ran in to collect it. Then the chief terrorist threatened to kill another hostage in half an hour if his demands were not met.

1

The moment had come for the police to hand over to the military. The police chief signed a written order passing command to OC 'B' Squadron, the senior SAS officer present, who gave his assault team orders for a deliberate option. The moment he had finished, the assault groups moved to their entry points.

Now it was just a question of waiting for my snipers to get as many terrorists in their sights as possible. Listening to their commentaries on the radio net, the OC suddenly called out the order we'd all been waiting for: 'I have control. STAND BY . . . STAND BY . . . GO!'

For the past two days an eerie silence had prevailed in the grounds of the old hospital. Now a volley of rounds went down and the whole place erupted into action. Two vehicles screamed up to the building and disgorged a swarm of black-clad assaulters. Explosive charges blew in the windows. Within seconds a Chinook helicopter was poised above the roof and more black figures were fast-roping out of it, to abseil down to the windows or enter through the skylights. Stun grenades blasted off; smoke poured out. The radio carried a babble of shots, shouts, explosions and orders.

In a matter of minutes the building had been cleared, the terrorists theoretically killed and the hostages rescued. The assault commander reported that he had control, and command was formally handed back to the police. Then the OC went in to start taking statements, and the exercise wound down. The guys were pouring with sweat inside their black kit, but elated that things had gone well. As always, the assault had been realistic in every detail, and had been excellent training.

'Well done, everybody,' said the OC at his preliminary debrief. 'That was pretty good.' Because we'd had three tough days in a row, and were now facing a five-hour run back to base, he didn't go into detail. Rather, he set 1100 on Friday morning as the time for the main wash-up in the squadron office.

'Thin out, guys,' said the sergeant major. 'On your bikes.'

So we packed our kit into the vehicles and set out for Hereford. But on the way events took an unexpected turn. It was 2 August 1990, and on the news we heard that Saddam Hussein had ordered the Iraqi army to invade Kuwait.

'So what?' said one of the guys scornfully. 'He's just a wanker.'

'Don't be too sure of it,' said someone else. 'It'll make big trouble, and the odds are we'll find ourselves in there. Maybe some of the guys have gone already.'

Speculation about Iraq and the possibility of war in the Gulf helped speed our journey home – but I don't think any of us realised just how Saddam's aggression against his neighbours was going to change our existence.

For the rest of that year our lives were dominated by uncertainty. Two squadrons – 'A' and 'D' – soon went out to the Gulf for build-up training; but until the last minute, we in 'B' Squadron were assured that we would not be going, as it was our turn to take over what are known in the SAS as team tasks – assignments for which small teams of men are needed in various parts of the world. Rumours began flying. As the likelihood of war increased, it was said that 'G' Squadron would go out to the Middle East as BCRs – battle casualty replacements – and since the commanding officer at Regimental Headquarters was ex-'G' Squadron, the story gained credence.

Different options were frequently discussed, one of them being that we might become sky-marshals on civilian flights to the Middle East – travelling ostensibly as normal fare-paying passengers, but in fact carrying weapons – to deal with any terrorist who might attempt a hijack. The idea seemed quite plausible; on the SP team we'd done any number of assaults on and inside aircraft, so that we were thoroughly familiar with the possibilities. But then the rumour died a natural death.

Throughout November and December, men were being selected for team tasks, and it was my luck to be chosen for an Everest expedition which a friend of mine, Harry Taylor, was planning. When I joined the Regiment six years earlier, he and I had found ourselves in the same troop. We partnered off together, and had formed a good rapport. He left the SAS in 1986, and by the autumn of 1990 he was preparing for his second attempt on Everest. On his first he had tried to ascend the unconquered North-East Ridge, but had been driven off by bad weather. Now his aim once again was to climb the North-East Ridge – Alpine-style, with a partner, Russell Bryce – but this time I would be coming up the North Ridge with Sherpas, bringing lightweight parachutes.

The plan was that I should meet the other two at the North Col; we would then climb to the summit together, jump off, and paraglide back down to basecamp. Everything was geared to breaking records: if I could reach the summit without oxygen, it would be a personal record for me; if the others came up via the North-East Ridge, they too would establish a first – as would we all by parachuting from the top. I was quite well qualified for the role, having done plenty of parachute jumps, and because I had spent eighteen months in the Alps on a German Army mountain guide course, during which time I became proficient at climbing in snow and ice.

In October the adjutant gave me permission to join the Everest party. Once my stint on the SP team was finished, he said, I could take three months off. I went to an exhibition in Harrogate where Berghaus, the mountain specialists, fitted me up with equipment. Already I had my mind focused on the Himalayas, and I was planning to start build-up training with hard walking in the Brecon Beacons early in the New Year.

Preparations for the Gulf were playing havoc with the annual rugby knockout competition between six squadron teams. Perhaps it was just as well, because so much needle develops during those matches that things become vicious, and guys are sometimes written off due to injuries for as long as six months. One of the players was a good friend of the England skipper, Will Carling, and invited him to bring the national team to train. The players could stay in the officers' or sergeants' mess, he said, and they would be saved the usual hassle of fans clamouring for autographs whenever they showed their noses out of doors. He also suggested that England might take on the Regiment in a friendly game. Carling came up with a couple of colleagues for a check round, but one look at a match between squadrons was enough. 'Not a chance!' they said. 'We'll not play this lot. There'd be guys left crippled all over the field.' So that little plan never came to fruition.

A week before Christmas, we were dragged into the Briefing Room at Hereford and told that half of 'B' Squadron was going to deploy to the Middle East after all. 'G' Squadron would take over the SP team. Everyone who had been detailed to go began laughing and joking, and saying, 'Great!' The guys still allocated for team tasks were seriously disappointed, and angled to join the Gulf party. But I think that privately most people were concerned that the conflict could develop into a big and nasty war. We reckoned that if Israel came in, Syria and Jordan might side with Saddam Hussein; things could easily get out of hand, and half the Middle East would go up in flames. There was also the threat that Saddam would use chemical or nuclear weapons.

I was excited by the prospect of war, but I hoped that if the deployment did come off it would be a quick one, so that I could return to the team training for Everest.

When I heard the news, I went home and said to Janet, my wife: 'Listen – we're heading out.' Being a calm, level-headed woman, she took it well. Normally, SAS guys say nothing to their wives and families about what they're doing, but in this case it was obvious where we were going: after Saddam's invasion of Kuwait, there had been so much coverage on television and in the newspapers – our destination could only have been the Gulf.

Christmas was not a relaxed time. The Regiment was stood-to throughout the holiday period, and we were busy getting our green kit ready. (In SAS terms, 'green' refers to normal military operations as opposed to 'black' work, like that on the SP team, for which you wear black gear from head to foot.) When you've been out of the system – that is, away from military duties – for a while, as I had, your kit's not as it should be, and it takes a couple of weeks of hard graft to get everything sorted out.

On the Alpine guides' course in France, Italy and Germany I had learnt German, skiing, climbing, mountain rescue work, weather prediction and how to clear avalanches with explosives, but no real soldiering. Before that, I'd done nine months on the SP team as an assaulter – so again there was no military work involved. After Germany, I returned to the SP team for another nine months, this time as Sniper Commander. So altogether I'd been in black roles for at least three years, and had not worried too much about having the right equipment at hand, all sorted into the correct places.

Now I brought my webbing and bergen home to paint them in desert camouflage colours. We were having an extension built on to our house, and a labourer called John was digging the footings. Seeing me at work outside, he came up and asked what I was doing.

'Just painting my webbing.'

'Those colours are a bit light, aren't they?'

'Well,' I said carefully, 'you'd be surprised. It works quite well.'

In fact he was right: I had the colours too light and sandy, as I was to find out to my cost.

One of the rules within the Regiment is that all married men should have life insurance. Jan and I had a policy already, so we were all right; but as soon as the deployment was announced, pressure to take out policies fell on those who weren't already covered. Naturally the insurance companies put up the shutters, having heard where we were going, and those who did get policies had to pay high premiums. The result was a minor panic: in normal times the guys try to get away without paying premiums, but now, with a war in prospect, the future suddenly looked very different.

On New Year's Eve, with my departure imminent, Jan and I got a friend to babysit our daughter Sarah, who was just over two, and went downtown to a bar. But after one drink we looked at each other, returned home, and sat at the dining-room table, discussing painful questions – What would happen if I didn't come back? Should she marry again? Where would Sarah go to school? – and so on. We stayed up until three or four o'clock, and became very emotional. I wasn't concerned about myself or about Jan, who I knew would be able to look after herself. The person I worried about was Sarah; if I went, what sort of a life would she have?

If the Gulf conflict were to escalate into a major war, the SAS would become a small cog in a huge machine. Until then – during my service, at any rate – we'd always been the ones who called the shots, who had responded to particular threats. Even in Northern Ireland, we could to some extent choose our own ground. Another advantage was that our physical appearance was always much the same as that of the natives. In Iraq we would be operating among Arabs, immediately recognisable as aliens, without any friendly forces or civilians to back us up. On top of these worries was the threat of chemical warfare. It was impossible to say how dangerous things might become, but the uncertainty alone was enough to put the wind up even seasoned operators.

Next evening Sarah's godfather, John, a friend of mine in 'A' Squadron who'd been my best man, came round to the house and wrote out an unofficial will – a letter saying that if he was killed, I (or Janet) was to make sure that his house was sold; £10,000 would go to Sarah, the rest of the money to his mother, his stereo to his brother, and so on.

Packing our kit took some time. All our weapons were bundled together and went separately, rolled up in canvas sleeves. When I asked the SQMS if he'd included pistols, he said, 'Yeah – twenty of them,' and that reassured me, since pistols were essential back-up weapons, which we would need in case our own weapons failed or if we were caught in a confined space like a vehicle or an observation post. Most of us would be carrying M16 203s – a combination of 5.56 calibre automatic rifle in the top barrel and grenade launcher below – or Minimi machine-guns. Both are over a metre long and awkward to handle or conceal at close quarters.

Personal equipment was our own affair. As I was sorting mine, I asked the SQMS if I could draw some cold-weather mountaineering gear.

'Nah,' he replied. 'You're going to the fucking desert, yer dick! It won't be cold there.' He laughed at my request as if he was the regimental expert on desert warfare. Little did he know what the winter in Iraq would be like. In spite of his brush-off, I kept thinking that we might end up at high altitudes, in the mountains of northern Iraq on the Turkish border, where snow might be lying. It was as if I had some premonition. But I did nothing about it, and most of us didn't take any cold-weather gear at all.

At a briefing early in January the OC came up with a statement to the effect that if war broke out we might find ourselves 300 miles inside Iraq, taking out various installations. We thought that could mean somewhere round Baghdad. Back at home, on an atlas, I drew a circle with a radius of 300 miles from Kuwait and the Iraqi border. Jan and I talked about the Euphrates, which runs out of Syria and right through Iraq until it joins the Tigris at Basra. From school Jan remembered that ancient civilisations had flourished in the fertile land along the two big rivers: they had been among the most important waterways then, and the land between them, known as Mesopotamia,

7

had been called the cradle of civilisation. I wondered idly what the Euphrates would look like now.

That evening I telephoned my parents. I always did this before going somewhere. I'd just say, 'I'm off,' and normally they'd reply, 'All right. See you, then. Take care.' But this time things were different. There was a feeling that the war might last a long time, and that it would turn nasty. Mum and Dad did their best not to sound upset, but when my younger brother Keith came on the phone he started crying, and it cracked everybody else off. I said, 'Eh – stop that. Everything's going to be fine.' But the conversation brought home to me the fact that we weren't playing any more.

At last we heard that we were to fly on the night of Saturday 5 January. Being one of the senior guys in the party, I went into camp to make sure that everyone was ready. One of the lads said, 'Bob and Rich are in the club, and they're shitfaced.'

'Jesus! Where's their kit?'

'They haven't packed it yet.'

I got one man to go to Bob's room and one to Rich's, telling them to pack everything they could see, and bring it up to the guardroom. Then another lad and I went down to the club and dragged the two boozers out. Both very short men, they were propping up the bar, pissed out of their brains and giggling like schoolgirls. The rest of us walked them slowly to the coach, laughing and joking to keep them quiet. They gibbered away happily to each other as we got them aboard and sat them down at the back – and away we went to RAF Brize Norton, everyone else very quiet, just chatting to each other, shooting the shit.

The Tristar landed at Cyprus to refuel, then flew on to the Gulf, where it taxied up behind a hangar. Getting off into the warm night, we found the OC, SSM and SQMS lined up waiting for us at the bottom of the steps, all wearing desert kit with shamags, or Arab shawls, wrapped round their necks like scarves. It was our first sight of anyone dressed like that, and it rammed home to us where we were.

A Hercules was parked alongside and we jumped into the back. Normally RAF crewmen are sticklers for the rules, and every time you board an aircraft they make you sit down and buckle up. But now, on operations, there were no seats or straps, so we pleased ourselves and sat on the metal deck for the short flight up to our Forward Mounting Base, known as Victor. The head loadie (loadmaster) said, 'Hold tight, because we're going to do an operational take-off.' The pilot revved his engines until they were screaming and the whole aircraft began to judder; then he let go his brakes and we were hurled forward and heaved into the air. Fifteen minutes later he went diving in and landed with a couple of heavy thumps and violent deceleration.

At Victor a hangar became our temporary home. A heap of bergens, weapons piled in big rolls, a stack of American cots, boxes of radios, medical kit, demolition equipment – everything looked as though it had arrived just that minute. We gathered round for a quick briefing from the SSM: 'No walking around in your shreddies when the RSM's about . . . There's a couple of you need haircuts . . . Don't go into the Int hangar unless you're invited . . . Let's have the hangar tidy, fellers . . . Keep your kit up together round your bed space . . . I want the place swept out periodically . . .'

Then the SQMS talked about the stores. 'OK,' he said, 'the stores are there. There's rations there, but I don't want you going into them. If you need any kit, come to me . . . the ammo bunker is next to the cookhouse . . . Cookhouse timings: six to seven breakfast, twelve to one lunch, six to seven dinner . . . Grab yourself a bed, get a space . . . We'll start training tomorrow morning.'

The OC also gave us a brief, which amounted to his personal perception of how the build-up to war was going. He said that plans for Special Forces were still fluid. 'A' and 'D' Squadrons were already well advanced with their build-up training for deployment far behind Iraqi lines, and were out in the desert doing a squadron range package – that is, putting in squadron attacks which use all weapons, including .50 Browning heavy machine-guns, mortars, LAW 90 rocket launchers, Milan anti-tank missile launchers, and – most effective of all – M19s, high-speed grenade launchers, in effect machine-guns firing bombs.

As for 'B' Squadron – the OC said he hoped to get us a few vehicles, which we would have to convert for desert operations. He promised to keep us updated on the way things were looking, then told us to get our heads down before we started training next day. We each found a cot and set it up against the wall of the hangar, with a six-foot table across the foot of the bed and mosquito nets rigged on poles above – and that was to be our home for the next ten days.

Morning revealed that we were well out in the desert, at one of several different camps dotted about a vast training area. Most of the desert was a flat plain of hard, beige-coloured sand, but every now and then runs of low dunes broke the monotony; on these ridges, which were maybe thirty feet high, a few tufts of dry grass and the odd tree were growing, and the sand was very soft, so that vehicles often got stuck. The wind had sculpted the sand into waves, which gave the landscape an attractive appearance.

Approaching Victor you came over a rise, and there was a high chain-link fence surrounding the large hangars and a runway, with sand-dunes lapping the perimeter wire. The base had been built as a parachute school; the hangars were for storage of chutes and other equipment and there were tall towers for hanging chutes to dry. At night the perimeter was brightly illuminated.

We began build-up training, and there was plenty to organise: radios, satellite communications, TACBEs, NBC drills. As a trained medic, I set up some medical instruction, teaching guys how to put drips in, how to pack gunshot wounds to stop bleeding, how to treat heat exhaustion. To demonstrate intravenous techniques, I grabbed a 'volunteer' from the front row, choosing someone lean, because he had prominent veins; tough though the SAS may be, some of them were also pretty squeamish, and it's not unknown for them to faint when it comes to injections.

Most of our training took place inside our hangar, but we also went on the ranges to zero our weapons, which included 203s, Minimi machine-guns (also 5.56 calibre), and the more potent general-purpose machine-guns (GMPGs, known as gympis), which fire 7.62 rounds, have a greater range and are harder-hitting than the Minimis. There was one set of ranges only a couple of hundred yards away, and a larger complex three hours out into the desert. We'd fired the weapons already on a gallery range in Hereford, but because they'd all been packed up, loaded and unloaded several times, we needed to zero them again.

The trouble was, we were short of ammunition. For our contact drills on foot – practising reaction when you bump into enemy – we had only thirty or forty rounds per man. In a full practice for a single contact – contact front, contact left or right, contact rear – you can easily fire a couple of hundred rounds. We drilled in groups of four or six, as if we were patrolling along. Cardboard targets would appear ahead, somebody would shout, 'CONTACT FRONT!' and we'd split into pairs to fight our way back, each pair covering the others as they moved. The SOP, or standard operating procedure, was never to go forward after a contact, always to move back. For one thing, we never knew the size of the force opposing us, and in a reconnaissance patrol there were too few of us to take on any major enemy unit. For another, we couldn't carry enough ammunition for a prolonged engagement. Working in small groups, our immediate aim was to shoot our way clear of trouble, which gave us a better chance of escaping uninjured. But now in training, with our severely limited ammunition, all we could do when someone called 'Contact!' was to go to ground and put in one round each; then we were out of rounds – and doing it dry is never the same.

At that stage we had no 203 grenades, and we badly needed some to zero our sexton sights – pieces of auxiliary kit that you can bolt on to the side of the weapon to improve accuracy. We hadn't been issued with these sights, but I'd had one for years and had brought it with me, so now I fitted it myself.

We seemed to be short of everything, not least proper desert vehicles. What we needed were purpose-built, long-wheel-base 110 Land-Rovers, known as 'Pinkies' ever since they'd been painted pink for the Oman campaign of the 1970s. 'A' and 'D' Squadrons both had Pinkies, which they had brought out with them; the vehicles had mounts for heavy machine-guns and posts for Milan anti-tank missile launchers. All we could get were short-wheel-base 90 Land-Rovers, which had no seat-belts or gun-mountings, and were derisively known as 'Dinkies'. We also had one bigger truck, a Unimog, to act as a mother craft, carrying ammunition.

Under the guidance of a sergeant from Mobility Troop, we got stuck in and stripped down the Land-Rovers, taking off the doors, tailgates, wing-mirrors and canvas tops, removing windscreens, fixing hessian over the lights and mirrors to prevent any reflection at night, and welding baskets for jerricans on to the sides. Somebody said that when the war was over, we would have to put the vehicles back together again, and we looked at each other, thinking, 'You bet!' But we kept all the pieces and piled them in a corner of the hangar. We also had three trials motorbikes, but only a handful of us had been trained to ride them. With bikes of our own at home, we had plenty of experience, and we took the Armstrongs out and practised throwing them around in the desert.

Even as we worked, we were looking at our Dinkies and thinking, 'Bollocks! This is crap!' When we practised navigation and drove about the sand-dunes, we wasted a tremendous amount of time getting bogged down and having to dig the Land-Rovers out. When we had a day doing vehicle contact drills, everything became farcical: we tried to fire the gympis off sandbags piled on the bonnet, which was hopeless, and when the drivers reversed hard into a J-turn, guys started being thrown out. With the whole squadron watching the range-work, a big Australian called Stan was flung out at high speed and cartwheeled half-way across the desert with his gympi attached to him, so that he was burnt by the hot barrel.

We laughed at the time, but underneath we were alarmed by the thought that we might be sent across the border in these vehicles and might have to use them for real: what looked funny now might easily be disastrous later. We also experimented with six of us standing in the back of the Unimog and firing from there: it was like the chuck wagon in a cowboy film, with the good guys popping off at the Indians. But we soon found that it was impossible to hit anything, because at any speed the vehicle bounced up and down outrageously.

In general, it was pathetic trying to operate with the wrong equipment, and altogether our training was poor. The other two squadrons had far better facilities. The reason for this was simple: they were the ones who were supposed to be going into Iraq; at that stage we were no more than BCRs. Nevertheless, we were still hoping that we'd be deployed.

Wild ideas started coming up. There was talk of 'B' Squadron parachuting into Kuwait City, which had been occupied by Iraqi forces. The idea was that we would capture a big block of flats and direct mortar and artillery fire on to Iraqi positions. Also, being snipers, we could fire from the building and take individuals out that way. The originator of this plan – whoever he was – didn't seem to have realised that once the Iraqis saw where we were, they would simply blow the shit out of the place – and we would have no means of escape. The RAF planners actively considered throwing us out of a Hercules at 400 or 600 feet (the usual height is between 800 and 1,000), and insisted that we made a practice jump at that height.

One suicide mission had been proposed for 'B' Squadron during the Falklands war, and now here was another. Half the guys were going to be knackered by the jump alone. On the SP team, I had been on one practice jump in which sixteen out of thirty men were injured – not killed, but put out of action. This time we had drawn and fitted the parachutes, and we were about to walk out of the hangar for the training jump when our own OC cancelled the option.

Immediately, another rumour came up, even crazier – we were to jump into Baghdad and take out essential installations such as power-stations. But soon it was found that cruise missiles could do the job from a distance of several hundred miles.

The desert around the base was exactly as I'd expected it to be – hot and sandy, with plenty of dunes and undulations to give cover. In spite of the limitations imposed by our lack of equipment it was good for training, and we were working long hours: up at six, train all day, have dinner, sit down for a couple of hours, and then, once it was fully dark, do a night navigation exercise, before going to bed at ten or eleven. Several of the guys had radios, and when the six o'clock news came on the BBC World Service, everyone would crowd round to listen. High-level diplomatic negotiations were going on in Geneva and elsewhere as world leaders struggled to avoid a confrontation, and from one night to the next the chances of war went up and down. For recreation, there was a school of card-players, and some people would read – anything from Shakespeare to *Viz* comics. I'd taken a load of paperbacks by Tom Sharpe, who always makes me laugh. On the whole, though, we were too tired to read or play, and we began to suffer from sleep-deprivation.

Then suddenly another job came up, for a team to go down and put extra security on the British Embassy in Abu Dhabi during a visit by Douglas Hurd, the Foreign Secretary. They picked five of us who had done the bodyguards' course and ferried us down there. In Abu Dhabi we had a look round the

Embassy, and settled into a flat-roofed bungalow within the grounds, which were maybe a hundred yards square, and beautifully kept – a huge garden with irrigated lawns, shrubs, flowerbeds and trees. The main Embassy building was two storeys high and quite large, and several other staff bungalows were dotted about. Local security was operating outside the walls of the compound, and we were to patrol inside.

Up at Victor we were banned from going into town, but here there was nobody to keep an eye on us. Hurd was not due to arrive until 6p.m., and we had a couple of hours spare. Also, we were dressed inconspicuously in casual civilian clothes – polo shirts and corduroys – so we took our chance and went into town for a look round.

It was strange, walking round the streets of a prosperous, gleaming new town, to find that everything seemed normal, with not a hint that a major war was about to erupt. It felt good to have a break from training, see a different culture, and eat different food. After a meal we did some shopping, and bought little radios, miniature binoculars and a camera. I also bought a couple of shamags for myself, and another four or five for the guys still at Victor. Then we slipped back to the Embassy in time for the arrival of our star guest.

When he came in, we saw him get out of the car and go into the building, so that we knew he was our responsibility for the time being. The situation, in the run-up to war, was enough to make anyone jumpy. We'd been getting reports which suggested that the Iraqis were capable of parachuting a special forces team into Abu Dhabi to take Hurd out – and at the time we had to treat them seriously. We thought they might have kamikaze types trained either to drop from the air or to come in by boat, because the Embassy was only about a hundred metres from the sea.

After dark the perimeter wall was illuminated by lights that cast deep shadows, so that it would have been difficult to spot anyone hanging about. In the middle of the night one pair of our guys was on patrol in the compound and the other three of us were asleep in the bungalow, when somebody suddenly began screaming 'CONTACT! CONTACT!' at the top of his voice. Still half asleep, we leapt up and cocked our weapons, bumping into each other as we rushed about trying to make out where the

14

enemy was. Just as we were about to burst out and sweep the compound, we realised that the person yelling was Paul, who'd been having a nightmare and had dreamt up the whole confrontation.

Somehow we settled down again, and in the morning, after Hurd had made an early departure, we whipped into Abu Dhabi again for breakfast of coffee and croissants. A couple of the guys bought telephone cards, so that they could call home. Back at Victor, nobody mentioned anything about having been in the town, and when I handed out the spare shamags, I said to the lads, 'Just don't tell anyone where they came from.'

That little episode left us even more exhausted, and we told the OC we needed a day off because we were knackered. He made a compromise and let us off a navigation exercise, so that we were able to get our heads down for an extra four-hour stretch.

The Regiment had established a Forward Operating Base at Al Jouf, an airfield in the north-west of Saudi Arabia, and we knew that if we were deployed across the border it was from there that we would go in. When the air war began, on the night of 16/17 January, with coalition aircraft bombing targets in Iraq, we expected to be deployed at any moment.

Although we didn't know it at the time, the Commander of British Forces in the Gulf, Lieutenant General Peter de la Billière – himself an outstanding SAS officer who had served in numerous earlier campaigns, from Korea to Malaya, Borneo, Oman and Dhofar – had been trying his hardest to persuade the American Commander-in-Chief, General Norman Schwarzkopf, to send us in. But Stormin' Norman had a hang-up about using Special Forces; he had seen the American Special Forces make a hash of things in Vietnam, and now he preferred to use conventional methods – to soften up the Iraqis with bombs, and then overrun their positions with tanks, without wasting highly-trained special troops. Besides, he could get all the intelligence he needed from satellites and reconnaissance aircraft.

In the end, however, DLB persuaded him that SAS patrols would glean useful intelligence if they were inserted deep inside enemy territory, and the C-in-C agreed to our deployment. Hardly had he done so when Saddam Hussein started putting Scud missiles down on Israel, and neither satellites nor aircraft could find the mobile launchers. Suddenly – and quite by chance – the regiment had a vital role to perform: to find the mobile launchers, put an end to the bombardment of Israel, and so prevent Israel entering the war with potentially disastrous consequences to the coalition.

Suddenly our future became more clearly defined. No longer mere BCRs, we were assigned a proper task. The big Special Forces punch was to come from 'A' and 'D' squadrons, who would go in as substantial motorised patrols, each heavily armed and half a squadron strong, tasked with finding the Scud TELs (transporter-erector-launchers) and calling in Allied aircraft to take them out. But the plan was that before the heavy mob was deployed, three eight-man patrols from 'B' Squadron, designated Bravo One Zero, Bravo Two Zero and Bravo Three Zero, would infiltrate deep into Iraqi territory and lie up in OPs (observation posts) to report enemy movement, especially that of Scuds. De la Billière believed that if we could establish OPs first, and start passing back useful intelligence, it would strengthen his hand in bargaining with Schwarzkopf and increase the chances of the big patrols being deployed. Naturally our own CO was as eager as anyone to get people in there.

For our patrol, Bravo Two Zero, members were selected from a nominal roll, and according to their particular skills: besides fighting power, we needed a demolitionist, a signaller and a medic (myself). Our main task would be to gather intelligence; our aim was to find a good LUP (lying-up position) and set up an OP. From there we would maintain surveillance on the MSR (main supply route) which ran westwards from the town of Al Hadithah to three airfields known as H1, H2 and H3, and along which it was thought the Iraqis were moving Scud launchers. Once established, we would remain in the OP for up to ten days, reporting enemy movements by radio or Satcom telephone, and calling in fighter-bombers to attack any worthwhile target. A subsidiary task was to blow up any fibre-optic communications links we could find. After ten days, we would either get a re-supply by helicopter, or move to a new location, also by chopper. Besides all our personal equipment, we would take kit for building the OP: 120 empty sandbags per man, vehicle camouflage nets, poles, and thermal sheets to put over the top of our structures, so that if Iraqis flew over with thermal-imaging kit they wouldn't be able to pick up the heat rising from our bodies.

To practise the task we'd been assigned, we went out into some sandhills and dug in OPs. Now it so happened that I was pretty good at this, having done a lot of it with the Territorial Regiment in Germany, where one of our main roles had been to construct OPs and man them for three weeks at a time. After the earth and rock of Europe, the sand of Arabia was a doddle. We began by digging a pit three metres by two. The sand kept sliding in, but once we were down to a reasonable depth we built walls of bags filled with sand, then laid poles across the top and covered them with thermal sheeting and sand-spattered hessian. At the front we left a slot for observation, camouflaged with strips of hessian like a net curtain, and a small aperture at the back, concealed by a flap of hessian covered in sand and glue.

The main object of the exercise was to work out what we would need to go to ground in Iraq, and the answer seemed to be plenty of sandbags and plenty of water. At the end of the day we all went round each other's OPs, and I am glad to say that ours was by far the best. Encouraged by the nature of the desert in the south of the Gulf, we decided that to build an OP in Iraq would be a viable proposition, and that we should be able to get away with it.

Each patrol's plan, in fact, was to put in two OPs, one covering the other, 50 or 100 metres apart and linked by telephone line. One would have an observation opening facing forward on to the MSR, and the other would be in front of it with the opening facing backwards, so that the guys there could watch the ground behind their colleagues.

It was when we started getting our kit together that the scale of the shortages finally emerged. 'Right,' we said to the SQMS, 'we need 203 rounds.'

'Well,' he replied, 'we haven't got any.'

'Why the hell not?'

'There are just none here.'

In that case, I decided, I wasn't going to carry the grenade-launching part of my weapon across the border, because it made the whole thing so heavy. The launcher, or lower barrel, is easily detached, and without it the rifle becomes considerably lighter and a joy to handle – but in that mode it needs a replacement stock, since the main stock comes away with the lower barrel. The SQMS told me I couldn't split my weapon, because he had forgotten to bring out the extra stocks.

In fact there were plenty of 203 rounds – but other people had them. One day I went across to see two friends in 'A' Squadron and found them sitting in their Pinkie. They were just about to move up to Al Jouf, within striking distance of the border. I said, 'Listen – we're flying up tomorrow, just after you. Is there any chance of you giving us some bombs?' John – Sarah's godfather – lifted up the seat, and underneath were boxes of 203 rounds. They brought out twelve and said, 'Here, take these.' So I went with both parts of my weapon fitted after all.

It was the same with claymore mines, which we wanted as a deterrent to put the brakes on anyone trying to come after us in the desert. (If you're being followed, you can put down a mine with a timer, and crack it off after maybe five minutes. Even if it doesn't do any damage it slows people down, because they wonder if there are more mines in front of them.) When we asked for claymores, the answer was that there weren't any, and someone told us to make our own out of ammunition boxes packed with plastic explosives and gympi link – the metal belt that holds machine-gun rounds together.

This was ridiculous: home-made devices like that are crude, large and heavy, and we hadn't got the capacity to carry them. Later we did make a single claymore out of plastic ice-cream cartons, and one of us took it in his bergen. In fact there was a whole tent full of claymores, but through lack of communication at various levels, they remained hidden away. In the end we were given a mixed load of stuff by the Special Boat Squadron: five claymores, a box of L2 grenades, one of white phosphorus grenades and some 66 rockets. We shared out some of this with the other two patrols, and I myself finished up with one L2 grenade and two white phos.

Yet another sore point was pistols. The twenty pistols packed and shipped for our own use simply disappeared, nicked for the other squadrons. The result was that the only guy in our unit with one was Vince, who had brought it with him from 'A' Squadron. We also asked for silenced pistols, and in particular for the make invented during the Second World War for Special

Operations Executive. Although fairly primitive, these have never been surpassed for sheer quietness. They come in two parts – the silenced barrel (a fat tube) and the pistol grip, which is also the magazine – and part of their secret is that they have so few working parts. They fire single shots only, and have to be reloaded manually, by undoing and pulling back a screw, which lifts the next round into the breech; but the quietness of the report is uncanny – no more than a *pffft* – and at close range the 9mm. slug is deadly. The other two squadrons had such weapons and as things turned out, there were several moments during my escape when I could have done with one; but again, we were told that none were available.

People started getting a bit pissed off with all these shortages, and one day in the hangar someone challenged the OC about them, saying, 'Look – we've got no pistols, we've got no grenades, we've got no claymores. You're expecting us to make claymores out of ammunition boxes, and it's bloody stupid, because they're not effective.'

The OC, who was doing the best he could, blew his top, and said, 'Listen, you're about to go to war. You'll take whatever you can get. You're not in Northern Ireland, where you can ask for any kind of asset. You've got to improvise. That's what makes the Regiment so good – improvisation.'

In fact the things we were missing were basic equipment which we should have had. Take the maps, for instance. The only maps we had were really poor and designed for air-crews; their scale (1:250,000) was so small that they showed few details, and although they might have helped navigators they were no good to people on the ground. To back them up, we badly needed satellite-derived information – but again, we were told that no satellite imagery was available. Our first escape-maps were also as old as the hills. Incredibly, they had first been printed in 1928, then updated for the Second World War; but at the last minute we were issued with newer ones, printed on silk, which we worked into the waistbands of our trousers.

Each of us was given a photostated indemnity note, in Arabic and English, promising £5,000 to anyone who handed over a co-alition serviceman to a friendly power. Deciding the document was rubbish, I threw mine away. Later, however, I changed my mind; because I couldn't speak Arabic, I thought I'd better have a note after all. So I got another member of the patrol, Bob Consiglio, to photostat a copy of his (with the serial number 075 in the top right-hand corner), and took that with me. We also signed for twenty gold sovereigns apiece, in case we had to bribe somebody or buy our way out of trouble. Of course we were supposed to return these after the conflict, but not everybody did.

At Christmas, back in Hereford, we'd had what was known as Cross-brief Studies, the formal review of what the Regiment had done during the past year, and a forecast of what it would be doing the next. Proceedings had finished with an address from the CO, who asked everybody except 'A' and 'D' Squadron to leave, and then made some pretty sombre comments. 'Look, guys,' he'd said. 'There's a good chance we're going to be at war, and it may escalate into something big. But if any of you look like getting caught, you certainly want to consider saving the last round for yourself.' Basically he'd been saying: 'Shoot yourself rather than get caught.'

Now, out at Victor, those words began to spread around. The Regiment didn't want anyone else to know that the SAS had been deployed, and we were supposed to be in isolation – not only within the camp as a whole, but also within squadrons. As soon as we were tasked, we should have been separated from everyone else and put into our own isolation pen. Our briefing room – in this case a tent inside the hangar – should have been secured by the Headquarter unit, and nobody should have been allowed in there except members of the patrol – because, if you're captured, the less you know the better. As it was, maps and papers were left lying about the floor, and everybody knew what everybody else was doing. Inevitably, people talked to each other, and the CO's advice leaked out to us as well.

For years people had reckoned that you'd be better off shooting yourself if the IRA got hold of you, and that black Africans would probably skin you alive. Now the same seemed to apply to the Iraqis. Guys went around saying, 'These people will carve you up if they get you. They'll have your bollocks off, for a start.' We were not to know that most of this was pure hype. The military capabilities of the Iraqis were also becoming wildly exaggerated, but our intelligence about the true situation was so sketchy that rumours kept building up.

While we were still at Victor, we were given jabs against anthrax, which made everyone feel like shit for three or four days, with bad bruising in the arm that had been injected. One man's arm remained black and blue for six weeks, and some people had muscle around the puncture actually go rotten three or four weeks after the jab. Several guys from 'A' Squadron had to be dragged back out of the field for minor surgery. I was lucky, and got nothing worse than a cold and a burning throat; I kept waking up in the night, coughing up lumps of phlegm the size of golf balls.

The patrol's principal task would be to man the OP, but there was also the possibility that we might be tasked to blow fibre-optic communication lines, one of which was thought to run alongside the MSR. Luckily one of our lads had done some moonlighting for a contractor laying fibre-optic cables, and he told us that we needed a particular device, like a metal detector, for tracing them – so we indented for one immediately. He also knew that if a cable is cut, the operators can send out a pulse of light which bounces back along it, giving them a precise indication of where the break is, so that repairs are fairly simple. We therefore worked out that, if we did blow a line, we would put anti-personnel mines around the break, so that when engineers came to repair it they would be taken out. We would also lay another, delayed-action device to blow the line again later. But the main aim of the exercise would be to kill as many skilled personnel as possible. Western technicians had poured out of Iraq during the past few weeks, and we knew that there must be a shortage of engineers; if we managed to kill the first wave coming out to make repairs, it was a good bet that the next lot, in true Arab fashion, would say they couldn't find the break, and the line would remain cut.

When I heard the code-word for our patrol – Turbo – I couldn't help laughing, because Turbo was the name of the best dog I'd ever owned. A black Staffordshire bull terrier of incredible strength, he was the most engaging character you could imagine: a desperate fighter and randy as a billy-goat, but deeply affectionate with humans, with a look in his eyes that would melt any heart. When I thought of all the scrapes he'd got me into, a warm feeling came over me, and I almost felt he'd become a member of the patrol.

At first we heard that Bravo Two Zero would be commanded by Bob Shepherd, an exceptionally level-headed Scotsman, always cheerful and smiling, who had been my instructor on selection. He had come out to Saudi with 'A' Squadron, but had recently been brought into 'B' Squadron to strengthen its middle management. The news of his appointment delighted us. By our standards Bob was quite old – thirty-six – but he was always closely in touch with the younger guys, and someone we could look up to and trust absolutely. Tall and strong, with swept-back dark-brown hair, he'd always been outstandingly fit. On the selection course he was probably the fittest instructor of all, but also one of the nicest; you could be sure he would never stitch you up, but would spend time helping you.

Unfortunately his command lasted literally a few minutes. Partly because of personality clashes, partly because he'd had experience with heavy weapons, he was kept back to work with the other squadrons – and his place was taken by Sergeant Andy McNab. Andy was then about thirty-two, a Cockney Jack-the-Lad with such a gift of the gab that he could talk his way out of any situation and tie you in a knot. Dark-haired, with a moustache, he'd done a lot of work in the Regiment and was a good demolitionist – but words came out of him so fast that you never quite knew where you were.

Paired off with Andy – sharing bed-spaces, vehicles, cooking equipment and so on – was Dinger, a lance-corporal of twenty-eight who'd been in the Parachute Regiment. A bit of a wild character, Dinger drank like a fish, smoked like a chimney, couldn't give a flying monkey's, and was always game for a fight. If you described anyone as mad, or as a joker, it would be him. Yet he was also a good family man, married with two daughters. Just before we left, one of his mates did him a really short crew-cut, which gave him an extra-youthful appearance.

The other sergeant was Vince, an older man, about thirty-five, a medic like myself, who tended to be a bit nervous and twitchy in his movements. He was tall and slim, with an athletic build; he had fuzzy, dark-gingery hair and a drooping, Mexican-type moustache. He came from Swindon, and was married with three children. He was putting a bold front on things, but I knew his heart wasn't in this operation. Only a few days before, we'd sat on his camp-bed and he'd said to me, 'I don't want to be doing this.' We discussed things a bit, and I said to him, 'Well – now that we're here, we'd better just get on with it, and hope we'll come out OK at the end.' I got the impression that he wanted to finish his time in the army and be done with the whole business.

A closer friend of mine was Trooper Bob Consiglio. Twenty-four years old, the son of a Sicilian father and an English mother, he was dark as any Italian and very small (only 5' 5") but incredibly strong, with a heart like a lion. He was the only guy ever known to have spent six months in Hereford without trapping a woman. He used to try like mad, every night, all night long, but he never made it. It seemed that his lack of height was against him. Girls somehow didn't realise what a good sense of humour he had; if ever someone was going to say something really daft, it would be him. He was a really nice lad, and would do anything you told him to; a hard worker, and a cheerful character. If you thought of Bob as a dog, he'd be a terrier.

Bob was endlessly good-natured, and, when he was the newest member of the troop, had taken a lot of stick from the rest of us. He didn't exactly look at us in awe, but he went all out to impress us, trying his hardest not to appear the dummy. The result was that we kept playing jokes on him. Once, when the staff sergeant was away and I was running the troop, we went climbing in Pembrokeshire, on the Welsh coast. I went into Bob's bag and took out one shoe. When we reached the foot of the hills he started to hunt about, and although he wouldn't say anything I could see him getting worried, thinking he'd left the shoe behind. I deliberately started to hustle him: 'Get your kit on. Let's go.'

'Can I climb in my big boots?'

'No – get your stickies on.'

He began muttering and hesitating, playing for time, but in the end he had to say, 'Listen – I forgot to put one of my stickies in.'

I pretended to blow my top at him, and he began to apologise. 'I'm sorry,' he said, 'I'll run back and get it.'

'Go on, then,' I told him. 'And make it fast.'

Away he went – and when he'd gone a few yards I shouted after him to come back.

No matter how much we used to pull the piss, when it came

to fighting, Bob wasn't frightened of anything. At Al Jouf he and I lived under the same vehicle cam net, and I said to him one day, 'Bob, if anything happens when we're in there, make sure you stick with me. Get on my arse when we're leaving.' And he said, 'Yeah – I will.' It wasn't that I didn't trust him to do anything by himself – though I did want to protect him, almost as if he were a brother. Rather, because he was such a brave little sod, it would be to my own advantage to have him close.

Twice Bob's size was Stan – a different character entirely. A Rhodesian who'd moved to Australia, he was over six foot tall, not that obviously muscular, but very, very strong, well-spoken, and a gentleman. Down under, he'd been at university, rowing in the university boat team, and then became a dentist, with a practice of his own in Sydney. But all he'd wanted to do was join the SAS, and gradually he had worked his way there. In Hereford he again had a dental practice, while at the same time serving in the Regiment. A single man, and very good looking, he became known in the camp as 'Dr Sex', such havoc did he create among the local girls. Nothing ever seemed to bother him; whatever happened, his voice kept the same tone, and he just got on with things. If he had a fault, it was that he was too nice, too placid and, for all his intelligence, perhaps a bit naive. He was another good mate of mine – and I wouldn't have liked to see him get angry, because he could be a formidable fighter.

The other two members of the patrol were Legs Lane – so called because he was tall and thin – and Mark, a keen New Zealander who had joined the squadron only a month before. Both were very quiet – Legs particularly so – and it was difficult to get much out of them; but both were good men, and Mark especially was always one to start straight in, game for anything. Legs was a key man in the patrol as he was carrying the 319, the main radio set.

Finally there was myself: a Geordie from near Newcastle, aged twenty-eight, and a corporal. During six years in the regular SAS I'd gained a good deal of useful experience in many countries, and at the beginning of 1991 I was physically the strongest I'd ever been, because during my last tour with the SP team I'd hit the weights and built up a lot of muscle on my upper body. The extra strength had been useful, because much of what you do on the SP team is bodywork – you're forever going up ropes or sliding down them, climbing into buildings, carrying guys, jumping off vehicles, pushing people away or restraining them. In all this, you're handling a lot of weight. In your black kit, you have your body armour, kevlar helmet and waistcoat loaded with ammunition, stun-grenades and axes, besides your machine-gun and pistol. With all the hours on the bench, and practical work, my weight had gone up from 11 to 12½ stone. Little did I know that the extra muscle was going to save my life.

In our last days at Victor we were busier than ever. Andy was getting the demolition kit sorted. I saw to the medical packs, Legs Lane to the radio. Everyone scrounged ammunition. We were told that when we moved up to Al Jouf we would go more or less straight in, so that everything had to be ready before we left. We were also told to leave all our non-essential kit behind.

We flew up on the evening of 18 January in three Hercules, staggered. On board were all the squadron vehicles and stores. The air war was then at its height, raging for the third night, and there was quite a high risk of being shot at en route. Through the headsets dangling from the walls in the back we tuned in to an American AWACS controller directing a US pilot with an Iraqi on his tail. The pilot was highly excited, and kept yelling, 'He's got us! He's locked on!' but the controller remained completely cool and talked him calmly through the turns: 'OK. Steady. I have you on radar. Steady. Bank left. Just bank left . . .' The American ended up taking the Iraqi out, and it was great to listen in; the pilot's excitement and fear and the controller's laconic replies brought home to us the fact that the war was going on in earnest. The sky was full of armed warplanes, all trying to blow the opposition out of the air. During the flight the SSM went round telling everyone to start taking their NAPs tablets, to combat the effects of nuclear or biological contamination. We were all saying, 'Yeah, yeah. OK.' But somebody muttered, 'These fucking things make you sterile,' so although a couple of the guys took the pills, the rest didn't risk it.

When we felt the wind at Al Jouf, somebody gasped, 'Jesus! It's a hell of a lot colder up here.' Because we'd been told we were going to deploy immediately, we'd left most of our warm kit behind.

The moment we landed, we began to unload our equipment

and pile it in a grassed area like a garden, about thirty metres by twenty, next to one of the hangars. Helping us was an officer who had been commissioned from the ranks, and had a fearsome reputation of being a real bastard. Everyone was in dread of him, even the majors. Now he was the quartermaster, but he got stuck straight in, and was carrying the long cardboard boxes of rations off the aircraft with us. He laid three boxes down parallel to each other in one layer, and three across them in the next tier. When Bob Consiglio started the third layer with a box lying in line with the one below, instead of across all three, the quartermaster took one look at him and said in a menacing voice, 'Get it right, cunt.'

Bob, not knowing the man from Adam, was about to say something, or even to grab hold of him. I looked at him and shook my head, silently praying, *'Please!* Don't say a thing, or he'll kill you.'

Someone told us we'd be sleeping that night in the grassy area; so we sorted out bivvy bags and sleeping bags, made a brew, and got our heads down in the open. The night sky was clear, and as we lay there we watched streams of B-52s crossing high above us, with fighters skimming like minnows alongside. The sight sent my mind straight back to the time when, as a boy, I'd watched television pictures of B-52s going over in streams to bomb Vietnam. Now, as the aircraft reached the Iraqi border, their flashing lights were suddenly extinguished, but we heard the roar of massed jet engines rumble away into the distance. It was comforting to know that our aircraft were bombing the shit out of the enemy, and we hoped they would do enough damage to make Saddam capitulate before we were even deployed.

Morning showed that the airfield was surrounded by security wire and primitive, flat-roofed wooden towers with glass windows, which reminded us of the German concentration camps we'd seen in World War Two films. Eight A-10 pilots were stationed on the base, flying their tank-buster aircraft in and out all the time. There were also a couple of small Saudi jets coming and going.

There was one main terminal, quite small, with a few other buildings attached to it. Our regimental head-shed and all our stores were there, but we were billeted on the other side of the airfield, where there was a cement building with a single washbasin and a hole in the ground to act as a toilet, which inevitably became blocked. The SSM had been told to bring the squadron tents, but he had decided that, because we were in the desert and the weather would be hot, we wouldn't need them. In fact it wasn't hot at all. It was bloody cold, and the dust was phenomenal. All we could do was sling cam nets from our vehicles for a bit of shelter, and we lived on the ground like pigs, huddled round the Land-Rovers. We had no tables or chairs, so we ate our meals sitting on the deck, with the dust blowing around everywhere, covering us, our kit and our food.

We'd hardly got our bearings when the RSM came across for a chat. He was a bit deaf, and as he was talking to one of the lads, a clerk from the HQ building came past and made some remark. The RSM thought he heard 'Good morning', so he politely said, 'Aye, good morning' back. In fact what the clerk had said was, 'Scud warning'. Suddenly, through the hedge, we saw groups of people running like hell, and one of the last of them yelled, 'There's a Scud coming in!' Some of the squadron stayed where they were, drinking their tea on the grass, not bothering. Others ran left and right for the shelters, some struggling to pull respirators on, others to don NBC suits.

Soon afterwards the all-clear came. We rapidly learned the drill: the operators in Riyadh were monitoring every launch and putting out general alerts, then a few seconds later, as soon as they had determined the missile's track, they began to call 'Stand down here, stand down there' to the areas not under threat. Every now and then the SSM would tell us to dig slit-trenches, but the guys just said, 'Ah, bollocks!' The airfield was remote and unimportant, and the possibility of a Scud landing on it was infinitesimal. When warnings came in the middle of the night, we soon decided to ignore them. The OC would run round all our positions shouting, 'Scud warning!' and he himself would run for the shelter. At first some of the guys did the same, but it soon reached the point at which we all just zipped up our sleeping bags and stayed where we were. In the end the OC went berserk and gave us all a bollocking – but then we deployed across the border, and that was the end of it.

We had no time for detailed planning – but that hardly seemed to matter, because we knew what we wanted to do, and the task seemed fairly simple. The site we had chosen for our LUP was opposite a slight bend in the MSR, at a spot where it looked from the map as though we could dig into the bank of a wadi and have a view straight up the gully to the big road.

If we saw a Scud on the move, we were to report it immediately by voice over the Satcom telephone, and follow up with a message on the 319, so that the sighting was doubly confirmed. Then aircraft would be launched or vectored to take the missile out. A brief on the missiles gave us an idea of what big beasts they were. Nearly forty feet long and three feet in diameter, they would look a bit like fuel-tankers when in the horizontal position on their trailers. Apparently the Iraqis' habit was to park them alongside embankments or under road bridges so that they were all but invisible from the air. When on the move, a TEL would always be accompanied by several other vehicles in a little convoy.

Privately, we agreed that if we did find a convoy we would allow a few minutes to elapse after it had gone past us – otherwise the Iraqis might pinpoint the source of the intelligence which had brought an attack down on their heads. There was also anxiety about what the Scud warheads might contain: if they were nuclear, or full of gas or biological agents, we didn't want to be around when they came apart. We were also nervous of using satellite communications, because they give a hell of a splash-off, and a good direction-finding station can locate a transmitter within twenty seconds. So we practised getting on the phone and putting over the bare essentials of a Scud sighting in as few seconds as possible.

Bravo One Zero and Bravo Three Zero had decided to take vehicles in with them, but at the last minute we opted to go without. Over the past few days the matter had been the subject of intense debate. Obviously vehicles would give the patrol far greater mobility and enable us to drive out of trouble and back over the border if things went wrong. On the other hand, they would be hard to conceal, and might easily give away our presence. At one point we were positively ordered to take them, but the order was rescinded, and in the end we elected to go in on foot. In Bravo One Zero and Three Zero the decision went the other way, and they took Dinkies with them. (The vehicles that we had prepared for ourselves were eventually used by 'A' and 'D' Squadrons.)

In our patrol, as usual, the matter was decided by Chinese parliament, with every man having his say. Opinion was evenly divided, and nobody insisted that vehicles were essential. Looking back, I realise that I had a strong influence on the decision. I had built countless OPs in Europe. In the Territorial Army I'd made more OPs than all the rest of the guys in the patrol put together, and I'd specialised in what we called hasty hides – we'd dig in, put logs across the top of the hole, and bury them. Altogether, I considered myself something of an expert at the job; but I had never operated in the desert, and just couldn't see a small patrol like ours escaping detection if we were saddled with vehicles. Looking back, I realise it was a cardinal mistake to go without. What we should have done was to drive in, install an OP with a couple of men, change them over every night, and pull off to a safe distance during the days, hiding the vehicles under cam nets in the bottom of some deep wadi. Mobility apart, the advantage of vehicles would have been that we could fit them up with powerful armaments, including heavy machine-guns.

The penalty of leaving our Dinkies behind was that we were saddled with huge individual loads. The average weight of a bergen was 60 kilos, or 150 lbs: with that lot on, you had to walk with your head down like a donkey, so that you'd be useless in a contact, and if you fell over you'd be knackered. No wonder straps were breaking and stitches starting to pull out.

But that wasn't all. Apart from the bergens, each of us had a belt-kit of pouches weighing 20 kilos, and a whole load more gear that wouldn't fit in anywhere else: seven days' rations in one sandbag, two NBC suits in another, an extra bandolier of ammunition, extra grenades for the 203 launchers, and a jerrican of water. Altogether we had nearly 120 kilos of kit apiece.

Talking to the RAF helicopter pilots who were going to fly us, we heard how they planned their routes into Iraq to avoid known anti-aircraft positions, and with their help we identified the precise spot at which we wanted to be dropped. At first we chose a point five kilometres short of our LUP, but later, because of the phenomenal weight of our kit, we changed our minds and asked to be put down only two or three kilometres short.

Arrangements for evacuation seemed straightforward enough. If we had not come on the air within forty-eight hours of being dropped off, a chopper would come back to pick us up. If we needed casevac, a heli would come within twenty-four hours of any call. If we had a contact and needed assistance, half the squadron would be on board the helicopter to pull us out.

The OC tried to reassure us. 'Don't worry,' he said. 'You've got your 319. You've got your Satcom. You've got your TACBEs. "A" and "D" Squadrons are going to be in your area. Also you've got your forty-eight-hour Lost Comms procedure, and your twenty-four-hour Casevac.' That all sounded fine – but, as will become apparent, things didn't turn out as we hoped.

One detail to which we should have paid more attention was our cover-story. We agreed that if we were captured, we would claim to be members of a medical team, sent in to recover downed aircrew – or possibly members of a team sent to provide security for medics, and that our chopper had been forced down. The general idea was to stick as close to the truth as possible, but to say that we were reservists or ordinary infantrymen, and that we'd been brought into the war because we worked in a medical centre. Yet we never had time to work things out in any depth – for instance, about which fictitious regiment we belonged to.

We went off in such a rush, in fact, that when we boarded the Chinook on the evening of 19 January, Andy went on getting his final briefing on the ramp at the back of the helicopter. (Bravo One Zero and Three Zero were to go in the next night.)

Guys from 'B' Squadron threw our kit into vehicles and came with us to the helicopter. Among them was Bob Shepherd, and as he helped me with my equipment I said, only half joking, 'Bob, I wish you'd fucking well failed me during selection!'

'Yes,' he said. 'So do I!'

I sensed a peculiar atmosphere. Nobody had much to say. As we were going on board, our mates were all around us, but I got the feeling that they thought this was a one-way ticket. Somebody said to me, 'This is bloody ridiculous – it's not on, to carry loads like this.' But by then it was too late to change things.

Off we went into the dusk, and after half an hour we landed at Arar, an airfield just inside the border, to refuel. When the pilot shut down his engines, we stayed where we were, in the back. Then came an incredible let-down. The engines started turning and burning again, we lifted off and were almost over the frontier when the pilot radioed for permission to cross – and it was denied. He came on the intercom to announce, 'Sorry, guys – mission aborted.' Because the Americans were saturation-bombing targets on our route, he had to deconflict and keep out of the way.

Having psyched ourselves up to a high level of preparedness, we somehow had to come down. Although everyone pretended to be disappointed, in fact the guys were immensely relieved. We all looked at each other, and grins spread over our faces as we headed back to Al Jouf.

Chapter Two

Contact!

As soon as we landed back, the guys started stripping their kit in an all-out effort to save weight. Until the final moment all eight of us went on sorting and repacking, throwing out anything that didn't seem essential as we tried to lighten our loads. Out went luxuries like sleeping bags and most of our warm clothes. We realised that the weather was much colder than at Victor, but we simply had to cut down on our weights, which had reached ridiculous proportions: our bergens were so heavy that the only way we could get them on was to sit down, settle the straps over our shoulders, and have a couple of the other guys pull us to our feet, as if they were hoisting knights in armour on to their chargers.

I became obsessed with the need for ammunition. Pressured by the thought that we were going to be on our own behind enemy lines, I left food out of my belt-kit in favour of more rounds. Normally I carried 24 hours' worth of rations in a belt-pouch – enough to spread over four days at a pinch – but now I reckoned that if we did get compromised, I could reach the Syrian border in two nights. All I would need on me in that case would be two packets of AB (army issue) biscuits; so I put the rest of the food into my bergen and filled my belt-kit with extra ammunition. Altogether I had 12 magazines of 28 rounds each, and also about 90 loose rounds, including a few armour-piercing, which I'd brought from Hereford.

One of the items I threw out was my brew-kit: tea-bags, sachets of coffee, orange powder, sugar and inflammable hexi-blocks. Since we were going in on hard routine – which meant no cooking, no fires and no smoking – I thought I would have no chance to use anything like that. Another serious omission was puritabs, for sterilising water. If we'd been going into the jungle, where you use local water all the time, I'd certainly have taken some – but I thought that in the desert we'd be drinking out of jerricans; it never occurred to me that I might have to rely on the Euphrates. Certainly we wouldn't risk drinking from wells: in the light of how Saddam had treated his own people, especially the Kurds in the north, there seemed a good chance that wells might have been deliberately poisoned.

Gradually more guys from Hereford floated in, building up the squadron's numbers, and at the last minute a British Telecom fibre-optic detector turned up, looking rather like one of the metal-detectors that treasure-hunters use to sweep the fields. We also got one Magellan GPS (global positioning system) – a hand-held navigation aid, not much bigger than a mobile telephone, which locks on to satellites as they pass overhead and gives you your position to within a few feet: altogether an excellent device.

The atmosphere in the patrol remained tense but cheerful. If the guys bitched, it was at the lack of equipment. Until the last moment we kept demanding satellite pictures of the area for which we were heading, and in the end some did arrive. They were of poor quality, but they appeared to confirm our decision to leave vehicles behind, since they showed that the desert was extremely flat and open. What we failed to realise, through lack of proper instruction, was that we were reading the imagery upside-down, mistaking low ground for high ground, wadis for ridges and so on.

As time ran out, I was thinking a good deal about escape and evasion. At one Int briefing I asked the officer if he had any in-formation about enemy movement or positions along the border with Syria.

'No,' he said, 'as far as I know, there are no defences along it.'

'Can you tell us what the border looks like?'

'Sorry – I just don't know.'

When we discussed crossing this border among ourselves, the guys began joking. 'Aye,' said someone from another patrol, 'if we get compromised, we'll all meet up at the Pudding Club in Istanbul (the café where, in *Midnight Express*, the guy says you can always leave a message).' For someone like myself with a sweet tooth, that seemed a good enough rendezvous.

The second time, our departure was set for the evening of Tues-day 22 January 1991. Just as we heard we were to fly that night, the mail came in. I thought, 'Christ – I don't want this.' I'd been waiting for the post, and normally I looked forward to getting a letter from Jan; but for the past couple of days I'd been trying not to think about home, because it upset me. So I read the letter quickly, and glanced at the new photos of Sarah, who was walking well and stringing quite a few words together. Then I put the letter and the snaps into the bag of equipment I was leaving behind in the SQMS's tent. Just seeing the pictures made me realise what I was missing, and what I might be throwing away.

Before we left, we had a big meal of fresh food, which we ate sitting on the ground – there still being no tables or chairs. Then came last-minute checks as we went through all our pockets to sterilise ourselves, and make sure that we were carrying no scrap of paper that would give away who we were or where we came from. The only identification I had on me was the pair of metal discs slung on a chain round my neck, bearing my name, army number, blood group and religion (Church of England). To stop them clinking, I'd covered them in black masking tape, and on each I'd taped a good-luck talisman. One was a new five-pence piece given to me by my mother-in-law, to accompany her Christmas present of a Samurai sword – for the Japanese reckon it's bad luck to give a sword without a coin. The other was a big old British penny which I'd found lying head-up in the sand of the training area near the camp at Victor. It must have been dropped there by a Brit many years earlier – and if that didn't bring luck, what would? I'm not really superstitious but thought I might as well give myself any advantage I could.

Again, our mates in 'B' Squadron came to see us off, and the atmosphere became fairly emotional. This time all three Bravo patrols were deploying simultaneously, in two Chinooks. Because we were sharing our aircraft with half of Bravo Three Zero, and they were due to drop off first, we hauled our own gear to the front of the fuselage, leaving room for four guys, their kit and two Dinkies at the back. On the tailgate one of the lads said, 'Hey – I'm getting a picture of you lot,' and he took the patrol photograph which appears in the illustrations.

Earlier, we'd been joking with the loadies, saying, 'Can't you damage this fucking chopper so that it won't take off?' Unfortunately, there was nothing wrong with it – but it was so heavily laden that the pilot had to taxi it like a fixed-wing aircraft in order to get it off the ground. Then, as he had it rolling, the tail came up a bit and we lifted away.

The noise in the back was horrendous: the roar of the engines, backed by the thudding *boop, boop, boop* of the rotors, made normal conversation impossible. But a few headsets, plugged into the intercom system, hung down from the sides of the cabin and made it possible to listen to the pilots talking. When we landed to refuel at Arar, the pilot shut down his engines, and I sat there thinking, 'I hope this damn thing doesn't start up again!'

Once again we waited where we were, and no one had much to say. My mind wandered back to the occasion when, on a training exercise with the SP team, we were aboard a Puma, going in to attack a runaway coach. In the back of the heli we were all dressed up in black kit with respirators on; two guys were sitting at the open door with the fast ropes bundled up under their legs. In front of me was a young Scots fellow, and when we went into a hard turn, I put a hand on the back of his equipment, to keep him steady. He shook his shoulder to show he didn't need holding. All of a sudden the noise changed to a high-pitched screech and the padding inside the roof started to fall off. The pilot had banked round so steeply that we were looking straight down at the ground through the open door. The Scots lad began yelling, 'Get a fucking grip of me!' In a couple of seconds it was clear that the aircraft didn't have the power to pull out of its turn, and we went crashing down on to a bank-side, bounced, narrowly missed some telephone lines and smashed down into a field. On the bounce, one of the fast ropes fell out and wrapped itself round a fence; it could easily have dragged the chopper back down, but as the aircraft was rising, the rope slowly uncoiled itself.

After the final impact we all jumped off and began running after the coach, continuing the exercise. But we'd only gone about twenty metres when someone stopped, threw his respirator off and shouted, 'What the fuck are we doing? For Christ's sake, bin the training!' We all stood round laughing, partly out of relief: having narrowly escaped death, we'd still been hell-bent on chasing the target. The Puma was written off, with its whole tail section cracked away. By a miracle, when it hit the bank, the rotor blades still had room to turn, because there was a ditch at the foot of the bank. If the ditch hadn't been there, the blades would have been ripped off, and we'd probably have gone in upside-down.

This time there were no such dramas. With the refuelling complete, the Chinook's engines re-started faultlessly and off we went. By then darkness had fallen, and we'd flown for only a few minutes when the pilot came on the intercom to announce, 'Congratulations, guys, we've just crossed the border. You're now in Iraq.' I thought, 'Great! This is cool, flying three hundred kilometres into enemy territory. Nobody else is doing this. Nobody else knows we're going in.' But at the same time I was thinking, 'Jesus! This is real! This is bloody dangerous.' During my time in the SAS I'd been in some hairy situations on exercises in various parts of the world, and on operations in Northern Ireland, but nothing as dramatic as this. This was the first time I'd been to war.

To keep under the radar, we were flying only ten or twenty metres off the ground. I took my hat off to the pilots, who were prepared to go into hostile airspace so lightly armed; apart from our own weapons, the only armaments on board were the two SA 80 automatic rifles which the loadies could fire through the portholes. SA 80s are poor-quality, unreliable weapons at the best of times, prone to stoppages, and it seemed pretty tough to have to rely on them. We'd told the pilots that if we were attacked when we landed, we would handle the firefight, and bring the aircrew back with us on our escape and evasion, so all they had to do was stick with us.

The red canvas sling-seats along each wall had been pushed back to make room for the vehicles, and we sat on our bergens, squashed into any space available, each man busy with his own thoughts. A good deal of room was taken up by the extra fuel tanks – two fat black cylinders, like propane gas containers. I had my back to one of them, with one of the Land-Rovers in front of me, chained down to D-rings in the floor to stop it shifting during the flight.

In the dim light I watched my mates' faces, all preoccupied with their own thoughts. Then in my headphones I heard the pilot start shouting. A SAM site had locked on to us. With such a heavy load, no violent evasive tactics were possible; what he did was to go right down and hover only a foot or two above the desert. He had chaff, which he could fire off if necessary, to confuse incoming missiles, but I felt quite scared by the realisation that someone else was in the driving seat, and I wasn't in charge of my own destiny.

Time slowed to a crawl. We seemed to hover for an eternity, and when I looked out through one of the portholes, I was appalled to see how bright the moonlight was. The desert looked totally flat, without cover anywhere. Then after a minute or two we lifted again and carried on.

In my head I ran over the rations that I'd chosen and stowed in a sandbag. Deciding what you're going to eat for ten days ahead isn't easy. We'd done it by breaking down standard army ration packs and laying out our selection for each day on the ground – Monday, Tuesday, Wednesday and so on. I knew from experience that when you're sitting around in an OP, boredom makes you want to eat; for most of the time there's nothing else to do. But I'd resisted the temptation to overload, and restricted myself to a daily ration of one main meal, two packets of biscuits, and some fruit like pineapple or pears in syrup. The main meals were boil-in-the-bag – things like beef stew, chicken and pasta, pasta and meat balls, bacon and beans – pre-cooked and sealed in tough silver foil sachets, which you could roll up and squash down. Because we would be on hard routine, I'd gone mainly for lighter meals like pasta, which are easier to eat cold than solid meat. We'd also done some swaps with the Americans on the base, and I had one MRE (meal ready to eat) of corned beef hash to make a change. But our own boil-in-the-bag stuff was good – tasty and satisfying.

I thought wistfully of the brew-kit I'd left behind. Most of the other guys had brought theirs, because for them brewing-up is an ingrained habit; they do it automatically whenever they stop for a break, as much for social reasons as the need for refreshment. But I, not being a great tea or coffee drinker, had decided to go without.

As for personal kit, I was dressed, like the rest of the guys, in regular DPMs (disruptive pattern material combat fatigues). We'd also been issued with lightweight, sand-coloured desert smocks which – unbelievably – dated from the Second World War. I had worked my silk escape map into the waistband that held the draw-string of my trousers, and taped the twenty gold sovereigns given each of us for E & E purposes on to the inside of my belt. On my head I was wearing a German Army cap – a souvenir of my Alpine guide course – and on my feet a pair of brown Raichle Goretex-lined walking boots, with well insulated uppers and soles, which I'd also acquired in Bavaria at a cost of more than £100. On my hands I had a pair of green aviator's gloves, made of fine leather. As useful extras I had the two shamags I'd bought in Abu Dhabi. One was very light coloured, like a biscuit, and I'd made vain efforts to darken it by dyeing it in tea. The other was thicker and altogether more suitable, being oatmeal and purple, with the design favoured by the special forces of Oman.

In my right arm I was cradling my chosen weapon, a 203, which I'd fitted with a makeshift sling made of nylon para-cord. Four of the patrol had 203s, and the rest Minimis, the allocation being determined largely by the other burdens that each of us was carrying. Since the 203 weighs 10 lbs and the Minimi 16 lbs, those with less to carry had the machine-guns. I, being the patrol medic and saddled with the 12-lb medical pack, had a 203, as did Legs Lane, who had the 30-lb radio. Stan, on the other hand, who was exceptionally strong, had a Minimi. On board the Chinook we kept the rifles loaded, with bullets up the spout and safety catches on, in case of sudden action.

Each of us also had a 66 rocket launcher – a brilliantly simple, disposable American device, which you throw away after firing. In its folded state it looks like a simple tube, with the rocket pre-packed inside it; you can carry it either slung over your shoulder on a strap, or, as I had mine, laid across the top of my bergen, under the flap. When the time comes to fire, all you have to do is pull out the second half of the tube to make a longer barrel, flip up the sight and pull the trigger.

As the chopper clattered on through the night, I was trying to think ahead, mainly about E & E. We should have had written orders, and a definite plan, but all that seemed to have been bypassed in the rush, and in the end everything had been word of mouth. The regiment's official line was that if the patrol was compromised, we should head back towards Saudi Arabia. But since Saudi would be nearly 300 kilometres off, and the Syrian border was only 130 kilometres to the west, we had already decided that if things went tits-up, we'd leg it for Syria (Stan had asked the pilots to measure the distance on their map, so that we knew exactly). That would make obvious sense – especially as the Syrians had publicly shown their defiance of Saddam Hussein by announcing that if they picked up downed aircrew from any of the allied nations, they would hand them back to the coalition forces.

Talking it over at Al Jouf, we reckoned that if we went all-out in light order, jogging and running, jogging and running, we could make the border in two nights. I'd even considered packing a set of shorts, in case we had to go for it. What we had failed to take into consideration was the lack of water; you can't jog carrying full jerricans, and there was no other source around. Nor had we bargained for the cold.

Five minutes out from Bravo One Zero's location, the loadie gave a thumbs-up signal. I unshackled the chain nearest to me, and smelt rather than heard the Land-Rover engine start up. One member of the other patrol, Paul, was wearing a single glove – for a special reason. Two days earlier he'd burnt the palm of his hand on a metal mug while making tea, raising a blister the size of a fried egg. The only treatment possible was to take the fluid out, apply some Flammazine ointment, and keep the wound clean. Paul wouldn't let the OC or the SSM see it, because if he had, he'd have been taken off the patrol. I found him holding his hand in a bucket of cold water, and as I dressed the burn for him, I said, 'Paul, you're an idiot. Just step down and let someone else go.' 'Not a chance,' he replied. 'I'm going.'

With two Land-Rover engines running, the back of the Chinook filled with choking diesel fumes. I began to think, 'I wish to hell they'd get out of here.' Then two fingers from the loadie indicated 'Two minutes to landing.' Then one minute. We felt the helicopter decelerate and settle into a landing attitude. All at once, with a bump, we were on the ground. The tailgate went down, the vehicles rolled, and the guys hustled out into the night. That was a tense moment, because it was perfectly possible that enemy were waiting to receive us. The rest of us were at the ready: we had our webbing on and weapons in hand. If the chopper had come under fire, we'd have burst out and gone to ground. But nothing happened. The tailgate came up. With some of the weight gone, the heli made a normal take-off, and we were away again.

Twenty minutes later it was our turn. We grabbed our own kit and dragged it to the edge of the tailgate. Soon the loadie gave us five fingers, then two. We pulled on goggles to keep flying sand and grit out of our eyes. As the chopper hit the deck, the tailgate went down. Cold air and dust came screaming in; particles bombarded my face, but thanks to the goggles I could still see. We tumbled out, dragging our kit. Above us was a horrendous sight. Two enormous blue fluorescent lights seemed to be blazing above the aircraft. For a moment I couldn't think what the hell was happening. Had we been caught by an Iraqi searchlight? I felt appalled that the illumination must be showing up for miles around. Then I realised that the downdraught from the rotors was raising a storm of grit, and as the grains hit the whirling blades they lit up with a bright blue glow. I thought, 'Bloody hell! Somebody's bound to see this.' The noise was terrible, too: the Chinook makes a dreadfully distinctive clatter – a *doo, doo, doo, doo* from the blades, backed by the piercing whistle of the engine exhaust.

While the racket still covered us, the guys with machine-guns snapped their belted magazines into place. Then in a few more seconds the heli lifted away into the night and was gone.

The contrast was extraordinary. For the last couple of hours we'd been in deafening noise. Now suddenly we were thrown into silence. The air was still, the night clear. We lay facing outwards in a circle on the desert floor; as the sound of the engines died into the distance, we heard dogs barking not far off to the east. Obviously they were round some building – and *they'd* heard us if nobody else had.

After the stink of exhaust in the back of the chopper, the air smelt incredibly fresh and sterile. There was no trace of any plant or animal scent. That clarity alone told us we were in the middle of a barren wilderness. With our goggles off, we had all too good a view of our surroundings. We'd landed in the middle of a dry wadi or river bed, maybe 200 metres wide. Scattered clouds were sailing across the moon, and in the clear intervals its light was very bright. It was brighter than I'd expected – altogether too bright. As our eyes adjusted, we could see that the wadi had walls five or ten metres high, apparently with a level plain above them on either side.

The MSR was somewhere up ahead of us, to the north, running roughly east and west across our front. The ground beneath us was dead flat, and consisted of hard-baked clay, but we found we were lying right between a set of tracks made by a vehicle whose tyres had sunk into the dry mud. I realised that the mud was only an inch or two deep, and that under it lay solid rock. There was no loose material with which to fill our sand bags.

For what seemed an age Andy just lay there, doing nothing. It's always essential to spend time letting your eyes adjust to night vision, but this was getting ridiculous. It had immediately occurred to me that if any Arabs had seen the chopper, they'd already be running or driving across the flats towards the lip of the wadi without us being able to see them. I had visions of people coming from all directions and suddenly appearing on the rim, against the stars.

Looking at Andy, I thought he seemed semi-stunned. 'For fuck's sake,' I whispered, 'let's get some guns on to the high ground.' So we sent out two lads, one on either side, to go up the wadi walls and keep a lookout.

Gradually the barking of dogs died away and left us in total silence. Our most urgent need was to get our kit out of sight, and we began dragging or humping it across into the shadow of the moonlight cast by the right-hand or eastern wall. Everything was black and grey, like in an old film. From the middle of the wadi that shadow looked solid and deep – a good place in which to hide. But when we reached it, we found it was an illusion. There was no cover of any kind, and in the daylight the whole river bed would be dangerously open.

In heaving and dragging our kit, we were inevitably leaving marks in the baked mud of the wadi floor. But it wasn't long before we realised we were much deeper in the shit than that. From our study of satellite imagery, we had expected the sides of the wadi to be made of sand. Far from it. They were slabs of rock, some smooth, some crumbling, with a jumble of loose lumps at the bottom. There was hardly a grain of sand in the whole area. We were on bedrock. Training in the dunes of the Gulf, we had built beautiful OPs with the greatest of ease, digging into the sand and filling as many bags as we needed. Here, without sand, our bags were useless, and we couldn't dig an inch.

One urgent necessity was to find out exactly where we were. So Mark got out the Magellan and plotted our position to within a few yards. Then we pulled in our two flanking guys, who reported that the desert on either side of the wadi ran away level in flat plains, without a stitch of cover.

Andy went forward with Mark to recce the ground ahead. As the rest of us lay waiting for them to return, we began to realise how cold it was. The wind bit through our DPMs and smocks, which were far too light for the job, in both weight and colour. They gave very little protection against the cold, and were such a pale sandy colour that they shone like beacons in the moonlight. Under mine I was also wearing a dark-green Helly Hansen sweater, but the combination was nothing like enough for the temperature, which can't have been more than a degree or two above freezing. Besides, the wind was producing a high chill-factor. Way down at Victor, several hundred miles further south, a good deal further south, the nights had been warm and the days hot enough to make us sweat. Nobody had thought to warn us that things would be different up here.

The dogs started barking again. It was hard to tell what had set them off this time – could they hear us, or was our scent carrying on the wind? We reckoned they were no more than four or five hundred metres away. That figured, because the satellite photos had shown irrigated fields and habitations within about that distance of our drop-off point. We just hoped they didn't come across to suss out what was disturbing them.

In twenty minutes Andy and Mark were back. 'Right,' Andy whispered, 'We'll head up here. Get forward up the wadi.'

Four of the guys struggled into their bergens and walked forward about 300 metres, then went to ground. We watched them lumber off like pale-coloured bears, their smocks glowing in the moonlight. As soon as they were settled, the rest of us moved up to join them. Then the first four went back and picked up the rest of their kit, including the jerricans, which were tied together in pairs with tape. Once they'd joined us, we went back – and so it continued for most of the night: shuttling forward, back, forward, back. It was knackering work, but I remember at one point seeing Stan stand up with his bergen on, belt-kit and all, and put two of the jerricans on his shoulders. Off he went, walking upright, with his Minimi held correctly in front of him – an amazing sight. I knew he was a strong guy, but this was incredible.

By 0500 we had moved about two kilometres to the north, and

were in the area selected for the OP. The sky in the east was already beginning to lighten. We were still in the wadi, and the walls were still bare rock, so that there was no chance of digging it. We sat around for a minute or two, discussing what to do. We couldn't stay where we were, because the ground was far too open. Then Andy went on round a corner with Stan and found that the wadi came to a dead end in a cul-de-sac no bigger than a good-sized room. The walls were fairly steep, but on the left-hand side, as we faced north, one massive slab of rock had fallen off the side of the ravine. The detached lump was about seven feet high, and lay a couple of feet clear of the wall, with a second, smaller rock near its foot, making some natural shelter. A few feet farther to the south there was an overhang going back under the wall. The floor was of hard-baked clay, with loose rocks and some stunted thorn bushes scattered about.

It wasn't a great hiding place, but it was the best we could find. So we went in and packed away all the kit for the OP, the poles and nets, because they were no use to us in this rock desert. We put the jerricans at the bottom, with the thermal sheets, cam nets and empty sandbags on top, to deaden any noise. Some of us sat on the cans, a couple tucked in underneath the overhang, and the rest settled around the rocks at various places. If we wanted to shift about, we went at a crouch or on hands and knees, but all movement was kept to a minimum.

The end of the wadi covered us from the north – the direction of the MSR – and we were reasonably well protected by the sides; but to our rear we were dangerously exposed. If anyone came up the river bed, following our tracks, they'd be bound to walk or drive right on top of us. 'This is no bloody good,' somebody muttered. 'If it looks bad in the daylight, we'll have to consider getting on the phone and getting relocated.'

Before dawn, we put out two claymore mines, about 50 metres down the wadi, with wires running back to our position, so that we could blow up anybody who approached along the foot of the eastern wall.

Within the patrol, Vince had been nominated as second-in-command, so if anything happened to Andy, he should in theory take over. Once we were on the ground, however, I found that I was emerging as more positive than him, and keener to take decisions. Apart from this, there was no definite command structure.

At first light Andy and I crept carefully up a small channel and lay at the top of the bank for a look around. Daybreak revealed that flat, grey-brown plains stretched away into the distance to the east and west. But there, straight ahead, only a couple of hundred metres away, was the MSR, running right and left across our front on a big embankment, like a long ridge. To the left, one harmless-looking civilian truck was parked on the edge of the highway; it had an open back and slatted sides, as if it was used for carrying animals. One or two other lorries rumbled along the road, but on the high ground to our right, another couple of hundred metres away, was something much more sinister: an anti-aircraft position. Through our binoculars we could see the twin barrels of guns, which we identified from our manual as SA 60s, poking up above the emplacement, and at least two Iraqis moving about.

The sight gave us a nasty jolt: to see those guns so close to us was bloody frightening, because they could only have been placed there to protect some installation from air-attack, and they showed that we were right on the edge of an enemy position. We knew we were going to have to be extremely careful.

We came back down and let the rest of the guys know that there were enemy within 400 metres of us. In the shelter of the wadi we heard the occasional vehicle go along the road, but we kept our heads down while we conferred in whispers about what to do. Clearly it was too dangerous to spend any length of time where we were, and the vital necessity was to get a message through to base, asking for a relocation or a return.

The trouble was, the 319 radio did not seem to be working. It should have been possible for us to communicate instantly with Forest Hero, the base station in Cyprus, and from there messages should have been back in Al Jouf within a couple of minutes. Any message from us would be passed straight to the CO or the Ops officer, whatever the time of day or night. But although Legs patiently tried different frequencies and experimented with various aerial arrays, he could not evoke any response. What we didn't realise till much later was that we'd been given the wrong frequencies – so Legs sat there, trying and trying to get through, assuming that this was one of those days (which you often get) when atmosphere conditions are bad, and radios just don't work. For the moment there was no serious worry, because we knew that as a fall-back we had the Lost Comms procedure whereby, if we had not come on air within forty-eight hours, a helicopter would automatically return, either bringing us a new radio set or armed with a plan to shift us elsewhere.

We took turns to go on stag, while the others had a meal or a sleep. We did an hour's guard-duty each, holding the clackers for detonating the claymores and watching the wadi. The rest of the guys, having had a sleepless night, were glad to get their heads down. It was so cold that several of them struggled into their NBC suits and lay around in them. We were all more or less hidden, and there was a good chance that if we kept still, even a man looking up the wadi from a distance would not have seen us.

Then, late in the afternoon, we heard voices. A boy of twelve or thirteen, his voice just breaking, began calling out, and a man answered him. Peering cautiously over the western rim, we saw the boy and the man – maybe his father – driving a herd of goats. They were walking across the plain, nearly parallel to the course of the wadi, but heading in towards us as they moved northwards, and calling the goats on as they went. The truck with slatted sides was still parked the far side of the MSR, so it looked as if the goatherds had come out to check their flock, or were about to load the animals up.

Either way, they were too close to us for comfort. We grabbed our weapons and lay like stones, hardly breathing, every man with a round up the spout. From the jingling of the goat bells and the voices, we reckoned the flock passed within fifty metres of our hiding place. As the sounds faded into the distance, we kept still, listening. Half an hour later, we crept to the top of the bank again to check what was happening: the truck had disappeared, and there was no sign of the goats – but where they had gone, we couldn't tell.

This place was decidedly bad news. There was so much activity in the area that it could only be a matter of time before we were compromised. Legs, cool as ever and lying in a hollow, redoubled his efforts to get through on the radio. Mark went over to help him, and the pair of them worked on the set, switching frequencies and rigging different aerials. Once you get through to base, you always feel better – at least you have contact. But now there was no response, and people began to grow apprehensive.

We were also getting frozen. At one point Andy came up to me and said banteringly, 'I hope your feet are cold.'

'Like fucking ice,' I told him.

'Good,' he said, 'I'm pleased to hear that – with those bloody boots on.'

I had the best boots of anyone in the patrol. One of the guys had ordinary army boots, and a couple were wearing jungle boots. Whatever we had, our feet were numb. Oddly enough, I didn't feel hungry, and all I ate during the day was a bar of chocolate and a packet of biscuits.

As soon as it got dark, we put out a recce party; Andy, Mark, Stan and Dinger decided to take a look round.

'We'll leave in this direction,' Andy briefed the rest of us in whispers, 'and we'll come back in the same way. The pass number's the sum of nine. We shouldn't be more than three or four hours. As we come in, the first man will walk down with his arms extended and his weapon held out sideways in his right hand.'

If the rest of us heard a contact, he went on, we were to stand-to, wait five or six minutes for the recce group to come through our position, and put fire down on anyone following them. If our own four guys didn't appear, we were to make for the drop-off point, and they would join us there.

They left at 2300, hoping that by then all the natives would have got their heads down. With the recce party gone, the rest of us took turns to do an hour's stag. Not a sound broke the silence; the night was utterly still, but not nearly so light as the one before, because the sky was full of clouds.

In the event, the recce party returned safely at 0330. They came back to the wadi from the agreed direction, but they were never challenged, because Vince, who was on stag, had fallen asleep. I happened to be awake and saw their black figures appear on top of the bank, against the sky. A moment later Andy was bollocking Vince for not being alert.

The recce group had found that the MSR was not a metalled road but a series of dirt tracks running parallel through the desert, and spread out across nearly a kilometre. They'd also discovered a single white post standing in the ground, about 300 metres from the LUP, but they could not make out what it was marking. Then they'd checked out a little tented encampment beyond the spot on which the lorry had been parked. It was a second AA position, with a few vehicles parked round it. When dogs started barking, they pulled off and moved round to see if they could find mounds or ditches or anything marking a fibre-optic line, but there was no sign of one. They also looked for a better position for us to move into – but, again, with no luck.

For what was left of the night they got their heads down, and the rest of us stagged on again. In the morning we at least felt confident that we had got in without anyone knowing we were there, but we had decided that it was too dicey to stay; there were too many people about, and we were too close to the site that the AA guns were guarding.

When I crawled round to where Andy and Dinger were sitting, I found them composing a message.

'What are we going to do?' I asked.

'We're asking for permission to attack the AA position.'

'What the hell's the use of that?'

'We might as well do something while we're here. Half of us'll sneak up the back and take the position out while the rest of you guard the kit here. Once it goes noisy, you get on the radio and call in the chopper to lift us out.'

As I listened, I was thinking, 'This isn't our mission. If we start messing around, they'll get annoyed back at RHQ.' In fact they'd get infuriated; to do something as reckless as that, outside our remit, would constitute a serious offence in regimental terms. It was pretty obvious that the installation which the AA positions were guarding must be manned by a fair-sized force of regular army or militia. Whatever the outcome of an attack, we would have to hustle back to the drop-off point wearing our bergens. With the sandbags and OP kit removed, their weight had come down to about 100 lbs each, so that they were more manageable – but a sudden pull-out such as Andy had outlined would mean leaving all the OP gear behind and giving away what we'd been up to. Until that moment we'd taken great trouble to leave no trace of our presence, pissing into a jerrican and shitting into plastic bags which, in an orderly withdrawal, we would take with us.

Another serious objection to the plan was the erratic behaviour of our radio. As far as we could tell, there was nothing wrong with it, but if we couldn't get through to base within the next few hours, we would have serious problems.

For the moment I didn't say anything. Instead, I went back and sat down beside Vince. When I told him what the others were planning, his eyes bugged out like a frog's.

Then, after half an hour, I decided, 'Ah, bollocks. We can't do this.' So I went back round the corner and told Andy it wasn't on. 'If there's something big there,' I told him, 'we're going to end up in the shit. Especially if that chopper doesn't come and get us. We're banking everything on that. If we can't raise base on the radio, or the heli can't get in, we're going to be screwed. Judging from what's happened so far, our comms are screwed anyway, so we're not going to get through.'

Dinger said, 'Yeah – you're probably right. We'll cancel that one.'

'And besides,' I told him, 'it isn't our mission to go and take out an AA position. Our mission's here, in the OP. If we can't stay here, we'd better go back.'

The others continued to fart around, and it wasn't until 1400 that they decided to drop the idea of attacking the AA site and go for a relocation. Having spent hours encoding a long message about the plan, they began to make up a new signal. But we still couldn't get through on the radio; by then the ionosphere had dropped, and contact was impossible. We also tried using our Satcom telephone. We didn't want to speak for long on it, because we'd been told that it threw off an enormous electronic splash, and that any call which lasted more than twenty seconds was liable to be picked up by direction-finding apparatus. So we switched the set to listening-wait, hoping to hear a call from base. Then occasionally we would come up on the call-sign with a quick request for a comms check: 'Hello Zero Alpha, this is Bravo Two Zero, radio check, over' – but nothing happened.

It looked as though we were going to have to rely on our Lost Comms procedure. That would mean pulling back down the wadi to the drop-off point, and being there when the chopper came in at midnight. Naturally we hoped that it would lift us out to somewhere more favourable, but, more likely, it would bring us a new radio: the CO would be advised that our set had gone U/S, and he would naturally want us to continue our mission.

Either way, after dark the whole patrol was going to move back, and we sat there thinking what a pain in the arse it would be to walk that distance humping our kit, and then hump it all the way back, just to pick up a new radio. We weren't looking forward to making the effort.

Then, about four in the afternoon, everything went to ratshit. Once again we heard the herder boy calling his bloody goats. This time he sounded closer, and coming directly for us. I'd been talking to Andy and Dinger about the radio, and I was under the overhang when the boy started shouting, from a point directly above my head, but some way out behind me. The three of us lay rigidly still – but when I looked across at Vince, on the other side of the rock, he was craning his head to see if he could spot the boy. Mouthing at him furiously, and giving tiny, frantic movements of our fingers, we tried to make him keep his head down.

If we'd all stayed still, we might have been OK. Nine times out of ten, if hidden people don't move, they get away with it. What betrays them is shape, shadow, shine, and above all movement. It's the same with birds and animals in a wood: as long as they keep still, you don't see them, but the instant one moves, that's it.

It was Vince who moved. At the time he didn't admit it, but later he came clean. Overcome by the temptation to see what was happening, he eased his head up until the boy caught sight of him.

At the time we weren't sure what had happened. All we knew was that the shouting stopped. There was no particular cry of alarm, but the sudden silence itself was ominous. It was pretty obvious that the boy had run off. I crawled round to Vince and hissed, 'Did he see you?'

'No, no, no,' he answered. 'We're OK.'

I left it at that, but I didn't believe him. Things were getting scary: there wasn't exactly a panic, but we knew we were about to be rumbled. I felt fear starting up in my stomach. Legs was still at the radio, trying to get through. 'What's happening?' I demanded.

'I'm trying,' he said. 'I'm trying.'

'Have you been on the guard net?' I asked him.

'No.'

'Well, get on the guard net and start tapping Morse.'

The guard net sends out new frequencies, and I knew that if we came up on it, we would compromise its entire operation for the current twenty-four-hour period. But in this emergency such a procedure was justified. Legs started working on the text for a burst transmission. 'High possibility compromise. Request relocation or expel,' his message read; but just as he was tapping it in, we heard the roar of a heavy engine and the squealing and grinding of what we thought were tank-tracks, approaching up the wadi.

That was when the adrenaline started to flow. There wasn't any more creeping about. We were all buzzing round. Wild thoughts raced through my mind: the damage a tank could do with one round into the end of the wadi – it would destroy us all. There's a form of anti-personnel round like a huge shotgun; if they whipped one of them up there, that was us finished.

'Get the 66s open,' somebody shouted, and we cocked our rocket launchers. The guys had spread out round the end of the wadi, lying behind whatever cover they could find. Dinger chose that moment to light up one of his filthy, home-rolled fags, amid strong protests.

There we were, waiting for this tank to come into view round the corner. Every second the squealing and grinding got louder. We were stuck, pinned like rats in the dead-end of the ravine. We couldn't tell what else might be coming at us over the flat ground above. The chances were that the Iraqis were deploying behind us, too; even at the moment, they were probably advancing on our position. A couple of hand grenades tossed over the edge would make a nice mess of us. Even so, if the tank came into view and levelled its gun on us, we'd have no option but to run up on to the plain, and chance it with the AA positions on the high ground.

By then it was 1700 hours, but still full daylight. Someone said, 'Let's get some water down our necks, fellers,' and everyone started drinking, because we knew that if we had to run for it, we'd need the liquid inside us. Other guys began frantically repacking their kit, pulling off the warm jackets they'd been wearing and stuffing them into their bergens. A couple of the lads struggled out of their NBC suits and stowed them.

No one gave any orders about what to do. We just decided

that if a tank or armoured personnel carrier came round the corner, we'd try to take it out, and then go past it down the wadi, using the dry watercourse as our escape-route. The rockets wouldn't have been much use against a tank, but they might have disabled it by blowing off a track.

So there we were, getting water down our necks and having something to eat. Then I looked round at the tail ends of the rocket launchers in front of me and said, 'Hey, fellers – watch the fucking back-blast on these things. I don't want my face burned.' When a 66 is fired, the danger area behind the tube extends for twenty metres. There was silence for a minute. Then, suddenly, out of fear and tension, everyone started laughing. They couldn't stop. I thought, 'This is bloody ridiculous. There's a tank coming round the corner, and here we all are, giggling like schoolgirls.'

Dinger pointed at my German Army cap and shouted, 'Hey, Chris, you look like Rommel.'

'Fuck off, Dinger,' I yelled back. He was dragging desperately on his fag. 'Put that fucking thing out!'

'Ah – fuck the SOPs,' he said, and everyone laughed some more.

I checked my 203 magazines again, tapping them on the bottom to make sure the lip was properly engaged in the breech. I had the mags taped together in pairs, head to toe, so that I could load the second instantly by turning the empty one upside down. Each could hold thirty rounds, but I'd only loaded them with twenty-eight, to leave the springs a bit looser and cut down the chance of a stoppage. The spares were in my left-hand lower pouch.

Then suddenly round the corner came . . . not a tank, but a yellow bulldozer. The driver had the blade high up in front of him, obviously using it as a shield; he looked like an Arab, wearing a green parka with the hood up. We all kept still, lying or crouching in firing positions, but we knew the man had seen us. He was only 150 metres away when he stopped, stared, and reversed out of sight before trying to turn round. Obviously a local, he must have known that the wadi came to a dead-end, and his only purpose in coming up it had been to find out who or what was in there. We held our breath as the squealing and grinding gradually died away.

51

For a minute or two we felt more relief than anything else. Then it was, 'Get the radio away, Legs,' and everyone was saying, 'We've got to go. We've got to go.' Dinger lit another fag and sucked on it like a dying man. Now we felt certain that the local militia must be deploying behind us, and one or two of the lads were being a bit slow, so it was 'Get a fucking move on' all round. We'd already decided to ditch the surplus kit we couldn't carry, but we pulled our bergens on and were ready for the off. As we were about to leave, I called, 'Get your shamags round your heads.' So we all wrapped our heads in shawls, in case we could bluff our way and pass as Arab soldiers, even for a few minutes.

As soon as Legs was ready, we started walking southwards, down the wadi, towards our emergency rendezvous point. Finding myself at the front, I led the patrol out. Call it arrogance, if you like, but I didn't trust anyone else to go first.

Dusk was already coming on, and I was hoping we could reach the drop-off point, less than two kilometres to the south, and put down enough fire to defend ourselves until dark fell – and then we'd have to wait until the chopper came in.

Moving out, I kept close in to the left-hand wall of the wadi, because that was the steepest, and in the lee of it we were out of sight of the AA guns. When I turned round, I found that the guys had opened up to a tactical spacing of maybe twenty metres between each; but I was thinking, 'If we have a nonsense here, we want to be tight together.' So I yelled back, 'Close up!'

The bulldozer had gone out of sight, but we were moving towards where we'd last seen it. All too soon the wadi began to flatten out, and on our left a long slope ran up to the plain above. As we came clear of the steep part of the wadi wall, I suddenly saw two Arabs on the high ground above us, guns down by their sides. They were barely 200 metres away, and were standing motionless. There was something oddly inert about their appearance; they showed no surprise and did not move as we walked into their view. Both were wearing dark overcoats on top of their dishdashes (native cotton robes), which reached down to their ankles. Also they had red-and-white shamags done up on top of their heads like turbans. I reckoned they were civilians or possibly militia.

'It's that sodding boy,' I said to myself. 'He's run like hell and tipped them off.'

'Close up!' I yelled again, because it was obvious the shit was going to go down. Next behind me was Bob Consiglio, and I shouted back to him, 'Fucking hurry! Catch up!'

We kept going. But the two Iraqis began to parallel us, moving forward. In case anybody hadn't seen them, I called back, 'We've got two on the high ground to the left, and they're walking down. Keep going.'

Behind me everyone started cursing. The tension in the patrol was electric. I felt fear rising in my chest. Afterwards, I realised that the two Iraqis were waiting for reinforcements to come up; also, they were probably a bit confused, not knowing who the hell we were. But at the time I was wondering if we could outrun them, or lose them somehow, without starting a firefight.

Then I blew it in a big way. I thought, 'I'm going to try the double bluff here,' and I waved at them. Unfortunately I did it with my left hand, which to an Arab is the ultimate insult – your left hand being the one you wipe your arse with. The reaction was instantaneous: one of them brought up his weapon and opened fire. Suddenly he was putting rounds down on us. We swung round and put a couple of short bursts back at them. Both dropped on to one knee to continue firing. As I stood there, I saw Vince take off down the wadi. In spite of the danger, there was something ridiculous about his gait: a pair of legs, going like the clappers under a bergen, and not making much progress either.

'Stay together!' I yelled. 'Slow down!' We began to run, turning to fire aimed bursts. The secret is to keep them short – no more than two or three rounds at a time. Otherwise the recoil makes the weapon drift up, and the rounds go high. We ran and fired, ran and fired.

Within seconds a tipper truck with metal sides screeched to a halt beside the two Arabs, and eight or ten guys spilled out of it. Stan also saw an armoured car carrying a .50 machine-gun pull up. Somehow I never saw that; it may have been behind a mound from where I was standing. Some of the Iraqis began firing from the back of the truck, others from positions behind it.

It looked as though there were about a dozen altogether. They had automatic rifles – almost certainly Russian AK 47s – and at least one heavy machine-gun. But their fire was inaccurate, and we could cope with them. In my mind they weren't the real threat. What worried me much more was the thought that a bigger force was probably driving round ahead of us, out of sight, to cut off our retreat.

Looking back, I found that our guys were running across the open ground, struggling under the weight of their bergens. Even though the packs weren't as heavy as before, trying to run with them was a nightmare. At one moment the patrol seemed to converge into a tight group, then we spread out again, some running, others taking turns to stop, turn and put down rounds, then run again.

If anyone says he's not frightened in a firefight, I don't believe him. I was shit scared, and so was everyone else. I know the SAS has a high reputation, but the guys are not superhuman: they may have enormous courage, but they are subject to the same fear as anyone else. The Regiment's strength lies in the fact that its members are highly trained to control their fear and respond positively to whatever threat they are facing.

In this contact, panic threatened. The flow of adrenaline was fearsome: you can do a lot when someone's shooting at you. But then you get desperate for breath, and your chest and stomach start to burn. On we went, legging it up the slope now, swivelling, shooting at the enemy as they ran back and forth between vehicles. Three times I saw men go down when I fired. One went down behind a mound and never came up. Two others rolled over as they were running. At one point there was a hell of an explosion from one of the vehicles.

Green tracer started coming across, whizzing past our heads. I could hear the odd *doof!*, then *crack!*, then *prooh!*. We were right in the open, like ducks in the water, with all this shit coming in. Whenever one of us stopped to turn and fire, the enemy seemed to concentrate on him, and we could see the tracer close in on the stationary target.

Luckily the Iraqis seemed to have the intention of coming after us. Rather than dropping down into the wadi, and putting themselves at a disadvantage, they preferred to stick to the high ground. As the tracer flew, I got out my TACBE, pressed the tit, and began screaming into it, 'TURBO! TURBO! This is Bravo Two Zero. CONTACT! CONTACT!' Andy was doing the same. He, I and one of the other guys had TACBEs set to American frequencies, so that we could speak to American pilots. The other sets were on British frequencies. Every one of them should have produced an answer within seconds. Every one of us expected to hear a voice come back out of the air – but nothing happened.

'My TACBE's fucked!' I yelled to Andy.

'Can't get through on mine, either.'

'Keep trying.'

Then somebody shouted, 'I'm ditching my fucking bergen!' Someone else yelled, 'You're fucking right! I am too!' Next second, I was doing it myself, fighting to get the straps off my shoulders. Then I was kneeling by the pack, struggling with the clips on the top flap to free my 66. My lungs and heart were bursting, my whole body heaving and shaking. I said to myself, 'Slow down, slow down – or you're done for.'

I got one clip undone. Just as I reached my hand towards the other, the thing exploded in pieces, hit by a .50 bullet. I never felt anything – no wind or burn – but if my hand had been four or five inches farther forward I would have lost it. The heavy round put the bergen down flat beside me. I leapt on it, grabbed the 66, whipped it over my shoulder, and started off again. Ahead of me to the right I saw big splashes of soil or rock coming up. I thought, 'Fucking mortars! Now they're firing mortars, and some dickhead has failed to take the pins out of the shells.' That's what it looked like: as if the Iraqis were forgetting to pull out the safety pins from their mortar rounds, so that the bombs were merely kicking up dirt and rock, rather than exploding. What had happened, in fact, was that the AA position had opened up on us, and rounds from those things were coming across as well.

By now we were walking. We couldn't run uphill any more. I remember Legs being just ahead of me, in the middle. But as I moved away from my bergen, I was thinking, 'What is there in there that I should have?' Then I remembered: it was the medic pack. 'Fuck the medic pack!' I shouted to no one in particular. When I'd gone about twenty metres from the bergen I said to Legs, 'Have you got the radio?'

'No,' he gasped. 'I had to leave it.'

'Fuck it,' I said. 'Keep going.' But then, suddenly, I thought, 'Jesus! My hip flask! The hip flask that Jan gave me for Christmas. Bloody hell – I'm not leaving *that*. The rest of the stuff is military kit, but that's mine.'

I don't know what happened. The sensible thing would have been to leave it behind. But something clicked, and without hesitation I ran back down the slope. As I reached the bergen, I thought, 'You idiot – you're going to get shot now.' I bent down, my back to the Iraqis, and I was thinking, 'You're not going to be walking far at all, because there's going to be a round come through you any second.' I imagined parts of my chest hurtling out in front of me, and wondered what they would look like. Would my clothes tear apart, as in a movie, and bits of flesh and bone fly out? But I stuck my hand into the top of the pack, found the flask, brought it out, stuffed it into a trouser pocket and started forward again.

By then I was finding it hard to walk. My breath was roaring in my throat. I had the sensation of suffocation. Never in training had I pushed myself so hard. I seemed to be going through the movements of breathing but getting no oxygen in. Yet fear was driving me on.

Then we were probably out of range, too far to have any real chance of dropping more of the Iraqis; but the occasional guy would still turn, put rounds down, and look to see where his mates were. The whole scene was becoming surreal. People didn't seem to be heading in any particular direction; they were weaving back and forth in front of each other, like eddies in a stream. I remember seeing Bob, who was behind me and lower down, throwing a couple of white phosphorus grenades to get some smoke up, and thinking, 'You brave bastard!'

I looked at Legs, and saw tracer going across the top of his head. Knowing that tracer flies higher than normal rounds, I couldn't understand how the other stuff wasn't hitting him. I thought, 'He's going to get it here.' Then I wondered if the Iraqis were firing all tracer, instead of one round in five, as we would. Then the stuff was coming past *us*. Andy and I were walking up together, and tracer was flying between us, rounds right between the pair of us.

At last we got over the top, into dead ground, and collapsed on to the deck. Andy gasped, 'Fucking hell! I don't know how we managed that.'

'Nor do I,' I said. 'But look at this – at least I got my flask back.'

'Where was it?'

'In my bergen. I had to go back for it.'

'Christ!'

I unscrewed the top, took a swig of whisky, which was six-teen-year-old Lagavulin, and handed it to him.

'Jesus!' he gasped, as he felt the impact of the spirit.

For a few seconds we lay there, trying to get our breath, and when we stood up again to see where the guys were, we were amazed to find everyone in one piece. I'd thought we must have lost two or three – but they all appeared and came round, just like that, nobody so much as touched. At the very least I'd been expecting to have to dress wounds – although, with the medical pack gone, there was very little I could have done except stuff holes with bandages.

Everybody was talking, but I can't remember what they said. It took us only a few seconds to reach a group decision. If our Lost Comms procedure worked, the Chinook would come in to the drop-off point at midnight; but now that we'd stirred up such a hornets' nest, and the Iraqis knew we were in the area, the chances were that they'd ambush the helicopter and shoot it down. We decided it was safer to make for the Syrian border. First, though, we'd head south and put in a dog's leg, as a feint, to throw the Iraqis off our track.

'Right,' I called, 'let's go.' Without consciously trying to take command, but wanting out of this bloody place, I led off, with Andy behind me and the rest in line. By then, we thought, we were out of range of the Arabs' original position, but some of them had worked their way round on to a closer ridge, and as we came up out of the depression they opened up again. Also, we were back in view of the anti-aircraft gunners, who resumed firing. Some rounds were going *boosh* past us, others landing ten or fifteen metres away – but we weren't interested; we just kept walking like mad. Then the vehicle with the .50 came up on to a crest and started cracking rounds over us again from a range of 400 or 500 metres, but luckily for us the light was dying, and the rounds were going far too high.

So we set off, and walked for our lives into the gathering night.

Chapter Three

Down To Two

Until we cleared the second long valley, the occasional AA round was still falling in. Some burst in the air with a puff of black smoke and a crack, and others hit the ground. Then we were in the clear, out on the barren gravel plains, and we headed due south, marching as fast as we could in single file. Every now and then we'd shout to Mark to get a fix, and he'd switch on his Magellan and hold it up until it locked on to a satellite. After a couple of minutes, he'd call, 'I've got one,' and the guys would go to ground while Andy and I closed up to look at the map and check our position. Mark would read off the coordinates from his little illuminated screen, look down at the map and say, 'OK, we're just there' – and we'd know our position, within ten feet or so. Encouraged by such precision navigating, we'd carry on.

It was a great shock to us that we seemed to have been abandoned by our own people. It's an unwritten rule of the Regiment that if guys need help, their mates come and get them. Wherever you are, even in the shittiest area in the world, if you get into a firefight and give a shout on the radio, they'll come and find you. Now we'd yelled ourselves hoarse on radios and TACBEs, and there had been no result. The disappointment was horrendous. When I'd got out my TACBE, I'd thought, 'This is my last resort,' and I'd fully expected to hear an AWACS pilot answer my call; I had no doubt that he'd have half the Regiment coming out in search of us. What we could not have known at the time was that the nearest AWACS aircraft was 500 kilometres to the east – about four times the maximum range of the TACBEs – and that we had been given the wrong radio frequencies, so that none of our calls on the 319 had gone through unscrambled.

Now, deprived of our food, water, warm clothes and other essential kit, we set our faces to the south. After half an hour someone shouted, 'We're getting followed up!' Looking back, we saw the lights of a vehicle. At first we couldn't tell whether or not it was moving, but then through Vince's night-sight we made out that it was definitely coming after us. In some places the desert was completely flat, with no features of any kind, and obviously the vehicle could make good speed across those pancake areas; but luckily for us there were also a lot of wadis, in which the going was rough and the driver had to crawl. There was no way he could still see us – the night was too dark for that – but he knew the line we'd taken down the first wadi, and he was driving on the bearing he had seen us follow, 180 degrees.

The ground varied from hard-baked clay to gravel and loose rock, on which our boots inevitably made a crunching sound. There was also the rustle of clothes and pouches rubbing on each other. We could have been quieter if we'd gone slowly, but the paramount need was for speed, and I pressed on as fast as I could in spite of the noise, with the other guys close behind, at intervals of no more than two metres between each man. All the time I was thinking that, because the AA positions we'd seen were obviously guarding something, the military there would radio ahead, organising searchers to come round in front and cut us off. We already knew that although the desert seemed so empty there were outposts dotted all over it, and we could have walked on to a position at any moment. There was also the risk of stumbling into a bedouin encampment.

After an hour, and maybe eight or nine kilometres, we stopped and came together in a group. Dinger took off his duvet jacket and started covering it with rocks.

'What the hell are you doing?' I asked.

'I'm ditching this fucker. It's far too hot.'

'Keep the damn thing,' I told him. 'Tie it round your waist. You're going to need it.'

Later he thanked me, and said I'd saved his life. But for the moment he cursed as we got going again. I kept thinking of all the stuff I'd left behind. I hated the idea of the Iraqis pillaging our kit. No doubt they'd already whipped the patrol camera away – but unfortunately for them none of the film had been exposed. And what would they make of Tom Sharpe's *Riotous*

Assembly? They'd also have got my dark-blue Patagonia thermal top, my bivvy bag, ten days' rations, the medical pack, a pair of land-line telephones, a couple of anti-personnel mines and some demolition equipment. At least they hadn't got my precious hip flask. With a flicker of satisfaction I remembered that we'd left the claymores and anti-personnel mines buried in the floor of the wadi, and wondered whether they'd taken any of the enemy out. I wished I'd kept more food in my pouches, and less ammu-nition. As it was, I had nothing to eat but two packets of hard, cracker-type Compo biscuits, five in each packet. At the very least we were in for forty-eight hours of hard going, on little food and water.

When you're moving in a straight line, and have a contact, it's usually the Number One who gets hit and, even if he isn't shot, it's Numbers Two and Three who have to get him out of trouble, a.s.a.p. On that march our SOP – which everyone knew by heart – was that if we hit trouble the lead scout would put a 203 round towards the enemy and empty a magazine in their direction. By that time Two and Three should already have gone to ground, and be putting rounds down. Number One would then spring back, zig-zagging, and go to ground himself, to cover the other two, while the rest of the guys fanned out. Equally, though, it was important not to panic and start firing at phantoms, as shots would immediately give our position away.

Contact SOPs were second nature. But Vince, who was Num-ber Two, kept dropping back, as if he didn't want to be near me. More than once he stopped and said, 'If we get a contact in front, whatever you do, don't fire back. You're better off sticking your hands up.'

I said, 'Hey – if we get a contact, I'm shooting. Because if we get captured, we'll get done.'

'Don't,' he said. 'If you shoot one of them, they'll kill the lot of us.'

'Bollocks!' I said.

'You've got to think about it,' he insisted. 'I'm not doing it.'

By that time the patrol had closed up again, and there was a bit of an argument. 'Get your finger out,' somebody told Vince. Nobody supported him. I just said, 'Stick behind me,' and led off again. A few minutes later a message came up the line, to slow down and stop. Somebody shouted, 'Stan's gone down!'

Stan! I thought, 'Jesus! He's one of the strongest guys in the patrol. What the hell's the matter with him?' I ran back and asked what was wrong, but he was on the deck and seemed to be nearly unconscious. All he could do was grunt. It was as if he was drunk, only half there. I'd seen students like that on selection courses, so knackered that you couldn't get any sense out of them.

'What's happened to him?' I asked the next guy.

'Dunno. He just went over.'

'Did he hit his head on a rock or something?'

'I don't think so.'

'Stan!' I said. 'What's wrong?'

He just went '*Urrrhhh!*'

One of the guys said, 'I reckon it's heat exhaustion. He's sweating like hell.'

'Never!' I said. 'It can't be. The night's bloody freezing.'

I'd been sweating a bit myself – but not that much. What we didn't know was that Stan was still wearing his thermal underclothes under his DPMs. He'd been caught out with them on when the contact started, and hadn't had a chance to take them off. The result was that he'd become seriously overheated and had sweated himself dry.

Anyway, we got out our water bottles. I tipped sachets of white rehydrate powder into four of them, and started pouring the water down his neck. He drank three bottles straight off – one of mine, one of Andy's, and one from one of the other guys: six pints at least. That should have pulled him round, but it didn't seem to have much effect. He was still dizzy and exhausted, not making much sense.

Somebody said, 'We've got to look for a safe spot and leave him. Find a hole in the ground.'

There was no way I'd do that. We couldn't leave one guy by himself – not when there were seven more of us, all strong and still fresh. I bent over Stan and said in a menacing voice, 'Listen: if you don't start walking, we're going to fucking leave you. Understand?'

He nodded and gave a grunt.

'Get up, then,' I told him. 'Get on my arse, and don't leave it. Just fix your eyes on my webbing, and keep that in sight.'

Someone said, 'OK, Stan – give us your kit.' Andy took his

Minimi, then said to me, 'Chris, take this,' and gave me his night-sight (generally known as a kite-sight), which Stan had been carrying slung round his neck.

'I don't want that fucking thing,' I protested. The sight weighed four or five pounds, and I thought it would be a pain to have it dangling on my chest. But I took it – and thank God I did, because without doubt it saved my life. I also took a box of 200 rounds for the Minimi and slung it over my shoulder.

We couldn't hang around any longer, because the vehicle lights were still bobbing about in the darkness behind us. I got hold of Stan again and repeated, 'Just walk behind me – and whatever you do, keep going.'

He went, '*Urrrhh*, yeah, yeah,' then he got up and we kicked off again. Once more I led, with Stan at my back, Vince behind him, and the rest of the patrol following. Lead scout is a tiring job, because you have to be looking ahead all the time; but, being quite observant, I reckoned that if there was something in front of us, I would see it as quickly as anyone else. Andy was in the middle, the normal slot for a patrol commander.

Every time we stopped for Mark to do a Magellan check, I'd say, 'Stan – lie down. Get your head down for a minute,' and he'd lie down without a word, as if he were semi-conscious, obedient as a dog. When we were ready to start again I'd give him a kick and say, 'OK, Stan, let's go,' and he'd get up again and start walking right behind me – only to fall back, farther and farther.

When this had happened two or three times, I tried to provoke some reaction by saying, 'Stan – if you don't keep behind me, and keep up with me, I'm going to leave you.' He did react in a way, by promising to fix his eyes on the back of my webbing, and not let that out of his sight. That kept him going for a while, but still, whenever we stopped, he would lie down like he was dead.

Once again the sky was partly overcast, but a cold north-west wind was keeping the clouds on the move, and whenever the moon came out, it lit up the desert brilliantly. Often I saw some dark object standing out from the background. Usually it was a mound or rock, but it could have been a building or a vehicle, and it needed checking. The moment I had a doubt, I'd stop, lie down and watch for a while, to see if anything moved – and whenever I did so, the other guys automatically went down too, flat on their stomachs, forming an arc.

The little binoculars we'd bought in Abu Dhabi were a distinct asset, as they drew in what light there was and often enabled me to work out what it was that I'd seen. But the kite-sight, or image-intensifier, proved a godsend. Basically a black tube, it was designed to fit on top of a 203, but it made the weapon heavy and unbalanced and I found it easier to put the sight up on its own, holding it like a telescope. To use it, I had to switch it on and wait ten seconds for it to warm up. It gave out a faint, high-pitched squeal, and produced a clear, fluorescent green, white-flecked picture of the ground ahead, with much more detail than the naked eye could pick out.

The more I came to depend on the sight, the more anxious I was that I might switch it on accidentally while walking and run the battery down, so as I was moving I kept a finger on the button, to make certain that it was turned off. The penalty of using the sight was that it reduced my natural night-vision. Whenever I'd taken a check round, and lowered the sight, I could see very little for a minute or two.

In spite of the danger, I enjoyed being out at night. We had done a lot of training in the dark, and I always felt safe, protected by the fact that nobody could see me. I thought of the time when I was a boy, out shooting pigeons with my father, and we were coming home in the dusk one evening. As we passed along the edge of a wood, I felt really frightened by the intense blackness under the trees. It was the sort of place where, in a children's book or a movie, witches would lurk. I said to my dad, 'I'd be scared stiff to go in there.'

'Why?' he said.

'Well, you can't see.'

'Come on, then.' He took my arm and walked in fifteen or twenty metres. I was terrified, and stuck close by him, holding his jacket so that he couldn't do a runner on me. Inside the wood, we sat down.

'Just keep quiet, and listen,' he whispered. After a while he said softly, 'There you are. If anyone was trying to creep up on us, we'd hear him. You can't walk through a wood at night without making a sound. What you've got to realise is that if there are people in here, and we can't see them, they can't see us either. This is the safest place to be.'

The lesson stuck, and I was never scared of the dark again.

At every halt Mark took a fix with his Magellan until we were confident about our route. But the vehicle lights were still coming up behind us, so we decided to put in the dog-leg. Until then we'd been heading back towards the Saudi border. Now we resolved to turn right – westwards – for a spell, then right again, and head northwards across the MSR which we'd been watching. The loss of our jerricans had forced us to modify our original plan of going north-west, straight for the Syrian border. Obviously we would need water, so we decided to aim due north, for the Euphrates, and follow the river out to the frontier.

So, after sixteen quick kilometres southwards, we turned due west and did ten kilometres in that direction, hoping that the Iraqis were wasting their time and resources by throwing out a cordon ahead of where they'd last seen us. The pace was very, very fast – speed marching, with everyone in line-ahead, going as fast as they could without running, probably at nine kilometres or six miles an hour. Now and then we crossed a dry wadi like the one in which we'd lain up, but for most of the way the desert was completely open, without landmarks, and we kept going on a bearing. Whenever we heard the sound of jet engines overhead, we'd switch on our TACBEs and shout into them – but answer came there none.

By the end of the ten kilometres westwards, the strain was starting to tell. We'd been moving at high speed, with fifty-pound belt-kits and our weapons, and we were sweating quite a bit in spite of the cold. That meant we were all thirsty, and soon we'd drunk nearly all our water. Whenever we stopped, we made sure to get more liquid down Stan's neck. He had kept going by sheer will-power; admittedly he had been relieved of the burden of his weapon, but even so, after such a collapse it was a major feat to maintain the pace we were setting.

As soon as we'd fully lost sight of the vehicle behind us, we made our second right turn and headed north, stopping frequently to check our position with the Magellan. This went on until we thought we were back within about seven kilometres of the MSR. Then, as we went to ground for yet another map-check, I said to Andy, 'Right: from now on, we're coming to the most dangerous bit. What I'll do is push as hard as I can until we've crossed the MSR. There could be people looking for us along it. If we get caught on those tracks, out in the open, we're going to be knackered. If there are any enemy on the ridge beyond the road, we want to be up on the high ground as soon as we can.'

'Yeah,' Andy agreed, 'push it out.' And he told everyone else, 'We're going to walk real fast until we cross the MSR. OK?'

So we started again, travelling at an even faster pace. By then I was using the kite-sight most of the time, with my weapon tucked under my left arm. It was awkward and tiring to walk in that attitude. After a while my eyes started to hurt as well, because looking through the sight continuously was like staring at a light. But there was no alternative. Soon I could make out the ridge on which the AA guns were mounted, and I kept scanning for lights or artificial shapes, focusing my attention on what lay ahead.

Disaster hit us without warning. We'd been walking for an hour since I last spoke to Andy, when at last we came to the MSR and started to cross the tracks. It turned out that there were about a dozen of them, running side by side, marked in hard mud, and they seemed to be spread over 200 or 300 metres. Out on that open expanse, obviously well used, I felt horribly exposed, so I turned up the pace even faster. Then, just short of the high ground, I looked through the night-sight yet again and saw what I thought was a building or vehicle. I couldn't be sure what it was, but the object certainly looked artificial, so at the foot of the slope I stopped to confer with Andy.

Looking round, I saw Stan behind me, with his head hanging down, then Vince . . . but no one else.

'Where the fuck's the rest of the patrol?' I demanded. Vince just said, 'I don't know. We've lost them.'

'What d'you mean, lost them?'

'They split off somewhere.'

Vince didn't seem too concerned. But I thought, 'Oh my God!' I was on the verge of panic, but all I said was, 'Right – let's get up on the high ground, fast.' I took one more look at the black object, decided it was a rock, and hustled forward as fast as I could. Just short of the top of the ridge I stopped again. Stan lay down like he was dead. Vince was completely zonked as well – he just sat there and couldn't speak.

By my calculation, it was at least an hour since the patrol had split. Looking back across the open gravel plains with the kite-sight, I had a clear view for miles. It seemed impossible that the others could have gone far enough to vanish. I kept scanning and thinking that at any second I would see five black figures trudging in single file – yet I couldn't get any movement any-where. Men walking in that bare landscape would have showed up large as life – but somehow the desert had swallowed them.

For a few moments I was dumbfounded. Then I thought: 'My TACBE and Andy's are compatible; if both are switched on at the same time, we should be able to talk to each other.' The SOP for this situation was that anyone in difficulties would listen out on every hour and half-hour; so I waited five minutes till mid-night, pressed the button and called: 'Andy! Andy!' No answer. I kept on for five minutes, fully expecting him to shout back, but no call came.

Things were going from bad to worse. We were down to three men; one of them was out of the game, and the other didn't want to be in it. We had only two main weapons: I had my 203, and Vince a 203 and a pistol. Stan had nothing but a bayonet. I felt a kind of jealousy and resentment start to burn inside me. The other group was larger, a stronger fighting force, most of them armed with Minimis. If anybody was going to get out, they were. I felt I'd much rather have been in their party than in ours.

Already thirst was a problem. We'd done a fearsome tab, and Stan had drunk all my water. We had also lost the Magellan, which was with Mark. From now on we'd have to navigate by map, compass and dead reckoning – and this depended on knowing how fast we were covering the ground. Experience told me that the error was likely to grow ever-larger as we became more tired and tended increasingly to over-estimate the distance we'd gone. I regretted never having done a course in astral navi-gation: I could recognise the Plough, Orion's Belt and a few other constellations, but that was all.

I looked round. Stan was asleep on the ground beside me, but Vince had moved off about fifteen metres and was squatting down. I thought he was having a shit, and that if he was, I'd better go across to make sure he buried it. But when I walked towards him, I found that what he was doing was burying his ammunition – a box of 200 rounds and a sleeve of 203 grenades.

'What the hell are you doing?' I hissed.

'I'm not carrying that stuff,' he said. 'It's too heavy. If we get into a big contact, we'll all be wasted anyway.'

'You've got to fucking carry it,' I told him.

'I can't.'

'Give us those rounds here, then.'

I was fuming. We only had the two weapons, and might really need the ammunition. But I couldn't turn round and order Vince to carry it. So I slung the 203 bandolier over my shoulder and let him bury the box. But I knew that from that moment I couldn't rely on him.

I went back, sat down, and waited until 0030. Then on the half-hour I tried the TACBE again – but still the night yielded no reply.

I felt angry as well as scared. I simply couldn't make out how the patrol had split. But whatever had happened behind us, I could see no future in sitting where we were; we had to get away from the MSR and put more distance behind us, in case the Iraqis tried to follow up. So we cracked on, walking again, with Stan on my shoulder and Vince behind him.

For the next four and a half hours, we slogged on and on. By then, on the high plateau, the ground was flat as a billiard table, but it was covered with loose rocks the size of your fist. These made the going rough, and I could feel I was starting to get blisters along the sides of my feet.

Every time I stopped to check our position, I'd say, 'Stan – just lie down,' and he'd lie down and go straight to sleep. If I tried to get Vince to help me plot where we were, he showed no interest in the map, because he was knackered, mentally as well as physically. I had a small torch attached to my compass, and I'd covered the lens with black masking tape, with just a pinhole in it, so that a very fine beam of light shone on the map. Whenever I tried to work out where we were, Vince would agree with anything I suggested. I would have preferred him to argue. I kept wanting him to say, 'No, look: I think we're *there*,' because it would have made me think harder – but he'd gone completely inert.

Anyway, we kept going until 0500, by which time we were all at the end of our tether. That was hardly surprising, as we'd covered the best part of seventy kilometres during the night. I was thinking, 'Dawn can't be far off. We'd better find somewhere to hole up for the day,' when we came across an old tank berm. This took the form of a bank of soil about six feet high, built in the shape of a big U or horseshoe with one end open, so that a tank could drive into it and be hidden from the other three sides. Just short of it, and leading into it, were two tracks about twenty-four inches wide and fifteen deep, where a tank had sunk into the ground on its way in or out.

There was no future in lying up inside the berm itself; the wind was blowing straight into its wide, open end, so that its walls gave no shelter, and anyone passing could look in. Equally, we couldn't lie outside the walls in the lee of the wind, because we'd have been in full view from the other direction. The only shelter from the wind, and at the same time cover from view, was in the tank-ruts outside.

'We're going to have to stay here,' I said, and we lay down in the deepest part of one of the tracks, head to toe, Vince at one end, me in the middle and Stan beyond me. Down flat, we were more or less hidden, but I only had to raise my head an inch or two to see out. It was a precarious refuge to say the least – and if anyone came to visit the berm for any reason, we would ob- viously be compromised.

While we'd been on the move, the wind hadn't seemed too cold; but now that we'd stopped putting out energy, it cut through our thin clothes viciously. That was bad enough, but when daybreak came I looked out, and the first thing I saw was heavy clouds piling in from the west, black as the ace of spades. I said, 'Oh, Jesus, fellers. The sky's really dark over there. It's going to piss down with rain.' Then I looked in the other direc- tion and saw something square, about 600 metres off. It was either a little building or a box-bodied vehicle, with antennas poking up out of it, and at least two men round it. This showed how right we'd been to remain alert during the night: here was some small military outpost, miles from anywhere – exactly the sort of place we might have walked on to.

Back at Victor we'd shared some jokes about how shy Arabs are about shitting. The SSM had told me that an Arab will walk miles rather than shit in front of his pal, and this berm seemed just the place one might choose. I couldn't see any old turds lying about, it was true, but the bank was just the right distance from the outpost. So I said to the guys, 'There's an enemy posi- tion across there. We're going to have to be careful in case one of the fellers there comes across for a crap. We'll have to take turns to stay awake. Vince, you do the first couple of hours' stag.'

Not that I'd worked out what we'd do if anybody did approach; we'd either have to leg it across the open ground or take the person out – and neither seemed a good option. There was no other cover for miles around, and if we killed anybody it would inevitably reveal our approximate position and throw away the advantage we'd gained from putting in the dog-leg. Nor did it seem likely that any of us would get our heads down, it was so bloody cold. The wind came knifing through my DPMs and smock, so I opened my canvas map case and laid it over my legs. Also I wrapped one shamag round my head, and pulled the other round my shoulders. Even then I was still freezing. But somehow I must have dozed off, because I woke up shaking violently, with what felt like pins and needles in my face. When I opened my eyes, I couldn't believe it: it was snowing, and we were covered in white.

Big flakes were teeming down, coating us with slush as we lay there. I thought, 'Oh, for fuck's sake!'

'Look at this!' I exclaimed bitterly. 'You'd think we were at the fucking North Pole.' Nobody answered, so I said, 'Vince, are you all right?'

He grunted something back.

'Stan, how are you feeling?'

'Oh, a lot better.'

That lifted me – just to hear him sounding more like himself. He seemed a hundred per cent livelier than he had been.

'Thank Christ,' I said. 'Well – get something to eat.' All I had was my biscuits, so I ate two of them, chewing slowly to produce saliva and work them down. Stan and Vince both ate something too.

'What was wrong in the night, Stan?'

'I had my thermal underwear on, Chris. Sweated myself dry. I didn't have time to take it off when the contact started.'

'You lucky bastard!' I said. 'Now, I mean.'

'I'm still fucking freezing, though.'

'So am I.'

The worst result of the night – though I didn't realise it immediately – was that I'd badly burnt my feet. At first I couldn't understand what had happened; my boots were well run-in and completely comfortable, and had never given me the slightest trouble. Later I realised that the problem was my socks. They were German Army issue, made of rough grey-brown wool, and because our build-up had been done in such a rush, I'd worn them for four or five days on end before the deployment. By the time we started walking, they were already stiff with sand, dust and sweat – and now, as a result, they'd chewed the sides of my feet into large blisters.

The normal treatment – which we'd used on selection courses – would have been to push a needle into each blister, extract the fluid, and inject tinc benzine, or Friar's Balsam. The process hurt like hell – it felt as if a red-hot poker had been laid against your foot – but it toughened the underlying skin enough for you to be able to walk on it. Even washing my feet and putting on plasters would have helped. But there, trapped in the tank-track, I couldn't even take my boots off to inspect the damage, let alone do anything to repair it.

From time to time we talked in whispers. At one point Vince said, 'I knew we'd been compromised in the wadi.'

'How?'

'That fucking goatherd – I saw him.'

'He must have seen you, then.'

'Must have.'

I cursed silently to myself. If Vince had admitted that at the time, we'd have got out of the wadi a lot quicker before the bulldozer appeared, and before the two guys appeared above us. We might even have made a clean break back to the drop-off area.

Now and then during the day we saw military-looking vehicles driving in the distance. I lay in the tank-track thinking, 'This is shite!' The snow turned to rain, then back to snow. Our ditch filled with water. The water dissolved the earth into mud, and soon we were wallowing in an icy quagmire. There was mud all over us, all over our weapons. We were becoming sodden with the filthy stuff. But all we could do was lie there in it, from six o'clock in the morning right through till dusk.

I'd often been cold before, but never in my life had I been as cold as that. The cold bit into our very bones. Time slowed to a crawl. Now and then we heard a vehicle drive past, but otherwise there was nothing to occupy our minds. I became so frozen that I didn't even want to move my arm so that I could see my watch, and I asked Stan what the time was. 'Twelve o'clock,' was the answer. Jesus! Was this day ever going to end?

Trying to escape from reality, I thought back to other times when I'd been frozen. Once when I was seventeen, on my first escape and evasion exercise with the Territorial SAS, up at Otterburn in the middle of the winter, I was caught by the hunter force of Three Para. They got us, gave us a good kicking, stripped us naked, tied our wrists and anchored us up to the chest in the middle of the river until we were completely numb. Then they took us into an insulated airborne shelter, with five gas heaters blazing, where the temperature was about 120 degrees. As our circulation got going again, the pain became excruciating – and it was then, when we were doubled up in agony on the floor, that they started interrogating us about who we were and what we'd been doing. As soon as we were warm and starting to recover, they put us back in the river and so began the whole process again . . .

In the tank-ruts, it was impossible to concentrate on anything for long, the discomfort was so intense. I tried to think of places where I'd been warm, like Africa, but I couldn't stay long in any of them. The one big plus was that Stan seemed to be back in his normal spirits. He'd brought a proper boil-in-the-bag meal in his belt-kit, and once he'd got that down him, he was ready to go. Vince, on the other hand, was feeling the cold worst of any of us. He wasn't whingeing, but he kept saying, 'Chris, I can't feel my fingers. I'm bloody freezing,' and I was saying, 'So am I. But we can't do anything, Vince. We can't move, so we've just got to stick it out.'

'Can't we cuddle in together?'

'Not yet. It's too dangerous to move.'

The temptation to get up and go, to start moving again, was colossal: anything would be better than enduring this agony. But one of the regiment's most fundamental SOPs is that during escape and evasion you don't move in daylight, and I decided that we must stick by it. If we were spotted walking, Iraqis would come at us from all sides. Grim as it was, I insisted we stayed where we were.

Then, late in the afternoon, Vince put the wind up me by saying, 'Look – I'm going down here.'

71

We had to do something.

'What's the time, Stan?'

'Four o'clock.'

'Let's cuddle in, then.'

Vince and I wriggled further down to where Stan lay, and the track was a bit wider. At that point we were all coming out into the open, but we took the risk and lay together, cuddling in for warmth, with me in the middle and the other two on the outsides.

After what seemed an age, I asked again, 'What's the time, Stan?'

'Five past four.'

'Fucking hell!'

This was real torture. It seemed like eternity, lying there caked with freezing mud, with icy water soaking through to our shreddies. Whenever the snow stopped, the wind would get up and bring on the rain, and then the snow would start again – as if someone was programming the weather to cause maximum discomfort.

At last, at about five-thirty, darkness began to fall, and we decided to crawl inside the berm so that we could shift around and get some feeling back into our bodies. But until we tried to move, we didn't realise what a state we were in. Then we found we were truly in the shit.

My fingers and toes were numb, but that was to be expected. It was when I went to stand up that I really got it: the pain in my knees and back was outrageous. I felt as if I had acute arthritis in my spine and hips. Suddenly I thought, 'Jesus, we really are going down here.' For a moment I was hit by despair.

Anyway, we dragged ourselves inside the berm and started trying to run back and forth, to start the energy going and get some heat moving inside our bodies. But my feet were still numb, and clay built up on the soles of my boots so that I could hardly make any progress. Our hands were so dead that we couldn't pick up our weapons – but luckily they had slings, and what we did was duck down, put our heads through the slings, and stand up.

As Vince did so, he said, 'Chris – I can't carry my weapon. I just can't.'

I heard a note of desperation in his voice, so I just said quietly,

'Stan, you take it for him.' So Stan took Vince's 203, leaving him with his pistol.

My memories of the next few hours are hazy, because I was being hit by hypothermia. All three of us were. But even though my mind was becoming clouded, I knew we had to keep moving.

'Right, fellers,' I said. 'We're going to have to start off again.' So away we went. I was stumbling with my weapon slung over my shoulder and my hands tucked under my arms, trying to get some feeling back into them. I kept thinking, 'If we have a contact, we're knackered, because we're not going to be able to shoot back.' I couldn't have pulled the trigger or changed magazines to save my life.

Stan and I were doing the navigating, but he was getting his compass out more often than I was.

'Where are we heading?' I'd ask, and he'd say, 'Due north. We're all right.'

Then the clouds thickened up. Another flurry of snow drove into our faces, hurtling in from the north-west, and soon we were tabbing over ground as white as on a Christmas card. One advantage of the blizzard was that it hid us; no one was going to see us while so much snow was falling. But equally, we ourselves were blinded, and could easily walk on to an enemy position without spotting it.

When the moon came out again, the desert was light as day, and I could read my map without the torch. Vince, who kept lagging behind, called, 'Hey, you're going to have to slow down. I need a rest.'

'Vince,' I told him, 'you can't rest. We've got to keep moving, see if we can warm ourselves up.'

The worst thing was that we were walking hard but not getting any less cold. Normally, after you've walked for an hour, your circulation's really going, and you're warm all over. But because our clothes were soaked through, and this bitter wind was blowing, the chill-factor was keeping our body temperature right down. Also, there was no fuel left in me to re-stoke the fires: I'd burnt it all up. I thought, 'If it's still like this tomorrow morning, we're all going to be dead.'

I knew that in our state, without warm clothes or shelter or food, we couldn't survive such conditions much longer. In fact I thought it was likely we would all die that night. I'd never experienced such pain from cold, such agony in spine and legs. In the course of training I'd had plenty of lectures on hypothermia, and now I recognised some of the symptoms in myself: disorientation, dizziness, sudden mood swings, outbursts of anger, confusion, drowziness . . . Normally a man in that state would be put into a sleeping bag or a space blanket and brought round – but here there was no respite.

So we kept walking – until Vince really started going down. 'Wait for me,' he called. 'You've got to wait.'

We waited a few times. But then I decided that shock tactics were necessary. I knew that at home he had two young girls and a little baby, and that he was nuts about his family. So I gripped him by the arm and said, 'Vince, if you don't fucking keep going, you're never going to see your kids. Think about your home. Think how they'll want you back. Now – get your finger out and start moving.'

'Listen,' he said, 'I want to go to sleep. I'm too tired. I've got to sit down.'

'Vince,' I said, 'we can't sit down. If we stop, we're going to fucking DIE. Get that? If we lie down and sleep, we'll freeze to death, and never know anything about it.'

We carried on walking for a bit, and then he shouted at me, 'Chris!'

'What?'

'My hands have gone black.'

I thought, 'Jesus! Frostbite!' My own fingers were still numb, and I wondered what state my hands were in under my gloves. I walked back to Vince and found him staring down at his hands. He was wearing black leather gloves.

'My fucking hands have gone black,' he repeated. 'My fucking hands!'

I realised his mind was wandering, so I just said, 'OK, Vince, put them in your pockets. Get them warm, and the colour'll come back to them. Come on now: keep up with me and Stan, mate. Keep going.'

At that point I can't have been thinking straight. What I should have done was to keep hold of him, or actually tie him to me. But that didn't occur to me, and I just kept walking. Stan and I would tab on for a bit, then wait for Vince to catch up.

74

Then the same again. I tried to alternate, being sharp with him one moment, kind the next. One minute I'd shout, 'Get a grip!' trying to spark him into action. Then I'd turn comforting, tap him on the shoulder, and say, 'Come on, Vince, keep walking. Everything'll be all right. We're going to get out.'

Vince's own behaviour was swinging wildly. Several times he started yelling out loud – which of course was bad for our nerves, as anybody could have heard him from hundreds of metres off. Stan hissed, *'Vince – be quiet!'* and he shut up for a while.

Because hypothermia was hitting us, our navigation had become erratic. For some time I'd had the feeling that I was drifting away from reality. The map was saying one thing, and what was happening on the ground seemed to be quite different. Somehow we were getting dragged off to the north-east all the time. I don't know why, but something in me kept pulling me that way.

I saw what was happening, and began to wonder – quite illogically – if I had a tendency to head north-east because I'd been born in the north-east of England. Basically we were wanting to head north-west, and we kept having to correct ourselves, constantly checking on the compass. Every few minutes Stan would say, 'Eh – we're coming off. We're coming off.' Then the clouds would open, and we'd get a glimpse of the Plough, and we could bring ourselves on course again. Then more snow flurries would come in, the stars would be blotted out, and we'd veer off once more. Because it was so cold, I had one hand in my pocket or underneath my arm. Whenever we stopped, the shivers came on, making it hard to concentrate on the map. Spells of weakness kept sweeping over us, fogging our minds still more.

Struggling as we were, we cracked on for a while – but then, as we stopped once again, we realised that Vince was no longer with us. When Stan shouted back for him, there was no answer. 'Chris,' he said, 'we've lost him.'

'We can't have,' I answered stupidly. 'He must be just behind us.'

We started back on our tracks. Naturally I was worried, but I felt bad-tempered about having to retreat. Where snow was lying, it was easy to follow our footprints; but then there were long stretches of bare rock from which the snow had been blown clear, and whenever we crossed one, we had to cast about on the far side, working forward and back to pick up our trail again. Now we realised how much we'd been veering about as we advanced, zig-zagging all over the place.

After twenty minutes there was still no sign of Vince. We called as loud as we dared, and we could see a reasonable distance – but I suddenly realised that our quest was hopeless. The truth hit me with a jolt: it was half an hour, at least, since we'd seen him, and we had no idea what he'd done. He might have walked off to the right; he might have walked off to the left; he might be walking straight backwards; he might have lain down in a hollow and gone to sleep. This last seemed the most likely; that was all he'd been wanting to do for hours – stop and get his head down. If he had curled up somewhere out of the wind, we could spend all night walking in circles and never find him, probably killing ourselves in the process.

'Stan,' I said, 'I'm making a decision. We're going to turn round and leave him.' I could feel my companion's hesitation, so I added, 'Fuck it – I'll take the responsibility. We've got to leave him, or we'll kill the pair of us.'

'OK, then,' said Stan. 'Fair enough.'

It was a terrible decision to have to take, but I saw no alternative. I kept thinking of the times I'd been out on the hills in Scotland, and the weather had turned really bad. In the Highlands, there'd always been the comforting thought that we could get into a barn or a bothy, or go to a hotel. The same applied in Norway – we could always take refuge in a hotel or a hut if things became impossible. But here there was no such facility: nowhere to go, nowhere to escape from the wind and snow, nowhere to dry our kit and warm up, nowhere to find food. I felt all the more certain that if conditions were the same in the morning, Stan and I would die as well. There was no way we would resuscitate ourselves with no shelter and absolutely nothing to light a fire with. So with heavy hearts we turned round and cracked on again, and left Vince on his own.

Chapter Four

Down To One

Our only hope was to get down off the high ground into warmer air, and gradually, as we tabbed on, we did seem to be descending. We never went down any steep gradient, but all the same it felt as if we were losing height. I hoped to God that Vince was doing the same – that he would find his way down off this cruel, high plateau, reach low ground somewhere, get his head down in a hollow, and wake up in the morning.

Our map showed a line of pylons running across our front, and another line that terminated in the middle of nowhere. So we thought that if we hit the first set of masts, and then the second, we'd know exactly where we were. But it didn't turn out like that. We only hit the one line of masts, and couldn't find any more. Later we discovered that the second line didn't exist except on the map.

But at least we seemed to be coming down. The snow flurries died out, and the wind became less bitter. Then through the kite-sight I saw a black-looking band running across our front. We sat down to study it, and presently made out that it was another main road. Approaching cautiously, we lay in a hollow which turned out to be full of mud: somehow, in the middle of the arid desert, we'd chosen a place like a miniature peat bog.

In front of us we saw a chain-link fence running parallel with the road, maybe ten metres on the far side of it, and shining faintly in the moonlight. Beyond the fence something pale was looming. It looked like a strip of concrete, and we thought we'd come on some form of installation. As I followed the line of the fence with the sight, I muttered, 'Christ – it must be a massive place. This bloody barrier goes on for ever.' Then at the last minute we realised that what we could see was a railway line, fenced to keep animals off the track.

The chain-link was only about six feet high. Any other time, we'd have scaled it in seconds. But we were that cold and pissy helpless we just couldn't climb it. Our hands and arms were almost useless, and wouldn't pull us up and over. Stan brought out his set of folding Leatherman pliers and, with an all-out effort to make his hands work, cut a vertical slit in the mesh. We knew it was wrong, and a departure from the SOP, because anyone who came along and saw the gap would realise that somebody had been through there – but it was the only way we were going to cross the track.

Anyway, we squeezed through the gap and found ourselves on the railway line. 'Jesus!' we thought. 'Shall we walk along it?' It would have been easy going, tabbing on the concrete sleepers. A check on the map showed that it ran straight to a town on the Syrian border. But then we reckoned that probably the line would be patrolled, or that someone on a train would be bound to see us. There was nowhere to hide near the track, and if a train came along, we'd be caught in the open.

We decided to continue northwards. At the fence on the far side of the line Stan gave me the pliers and said, 'Your turn.' My fingers were so numb that I could hardly grip the handles, and putting pressure on them hurt like hell. But wire by wire I cut a slit, and we wormed through, pulling the chain-link back into place behind us so that the gap wasn't too obvious. With any luck it would be days before anyone noticed the damage.

Leaving the railway, we found a big, rounded hill ahead of us and started up it. A few yards short of the summit we stopped, both in the same stride. In that split second we'd spotted that AA gun barrels were pointing into the sky no more than four or five metres in front of us. Standing still and staring at them, we realised we could see the top of a wall of sandbags, almost under our noses. Obviously there were Iraqis inside the sangar but, thank God, they seemed to be asleep.

Without a word, without turning, we back-tracked down the slope, inches at a time, watching for any movement to our front. Nothing stirred. Once we were clear, we pulled away eastwards in a big loop, leaving the mound on our left, and then came back on to our northerly heading. But the incident gave us a fright, because we'd been walking carelessly, not worrying about the scrunching noise our boots were making on the loose rock and gravel.

By the early hours of the morning we were back into a system of shallow wadis and dry channels maybe thirty feet wide, but only two or three deep. These river beds were full of little bushes which threw thick, black shadows in the moonlight, so that every hollow seemed to be full of quite dense vegetation. I thought, 'Great – we'll be able to get our heads down in here. It should be warmer, too.'

About 0530 we started looking for a place to lie up, and settled in a hollow. As I lay down next to Stan, I pulled out my hip flask and offered it to him. I thought the dickhead would realise what was in it, but no: he expected it to be water. I watched as he put it to his lips, and then – his face! His eyes bulged. He went *pwhhhoohhh! mphhhh!* and then 'Fucking hell! What the hell's that?'

'Whisky, you clot!'

'Bloody hell! I thought it was water.'

'You dick, no.' I took a sip myself and told him, 'That's the last time you're getting offered any of this stuff.' So I whacked the flask back into my pocket. Stan took off his webbing and laid it down in the middle of some bushes, and we cuddled down together on top of it. It was really embarrassing, because we were front to front, with our arms round each other, and we had to take turns on whose head was at the bottom.

So we lay there, shuddering, drifting off into sleep, waking with a start, shaking all over, until dawn broke. By then I was bitterly regretting some of the mistakes I'd made in choosing and packing my kit. Apart from the brew-kit, which would have been a great morale-booster, I should have had a Goretex bivvy bag or at least a space blanket in one of my pouches.

When daylight came, we found that some of the mud had dried on us, aided by our body heat, and our clothes were all stiff and covered with ice-crystals, as if they'd been left out on a frosty night. Looking up, I saw that the sky was clear and blue, and thought, 'Thank God, it's going to be a fine day.' Light revealed that the bushes which had looked promising at night were nothing but thorny skeletons, eaten down by goats; there wasn't a leaf on them, and they weren't going to hide us from anyone. So we crawled across and tucked ourselves into the wall of a wadi that ran north and south.

At ten o'clock the sun came up and shone on us as we lay

against the western wall. I'm sure that saved our lives. One more wet, windy day, and we would just have drifted off into unconsciousness and never come round. The sun never felt very warm, but it definitely made the air less cold, and we began to sort ourselves out a bit. We took off our webbing, and I spread out my map case to dry. We also cleaned the mud off our weapons and reloaded magazines. I found I'd fired about 70 rounds during the contact. Stan produced a sachet of American corned-beef hash from his belt-kit, and as I watched him eat it, I was thinking, 'Why the hell didn't I bring my own rations with me?' All I had was two biscuits, my last.

At one point I said, 'Stan – can you tell me, what the fuck are you doing sitting in the middle of Iraq? You're supposed to be a dentist, with a Porsche 911, living in the middle of Sydney – and now you're in fucking Iraq, with nothing!'

'You know, Chris,' he replied, 'I'm asking myself that, right this very minute' – and he burst out laughing. 'I bet we look a bloody state now.'

'Too right we do.'

'What about *you*, then? What are *you* doing here?'

It was a good question – and when I thought about it, I saw that my involvement in the SAS could be traced back to my love of being in open country. It was that, more than anything else, which had determined the course of my career.

I grew up in Rowlands Gill, a small village in the country just outside Newcastle, and went to the junior school there. From our house, I could walk straight out across the fields and into the forest, and the result was that as a kid I was constantly playing in the woods, making camps and sleeping out. My father worked on construction sites, driving plant machinery, but he generally got laid off during the winter, when work on the sites shut down, and that suited him fine, because all his life he'd been keen on shooting. He'd been brought up in the hamlet of Blanchland nearby, where his uncle had been a gamekeeper, and he'd spent his own boyhood roaming the woods and fields. He'd take me with him out into the country round Rowlands Gill, where he had permission from the farmers, and also near Blanchland, where he was friendly with a farmer called Clive. We used to build hides, in which we'd wait for pigeons, or ferret rabbits out of burrows in the hedges. On winter evenings we'd stand in the woods and flight pigeons as they came into roost.

My dad had a five-shot Browning automatic 12-bore. Once, as we came round a corner, we saw five rabbits on the edge of a field. He got them all, one after another. With feats like that he soon became my hero, and I loved every minute of our expeditions.

Whatever we shot, we ate. My dad would skin the rabbits or pluck the pigeons – as well as the odd pheasant, partridge and grouse – and my mum would cook them. I used to listen fascinated to the stories he told about himself and my cousin Billy, and the times they used to go shooting together as young men. In time I came to resent the fact that Billy seemed closer to him than I ever was, and had got a lot more out of him.

But then came a great change. Some time in his thirties, my dad decided it was wrong to shoot birds and animals, and stopped altogether. By then I was mad keen, and kept suggesting we should go out, but he said, 'No – you're better off just watching them or taking pictures, capturing them on film. If you want to go, shoot with a camera.' It may have been something to do with the fact that myxomatosis was at its height. The sight of sick rabbits blundering about, bouncing off each other, with their eyes closed by purulent swellings, disgusted him, and he was upset by the thought of so many animals dying in pain. As we drove into Blanchland, he'd say, 'God – that bank used to be *covered* with rabbits, and now there's nothing.' He may have thought that if he laid off, it would help the rabbits recover.

At an early age I started asking if I could have an air-rifle, and my parents kept saying no. At one point my dad bought me a .410, but I was only allowed to take it out with him, under close supervision. Later, when I was thirteen or fourteen, I saved up my pocket money and asked again if I could buy an air-rifle. Still the answer was no, so my brother Keith and I went out with some older boys and bought one, a BSA .22. I kept the precious weapon in the loft, along with a few dirty magazines and bottles of cider that we'd managed to tuck away.

Again I asked my mum, 'Can I buy an air-rifle?' and when she answered, 'No,' I said, 'What if I just get one?'

'You wouldn't be able to keep one in *this* house, without your dad and me knowing.'

Keith and I were looking at each other, thinking, 'Yeah – right!' What we used to do was smuggle the air-gun out over an outbuilding at the back. Keith would wait on the ground, while I climbed out of my bedroom window and handed the gun down to him. Then we'd run off into the woods and go shooting.

One day, as I came home from school, I found that Keith had got there before me; he grabbed me, his face all fearful, and said, 'Dad's just bought a new TV, and the man's in the loft, putting up the aerial. You'd better get up there quick.'

The hatchway going up into the loft was in my bedroom. I stood there with Keith, waiting anxiously, when my dad called cheerily up to the fitter from downstairs, 'I don't suppose there are any bottles of beer hidden up there?'

'No,' the man answered, 'just a couple of dirty books and . . . some cider.'

Keith and I stared at each other in horror. Luckily my Dad took the answer as a joke and started laughing. The aerial guy said, 'No, no – there's nothing up here.'

The rifle was never discovered – but when I was sixteen or so I declared it, and by then it was too late for anyone to worry.

My Mum came from Lynemouth, a mining village on the coast of Northumberland. A quiet, very modest woman, she had the patience of a saint, and a tremendously strong sense of right and wrong. Nothing on earth would make her break the law – and sometimes she drove the rest of us crazy by her insistence on absolute honesty, even in the smallest things. But I grew up with enormous respect for her integrity. In bringing up three boys, without any modern appliances, she worked all hours of the day – and I'm ashamed to think how little help we gave her.

At school I was quite soft, and used to get bullied. If a girl started making up to me, I'd have the shit kicked out of me by someone else who fancied her. If there was going to be a fight, it took place when school finished. There'd always be a big crowd gathering at the gate, waiting for the action, and I'd be nearly crapping myself as I approached. Sometimes if my brother Keith got the worst of an argument, he would say, 'Right – my big brother'll see to you.' Then he'd find me at playtime and say, 'By the way, you're to have a fight tonight.' Sometimes I'd go over the back fence and do a runner across the fields to avoid facing the music.

But then came a transition. When I was sixteen I decided that this sort of thing had to stop, and I began fighting back. It wasn't a personality change; just that I went on to the offensive. I realised that if you have a fight, you probably get hurt, but it doesn't last for ever. Listening to my dad, and taking a grip of myself, I put a stop to the bullying.

I also started judo lessons, and couldn't get enough of them. At first, for a couple of months, I was taught by a Japanese who practised a pure form of the ancient martial art, but then I progressed to an instructor in Newcastle, an ex-Olympic champion who taught me to fight dirty – how to disable an opponent by kicking him in the balls, and how to knock somebody's head off. I became so keen that I'd go into town almost every night, and I started winning competitions; in my first fight I floored my opponent within seconds, and hurt him quite badly. But I gave up judo when, in a fight with a bigger boy, my clavicle became detached from the rib cage. Although I finished the fight, I lost on points – and afterwards the injury caused me so many problems that I thought I'd better stop.

I found judo a wonderful means of channelling aggression to a useful end. Not that I see myself as aggressive – determined, yes, perhaps a bit short-tempered, but not aggressive. If things start going wrong, and I tell someone not to do something, and he does it again, I might have an emotional outburst – but on the whole I'm easygoing.

With a jolt I remembered the sick fear I once felt when I was a kid of about thirteen. We were playing Knocking Nine Doors, and a big guy rushed out and chased us down the street. He was known as a really hard man, and when we belted on his door, he was waiting behind it. He flew out, and we went hurtling down the road. He chased us for a couple of hours, and the terror I'd felt then was exactly the same as what I experienced during the contact in the wadi.

That wasn't by any means the only time I'd been on the run. Once my younger brother Keith and I had been playing football with some boys in Blanchland. I must have hurt one of the locals in a tackle, and he went off in a rage. Later, Keith and I set out with our cousin to get conkers. I'd just climbed the tree and started hitting the conkers down, when Keith gave a hoarse cry: '*Chris – look!*' Peering down through the leaves, I saw a gang of ten or twelve kids from the village, all armed with sticks, heading for us at a run.

'There they are!' the raiders shouted as they spotted us. 'There they are!'

I jumped down from the tree. 'You run back up home that way,' I told Keith, and I took off in the other direction. The pack came after me – and it was like hare and hounds for the rest of the day, four hours at least. I ran until I thought I was going to die. I ran through the forest, waded the river, ran up on to the moors – and still the little bastards were after me, determined to get me. In the end I spotted a neighbour of my aunt's, a man who worked as a gamekeeper. I came tearing down the road with the hunters close behind and threw myself into his arms, unable to speak.

I hated school work. I was all right at maths and technical drawing, but never much good at basics like reading and writing, and I took little interest in most of my lessons. Part of my trouble, I suspect, was that the school was in a period of transition, changing from grammar school to comprehensive, and the teachers were not interested in the less able children, so that it was easy to sit at the back of the class and do whatever one wanted.

Afterwards, I bitterly regretted my lack of motivation, especially when I found that, as an adult, I had a perfectly good brain. When I joined the army, I realised I had to pass the exams in order to survive, and so I really got down to work. I found the German course, which I took before going on the Alpine guides' course, a severe effort, as I had no real grounding in English grammar and vocabulary, let alone German. So I had to learn English properly first – and there I was, sitting alongside brigadiers and colonels in Beaconsfield, struggling to keep up. But in the end I surprised myself by passing, and in Mittenwald I went on to receive lessons in Bavarian-accented German on the weather, rock-formations and so on.

As a boy, though, I was more interested in making a camp in the woods or racing about with the other kids on the estate at home than in going to school; every now and then I'd play truant, or try it on at home by pretending to feel ill.

My father never took much interest in my education, and it was my mother who always read my school reports first. She was forever disappointed – and I'd beg her not to show them to my dad. After reading one report, she made an extraordinarily prophetic remark. 'Chris,' she said, 'I hope you've got a sturdy pair of boots.'

'Why?' I said.

'Because you're going to have to do an awful lot of walking one day.' She meant that I'd have to walk round looking for jobs, and she started singing that song, 'These Boots are Made for Walking'. I remember pulling faces behind her back, mouthing, 'Shut up! Shut up!' – but she went on singing and laughing.

By the time I was sixteen, all I wanted was to join the army. I didn't get much encouragement from my dad, because when he'd been caught for National Service in the Royal Horse Artillery, he hadn't liked the army one bit. Probably it was because he was the youngest child, and a bit spoilt. The sudden strict discipline kicked him into shape, but also it gave him an unpleasant shock, and once he came out he had nothing more to do with the military.

At least he didn't oppose me when I wanted to join up. At the local recruiting office I did the first tests to become a boy soldier, and passed them fine. For the final tests I was due to travel to Sutton Coldfield, but because I went down with jaundice, I missed the interviews. I felt destroyed at having lost the chance of joining. I remember lying in bed, feeling lousy, and seeing two men in uniform, an officer and an NCO, come to the house, to tell my parents that the army suggested I should join up for man's service when I was seventeen or eighteen.

Luckily at that point my cousin Billy was in 23rd SAS, the territorial unit, and one day he said, 'Well, why not come up, and we'll get you out on a couple of weekends? Then you'll see what it's like to be in the army.'

Until then I'd only been in the Air Cadets, and knew practically nothing. When Billy came down to pick me up, I was still at school. I said, 'What do I need?'

'Oh, just get a set of spare socks.'

My mum was clucking round me, getting out tins of soup and making sandwiches, but Billy said, 'Don't worry – he'll be fine.' So we went up to Prudhoe, in Northumberland, where 'C' Squadron of 23 SAS had its base. At that time – the late 1970s, before the siege of the Iranian Embassy in Princes Gate – the

SAS was nothing like as well known as it later became; but the Regiment was flourishing, and there was much territorial activity. I was just a naive lad of sixteen, and as I walked through the doors of the drill hall, I saw all these guys who looked tremendously old. Probably their ages ranged from thirty to forty-five, and a lot of them had seen service in Suez and other campaigns, having served in the regular army. No doubt I looked a bit of a twerp to them. But nothing could damp down my excitement; when the SQMS took me into the stores and gave me a camouflage suit, a set of webbing pouches, a poncho and a bergen, I was over the moon.

A bunch of recruits had assembled for a weekend's training – some were civilians, others from regular army units. Their average age must have been about twenty-five. As I arrived, they were about to have a map-reading lesson, so I sat down with them and did that. Next, we all scrambled on to trucks and drove up to Otterburn, where we walked out on to the moors. 'Right,' somebody said, 'tonight we're going to sleep against this wall, under ponchos.' I thought it was terrific – to spend the night outdoors. I was so excited that I couldn't go to sleep, and I lay for ages gazing up at the stars.

Next morning, after no more than a couple of hours' sleep, I was up early, and we spent the day walking. We'd walk for a while, have something to eat, get another lesson in map-reading, then go on again. The exercise ended with a long hike, which left me knackered. Back at Prudhoe, I thought, 'Well – that was great. But that's it.' I imagined that after my introduction to the army, I wouldn't be asked again. But luckily for me the OC happened to be there. He was a scary-looking guy, with ginger hair and little milky-bar glasses, and looked a right hard nut. He came over to speak to me and said, 'You're Billy's cousin, aren't you? Would you like to come back up?'

'Fine,' I said. 'Great.'

'Good,' he replied. 'But you must understand that you won't be on the books. You shouldn't be here, really, because we're breaking the law. If anything happens, you won't be able to lay claim on the army.'

That didn't worry me one bit, and from then on I went up to Prudhoe every weekend. The selection course went on over a period of three months, with the recruits assembling only at weekends. At first the group had consisted of sixty people, but every week a few of them decided they'd had enough and threw their hand in. Whenever I got out of the wagon at the start of a new exercise, the number had gone down. But for me things became more and more exciting, because we went from being in a big group to working in pairs, and in the end I was on my own. It was a big thrill when someone told me to walk alone from Point A to Point B; I had become confident with my map-reading, and between Friday night and Sunday morning we'd cover up to 60 kilometres, carrying a bergen. On the last weekend of the course there were only four of us left, and I was the only one who finished the march.

Completion of that march was the prerequisite for going on to a Test Week in Wales. Normally, anyone who passed would be tested for two weeks down the Brecon Beacons. But I was too young to go, and they told me that I wouldn't be ready to take selection for 23rd SAS until two more territorial selection courses had gone through. In other words, I was going to have to wait a whole year.

That was disappointing, but I was so keen that I volunteered to keep going out on the territorial weekends when the next course started. By that time I knew all the routes, and I could run from one check-point to another without having to consult a map. I'd also learnt how to cut corners and cheat a bit. At the end of that course only one man passed: he and I were the sole survivors.

By then I'd become a bit of a joke in the Squadron. None the less, on the third course I had a still greater advantage. I was so fit, and knew the ground so well, that I finished each leg before the other guys were half-way.

Now at last I was old enough to go down to Wales for the Test Week. After two weeks on the hills, based at Sennybridge, I passed out and at last became a member of 'C' Squadron. My aim, of course, was to join 22, the regular SAS; normally, to do that, you have to enrol in another regiment first, and then obtain secondment. My best course seemed to be to join the Parachute Regiment – but all the guys said, 'Don't bother with that. Once you've served here in 23 for a bit, you can go straight on to selection for 22.' Apart from that, 22 were holding a lot of courses and exercises down at Hereford, and there were often spare places – so I was going south a good deal.

Between all my outdoor activities at weekends, I had various jobs. I worked in a fibre-glass factory, then in a garage, where I got an apprenticeship as a mechanic. But I really had very little interest in the work. Instead of concentrating on the job, I'd be thinking about morse code or demolitions, and in the evenings I'd listen to tapes or study manuals on such subjects. The result was that I could never hold down a job for long; I was always wanting to go off with the TA, and my employers wouldn't give me the time. Someone would ring up from Hereford and say, 'Right, we've got three slots here on a jungle trip. Send two guys down.' But if I went into work and said, 'Listen – can I have four weeks off, from tomorrow?' of course the answer would be no. One day I went in knowing there was a possibility of an exercise in Belgium. After that I was planning a summer holiday in Greece, and immediately after that, there was an exercise in America which would last six weeks. When I asked my manager if I could have the time off, he said, 'Not a chance,' so I said, 'OK – stick your job,' and packed it in.

During the exercise in Belgium our patrol commander began breaking SOPs by walking during daylight. We were moving up the edge of a field on a hot, sunny summer's day when suddenly we got a contact. As I was coming over the brow, a line of red berets popped up out of the golden corn, and we were captured by Belgian paras. I spent my eighteenth birthday being interrogated, put through TQ (tactical questioning) in stress positions, and I thought, 'There's no way I'm ever going to get captured again.'

Back from exercises, I started labouring on building sites for a friend of my father who had his own business. He allowed me to work for him more or less when I wanted, and the money was all under the table. If a TA exercise came up, and I wanted three weeks off, there was no problem.

By this time I was extremely fit. Every day I'd do a ten-mile run, followed by a 16-mile bike ride, and then swim for a mile, and run the three miles home. I seemed to go through this routine with the greatest ease, and maintained it for months on end. Out running, I had the lovely feeling that it was no effort, but that I was coasting comfortably through the country lanes. One day, for some reason, I didn't go out – and in the house I simply couldn't sit down. My mum was cooking dinner, and I was driving her crazy by jumping up and down. 'For God's sake, go for a run, will you?' she said, and I ended up doing just that – and after ten miles I felt fine.

When I asked at Hereford to go on selection for 22 SAS, there was no problem. But first I was taken on an LTM (laser target marker) exercise by Jack, one of the permanent staff instructors. It was here I met a few of the Regiment's characters, not all of them admirable. We went out to the Black Forest in southern Germany, where our patrol's task was to put a marker on a farm building, so that a jet could fly across and bounce a signal off the target. I was mustard keen, but there was a guy from 22 who just sat out in the middle of a field smoking, not bothering even to unpack his equipment from its plastic bag. I didn't think that was very professional, and when he said, 'You're a dickhead to get your LTM out – you'll just have to clean it,' I felt quite annoyed. I couldn't see the point of going to Germany and being deployed into the field, and then not doing the exercise properly. Later someone explained that I was doing what I was doing as a hobby, and that once I'd joined up it would become a job and I'd think differently. But Jack turned round and said, 'Don't take any notice of what happened here. That isn't the Regiment.'

At last the time came for me to go down to Hereford and take the 22 Selection course, which was spread over six months. We did four weeks on the hills, two weeks' tactics training, five weeks in the jungle in Brunei, then combat survival followed by continuation training. In the hills there were some days when I felt we were being crucified, but on the whole it wasn't too bad. In tactics training, I found I was confident with a weapon, but I was shocked by the state of some of the troops who came up: their weapon-handling drills were poor, to say the least.

In the jungle we were put into six-man patrols, and sent to live in a basecamp from which we moved out every day to do range work, navigation or RV drills. I found it tough going. Navigation posed no problem, and I discovered that I could mix with other guys easily enough; but I didn't like the physical difficulties of living in the jungle, where you're wet, filthy and stinking for weeks on end. Also, I had difficulty assimilating spoken orders. Many of the other guys had led patrols in Northern Ireland, and some had been in the jungle before, so that they were all more experienced than me.

Back at Hereford, at the end of the course, we were all taken into the camp cinema. Nothing had been said about who had passed or failed. Then the sergeant major, whose sense of humour was all his own, announced that he would read out a list of names. The people on it were to go back to the accommodation block, wait there, and return in fifteen minutes' time. He read out twenty names, including mine – more or less half the people on the course. Had we passed or failed? Nobody knew. We walked across to the accommodation block silent and numbed. Then someone said, 'Well – hell! So-and-so's a wanker, and he's still over there. *He* can't have passed.' Somebody else said, 'But Smith's over there too, and he's a good bloke.'

Returning to the cinema a quarter of an hour later, we found that the other half of the course had disappeared, and we sat down again. The sergeant major stood up and said, 'Right, you lot. You haven't passed . . .' There was an intake of breath, and a pause long enough for everyone's heart to hit the floor before he added, 'yet.' Faces lit up. Everyone burst out laughing. There was continuation training to come – but so what?

We did combat survival – in which six more of the guys failed – and after that, build-up for Northern Ireland and the counter-terrorist team. Then at last the survivors passed, and we were given our berets.

Normally, before joining the regular SAS, a soldier would have to put in three or four years of TA courses and exercises; but I had already done seven years as a territorial, and so was able to skip that requirement. It was a tremendous thrill for me. I'd achieved the goal on which I'd set my heart. But I soon found that the regulars were not particularly pleased about TA guys coming into the Regiment by the route I'd taken – as they saw it, by the back door. Some people thought of the TA in terms of *Dad's Army*, and didn't realise that I'd already done more work than many members of 22. So one or two of the guys gave us newcomers a hard time, forcing us to prove ourselves even more. For instance, when I did Junior Brecon – a six-week tactics course aimed at anyone who had not been in an infantry unit – someone told me, 'Go down there, and make sure you get a distinction.'

Luckily I managed to do just that – and from then on, everything was fine. I soon developed fierce loyalty to the Regiment, and saw that anyone who worked really hard to achieve his best earned a lot of respect and credibility within the unit. I realised that in any small group the key thing was to keep tight, and for everybody to work as one; by that means, sticking together, you can get through quite a lot.

Next stop for me was the Parachute Regiment, which I joined as my parent unit. After Christmas at home I reported to Aldershot with Barry Hilton, who'd come from the Navy, and also needed a parent unit. I'd had a real skinhead haircut, because I knew the other recruits would be the same. Barry turned up with long hair. We went in to see the Company Sergeant Major, who acted the part for all it was worth. He had the pair of us standing in front of him and said, 'OK, I want you to come back to me in uniform.' Glaring at me he added, 'And make sure that tart's had a haircut.' Then we were marched out.

Round at the hairdresser's, Barry only had a trim. 'Jesus!' I said. 'Get a shorter cut.'

'Not a chance,' he answered. 'I'm in the Regiment now. I'm not getting my hair cut for anyone.'

'Oh, for God's sake! Please, just get one, or we're in for some flak.'

When the CSM saw us again, he said, 'Right, I told you to get him a haircut,' and he started bollocking me.

After that short, sharp introduction, we started working with the recruits, lads straight from civvy street who looked up to us because of our experience. Unlike the SAS, where you're left largely to make your own decisions and make sure that you turn up in the right place at the right time, here people were yelling at us the whole time. The activities were all done in groups: team running, a steeplechase, a log race, the assault course and so on. There was always someone on top of us, kicking us to get from A to B, and some of the young guys of seventeen and eighteen began getting hammered. The instructors just beasted them, hitting and kicking them so that they were frightened and didn't learn anything.

Being five or six years older, I found I could cope pretty well. I was living in a room with eight or nine recruits, and in the evening I used to teach them map-reading. One instructor was having trouble with his wife; now and then she'd kick him out of the house, and he'd come down to live in the accommodation block. To relieve his feelings, he'd knock a couple of the young lads around. One night he came in screaming and shouting. I walked up to him and said, 'Hey, cut it out now, or I'll go and see somebody.' He didn't know what to say, because to all intents and purposes I was an ordinary recruit – but he knew I'd passed SAS selection, which he would probably never get through. He just muttered something, slammed the door and got his head down.

I realised how bad the atmosphere was one Saturday, when most people had knocked off for the weekend. I had collected the lads who were left behind and taken them map-reading in a training area called Long Valley. I told one of them, 'Right – you're leading the way now. Can you use a compass?'

'Yes, yes!' he said quickly. But it was quite clear that he couldn't, and when I asked him why he'd lied, he said, 'I thought you were going to hit me.' That was the mentality they'd got into.

Another day one of the instructors came up to us and said that his mother was ill and he ought to go home, but he had to give a lecture that Friday evening on the gympi, the general-purpose machine-gun. I volunteered to take the period in his place. While I was in the middle of my talk, in walked the OC of the camp. He sat there and listened, and at the end, thinking I was one of the regular instructors, came up to tell me off for being improperly dressed (I didn't have my belt on or my wings up). I apologised and said, 'I'm Private Ryan from Hereford.'

'What are you doing here?' he asked.

'Just working with the guys.'

'You're wasting your time down here.'

I believe he telephoned Hereford and said he was going to send us back – but outside events accelerated our return anyway. At that time, law and order were breaking down in Aden, and the order was given to evacuate all British personnel; the QE2 was going in to pull them off the beaches, and 'B' Squadron was detailed to parachute into the sea to secure the beach-heads. Everyone was loading up, and my sergeant major rang the Parachute Regiment, asking to have us back immediately, as he needed everyone he could get.

The original intention had been that Barry and I should spend three months with the Paras – but now we were leaving after only eight weeks. In the morning we had to say goodbye to the CSM. I knew Barry hadn't enjoyed himself at all, so as we were about to go in I told him, 'Whatever they say, just tell them you've had a good time. Say you thought it was great, and you've learned a lot – because that's what they want to hear. Then we'll leave.'

'Yeah, OK,' he went.

So we marched in and stood to attention in front of the OC, with the CSM behind us.

'And did you learn a lot?' the OC asked.

'Yes,' I said, 'a great deal.'

'And how about you?' he asked Barry. 'What do you think?'

'I think it's a load of crap.'

Fucking hell! The CSM was right behind us.

The hair on my neck stood up, and I started shaking.

'RYAN!' roared the sergeant major. 'Atten-SHUN! About TURN! Quick MARCH!'

Out I went in double time, with the others yelling at Barry behind me.

Back in Hereford, we found that the trouble had run ahead of us. The OC saw us, also with the sergeant major in attendance.

'One of you two didn't enjoy himself down there,' said the colonel. 'Who was it?'

We stood there looking at each other. Inside I was screaming, 'Come on, Barry, say something!' I thought, 'You wanker!'

Then the OC said to me, 'Chris – thin out. You've got to go to "B" Squadron.' So off I went, and Barry got a terrible bollocking, because obviously they knew already what he'd been saying. Looking back on my stay with the Paras, I realise that all the ferocity and bullying had the desired effect, in that they produced a breed of fearsome fighting men – as testified by the actions at Goose Green in the Falklands, and many other campaigns.

As soon as I joined 'B' Squadron I did a couple of exercises with Government agents in the United Kingdom and Europe. In one, which was highly realistic, we flew into Jersey in the middle of the night, our helicopter landing in a public park, to kidnap an industrialist who – according to the scenario – had been in touch with the Russians and was liable to defect. Wearing civilian clothes, we booked into hotels and made contact with agents who already had the target under surveillance. Then, having hired a van, we snatched him as he came out of a restaurant late at night. After a quick transfer to a car, we drove to a pre-designated pick-up point on the coast and the helicopter, which had been cruising out of sight off-shore, slipped in at wave-top height to land on the beach and collect us.

That was the first time I'd been exposed to anything of the kind, and I thought, 'This is for me!'

Next I went on to the SP or anti-terrorist team, and found it really exciting. Part of the team was on stand-by the whole time, for immediate response to a threat like the hijacking of an aircraft, and we all trained to a very high level, each guy putting down at least a thousand rounds a week.

Within the squadron I found a wide mixture of people. Some guys were really quiet and tended to withdraw into themselves; but the chief requirement was that everyone should mix and get on with each other, so that they could work together under extreme pressure. Everyone was highly motivated by pride in the job and the determination to be best – and with a lot of healthy young guys thrown together, the competition was intense. At times when nothing much was happening, this could lead to back-stabbing and unpleasantness; but when things were moving, and the guys were working together, nobody could compete against them.

One thing I couldn't help noticing was the speed at which people seemed to age. Guys of twenty-three or twenty-four were still relatively fresh-faced; but by the time they reached thirty, a lot of them were wrinkled, with their hair turning grey. By that age nearly everyone had some injury – broken legs, broken wrists, back strains, hearing problems brought on by firing weapons and detonating explosives . . .

As I lay against the bank of the wadi, Hereford seemed a long way off. I took off my boots – one at a time, in case we were surprised – to have a look at my feet. As I thought, they were badly blistered along the sides, especially round the ball, and on the heels. But I had nothing to treat them with, and could only put my boots back on again.

We'd become so confused during the night that it took us

some time to work out which day this was. We decided it was the morning of Saturday 26 January. Time passed slowly, but we weren't too uncomfortable. The sun was reviving us, we were chatting in low voices, and our spirits were kept up by our belief that the Euphrates was only just over the next hill to the north. Because we'd walked all night, I knew we'd covered a long distance, and thought we must be within a couple of kilometres of the river. We said to ourselves, 'We'll hit the river, get some water, and walk out into Syria – no problem.' We managed to convince ourselves that we were safe for the time being. We'd put so much ground between us and the scene of the contact that we didn't think anyone would come looking for us.

Of course, we were wondering about Vince. I hoped against hope that, like us, he'd come down off the plateau and found a warmer place; but in my heart of hearts I felt that he was dead. I imagined him lying down in a hole among the snow, falling asleep, and drifting away, without any pain or knowledge of what was happening. At the back of my mind I kept hoping that we would see the rest of the patrol appear – that we'd hear one of them say something and they'd pop up out of the ground.

Together we did a map appreciation, trying to work out how far we'd come in the night. There was no feature on the ground that we could identify, but we knew that we'd been on the move for eleven hours. Some of that time had been spent backtracking in search of Vince, but we calculated we must have advanced about forty kilometres. We thought that one more good night's push would bring us to the Syrian border.

We spent a profitable hour cleaning our weapons, which were covered in mud and grit, doing them one at a time in case we got bounced. In my right-hand pouch I had a small but comprehensive kit – pull-through, four-by-two cleaning patches, oil, rag, and a tool like a pocket knife fitted with screwdriver, scraper and gouge. With this I gave my 203 a thorough going-over. I pulled a piece of four-by-two through the barrel, cleaned and oiled the working parts, and checked the loaded magazines to make sure no grit had got in among the rounds. By working carefully, I stripped the weapon and reassembled it making hardly a sound.

Then, at about midday, we heard the noise we'd already learned to dread: the jingle of bells. Fucking goats! Again! We went down flat with our weapons and looked along the little valley. There they were, a scatter of brown, black, grey and dirty white animals, coming slowly into the wadi from the north-east. Then their minder appeared and sat down on a rock in full view, only fifty metres away. He was a young man with thick, curly black hair, and stubbled cheeks, dressed in a big old overcoat of what looked like dark grey tweed. There he sat, day-dreaming, kicking his feet, chewing on stalks of dead grass.

The goats began feeding our way. Stan and I lay still with our 203s ready. 'Right,' I whispered, 'if he comes up on us, we're going to have to take him out.'

'Wait a minute,' said Stan. 'He might have a land cruiser, or even a tractor – some vehicle he'd lend us.'

It went against the grain to kill a civilian. But I felt certain that if the man saw us at all, he'd go back to the nearest habitation and give us away. It flashed through my mind that we could tie him up – but if we did that, he might die of exposure. I thought, 'He's either going to escape or die – so we might as well do him now.'

The goats kept feeding and moving towards us. I began to fancy eating one of them, a young one – goat steak. Goat curry – even better. Also, I liked the look of the coat the guy was wearing – it was obviously a hell of a lot warmer than anything I had on.

The lead goats reached our position, walking on, stopping, nibbling. When they saw us, they jerked their heads up, but that was all – a jerk, and on they'd go, meandering past within a few feet of our faces. All this while the herder was sitting there, looking up at the sky now and then, but basically doing nothing except minding his herd and his own business. Certainly he hadn't locked on to anything.

'He's bound to come after them,' I breathed, 'and if he does, we'll do him.'

We didn't want to fire a shot, for obvious reasons, but both of us had knives. Mine was a folding knife – a good one, but with relatively small blades. Stan had a k-bar bayonet on his webbing with a six- or seven-inch blade. 'I'll grab him,' I muttered, 'and you run up and stick him.'

But Stan, being a gentleman and a good soldier, wasn't happy. He didn't want to kill an innocent civilian. 'Shouldn't we take the chance of seeing if he's got some vehicle? We could nick it and drive off.'

'No, we'll do him.'

Then the man stood up. On his feet, he looked quite a big guy – about the size of Stan, and hefty with it. Immediately I changed my plan. 'Fuck it,' I whispered. 'Stan, give us that knife. You grab him and I'll do him.'

'No,' Stan muttered. 'I don't think . . . You're not having it.'

'Then *you'd* better do him . . .'

Suddenly it was too late. With the guy nearly on top of us, Stan jumped up and grabbed him.

'Siddown, mate!' he said loudly. '*Hurrh!* How're you doing? Good? Right! Siddown!'

The guy jumped and let out a stream of Arabic, but Stan forced him down on the bank-side. I sat down too, staring at him. He was only a young fellow, in his twenties, but of low intelligence, I guessed. He was dressed like the village idiot, dishevelled, with several ragged jumpers under his overcoat, and dirty bare feet in slip-on leather shoes. He kept looking at me, but I didn't say anything.

Stan did all the talking. 'Car?' he said. 'Tractor?' He made driving motions with his hands. 'House?'

He drew in the air, but our visitor didn't understand a word of English. All he said was, '*Aiwa. Aiwa*' – 'Yes. Yes.' It was *aiwa* to everything. In between, he jabbered Arabic and pointed down the wadi.

'Where's there a vehicle?'

'*Aiwa.*'

'How far to walk?' – with walking motions.

'*Aiwa.*'

I exclaimed, 'Ah, bollocks, man, he's just saying yes to everything.'

After a bit Stan said, 'Listen – I'll go with him and see if we can get a tractor.'

'Don't do it!' I said fiercely. It seemed incredible to me that Stan should want to go off with a total stranger. I reminded him that we were aliens in a foreign country, where we had no business to be. I knew we'd get no friendly help from the Iraqis. The natives weren't going to do us any favours. Quite apart from being enemies in war, we were infidels. This man would sell us down the wadi – but Stan couldn't seem to see that.

'Listen,' I said. 'Suppose this was World War Two, and we were a couple of German paratroopers, lost in the Welsh mountains. We meet this farm lad and try to chat him up. Of course he says he's going to help us. But what does he want really? To get us in the nick. Nothing else.'

Even that didn't change Stan's mind. 'It's OK,' he said. 'I'll take the risk and go with him.'

'Stan! You're fucking not. You're staying here.'

'Chris – I want to go.'

This was a big shock to me. I thought he was crazy. But I couldn't force him to stay, because that sort of thing doesn't hold water when you're on the run. So I said, 'Well, OK. I can't order you, because we're on our own. But listen, mate: I don't *want* you to go. It'll mean us splitting up. You'll be on your own. You're making a big mistake here.'

'No, no,' he said. 'What I'll do is leave my weapon and webbing with you. Then I won't cut such an aggressive figure. I'll just walk next to him. Why don't you come too?'

'Not bloody likely! I disagree with what you're doing. It's dangerous, and stupid too.'

But I could see that he was determined, so I said, 'Well – I'll wait here for you till six-thirty, last light. If you're not back by then, I'm off on this bearing.' And I gave him the northerly course we'd already decided on.

'Fair enough,' he said.

'Go on, then. When you're out of sight, I'll take your weapon and webbing fifty metres up that dry stream bed, and hide them there.'

'Yeah – OK.'

So Stan stood up with the Arab and said, 'Come on, cobber. Let's go,' and the two of them started walking off, with the Arab whistling for his goats to follow. I crawled down to the bottom of the wadi and sat and watched them. When they'd made a couple of hundred metres, I suddenly thought, 'NO! This is wrong!' and I yelled out, 'STAN! Stan, come back here!'

Back he came, almost running.

'For Christ's sake, think about what you're doing,' I told him. 'Leave your webbing if you like, but at least take your weapon.'

'I don't want to look too aggressive.'

'Sling it over your shoulder, then, and carry it down the side of your body – but have it with you. And if you change your mind when you get back down there towards him, just drill him, like I said. Put one into him, and we'll sit the day out together.'

But Stan was overboard about his new friend. 'No, no, Chris,' he said. 'He's quite all right. He's offered me food.'

'What food?'

'It's only a few berries.'

'Bollocks to the berries,' I said. 'Just drill him.'

'No – I trust the guy. He seems like, you know, friendly. If we get to a vehicle, I'll give him a sovereign.'

'Drill him,' I repeated. 'Go back and shoot the bugger.'

But Stan wouldn't have it. Away he went with the Iraqi, meandering down the dry stream bed. For nearly a kilometre he remained in sight. He'd wrapped his shamag round his head, and from a distance he looked quite like another Arab. I could see the two of them trying to chat together, matey as anything. In the end they went round a bend to the left and disappeared.

'Jesus!' I thought. 'Now I'm on my own.' I wished I hadn't let Stan go – but for the moment I didn't feel too worried. I found it difficult to keep still. For a few minutes I'd sit against the bank in the side of the wadi; then I'd come up on to a mound in the middle of it and scan with my little binoculars. Looking straight down the line of the watercourse I could see for miles, up on to a big hill in the distance. Again and again I looked for the two men walking up there. Then I'd go back into cover.

Time crawled by. After a couple of hours I took Stan's webbing and tucked it into the side of the stream bed, where I'd told him it would be. On top of it I left four of the extra 203 rounds which I'd taken from Vince during the night. Then I had nothing to do but wait for dark.

As the hours dragged past, I grew more and more jumpy. Several times I imagined I heard something. Whenever that happened, I'd creep round to one side of the mound and look out, hoping like hell that I'd see Stan returning.

Dusk came on. By 1730 I was in a state of high anxiety. Very soon I was going to have to make a decision. I was hungry and thirsty and cold, and on my own. Six o'clock came, and I thought, 'Jesus, this is it.' I took one last look back down the wadi. Night had come down, and there was still no sign. I still kept hoping I'd see the lights of a vehicle heading out – but no.

99

It was a tough decision. My last friend had disappeared. He could still be on his way back. But when 1830 came I thought, 'This is it. You can't sit around here any longer.' So I checked my compass and started walking north.

For fifteen minutes I tabbed it steadily over level, open ground, with darkness settling in on the desert all round me. Then I happened to look over my shoulder, and I saw a set of headlights coming up the wadi I'd just left. 'Bloody hell!' I thought. 'Stan's got a vehicle after all. Brilliant!'

I started running back as fast as I could. I must have been half-way back to my start-point when suddenly I saw that it wasn't one set of lights coming towards me, but two. Immediately I thought, 'Shit – he can't have two vehicles. He must have been captured, and this is the enemy. If he'd been on his own, he'd never have brought two vehicles.' So I turned and ran north again.

Already I was out of breath. Glancing back over my shoulder to check the vehicles' progress, I searched desperately for cover on the flat plain. A burning sensation seared the top of my throat and forced me to slow down. Behind me, the vehicles had driven up the side of the wadi and were heading straight across the open desert for me. Then the clouds parted and the moon shone through, lighting the place up like day. It may have been my imagination, but my smock seemed to have become luminous, shining like an electric beacon. The old adrenaline had started up, and my heart was going like a sledgehammer. Then I saw a little bush with a shadow behind it, and threw myself down into that tiny patch of black.

As I lay there panting, I frantically sorted out my kit. I checked the magazine on the 203, and piled spare mags in a heap beside me. I opened out the 66 so that it was ready to fire. I even bent together the ends of the safety pins on my white phos grenades, so that I could whip them out quickly if need be.

For a moment I got a respite. The lights swung round, whipping wildly up and down as the vehicles went over bumps, and headed back into the wadi. There was a lot of banging of doors. Obviously some guys had got out to have a look round the place where the goatherd had found us in the morning. I squinted through the kite-sight, trying to make out what they were doing, but the glare from the lights shone everything else out. Then the vehicles moved off again and started driving about the floor of the wadi.

The moment the lights were away from me, I picked up my kit, stuffed things into the webbing pouches down my front, and legged it. Now I was really running, looking right and left for cover – and suddenly the lights swung round and they were coming for me again. I dropped down and got my kit out once more. I set up the 203 with the battle sight, and as I piled the spare magazines, it went through my mind that this was just like range practice. I cocked the 66 again, lifted the bomb sights on the 203, and waited.

Whether they'd seen me or not, I couldn't tell. But they were driving towards me at a steady roll. I got the 66 lined up on the leading pair of lights – and then I became aware of this amazing noise: *ke-kik, ke-kik, ke-kik, ke-kik*. It sounded like a steam train, and I thought, 'Jesus! Here's another vehicle, and the engine sounds really rough. Where is it? Where's it coming from?' When I closed my mouth, I couldn't hear the noise any more. I strained with my ears and wondered, 'Have they switched off, or what?' Then I opened my mouth to breathe, and it was *ke-kik, ke-kik, ke-kik* again. Suddenly I realised that what I could hear was the accelerated pounding of my own heart.

The lights were still coming. Obviously the vehicles weren't going to stop. Someone on board must have realised that I would be heading due north, for the river, and they were driving on that bearing. The wagons were rolling at maybe 15 m.p.h., and the lights were quite steady. They would pass so close that there was no chance of them not seeing me. It was going to be them or me. I hugged the ground and tried to stop myself shaking. An age seemed to pass as the vehicles ground on.

Now I thought, 'This is it. You're going to get killed here.' The worst thing was that I suddenly saw an image of my daughter. 'I'm going down here,' I thought, 'and Sarah will never know how her dad died.' I felt sudden fear that if I did get killed, she wouldn't remember me. She would never really know who her father was or what he'd been like. She was never going to understand how or where my life had ended – and I found that desperately sad.

Fifty metres, and they kept coming. Two Land-Rover-type

vehicles, advancing at a purposeful crawl, obviously in search of me. I couldn't tell how many men they might contain. I held the sight of the 66 aligned between the front pair of lights. When they were twenty metres off, I pulled the trigger.

Whhoooosh! went the launcher, right in my ear. Out front there was a big *BANG* as the rocket took the vehicle head-on. Oddly enough, I remember no flash, just this heavy explosion, and a cloud of white smoke billowing out in the moonlight. The vehicle rolled to a stop. I dropped the 66, grabbed the 203 and lined up the grenade sight on the second pair of lights, a few yards to the left of the first. From maybe forty metres I smacked that one right in the bonnet. Then I was up and running towards the enemy.

In a moment I had reached the first vehicle and put a burst into it. Coming to the second, I sprayed it all down the side, through the canvas back. Then I looked into the back and put another burst in. There were men in the back wearing dish-dashes. I let off another burst over the backs of the front seats into the driver's compartment. Then I had to change magazines. At the front again, I put more rounds into the first vehicle. Suddenly I thought, 'Fucking hell! I've left all the other magazines.' I sprinted back to them, snatched them up, stuffed them down the front of my smock and ran.

I ran till I thought my heart was going to burst. I imagined that everybody was on to me and chasing me. The moon was so bright that I felt as if a spotlight was beaming down on me. I was swept up in panic, just as I had been when chased as a kid. It was as if I'd been found out, and was on my own. I ran till I had to slow down, because I was feeling like I had during the initial contact: my throat was heaving, my chest exploding, my mouth dry as the desert. I'd had no water all through that day, and soon I was so knackered that it was painful even to walk.

All the time I was turning to look behind, to see if any more lights were coming up – but nothing showed. At last I thought it was safe to stop, sit down and sort out my equipment.

After a contact like that, it takes time to recover. Gradually I chilled out and got myself together. One minor improvement was that I had less to carry: once I'd fired the 66 I threw away the tube, which was useless to the Iraqis.

Walking again, I kept on for a couple of hours towards the

north. All the time I was wondering what had happened to Stan, and hoping to hell he hadn't come back in one of the vehicles. Or had he sent them up to me? No, I decided: he couldn't have. It must have been the goatherd who brought the Iraqis back to the wadi; no one else could have directed them on to my position with such accuracy. Thinking over our confrontation with him in the morning, I realised I should have done him there and then. Of course I should. My intuition about him had been right. I should have done him with my own knife, but he was a big guy, and somehow, with Stan not keen, it hadn't been on. Then I should never have let Stan go off with him: I should have put a round through the bugger myself. But then, if he had come back in one of the vehicles, maybe in the end I'd done him after all – because I don't think anybody in either of them could have survived.

The question was, what had happened back on the site of the contact during the last couple of hours? If anyone had got away from one of the vehicles I'd hit, or if someone else had found the wrecks, word might have gone out that another enemy soldier was on the run. People would surely guess that I was heading for the Euphrates. From the firepower I'd put down, they may have thought that there were several guys at large.

I tabbed on and on through the moonlight. Now the desert was rolling in gentle undulations, and I believed that the river was going to appear over every rise. Then, away to my right, I heard dogs barking, kids shouting, grown-ups calling. As I went down on one knee to listen, I saw the red tracer of anti-aircraft fire going up in the distance. Obviously there were habitations somewhere close to me, and the people I could hear were watching that nice firework display on the horizon. Then I heard the far-off roar of jets; I couldn't see them, but the sound of their engines was unmistakable. They must have been miles off, attacking some target, and the red tracer was curving silently up towards the stars.

Half an hour later I spotted a glimmer of light ahead. The kite-sight picked out three stationary vehicles, with light coming out of the side. I went down and watched for signs of people on foot, in case a mobile patrol was being deployed to cut me off. Men on foot could be strung out in an extended line, sweeping the desert ahead of them. After a careful search with the kite-sight, back and forth, I saw nothing more, so I boxed the vehicles and carried on.

Again, as I came to the top of a rise, I was convinced that I must find the Euphrates in front of me – but no. The next thing I saw was a set of pylons. I'd been expecting them for some time, because they were marked on my map. Beyond them was an MSR, and some fifteen kilometres beyond that, the river. When I sat down under the power-lines and scanned ahead, I found I could see the road, and a wide-open flat area beyond it – but no water. By then it was two in the morning, and nothing was moving on the highway. Coming down to the MSR, I found this was metalled. By then I was almost on my knees, and when I found a culvert under the road, I crawled into it and stretched out. All I could think was, 'I've got to get my head down,' so I took off my webbing and lay on that. I was also desperate with thirst, and I kept tipping up my two water bottles to see if I could get a drop out of them – but not one. I felt relatively safe in the culvert and closed my eyes – but anxiety was gnawing at me, and so was the cold.

Within ten minutes I was shaking all over, too frozen to stay still any longer. On again, then. From the map, I thought that if I crossed the MSR and kept heading north, I must hit the Euphrates, flowing from north-west to south-east. From talking about the river to Jan, I knew that in Biblical times it had been a mighty waterway, and I assumed that it must still be pretty big. But what I hit next was a huge system of dry wadis, with steep walls up to twenty metres high, all made of dead rock. Obviously they'd once been a river bed. Maybe in wet weather flash floods would turn the channels into a rushing river again. I was gagging for want of water, and getting so confused in my mind that suddenly I thought, 'Jesus – I hope this isn't the Euphrates. Surely it can't have dried out since the Bible? If it has, I'm fucked.'

Panic was making me walk faster and scrabble down through the tumbled, loose rock. I kept thinking, 'There's got to be water at the bottom of this.' At its lowest point the river bed seemed to open out, and as I looked down through the kite-sight, I made out a line of palm trees running across my front from left to right. Also, away to my right, I could see the houses of a village – pale, flat-roofed blocks glowing in the moonlight, with a breeze-block wall running down one side, and the shapes of cultivated fields outside it. I still couldn't see any water, but I thought, 'This has got to be the river – the Euphrates at last. Great!' I started walking down towards the trees, which I presumed were growing on the bank.

The closer I came, the warmer the air seemed to be – or at least, the atmosphere seemed stiller and calmer. I kept about 300 metres from the breeze-block wall, but dogs came out and started barking. As there was no wind, they could hardly have smelt me. More likely, they had picked up the noise of my feet, first on the rock and then in the dry grass of the fields. The houses were dark; they may have been blacked out, but probably the people in them were asleep.

Moving parallel to the boundary wall, I made my way carefully down to the river through oblong fields. No crops were sprouting as yet, but the ground had been well tilled, and the fields were divided up by irrigation ditches, with grass growing on bunds. I tried to keep out of the fields, for fear I would leave footprints in the soft soil. Rather than cross the cultivated areas, I kept to the ditches, which as yet had no water in them.

At last, between the trunks of the palm trees, I saw water. Irrigation pumps were working all along the bank: the night was full of their quick, steady beat – *boop, boop, boop, boop*. I could hear many different pumps working up and down the valley. For several minutes I kept still, watching for any movement. The cultivation seemed to end about ten metres from the edge of the water, and my kite-sight revealed piles of cut bushes, each about two metres square, sticking out from the bank into the stream, one about every fifty metres. At first I couldn't make out what they were for, then it occurred to me that they were probably makeshift jetties, for men to fish off or to bring boats alongside. In any case, using one for cover, I crept right down to the water's edge.

Crouching next to the pile, I got out my water bottles, but found that at the bank the water was only a few millimetres deep – a thin skin over mud. I tried to wade out, but I hadn't taken three steps before my feet plunged deep into silt. In a second I was up to my knees, then up to my bollocks. I thought, 'Jesus, I'm sinking!' I threw my rifle back on to the pile of bushes and dragged myself out, soaked up to the waist and coated in slimy, silty mud.

For my next attempt, I crawled out over one of the platforms of bushes. As my weight came on to it, the whole structure sank into the stream. I could feel water coming through my clothes at the front – legs, crutch, chest – but I filled both bottles, crawled back out, and drank one down.

I swallowed and gasped and choked, trying to stifle the noise. The relief of getting water down my neck was incredible. I shone my torch beam down the neck of the full bottle, and saw that the water was black and foul-looking, but it tasted quite good. I crawled out to fill the empty bottle again.

At that point the river was a couple of hundred metres wide, and I could see no buildings or cultivations on the far bank. In the moonlight the land beyond glowed white, as if it were encrusted in salt. Because there seemed to be no habitations over there, it occurred to me that I might swim across and make better progress along the far side. I'm a strong swimmer, but I thought that to go in with my weapon and webbing would be asking for trouble. The water was icy cold, and although the surface was smooth, I could see that a strong current was flowing out in the middle of the stream. If I'd got into difficulties half-way across, that would have been it.

By then it was nearly five o'clock, and I needed somewhere to basha up for the day. I moved cautiously out between scattered houses, up to a dirt road. Again a dog started barking, so I waited a couple of minutes before going on up into the dry wadi systems. Once into the rocks I turned on my TACBE and tried speaking into it. Getting no response, I left the beacon on for a while. As I climbed, the rocky channels grew steeper and steeper, and a couple of hundred metres above the road, they came to a dead end. There I found a rock a couple of feet high which was casting a black shadow in the moonlight. I curled up beside it, with my map case beneath my legs, one shamag round them and the other round my head, and lay there feeling relatively secure in that patch of deep darkness.

Before settling down, I gave myself the only treat at my disposal: I got out my flask, and took a nip of whisky. The old Lagavulin burnt as it went down into my empty stomach, but it gave me a momentary lift. I was so exhausted that in spite of the cold I kept falling asleep, only to come round with a start a few minutes later, racked by shudders. It was a real pain to be wet again; having spent hours with Stan getting dry, I was now soaked all up the front, with my sodden clothes clinging to me, and the damp intensifying the cold.

When first light came, with dawn breaking early under clear skies, I realised that I wasn't really in any sort of cover. At night the shadow of the rock had looked comforting; if someone had walked past in the dark, he wouldn't have seen me. Now I found I was lying out in the open.

Looking up on to the north bank of the wadi, I saw a hollow among some loose rocks. I walked up to it, lay inside it, and piled up a few more rocks at either side to break my outline. That was the best place I could find in which to spend the day – and that was when it really hit me how much I was on my own.

Chapter Five

Boxing Clever

In the days and nights that followed, there were several moments when morale plunged to rock-bottom – and this was one of them. A wave of loneliness swept over me, as I realised that I was utterly alone. I thought, 'This can't get any worse.' I was hungry, wet, tired, cut off from all communication with friends, and still far inside a hostile country.

'If things get on top of you,' my mum always used to say, 'have a good cry.' So I lay there in the rocks and tried to cry – but I couldn't. Instead my face crumpled up and I started laughing. 'Dickhead!' I thought. 'Here you are, deep in the shite, and all you can do is laugh!' But somehow it did the trick; it let go the tension and sorted me out. I daydreamed wistfully about the glorious puddings my mum used to make – particularly her rice pudding, with its thick, sweet, creamy inside, and its crust baked to a crisp golden brown. I could have done with a helping of that, there and then. But from that point I wasn't bothered about being alone. I seemed to have made a transition into feeling that I'd been on my own for the whole trip. I was used to it now – all I had to do was get on with heading for the border.

It was the morning of Sunday 27 January, my third day on the run. I would have liked to let my feet breathe, but that would have involved too great a risk. I had to be ready to leg it at any minute: so it was one boot off, one sock off, check that foot, and get sock and boot back on. Then the other foot. The blisters looked bad; they had long since burst, and the underlying skin was raw and bleeding. My toenails had started lifting, and there were blisters under my toes. I had no means of treating them, and could only hope that my feet would hold out until I reached the border.

With my boots back on, I devoted the best part of an hour to

cleaning my weapon. Again, I took care not to make any noise
that would carry. If you release the working parts of a 203
normally, they snap forward with a sharp crack, but if you
handle them gently, you need make scarcely a sound. Once I
had everything squared away, I lay back with my belt undone
but my webbing still in place, straps over my shoulders, so that I
could make a rapid getaway if need be. Even down there, almost
on the level of the Euphrates, the air was still icy cold, and I shivered continuously. I lay on one side, with my hands between
my legs, tucked in under one big rock, with smaller rocks pulled
into position shielding my head and feet, and bare rock beneath
me.

From time to time I dozed off, but always I woke with a start a
few minutes later, shaking all over. It was my body's defence to
bring me round like that: if I hadn't kept waking, I would have
drifted off and been gone for ever. Aching from contact with
the rock, I would shift about, trying to find a more comfortable
position. There was always a pebble or bump of rock digging
into some part of me, and the pressure-points on the outside of
my knees, hips and spine had already begun to rub sore.

The drink had made me feel better in one way; the trouble
was, the intake of all that cold water had given me the shivers,
and all I wanted to do was press on again, so that I could warm
up. The hardest thing was to keep still in daylight. The urge to
start walking, to make progress towards the border, was almost
overwhelming.

Below me, the wadi dropped towards the river in a V-shape,
snaking left and right. Its flanks consisted of tumbled grey-
brown rock, devoid of vegetation, but the bottom of the channel,
where water would run after rain, had smoother sides. There
was nothing whatever alive to keep me interested: no bird or
animal, nothing moving. Boredom soon became another powerful enemy: it took all my will-power to resist the urge to move
on, or even just to have a look round.

The day was quiet: I never heard voices or traffic movement,
but now and then the wind would stir among the rocks and I
would come fully alert, looking round, wondering if a person or
an animal had shifted. From where I lay I could see what looked
like the remains of an ancient viaduct, jutting out from the bank
of the river into the water. There were three tiers of pale yellow

arches on top of each other, and they looked as though they were made of stone. I'd spotted the structure when I was getting water, and now, if I lifted my head, it was still in sight. I wondered how old the remains of the bridge were, and whether they could date back as far as the Romans. Round the base of the arches the water was obviously deep, for through my binoculars I could see the current swirling fast. The river was brown with silt, a strong contrast with the salty-looking land on the far bank.

What kept my spirits up was the thought that I must be close to the Syrian border – within no more than thirty or forty kilometres. Looking at the map again and again, I worked out that I was much farther west than I had thought I was. I reckoned I was within one night's march, possibly two, of safety.

Until then, the longest I'd ever gone without food was four days, on combat survival training in Wales. Even then, an agent had brought me one slice of bread or a little piece of cheese every twenty-four hours – but I remembered feeling pretty weak at the end. The furthest I'd ever walked in one march was 65 kilometres – the final march on Selection. Now, I reckoned, I'd covered about 150 kilometres in three nights, and already it was five days since I had had a proper meal – the big blow-out at Al Jouf. With my biscuits finished, I inevitably began to worry about how long my strength would hold out. How long could I go on walking? Would I slow right down, or even be unable to keep going at all?

I knew from weight-training, and books about the subject, that when the body is under stress it starts to burn its own muscle, trying to preserve fat for emergencies. I was carrying very little fat anyway – so the only realistic prospect was that my muscles would deteriorate quite quickly, especially as I was burning yet more energy by shivering all the time. In lectures on combat survival we'd been told that a man lost in the desert can only survive for a day without water – but this wasn't by any means a typical desert, and the temperature, far from dangerously high, was threateningly low.

Of course I kept wondering about the rest of the patrol. I greatly feared that Vince was dead, and in a way I felt responsible. Lying all day by the tank berm had undoubtedly contributed to his collapse, and it was I who had decreed that we should follow SOPs and stay there. If we'd been a bigger, more heavily-armed party, we might have risked moving to somewhere warmer in daylight – and that might have saved him, at any rate for the time being. Then, in the night, I should have tied him to me. As a qualified mountain guide, I could have handled the situation better. But at the time I'd had a lot on my mind. I myself was going down with exposure, and not thinking as clearly as I might have.

Vince had been fit, but he had carried no surplus weight. Taller than me – maybe 5' 11" – he was skinny, with the build of a runner. In fact, as we'd sat discussing what might happen if things went wrong, he'd told me he reckoned that if he stripped down, he could run and walk thirty miles in the night, so that he should make Syria in two nights at most. The trouble was that, like the rest of us, he hadn't reckoned with the cold. Exposure can catch people in different ways. Even when I started to go down, and was slipping back and forth between feelings of drunkenness and being clear-headed, I still knew what was happening to me. I don't think Vince did; he was deteriorating so fast.

What about Stan? It seemed certain that he'd been captured, and I could only hope he wasn't having too bad a time. As for the other five – I reckoned that the chopper must have come back and lifted them out. I felt sure that the aircraft had been inbound towards our original position, following normal Lost Comms procedure, and that it would have flown around until the guys made contact with the pilot. 'By now,' I thought, 'those lucky sods are sitting back in base, pissing themselves with laughter.'

Trying to concentrate on pleasant subjects, I thought about my family – about Sarah and Jan, and, before Jan, Susan. During my time with 23 SAS, I was engaged to a pretty, tall, blonde woman called Susan who lived in the same village. I met her while I was still at school, and for seven years we went everywhere together, even on holidays. She had a job as receptionist for a firm of lawyers in Newcastle. We'd meet for lunch, and often she'd come back from work to stay the night at my home. In the evenings I wasn't interested in doing anything except listening to Morse code or reading through my technical manuals, but she'd sit around patiently enough.

My mum kept saying that I was too young to get married – and I was certainly too inexperienced. What she was trying to tell me, but couldn't in so many words, was that I ought to go out and sleep with other women, and live life a little rather than tie myself down with the only girl I'd ever known. 'You're a man now,' she'd say, 'and you've got to get around a bit.' I couldn't understand what she was on about – but now I see how right she was. I was extremely naive, having been strictly brought up never to drink or smoke, and my horizons were very limited.

When my selection course for 22 SAS was in the offing, Susan and I planned to get married and move south – provided I passed. Once in the regular SAS, I'd be on a good wage, and everything would be all right.

Or so I thought. In fact, with my own move south all that went by the board. Suddenly I was thrown into the company of guys of thirty, who were constantly going out humping and drinking, and it was a real eye-opener for me. Hereford was alive with young, single girls, all determined to latch on to the guys in the Regiment. With a new intake, especially, their behaviour became outrageous. Rapidly I saw the other side of the coin. My long-standing engagement seemed like a big mistake, and I started to play the field like everyone else.

The difficulty was to break the news to Susan. After returning from the Parachute Company to the Squadron, I did a couple of short exercises, and then went on a three-month trip to Botswana. Immediately after that I joined the SP team, which meant that for nine months I was on thirty minutes' notice to move, and couldn't leave Hereford. The result was that I didn't visit home for more than a year. Susan and I did talk on the telephone, but in the end she wrote saying, 'This is no good, and I think it's best if we finish.' So I took the easy way out, rang her, and said I agreed.

At least the break meant that I was unattached when I met Jan. That was in 1986, when she was serving in Queen Alexandra's Royal Army Nursing Corps, and working as matron in charge of the hospital at Airport Camp in Belize. I was out there on a three-month deployment with a troop called F Company, which organised jungle training courses for the resident British battalion, and also gave guys new to the SAS their own first jungle experience.

One of my jobs was to run a range, and when I saw this gorgeous blonde walk past our accommodation on her way from the hospital to the officers' mess, I immediately decided to invite her up for some pistol shooting. The only slight difficulty was that I didn't know her name – so I decided to cast my net wide.

The sergeant in charge of the hospital was a bit of an SAS groupie, always snivelling round the guys, so I asked him if he'd like to bring his staff up to the range. He made enquiries and reported that his people were keen. When I asked who was coming, he gave me a list of names – but this still didn't tell me what I wanted to know, as it just said 'Major This' and 'Captain That'.

'Have you got a woman in there?' I asked – knowing full well there was one.

'Oh yes – that's Captain James, the matron.'

'Well – invite her too.'

He went round and asked her, and the answer was that she'd be along as well.

We set the ranges up, and I had all the guys detailed off so that I'd be free to grab the matron and give her some personal instruction. Alas, she failed to appear, and I stumped off in dudgeon. But just as I set off across the football field, I saw her coming in the opposite direction. 'Damn!' I thought, 'I've screwed this up.' As we passed each other, I said 'Hello,' and when I saw her reach the range, I ran back, pretending I'd been to fetch something. Then I grabbed her and took her to one side, inviting her for a drink.

Back in England we met up again, and we saw a good deal of each other when I did my training to become a medic. For a month I was attached to the John Radcliffe Hospital in Oxford, where she also had trained, and as she was stationed at Wroughton, only an hour's drive to the west, she would come up in the car to collect me whenever I had time off. We got engaged in September 1987, and married the following summer.

My medical training was thorough and lengthy. It began with an intensive six-week course in Hereford, where we learnt about anatomy and physiology, and the role of drugs. Then I picked a hospital – the John Radcliffe – to which I was posted for four weeks. My introduction to the place was breathtaking. The day I arrived, the sister – who came from Hereford and knew who I was – introduced herself and immediately said, 'Would you like to see something interesting?'

'OK,' I agreed cautiously.

'Get your white coat on, then, and go through those double doors.'

Inside was the resuscitation room of the emergency theatre. I thought I was going in to watch a video or listen to a lecture. Not at all. As I walked through the doors, there was a lump of meat screaming on the table, with two doctors and three or four nurses working on it. The man, a road casualty, had compound fractures of the legs and arms, as well as big gashes in his face and on his chest.

After that brisk introduction, I was partnered off with a house doctor and put into the Accident and Emergency room. I'd go into the little cubicle with my mentor, and be introduced to the patient as another doctor or a consultant. I'd watch and listen as the proper doctor made his diagnosis; then, after we'd come out, he'd ask me what I thought ought to be done. If I produced the right answer, he'd say, 'OK – go in and do that,' but if I was wrong, he'd make alternative suggestions. It was excellent hands-on training, and we had at least one serious road casualty every week, so that I got plenty of practice.

Another useful ally was the matron in charge of the maternity ward. Often she would make sure that the mother-to-be didn't mind a colleague being present, and then bleep me so that I could go in to watch the birth, whether it was natural or Caesarean section.

I was put to live in the nurses' accommodation block, where three bedrooms, a bathroom and kitchen were arranged as a kind of flat. When we arrived, someone said, 'Oh, good, here's our bouncers for the next four weeks.' When I asked what she meant, it turned out that at least once a week a nurse would be attacked, probably by a patient.

Sure enough, one night a drunk came in with his wrist and hand badly cut after punching his fist through a kebab shop window. A nurse began cleaning his wounds, taking splinters of glass out of his hands. Suddenly he went for her, yelling out that she had hurt him. He got her by the neck and slammed her up against a wall, trying to strangle her. Another of the girls came screaming into my room. I pulled on my white coat and ran. It was a horrendous sight. The nurse was up against the wall, with blood all over her face and neck and down the front of her uniform. I thought the guy was murdering her, so I dragged him off and hit him. He looked amazed and said, 'You can't do that. You're a doctor.'

'Just watch this, then.'

Wham! I smacked him again, and put him down with a kind of anaesthetic quite new to him. All the time another of the nurses was crying out, 'Don't hurt him! It's all right.'

'Come on!' I said. 'He *was* trying to throttle her.'

Another phase of our medical training was to watch post-mortems being carried out in the mortuary at St Mary's Hospital, Paddington, and to practise for live operations by doing things like putting in chest-drains or carrying out tracheotomies on the corpses. Again, my first exposure to this peculiar world was a bit of a shock. One day our instructor said, 'OK – there's some bodies you can work on.' There were four old people, one middle-aged man who had hanged himself, another man in his thirties, and a boy of nine or ten, who'd fallen downstairs through a window, so that a piece of glass had pierced the top of his skull. Otherwise there wasn't a mark on him, but strangely enough, there was a rush for the older bodies – nobody wanted to touch the kid. Another day the pathologist brought out the body of a man who'd been in the Thames for three weeks. His skin and clothes were all the same colour – a slimy green – and all round the corpse was a solid wall of stench.

Back at Hereford, I sat various written and practical tests, and so became a qualified medic – though I had to re-qualify by doing a short refresher course every year . . .

Jan and I were married in Hereford during the summer of 1988, and our first child was due early in 1989. But during December, because Jan's blood-pressure kept falling, she was taken into hospital. Being a theatre-sister herself, she knew the score pretty well, and about three weeks before the baby was due she asked for it to be induced, because she knew I'd be leaving the country early in the New Year and she wanted to have it while I was still around. The doctor declined absolutely; but her blood pressure continued to rise and fall, and while she was in for a check during the morning of 21 December, the surgeon told her she must go for surgery immediately, because the baby's umbilical cord was being twisted and compressed, and cutting off the blood supply.

At 9a.m. she rang me at home and said she had to go for a Caesarian section straight away. In the background I could hear the surgeon saying, 'If he wants to be in at the birth, he'd better get down NOW, because you're going straight in.'

I was still in bed, recovering from a late night. I leapt up, threw on the first clothes I could find, jumped into the car and raced through Hereford with headlights and flashers blazing. As I ran into the hospital I saw Jan being wheeled past on a trolley.

The surgeon asked if I'd done the medical course, and when I said I had, he said, 'Come with me, then.' He took me into a room and got me dressed up in green theatre clothes. Then we went through and found Jan already on the operating table. They'd given her a spinal anaesthetic, which left her numb from the waist down but fully conscious, and she was keeping up a running discussion with the surgeons.

'What layer are you going through now?' she asked. I kept looking at her and saying, 'Please shut up!' But she was determined to talk the surgeon through his task. Then suddenly she said to me, 'Just watch your feet. Stand back a bit, or your wellies are going to fill.'

I stepped back, and a few seconds later the surgeon cut through the amniotic sac, so that the fluid flowed out. All I remember after that is this thing like a little alien being pulled out of Janet's belly, screaming.

The baby, a girl, was all but full-term, and perfect – but if it hadn't been for the hospital's prompt action, we might have lost her. We had decided that if we got a boy, he would be Stephen, and a girl would be called Sarah. So Sarah she became. Although Jan was in real pain the next day, she came home a couple of days later, and recovered quickly.

After little more than a week at home with her, I had to leave to go on the German guides' course – which meant that I was away for three months at a time, and could only come back for a week or 10 days before leaving again. The result was that there wasn't much bonding between myself and Sarah until I finished the course. It was sad, because although I had a daughter, she meant little to me. But then, in May 1990, I came home for six

116

months, and after a couple of weeks Sarah suddenly latched on to me. Belatedly I realised what I had, and we became tremendously close.

To me, she seemed the perfect child. Of course my opinion may have been prejudiced by the fact that she looked very much like me, with clear blue eyes, and hair that gradually turned darker as she grew older. But from an early age she was exceptionally well behaved. We only had to tell her once not to do something, and she never did it again. She was never afraid of the dark, but slept right through the night without any light on. Best of all, she was always glad to play on her own. She seemed to have inherited my gift of wanting to get on with life, and to try her hand at everything. Although so good, she had an independent mind, and would happily spend hours on her own, drawing, painting and singing away to herself. She was also a bit of a tomboy, and was often covered in cuts and bruises from falling out of trees or off climbing frames. I smiled to myself as I thought how she would sit in the dog-basket, cuddled up with Jessie, our other Staffordshire bull terrier, reading her picture-books . . .

Up in the rocks, something near me stirred, jerking me back to the Euphrates. I sat up and looked round, holding my breath, listening. Goats? A dog? A human? In a moment or two I was reassured; there seemed to be nothing close to me, and the movement had been only that of the wind. But thank God – at last the light was starting to fail. It wouldn't be long before night came and I could continue on my way.

What I had no means of knowing was that, during that day, the other guys in the patrol had been captured close to the river at a point about 100 kilometres nearer to the Syrian border. As a result of contacts with them, some 1,600 Iraqi troops had been deployed to look for other coalition soldiers on the run, and the civilian population along the river had been alerted: not only the men, but the women and children too had been ordered to turn out.

I came out of my hiding place not long after dark, and began heading north-west, keeping as close as I could to the edge of the cultivated land, where the going was easiest. I was walking more carefully now, because I was in a populated area. I was probably down to three or four kilometres an hour. Occasionally, for a change, I rested the 203 over my shoulder, but for most of the time I held it in both hands, with the weight taken by the sling of paracord round my neck. That way, the weapon was less tiring on my arms, but it was also at the ready: I could have aimed and fired a shot within a second.

Soon I found that there were amazing numbers of Arabs out and about. Every half hour or so I'd come across a group standing or sitting around, chatting in quiet voices. Several times I picked up the glow of a cigarette and had to box round it. Often I just smelt smoke, either from cigarettes or from a fire or stove, and pulled off without seeing anything. (The smell of Arab cigarettes is harsh and distinctive.) I didn't know what the norm was, but it seemed odd that so many citizens should be out of doors on a freezing winter night.

Again and again I saw or sensed people ahead of me, brought up the kite-sight for a better look, and had to make a detour. In the end my lack of progress became quite frustrating, and I started to think that if things were going to be like this all the way to the border, I would never get out. I would become too weak from lack of food, and would end up getting captured.

During that night I was on the move for eight hours, and must have covered thirty or forty kilometres, but I made only about ten kilometres towards the frontier. I would walk gently forward for a while, see someone, back off and box them. Immediately I'd come on someone else, box them, and carry on. It was zig-zag, zig-zag all the time, five or ten steps sideways for every one forward.

I found it incredibly difficult to maintain concentration for any length of time. Wild animals like antelopes and deer, which are preyed on by carnivores, have the ability to remain on the alert for hours on end – and in fact their lives depend on it. But humans have lost the knack, and it takes conscious effort to stay at a high pitch of watchfulness.

Often I found I was having silent conversations with myself.

'I'll walk as far as the top of that hill,' I'd say. 'Then I can have a rest.'

Soon I'd ask, 'How the hell did you get yourself into this mess? And where have the others got to now?' Casting ahead in my mind, I wondered what the border with Syria would look like, and how I'd cross it. People and personalities from my past kept drifting into my head: my mum and dad, my brothers, my schoolteachers. I'd wonder what they'd be doing at that moment – and I longed to tell them where I was. I imagined how surprised they'd be if they knew what I was doing. Often I heard their voices, and these became so real that I'd forget about my own security and pay no attention to my surroundings. Suddenly I'd come to and realise that I'd covered a kilometre or more in a dream.

Whenever I passed a house, the dogs would start barking, and the noise would ricochet down the valley: one lot of dogs would alert the next, and they'd start up before I even reached them. Those tell-tale alarm calls progressed along the river ahead of me, and to my ears they sounded as loud as the wail of a siren.

The dogs were an infernal nuisance. As I was skirting one village, above me on a mound, I looked up at the houses – square, dark silhouettes with flat roofs and no lights showing – and saw a whole pack of them coming down, barking their heads off. Through the night-sight I watched them make straight for me. One ran up to within 10 feet, with three or four more close behind it. If I stopped, they would stop, and also they'd stop barking. But the moment I threatened them or moved, they'd bark like hell again and creep on some more, stalking me.

I kept looking anxiously up at the houses, expecting lights to come on at any second. I felt like the Pied Piper, with all the dogs following me. I kept thinking furiously, 'Oh, for God's sake, SHUT UP!' I stopped, picked up a rock and hurled it. The pack ran away for a few metres, only to close in again. As I cleared the houses, they followed for a couple of hundred metres, then stopped, and stood or sat, watching and barking until I was out of their sight. Then, when my nerves were well in tatters, they'd turn back and troop home. The one saving grace was that their owners seemed to pay no attention whatever. So far as I could see, nobody ever came out of a house to investigate the cause of the commotion.

For a while I stayed as close to the river as I could, partly for navigation, partly so that I could get more water in due course; but then, deciding I was too close to the inhabited stretch, I drew away to the south again and returned to the edge of the desert, where sharp, bare rock seemed to predominate. There I started cross-graining through the wadis, which were running down towards the Euphrates at right-angles to my line of advance. All the time I was trying to find a safe compromise, far enough from the river and its habitations, but at the same time out of the wadis, so that I wasn't forever scrambling up and down.

By five in the morning I was starting to worry about finding somewhere to lie up for the day. At 5.30 it was still fully dark, but when I came to the top of a cliff looking out over the river, something made me decide to scramble four or five metres down the face. There I found a ledge, and at the back of it a nice flat area, with a crack going back underneath the cliff. That seemed as good a refuge as any, and I lay in it until day broke.

When the light came up, I found I could look straight down into the river on my side, and that on the opposite bank there was a small village. The houses were simple, single-storey structures, mostly built of breeze blocks, with flat roofs. They stood in areas of dirt, with not a sign of a garden. Soon, as I watched through binoculars, people started to come out and walk up and down, going about their daily tasks. There seemed to be very few men, but plenty of women, all dressed in black robes from head to foot and heavily veiled: groups of them came down to the water's edge to fill their buckets. Surprise, surprise, the place was alive with dogs. I watched the comings and goings out of sheer interest, but also I was looking for any abnormal activity which might suggest that the area was on the alert – military vehicles driving about, or troops on the move. I was annoyed not to have the camera which I'd left in my bergen: with it, I could have taken pictures of the village and the river.

Two men spent the whole day fishing, paddling up and down in a boat, dropping off gill nets, going round, and pulling in fish. On each pass they let themselves drift maybe a hundred metres downstream. The speed at which the boat picked up confirmed that the current was strong, and I felt all the more glad that I hadn't tried to swim across. In daylight the water looked a dark-brown colour, and a good deal of rubbish was floating about inside my bottle; but the sight of the shining fish reassured me: if they could live in the river, I thought, the water couldn't be too bad.

All that day – Monday 28 January – I lay on the ledge, with

my webbing under my head as a pillow. Up there in my vantage point, under the overhang of rock, I felt secure, almost peaceful. It was the sort of place, I thought, in which an eagle or a peregrine falcon would nest. My main enemy was boredom. I spent hours studying my map, trying to work out exactly where I was. Again I managed to convince myself that I was well to the west of my true position, and a great deal nearer the border.

Throughout all the hours of daylight there was never a movement close to me, either above or at the sides – just the activity in the village across the water, with the odd car coming in and out, and the people going steadily about their business. From among the ploughed fields below came the constant sound of an irrigation pump – a distinctive *dyoot, dyoot, dyoot, dyoot*, the only noise in the valley. It was great to have a live cabaret to watch.

I tried not to think about food, but inevitably, with all that time on my hands, it had become a major preoccupation. Every one of those houses opposite had food in it, even if it was only flour or bread. But for the dogs, I could nip into one under cover of darkness and steal a loaf. In my mind I kept seeing the sachets of fruit that I'd left in my bergen. What wouldn't I give for some pineapple in syrup? 'When I get out of here,' I thought, 'I'm going to eat a gallon of ice-cream.'

All the dogs made me think of Turbo, my Staffordshire bull-terrier. What a character! What chaos there would have been if he'd been with me! He'd have fought every dog along the Euphrates, and sent the whole lot packing.

A friend in the squadron had got him for me. He was supposed to have been eighteen months old when he came; but he already had grey hairs on his muzzle, and healed-over scars on his face – which made me think that he was a good bit older than he was supposed to be, and also that he'd been entered in fights. His official documents turned out to be extremely elusive, and we never did establish his age properly.

When we first had him, he couldn't pass another dog without looking for a fight. If I took him walking on a lead, and we met another dog, Turbo would apparently pay no attention. But the moment I let him off, he'd turn back, go like hell and get stuck in. In this way he managed to start dozens of battles – although after a while he seemed to settle down.

Alas, he came to a sad end. When we moved house, the

change of routine seemed to upset him. Until then he had always been the cleanest dog you could imagine, but now he began to wet indoors – and when Jan came home with the infant Sarah, he growled at the baby.

That put us in a fix. We couldn't give him away, because we couldn't be sure how he would behave with someone who didn't know him; even though he meant no harm, he was strong enough to knock small children over, and generally be a nuisance. So we decided with great sorrow that we would have to put him down. Remembering how my father had always shot dogs when they became too old or infirm to carry on, and hating the idea of taking Turbo to the vet, I resolved to do the deed myself. So I got a pistol and drove out to the range – but then I looked at him and thought, 'Jesus, I can't do this.' So I reprieved him and brought him home.

All too soon he growled at the baby again, and I decided his time had come. I drove him out into the country with a .357 pistol in my trouser pocket. But when I jumped out of the car and said, 'Come on, Turbo!' he just sat bolt upright, gazing ahead. Normally he'd rush out at the first opportunity, but he knew something was up. In the end I shouted *'Cats!'* and out he hurtled, between my legs. I put one round straight down into the top of his skull but he stayed on his feet, his tail wagging against my knees. A split second later I gave him another, and then, as he was still standing, I put one between his eyes. Poor Turbo! I brought his body home and buried it in the garden.

From my perch on the cliff face, I watched the shadows lengthen in the village opposite. Gradually the grey-brown fields beyond the houses faded into the dusk. As evening came on, I began itching to get going again, and had to hold myself in check. When darkness fell at last, I moved out, climbed to the top of the cliff and started walking. That night, thank goodness, activity seemed to cease as people disappeared into their houses, and after dark there was nobody about. But to keep out of the way, I pushed up towards the wadis, between a line of pylons and the main road. Up there, I found myself in steep country. I kept coming to what looked like small quarries, so that I'd have to climb down, walk across a flat floor, then scramble up again and along the top. It was really tiring, and my feet had become seriously sore. After my prolonged study of the map, I thought I'd identified the spot I'd reached – a big bend in the river with a village on it. This looked only about a day's walk from the border – a fact which lifted my morale and gave me strength.

Again I walked all night. The occasional car went along the MSR, which was three or four hundred metres down to my right. Some had headlights on, others were driving blind. At some point late in the night the headlights of a car illuminated a motorway-sized sign. I was too far away to read the names, but I got the idea of moving down to the road so that I could check what the sign said.

It was then that I saw the only wild animal in the whole of my trek. As I dropped towards the road I looked through the kite-sight, and there, on top of a mound, stood a big fox, staring down at me. I knew what he was from his sharp-pointed face and sticking-up ears. For a whole minute I watched him, and he never moved; then I went on, and left him in possession of his territory. In that fox I recognised a fellow creature of the night. I bet that, like me, he lay up all day and came out only when darkness fell. He can't have been as short of food as I was, but I found it hard to imagine what he lived on, because never in all my time on the move or lying up did I see any form of rodent.

Closing on the sign, I peered up at it and made out the legend – in English as well as Arabic – AL QAIM 50; NEW ANA 50. New Ana was behind me, and I'd known for some time that I was heading for Al Qaim – but 50 kilometres! That was a massive blow to morale. I'd imagined I was almost at the place. Sitting there in despair, I thought, 'I'm never going to finish this damn walk.' When I got out the map and pinpointed my position, I saw I was still 80 or 90 kilometres from the border – at least two days short of the spot I thought I'd reached.

I couldn't believe it. I felt as if I'd had a kick between the legs, and sat down on the side of the road, staring at the sign. But the evidence was there, and everything fitted together, as I worked out where I was and where I'd been. The reality was intensely depressing.

There was nothing for it but to keep going. Weighed down by exhaustion, thirst and fear, I started moving along the line of the MSR. I was only a hundred metres from it when I heard a drone from somewhere along the road behind me. I went to ground and lay listening. The noise was coming from miles away to the east, but it grew steadily until it seemed to fill the night. Presently a four-ton wagon went past – but still the heavy drone was increasing. I moved down to the edge of the road and hid in some rocks, looking along the highway through the kite-sight. For minutes I couldn't see anything. Still the noise built up. Then, as I scanned for the twentieth time, I saw a black dot, which grew bigger and bigger until it resolved itself into a massive vehicle, filling the sight. With a tremendous roar it came level, and suddenly I realised I had a Scud going by me. The TEL vehicle was a huge articulated truck, with the missile canopied-up under tarpaulins on its trailer, and a convoy of smaller trucks behind it, all heading out towards the Syrian border. In one of them, with an open back, I could see a whole gang of squaddies.

'Jesus!' I thought. 'That's what I'm here for – to find Scuds!' I never imagined I'd get as close to one as this. Should I have opened fire on it? I couldn't have destroyed the missile, but a grenade from the 203 into the front of the truck might have put the launcher off the road. Yet I would have marked my position, and the guys in the convoy would have been on top of me.

If only I could report back what I'd seen: this was exactly the information the coalition needed. I whipped out my TACBE, switched on and spoke into it, but as usual got no response. I was left with the mortification of hearing the drone of the engine and big tyres gradually fade into the distance. I imagined the drama of a couple of A-10s coming in to take the launcher and missile out – but it was not to be.

Then again I felt crushed by the disappointment of finding myself so far from safety. How could I have miscalculated so badly? I cursed the wretched, useless map.

On the move once more, I crossed the MSR, so that I was between the road and the river, which at that point were maybe fifteen kilometres apart. Now the ground was really flat, and again I started crossing ploughed fields. It was time to look for a lying-up position, but here in the farmland I couldn't see any rough, broken areas. So I planned to move back across the road and regain the higher ground beyond. Then I came to a culvert, about six feet high and eight wide, underneath the highway, obviously built for pedestrians and animals to walk through.

I was feeling so knackered and let-down that I decided to lie up in the tunnel. It was a bad decision, but I can see why I took it. I was thinking, 'You're going down. You're not going to last much longer. Why not take a vehicle and drive to the border?' The culvert would make a good base for such a hijack.

I sat there in the tunnel having this discussion with myself. My lazy side was saying, 'Just do it: grab a vehicle and drive out.' The other side was saying, 'What happens if there's two people in it? How are you going to make them stop? What if there's only one man, and he just drives on? Once you've been seen and reported, that's you finished.'

I went through the scenario again and again. I imagined myself standing on the road, putting one hand up, levelling my weapon – and the car accelerating past. Then I'd have given my position away and lost all the advantages I'd so painfully built up. Suddenly I thought that if Stan had still been with me, the idea would have been even more tempting – but even if we got a vehicle, the chances were that we'd drive into a control point.

I decided not to risk it. But I'd landed myself in a hell of a place. While I'd been dithering, the sky had begun to lighten, and it was already too late to move on. Safe or not, the place was horrendously uncomfortable. The wind was blowing straight through that culvert as if from the North Pole. Soon I was absolutely frozen. I tried moving rocks to make a little shelter, yet still the wind whistled through the gaps. In the gloom I could see that bushes were growing in the floor of the tunnel, and I thought that maybe I could pile some into a barrier; but when I grabbed one, I got a handful of vicious thorns. There seemed to be no way of improving my shelter, so I lay down, determined to stick it out.

Just at full daylight, I heard the sound I wanted least in the world: goat bells. I'd had enough of goats and goatherds already. Looking through the tunnel towards the river, I saw the lead animal come into view, heading confidently into the culvert, obviously on its way through. I just had time to scoot out the other end of the tunnel and up the sloping embankment of the MSR. As I ran towards the top of it, a car was approaching at speed, so I flung myself into a shallow ditch which led down the bank at an angle from the road-edge.

There I lay on my back, trapped, looking straight down over

my boots to the top of the culvert exit. In a few seconds the lead goat emerged below me, not three metres away. More and more goats came into view, pushing and jostling. Their stink rose all round me. Last came the goatherd, an old man wearing a long, woolly coat over several other layers, with a white shamag wrapped round the top of his head. He was leading a donkey, which had a blanket over its back, and five or six dogs jostled at his heels. As he walked out, the top of his head was barely three feet below my boots.

I lay rigid, with the 203 down my front, praying that he would not look back, and that the dogs would not get wind of me. Had they done so, I'd have had to drill him. Little as I wanted to kill an innocent civilian, I was desperate. If I had shot him, I would have been in a dire position: I'd have had to run off into the wadi system with the pack of dogs after me, and even if I'd made a temporary getaway, the old man's death would have put down a great big marker. Obviously he came out that way every morning, and people would be expecting him back.

How the dogs failed to smell me, I still cannot imagine – unless my scent was obliterated by the stink of the goats. I held my breath as the party moved slowly away, up into the wadis. The old man never looked back, and the jingle of bells faded among the rocks.

I couldn't go back into the culvert, because it was clear that at some time during the day the flock and their keeper would return. Equally, I couldn't move down anywhere below the road, because the farmland was too open, and too full of people at work. Besides, I felt sure that there must be a village, or at least a few houses, not far off.

I lay still and watched the goats until they were out of sight. My mind was racing. There was only one way I could go – up into the wadis. But traffic had started to build up on the motorway; every other minute a vehicle came past, and if I began moving up on to the high ground, there was every chance a driver would see me from the vantage-point of the elevated embankment. I kept imagining what would happen if somebody spotted me and raised the alert. The hunt would be on, and, because it was still just after dawn, the searchers would have all day to catch me.

I decided to take my chance and make a go for it between cars.

I rolled over on to my belly, slung the 203 on my shoulder, slithered down the embankment and began crawling up a dry river bed. Every time I heard a car coming, I went to ground, scared stiff that I would be seen. After a hundred metres I came up into a crouched stance, scuttled upwards and got round into the beginning of the wadi system, maybe 500 metres from the road. Then I walked until I found a hollow in the ground, and lay down in that.

There I was, stuck again for the hours of daylight. As a hideout, my hollow was far from ideal. Although I couldn't see the road, I had a reasonable view downhill maybe 200 metres, but behind me the outlook was blocked by a mound. If anyone had come along, I wouldn't have seen him until he was on top of me. This kept me fully on edge. Any sound made me whip round, even if it was only the wind passing over the rocks. My entire world was one of barren, grey, broken rocks, with nothing but the occasional withered bush to break the monotony, and nowhere to hide in an emergency.

I calculated that this was Tuesday January 29, and a map check showed that I was still at least 70 kilometres from the border. Working backwards, I realised that due to hypothermia Stan and I had miscalculated on our last night together, and we'd gone in a much more northerly direction than we'd supposed.

By this stage even keeping still had become painful. Because of the cold, I had to maintain a foetal position, with my knees tucked up to my chest, lying on one side or the other, and I'd lost so much weight that my pressure points had become very sore. I could see that the day was going to be a long one.

Chapter Six

Echoes Of Africa

There was something spooky about my surroundings. The wind blowing through the rocks of that huge wilderness took my mind back to another desert, another time. Africa . . . the Kalahari. My thoughts floated away to the time when 'B' Squadron was deployed on a three-month training exercise, my troop staff sergeant was killed, and we all became caught up in what felt like voodoo or black magic.

For the various parts of the exercise, the squadron had spread out over a wide area. The Air Troop went free-falling; the Boat Troop splashed around in the swamps which were ideal for their purposes; the Mobility Troop drove around the Kalahari desert; and the rest of us went climbing in the Tsodilo Hills. That was my first trip abroad with the Squadron, and the fact we lost one of our guys within days brought home to me how dangerous and close to the mark our training was.

On our first evening in the country, before the troops split up, we had a brief on snakes from an African called Lazarus who'd been a sergeant in the police force. Later we realised what a bullshitter he was when he told us that his skin had originally been as white as ours, and had gone black from exposure to the sun. But when he first started releasing snakes from a sack to show us the various kinds which we might come across, we didn't know what to make of him.

He brought out a spitting cobra, holding it by the throat, and said that if you gripped it like that, it couldn't spit. 'Watch that bloody thing,' growled the SQMS, 'because if it does spit, and the stuff gets in your eyes, you'll have problems.' Sure enough, as Lazarus came past me the cobra spat, and although I closed my eyes, some spit landed on my arm and the side of my face. I wiped it off immediately, but wherever a drop had touched it took the pigment out of my skin. I was left with pale dots all over my cheek, and a patch the shape of the British Isles on one arm.

As a grand finale Lazarus produced an Egyptian cobra – a massive creature, twelve or thirteen feet long – which he set down on the ground. We were gathered round in a circle, and he said, 'Stand still, and let it go through your legs.' All was well until one guy moved – whereupon the cobra chased him. The man ran up on to a water bowser, and the snake wrapped itself round one of the axles, baring its enormous fangs as Lazarus heaved on its tail, trying to drag it off. In the end he got it back into his sack, but it was amazing that none of us had been bitten.

After that little introduction, our troop moved up to the Tsodilo Hills. Our camp was maybe half an hour's walk from the base of the biggest hill – an outcrop of bare, blue-grey rock which rose abruptly in tiers out of a dead-flat plain. From a distance the hill looked strange but not particularly impressive: only when we got closer did we realise that some of the tiers, which went up in vertical rock faces, were 100 or 200 feet high.

In the evening, as we sat round the fire, one of the guys said, 'I'm going out shooting – does anyone fancy coming?' Nobody could be bothered. So he went out on his own, and presently he came back with a small, furry animal, about the size of a hare. A few Botswanan soldiers had been attached to us for training, and when he offered the animal to them, there was a big commotion. The Botswanans were with some Bushmen, who became very agitated. The little men raised a hubbub, rushed about and began lighting more fires. Via the Botswanans, the message came back to us strongly that we shouldn't kill any more animals as it was dangerous, and would provoke the spirits who lived on the mountain.

Next morning we had a brief on the climb. Ian, our mountain guide, had worked out that rain was probably going to come in during the afternoon, so he told everybody to be off the rock by midday. Then he split us into climbing pairs, and sent us off. I was with Ian himself, and when we reached the first of the rock faces, he began showing me how to use various aids, particularly devices called friends, which expand and lock themselves in position when you hammer them into crevices. The mountain rose in a series of well-defined vertical faces and horizontal ledges, almost as sharp as a huge staircase.

Joe Farragher – a staff sergeant and a big, heavy man of about 17 stone, strong as an ox – went off climbing with a guy called Trev, who soon stepped off a rock, and, although he only fell a couple of feet, put his back out, so that he had to be carried all the way back to camp. As a replacement, Joe got the young Rupert to go climbing with him. By the time he left for his second attempt, it was already 11a.m., and he shouldn't really have returned to the mountain, because it was a good half an hour's walk from the camp, and everyone had been told to be off it by twelve.

Anyway, Ian and I were climbing away when suddenly we heard yells from round the corner. It was the officer, shouting down that there'd been an accident. Ian got both of us down on to a ledge, and we hurried round, to find Joe lying on the rock, having fallen about 75 feet. We ran up to him, and I tried breathing into his mouth to give him CPR – but there was frothy red blood coming out of his mouth, and when I touched the back of his head under his climbing helmet, it felt like a broken eggshell. He was obviously dead, so we shouted down to some others to send for the Alouette helicopter, which was on stand-by.

Soon the chopper came in – but further dramas began immediately. The ledge was too narrow for it to land, and the face of the mountain was so steep that the pilot had difficulty hovering close enough for a doctor to abseil down. The heli began rocking, so that the doctor was swinging in and out – if he'd missed the ledge, he'd have gone down a couple of hundred feet. The pilot began making energetic cutting motions, telling the loadie to sever the rope – but in the end the doctor got down safely.

After he'd pronounced Joe dead, we trussed his body into an old stretcher and prepared to lower it down the face. The drop was so long that we had to tie two ropes together, and Ian asked me to abseil down first, to make sure that we could get our figure-of-eight linking device past the knot. I was feeling quite shocked, but also excited to be involved in a real rescue. As I went over the edge, I wasn't sure where I was going to end up, but luckily it turned out that the knot was level with another flat ledge, so that passing it was easy.

It should have taken no more than half an hour to get Joe down; but everything seemed to go wrong. Ropes kept getting snagged or broken, and several times the body nearly fell out of the stretcher. We had to keep tying him back in, and it was awful to see a person we had known and liked trussed up like a stuffed chicken. Like the rest of us he was wearing shorts and a T-shirt, and by the time we got him down he was in a mess, with his skin all scraped. Altogether we struggled for eight hours, and darkness was falling when we reached the plain.

That evening we were all pretty subdued, and we didn't feel any better next day, when the Alouette which flew the body out broke down. Then we heard that while the guys from the Air Troop had been free-falling, the engines of their C-130 had caught fire, and the aircraft had had to land.

We were starting to wonder whether there was some jinx on the exercise when one of the Air Troop produced a paperback copy of the South African explorer Laurens van der Post's book about the Bushmen, *The Lost World of the Kalahari*. 'Listen to this,' he said, and he read out some passages describing how the author had come to this very area, maybe forty years before, in search of Bushmen. When members of his party killed an antelope and a warthog, everything went belly-up: wild bees attacked the camp at sunrise – not once, but every morning – even though it was highly unusual for them to fly at that time of day; when the expedition's cameraman tried to film some ancient cave paintings, the movie-camera repeatedly broke down; their tape-recorder also ceased to function. In the end van der Post became so scared that he decided to leave the area immediately.

First, though, he got his guide, Samutchoso, to communicate with the spirits. After the man had gone into a trance, the answer came back: 'The spirits of the hills are very angry with you, so angry that if they had not known your intention in coming here was pure, they would long since have killed you. They are angry because you have come here with blood on your hands . . .'

To win forgiveness, van der Post wrote a letter addressed to 'The Spirits, The Tsodilo Hills', in which he humbly begged pardon. As 'an act of contrition' he promised to bury the note at the base of the great cave painting which he had found. He then got all his companions to sign the letter, sealed it in an envelope, and placed it in a lime-juice bottle, which he duly buried in the cave. Thereafter he had no more trouble: his Land-Rovers started without difficulty, and the expedition moved on.

His experience sounded uncannily like our own, and the death of that one animal seemed to have put us under the same spell. We decided to go and look for the cave, and I walked round the mountain with one other guy, Merv. We found the place easily enough – at least, we found *a* cave, in which there were primitive red paintings of animals on the walls. I thought it looked a bit creepy, and didn't fancy walking in; but Merv decided it was all right – so we went in, and at the back we found a green bottle, corked up, with a piece of paper inside.

Back at the camp, we reported on what we'd found. People made a few jokes, but Harry (the Everest climber, who had spent a lot of time in mountains, and felt sympathy for the people who lived in them) suggested that we should write a note of our own, apologising for the death of the animal, put it in another bottle, and leave it in the cave.

When our message was ready, Merv and I went back to the cave with it. The old bottle was still there – but something very strange had happened. Although the cork was still in place, the paper inside had been shredded, as if by a hamster. Of course we were disconcerted. Then we thought that some of our own guys must have been pissing around. Anyway, we left our bottle beside the first one, and went back to the camp – only to find that nobody else had been near the cave.

Whatever had happened, the atmosphere was becoming tense. That night, as we sat round the fire, the sergeant in charge announced that we would abandon the climbing equipment that was still on the mountain: if anyone else wanted it, they could have it. But in the morning we went up to look at it again, and when we studied the place where Joe had fallen, things somehow didn't look right. There seemed to be no reason for the friends to have pulled out, as they had, all three at once; so we sent for Ian, the expert. He came up, and also thought there was something wrong; he agreed that the friends should never have come out.

During the recovery of Joe's body, the sergeant had come down and told me to take pictures of the body and the ropes. I got some photos, took the film out and handed it over. Now, with Ian there, I took more pictures of the ropes.

By then everyone was becoming nervous. The place had an unpleasant atmosphere; we felt as though we were being watched. Even off the mountain, mishaps kept occurring. A herd of goats came through the camp and wrecked the tents, knocking everything over and chewing up our clothes. One of the Mobility Troop fell off his motorbike and broke his collar-bone. The Boat Troop was attacked by a hippo, which bit off one of the twin tails of a Gemini inflatable. The bang scared the animal off, but the boat was finished. When the RAF flew a Hercules over the top of the mountain and tried to throw out a wreath for Joe, it blew back into the aircraft. So they flew over again, and twice more it came back in. You could, at a stretch, explain that in terms of air turbulence, but it seemed uncanny, and only when they were three or four miles from the mountain did the wreath finally stay out and float away.

All this could have been coincidence – but there was no doubt that the Bushmen believe in the power of the mountain spirits, and by the end of the exercise I was well on the way to doing the same. Though not religious, I appreciated for the first time the sheer strength of some people's beliefs, and began to feel that there were forces at work which we Europeans simply didn't understand. Through the Botswanan soldiers, the Bushmen kept sending us the message. 'Whatever you do, don't kill anything else.' We didn't tell them about our own bottle.

One of the guys came with me to consult a witch doctor in the nearby village and find out what fate had in store for us. After we'd dropped a few boxes of rations in payment, a skinny, middle-aged man, wearing nothing but a loincloth, came out of his mud hut carrying a small leather bag. Having swept a patch of earth clear with one hand, he tipped six or eight bones on to it, and sat staring at them for fully half a minute, muttering to himself. Through the Botswanan who was with us, the message came back that we had nothing more to worry about, and we started to feel happier.

With our squadron exercise finished, we drove away, and as I looked out of the back of the Land-Rover at the mountain, I still had the feeling that there was something there, watching us, glad to see us go. We were told not to mention the story back in

Hereford, for the sake of Joe's family. But that was the first incident for me in which I'd seen someone killed, and it stuck in my mind for ever.

Remembering Africa helped pass the day. But cold, hunger, thirst and the pain of lying on rock continually reminded me I was in Iraq. Somehow the hours dragged by. At about five in the afternoon I moved up to the top edge of the mound and lay there gazing into the distance. Ahead of me, in the direction I needed to go, ridges of bare rock rose one behind the other, greyer and greyer as they stretched to the horizon. Close at hand the ground was rolling, and on my left hills climbed steeply towards a high plateau. Looking west, I could see an old stone fort perched on one of the ridges running up from the river valley; it stood in an elevated position, and obviously commanded phenomenal views. I worried slightly that it might be a manned border post, but somehow the sight of that man-made structure gave me a lift. The fort made a sudden contrast to the barren wastes of the desert.

I realised that, as I grew weaker, I was covering the ground more slowly, and not making the progress I expected. All the same, after studying the map on and off during the day, I reckoned that one good night's march would take me across the frontier.

Then a simple event gave my morale a tremendous boost. Never mind wind-noises: I really *did* hear a movement close at hand. Once again goats came into view below me, and I held my breath as they grazed along the contour. Then I saw their herder, working round the slope below me. Keeping well down behind a rock, I watched him. The goats traversed the lower side of the mound, away from me, but the man whipped round my side of it, out of sight of the road. As I looked down, from about a hundred metres away, he whipped up his dishdash, squatted down and had a big old shit. Then, quick as a flash, he wiped his arse with his left hand, gave it a brisk scrape on a rock, and was off, running back to catch up with his flock.

Again I remembered how, back in the Squadron in Saudi, the SSM had said to me, 'You'll never see an Arab have a shit.

They're that bloody shy about it. It's like seeing a rocking-horse shit. It just doesn't happen.' But here it was, happening right in front of me, and I lay there doubled up with silent laughter. 'Wait till I get out of here!' I thought. 'I'm going straight to the SSM to tell him what I've seen.'

Chapter Seven

Over The Border

The crapping Arab made my day. My morale had been down, but suddenly it was back up again. I couldn't stop laughing. A simple thing like that brought me right back on line. Once again I was full of anticipation, waiting for the time to be off.

Water was an urgent necessity. On the map I'd found a pumping station, and I felt I must have a good chance of getting a drink there. Surely a pumping station would have clean water coming out of it? Also I was buoyed up by the hope that I hadn't far to go. I really felt good. I said to myself, 'Eh – you're near the end here!'

This was my sixth night on the run, and in six nights and six days I'd had nothing to eat but two packets of biscuits. I was seriously dehydrated, and my feet were in ribbons. Even so, I felt pretty good, and had that sense of excitement mixed with apprehension that you get before a race or a big football match.

All I had to do was go down to the pumping station, get water, and carry on. By then I'd be only about ten kilometres from the border, and I would either cross it that same night, or reach it the next day.

The sight of the big hills in the distance made me think of the mountains of Wales, and I felt glad that I wasn't on ground as steep as the Brecon Beacons. Seeing how far I still had to go, I reckoned I'd never make it if the slopes were as tough as on Pen-y-fan or its neighbours. The desert might be harsh and hellishly dry, but at least it was reasonably level.

Things didn't work out as easily as I had hoped. I waited till dark and then started walking, but after only a hundred metres I came round a corner and found a small tented encampment to my right, obviously Bedouin, the nomadic herdsmen of the desert. Several dogs began barking, and through the kite-sight I

136

could see two tents and one vehicle. But nobody came out for a look round, so I moved carefully away to the left, boxed the position and carried on.

As soon as I could, I swung down to the right, heading for the pumping station. I began to follow a line of telegraph-poles, which made navigation easy. But by then my feet had become really sore, and I had to keep stopping. I forced myself to do ten poles between each rest – ten lots of 150 metres, every one of them a major effort. According to my map, I was heading for a point at which the telegraph lines crossed a run of pylons. In due course I saw the pylons, coming in on my right. The wadis to my left were getting deeper, the sides steeper. Then I saw that instead of crossing the telegraph line, the pylons were set out parallel with it. The map wasn't making sense. So I said to myself, 'Bollocks – I'll just cut down to the right and head for the river.'

I peeled off the high ground and started on another bearing, confident that I'd hit the river sooner or later. As I went down I spotted a square, white building with a flat roof – the pump house. Coming close, I saw that the end facing me was open, and that a lot of pipes ran in and out of it. There was one main pipe, which I guessed was bringing water from the river, and several smaller ones.

By then I seemed to have grown careless. Whether or not it was the result of exhaustion, I don't know, but I was getting almost blasé. When you're that tired, it's all too easy to decide you'll do yourself a favour, sling your weapon over your shoulder instead of carrying it at the ready, and just saunter along. It's hardly a conscious decision to lower your standards and sink from very, very cautious to plain un-cautious; it's just something that happens gradually, without you noticing.

In any case, I walked straight into this place, lulled by the fact that it was silent and no machinery was working. I wasn't crash-banging about, but I didn't case the building as carefully as I might have. I even got my torch out and shone it around, because I could hear water dripping from a pipe. There it was – a steady drip, glistening in the torch beam.

Then, as I started getting my water bottle out, I looked up and noticed a little glassed-in hatchway on the back wall, with a red glow coming through it. Standing up to peer through, I saw a small electric fire with a bar glowing. Across from it lay an Arab, huddled down in a parka and sleeping bag, dossing on a camp-bed. He was separated from me only by the thickness of the partition wall.

'Jesus Christ!' I thought. 'I've walked right into this. What the hell am I doing in a building anyway? I've dropped a bollock here.' I tiptoed out, without any water, and crept away. I tried to give myself a shake-up. 'Well, come on. Screw the nut.' It took a fright like that to wake me up. Things had started to seem too easy. I was making good progress. The border was only a short distance ahead. Nobody had challenged me for a while, and I'd started to switch off my defence mechanisms.

Getting over the fright, I moved on in a state of maximum alert. I held my weapon at the ready, and moved very slowly, scanning constantly. But I was hardly clear of the pump house when, from high ground to my left, an air-raid siren went off. The noise started low, wound up to a high note, then swung down again. I hit the ground, thinking I had tripped some alarm, and lay there listening. Up and down went the metallic scream, swooping high and low. As I searched through the kite-sight, scanning the high ground, I made out anti-aircraft positions with gun barrels showing against the sky and black figures running round them. Then I saw tall, lattice-work towers, maybe a couple of hundred feet high, with what looked like cables slung between them. They seemed to be part of a communications network, and when I heard a drone start up, I thought the noise was coming from generators. I reckoned I'd walked into some sort of signals base. How the hell had I got in among all this without seeing anything? I certainly hadn't crossed any fence or other barrier, but somehow I had landed in the middle of the complex.

I knew I wasn't far from the river; vegetation started only a couple of hundred metres below me, and I thought that must mark the bank. I lay still until the all-clear went up – a noise like a Second World War siren – and everything quietened down. Whatever had caused the alert, it hadn't been me. When I reckoned it was safe to move, I got up and set off cautiously towards the river – only to see a group of five men walking. Back on the ground, I lay still until they had passed and disappeared.

Desperate though I was for water, I decided I had to get out of this thickly populated area. I had seen from the map that the river bent round, and thought I could hit it at another point not far ahead. But now I seemed to be in the middle of numerous scattered positions, and I had no option but to weave my way through them.

I crept onwards. To my front I saw something sticking up into the sky. Peering through the night-sight, I realised that it was the barrel of an anti-aircraft gun. As I looked down, I saw its circular emplacement right in front of me.

I pulled back, boxed it and moved on with every sense at full alert, threading my way forward between buildings which showed up here and there, pale in the moonlight. The place was extremely confusing, as it didn't seem to be laid out in any regular pattern; perhaps because the ground undulated so much, the dirt roads were neither straight nor at right-angles to each other, but coming in from all directions. On the ground, insulated land-lines were running all over the place. I thought of cutting them, to put local communications out of action, but knew that it would only draw attention to my presence. My map was far too large-scale to show details that would have been useful to me, and it no longer bore any relation to the ground.

At one point I could see a big cliff coming round in front of me, like the wall of a quarry – but of course there was no sign of that on my sheet.

Then – wonder of wonders – I reached a stream, with vegetation growing beside it. The water looked crystal clear, and the moonlight shone through it on to a white bottom. I thought, 'Jesus! I'm in luck here. A spring of clean water, flowing down into the Euphrates.' The whole place was so dangerous that I didn't go down for a drink; I just filled my bottles, popped them into my side-pouches, and moved quickly away.

Just as I left the stream I saw a file of seven men walk across my front, two or three paces apart. They were moving carefully, obviously on patrol. I froze, thinking, 'If they've got a dog, it's going to pick up my scent now.' But no – they disappeared, and I moved out on a bearing, going very slowly.

Again I came across an anti-aircraft position; this time I was so close that I peered over a wall of sandbags and saw three men lying on the ground in sleeping bags. For a moment I felt stunned – so close were they, right under my nose.

I seemed to be glued to the ground, staring. Then I felt a surge of fear, rising like acid from stomach to throat. The thought flashed into my mind that if I'd had a silenced weapon, I could at least have taken out anyone who spotted me. But nobody had: the men were all asleep, and within a few seconds I was creeping slowly away.

The next thing I hit was a vehicle laager point. Mounds of rock or minerals stood about, as if in a quarry. As I came creeping round the side, I walked right up to a Russian-made Gaz 80 jeep, only four or five yards away. Again, I got a bad fright. I couldn't see through the vehicle's windows; for all I knew it could have been full of people. For a few seconds I held my breath, 203 levelled, waiting for it to erupt.

When nothing happened, I turned to go back. I found I'd passed other vehicles and wandered into the middle of this park without seeing it. There were four-ton trucks with the canvas backs off, some with the canvas on, buses like ordinary coaches, double-deck car transporters – none of them had armour or weapons fitted, but this was a big collection of general transport. How I'd penetrated in among all these without noticing them, I couldn't explain. With hindsight, I realise that my concentration was coming and going, functioning at one moment but not the next. At the time I merely felt bewildered.

No matter how I'd got in there, I had to get out. Ahead of me were houses, with light coming from one window. Silhouetted figures were moving across it, and I could hear voices calling. I pushed off to the right, sometimes walking on tiptoe, often crawling on hands and knees.

I boxed that particular group of buildings; then ahead of me lay a single, big, whitewashed house, with a steeply-pitched roof and a pale-coloured wall maybe a hundred metres long running round its garden, and trees and shrubs sticking up over the top of it. To the left were two other buildings with lights shining from them and people outside, talking and shouting. I think there was also music playing on a radio.

The big house was easily the most impressive I'd seen, and by far the best maintained. High on one wall, beneath the apex of the roof, was a mural, an outsize portrait of Saddam Hussein. In the dark the colours were indistinct, but I could see that it was a carefully painted head-and-shoulders representation, which showed the dictator bare-headed, wearing military insignia on his epaulettes. The picture reminded me of the violent murals I'd seen in Northern Ireland, and for several seconds I stood looking at it, thinking, 'You're definitely in the wrong place now, mate!' What made me stand there gawping, I can't explain. Again, as in the pumping house, I seemed to have grown blasé; it was almost as if I thought I'd become invisible, and didn't need to hide any longer. After surviving so many close encounters, I felt that nobody could see me, and I needn't be so careful any more.

Anyway, as I stood there, a man came round the corner, only fifty metres away – a dark figure, silhouetted against the light. Instinct, rather than any conscious decision, made me control myself. I felt a surge of fear, but instead of bolting I simply turned away and walked casually round the side of the house. In two steps I was out of sight. *Then* I ran. As I sprinted, I told myself, 'For God's sake, screw the nut. Take a grip.'

The man had seen me. I knew that. But he didn't seem to have followed up. Round the back of the building I spotted a ditch running along the side of the road. I dived into it, and as I lay there two family-type vehicles, like Espace vans, came rolling down. At their approach, the big house suddenly burst into life: security lights blazed on, and people poured out to meet the vehicles, both from the building and from pill boxes at the gates. A man got out of the vehicle, and four of the other guys bodyguarded him into the house. As soon as the party was inside, the lights went off, so that the place was plunged into darkness again. It crossed my mind that this could be Saddam himself. The house was an impressive one, and well maintained. Was this his secret hideaway? Then I realised that he would never draw attention to himself by having his own portrait on the wall; more likely, this was the home of the local governor, or some similar official.

The whole incident took only a few seconds, and it left me thinking, 'What the hell is this?' I seemed to have strayed into a nightmare, with unexplained people and events popping up all over the place. I saw that I must have walked right past the sentries in the pill boxes. Again I realised how dangerously I was switching off. In my head I began having a conversation with myself.

n't believe I did that.'

bloody did! Switch back on.'

By this time I'd been in this complex – whatever it was – for five hours, trying to find my way out. Time was cracking on. According to my route plan, I should already have been on the border. Something had gone far wrong with my map-reading, and I was faced by the prospect of having to lie up without food for yet another day. Oddly enough, I never felt desperate with hunger, I never got pains in the stomach. My biggest worry was that I was gradually growing weaker – less able to walk, less able to concentrate.

My immediate plan was to creep back up to the road and go somewhere beyond it, clear of the buildings, so that I could sneak another look at the map; but before I could move, I heard footsteps and voices coming down the path towards me. By the sound, there were two men at least. I was crouching in a corner beside a mound, without cover, and they were coming right on top of me.

My survival instinct took over – instinct sharpened by years of training. Whoever these guys were, it was going to be them or me. To fire a shot in that position would have been fatal, so I quietly laid my 203 down and got my knife open in my right hand. As the first man came level with me I grabbed him, stuck him in the neck and ripped his throat out. He went down without a sound. When the second man saw me, his eyes widened in terror and he began to run. But somehow, with a surge of adrenaline, I flew after him, jumped on him and brought him down with my legs locked round his hips. I got one arm round his neck in a judo hold and stretched his chin up. There was a muffled crack, and he died instantaneously.

When I got back to the first, he was still quivering. I could feel hot, sticky blood all down my front. There hadn't been a sound. Now I had two bodies to dispose of. To leave them where they were would advertise my presence to all and sundry, but if they just went missing, the chances were that nobody would raise the alarm for a few hours at least.

Luckily the river was less than a hundred metres off, and a gentle slope covered by small, loose rocks led down to it. Luckier still, the bank was screened by a stand of tall grass. Each body made a scraping, rattling noise as I dragged it over the rocks; but I got both to the edge of the water, one at a time, without interruption. Then I loaded them up with stones inside their shirts, dragged them into the water and let them go.

Knowing my bottles were full, I didn't bother to drink any of the dirty water in the river. The encounter had roused me to a high state of alert, and it had all taken an hour. Now my urgent need was to clear the complex before daylight.

Moving silently, I worked my way up to a road that ran along the contour. Under it I found a culvert, and I thought I'd crawl into it for a look at my map; but as I came to the end of the tunnel, I heard a kind of growling. Thinking there must be some animal under the road, I tiptoed forward and peered into the pitch darkness. I couldn't see a thing. Suddenly I diagnosed the source of the noise: it was some local, snoring. I felt slightly annoyed that an Arab had already nicked the retreat I fancied. Probably he was a soldier, and supposed to be on stag. Lucky for me, then, that he'd decided to have a kip. Creeping back out, I climbed up on the side of the road and crossed over.

As I did that, I heard a shout from down by the houses where I'd heard people talking. I didn't think the yell had anything to do with me, but I ran across the road, made about fifty metres into the rocks and dropped down. A man came running up the road, which was raised about six feet above the ground. He stopped right opposite me and stood staring in my direction. Evidently he couldn't see anything, and he ran back. A moment later, a blacked-out land-cruiser roared past, its engine screaming in second gear, straight up the road to the junction with the MSR, and disappeared.

For nearly half an hour I lay still, letting things settle. After getting that fright, and the violent expenditure of energy, reaction set in and I felt drained of strength. But I couldn't stay where I was, so I began to work my way round the rocks. On my left was a run of chain-link fencing, quite high. So that side of the complex was protected, anyway.

Coming to a corner of the barrier, I went up on to the MSR and crossed over. As I did so, I looked to my left and saw three guys manning a vehicle control point on the junction of the road coming up from the complex. Dodging back up a wadi, I peeped over the side and saw a line of anti-aircraft positions facing towards the Syrian border.

I pulled back again, stuck. The ground there was almost flat. I couldn't go forward, and I couldn't go back. Dawn was approaching. My only possible refuge was another of the culverts under the road. I found three tunnels, each about the diameter of a forty-five gallon drum and maybe 10 metres long. The first looked clean, and I thought that in daylight anybody looking in one end would see straight through it. The second seemed to be full of dead bushes and rubbish, so I crawled in and lay down.

In the confined space, I realised how badly I was stinking. But my surroundings were no better: there was a powerful stench of decomposing rubbish and excrement.

I was desperate for a drink, and looking forward to one with incredible anticipation. But when I went to compress the plastic clip that held the buckle on my webbing pouch, I found that my fingers were so sore and clumsy that I could scarcely manage the simple task. Gasping with pain, I used all my strength to force the clips together. Then came a horrendous disappointment. Bringing out one bottle at last, I opened it and raised it to my lips – but the first mouthful made me gasp and choke. Poison! The water tasted vicious and metallic, as if it was full of acid. I spat it straight out, but the inside of my mouth had gone dry, and I was left with a burning sensation all over my tongue and gums. I whipped out my compass-mirror, pointed the torch-beam into my mouth and looked round it. Everything seemed all right, so I took another sip, but it was just the same. I remembered that when Stan had collapsed during the first night on the run I'd put rehydrate into my bottles, to bring him round, and I wondered if the remains of it had somehow gone off. Then I tried the second bottle, and found it exactly the same. I couldn't make out what the hell had gone wrong. Whatever the problem, the water was undrinkable, and I emptied the bottles out.

'Now I *am* fucked.' I thought. I was in a really bad state. It was eight days since I'd had a hot meal, two days and a night since I'd had a drink. My tongue was completely dry; it felt like a piece of old leather stuck in the back of my throat. My teeth had all come loose; if I closed my mouth and sucked hard, I could taste blood coming from my shrunken gums. I knew my feet were in bits, but I didn't dare take my boots off, because I feared I'd never get them on again. As for my hands – I could see and smell them all too well. The thin leather of my gloves had cracked and split, from being repeatedly soaked and dried out again, so that my fingers hadn't had much protection. I'd lost most of the feeling in the tips, and I seemed to have got dirt pushed deep under my nails, so that infection had set in. Whenever I squeezed a nail, pus came out, and this stench was repulsive.

With my extremities suppurating like that, I wondered what internal damage I might be suffering, and could only hope that no permanent harm would be done. With the complete lack of food, I'd had no bowel movement since going on the run, and I couldn't remember when I'd last wanted to pee. I yearned for food, of course, but more for drink – and when I did think about food, it was sweet, slushy things that I craved. If ever I found myself back among rations packs, I would rip into the pears in syrup, ice-cream and chocolate sauce.

I felt very frightened. First and most obvious was the danger of being captured – the fear of torture, and of giving away secrets that might betray other guys from the Regiment. Almost worse, though, was the fact that I could see and feel my body going down so fast. If I didn't reach the border soon, I would be too weak to carry on.

Twisting round in the cramped space of the drain, I got out my map and tried for the hundredth time to work out where I was. It was now the morning of Wednesday 30 January. What options were left to me? Already light was coming up, and whatever happened, I was stuck in the culvert for that day. When dark fell again, I could try to sneak back down to the river, cross over and go along the other side – but it seemed a far-fetched hope. In any case, I'd built up a deep dread of going anywhere near the river. Every time I'd tried it, something had gone wrong; one more attempt, and I might easily be captured. At the very least, I still had thirty kilometres to go. How long could I hold out? I just couldn't tell what my body was still capable of.

First, I somehow had to get through eleven hours of daylight – eleven hours, when every waking minute now was agony. At least I was out of the wind, and less cold, so that I could drop off to sleep. I'd go straight off and be fast asleep, and start dreaming, usually about the squadron. I was with the rest of the guys.

They were all round me, talking and laughing, getting ready to go. We didn't seem to be in any particular place – unless it was the actual place I was in – but their presence was completely real. Then suddenly, maybe ten minutes later, I'd wake up, shuddering violently, hoping against hope that my mates were still there, and fully expecting that they would be. The dream had been so strong that I felt certain I'd find people lying near me, moving around, and that we were all together. Then I'd open my eyes and realise that I was alone in the culvert with no one to talk to. It was a horrible let-down.

Sometimes, also, I was at home in England with my family. Every time I fell asleep, the hallucinations grew more vivid. The most worrying feature was that I'd become confused between Jan – my wife – and Susan – the woman I was engaged to for so long. I kept trying to imagine Jan's face, but the awful thing was that I couldn't remember what it looked like. I was aware that I should remember her perfectly well, but I just couldn't see her, and I couldn't have described her to anyone else. I knew that she had blonde hair, but that was all. It was terrible to be aware that my own mind was going.

Instead of Jan, I was seeing Susan all the time. I saw her sitting on a fence, or in our house at Rowlands Gill. When I saw little Sarah, it was on Susan's knee that she was sitting.

I saw our home at Christmas, with all the decorations up – and the confusing thing was that this part of the dream reflected reality, not fantasy. The three of us had been sitting at the round table in the living room, and Jan had said, 'Chris, will you switch the Christmas tree lights on?' But little Sarah had jumped up and toddled across, saying, 'No, Daddy, I'll do it' – and she went over and flicked the switch. Now, in the filthy culvert, I saw the whole scene again and heard her baby voice saying, 'Daddy, I'll do it.'

For hours I lay there, drifting in and out of consciousness. At one point I suddenly found myself thinking of the Killing House – the special building at Hereford which the counter-terrorist team uses for a lot of its training. The walls are hung with sheets of rubber – so that live bullets can be fired without danger of ricochets – increasing the sense of claustrophobia. Visiting VIPs are often taken into the Killing House for demonstrations, which usually begin with pistol shooting. My speciality was always these pistol demos, in which I would fire at a 'Hun's Head' target (like a man wearing a German helmet) while rolling around the floor – and expect not just to hit the target, but to put all the rounds through the same hole.

Next, visitors are usually taken into another room and placed in one corner, behind white tape. Touching the tape, on the outside, would be one figure target. Next to that would be a live man – described as the hostage – sitting at a desk, and on his other side, a second figure target. The soldier in charge of the demo stands behind the hostage, commentating, and explaining that members of the SP team are planning to snatch him to safety.

One day the visiting VIP was none other than the Prime Minister, Margaret Thatcher, who was shepherded into the corner behind the tape, together with two bodyguards. The team commander gave his usual spiel, waffling on about the SAS until, with deceptive lack of emphasis, he said, 'Our success depends on three factors, which happen to have the same initials as the Regiment: Speed, Aggression and Surprise.'

On the word 'surprise' a loud explosion blasted off outside the door, simulating the demolition of the hinges. Two men in black ran in, armed with MP5s. Each put a burst of live rounds through one of the targets, so close to the visitors that they could feel the wind of the bullets. A third man dashed in, seized the hostage and dragged him away so quickly that, in the violent storm of noise, nobody noticed he had gone. In seconds the raid was over – and the only visitor still on her feet was the Prime Minister. Both bodyguards had hit the deck. As the smoke was clearing, she turned to them and said, 'What *are* you doing? For God's sake stand up!'

It must have been my claustrophobic surroundings in the culvert that brought back the scene so clearly. Yet another star visitor was the Princess of Wales, who came down with Prince Charles not long after they had been married. Her hair was longer then, and although she dressed up in black to take part in an assault on what was known as the old embassy building, she declined to put on a respirator or pull her hood into position.

As she came out after the attack, one of the guys asked, 'How did you find that?'

'It was great,' she replied, 'but I couldn't understand why someone kept hitting me on the back of the head.'

'You will when you look in the mirror,' he told her. What she didn't realise was that her hair had caught fire, and her neighbour had been beating out the flames. It was this slight setback that accounted for the much shorter hairstyle that she adopted for her next official trip.

Such memories helped a few minutes go by. But all too soon I was back in the reality of the drain. I wasn't worried by the occasional rumble of a car going past above me, but soon I began to hear other movement: scurrying, scuffling noises, as if troops were running around. I thought, 'Here we go. The next thing is going to be somebody at either end of this fucking culvert, and I'll be caught like a rat in a drainpipe.'

Every time I moved, dust rose around me and filled the tunnel, half choking me and making my tongue cleave to the back of my throat even more stickily. From the scrabbling, it sounded as though squaddies' boots were moving everywhere. I reckoned that the bodies had been discovered, the alarm had gone up, and that a search-party was closing in on me.

Most of the noise was coming from the end towards which my feet were pointing. I tried to turn my 203 to face the disturbance, but the drain was too narrow and I couldn't bring the weapon to bear. Now was the moment I needed a pistol, or better still a silenced one.

The scrabbling noise came closer. I tensed myself, certain that a man would stick his head into the end of the pipe at any second. If he did, my only option would be to try to scuttle out the other end. But what did the intruder turn out to be? A frigging goat!

A herd was being driven up the side of the road. I watched their legs move steadily past, and the scrabble of their feet on rocks, echoing through the tunnel, sounded like a whole company of squaddies on the move. Again I was terrified that they might have a dog with them; if they did, it would surely get my scent.

Tortured by thirst, by noises close at hand, by phantom scenes from home, I somehow stuck out the day. That was the lowest point of my whole escape. I'd lost so much weight that lying down became ever more agonising. Whatever attitude I

148

adopted, bones seemed to be sticking out, with no padding to cover them, and every five or six minutes I'd be in such discomfort that I'd have to turn over. Spine, hips, ribs, knees, elbows, shoulders – everything hurt, and I was developing sores all over. I kept telling myself, 'You've got to clear that border tonight, whatever happens.' But first I somehow had to escape from the trap in which I'd landed myself – and if the night turned out clear again, I didn't see how I was going to avoid the VCP.

Eventually darkness fell, and when I poked my head out of the end of the culvert, my morale took a lift again. Until then the nights had been clear, but this one was black as pitch, with the sky full of storm clouds that looked so threatening I even thought it might rain. The very idea of moisture was exciting. If rain did come, and I turned up my face, at least my parched mouth would get some refreshment. Maybe I could even collect water by spreading out my map case.

I crept out of the culvert. The night was so dark that when I looked in the direction of the VCP, I couldn't make it out. Moving closer, I found that the guards were still standing there, so I eased away until I could no longer see them, and when I was half-way between them and the anti-aircraft positions, I started walking at full speed.

Thank God for the darkness. Behind me nobody moved, and I got clean away. I'd been going for nearly two hours, parallel with a road, when all of a sudden a blinding flash split the darkness. Convinced I'd walked into ambush lights, I flung myself down; but then from behind me came a heavy explosion, and I realised that an air-raid was going in on the installation I'd just left. The same thing happened twice more: a flash, and a few seconds later a really big, deep *boom*. I kept thinking, 'If this hadn't been a dark night, that's where I'd still be.' What effect the bombs were having I couldn't tell, but the explosions sounded colossal, and I thanked my lucky stars that I'd been able to move on.

Occasionally, far away to my left, I saw anti-aircraft fire going up into the sky, and I guessed it must be coming from the airfields designated H1 and H2. No sound carried over that distance, so the tracer arched up in perfect silence – but at least it meant that the bases were under coalition attack. I knew that

'A' and 'D' Squadrons were operating in that area, and hoped it was they who were hammering the Iraqis.

I knew from the map that the Iraqi town of Krabilah should be coming up on my right. Krabilah lay on the border, and there was a Syrian town beyond the frontier. The thought of it kept me going, but only just. By now my feet were so bad that whenever I sat down for a rest they went from numb to excruciating. Upright, I couldn't feel them much; sitting, I thought they were going to burst. Several times I sat there thinking, 'Fucking hell! I can't take much more of this.' Then the pain would ease off, and I had a few minutes of bliss, with nothing hurting.

The worst bit came whenever I stood up again, and the pain just exploded. Starting off, I couldn't help gasping with the sheer agony. I had to shuffle my boots along the ground like some old comic, and I kept thinking, 'If anyone sees me, doddering along like this, I'll look a right idiot.' It wasn't till I'd taken about ten paces that my feet seemed to go numb again, and I could walk out. Occasionally I'd hit a sharp stone or rock – and boy, was that sore.

Never in my life had I been so exhausted. Often on selection and afterwards I thought I had pushed myself to my limit – but this was something else. I had sunk to an altogether different plane of tiredness and debilitation. The temptation to stop and rest was almost irresistible, but I knew that if I did I would never reach the border before my body gave out.

Helping me, I'm sure, were the years of training that I'd put in: not just the physical fitness which I'd built up, but the mental toughness, which life in the SAS had given me. Always competing with other guys as good as or better than myself, always determined to come out on top, I had learnt to push myself beyond what seemed to be possible. I was used to being hurt, and knew that I simply had to walk through the pain.

I couldn't fall back on religious belief to sustain me, because I didn't have any. As a child I'd gone to Sunday school, but only because someone would read us a story and we played games. In school proper I'd had religion thrown down my neck until I was sick of it; but as an adult I found I was unable to believe in God, seeing how much misery and disease and poverty there are in the world. At the same time, I think that humans do need to believe in something or someone. When you're in trouble you'll always cry for somebody – whether it's God, your mother or your wife. In those dire straits I believed in my wife and child – and the person who dragged me out of it was Sarah.

Without warning, the hallucinations began again. Suddenly, out in the middle of the black Iraqi night, there she was, walking in front of me, dressed in the purply-blue top and yellow bottoms, all covered in dots, that she'd worn at Christmas. The image I had of her, and the angle from which I could see her, were exactly the same as they'd been in Hereford. As I hobbled over the rocks and gravel, she somehow kept ahead of me, toddling on, leading the way through the dark. There seemed to have been a complete reversal of roles. Now she was the one who had confidence; I was the one who was afraid. Time and time again I heard her say, 'Daddy, do it.' Her voice was so clear that I thought I could pick her up in my arms. Time and time again I reached out to touch her. I felt that if I could catch hold of her hand, she would pull me out of trouble. Throughout that endless night I was on the verge of tears when I found I could not reach her. And yet, even when I realised she was not there, I knew that it was only the thought of her, and my need to see her again, that were keeping me going.

Towards the end I was stopping and resting on my feet. Because they were so agonising if I sat down, I took to reading my map standing up – which was not a good idea, as my torch was up in the air instead of close to the ground. I'd walk until I was really knackered, then prop myself against something so that I kept the pressure on my feet.

I was so far gone that when I reached some houses I was on the point of giving in. 'If only I were in England!' I thought. 'There'd be milk bottles standing on the doorstep, and a milk-float coming past in the morning.' How many bottles of milk could I have drunk straight down?

I watched the houses for a while. They were only small places, but I'd find water in them, for sure, and food. Suddenly I decided I'd had enough. 'Bollocks to it,' I thought. 'I'll go in, and if I have to, I'll do the people in there. I'll get something to drink and take their vehicle.'

I slid along one side of the nearest house, and found a window in the wall. It had iron bars down it, with a hessian curtain inside. Music was being played inside the room, and a candle or oil-lamp was flickering. I went past the window and reached the front of the building. Outside the door stood a car. 'Now!' I thought. 'Just let the keys be in it!' As I came round the corner I looked down, and there was a blasted dog, lying outside the door. The moment I saw it, it saw me and went berserk, barking frantically. Back I scuttled, along the side of the house, and away off into the wadis. The dog came out, and more dogs from the other buildings joined it. They followed me for about a hundred metres, barking like lunatics, then stopped. Oh for Turbo, I thought. He'd sort them.

Up in the wadis, I came to a railway line, scrabbled under it through a culvert, and was back in the desert. With a jolt I realised that this must be the same railway that Stan and I had crossed all those nights earlier. If only we'd tabbed straight along it, we'd have been out of Iraq days ago.

Galvanised by my latest fright, I kept walking, walking, walking. According to my calculations, I should have been passing Krabilah on my right, but there was no sign of the town. What I didn't realise was that every house had been blacked out because of the war, and that I had already gone clean by the place in the dark.

I reached a refuse heap, where loads of burnt-out old cans had been dumped in the desert, and sat down among them to do yet another map-study. I couldn't work things out. Where was the town, and where was the communications tower which the map marked? Where, above all, was the bloody border?

I started walking again, on the bearing, and as I came over a rise I saw three small buildings to my front. With the naked eye I could just make them out: three square bulks, blacked out. But when I looked through the kite-sight, I saw chinks of light escaping between the tops of the walls and the roofs. As I sat watching, one person came out, walked round behind, re-appeared and went back indoors. I was so desperate for water that I went straight towards the houses. Again, I was prepared to take out one of the inhabitants if need be. I was only fifty metres away when I checked through the kite-sight again and realised that the buildings were not houses at all, but sand-bagged sangars with wriggly tin roofs. They formed some sort of command post, and were undoubtedly full of squaddies. Pulling slowly back, I went round the side and, sure enough, came on a battery of four anti-aircraft positions.

If I'd walked up and opened one of the doors, I'd almost certainly have been captured. Once more the fright got my adrenaline going and revived me.

On I stumbled for another hour. My dehydration was making me choke and gag. My throat seemed to have gone solid, and when I scraped my tongue, white fur came off it. I felt myself growing weaker by the minute. My 203 might have been made of lead, such a burden had it become, so much of the strength had ebbed from my arms. My legs had lost their spring and grown stiff and clumsy. My ability to think clearly had dwindled away.

At last I came to a point from which I could see the lights of a town, far out on the horizon. Something seemed to be wrong. Surely that couldn't be Krabilah, still such a distance off? My heart sank: surely the border couldn't still be that far? Or was the glow I could see that of Abu Kamal, the first town inside Syria, some twenty kilometres to the west? If so, where the hell was Krabilah? According to the map, Krabilah had a communications tower, but Abu Kamal didn't. The far-off town *did* have a bright red light flashing, as if from a tower – and that made me all the more certain that the place in the distance was Krabilah.

Morale plummeted once more. Like my body, my mind was losing its grip. What I *could* make out was some kind of straight black line, running all the way across my front. Off to my left I could see a mound with a big command post on it, sprouting masts. Closer to me were a few buildings, blacked out, but not looking like a town.

I sat down some 500 metres short of the black line and studied the set-up through the kite-sight. Things didn't add up. With Krabilah so far ahead, this could hardly be the border. Yet it looked like one. I wondered whether it was some inner frontier-line which the Iraqis had built because of the war, to keep people back from the border itself. Suddenly I thought of the Int guy back at Al Jouf, unable to tell what the border looked like. 'What an arsehole!' I thought. 'He should have known. That's his fucking job.'

Whatever this line ahead of me might be, all I wanted to do was get across it. I was gripped by a terrific sense of urgency, but I forced myself to hold back, sit down and observe it. 'This is where you're going to stumble if you don't watch out,' I told myself. 'This is where you'll fall down. Take time over it.'

There I sat, shivering, watching, waiting. A vehicle came out of the command post and drove down along the line – an open-backed land-cruiser. Directly opposite my vantage-point two men emerged from an observation post, walked up to the car, spoke to the driver, jumped in, and drove off to the right. It looked as if the Iraqis were putting out roving observers to keep an eye on the border. I couldn't tell whether this was routine, or whether they suspected that enemy soldiers were in the area; but after a few minutes I decided that the coast was clear, and I had to move.

At long last I came down to the black line. Creeping cautiously towards it, I found it was a barrier of barbed wire: three coils in the bottom row, two on top of them, and one on top of that. Having no pliers to cut with, I tried to squeeze my way through the coils, but that proved impossible: barbs hooked into my clothes and skin and held me fast. I unhooked myself with difficulty, and decided that the only way to go was over the top. Luckily the builders had made the elementary mistake, every twenty-five metres, of putting in three posts close to each other and linking them together with barbed wire. Obviously the idea was to brace the barrier, but the posts created a kind of bridge across the middle of the coils. I took off my webbing and threw it over, then went up and over myself, sustaining a few lacerations but nothing serious.

Still I could not believe I was clear of Iraq. The barrier seemed so insignificant that I thought it must only be marking some false or inner border, and that I would come to the true frontier some distance further on. The real thing, I thought, would be a big anti-tank berm, constructed so that vehicles could not drive across. Maybe this was why I had no feeling of elation; for days I had been thinking that, if I did manage to cross the frontier, it would be the climax of my journey, but now I felt nothing except utter exhaustion.

With my webbing back in place, I set off yet again on the same bearing. Never in my life, before or since, have I pushed myself so hard. I think I was brain-dead that night, walking in neutral, moving automatically, stumbling grimly onwards. Once or twice Sarah returned to keep me company and lead me, but mostly I dragged myself on without hearing, seeing or thinking.

154

In the end I could go no further. I simply had to sit down and rest. I took my weapon off my shoulder, and just as I was lifting the night-sight from where it hung round my neck, I seemed to click my head, and felt what I can only describe as a huge electric shock. I heard a noise like a ferocious short-circuit – *krrrrrrrrk* – and when I looked down at my hands, there was a big white flash.

The next thing I knew I was sitting in the same place, but I couldn't tell if I had been asleep, or unconscious, or what. I was aware that time had passed, but had no idea how much. Nor did I know what had happened to me. But it was a weird feeling, to have been out of the world for a while.

I got my kit back on and stood up. This time my feet were real torture, and I was barely able to totter forwards until they went numb again.

It was still dark. The night seemed very long. Nothing for it but to keep going. Was I in Syria or Iraq? Couldn't tell. Better steer clear of the odd house, then, because every one had a dog. What would I do when it got light? Didn't know. Couldn't think. Should be in Syria.

I woke up a bit when I found I was crossing vehicle tracks – many wheel marks imprinted in dry mud. Then after a while I thought I heard something behind me. As I turned to look, the same phenomenon hit me again: a big crack of static in the head and a blinding flash. This time I woke up on the ground, facedown, and I said to myself, 'Jesus! You picked a stupid place to fall asleep. Get a grip.'

On my feet again, I checked my weapon to make sure I hadn't pushed the muzzle into the ground as I fell, and went forward once more. Now I was walking towards a red light, which never seemed to get any brighter. I would approach the next crest in the ground thinking, 'When I get there, the light will be close in front of me.' But that never happened. The glow must have been miles away.

All this time, although I did not know it, I was drawing away from Krabilah, which lay down to my right in the darkness. I had walked clean past it without seeing the least sign of it. But that was hardly surprising, because things were becoming blurred now. I was in and out of wadis, staggering on. I was on a flat area with more tracks. Presently I came to the wall of one

155

wadi and had another attack: a big crack in my head, the same *krrrrrk* of static, a flash . . .

The next thing I knew, I came round to find my nose blocked and aching. How long I had been unconscious I could not tell. But dawn had broken, so I presumed that an hour had gone by, at least. In my compass-mirror I saw that blood had run down my cheeks and neck, matting in the stubble. Somehow I'd fallen flat on my face.

I propped myself against the rock wall. If ever I had come close to dying, it was then. I seemed to have nothing left. My strength had gone, and with it the will to move. I lay back with my head resting against the rock, feeling almost drunk. Now that daylight had come, I knew I ought to lie up. But no – I couldn't last another day without water. For minutes I sat there in a heap. Then I got out my precious flask and drank the last little sip of whisky. It tasted horrible, like fire. I was so dehydrated that it burnt all the way down into my stomach, and left me gasping and desperate, so that I wished I'd never drunk it.

Then suddenly, to my indescribable relief, out of the wadi wall came Paul, the guy in Bravo One Zero who'd burnt his hand before we left. He was dressed in green DPM, not desert gear, and stopped about twenty feet away from me.

'Come on, Chris,' he said, 'hurry up. The squadron's waiting for you.'

It seemed perfectly normal that the squadron should be there. Painfully I levered myself to my feet with the 203 and shuffled down the wadi, expecting to see the rest of the guys lined up, sorting themselves out, ready for the off. In my mental picture, everyone was in as bad a state as I was – knackered, but preparing to go. Yet when I came round the corner, there was nobody in sight.

To this day I swear that Paul walked out in front of me. I thought I was *compos mentis*, and seemed to know what was happening. I knew I'd passed out. I knew I had fallen and hit my nose – but now I was fully conscious and alert again. I even heard the sound of Paul's boots as he came towards me over the gravel in the wadi bed, and for a few moments I thought my nightmare was over. I thought help and salvation had come. Far from it. I was still on my own. Disappointment dealt another crippling blow to my morale. What the hell was I to do now?

I sat down, trying to get myself together. It was early morning on Thursday 31 January. I'd been on the run for eight days and seven nights. It was ten days since my last proper meal, six days since I'd finished my biscuits, three since I'd had any water. My body wasn't going to last another day.

In a futile gesture I pulled out my TACBE, switched it on and let it bleep away. Then I looked up and realised that in the middle distance, about a kilometre away, there was a barn or house – a combination of both, standing out on a rise in the middle of scruffy fields in which rocks poked up out of the bare grey earth.

As I stood watching, a man came out of the house and walked away with a herd of goats. The people living in that barn must have water. I decided that I had to get some, whatever the cost. If I was in Syria, the people might be friendly. If I was still in Iraq, I was going to have to threaten to kill them, get a drink, and carry on. I'd made up my mind: I was going in there, and I'd kill everybody if need be.

Chapter Eight

Safe Or Sorry?

I left the TACBE on in my pocket as I started forward. *Beep*, it went, *beep*, *beep*. I began closing on the barn. The building was made of dirty-white stone, with a low wall running out of its right-hand end; and the doorway was open. Outside it was a young woman with a black scarf tied round her head in a band, bending over a wood fire and holding what looked like an upturned wok. I could see that she was cooking pieces of dough, like nan bread, spread over the shallow cone of hot metal. Two or three children were playing in the open.

The woman saw me coming but did not react much. As I approached, my weapon in my hands, she lifted her head and called into the house. I was only five or six metres off when a young man came out – a fellow of maybe eighteen with dark, curly hair. He touched his chest and then his forehead with his right hand, nodding in typical Arab greeting.

I went up and shook his hand, and pointed at the ground, asking, 'Syria? Is this Syria?

He nodded, repeating, 'Seeria! Seeria!' Then he pointed over my shoulder and said, 'Iraq. Iraq.'

I looked back the way he was gesturing, and in the distance behind me, over the mounds to the east, I saw a town with a mast. Krabilah! Looking westward, I saw another town, also with a mast. Abu Kamal! The one to the east was miles behind me. Both bloody towns had masts! I realised that I must have passed Krabilah early in the night, and that most of the walking I'd done since then had been unnecessary – nothing but self-inflicted torture. That line of barbed wire had been the frontier after all. I'd been in Syria for hours.

The young man could see the state I was in. A worried look came over his face, and he began touching my hands. He took me by the sleeve and drew me into the barn. In the middle was a round oil stove with a glass door and a metal chimney that rose straight through the roof. At the far end of the room lay rolls of bedding and some straw. There was practically no furniture, and it was obvious the people were very poor. A woman with tattoos on her face sat breast-feeding a baby, and did not move as I came in.

I sat on a mat on the ground next to the stove with my weapon laid across my lap. The young man looked at me and asked in gestures if I wanted something to eat.

'Water!' I croaked, tipping up an imaginary glass. 'Water!'

A moment later he handed me a shiny metal bowl full of water, which tasted incredibly fresh and cold. Never in my life had I had a more delicious drink. I tipped it straight down my neck. The boy brought another bowlful, and I drank that as well. Next he gave me a cup of sweet tea, thick with dissolved sugar, and I put that down too. Then the woman came in with some of the bread she'd been making, and gave me a piece. It was still hot, and smelt delicious, but when I bit off a mouthful and tried to swallow it, it locked in my throat and would not go down.

I had to get my boots off. It was four days since I'd seen my feet, and I was dreading what I would find. As I undid the laces and eased the boots off, the stink was repulsive. Like my hands, my feet were rotting. I smelt as if my whole body was putrefying. When the man saw the state of my feet, with pus oozing along the sides, he let out a yell. The woman who'd been cooking came up with a wide bowl like a dustbin full of cold water and began to wash my feet. All my toenails had come off, and my toes were numb – I couldn't feel them. But the water stung the rest of my feet like fire.

In spite of the pain, I forced myself to scrape the pus out of the cuts along the sides and round the heels. I also washed the blood off my face. With that done, it was bliss to lie back with my bare feet raised to the warmth of the stove and let them breathe. Another girl appeared from outside, took my socks and rinsed them through. When she brought them back, of course they were still wet, but I pulled them on, and got my boots back on as well.

In sign language, and by making aircraft sounds, I tried to indicate that I was a pilot and had been in a crash. Then I made some siren sounds – *dee-dah, dee-dah, dee-dah* – to show that I wanted to go to the police. A boy of about six had been drawing pictures of tanks and aircraft on sheets of dirty white paper. With my numb fingers I drew a police car with a blue lamp on the roof. Suddenly the message got through: the young man nodded vigorously and pointed towards the distant town.

'Go to the town?' I suggested, and I made driving motions. 'You have a vehicle?'

Again he nodded and pointed. What he meant – I soon found out – was that we should start walking down the road towards the town and thumb a lift.

With the water and tea inside me, my body seemed to have switched back on. My drowsiness and disorientation had vanished. I felt sharp again, as if there was nothing wrong, as if I could do the whole walk again. Everything seemed so relaxed that for a while I just sat there, recovering.

The old man came back with his goats and stood looking at me. Then, to get some action, I dug a sovereign out of my belt and showed it round. I started saying '*Felous, felous*' – 'money, money' – and pointed to the goats, then back at the coin, trying to put over the idea that this represented many animals, or a lot of cash. 'Bank,' I said, 'bank.'

The appearance of the gold galvanised the young man. All at once he became hell-bent on going into town. Maybe he thought that if he escorted me in I would give him the money. Soon everyone was staring at the sovereign. Another girl came in, and somehow I knew she said, 'He's got more on him somewhere.' The old man appeared with a gun – some ancient hunting rifle. 'More,' he said, 'more' – and by gestures he showed he wanted another coin, to make the girl a pair of earrings. Then he started demanding gold for the other girls as well.

'No, no, no,' I said. 'This is for goats, clothes and stuff. No more.'

The Arabs began muttering to each other. For half an hour things remained tense. I lay with my feet against the oil fire, warming up. It was the first time in a week that I hadn't felt half frozen. I had begun to hope that I could sleep in the farmhouse that night; I wanted to tell them, 'Wait awhile – just let me rest here.' But the young man had become determined to go into town, and indicated that I should come outside.

I decided not to wait any longer. But to present a less aggressive figure, I took off my webbing and smock, so that I was left wearing my dark-green jersey and camouflage trousers. With signs I asked the man for some sort of bag. He produced a white plastic fertiliser sack, and I put my kit into that. I then slung the sack over my shoulder and we set off along the road.

Soon I thought, 'It's hardly the thing, to walk into a civilian town carrying a rifle,' so when we'd gone about two hundred metres, I broke my weapon down in two and put it in the bag. I still had my knife, but in this situation I could have done with a pistol – an inconspicuous weapon, which would have come in handy during the emergency which followed.

The young man led off quite fast along the dirt road and I shuffled behind him, in too much pain to move quickly. Every minute or two my companion stopped and waited for me to catch up. Then, seeing I was in difficulties, he took the bag off me, and without the weight I made better progress. I kept saying, 'Tractor? Where's a tractor?' – and I presume he was saying in Arabic, 'One'll come soon.'

Wagons were rolling out from the town, and presently one stopped: a land-cruiser loaded with bales of hay. The driver could speak a little broken English. He said he was a camel farmer, and asked who I was.

'My aircraft's crashed,' I told him.

'Your aircraft? Where is it?'

'Over the hill, over there. I need to go to the police.'

'OK. I'll take you.'

He swung his vehicle round, and I got into the middle of the front seat, between him and the young man. In a minute or two I was regretting it, because he started making aggressive comments: 'You shouldn't be here. This is our country. This is a bad war.'

I just said, 'Yeah, I know,' and kept as quiet as possible. Soon we hit the edge of the town, which proved a severe disappointment. I'd been imagining a fairly sophisticated place, with banks and shops and other signs of civilisation. This place had nothing but crude houses made of grey breeze blocks, with heaps of rubbish lying round them. There was no vegetation, and not a sign of a garden. The only form of decoration was the odd burnt-out car. One thing that did surprise me was the extent to which the Syrians resembled Europeans – and I was startled by the sight of two men with flaming, carrot-coloured hair, one of them sporting an equally red beard.

My driver pulled up outside a house on the left-hand side of the road and beeped his horn. Out came an Arab dressed in a black dishdash. There was a bit of an exchange between the two; then the driver said something to the young farm lad, who got out of the truck. I felt helpless, because I saw fear in the boy's face, and didn't know what was happening.

'Everything all right?' I asked, but the driver spoke sharply to the lad, who set off walking, back towards home.

The two of us went on into town, and the driver started niggling again. 'You want to go back to Iraq?' he said, and roared with laughter. 'I should take you back.'

'No, no!' I said. I brought out my idemnity slip, written in Arabic as well as English. The letter promised £5,000 to anyone who handed me safely back to the coalition. The driver snatched it and began to stuff it into his pocket, as if it was actual cash.

'You don't understand,' I said. 'I have to be with this piece of paper. Me and the paper at the same time. You only get the money if the two are together.' I took it back from him and put it away.

'OK,' he said, 'OK.'

At least he stopped talking about taking me back across the border. But then he asked, 'You have gun?'

'No,' I said. 'No gun.'

We came to a petrol station, and he pulled up. On the other side of the pumps was a car with a gang of young lads round it. The driver touched my bag, with all the kit in it, and asked, 'What all this?'

'Nothing, nothing. Just my things.'

He reached over to pat me on my stomach, to feel if I had a weapon concealed about me.

'No,' I protested. 'I've got nothing.'

Suddenly he called out to the lads by the pump, and one of them came over. The boy stood by the window and didn't look at me, but kept his eyes straight down on the bag. The driver went on talking to him – until suddenly he ran off into the building.

I thought, 'There's something going on here. There's going to be a lynching party coming out. They're going to do me for my weapon, or put me back across the border.'

It was time to go. I opened the door, grabbed the bag and began to get out. At that moment the driver seized my left arm, trying to restrain me. I dragged him across the front seat and half out of the cab. When I kicked the door shut, it caught his head in the opening and he had to let go of me. He let out a yell, and I took off.

Fear boiled up in me again, almost worse than before. Away I went, running up the street, with the plastic sack in one hand. At least, I thought I was running – but when I turned round I saw a load of old guys easily keeping pace with me. I was running in slow motion. I couldn't go any faster.

Soon there was a big commotion, and a crowd of over a dozen people coming after me. They were barely thirty metres behind me and closing fast. I thought, 'You're screwed here.'

Instinctively I knew that in those Arab border towns everyone is related to everyone else. Although some of these people called themselves Syrians and some Iraqis, they probably all belonged to the same families, and had cousins or even brothers on the other side. I'd seen it on the border between Saudi and Iraq: guys from both sides were driving across to the frontier posts opposite, just to have tea with their friends. Whenever they got a stand-to, they'd merely disappear back.

Now, somehow, these Syrians knew I had a weapon in that bag. They were out to get it, and then to throw me back into Iraq, or worse. A terrific atmosphere had suddenly built up. The pavements were full of people, and the ones on the other side of the road were all looking, alerted by the noise. Ahead of me, more pedestrians were staring. I kept hobbling and staggering along, hampered by the plastic sack in my right hand. I couldn't even wave my weapon in threat, because it was stripped down.To have reassembled it would have meant stopping for at least a minute, and by then the mob would have been on top of me.

Then, as I turned a corner, a miracle: there stood a man with an AK 47, wearing chest webbing. He was right next door to a pillar box, obviously on duty. It flashed into my mind that this might be the Iraqi border post, but it was too late to worry.

'Police?' I shouted. 'Police?'

I don't know what the guy said. I'm not sure he said anything at all. He just pulled me through a gateway and into a walled garden. I saw bunting of triangular flags over the entrance, vegetation all round, and a big bungalow. He had me by the arm and the scruff of the neck, and ran me into this enclosure, out of reach of the crowd in the street, who by then were yelling for my blood. What his motives were, I'll never know. He may have been trying to save me from the mob, or he may just have thought he'd grabbed a prisoner.

Inside the bungalow a man sat behind a desk, smoking. He was wearing a black leather jacket. So were all the other men in there – black leather bomber jackets and jeans – and they all seemed to be smoking. Nobody spoke a word of English. There was a lot of pointing. I said, 'I'm a helicopter pilot,' and made chopper noises, whirling my hand round to indicate rotors, and then diving it down to show that I had crashed.

Very soon they'd opened my bag and got out the 203, together with my webbing. Then the driver who'd given me the lift rushed in and let fly a volley of Arabic, jabbing his finger in my direction. I felt another surge of fear, and motioned to the bomber-jacketed guys, 'Get him out!' They bundled him into another room, protesting all the way.

The air was full of animosity, but I couldn't tell which way it was pointing. These leather-clad guys obviously had no time for the driver, but they didn't like the look of me either. I couldn't blame them. My hair was matted with dirt; my face was emaciated, eyes staring. I had ten days' growth of beard. I was filthy and stinking. I was also an infidel.

They started stripping my kit, and pulled out the two white phosphorus grenades. One of the guys, who was smoking a cigarette, held a grenade up and asked something in Arabic, obviously 'What's this?'

'Smoke,' I told him. 'For making smoke' – and I waved up clouds of the stuff in mid air.

They started lobbing the grenades round, one to another, catching them like cricket balls. The safety pins, which I'd loosened before our first contact, were hanging out. I knew that if one of the grenades went off, it would kill us all; so I made to stand up and grab them. The movement did not go down well. The instant I was half-upright, three guys pulled pistols and levelled them at me, yelling at me to sit down. So I sat back, and everything gradually calmed down. The man who'd finished up with the grenades brought them over, and let me push the pins back into place.

By then the others were ripping out all my kit: the kite-sight, my little binoculars, my fireflies (the lights which give a high-intensity flash and have infra-red filters for bringing aircraft on to you). All my stuff was disappearing, and I thought, 'I'm not going to see any of this again.' None of it was particularly valuable, but I'd become quite attached to it, having carried it all that way, and now it was being stolen in front of my eyes.

After about twenty minutes I was taken through a door into another room, and in came a man of fifty or so, wearing a grey suit. He was very calm, as if nothing bothered him, and he looked exactly like a Middle Eastern version of the actor Anthony Hopkins. He sat me down at a table with a piece of paper and said, 'Details? Name? Birthday? Country?'

I wrote down, 'Sergeant Chris Ryan, 22 Turbo Squadron, Para Field Ambulance,' and my date of birth – and left it at that. 22 Para Field Ambulance didn't exist, but I thought that if I finished up in a prison camp, and the number, combined with the word 'Turbo', reached the coalition, somebody would click on to the fact that I was a medic in 22 SAS. I gave my rank as sergeant because I knew it would command a bit more respect than if I said 'corporal'; besides, in the SAS corporals get sergeants' pay.

While I was writing, another man gave me a cup of coffee, and I drank it. It was thick and bitter, Arab-style, and made me feel thirstier than ever. The Hopkins character took the paper, went out, then came back in and beckoned me to follow him. I stood up, and as I reached the door two other guys were waiting. I felt as if I was going to run the gauntlet, but they grabbed me by the arms and pulled me into a different room. There they pointed down at a white dishdash and motioned me to put it on.

By then I was really scared. What the hell were they doing, making me dress up like an Arab? The dishdash came down to my feet. Someone came in with a shamag and wrapped it round my head. At first I could just about see out, but then they pulled it right down over my face. Nobody told me where

I was going or what was happening. I felt panic rising. Inadvertently I had handed myself over to these bastards, who had complete control of me.

I saw my bag of equipment go out the door ahead of me. A land-cruiser pulled up outside. Two men armed with AK 47s came in; there was an exchange, and I was passed over to them and marched out. One man climbed into the driver's seat, I was pushed into the middle, and the second man got in on my right.

As we came out of the police station, I held my breath. I felt certain that if we turned right, we would be on our way back to Iraq. If we turned left, there was a good chance that the Syrians would be keeping me.

We turned left. I breathed again. Then we set off at high speed, along rough streets full of kids playing. The fact that humans were in the way didn't deter the driver; he just kept going, with one hand on the horn, swerving in and out of the vast potholes. After a while the passenger made signs to ask if I was hungry. I said 'Yes' and nodded, so the driver stopped and waited while his mate ran out, returning with a bag of apples.

When I ate the whole of the one he gave me – core, pips and all, everything bar the stalk – both Arabs stared at me. The one on my right hadn't touched his apple, and he gave it to me – so I ate that too, core and all again.

On we went, missing hundreds of dogs by inches. We swerved to avoid any number of dead ones, too. Next we cleared the town, came on to a metalled road and down into a big valley. Then we were out in the desert, on a road that ran straight for miles.

I knew my bag was in the back, but I couldn't tell how much of my kit was still in it. I tried talking, and asked where we were going. 'Damascus?' I suggested. 'Damascus?' But my question produced no answers, so I shut up. At one point, to my right, I saw ancient ruins, but, in the state I was, they didn't interest me much.

Ahead of us I saw two dark-blue Mercedes parked on the side of the road, with a group of six men standing round the cars. As we came towards them, my escorts started jabbering to each other. Obviously this was some pre-arranged rendezvous. We began to slow down. Fifty metres short of the cars, I could see that one of the waiting men had a pistol in his hand. Suddenly the guy on my right pulled up my shamag, quite roughly, so as to blindfold me, and grabbed hold of my arm. I thought, 'Fucking hell, this is an execution squad!'

We came to a halt. I was dragged out, run up to the back of one of the Mercedes, thrown down on my knees. Somebody pushed my head forward, and one of these twats came and stood behind me.

Silence followed. Nobody moved or spoke. I thought I was going to die. Until then I'd always reckoned that if anything like this happened to me, I'd make a last-ditch run for it. Watching films of the Holocaust, and imagining I'd been caught by the Nazis, I'd seen myself putting up a last-second fight. But now it wasn't like that. Physically incapable of running, I just knelt there waiting for the bastard to shoot me in the back of the head. It was a terrible feeling, to be on my knees, waiting for someone to do that to me. But I didn't get scenes from my life flashing through my head, like you're supposed to. I just felt annoyed that I'd given myself up to these rotten people.

The silence seemed to last for ever. In fact it probably went on for less than a minute. Then there was a movement. Hands either side grabbed my arms, stood me up, moved me forward and threw me into the back of a car. The doors slammed and we drove off.

Now I had three escorts, all in western civilian clothes. On my left sat the youngest, a skinny fellow with a thin, weasly face and a straggling moustache – the sort of looks that annoy me. He struck me as a weak character. The driver was quite a big fellow, dark, good-looking, maybe my own age, and wearing a black leather jacket. His front-seat passenger was about forty: chubby, and going thin on top, he wore a green safari-type jacket with patch pockets. All three had ties, but they had pulled the knots loose, and in general their appearance was scruffy.

Who *were* these guys? Police, I hoped. But they gave me no clue as to their identity – and why were they messing about so much? In my state of exhaustion and confusion, I didn't know what to think. Of course I considered trying to take them out. I still had my knife on me – but the car was travelling fast, probably at 70 or 80 m.p.h. for most of the time. Also, there was another car escorting us, and police outriders. The desert we were going through was very open, with nowhere to hide.

My shamag was still on, but the guy in the passenger seat pulled it down far enough for me to see. Then, leaning over into the back, he began to strip-search me: he took off my ID discs by pulling the cord over my head, unclipped my belt, undid my boot laces, removed my watch, emptied my pockets, took my notebook and map. One thing which escaped him was my belt, which had 19 gold sovereigns taped to the inside.

That was another frightening moment, when I felt his hands on me. The guy on my left was holding my arm, and I was thinking. 'Jesus, if I'm going to safety, they shouldn't be doing this to me.' *Could* these fellows be the Syrian police? Or who were they? Why were they behaving like this? It was all very strange and alarming.

Presently they blindfolded me again. They talked a bit among themselves, and played loud Arab music on the stereo. Also, they chain-smoked. Soon I was in agony. In the warmth of the car – the highest temperature I'd been in for days – my feet and knees began to swell. Probably being static contributed to the trouble, and the pain became excruciating. I kept trying to ease the agony by shifting around, but all the time I was finding it harder and harder to breathe. I wasn't exactly hyperventilating, but I'm sure fear was contributing to my problems, and I was being choked by the filthy smoke.

I started feeling claustrophobic, and said, 'Can't you take the blindfold off?' Until then, whenever I'd tried to pull the shamag off my face, the guy in front had twitched it back, but now he seemed to realise that I was in trouble, and let it drop out of the way. I saw that the second Mercedes was ahead of us, and that whenever we came to a village, our outriders went ahead on their motorbikes to seal off any side-roads, so that we could go speeding straight through. Then they'd come howling past us and take the lead again.

The scrawny fellow next to me kept poking me in the ribs and going on about the war, making banal, needling remarks in broken English. 'What were you doing in Iraq? You shouldn't be here. Do you like Americans?'

At any other time I'd have thumped his block off – and I don't think he'd feel very well if I saw him today. As it was, I grunted monosyllabic answers, anxious to give nothing away. I still didn't know who these people were, or what they were doing. I felt fairly confident they weren't taking me to Baghdad, but I thought they might be going to hand me over to some extremist group as a hostage. I knew that both John McCarthy and Terry Waite were being held by guerrillas. In my confused state, I couldn't remember who it was holding them – was it Hizbollah? – but I began to think I was going to end up with them.

Sometimes our driver would overtake the other car and lead for a while. Every time we came to a village, one of my escorts would pull the shamag over my eyes so that I couldn't see any names.

After four or five hours we drove down a broad valley, with steep sides set back maybe a kilometre on either side, and high ground rising beyond them. Then, looking ahead, I saw a motorway sign coming up – and all it said, in enormous letters, was BAGHDAD, with a big arrow pointing from right to left.

When I saw that I felt that I'd gone through the floor and my arse was getting dragged along the ground. Just as I spotted it, the driver said something to the fellow beside me, who started poking me in the ribs, cackling, 'Yes, you right. You going Baghdad! You going where Baghdad is.'

I was growing angry – partly with the idiot beside me, partly with myself. How the hell had I ended up in such a situation? All my effort in walking so far seemed to have gone for nothing. Why had I given myself up to these dickheads? Why hadn't I tried to pinch a vehicle and drive myself to Damascus?

The front-seat passenger turned to me and said, 'Yes – we're Baghdadis.'

Then the driver pointed at his own backside and went, '*Ee, ee, ee, ee,*' watching me in the mirror as he did so, obviously meaning that my bum was twitching.

He never realised what a good turn he did me by making that stupid gesture. All at once he infuriated me and steeled my resolve. I thought, 'Fuck you! I can take anything you cunts can give me. I'll keep my mouth shut and take whatever's coming.'

I began struggling to reorientate my ideas. I had to accept that I was going to a prison camp. I was going to be interrogated. I was going to get a bad kicking, a beating. 'Think your thoughts,' I told myself. 'Get organised.'

169

I still considered doing a runner, but it was impossible. I was physically knackered, and wouldn't have gone a hundred yards. 'It's no good,' I told myself. 'They'll have you.' Instead, I sat still, trying not to annoy my escorts by fidgeting; but every part of me was aching: back, shoulders, knees – but worst of all, my feet.

With the view cut out by the blindfold again, I kept trying to visualise where we were. On the highway to Baghdad, I felt certain. But which way did it go? Had there always been a highway to Baghdad, right from Biblical times? And did it run through Jordan, or what?

Exhaustion began sweeping over me again. Although I'd drunk the water and coffee in the barn that morning, I was desperately in need of food, and more liquid. I had been weakened more than I realised. My mind was so confused that I couldn't remember the simplest details of everyday life.

Through my blindfold I could see and feel that we were heading towards the sun, and that hour by hour the sun was going down. But what did that mean? Did the sun set in the east or in the west? Unable to remember, I tried to think back to what used to happen when I was a kid. Gradually I got it: from my bedroom at home I could see the sun coming up over Gibside, the big country estate on the far flank of the Derwent valley where we lived. I tried to project myself out into the sky above our home, so that I was looking down on the house. 'Yes,' I thought, 'the sun's coming up over there. That's the direction of Newcastle, and, further off, China.' That meant the sun rose in the east, and set in the west. Now we were heading into the setting sun: therefore we must be driving west. In that case, I told myself, we couldn't be going to Baghdad. Desperately I tried to visualise the map and remember which part of Syria Damascus was in.

For the final half hour or so they kept my head wrapped up. Then darkness fell, and still we went on driving, until in the end we hit the outskirts of some town or city. By then the blindfold was off again, and I started to see signs saying DAMAS. 'Jesus,' I thought. 'Can this really be Damascus?' As I saw more and more signs saying DAMAS, I began daring to hope that it was the Syrian capital.

My escorts started to smarten themselves up. They put out

their cigarettes, turned off the radio, slid their ties tight, and straightened their clothes, as if preparing to meet somebody important. All that alarmed me. What were they getting ready for?

Then, on a piece of waste ground, we pulled into the kerb, behind yet another Mercedes, and my front passenger got out. His place was taken by a much older guy, of maybe fifty, well dressed, and balding a little. His dark suit gave him a sombre appearance, but at least he looked cool and calm. The other two characters in my car were obviously in awe of him; as he walked towards us they stopped chattering, and more or less sat to attention, hardly daring to breathe.

The new man got in, closed his door and gave one curt instruction, hardly more than a grunt. We moved off towards the city centre. Every now and then he snapped a direction at the driver, very abrupt: 'Left . . . right,' and that was all. After about five minutes he turned round and asked in English, 'Are you OK?'

I nodded and said, 'Yep.'

'Won't be long now.'

Then he picked up all the things they'd taken off me – watch, ID discs, bootlaces and so on – handed them back and said, 'These are yours.'

I thought, 'What the hell's going on? What was the point of taking it all off me in the first place?' There'd been so many changes of mood. First there'd been the farm boy, definitely friendly. Then the driver of the truck had turned hostile, telling me I had no business to be in Syria. Then the policeman on duty had saved me from the mob. Next the twats inside the station had tried to steal all my kit – hostility again. Then the guy who made me write down my details seemed to be back on my side. A few minutes later my escorts were giving me apples to eat. Then it was into the mock-execution, and more sick jokes about going to Baghdad. No wonder I felt confused.

Anyway, I started getting my kit back in place. I put away the maps and knife, and got the ID discs back round my neck; but by then my feet had swollen up so much that I couldn't get my boots on, so I didn't bother threading the laces.

All this time we were driving through the city, and I could tell how scared the driver was of our new passenger, purely from his reactions. He kept glancing fearfully sideways, looking for new instructions, and always at the last possible instant the man would bark at him, 'Left!' or 'Right!'

At last we came to a big modern building, probably ten storeys high. There were guards in green uniforms and armed with AK 47s on the gates, on the walls, everywhere: not the sort of place you could break into, or out of, in a hurry. Before I had time to wonder what it was, the gates swung open in front of us, and we drove into a courtyard.

Chapter Nine

Guest Of The Government

All my escorts got out. For a moment I was left sitting in the back. When I went to move, I found that my knees and ankles had locked solid. The older guy saw me struggling and clicked his fingers, whereupon the other two more or less lifted me out of the car, propped me up, and helped me – practically carried me – up a long flight of steps to the glass doors. They can't have enjoyed it much, because I was stinking like that three-week-old corpse I once saw and smelt in London.

After a few steps my legs began to function again, more or less. We shuffled into a big reception area, where everything looked efficient and well-guarded. Sitting at the desk was a man in uniform, with a peaked cap with a red band round it, who came to attention as we entered. Then it was into a lift, up a few floors, and out again. As the doors opened, we were met by a smartly-dressed, clean-shaven man in a dark-blue blazer, stripy tie and blue shirt. Beside him, hovering deferentially, stood another man, about the same age, but chubbier and less smart.

The boss-figure was an impressive character: in his mid-forties, he had a smart haircut, looked crisp and effective, and possessed obvious authority. I hadn't a clue who he was – and he did not bother to enlighten me. Only later did I discover that he was head of the Mukhabarrat, the Syrian Secret Police. For the moment I felt screwed up, unable to decide what the hell was happening.

The boss smiled, reached out, took my hand, and said in English, 'Welcome to Damascus. Welcome to Syria.'

The interpreter said, 'Come in, please,' and ushered me in.

Where was the catch? What were these buggers up to? It was horrible to be so unsure. I was desperately trying to think of all my options, and bloody fast, so that I didn't get caught out.

I followed them through into some kind of office and sat down on a Chesterfield. I could see the boss sniffing, and not liking what he was getting. Suddenly being in a clean environment, I could see what shit order I was in: my hair was matted, my hands and face were filthy. There was brown, dried blood on my DPMs. The boss himself took off the shamag, which was still wrapped round my head, and spoke sharply to the interpreter, clearly saying, 'Get this stuff off.' Someone else helped me out of the dishdash. Another guy brought in my bag and put it under a table. Then, through the interpreter, the boss said, 'Would you like to get cleaned up?'

'Yeah,' I said. 'Good idea.'

'Come with me.'

The interpreter's English was first-class, and he seemed very friendly. I thought, 'You'd better start playing a game, here,' and tried to appear grateful; but I still had no idea what was going on, and I expect I looked shell-shocked. Part of my mind was wondering what was going to happen, part trying *not* to anticipate, for fear of being disappointed. I had time to glance round the walls and noticed a gold-plated AK 47, as well as pictures of Assad, the Syrian President. A large, leather-topped desk stood in one corner, covered in ornaments and paperweights. Two or three settees were set out round a coffee-table. The whole room spoke of money and good organisation.

With the boss leading the way, followed by the interpreter, we walked out of the office, through a living room and into the bedroom, where some exercise machines were set out. Then we went into the bathroom, which had a big corner bath, a shower, a toilet, a pedestal basin with a mirror on the wall above it, and shelves full of toiletries. Everything was clean and glitzy, in an Arab way, with gold-plated taps and cupboard handles.

The boss walked around, fitting a new blade into a safety razor, putting some shampoo ready. Someone turned on the bath, and through the interpreter he said, 'This is all my stuff. Just use it, please.'

He went out and left me alone. There I was, in this luxury bathroom, with hot water running . . . It was then that I looked in a mirror and saw my face. Jesus Christ – what a sight! I was gaunt as a skeleton; under ten days' growth of beard my cheeks were hollow, and my eyes seemed to have sunk into their sockets. My hair was matted with every kind of filth.

I felt stunned, unable to make out what was happening. One minute I'd been gearing myself for prison; now I was being cosseted in a high-class apartment. But whatever else lay ahead, there was no reason not to have a bath. I started slowly undressing, and took off my shirt.

Looking in two mirrors at once (one in front, one behind), I caught sight of my back, and I could hardly believe it. My ribs and spine and hip-bones were all sticking out, as though I'd been starved for weeks. I could see every rib going round and joining my backbone. It was a shock to realise that I'd been living on my own body. In walking nearly 300 kilometres, and shuddering with cold for countless hours, I'd burnt away all the muscle which I'd built up during my time on the SP team.

In the mirror I saw a young boy coming in holding a tape-measure, and the interpreter behind him.

'What's going on now?' I demanded.

'We'll just take your sizes,' said the interpreter, and the boy started measuring me, round the waist, down the leg, under the arms, with the interpreter writing down whatever he called out.

'What the hell's this?' I was thinking. 'For a fucking coffin?' But I didn't ask – partly out of fear that I would find out something bad. Then the man who'd met me with the car also appeared, and asked what my shoe-size was. When I told him, 'Eight, eight and a half,' he said to the interpreter, 'He looks like a 42.' He then left, and I didn't see him again.

The boy soon legged it, and as I was getting my trousers off, in came another guy with a cup of Turkish coffee. I drank a mouthful of it, but it tasted like cough medicine and made me gag. 'Water!' I croaked, and made drinking motions.

I edged myself over the bath and lowered myself in carefully, backside first, keeping my feet out of the water. Then I gradually submerged them. As the heat hit the cuts, the pain was horrendous. After a few seconds I lifted them out again, then tried to lower them back into the water. I lay there with my legs elevated as I washed myself and shampooed my hair. Soon the water was absolutely black, so I got out, pulled out the plug, and started to fill the bath again. As I was doing that, the interpreter came back, and when he saw me, he said, 'Oh – excuse me. We have a shower, if you'd like to use it.'

'It's OK, thanks. I'm going to have another bath.'

175

I got back into clean water, and again the pain in my feet was terrific, as if needles were being driven into them. Apart from the cuts along the sides, they were discoloured, with red and blue patches. All I could do was lie there and bite my tongue. Then the burning ache seemed to subside, and I started to enjoy the hot water.

The interpreter sat down by the bath with his note-pad. 'Right,' he said, 'can you tell me what happened?'

'Play it like you're frightened,' I thought. 'Well,' I said, 'I'm a medic. I was brought in from the TA, and I was on board a helicopter going in to retrieve – '

'The TA?'

'The Territorial Army. The reserves. As I said, I was going in to retrieve a downed pilot, and something happened. There was a big bang, the helicopter crashed, and I just ran for it. We came down, and I was really scared. I didn't wait for anybody else . . .

'Keep it light,' I was thinking. 'Pretend to be nervous.'

'How long ago?'

'Three days, I think.'

'Whereabouts was the crash?'

'I don't know. I just ran. I had no idea where we were. I ended up with a goatherd.'

'What sort of helicopter was it?'

'A Sea King.'

'What did it look like?'

'Just a helicopter . . . Single engine.'

The interpreter had been watching me closely, and now he just said, 'OK,' and left the room. I had the strong impression that he hadn't believed a word of what I'd told him. Too bad. I climbed out of the bath and got my beard off with a couple of shaves. Without the stubble, I looked very thin and tired. My lips were cracked and broken, but no more than if I'd been in the sun too long.

As I was drying myself, the boy who'd measured me brought in a set of clean white underpants and vest and laid them on the toilet seat. Also, he picked up my own stinking kit, and took it out.

Spotting a pair of scales, I stood on them. At first I thought the needle had jammed, so I shook the platform about – but no:

it stayed steady on 63.5 kilograms. I knew exactly what my weight was when I'd left Saudi, and I could hardly believe it. Ten days earlier I'd been 12 stone 8, or 176 lbs. Now I was 10 stone, or 140 lbs. I'd lost thirty-six pounds.

I pulled on the clean underwear and walked out into the bedroom, and there – for Christ's sake – was a brand-new dark-blue pin-striped suit, together with a white shirt and a tie. By then it was 11 o'clock at night, but I realised they must have knocked up some tailor, and he'd run the suit together in half an hour. There was also a pair of black slip-on shoes. I put on the shirt and the trousers, but they were inches too big round the waist. The boss was watching me, and when he saw that something was wrong he went berserk, yelling at the young guy who'd taken the measurements. The boy was crestfallen and cowering, not daring to look up.

Anyway, as I took off the trousers and handed them back, the boss noticed the state of my feet. He telephoned for a medical orderly, while I sat on the edge of the bed and waited. Soon a medic appeared. He cleaned out the cuts with a lotion that stung, and put plasters on, but he made such a mess of the job that I reckoned I could have done better on my own. If they'd had any zinc oxide tape, I'd have taped my feet right up. Also, I knew I needed some antibiotics. By then my ankles as well as my feet were swollen, and the new pair of shoes wouldn't go on.

By the time the medic had finished, the trousers reappeared with the waist taken in. So I put them on, and the tie. The boss kept asking, 'D'you like the tie?' and I said, 'Yes, thank you. It's fine.'

'I think it's great,' he said. 'I picked it out myself.'

In fact it was a horrible mess of grey and red. The jacket of the suit fitted quite well, but because I couldn't get the shoes on I stayed in stockinged feet. Then suddenly I thought: 'Jesus – I know. It's a press conference. They're dressing me up for a staged press do. I'm going to walk into a room full of lights and reporters and cameramen. They'll all be asking questions. What the hell am I going to tell them?'

I hadn't a clue what was happening in Iraq. I presumed that the air-war was still in progress – but whether or not the ground-war had started I couldn't tell. I didn't even know what had become of the rest of my patrol. If I said the wrong thing now, I might blow the whole SAS operation in the Gulf. I might blow the fact that the Regiment was in Saudi. Did the Syrians realise I was in the SAS? Maybe I should tell them the truth, in the hope that they'd keep it quiet. One way or another, I could be in trouble.

Before I had time to worry too much, they ushered me back into the sitting room and the boss told the interpreter to switch on the TV. He tuned to CNN, and I soon saw that the air-war was still on – allied aircraft bombing Baghdad, and so on – but there appeared to have been no major action on the ground. Then the interpreter began to recap on what I'd told him.

'So you were a medic on board a helicopter.'

'That's right.'

After a bit of chit-chat he asked, 'Are you hungry?'

Hungry! In the past eight days I'd eaten two packets of biscuits and two apples. 'Yes,' I said, 'I am.'

'Just a minute, then.'

He let me watch CNN for a while, then led me through to the other lounge. I could move slowly without too much discomfort; my feet felt quite easy on the carpet, but I was sore and stiff all over. In my brief absence someone had set out a feast on a table. There were kebabs, steaks, rice, salads, bread, fruit. The interpreter kept saying, 'You must be starving,' and he heaped a pile of food on to my plate. The smell was fantastic, but when I cut into a steak and took one bite of it, it seemed to stick in my throat and I couldn't eat any more.

I just sat there drinking pints of water, until the boss asked, 'Is the food bad?'

'No,' I said. 'It's just that I'm not as hungry as I thought. More thirsty. I'm sorry.'

The other two had been eating, but I got the impression they were only doing it to be polite, and as soon as I gave up, they did too. Back in the other room, the interpreter asked, 'Well – what would you like to do now?'

I knew that a British Embassy had been hastily set up in Damascus when the Gulf War looked likely to break out, and I was on the point of asking to be taken there when the interpreter suggested, 'How about seeing some Syrian night life?'

'What?' I was astounded. Didn't these guys realise what a state I was in? I was making sense to them, but only just.

'No thanks,' I muttered. 'I can't walk.'

'Well – d'you need anything? D'you need to spend time with anybody?'

It was incredible: here the interpreter was, apparently offering me a woman. By then I'd seen the hand of God, and I was in no mood to muck around. I thought, 'Go for it,' and asked, 'Can you take me to the British Embassy?'

'Oh?' he seemed rather surprised. 'You want to go there?'

'Yes, if it's possible.'

'OK.' He began making phone calls. While he was doing that, I was led across to a table – and there was all my kit which had been taken away in the police station, and which I thought had been stolen piecemeal.

'Well,' said the interpreter, coming over, 'is everything there?'

I made a check, and found everything present – weapon, ammunition, kite-sight, even the white phos grenades.

'Yeah,' I said. 'It's all there.'

'This is interesting.' He picked up the kite-sight. 'What's this?'

'Oh – just a thing they gave us so that we could see in the dark.' I felt sure he knew what it was, so I showed him how to turn it on, and he stood there looking out of the window with it, down into the courtyard.

'Brilliant!' he said. 'I'll have everything packed away for you.'

I believe they knew exactly who I was, but they were playing along with my story. Then the interpreter asked whether I wanted my clothes washed, but I said, 'No thanks – just put them back in the bag.' So the young guy pushed everything back in, and I sat down again.

'You know,' said the interpreter keenly, 'I've always wanted to come to England for a holiday. Where do you live?'

'In Newcastle,' I said. 'With my parents.'

'Oh, I'd love to come there. Can you give me your telephone number and address? Maybe you could show us the sights and return our hospitality sometime? Could I give you a ring?'

I made up a number, giving the Rowlands Gill code with changed digits, and a dicky address. I thought, 'Jesus – you're digging yourself in deep here. If he asks you to repeat that number, you're going to be in the shit.' But once again, they didn't seem to question what I said.

'By the way,' the interpreter added, as we were waiting. 'Did

179

you see anyone as you crossed the border? Did anyone meet you?'

That made me think they must have had people out on their own side of the frontier, watching, and waiting to receive escapers. But I replied, 'No. I didn't see anybody.'

'So you found the police station yourself?'

'That's right.' I told them more or less what had happened at the farmhouse.

'And this young boy who took you in – where was his house?'

I tried to describe the location, and the boss promised to send someone to thank the people there. Then he said, 'How was your journey after that?'

I thought, 'If I start saying what the bastards did to me in the desert, he may keep me here for days, until he's had the guys dragged in.' So I just said, 'Oh, it was fine, thanks. No problem.'

There was a knock at the door, and in came the driver of the car, actually cowering, dry-washing his hands in front of him, with his head hanging down. Until then, I'd only seen orientals do that, and it made me wonder, 'Who *is* this boss guy? What does he do to people to make them behave like that?'

The interpreter gave me a piece of paper with a telephone number on it, and said, 'If you have any problems in Damascus, ring this number and ask to speak to me.' I put the note in my pocket and tucked my new shoes under one arm. Then I shook hands with the boss, who patted me on the back. 'The car will take you to the British Embassy,' he said, 'and staff of the Embassy will meet you there.'

I limped downstairs and found a Mercedes waiting. In we climbed, and the driver set off.

The Embassy was a disappointment. Instead of the grand house in a walled garden which I'd visualised, thinking of Abu Dhabi, it turned out to be an undistinguished office building in a row on a street, with guards on duty in pillar boxes along the pavements. There seemed to be a heavy presence of men with weapons, dotted all over the place in ones and twos. As we pulled up, I grabbed my bag, thanked the driver and got out.

A young man was standing on the steps, waiting to meet me. He introduced himself as the Second Secretary, and I soon saw that he was a switched-on lad – tall, dark-haired, wearing glasses, in his early thirties, and quite smart-looking. With him was the Defence Attaché, older, clearly a Rupert of sorts, and a bit of a stuffed shirt – fortyish, short, dark-haired as well.

'Who are you?' he asked.

'Sergeant Ryan from 22 SAS,' I told him.

'OK – upstairs.'

I dragged myself up one flight and sat down in a room. What with the state of my hands, and blood oozing out of my stockinged feet, you might have thought the DA would dispense with formalities. Not at all.

'Right,' he said, 'I'm just going to ask you a few questions, to verify who you are – make sure you're not a plant. What's your parent unit? Who's the commanding officer?'

I stared at the guy and said, 'Listen – don't start this fucking shit with me. I'm from 22 SAS, and I've been on the run for eight days. Just get a message back to High Wycombe.'

That woke him up. He gave a kind of choke, and the Second Secretary told him, 'Look, cool it.' The DA seemed to have no inkling of what had been going on behind the scenes in Iraq, but I got the impression that the Second Secretary had a pretty acute idea.

'There's nobody else come out, then?' I asked.

The DA stared at me. 'No – you're the first we've seen.'

By then it was 1 a.m. I gathered that the diplomats were living in a hotel just down the road, and that they'd been out at some function, but had been recalled by a message from the secret police.

The Second Secretary asked, 'Can you tell us what happened?'

So I gave them a broad outline of the story: how the patrol had been deployed and had a contact, how we'd legged it through the desert, split up, lost Vince, moved to here, had another contact, and so on.

The DA seemed amazed that anyone should have walked out into Syria. 'Nobody had told us you were anywhere near the border,' he said. But then he let on that, a few days before, he'd had a visit from two British guys doing some sort of a recce. When I heard their names, I realised they were from the Regiment, and that they'd been making a security assessment. When I said I knew both of them, things began to make more sense to him. He warned me that the building was probably bugged, so that the Syrians were listening to every word we said. I just hoped they'd packed up for the night. Otherwise they'd immediately know that I'd been lying an hour or two earlier.

The DA wrote down some details of what I'd told him and brought in one of the communications clerks, a girl, who encoded a message and sent it off to the UK command centre at High Wycombe.

Things were getting a bit ridiculous. The DA kept calling me 'Sergeant Ryan'. I was calling the Second Secretary 'John', and he was calling me 'Chris'. Anyway, with the message sent off, I reassembled my weapon and secured it, together with my ammunition, grenades, TACBE and kite-sight, in the strong room, and saw everything locked up safely. Then they told me that I could spend the rest of the night in the Meridien Hotel, just down the road, and said they'd put me on the British Airways flight to London the next day. They evidently felt that the hotel would be secure enough, but they told me to stay in my room, and to order meals through room-service.

London! That wasn't what I wanted at all. My only concern was to get back to Saudi and find out what had become of the rest of the patrol. But before I could protest they were asking if there was anyone I'd like to phone. I thought, 'If I'm going back to UK, I'll let Jan know.' So I said I'd call my wife.

I realised that if I did fly in to London, I'd only have a very short time there – the Regiment would want me straight back in Saudi, for debriefing; if I got to Hereford at all, it would be for just one night. But Jan didn't even know that we'd been deployed over the border, and I didn't want anyone else to know it either. So I thought things through a bit, working out what I could say and what I couldn't, and put in the call, with the Second Secretary sitting beside me.

Jan sounded quite surprised to hear my voice.

'Hi, Jan,' I said, forcing myself to sound casual. 'I might be coming home tomorrow.'

'Great! How's it going?'

'Fine. No problem.'

'Why are you coming back, then?'

'Just to pick up a bit of kit, you know, and escort it back across. I might only be there half the night. A couple of hours, even.'

'Oh, great!' she said. 'Great! So – that's it.'

'Everything fine there?' I asked.

'Yeah – everything's boring. You doing anything?'

'No,' I said. 'Everything here's cool. The only thing is – don't tell anyone I've rung. Just don't tell anybody I've been in contact.'

The Embassy guys offered to get a taxi down to the hotel, but as it was only a couple of hundred metres away, I said I could walk. Yet when the DA set off at a normal pace, I couldn't keep up with him. I padded slowly along the pavement, and anyone I passed looked down at my stockinged feet in some surprise. As we arrived at the hotel, the porters standing around in the lobby also glared at my feet in disdain. The Second Secretary said, 'We may have a bit of trouble here, as you haven't got a passport; they don't normally let anybody book in without identification. But I'll see if I can square it away.'

The guy on the desk wasn't amused. 'No, no,' he kept saying. 'No passport, no room! He cannot book in.'

The Second Secretary began muttering about going back to the Embassy and spending the night there. He said that to get a passport made out he'd have to contact the chargé d'affaires. A photo would have to be taken, and it couldn't be done until next morning.

Then I said, 'Listen – I've got a telephone number from the police. The boss guy said if I had any trouble, I was to ring them.'

'No, no,' said the Defence Attaché hurriedly. 'You can't do that. Don't ring them. Don't involve them any more. In fact we've got a cellar bedroom in the Embassy, and you can sleep down there.'

'No,' said the Second Secretary. 'The place is filthy. He can't go in there.'

'Nonsense!' barked the DA. 'He's just roughed it for eight days. He'll be all right.' Then he added, 'At a pinch, he can have my bed.'

What I didn't realise until later was that the man had two double beds in his hotel room – but of course, because he was an officer and I was an other rank, he didn't fancy having me sleeping in there.

We didn't seem to be getting far, so the Second Secretary said,

'Where's that telephone number?' He got on the phone to my friend in the secret police, and within five minutes two Mercedes screeched to a halt outside. A swarm of men ran in. It looked like a raid by the SS; some of them were wearing long black leather trench-coats. With them was the interpreter. He came running up to me, grabbed me by the arm and moved me to one side. 'Chris,' he said quietly, 'in two minutes you're going to sign the book. Sign with a name that you can remember, and give any address you can remember. Everything will be all right. If you get any more trouble, ring me again.' He then had a word with the Second Secretary.

I turned round, and there were three blokes giving the piss to the hotel manager behind the desk. His eyes were going round in circles, and he was nodding like a robot. Then the secret police party walked out. 'I'll see you later,' said the interpreter, and he was gone.

I went back up to the desk.

'Yes, yes. Sign here, please. Anything I can do for you, sir?' I gave my surname as Black, and made up some address near Newcastle. The man snapped his fingers for a porter, and two guys grabbed my bags. The diplomats said, 'We'll see you in the morning,' and up I went.

By then it was after 2a.m. and the past twenty-four hours had been the longest of my life. I'd really been looking forward to getting into that room. Once I closed the door, I thought, I'd be free of worry and danger for the first time in ten days. I'd be able to lie down, chill out, and go to sleep. But it didn't work out like that. As soon as I was alone, I started worrying about the rest of the patrol. I'd hoped that some of the guys would have escaped into Syria ahead of me. Either that, or they would have been lifted out by chopper, back into Saudi; but now this possibility seemed unlikely. If the five had been rescued, and three guys were still missing, the Regiment would surely have alerted the Syrians to look out for us, and warned the Damascus Embassy. I'd come up like a bad penny, but nobody else. What had happened to the others? Were they dead, or hiding up somewhere? Were they still on the move? If they were, they must be in a bad way by now.

I was so wound up that I felt I was still on the run. I got out my notebook and began scribbling reminders about what I'd done. I'd brought the book with me in case I had to take down a radio message or compose one, but in fact, until then, I hadn't made a single entry, for fear that I might be captured. But now I went back one day at a time, logging details to refresh my memory, and working out where I'd been at various times.

The DA had warned me not to go downstairs for breakfast, in case press reporters had come into the hotel overnight. Instead, he said, I should get anything I wanted on room-service.

So I lay on the bed, my feet propped up on pillows to help bring the swelling down – and all I wanted to do was drink. I had a craving for sweet drinks, particularly. When I looked at the room-service menu and found that they did ten different kinds of fruit-juice cocktail, I phoned down to a waiter and asked for one of each. 'Can you send them up?' I asked.

'Yes,' said the guy, 'but how many for?'

'For one person.'

'So which one do you want?'

'I want every single one. I want numbers one, two, three – '

'For how many people?'

'For one person.'

'Yes, but which one do you want?'

'SEND THEM ALL!' I yelled.

What do you think? The waiter came up with one drink! So I said, 'Fucking hell!', swilled this thing down, phoned up again and said, 'I want every single cocktail.'

'For how many people?'

'For ten people.'

This time the guy came up with ten glasses, and I went *whack, whack, whack* – straight down with the lot.

Then, lying in bed, I thought, 'Jesus, I need a piss.' But when I put my legs over the side of the bed, the pain in my feet was outrageous. I felt that they were going to split open – I really thought that the skin would rip, and flesh would burst out. I even considered slitting them to relieve the agony. I was nearly crying with it. As I crawled across the floor on hands and knees, I thought, 'This is bloody degrading! How much lower can you get? You're on your hands and knees in the shithouse!' But there was no other way.

I reached the bog and dragged myself up on to the seat. But immediately it happened again: the pain in my feet was so intense that I lost all feeling in my bladder, and couldn't pee. On the floor again, I crawled back to my bed and lay down. As soon as my feet stopped hurting, after about a minute, I wanted to pee again. Then I saw a metal wastepaper bin on the floor beside the bed, so I pulled it over and leaned over and pissed in that, and at last I could get my head down. But still I was tossing and turning, tossing and turning, my mind full of disturbing images – of my comrades wandering in the desert, or, worse still, being killed.

In the end, though, I fell asleep – only to be dragged back by the phone ringing. By then it was after three, and here was the Defence Attaché on the line, sounding ridiculously conspiratorial.

'What happened to the Charlie Oscar Delta Echo Sierra?' he breathed.

I said 'What?'

He repeated himself.

'What the fuck are you on about?'

'What happened to the *codes*?'

Suddenly I realised that he was trying to be covert, spelling out 'codes' like that. Also I realised that it must be High Wycombe who were asking for the information; whenever we encrypt a message, we put it into code, then burn the cipher and smash the encryption device. In fact, Legs had carried our cipher equipment. He had burnt the codes and smashed the Emu.

'One of the other lads had them,' I said. 'He burned them. I never had them at all.'

'OK,' he said, and rang off.

That was when I knew for sure that nobody else had come out.

In the morning I ordered breakfast from room-service, and ate some fruit salad and a roll. I still didn't want anything substantial, but I drank pints of fruit juice and tea. Compared with the day before, I felt quite good. Then the Brits came to collect me, and I hobbled back to the Embassy, shuffling along the pavement in my stockinged feet, with my shoes under my arm.

By the time we arrived, the place seemed to be full of people. The chargé d'affaires had appeared, and there were two British girls on duty, one dealing with communications, the other a typist. I chatted to them for a while, then they put me up against a wall in my shirt and tie to take a black-and-white passport photograph with a Polaroid camera. 'Better be careful,' somebody said. 'We've only got two frames left.' But the first shot came out well, so they trimmed it, stuck it into a blank passport and stamped it. There I was, fixed up with a ten-year passport. The whole thing seemed so amateurish that I felt I was being given a Second World War escape kit.

During the morning some questions came back from High Wycombe about the locations I'd mentioned, and the fact that I couldn't even work out the latitude and longitude showed what poor shape I was in. The DA had to do it for me. When I mentioned to him that I'd walked through some installation which looked like a signals complex, the Second Secretary said, 'No, no: that's the yellow cake processing facility at Al Qaim.' He knew everything about the place – even the number of the Iraqi regiment guarding it. The latticework towers I'd seen on the high ground were for defence, not communication: apparently what I'd thought were cables slung between them were in fact chains, to prevent attacks from low-flying aircraft.

'What's going on there?' I asked.

'We don't know exactly. Some sort of nuclear processing.'

'Bloody hell! I drank some water coming out of that place, and it tasted terrible.'

'Effluent,' he said. 'Nuclear effluent.'

I felt my insides go cold. Had I swallowed some radioactive waste and contaminated myself, maybe with fatal consequences?

During the morning a fax came in from High Wycombe saying: 'Has Ryan spoken to anybody? Has he had contact with anyone?' The Second Secretary asked if I wanted him to record the call I'd made to Jan. I said, 'Well, yeah. I've got nothing to hide,' and I gave him Jan's name and telephone number. Within an hour of that fax going back to High Wycombe, the regimental Families' Officer was round at our house in Hereford, banging on the door.

Of course Jan was upset, because if he comes round like that, it usually means your husband's dead.

'What do you want?' she demanded, immediately deciding to cover up.

'Have you just spoken to your husband?'

'No.'

'He's been on the phone to you.'

'No he hasn't.'

'I know he has. He's phoned you.'

'Well, yes. He said he's coming back to get some kit.'

'What else did he say?'

'Nothing.'

But the officer kept on with his questions, until Jan wondered what the hell was going on, and began to feel sure that something bad had happened to me.

In Damascus, I knew nothing of this, and we headed down to the airport to buy a ticket and get me on the flight to London. I'd bent in the heels of my shoes, so that they were like slippers, and occasionally I put them on; but my feet were still very painful, and mostly I was padding around in my socks. I got as far as the check-in desk, but there the guy stopped me because I didn't have a stamped visa showing when I'd entered the country. That was it; there was no arguing with him, and I ended up back at the Embassy.

The chargé d'affaires said, 'Right, it looks as though you'll be here for a couple of days. I'll give you some Syrian money, so that you can go and do a bit of shopping.' First, though, I went off with the Defence Attaché to see about a visa. We visited a building which was like a honeycomb of little offices, dozens of them, some with room for little more than a six-foot table, a chair and space for one person to stand up. Everyone was in military uniform. We went from one room to another, and one official after another said, 'Oh, no – it's the other one,' and directed us to somebody else. The DA showed tremendous patience, and in all we saw about twenty people. The last official said, 'Well, if you haven't got an entry visa, you can't leave.'

So we'd wasted the whole morning. I said to the DA, 'Why not phone my friend in the police again?'

'Oh no,' he said, 'We can't do that.' So I waited till I was away from him, and asked the Second Secretary the same question. He put through a call, and very soon a message was on its way from the police to the visa building. When we next went down, I collected my exit visa without difficulty.

The next flight out was in two days' time – but now things had changed. Instead of returning to the UK, I was told I'd be flying to Cyprus, where I'd be put on to a Hercules that was coming across from Riyadh. From Cyprus I was to fly to the Saudi capital, spend one night there, and then return to the squadron at Al Jouf. That suited me much better; there was nothing particular on at home, and I wasn't interested in going there. All I wanted was to get back to the squadron, so that I could find out about the rest of the patrol, and brief any other guys who might be going in.

That evening, back in the hotel, I had a meal in my room and went to bed. But still I couldn't relax: the missing guys were too much on my mind. It felt really bad to be sitting in Damascus, unable to contribute any information which might help with their recovery.

Back in the Embassy next day, I was shooting shit with the two girls. One of them, who was quite good looking, said, 'I've got a Walkman in the flat. Why not come down and listen to some music?' I said, 'Oh – great!' and we went downstairs into her living room. I wasn't sure what her interest in me might be, so I started talking about Jan and Sarah, to show her how the land lay. As we sat there chatting, I said, 'D'you mind if I take off my shoes and socks, and have another look at my feet?'

By then the cuts had dried up a good bit, but they still weren't a pretty sight, and when I stripped my feet off, she was horrified. Until then, I don't think either of the girls quite realised what I'd been through. They imagined I'd just been for a bit of a walk. Anyway, they were full of sympathy – and it was good just to sit there and let my feet breathe.

My fingers were nearly as bad as my feet. I still had no feeling in the tips, and when I squeezed my nails, pus kept oozing out. So I asked if she'd got a scrubbing brush, and went to the basin and scrubbed my fingers really hard. It was total agony, but I got the dirt out from under the nails, and all the pus, until blood was running freely. Then I rinsed my hands off, and from that moment the ends of my fingers began to heal up well. Obviously I should have seen a doctor, but the Embassy had no medic in residence, and a message from High Wycombe had specifically forbidden me to make contact with anyone outside.

The Embassy people did their best to entertain me. The DA's assistant, a sergeant, took me out for a drive round the heights of Damascus and showed me some of the military installations. Chatting about my escape, he said, 'God – you're going to get a medal for this.'

'Why?' I said. 'It was nothing special.'

Until that moment it hadn't occurred to me that I'd done anything exceptional. I'd just been for rather a long walk. The job we'd been tasked to do had proved rather more arduous than expected – but I'd had to go through with it all the same.

Back in the Embassy, one of the girls said, 'Would you like to go down the Street called Straight?'

'What's that?'

'You must have heard of it. It's mentioned in the Bible, and runs right through the city from east to west.'

I said, 'Yeah, OK.' So we walked down there and wandered through the casbah. I wasn't particularly interested, but the girls were all excited by the place's history. They started telling how, when the king died, and a new one succeeded, everyone squeezed off their old guns into the air, through the roofs of the covered market, and how one day after a heavy blast-off seven or eight people were killed by rounds falling back to earth. Certainly there were plenty of holes in the curved glass panels of the roofs.

I felt I was becoming a tourist, and to complete the picture I bought some clothes – a set of dark blue cords, a shirt, sweatshirt and track-suit bottoms. I also bought a bag to put my spare clothes in. We went for a couple of meals; at one I put away three helpings of chocolate ice cream in quick time. The girls kept looking at me as I got the stuff down my neck. Now that my appetite was returning, I had a craving for anything sweet and sloppy.

When the time came to leave, my weapon and ammunition obviously had to stay behind, but I wanted to take the TACBE and the kite-sight, because I knew that those things were in short supply back at the squadron. But the Second Secretary made me leave them, in case they aroused suspicion and got me pulled in for questioning at the airport.

When I went to board the Syrian Airlines aircraft I kept my bag with me, but as I reached the top of the steps, the steward said something aggressive to me in Arabic and threw it back down to the ground. As I went in through the door, I could only hope that someone would put it on board. On the plane, my seat was right at the back. As soon as we were airborne, with the no-smoking lights still on, everyone lit up. I've never been on an aircraft so full of smoke; you couldn't see from one end of the cabin to the other. But the relief of leaving Syria made up for everything. Even in the hands of the Embassy people, I'd never felt entirely safe. Damascus had a volatile, feverish air about it, and memories of the mock-execution out in the desert kept me on edge.

It seemed crazy to be flying to Cyprus, for the island lies more or less due west of Damascus, and it was east that I wanted to be heading. But the flight lasted less than a couple of hours, and soon we were coming in to land at Larnaca, with my mind racked by anxiety about what the score was in the squadron.

Chapter Ten

Back To Base

One good move the Defence Attaché had made was to jack up someone to meet me. He'd spoken to a friend in the RAF who was stationed in Cyprus, and arranged a pick-up. He hadn't said who I was, just that someone was on his way through.

When my bag came off the conveyer belt it had crosses of tape stuck all over it, and I was pulled to one side in the Customs. 'Open your luggage, please,' said the officer, and then it was, 'Why have you got all this army equipment? Where've you come from? What have you been doing?'

I said, 'I'm a British soldier, and I've been in Syria, working for the British Embassy in Damascus. Now I'm coming back to the base at Akrotiri.'

'Is anybody meeting you here?'

'Yes. There's a guy outside from the Joint Intelligence Company.'

The customs man looked into my water bottles, little knowing they could well be radioactive. Then he searched my kit, handling everything. I began to think it was just as well I didn't have the kite-sight and TACBE after all.

As I came out, I spotted a guy wearing a Barbour jacket, and I thought, 'You're obviously a Brit.' So I walked up to him and he immediately said, 'Chris?'

'Yeah. Hello.'

'Good. I'm Brian.'

As he led me across to a car, he said he was taking me down to a family who'd agreed to put me up, and once we were rolling he asked if I needed to see anybody.

'Yes,' I said. 'I need to see a doctor.'

'What's wrong?'

'Well, for starters, I think I drank some poisonous water. Also, my feet are in bits. Look at that.'

192

I held out my hand to show him my fingers, which had not only lost all feeling in the tips, but now seemed to be turning blue. I saw him looking at me strangely, but I didn't enlighten him about where I'd been.

We drove into a nice-looking housing estate, with guards on the entrance, and I was met by an RAF officer, who introduced me to his Scottish wife and their two young kids. No questions were asked; obviously they'd been briefed. They just welcomed me and sat me down, and the wife said, 'Can I make you something to eat for tea?'

'Well, thanks.'

'Right,' she said. 'It won't take a minute. *EastEnders* is on the telly.'

So there I sat watching *EastEnders*, and eating eggs, beans and chips, and thinking, 'This is outrageous!' It was really weird. Then a doctor turned up, the wife sent the children out, and the doctor took a look at me, asking what was wrong.

'It's my fingers,' I told him. 'I can't feel them much, and they keep going blue.'

He did the squeeze test a few times and said, 'Well, the colour seems to be coming back. I think you've got a bit of frost nip, that's all.' Then he looked at my feet, cleaned them up as much as he could, put zinc oxide tape on them, left me some spare tape, and said, 'There's not a lot I can do for you. Is there anything else wrong?'

'Well, I was round a chemical plant, and drank some of the effluent. Could that be having an effect on my hands?'

'I don't see how it could. But you ought to have blood tests and other checks when you get back.'

When he'd gone, the woman gave me a beer, which went down well, and we sat around chatting. Then, just before eight, the husband said, 'Right, I'm off to work. I'll be back at four in the morning to pick you up.'

I thought, 'Jesus, you're trusting – disappearing like this, leaving a stranger in your house with your wife and kids!' Anyway, off he went, and because I knew I wasn't going back to the UK after all, I thought I'd better call Jan to say that plans had changed. I asked the wife if I could use their phone, and she said, 'Carry on – as long as you like.'

So I dialled through and said, 'Jan, I'm not coming home after all.'

'Oh, God!' she exclaimed. 'What's happened?'

'Nothing. It's just that they don't need the kit fetching.'

'Listen,' she said, 'the Families' Officer's been round here asking questions. What the hell's going on?'

'Nothing. Everything's all right.'

'There's things *not* all right, I know.'

'Everything's all right,' I repeated – but still she wasn't satisfied.

'Are you injured?'

'No, no. Not injured. Listen. There's been some trouble, but I'm all right. You remember the place we were talking about?'

'You mean the river?'

'Yes, but keep quiet.'

'Well?'

'I was along there.'

'How many?'

'Seven others.'

'What are their names?'

'I can't tell you. I'm the only one that's left. But I'm fine. Whatever you do, don't tell anybody I've been on the phone again. Everything's cool. It's just that I'm not coming home now. I'm going back across there.'

That was when the old tears started. She kept saying, 'Something's gone wrong, I know,' and I was repeating, 'No, no. Everything's fine, I promise you. I'll phone again in a couple of weeks.'

I rang off feeling pretty shattered, and took a minute to get myself together. Then my hostess said, 'You can sleep in that bedroom there. Would you like to get your head down?'

'Great,' I said. But first I went to have a bath, because I'd got so sticky on the aircraft. When I stripped off, what should I find but that my legs had gone blue as well, worse than my hands! For a few seconds I was horrified – then I realised what the problem was. The dye had been coming out of my new Syrian cords, on to my hands as well. What a dick I felt, after that scene with the doctor. At least I knew why I kept turning blue. But no matter the colour, my hands weren't right; my fingers were still feeling woody.

I got my head down, and the next thing I knew, my host was knocking on my door at 4 a.m. His wife was already up and had made a cup of tea; she was waiting for us downstairs, and as we went out I thanked her for her hospitality.

At Akrotiri airbase we were confronted by the inevitable stroppy little RAF corporal, who sat there saying, 'Where's your ID card?'

'I haven't got one.'

'Passport?'

'Haven't got one.' (I had the passport which they'd made out for me in Damascus, but I wasn't going to show it to this prick.)

'Name?'

'There's no name.'

'Well, who are you?'

'I'm a person that's getting on this flight.'

Behind me was the squadron leader who'd been looking after me. He was carrying my bags, and now he said, 'It's all right. He's going on this flight. I'll vouch for him.'

'OK, Sir,' said the corporal, and we walked through.

By then the flight crew had assembled, and the chief loadie – the flight sergeant in charge of the back of the Hercules – had heard all this. He was quite a big half-caste lad, and he stood there watching.

The squadron leader came in, put my bags down and said, 'You'll be going aboard with this flight crew. Soon as they go, you get on too.' He went across to them and said, 'That's some extra luggage you've got.' Then he shook hands with me, and I thanked him, and he left.

The flight crew were all laughing and joking together. I sat by myself across the room, and after a few minutes the flight sergeant came across and said, 'Who are you, then?'

'I'm not telling you.'

'What?'

'Mind your own business,' I said, and looked down.

'Who the fuck d'you think you are?'

'What the fuck's it got to do with you?'

'Uh,' went the flight sergeant, 'if you don't tell me who you are, you're not getting on my aircraft.'

'If I don't get on,' I told him, 'I guarantee your career will fucking *end* when this aircraft touches down in Riyadh. Now stop asking questions.'

It was out of character for me to be so aggressive, but I'd had enough of all these dickheads, and someone like that wasn't going to stop me getting back. I felt I'd been through so much that I wasn't going to bow down to anybody.

I could see he was annoyed, but he was a bit rattled too. He just said, 'OK,' and walked away. These exchanges weren't bantering, there was needle in them – but they were typical of what happens if someone tries to push an SAS guy. It's a privilege, a sort of power for people in the Regiment – they don't have to tell outsiders anything. With officers, obviously, you're polite, and if they ask for your identity, you just say, 'Sorry, sir, I can't tell you.' Most people have the sense to back off if you tell them in a civil way that they don't need to know, and suggest they leave it at that. But there are always one or two who push and push, until it comes to the point when you're saying, 'Hey, fucking sling your hook.'

The back of the Herc was packed full of equipment, netted and strapped down on pallets. As I sat on one of the web seats, the first person I saw was Mel, a young signaller from 22 SAS. I thought, 'Great – the first friendly face, the first person I know,' and sat down next to him. It turned out that he was escorting some equipment across, so that he'd had to stay on board during the stop-over.

The flight sergeant knew where Mel came from – so when he saw us together, he realised that I was SAS and that he'd put his foot in it.

Anyway, Mel and I got talking. 'Have you heard anything about what's going on over here?' I asked, and he said, 'No, not a thing.' So I told him a bit about what had happened. It was a terrific relief to be able to talk to someone I knew.

Presently we took off, and four hours later I landed in Riyadh for the second time. The airport terminal was in complete disarray, full of military personnel, with areas hessianed off, control points set up, and people buzzing in all directions. I was puzzled to find that no one had come to meet me. The other passengers disappeared, and I was left sitting in the reception lounge on my own. Then at last a young man, in uniform but wearing no badges, came up and said, 'Are you Chris Ryan?'

'That's right. Who are you?'

'I'm taking you somewhere.'

'No you're not. Who *are* you?'

At last he gave me his name – Corporal Smith.

'And who are you working for?'

'Taff,' he said, naming the acting quartermaster.

'OK,' I said. 'That's fair enough.'

As we drove off in a white land-cruiser, I asked him if there'd been any news about the patrol.

'Not a word,' he said.

'Jesus Christ!'

I asked about Scuds coming in, and he said that one had landed close to the airport a couple of nights back. He took me to a big, plush, modern hotel, where a room had been reserved for me. The place was full of RAF aircrew in their flight-suits, with pistols showing in holsters underneath. They didn't realise how well off they were, fighting the war from such a luxurious base.

I went up to my room and lay down. I was still feeling weak, and lacking in decision. I only had to walk a hundred metres before I was out of breath, and felt like an old man. Within half an hour there came a knock on the door, and there was the former sergeant major, newly commissioned as Quartermaster. I'd hardly come across him before, but I knew he was a fairly unapproachable character, and he greeted me with a typically gruff, 'Ullo, Chris.'

He sat down and said, 'Right – I know everything's secret. But are you all right?'

'Yeah,' I said, 'I'm fine.'

'Are the rest of the lads OK?'

'I don't know, Taff. It's more than a week since I saw them.'

He told me that the Director and Assistant Director – the brigadier and colonel in command of Special Forces – wanted to debrief me. But before they arrived, he suggested I went downtown and got a brew, so he sent an assistant round with the equivalent of a couple of hundred pounds in local currency. Filling in time, I went out and bought a Walkman, some music tapes, including one by Eric Clapton, and a small radio. We then went to a burger bar, where we found a gang of young Americans wearing T-shirts with motifs on them like DEATH BEFORE DISHONOR, and that sort of crap. They were in high spirits, and going on about the war, but I couldn't help thinking, 'What a bunch of dickheads! They haven't a clue what's going on out there.'

I heard that the two guys from 'B' Squadron who'd done the recce in Syria were back in Riyadh; so I went round to see them, and immediately asked for news. All they'd heard was that I'd come out; they couldn't even discover the names of the people who were missing, such was the secrecy that had been clamped on everything. It was great to talk to them, and after some chat they suggested we should go out for a meal.

'Why not have it at my place?' I said. 'I can get it on the room.'

So all three of us came back to my room and ordered mixed grills. Just as we'd finished eating, a message came to say that the Assistant Director was downstairs, on his way to see me. Ignoring my pleas for them to stay, the other two promptly scarpered.

After a brief opening chat, the Colonel said, 'I don't really want to know what happened. But have a good long think, because you're going to be questioned about why you ran away.'

I thought he was implying that we'd all been cowards. I was too stunned to say anything except, 'Yeah – OK.'

Only when he'd gone did I start to burn with resentment. That seemed to me a very strange thing for anyone to have said, let alone a senior Special Forces officer who didn't yet know exactly what had happened. Anyway, he told me that the Director was on his way to see me, so I waited up, and it wasn't until about one in the morning that the Brigadier came rolling in. He said nothing about us having run away. On the contrary, having been a 'B' Squadron man himself, he saw my escape as a feather in the squadron's cap, and congratulated me. First thing next morning, he said, I was to fly up to Al Jouf on a Hercules.

I couldn't come to terms with the fact that there was no news of the others. Because the Iraqis had not announced the capture of any prisoners behind the lines, it seemed more and more likely that they were all dead. The worst thing was that people kept coming up to me and asking, 'Well, what do you think happened to them?' I had no idea: all I could do was repeat the story of the contact and the break, and I told it so often that I was starting to do it parrot-fashion. Beyond that, I wanted someone to tell *me* what the score was.

In the morning I dressed in my clean uniform, which had been through the washing-machine at the embassy in Damascus, and I felt fresh and good to have it on again. My feet were still pretty sore, but I got my boots back on, and so looked quite presentable.

As the aircraft landed at Al Jouf I was so excited by the thought of seeing the guys again that I went and stood on the tailgate as it was dropping down, all teed-up to rush out and greet them. But to my surprise there was only one man there – Geordie, the SSM. It turned out that he had told everyone else to keep away, in case I was overwhelmed by emotion. In fact three of the guys had ignored his instructions and were hovering in the background. As I walked out, they came racing across and surrounded me, hammering me on the back, and calling out, 'Well done!' For a minute or two I couldn't really speak. Bob Shepherd was so shattered by my appearance that he burst into tears. In place of the fit, bouncing young fellow he'd seen off a couple of weeks earlier, here was a prematurely aged cripple, broken, bent and shuffling; as he graphically put it, a bag of bones. He was so upset that, instead of driving back to 'B' Squadron's location, he took a solitary walk round the airfield to sort himself out.

Geordie thinned the guys out, took me to one side, and said, 'Right. We've got to go in for the debriefing.'

The head-shed was housed in tents alongside the permanent control-tower buildings. Before we went in, the SSM asked if there was anything I wanted to tell him. I said, 'Yeah, there's quite a bit. I'll tell you what actually happened, but I'm not going to tell the CO.' So I told him about Vince losing heart. 'If Andy or any of the others come out, they'll confirm it,' I said. 'Until then, we'll just leave it. There's no need to say it was his fault.' The sergeant major said, 'Fine,' and so we went in.

We went down with a sergeant from the Int section, a nice guy, who asked me to tell the story while he wrote it down. I was a bit put out by the sight of the CO, sitting on a chair and reading *The Times* at the other side of the tent, but paying no attention to me. Then the Ops officer walked past, and he didn't say anything either. I became more and more convinced that in their view I'd done something wrong.

Anyway, I got on with the debriefing, and in the middle of it half the squadron came back from the ranges, together with the OC. His behaviour was entirely different. He grabbed me, shook hands, and said, 'It's really great to see you! Terrific that you're back! Is there anything I can get you?'

I said, 'No thanks – I'm just talking to this Int guy.'

'Right – as soon as you've finished here, we'll get you across to the squadron, because everyone's dying to hear what happened.'

The debrief lasted two hours. Once it was over, Geordie drove me round the airfield to the squadron location, pointing out how all the light assault vehicles had been written off in training. On the way he asked, 'First things first: d'you want to go home?'

'No,' I said, 'I want to stay here and find out what's happened.' The last thing I wanted to do was desert the team.

Geordie also gave me amazing news about the other two Bravo patrols: they'd both come straight back. When Bravo Three Zero took stock of their location, the commander immediately decided that the area was impossibly dangerous. There wasn't enough cover to conceal the vehicles, and without further ado they began to drive back towards the Saudi border – a journey which took them two nights. Afterwards the commander was fiercely criticised, not least because he ignored an instruction to RV with 'D' Squadron – who were already in Iraq and needing reinforcement – not far off his route.

Bravo One Zero stayed an even shorter time. When the Chinook landed at their drop-off point, the pilot said to the leader, 'Pete – d'you want to have a look around while I hang on a minute? We crossed a road about fifteen miles back, and I can still see the lights of vehicles along it, the desert's that fucking flat. I can't see any depressions or wadis for miles. It's like a billiard table.' To prove his point, the pilot flew twenty kilometres up and down, trying to find some broken ground into which he could drop the patrol, but the desert remained horribly bare.

Pete took a decision which struck me as immensely courageous. 'Right,' he said, 'we're not staying here. We're flying out.'

Back at Al Jouf he was ridiculed and accused of being a coward – the word was actually used. But I and many others reckoned that of all the decisions taken by the three patrol commanders, his needed the most balls. To have stayed where he was would have been suicide – a replica of what had happened to us, if not worse. A year later people would start to say: 'Well, maybe he did the right thing after all' – but at the time he suffered.

Anyway, it was a big surprise for me to hear that all three OPs had been eliminated, for one reason or another. With Bravo Two Zero, it turned out that the comms failure had been due mainly to the fact that we'd been given the wrong radio frequencies. This was not the fault of anyone in the Regiment, but of the signal unit attached to us. The result was that although three of Legs' messages got through in garbled form, no reply ever reached us. I also found that we'd been seriously misled about the performance of our TACBEs; their effective range was only about 120 kilometres, and the closest most coalition aircraft were flying was 500 kilometres to the east. During the night of 24 January – our first on the run – one American F-15 pilot did pick up a call from Andy, and he passed it on to an AWACS aircraft. But because the call originated from a location which our head-shed was not expecting, it only caused confusion.

When the patrol went missing, tremendous pressure built up among the rank-and-file of the squadron to mount a rescue mission; volunteers were determined to make a box-search. When the CO refused to commit one of his few precious helicopters immediately to the task, some of the guys were on the verge of mutiny. But middle and senior management saw that, in the circumstances, the CO was right to delay a search until the patrol's situation became clearer.

The main problem was that the regimental head-shed was expecting us to strike back for the Saudi border in case of trouble, whereas after our initial feint we had set off in exactly the opposite direction. By 26 January, even though no explicit message had been received from us, it was clear that something had gone seriously wrong. At 1745 that evening a Chinook took off from Arar, with five members of the squadron on board, in an attempt to pull us out. That mission was aborted when the weather closed down. Another took off the next day – a joint Anglo-American team on board an MH-53 – which completed its planned route and approached to within five or six kilometres of our original emergency rendezvous before flying down what seemed the most likely escape-and-evasion route to the Saudi border, and almost running out of fuel in the process. A third search-and-rescue mission was mounted on 30 January, but this was also aborted when the pilot fell ill. The CO continued trying to arrange further searches until, in the early hours of 1 February, he heard that I had turned up in Damascus – whereupon it became obvious that none of the patrol could still be trying to return to Saudi.

More cheerful news was that 'A' and 'D' Squadrons had crossed the border in force just one night after our insertion, and that with their heavily-armed Pinkies they were creating havoc among mobile Scud launchers and communications towers. Their key weapon was the M19 – in effect, a machine-gun firing bombs at the rate of three or four per second. The ammunition was the same as in our 203s, except that the rounds contained more high-explosive – and when volleys of those things began bursting all round them, the Iraqis turned and ran. Details of the marauding operations had yet to emerge, but the squadrons' communications were working well, and from their operational reports it was clear that everyone was having a ball.

By the time I returned to Al Jouf, 'B' Squadron had tents, and life was much more organised. The OC and the SSM had organised a camp-bed for me – an American cot – in their own tent, which had a heater. I was amazed by the care with which Geordie was looking after me: before our deployment he'd seemed out of his depth, but now he was well in control, and really mothering me. He put my kit on the bed and said, 'Right, d'you mind speaking to the guys?'

'No, no,' I said. 'That'll be fine.'

An hour later they had a big map set up at the back of one of the tents. I stood at the front, and twenty of the guys came in to sit on the ground and listen. As I told them the story they kept perfectly still, absorbed, and remained almost totally silent – but I could tell from the occasional muttered curse that they felt what it had been like. When I described how it had snowed, and how cutting the wind had been, they knew I wasn't exaggerating, because at Al Jouf the weather had grown even colder since I left.

Afterwards the OC and the SSM made me dinner out of ration packs. Then we had to go back across to the headquarters, because the CO wanted to see me at 2300. I thought, 'Oh, God! Not again! Why the hell didn't he listen in while I was being debriefed?' But across we went to one of the control rooms, and I was there until two in the morning. At the end he asked, 'Is there anything you think you should have done?'

That nearly cracked me up. I almost burst into tears as I said, 'I should have tied Vince to me.'

'Listen,' said the CO. 'It wasn't your fault.' Then he asked if I'd mind going up to Arar, to talk to 'A' Squadron of Delta Force, the American Special Forces unit, which was about to deploy behind the lines. It meant leaving at 0530 – in about three hours' time – so we went straight back to our tent and got our heads down.

As I climbed into my sleeping bag, the CO draped a big goat-herd's coat over me. I felt like a little kid.

Apart from my night in Cyprus, that was the first time since the contact that I slept soundly. I don't know whether it was because I felt secure at last; for whatever reason, I went out like a light, and the next thing I knew, Geordie was shaking my shoulder. He'd already cooked a fried breakfast with the light on, but I'd been out for the count and hadn't noticed a thing. So we had sausages and bacon and a cup of tea, and set out at 0530 in a Land-Rover, accompanied by Gus, an American liaison officer.

All the way up, as it got lighter, Gus was picking information out of me. We'd met in Hereford, when he'd come to the UK to command one of the squadrons. At that time I was Sniper Team Commander, in charge of all the high-rise options – climbing and abseiling on the outsides of buildings, inside lift-wells, or ascending glass buildings on suckers. We were hosting the Delta Squadron, and Gus and I seemed to spend all our time together in the backs of vehicles. Now we were in a vehicle again – but at least this time we could have a useful conversation. Delta's target was the area round the nuclear refinery, and whenever we came to a new kind of terrain during our drive, he asked if the ground where they were heading resembled what we could see. I told him, 'At X it's *that* colour exactly,' and, 'at Y it's like *that*.'

The journey took nearly three hours. Then, in the control room at Arar, I met Major General Wayne Downing, commander of US Special Forces, who'd recently flown in to supervise operations. Slim, fit-looking, with a crew-cut, he was the epitome of a successful American soldier. He shook my hand and introduced me to four or five other officers. Then we sat down on Chesterfields round a coffee-table. Downing thanked me for coming up, and I told them what had happened. Again, at the end, there was silence. Then Downing said, 'That's the most amazing story I've heard in years.' There was a pause, and he asked, 'What have the doctors said?'

'Well – I haven't seen a doctor yet.'

He seemed shocked. With a look of worry and embarrassment, he said, 'I sure am sorry to have dragged you up here. You ought to have seen a doctor before you came. Tell you what, though: we've got some go-faster surgeons on the base. I'll have one of them look at you.'

I wasn't quite sure what he meant by a 'go-faster' surgeon, but I went to see one of them willingly enough. A quick examination confirmed that I had frost-nip in my fingers and toes. The doctor said that my feet would heal up in time, but that I needed some dental work done. When I told him about the nuclear effluent, he said I certainly should have a blood test.

When I got back to Downing, he said, 'I know I'm asking a lot, but will you talk to 'A' Squadron? They're deploying tonight, and I know they'd appreciate it. You could probably give them a load of help.' Of course I agreed. So I told the story yet again, this time to about forty guys, and at the end they burst into applause, with everyone wanting to shake my hand.

Before I left, I went to see Downing once more, and he asked, 'Is there anything you need?'

'Well, yes,' I said. 'Have you got any of those large water bottles, and a rucksack and stuff like that?'

'Sure have. You'd better go see the quartermaster.' So I did – and I came away with a vehicle nearly full of new kit, an embarrassing amount. Finally Downing sent me into a command room, full of signals equipment, where I found an SAS officer who'd been attached to the American Special Forces. I got talking to him about our patrol, and he said the mission had been sent off without proper briefing. His point was that the Americans could call up satellite imagery of any particular area within twenty-four hours of any request. When I asked why we hadn't done that, he could only attribute the failure to rivalry between Brits and Americans, or a reluctance on the part of the Brits to tell the Americans what they were doing.

Back at Al Jouf, I found myself endlessly speculating with other guys in the squadron about what could have happened to the rest of our patrol. I said I believed in my heart of hearts that Vince was dead, and Stan the same – or possibly captured. But I couldn't understand why the other five hadn't come out, or why there was no news of them. My own emotions were barely under control. On one occasion we were talking in a tent, and I found it was getting too much. I suddenly felt choked and said, 'Ah, listen: I'm off,' and went out. One of the others ran after me and put his arm round my shoulders. 'Don't worry,' he said, 'just get it off your chest.'

People began to assume that the rest of the patrol had been written off, and I heard that I would probably have to go on a tour of New Zealand, Australia and all round England to talk to the families of the guys we'd lost. The OC told me to stand by for the trip as soon as I got back to the UK. He said I wasn't to worry about it because the CO, the adjutant, the Families' Officer and OC of the squadron would all be there; I wouldn't have to do it by myself.

In spite of emotional swings, I felt reasonably well – so much so that, when 'B' Squadron began getting ready to drive into Iraq as the security force on a major re-supply for 'A' and 'D', I asked the CO if I could go with them. Luckily he realised that I was a long way from being fit, and said, 'Not a chance.'

The re-supply proved a memorable expedition, and when I heard how it went I was sorry to have missed it. 'B' Squadron provided security for a column of 10 three-ton trucks, and this gave about a dozen of our guys a chance to take part in the war. The party included specialists such as REME fitters and a Royal Engineer who was expert in the repair of Magellans.

The column was commanded by a major called Bill – a really strong character, much respected, with a wealth of experience going back to the Oman campaign of the 1970s. The final briefing which he gave in the middle of the night, in a wadi just short of the border, will never be forgotten by those who heard it. With everyone gathered round in a huddle on the ground, muffled in the long Arab coats they'd bought in the souk, he put over his objectives with inspiring vigour and precision.

'We stop for nothing,' he announced. 'Effective enemy fire is when rounds are coming through your windscreens.'

The SSM of 'B' Squadron, who was driving a Land-Rover, and thought he could score a point, said, 'I don't have a windscreen.'

'OK, then,' replied Bill instantly. 'When you've got rounds coming through your goggles.' After that, there were no more questions, and the column crossed the frontier at 0300, with a couple of Land-Rovers leading the way, four motorbikes behind them to relay messages back if need be, and the trucks following at twenty-metre intervals. During the hours of darkness they made slow progress, as the terrain was rough and difficult; they were driving without lights, and the lorries bounced around violently over the rocks. But with the advent of daylight they forged ahead, sometimes reaching 80 or 90 k.p.h. over smooth stretches.

Their route lay up two main wadis which, on previous days, had been swept by Jaguar or Tornado aircraft making low-level passes to confirm that Iraqi troops had not moved in. On its way the convoy passed numerous little Bedouin encampments. A few of the goat-herders still had camels, but most were motorised, and some owned big Mercedes trucks. Bob Shepherd, who had learned to speak Arabic for the Oman campaign in the 1970s, several times stopped to pass the time of day, and generally found the people friendly. Stan, whom he knew well, was much on his mind, and he kept hoping that one of the herdsmen might have news of him.

The rendezvous with elements of 'D' Squadron was at a Y junction, where two wadis ran together. After a run of 180 kilometres, the column reached it at about 1530. The scouts took them forward to a deep, steep-sided wadi, and for the next twenty-four hours the trucks lay up there out of sight, while everyone else came in off the ground in small parties to collect supplies of food, water and ammunition. There was plenty of fresh food – meat, bread and fruit – but most of the guys were happy with the boil-in-the-bag rations. There were also numerous broken vehicles for the REME mechanics to repair.

When the time came for the column to return, Bob jumped

ship, unilaterally transferring himself to 'D' Squadron for the remainder of the operation. Back at Al Jouf he'd been told that if he did this he would risk being RTU'd, but he was determined to take part in the war. As he said, 'This was what I joined the regiment for. This is my big chance.'

On only his second day with his new unit, 'D' Squadron had a major success. It was a bright morning, and by noon the desert was shimmering under a heat-haze as eight SAS vehicles cruised forward on the lookout for targets. The raiders saw what they thought was an enemy convoy. As they crept closer, they managed to convince themselves that they could identify two tanks and one other vehicle, all moving very slowly. Then, at a range of only two kilometres, they realised that what they could see was a couple of tarmac-laying trucks which were not moving at all; they had been working on a road, but had been abandoned for the time being.

Later that day the marauders came on the real thing: two TELs – transporter-elevator-launchers – with their Scud missiles in the horizontal attitude. They were about twelve kilometres off, but by then the shimmer had gone, and with their telescopes and binoculars the SAS were able to identify them clearly. A quick radio call whipped the coordinates back to base, and a pair of F-16s were scrambled. The TELs looked as though they had just come out to firing positions, and were about to set up for a launch at last light, so that they could run away in the dark if anyone spotted them. A number of smaller vehicles were active round them, but after the SAS had observed them for about forty minutes, moving slowly closer, they all suddenly began to drive away. Clearly they had spotted the dust cloud raised by the approaching enemy, and they were off. For the Scuds, however, it was too late. At last light, before their crews could get them moving, the F-16s came in to hit them with missiles and 1,000-lb bombs.

For the onlookers, who by then had moved up to within about four kilometres, it was a phenomenal firework display. Evening haze obscured details on the ground, but the sky lit up with giant flashes, the impact of the bombs made the ground shudder, and the heat from the explosions could be felt. The SAS, talking to the pilots, told them that other Iraqi vehicles had pulled off in a particular direction, and sent them in pursuit. Yet it was not until the next day that they realised the full success of the operation. Only then did they hear that the total bag of Scuds in that one place had been seven or eight. The two they'd seen had been the outliers of the group.

That was just one of many successes. Whenever our guys put in an attack, the Iraqis almost always held or ran away; they hardly ever pushed out. The sight of a dust cloud approaching, and the knowledge that it contained formidable firepower, was generally enough to send them running. The SAS tactics were to hit hard and disappear quickly. A typical attack would begin with a salvo of 81mm. mortars. As the bombs were falling, the assault party would be creeping in to open up with .50 machine-guns and M19s, as well as twin and single gympis. Once, because of the lie of the ground, they had to dismount and take out bunkers on foot.

Much of the terrain in which the squadrons operated was exactly what I had gone through: a moonscape of black or dark-grey rock and rubble, with large boulders dotted about. At night the units would run back and take up a defensive position, either in a wadi or in the open. If it was the latter, they would make what's known as a fish-hook, driving round in a big loop and coming back almost to the point at which they had swung off their original course, so that they could ambush anyone following up their tracks.

Each unit had been allocated a block of territory which it was to search, and gradually, as the guys developed a feel for the ground and for the behaviour of the Iraqis when under attack, they evolved an effective pattern of activity. Generally they would lie up for most of the day, and then, in the afternoon, push out a couple of recces to see what they could find. If they came on to anything, they would take it on just before last light, so that they had time to destroy it, defend themselves and pull out.

Their main targets were the towers designed for reporting air movement. Made of wood and steel, about ten metres high, they reminded everyone of World War Two goon towers set round prison camps. They were defended by forces of no more than platoon strength – about thirty men – most of whom ran away as the vehicles approached. At one, eight Iraqis were taken prisoner. When Bob questioned them, they said exactly what they were doing. They also said that their officer had run away with the radio set, an event that was more or less an SOP for them. They were very frightened, and wanted to go with the British. When they asked where the Brits were going, Bob told them, 'Baghdad.'

'Why?'

'To kill Saddam Hussein.'

'Good!'

Because the guys were low-level squaddies, there was nothing to be gained from sending them back to Saudi. Therefore, after the towers had been blown up, and the weapons and communications equipment destroyed, the SAS walked the prisoners about a kilometre out into the desert and left them there with a bucket of water, confident that their own people would come and rescue them before they suffered any serious hardship. Only once did our forces come up against hardened troops, defending a permanent signals outpost. The place had been hit at night by coalition aircraft, and a request came for close-up damage assessment. For once the SAS pushed their luck too hard: they found themselves facing a large force of troops who were determined not to move.

At about 2200 a gang of four left their vehicle and went in on foot, trying to establish how big the station was. Much of it turned out to be underground, in bunkers, with the defenders in slit trenches. Challenged in Arabic, the intruders replied in kind, but immediately came under fire, and the sergeant major was hit in the back. A round went in just beside his spine and came out through his stomach, luckily without hitting any bone. He was carried out of immediate danger by a small lad called Ben (who later won the Military Medal for his gallantry), while their two colleagues gave covering fire. The four of them pepper-potted back to the vehicle, the Land-Rover returned to the rest of the formation, and the whole lot moved off about five kilometres before taking up a position for the night.

That same night, further north, the American Delta Force had a big shoot-out and sustained a couple of casualties. Next day a helicopter came in to pick them up. The Americans offered to collect the British sergeant major also, but he declined the lift because, along with the OC, he was leading his gang and wanted to stay on the ground. His sense of duty saved his life –

for as the helicopter which would have taken him came back into Arar, it crashed just short of the base's perimeter, killing everyone on board, including some of the guys I myself had briefed.

The SSM claimed that his wound was not too bad, but by the time two more days had gone by, he was exhausted and glad to be evacuated. The chopper which recovered him also took out the body of the only member of 'A' Squadron to be killed in the entire six-week operation.

When the Iraqi ground forces surrendered, on 28 February, 'A' Squadron immediately returned to Saudi territory, but 'D' stayed on for a few more days, lying low and keeping abreast of events by listening to the BBC World Service. For them, the ceasefire was something of a disappointment, because they had been planning a joint operation against a number of towers with Delta's Minibugs, their small strike helicopters. With the end of the ground war, this was called off. After three days they pulled back and drove, union jacks flying, down the wadi which they had used as their route in, with A-10s doing rolls and somersaults overhead.

Much as I would have liked to take part in all this, I knew I was still a long way from being fit. So when the CO suggested that I should go down to the rear base for three days' R & R and then maybe be deployed again, I was staggered. I looked at him and nodded, but I was thinking, 'Not a chance! There's no way I'm going back over there.'

Anyway, I went and packed, and as we were driving towards the control tower the OC suddenly said, 'I think that's your aircraft!' A Hercules was already taxiing into position for take-off, but he screamed across and scorched the Land-Rover to a halt right under its nose. When I got on board, who should I find in charge but the big loadie I'd encountered at Akrotiri airbase. This time he knew all about me, and apologised for his surly behaviour in Cyprus.

Back in the hangar where we'd lived when we reached the Gulf, I got myself a bed-space and went in search of the kit I'd left behind – only to find that in my absence someone had been through it. I'd lost a bivvy bag, an American poncho liner, and a few other things. I felt certain that none of the badged SAS guys had done it, and blamed one of the men attached from other units. I had a brief panic when I thought that my original escape map, with the names of the patrol written on it, was among the things that had been stolen; but then I found it, and kept it secured.

The cookhouse at Victor was about 200 metres from our hangar, and by the time I had covered that short distance, I felt knackered and had to sit down. I was still eating small amounts of food, and putting weight back on very slowly. As soon as I started chewing anything at all hard, my gums would bleed, so that I always had the taste of blood in my mouth – and as I hate raw meat, it made me feel sick. Observing myself in the mirror, I thought, 'You look like a fucking vampire!'

Altogether I spent two weeks with them, not doing much: eating, sunbathing, listening to music, trying to recover. I felt dazed, and I was shocked at how long it took me to regain strength. When I went to a gym and got on the bench, trying to lift some weights, I realised how weak I had become. I couldn't even do a dip. It was soul-destroying to have become so feeble.

A young troop officer who was running an anti-terrorist team told me I could take charge of the sniper team.

'No way,' I told him. 'I'm going into town for a couple of weeks to recuperate.'

'No, you can't.'

'Bollocks. I'm going. I'm not fit to work at the minute.'

Next morning two of the guys gave me a lift down, and as we went into a shopping centre, out came a man called Kev, with whom I'd passed selection. Somehow the sight of him was too much for me. I burst into tears. He grabbed me, pulled me to one side, and took me round to his accommodation in an army camp on the outskirts of the city, where I stayed for the next few days. That first night I went downtown with him to a disco. Life here didn't seem to make sense: with the air-war still in full swing, and the ground campaign coming up, everyone was drinking and dancing.

After a few days I felt stronger, and went back to Victor to take over the sniper team. We started work, living in a tented camp, but I found that the Arab food didn't agree with me. It began to go straight through me, and I started losing weight again. At the same time, preparations were in hand for a body-guard team job in South America, and I was told to learn Spanish. I was given a one-to-one tutor from the Army Education Corps, but I found it impossible to concentrate. In Bavaria I had had no trouble learning German, and I thought I was quite good at languages; but now I couldn't remember a thing, or even string a simple phrase like 'Good morning' together. My head felt numb; words went in one ear and out the other. I did so badly that my instructor soon got annoyed. 'Listen,' he said, 'have you got the slightest interest in what you're doing?'

'*You* fucking listen,' I answered – and I told him what had happened to me. He immediately apologised, and said, 'You shouldn't be doing this. You can't concentrate.' He got hold of a young Rupert and told him to have me taken off the course.

Because my teeth were still so slack, I made arrangements to see a dentist. Before my appointment, I was warned that I mustn't under any circumstances tell him where I'd been. But when I got into the surgery, the dentist proved a really sensible, nice guy. A New Zealander, he asked me to fill in a form confirming that I didn't have AIDS, and so on. Then he asked his assistant to leave the room, and said, 'There's obviously something wrong.'

'Yes,' I said, 'I've had a bad eight days.'

'I should say so. What do you do for a living?'

'I test Land-Rovers.'

'OK. I'm not interested in what you've done. But your mouth's in a serious state. Your gums show signs of malnutrition; they're receding – that's why they're bleeding. I can see the roots of your teeth. There's a chance you'll lose a few. I'll have to take two out, anyway. Meanwhile, rub this paste in.'

Noticing that I wore a diver's watch, and that the rubber strap was loose on my shrunken wrist, he said, 'Oh, by the way: I've got a watch like that, and if you like I can cut the straps down with one of my files.' It seemed funny that the instruments he used on people's teeth were equally good for fixing watches.

To this day my gums haven't fully recovered; some teeth are still loose. Otherwise, I made a full physical recovery. It took six weeks for feeling to come back into my fingers and toes. A blood test taken in a makeshift hospital on an American airbase revealed nothing wrong – but evidently the doctor who did it missed something, because another test, carried out in the UK, showed that I had a blood disorder, caused by drinking dirty water from the Euphrates, as well as an abnormal amount of enzymes in my liver produced in reaction to poisoning. I was also tested for radioactive poisoning, but there appeared to be no contamination. One doctor, talking about weight loss, told me that it was safe to shed one pound of meat a week. When I told him I'd lost thirty-six in a week, he said, 'It's impossible.' I said, 'It bloody well happened.' To which he replied, 'Well, that's not good.'

The psychological scars took far longer to heal. In the Gulf I began to suffer from a recurrent nightmare, in which I walk through the dark along a road. Ahead of me I see two hooded figures, dressed in black, on top of a mound. I know they're the two men I killed in the nuclear complex, but still I go up to them to ask directions. The night is very dark, and it's as if black rain is falling. As I come close, I see the eyes of the second man, wide with fright, and at the last second a knife-blade flashes as he makes a lunge at me. At that point I wake up, sweating with terror.

When the dream began, I realised that it was caused by feelings of guilt. I phoned Jan and said, 'I've done something terrible.' She understood exactly, and said, 'Forget it, forget it. Don't say anything.' But I was also plagued by worries about Vince. There was I, a fully trained mountain guide, thrown into a situation where we were all going down with exposure, and I'd failed to do the obvious thing of tethering him to me and dragging him on a leash. Even if I'd just held him by the hand, or kept him in front of me where I could see him, I might have saved him. I knew the reason was that I had been suffering from exposure, too – but that couldn't bring him back. On the other hand, he might have slowed us down so much that the cold would have got the better of us all. Again, if we'd stayed together as a group, I think we'd probably have been captured, because you tend to talk each other into actions which you wouldn't take on your own.

On 24 February, the ground war was launched at last. I spent the time glued to CNN television. There was one big set in the corridor between the hangars, with a few settees and chairs in front of it, and guys were watching at all hours of the day and night, often falling asleep where they sat. When the coalition began taking prisoners, we couldn't believe the numbers: 20,000, 40,000, 50,000 – we kept a scoreboard.

In five days, unbelievably, it was all over. The squadron came back from Al Jouf to Victor, getting ready to go home. Moves were being made to bring 'A' and 'D' Squadrons back as well. Then the OC said that as soon as an aircraft to the UK became available, I would be on it.

Just after the ceasefire I was in one of the hangars when somebody rushed in, shouting, 'Hey! We've seen Dinger on the telly!'

Electrified, I ran back with him to see if I could catch a glimpse. There'd been shots of the Iraqis handing over allied prisoners.

'Are you sure it was him?'

'Yeah, yeah, it was Dinger all right.'

We sat there waiting for the next news programme. When it came on, someone shouted, 'There he is!' Sure enough, it was Dinger – and a moment later we saw Stan as well. Both were in Baghdad. They were wearing orange prison overalls, sitting at a table, on their way to being handed over to the Red Crescent. It was easy enough to spot Dinger, but Stan was harder to pick out, because he had lost a lot of weight and had become quite gaunt.

Just to see them was intensely exciting. We knew those two were safe – but what about the others? We were pretty sure that one man in 'A' Squadron, Jack, had been killed, because he had been seriously wounded and left for dead – but from Bravo Two Zero there were still five to account for: Bob, Vince, Legs, Mark and Andy. We asked the sergeant major what was happening, but he wouldn't tell us anything; then we heard through the regiment that the Iraqis had four more prisoners to release. We reckoned that meant one of our guys must have died.

Details trickled out slowly. The first to reach us, via Dinger, was that Legs had died from hypothermia after trying to cross the Euphrates. We therefore presumed that the other four would be coming out. Then, to our amazement, we heard that Jack had survived, and was about to be released. That meant that another of our own lot must have gone down. Rumours flew about, but there was no official information. Then some guys were detailed to pack their kit and stand by to fly into Riyadh, so that friendly faces would be there to greet the prisoners when they returned, and sit with them in the aircraft when they flew on to hospital in Cyprus.

'D' Squadron was still inside Iraq, in case anything cracked off again, but 'A' Squadron arrived back at Victor, and there was a lot of in-fighting in their hangar as scores were settled and frustrations worked off – something that occurs a good deal in a unit full of very strong characters. The guys are so well trained that during operations they keep control of themselves, whatever happens – but once they are back at base they're quick to vent their displeasure on anyone who's done something stupid or unnecessarily dangerous. When I went in to see my friend John, I found three or four guys lining up to kick the shit out of one of their mates. I let them get on with it, keen to hear John's amazing story.

Together with two mates, John had been going forward in a Pinkie at night to recce an enemy camp, when their wheels became entangled in barbed wire. In the dark, they had motored right into a defensive position among slit trenches. When a man popped out, John shot him at point-blank range – but at the noise the whole place erupted. When soldiers popped up out of the ground, he despatched them straight away; but as the driver tried to move off, the wire caught up round their axles and gave off such a shower of sparks that it made them an illuminated target and attracted a hail of Iraqi fire. The Land-Rover was riddled with bullets. The big Mira sight on top of it came off and hit the driver on the back of the head, and he was driving semi-conscious. In the end he stopped, so that two of the crew could get down and try to cut the wire away, while Jack gave covering fire from the vehicle.

While doing this, he was badly wounded by a rifle bullet, which travelled nearly the length of his leg, through ankle, calf and thigh. The other two abandoned the stricken vehicle. The driver was still semi-conscious, so John carried Jack as far as he could, stopping every now and then to pick off a couple of the Iraqis who were following up. Soon Jack had lost so much blood that he was convinced he was going to die, and since the Iraqis were pursuing them with vehicles, using their headlights, John decided to leave him. He got out his pistol and said, 'Jack – if

215

you want, I'll shoot you.' But the wounded man, with his mind wandering, said, 'No, no, no – the squadron will come and get me. You carry on.' So John left him with a 66 and ran off.

All night, on and off, Jack struggled to pull the 66 out to its cocked position, so that he could take out any vehicle approaching him; but in his weakened state, he lacked the strength to manage even that simple operation. In the morning the Iraqis swept the whole area with a search-party and found him lying in the desert, saved by the tourniquets which he himself had bound on as he slipped in and out of consciousness. The surgeon who operated on him had left London just before the war started, and did a brilliant job. His leg was saved, and British doctors later said they couldn't have treated it better. John and his friend were picked up by their own colleagues next day, when they made radio contact with an A-10 circling overhead. By giving a sequence of bearings, they enabled the pilot to pinpoint their position, and he in turn guided the squadron on to them.

'B' Squadron were the next to return to Victor, and we had a couple of nights on the town. We were told to be back in camp by 2300 hours, but since things didn't liven up until then, John and I decided to ignore the minibus when it came to collect us. Instead, I asked a nurse whom we'd befriended, Annie, if we could get our heads down in her flat, rather than go to the expense of a hotel. She said, 'Fine,' so we got ourselves shitfaced, and some time in the early hours collapsed on to her settees. When we came round at 9.00 the next morning, we knew there'd be trouble in store; but when we walked round the corner to the pick-up point, there stood a troop staff sergeant and a sergeant from 'A' Squadron. We felt a lot better, finding we weren't the only offenders, and in fact when we got back to camp, nobody said a thing.

Very soon after that, a message came telling us to pack. I would be on the first aircraft going home, together with the OC, SSM, and a couple of people needed for team jobs. So we left Arabia. When the Hercules landed at Cyprus and we walked into the terminal, someone said, 'Oh – we've just had some of your guys come into the hospital.' Immediately the OC got on the phone, but – quite rightly – security was tight and nobody was being allowed to speak to the released prisoners, so he had some trouble getting through. In the end he managed it, and I spoke to both Dinger and Stan.

Their voices sounded a bit flat, and I could tell they'd been through a lot; they weren't their normal bouncy selves. But Dinger said, 'Look – I owe you a pint for making me keep my jacket. I reckon it saved my life.'

'That's all right,' I said. 'But what happened? How did we split?'

'We heard an aircraft and went to ground. But I can't say much now. We'll see you when we get to the UK.'

Obviously he didn't want to talk on the phone, but I asked, 'Who else is coming back?'

'Andy and Mark.'

That was all he said. But it meant that, besides Legs, Bob Consiglio had gone. I felt very sad about Bob, good, tough little guy that he was – and immediately I wanted to know what had happened to him.

I also had a brief word with Stan. 'Ey,' I told him. 'You dropped a bollock there.'

'I know,' he agreed. 'I owe you a few pints on that. I should have stayed with you. I bloody well should have stayed.'

Chapter Eleven

Counting The Cost

As we came in to land at Lyneham, the OC was worried that the press might be waiting for us. With our suntanned faces, we were obvious targets. He asked if I had a hood on my jacket. 'You may have to lie on the floor,' he said. But in fact there was nobody waiting for us. My main worry was that the Customs man would drop on my aluminium trunk, which contained a good deal of music equipment.

'Right,' he said. 'I know all the squadrons from your regiment are coming back. You're the first man through. Do you have anything to declare? And remember – if I find you're not telling the truth, I'm going to strip all the squadrons.' I looked him in the eye and said, 'No – I've nothing,' and he let me through.

At the guardroom in Hereford I found a message telling me to go straight to the doctor. I went round the corner on to the quadrangle, and there was Janet. It wasn't the moment for an emotional meeting; it could have been an ordinary weekend. She ran over, greeted me briefly, and came with me to see the doctor, who had arranged an appointment for me that same day at the Queen Elizabeth Hospital in Woolwich.

First, though, we drove home for my reunion with Sarah, who was being looked after by Jan's parents. It was a terrific moment. I'd been away two months, and was worried that my daughter might not remember me. But Jan told me that every night when she went to bed, she'd kissed a photograph of me and said, 'Goodnight, Daddy.' Now as we reached home she shouted, 'Hello, Daddy!' and jumped into my arms.

Once we'd got sorted out, we drove up to London, and reached Woolwich about 5p.m. I don't know what people had been expecting, but they'd scrubbed out an isolation ward for my sole benefit, and when I stuck my head round a pair of

218

double doors, someone shouted, 'Get out! Get out!' as though I was going to contaminate the whole building. When I said I was from Hereford, they replied they'd been expecting someone to turn up in an NBC suit, glowing all over. By then the surgeon had got fed up with waiting for me, and had left; when I spoke to him on the telephone, he was not very polite. 'I've been waiting for you since nine o'clock this morning,' he griped.

'Well,' I said, 'I'm here now.'

'All right, then – I'll come back in.'

Even in the flesh he wasn't very happy at first. But when I told him I'd gone eight days without food, and might have been contaminated in a nuclear refinery, he became a different man, and asked me to report for tests in the morning.

We booked in for the night in a hotel on Blackheath Common. It was the first chance we'd had to be alone and talk the whole thing through. We went for a walk, and then, as we lay in bed, I told Jan the story.

Next day, the tests lasted all morning and into the afternoon. At the end, I went back into the isolation ward, and the doctor came in and said, 'You'd better take a seat.' His face was sombre – as if he had really bad news. Jan was outside, looking in through a glass screen.

'You've got a viral infection,' he said – but I thought he'd said 'a *venereal* infection', and nearly died. Naturally Janet and I had slept together the night before, and I thought, 'My God, surely I can't have given her a dose?' I prepared to defend myself hotly, saying I must have caught it off a toilet seat, but he saw me looking worried and asked, 'What's wrong?'

'Did you say *venereal*?'

'No, no – *viral*. I said *viral*.' He laughed and said, 'It's just a viral infection which will work its way through your body.'

He also found that I had a blood disorder, and enzymes in my liver. On the nuclear front, he did mention leukaemia, but brushed aside the possibility. Naturally that worried me, as I thought the army might be sweeping the subject under the carpet, rather than facing the truth.

After that we returned home, and 'B' Squadron went on three weeks' leave. For me, the prospect of the Everest expedition suddenly revived when Harry Taylor, who was still making his preparations, turned up at the house.

'You still on?' he asked.

'Damn right I am.'

I was feeling better every day, and couldn't turn the offer down. Harry said he would make special arrangements whereby I would stay at the basecamp for as long as possible and, as he put it, fatten myself up for a walk straight through all the intermediate stops – an opportunity most people never get. Usually on that kind of expedition you're sherpaing all the time, feeding the camps, building platforms for the real climbers, and then at the end the leader picks the two fittest guys to walk through. But now Harry said, 'It'll be a hell of a thing, after what you've just done, to walk straight through to the top.'

The temptation was tremendous. A glamorous adventure like that seemed just what I needed to take my mind off the Gulf and its aftermath. After a chat, we went down to a bar in Hereford to discuss things further. One reason he particularly wanted me to go was that I had medical training, and could act as expedition doctor.

As Harry and I returned home, we found the OC there. He said the army had decided to give all the survivors of the patrol a thousand pounds each, so that we could go on holiday. It was the first time the Regiment had ever done such a thing.

'Oh, great!' I said, without thinking. 'We can use that money for the expedition.'

'No way!' said Jan.

An argument set in between her, me, Harry and the OC – Harry and myself against the other two – and in the end I lost. At the end the OC said, 'I'll tell you something now. You're not getting permission from the Regiment to go on this expedition.'

'OK,' I agreed. 'Fair enough.' So instead of going to the Himalayas, I went with Jan for two weeks' holiday in Tenerife, the only place where we could book up at short notice.

In retrospect, I can see it was a mercy that I didn't go to Everest, as I simply wasn't fit enough. The party went up the North-East Ridge as planned, but Russell Bryce fell ill with altitude sickness and a stomach complaint, so that they had to return. The guy who took my place, an Australian, tried to climb the North Ridge, but turned back just short of the North Col with frostbite in his nose and fingers. The weather was horrendous. When I heard all that, I thought maybe I was well out of it.

All the same, lying by the pool in Tenerife wasn't quite the same thing, and after a short time I began counting the days till we got back. Jan and I realised we had made a mistake in not taking Sarah with us; if she'd been there, she'd have entertained us both, and stopped us from getting bored. In purely physical terms I was making a good recovery, but the psychological damage I had suffered ran deeper than I realised.

Bit by bit, we pieced together what had happened to the rest of the patrol. I'd only been home about three days when Stan phoned and came round to our house. He said the worst thing he'd ever done in his life was to ignore my warnings in the wadi. He apologised for having been an idiot, and promised that if ever we found ourselves in a tight corner again, he'd do what I told him.

After he had left me, he told me now, he walked for about four hours with the goatherd. Towards evening they sighted a small group of buildings, with vehicles outside them. The Arab pointed to them, and Stan went down on his own. As he arrived, an Arab in a fine-looking white dishdash came out of the building, heading for a Toyota land-cruiser. Stan tried to engage him in friendly chat, but the man made a dive for the vehicle. Thinking he might have a gun there, Stan fired a single shot through the window and dropped him. The report brought about eight militiamen, armed with AK 47s, hurtling out of the building, and a firefight broke out. Stan dropped the first, and the second, but then his ammunition ran out, so he leaped into the vehicle. The key was on the floor, under the body of the first Arab, but before he could start the engine the windscreen smashed in on him and a weapon was stuck into his face. Guys dragged him out and were immediately on top of him – so that was him captured.

After what he described as 'an incredible display of uncontrolled firing into the air', the militiamen bundled him into another car and drove him into the nearest town. At first he was treated well, given tea, and questioned by relatively civilised officers who spoke good English; but later he was kept blindfolded, starved, and beaten so badly that he sustained a depressed fracture of the skull.

His cover-story, about being a medic on board a chopper on a rescue mission, held longer than anybody else's. In particular, he said he was a dentist – which he was – so that when the Iraqis actually brought patients in to him, he was able to look at their mouths and give a diagnosis that was completely plausible. One of the interrogators then asked him where he had worked in London – and when he gave the number of some orderly room, the Iraqis went so far as to ring it to find out if the details were genuine. Early in February he was moved to a basecamp near Baghdad and reunited in a cell with Andy and Dinger.

Of course Stan and I indulged in a lot of speculation: if we'd done this, if we'd done that; if we'd stayed together; if we'd walked down the railway line. In fact, if there'd been two of us, I think we'd both have been captured. Lonely as it was to be on my own, I was probably better off. Psychologically it was bad, but physically it was safer. There was only one person to hide, one made less noise than two, and there was no chance that the pair of us would talk ourselves into doing something stupid. On my own, I was more careful than I might have been with a partner. If there'd been two of us, we probably would have broken into a house in search of food, and that might have led to our capture. Being alone was what saved me. That said, I would have given anything for a companion.

Happily, Stan made a full recovery. He'd had a hell of a battering, but his equable character seemed to enable him to bounce quickly back to normal. Thinking over his final firefight, he realised it had been Vince's weapon that he was using, and Vince could never have reloaded with a full magazine – which would have held up to thirty rounds – after the initial contact. We assumed that after he had been captured, the goatherd must have come down to the buildings where the firefight took place, told the militia that there was a second runaway out in the wadi, and directed the party that came in search of me.

After our return to the UK, Stan and I remained on close terms. Andy was a different matter. When he got back, he didn't seem to want to make contact. Several times I phoned his house in Hereford, but I always spoke to his girlfriend, and he never returned my calls. That seemed strange to me. I couldn't make out why he was being so stand-offish. It was as if he didn't want to come round and face me.

It was inevitable that we would meet sooner or later. Sure

enough, on one of our first days back at work, we bumped into each other in the OC's office on the squadron. When I saw him, I went, 'Hey!' and he just looked up and nodded. There was no handshake, no 'Glad to see you back' or anything like that. I was disappointed that a mate of mine could behave in that way, and I could only put it down to jealousy and the fact that I'd got away while he was caught. Thereafter, we'd talk about it if we were thrown together, but we never met for a drink to shoot the shit. To me it was pretty sad that anyone could carry on in a way so alien to the spirit of the Regiment, which values companionship and loyalty above everything. A psychiatrist who had us all in for a talk told us that after what we'd been through together, we'd remain very close to each other – and indeed his words applied to everyone except Andy.

As to the reason why the patrol originally broke in two – that was never satisfactorily explained. What happened, unbeknown to me, was that Andy, who was four back down the column, heard a jet overhead, and immediately went down on one knee in an attempt to contact the pilot on his TACBE, calling out to Vince ahead of him, 'Go to ground!' He was so busy trying to raise the pilot that he didn't realise Vince had never heard his call, and had carried on. The rest of the guys, who had gone down behind Andy, were all watching their arcs, as they should have been, so that they noticed nothing either.

Up front, I'd heard nothing. How I missed the sound of an aircraft, I can't imagine – it was the one noise we were all longing to hear. Whatever the reason, I'd gone on walking as hard as I could. Whenever I glanced over my shoulder, I saw Stan behind me, and Vince behind him, and I never had an inkling that anything was amiss. Then again, how we became so widely separated we've never managed to work out. Andy told me that after trying to contact the aircraft he'd heard, his party saw movement up ahead. As they went to ground and watched, three figures came walking across their front. His own guys weren't sure if the men were friend or foe, but they assumed they were an Iraqi patrol and didn't challenge them, letting them disappear into the night.

In any case, the five picked themselves up and started walking to the north-west, and when dawn came they laid up for the day in the lee of a mound, where they destroyed the encrypting unit for the radio – no easy task, as it was in a soldier-proof metal casing. They also burnt their code book. Because they had no use for Stan's Minimi, they stripped it into pieces and scattered the parts over a wide area of desert. Luckily for them, they had ignored the orders for maintaining hard routine – no cooking or smoking – and they'd all brought brew-kits, so that they were able to make themselves hot drinks. Even so, because of the snow, rain, wind and bitter cold, Mark began going down with exposure, so the group decided to risk a daylight move. They got up and made good progress until they reached a main road, where they planned to hijack a vehicle.

With Bob playing the part of a wounded man, and leaning on Andy's shoulder, they flagged down a car which turned out to be a taxi. As it stopped, the other three came up out of cover and surrounded it. Evicting the driver and two other passengers, they took one man with them, because he looked so scared that they thought he might help, and set off westwards along the highway.

All went well until they reached a VCP. Some way short of it they got out of the car, having – as they thought – arranged with their driver that he would drive through the control and pick them up on the other side. In fact he shopped them, and they had to take to the desert, boxing the VCP on foot.

Back on the MSR further west, they tried to pull the same wounded-man dodge again, but all the drivers were going, as Andy put it, 'like madmen', and three successive attempts failed. Leaving the road again, and moving north towards the Euphrates, they found themselves in an area of habitation. By then they reckoned they were only ten kilometres from the river; but behind them military vehicles began to pull up on the highway, and troops poured out and opened fire. The rounds went well over them, but then three or four anti-aircraft guns opened up as well. On the whole this was helpful, as it made locals think an air-raid was in progress, and put them into shelter.

From a high point the patrol saw that the town of Krabilah was in fact joined up with Abu Kamal, and that the built-up area extended right across the border. Reaching the bank of the Euphrates, they took a fix with their Magellan, and this confirmed that they were only ten kilometres from the frontier. By then it was dark. They considered trying to cross the river, but concluded that the risk of going down with exposure was too high. In the end they decided to keep heading west, with the hope of reaching the border that night.

Inevitably, they came on enemy positions; contacts ensued, and the firing brought all the defenders to a high state of alert. Creeping, crawling, working their way forward through ploughed fields and along hedges, they made slow progress. Andy, Mark and Bob had a contact during which Bob got split off and ended up in a contact of his own, when he held the Iraqis off for thirty minutes, single handed, before he was shot and killed outright. To have defended himself like that for half an hour, against a force of maybe a dozen Iraqis, was one hell of a feat. At the end, I feel certain, he must have run out of rounds. God knows how many Iraqis he took out: a lot, I know. After the war he was awarded a posthumous Military Medal.

With Bob cut off on his own, Mark got shot in the arm and ankle, and he and Andy split up. In the end Andy was captured only a couple of kilometres from the border – and he must have been somewhere very close to the line of my own route.

Legs and Dinger, on their own now, went towards the Euphrates, but soon ran on to another enemy position. Suddenly they heard a weapon cocked, and something shouted in Iraqi, from only ten metres ahead. They let fly a hail of automatic fire from the 203 and Minimi, and received only half a dozen rounds in return. Pulling back, they retreated to the river bank. By then enemy were closing on them from the east, firing occasional bursts. Finding a canoe moored to the bank, they tried to release its chain but could not manage it, and slipped into the water, planning to swim across. Soon they came to land again, only to find that they were on a spit or island, with the main channel still to cross. Only 200 metres upstream, a big road-bridge spanned the whole Euphrates. They could see several vehicles parked on it, and numerous people, some shining flashlights down on to the water. Elsewhere, intermittent firing kept breaking out.

After waiting an hour, during which they became increasingly cold, they decided their only option was to swim the second channel. Luckily Legs had found a polystyrene box, and they broke this into pieces, which they stuffed into the fronts of their smocks to increase their buoyancy. Then they waded out and swam.

The water was icy, the current strong; they found it hard to make progress, and had to let go their weapons. Legs, who was going down with hypothermia, began to fail. When he fell back, Dinger got hold of him and towed him on. Reaching the far bank, Dinger dragged him out, only to realise that he had become incoherent, and could not walk.

Daylight revealed a small tin pump house some fifteen metres from the shore. Dinger pulled Legs into it, but he was so far gone that he kept trying to crawl back into the river. Inside the shelter Dinger lit his remaining hexi-block and brewed up a cup of hot water, hoping it would revive his companion. Legs, however, was making no sense, and instead of drinking the hot water, he hit the mug away. When the sun rose, Dinger dragged him out into it, in the hope that it would warm and dry him, but he was too far gone; his skin remained cold, and his eyes flickered meaninglessly back and forth.

When farmers appeared and started to work in the fields, Dinger pulled him back into the hut. Then at mid-morning a man with some children in tow came within ten metres of the pump house. Seeing that he was about to be compromised, Dinger showed himself to the farmer, whose response was to lock the two fugitives in and run off shouting. By that time Legs' smock was dry, but he was slipping into unconsciousness. Clearly he could not move, so Dinger burst his way through the roof of the hut and made off towards the north, away from the river, in the hope that he'd pull the enemy away from Legs and give him a chance to recover. Almost immediately he was spotted and followed by a posse of locals, who soon swelled into a crowd. He tried to do a runner, but was caught by the mob, one of whom proposed to cut off one of his ears. The guy was actually holding his ear when he managed to bring out one of his sovereigns. The people fought over that, but then realised he had more, and he started handing them out, which cooled them down. Then they walked him into a village, where the people went wild and beat him to the ground before he was handed over to the police. While in the police station, Dinger saw Legs being brought in on a stretcher. He was quickly cross-loaded into an ambulance and driven away, but although Dinger watched closely, he saw no movement, and feared that his companion was already dead. So ended a gallant escape attempt.

226

By the next night, when I had my own contact and made the Euphrates, the survivors were in gaol, and being questioned by officers who'd been through Sandhurst. But the Iraqis had evolved their own kind of interrogation techniques. All the survivors were brutally beaten for several days, partly in the course of interrogation, partly by their guards, who hit them casually whenever they saw a chance. Even Mark was beaten between operations on his wounded ankle. The Iraqis were greatly agitated by their belief that the prisoners were Israelis, and when Andy tried to convince them that he was not by showing them his foreskin, they were astonished. Our guys stuck to their story of being a medical team for as long as possible, and then fell back on controlled release of real information.

Back in the UK, I was glad that I had been tortured by weather, thirst and hunger rather than by human beings. But all of us had suffered, and all reacted in different ways. Stan bounced back quickly. So did Andy. The worst affected was Dinger. I believe he felt exactly as I felt – that all he wanted was to be back with the guys, working among them. But because he'd appeared on CNN television news, the head-shed decided that his security was blown, and sent him off to a safe house in the middle of Wales.

That was the last thing he wanted. It was as if he'd been transferred from one prison straight to another, and soon he was desperate for company. He phoned me and said, 'Chris – for Christ's sake come up and see me, or get the guys over. I'm cracking up here.' I went into the Squadron and asked if we could go, but they said, 'No visitors. No one's to go up.' So I had some long chats with Dinger on the phone, and got his version of events.

It took him a long time to recover. For a year, at least, he remained very emotional, and to me he looked like a lost boy, on the point of panic. Because the press found out where he lived, and took to hanging about outside, he had to move to a less nice house. But eventually he settled down again.

As for me – I tried to persuade myself that all was well, and when the psychiatrist asked if everything was all right, I just said, 'Fine.'

'Sleeping all right?'

'Fine.'

In fact I was still being troubled by the same recurrent nightmare. But if I wanted to talk about it to anyone, I preferred to talk to Jan, to my mother, my father or my brother, rather than to someone who didn't know me.

One day I was lying in bed at about eleven in the morning, when I got a telephone call from the guy who had been Vince's next-door neighbour. 'Chris,' he said, 'the family's all here waiting for you to come round. They've asked me to make contact with you. I'll come and pick you up.'

'Is the CO and everybody there?' I asked him.

'I think so, yes.'

'OK,' I said. 'I'll get ready.'

A few minutes later I was there, but I found that the only other outsider present was the CO's wife. As soon as I walked into the room, she stood up and legged it. I was left with Vince's Mum, his Dad, his widow and three of his brothers. Everybody was looking at me, and I was looking at them. It was a horrible feeling, to have to sit and tell them the story.

The father said, 'You've come round to tell us what happened.'

'Yeah, OK. D'you want me to tell you, and then you tell the family – because it's quite distressing?'

The man went, 'No – just tell us all together.'

Until then the Regiment had said, 'You don't tell anyone anything about what happened on this patrol. There's nothing to come out.' Well – I was there, and I thought, 'Bollocks – I'm going to start from the beginning.' So I sat down with them and told the story.

I left out some details about Vince not wanting to be there, and just said he had died of exposure during our second night on the run. The family were pretty stunned. I hardly knew what to say, because I was in a difficult position.

One of the brothers turned round and said, 'How come *you* didn't die, then?'

I said, 'Well, I was lucky. Exposure can take you at different times.'

'But my brother was really strong,' he protested. 'He'd worked in the snow loads of times and survived.'

I don't blame them for wanting an explanation. But I legged it as soon as I could.

228

The Iraqis had returned the bodies of all the dead men, and five or six days later we had the funerals. It was a harrowing occasion for everyone, as we'd all lost close friends or relatives. The survivors of the patrol gathered together – and then Vince's father and brothers came across towards us. When one of the brothers accused me of not telling the truth about Vince, I took a deep breath and walked away. Andy McNab grabbed the man and said, 'Just watch your mouth. That's enough.' I knew why the brother had thought that: some newspaper had reported that Vince had been captured and tortured by Iraqis, so that everything had become confused. I think the family had had this image of a super-hero – someone who could never be taken, who was indestructible. It was difficult for them to believe that two of the patrol had frozen to death in the desert.

Then everything died down until about three months later. One evening I was in a bar with my wife and I saw this man come in. I said to Jan, 'Jesus, I know that guy, but I can't think who he is.' The fellow kept staring across at me. I thought he looked like an old-time Regiment guy. Then I realised: it was Vince's father, together with the brother who had challenged me.

By then the inquest had taken place. We'd all had to go to Oxford and give evidence from behind a screen. A pathologist had given his report – but the family had never seen Vince's body. So anyway the father came up to us in this bar and said, 'Chris, I need to talk to you.'

I thought, 'If the brother says anything, I'm going to drop him.' For a moment I stood there looking – but Jan must have seen my reaction, because she came straight over.

The father said, 'Listen – did you tell me the truth about Vince?'

'Yes,' I said. 'I've nothing to hide. In my heart of hearts, I know he died that night.'

'Well – you said Vince died on 25 January. I've just been up to the Regimental graveyard, and on his plaque they've got him dying a month later.'

'That's got to be wrong, then,' I said. 'I can give you my word it was that second night.'

I could see that the father was really distressed. As far as he was concerned, things didn't add up. No wonder he thought a cover-up had been staged. I knew 'A' Squadron was having a party up in the camp, and knew there would be someone there who could confirm my story – so I offered to take father and son straight up. Jan came with us. We jumped into a taxi and legged it up towards the camp. On the way I made the driver stop at the regimental plot and wait while I ran in and looked at the stone. Sure enough, the dates were wrong, not just for Vince, but for all three of them, Bob and Legs as well. Someone had made a terrible cock-up.

I took Vince's people into the club, got hold of the sergeant major and told him what had happened. He promised to sort it out, confirmed the real dates, and apologised to Vince's family. Next morning I went in and told the Families' Officer – and in due course they got new gravestones and changed the plaques.

Some aspects of the aftermath were less gloomy. As I was walking through the camp one day, the Quartermaster – who'd been the RSM when I passed Selection – shouted across at me, 'Hey, Chris – come 'ere!'

In his office he said, 'What happened to your sovereigns?'

'Oh,' I said, 'I lost them during the contact.'

'Well – I've got a list of the kit you lost during the contact, and you must have had a bergen the size of a bloody caravan.'

'Why?'

'Look at this.'

The list was a mile long, a complete farce. It included things like mountaineering boots and a Lacon box – a big metal container. What I didn't realise was that the SQMS had written off mountains of stuff without telling me.

'This includes everything I took to the Gulf when we went out,' I said. 'Not what I had in my bergen. When I got back to Victor, the Lacon box had gone missing and I'd lost the lot.'

'All right,' he said. 'Write me a note saying how you lost your sovereigns, and we'll forget about the rest.' In fact I had distributed the remaining sovereigns to those who I thought most deserved them – the other survivors of the patrol and members of my family.

With 'B' Squadron settled back in Hereford, Jan and I threw a party at home. Somehow 110 people crammed themselves into the house, and at one point the OC sighted my escape map, by then framed on the wall, with three sovereigns mounted in the surround.

'Chris,' he said. 'I thought you'd lost them all.'

'Yes,' I said.

'Well – you've got three up there. You shouldn't do that . . .'

'Yeah – right!' And that was the end of it.

Chapter Twelve

Wash-Up

Only six weeks after the squadrons returned to Hereford, there took place the Regiment's 50th anniversary celebrations. Unfortunately the founder, David Stirling, had recently died, but many veterans of the Second World War took part in the festivities, and everyone said how strange but also satisfactory it was that in Iraq the SAS had reverted to its original role as a long-range desert group, operating heavily-armed, motorised patrols in enemy-held territory.

We owed the fact that the patrols were deployed to General de la Billière's enthusiasm for Special Forces, and to his understanding of their capabilities. But it was largely luck that the SAS played such a crucial role. DLB had been advocating their insertion for general intelligence-gathering purposes, but as it turned out, their arrival in the Western Desert abruptly cut off the stream of Scud missiles which Saddam Hussein was directing at Israel, and so, by a hair's breadth, kept Israel out of the war. If she had come in, the results would almost certainly have been disastrous, because some or all of the Arab nations would have refused to fight alongside Israeli forces, and the coalition would have disintegrated before the ground war began.

The role Special Forces played in the war was, therefore, outstanding. All the same, to lose three out of eight men in one patrol was a severe blow to the Regiment, and the disaster led to various internal reforms. Oddly enough, the survivors of Bravo Two Zero were never brought together for a formal debriefing: instead, we were all asked to write reports of what had happened, and these were collated at regimental level. I also had to give a five-minute talk to the Regiment as a whole.

In retrospect, it was clear that shortages of ammunition and equipment had had little material effect on the outcome of events. They had worried us, certainly, but they had not contributed to the patrol being compromised. The most serious deficiency lay in our maps, which were totally inadequate, and in the lack of accurate intelligence about the physical nature of the area into which we were deployed. If we'd known there was no sand, we would obviously have made some alternative plan.

Another fact which became clear was that we should have compiled a formal written E & E plan before we deployed. If we'd done that, and made it clear that in the event of trouble we were going to head for Syria, we'd have had a much better chance of being picked up by the searching helicopters. It was also clear that we seriously over estimated the capabilities of our TACBEs – and the fact that we were given the wrong radio frequencies was simply a mistake, probably due to the speed at which we had to prepare. As to the way the patrol split, I see no point in blaming anyone. It was just something that happened, at a moment when we were all under maximum stress.

In Hereford, together with the Int Officer and a decent map, I worked out the exact distances I had walked. On the first night, before and after the split, we covered 70 kilometres. On the second night Stan and I made forty, losing Vince in the middle. On the third I walked another forty to reach the Euphrates. The fourth night was the most frustrating, as I had to cover forty kilometres in zig-zags and boxes to make only ten towards the border. On the fifth night I advanced thirty kilometres and then did another five or six during the day, up into the wadis. The sixth night took me into and out of the nuclear refinery – another thirty. The last and most terrible night I did between forty and fifty – most of them unnecessarily. The total came to 290, or just under 200 miles.

I found that people were beginning to compare my escape with that of Jack Sillito, who trekked for more than 100 miles through the Western Desert of North Africa in 1942, having been stranded behind German lines. In spite of the fact that all members of the SAS are supposed to know their regimental history, I must confess that I had never heard of Sillito until somebody pointed out his name in a 50th-anniversary account of the Regiment by the cartoonist Jak. Without realising it, I had easily beaten Sillito's distance, walking nearly twice as far. But in fact the two escapes were made in widely different circumstances.

Whereas my main enemy was cold, his was heat, and he had no river to give him water or guide him. Instead, he navigated by sun and stars, and scrounged liquid from condensation in abandoned jerricans.

At the end of June I heard the good news that in the Gulf War honours list I had been awarded the Military Medal. Many of my SAS colleagues also received decorations, and the tributes to the Regiment which flowed in were enough to make anyone feel proud. In a personal letter to General de la Billière, General Norman Schwarzkopf described the performance of 22nd SAS as 'courageous and highly professional'. He recorded that the activities of 'A' and 'D' Squadrons, combined with those of Delta Force 'A' Squadron, had convinced the enemy that in Western Iraq they were facing forces more than ten times the size of the units actually on the ground. He also stressed the very high value of the briefings which SAS personnel gave to the US Special Forces before they were deployed, and said that if it had not been for these 'thorough indoctrinations', the Americans would have suffered many more casualties.

I myself received several flattering letters from senior officers. 'Your personal bravery, sound judgement and quite outstanding resolve were an example to all SAS soldiers,' wrote Field Marshal Lord Bramall, former Chief of the Defence Staff, and by then Colonel Commandant of the SAS. 'Your escape is a classic of its kind, and worthy of national recognition.' At the end of the typewritten letter the Field Marshal added in his own hand: 'What a feat of courage and endurance. Well done indeed.'

The Director of the SAS wrote in similar terms, saying that my escape 'more than proves that our E & E training is fully justified'. Another stirring tribute came from Colonel J.A. McGregor, who wrote on behalf of the Parachute Regiment to say that 'undoubtedly Airborne Forces are very proud of your dedication and professionalism, and you will certainly inspire others to follow in your footsteps'. Yet for me the most pleasing of all was a note from General de la Billière, thanking me for my 'personal support' while under his command, and saying how delighted he was that my operational work had been recognised by the Queen.

Later, in a presentation copy of *Storm Command*, his book about the Gulf War, he wrote, 'You have personally made SAS history.' For us survivors, a particularly memorable day was the one on which he brought General Schwarzkopf to Hereford. The big American couldn't have been more friendly or informal: he shook hands with each of us, sat down for a debrief, signed our escape maps, and was exceptionally generous in his praise of what the Regiment had achieved.

My involvement with American Special Forces was renewed when Major General Wayne Downing asked me to go across and give a talk to their Training Wing about lessons learnt in the war. The guy who picked me up at the airport didn't know what I'd done, and began talking big about some escape-and-evasions in which his people had been involved. 'We had one of three, and one of seven,' he told me proudly.

'Seven what?' I asked.

'Seven hours – it was quite something.'

'Great!' I said. 'I've just done one of seven *days*.'

After that initial hiccup, the Americans looked after me magnificently. Among other facilities, they showed me a big interrogation centre out in the middle of Fort Bragg, built to look like a Vietnamese camp. When my guide said casually, 'By the way, we've arranged for you to spend a couple of days going through it,' I nearly died. 'There's no way I'm entering that place,' I told him. 'I'll walk round it, but that's all.'

More to my liking was a vertical wind-tunnel, designed to teach free-falling techniques. I'd never done any free-falling, but the Americans soon had me in the tunnel, where a powerful rising column of air, created by a jet engine, enables you to learn how to become stable and manoeuvre before you jump out of an aircraft. My hosts were hell-bent on arranging a full course for me, and actually did so – but unfortunately my own training commitments prevented me taking up the offer. When I came to learn free-falling proper, I found that my half-hour in the tunnel had given me a tremendous advantage over other beginners, and that on only my second jump, from 12,000 feet, I was immediately stable.

My trip to America was good fun, but I was amazed to learn that an F-15 E fighter-bomber had been shot down by a surface-to-air missile over northern Iraq on 19 January – three days before Bravo Two Zero had been deployed. The target had been the nuclear refinery at Al Qaim, and the pilot and navigator had landed by parachute next to the very power cables which I had followed. The downed aircrew had managed to contact another pilot with their TACBEs, but in trying to escape, they walked up to three buildings which they thought were houses – only to find that they were bunkers housing the troops from the nearby anti-aircraft position. It was extraordinary to realise that these were the buildings which I myself had approached, and had sheered off in the nick of time. I also learnt that Al Qaim had been one of Iraq's main Scud-holding areas.

I found all this fascinating – but also it was disturbing that none of the information had been passed to us in Special Forces, before we were sent across the border. We had not even been told the refinery at Al Qaim was one of the Americans' main targets. Looking back, it seemed all the more incredible that I had come through unscathed. First, the Americans had repeatedly bombed the plant. Then the aircrew had been captured near it. Then Andy and the rest of our patrol had been picked up or killed close by. The very night I passed through the complex, the Americans bombed it again.

Had I known how hot the area was, I would never have gone near it.

For a while after our holiday in Tenerife, my relationship with Jan was all right. I was kept busy on exercises, and seemed to be more my old self. Then in August 1991 I and one other guy were detailed at short notice to go out to a central African country, where the political situation was deteriorating fast and people were needed to guard the British Embassy and evacuate the ambassador, together with his remaining staff.

Jan was furious that I, out of everyone available, had been selected for what was obviously a dangerous task. But in fact the team grew from two to four, and then to eight.

By the time we flew out, things had become so bad that there was a strong possibility that we might have to stage a fighting withdrawal across a large river into the friendly state next door – but the limitations on our equipment raised uncomfortable echoes of Bravo Two Zero. We decided we would need anti-personnel mines, 66s, a 7.62 gympi, claymores . . . and the Government turned round and said, 'We can't send you with all that; you'll take pistols and 9mm. sub-machine-guns.'

236

Those would be little good against a crowd on the rampage. We arrived in Africa to find the atmosphere highly volatile; riots and looting were being orchestrated by the military, but things seemed to cool down as quickly as they heated up, and it was impossible to tell what would happen next. An operation that was supposed to be over in three days ended up lasting three months – and three very long months they seemed.

One by one the other nations pulled out – first the French, then the Belgians, then the Americans, leaving us on our own. The British Ambassador was constantly talking over a satellite telephone to Douglas Hurd and other leading figures at the Foreign and Commonwealth Office in London, but the message didn't seem to sink in at the other end. Even when we'd reported a major riot within 200 metres of the Embassy, London kept asking, 'Yes – but what's the atmosphere like?' The straight answer was 'Bloody dangerous!' and we felt like saying, 'For Christ's sake get us out of here.'

The reason we stayed so long was that the diplomatic complex was brand-new – a £5 million building which dealt with five of the surrounding African countries. Outside it, the place was in chaos, with inflation raging, and food running out. Outside, the hospital lepers were carrying off the bodies of patients who'd died, to eat them, and they were even scrounging the limbs of amputees.

One night things seemed so edgy that we told the staff to collect their possessions, leave their houses, and gather in the embassy itself. The manager heard that people were raiding his home, and came running for help. Gary, who was in charge, got the team together, but I said, 'What's the point of going up there, just to save a load of crap? There's nothing worth having.'

But Gary said, 'No – we've got to do it.' So we put on our ops waistcoats, collected our MP5s and pistols, with night-sights, and drove down a back-alley between whitewashed buildings. We could hear the rumble of the crowd in the distance; when the vehicle stopped, and I lifted my kite-sight, I could see several hundred people, all looking at us.

'If they've got weapons, we're knackered,' I said. But we got out and started walking down towards them. At our approach they fell back, tripping over each other. The noise of so many people moving was enough to scare the pants off you. Then the

237

manager went running into his house, and back out again with a single pair of trousers in his hand. As he jumped into the vehicle, he was yelling, 'Let's go! Let's go!' The second we moved off, the crowd erupted. They poured over his house, into it, through it, like ants, and ripped the place to shreds.

Back in the embassy I was furious with Gary, effing and blinding. 'Cunt!' I stormed. 'We could all have been killed, just for a pair of trousers!' Poor Gary did his best to soothe me down, but I stormed off to my room still in a rage.

The situation was frightening by any standards – there are few more alarming sights than that of an African mob on the rampage – but on a personal level I was becoming worried, because my own behaviour had grown noticeably erratic. The other SAS guys noticed that I wasn't my normal self; I would refuse to carry out quite reasonable requests, and often gave way to outbursts of anger.

In the end, in November, the Ambassador heard that I had been summoned to go to Buckingham Palace to collect my Military Medal. Because a young secretary needed escorting home, he asked me to go with her.

At the airport check-in, the official told me to open my suitcase, and also my Lacon box, in which I had several native clay masks which I'd bought in the market. He started unwrapping the masks, and said, 'These are works of art, which you're taking out of the country. I need money off you.'

'No, no,' I said. 'They're not worth anything. You can buy them everywhere.'

'I need money,' he repeated.

'Well – I haven't got any.'

For some reason I went into a deep panic, as if I was physically scared of the man. He became so upset that he threw my case off his desk, so that my things went all over the floor. If I'd been myself, I'd just have said, 'Sling it. You can have the lot,' and I'd have left everything where it lay. As it was, I behaved as if these things were all my worldly possessions, and grovelled about trying to get them re-packed. Behind me came some Japanese people with a television set packed in a wooden case. Again the man demanded money, and when they said they had none, he ripped the packing to bits and threw the television aside, so that it had to travel without protection. God knows what state it was in when it arrived at the other end.

Altogether, the atmosphere was horrible – and in the VIP lounge the security people were into my briefcase, demanding money again. (The girl I was supposed to escort had to fly economy, so that she was already checked in.) During the flight I was so wound-up that I spent a lot of time in the toilet, being physically sick. I couldn't eat or drink anything, but sat there feeling ashamed of myself at being so frightened.

Back home, my symptoms grew even worse. When I was under pressure at work, a rash like psoriasis came out on my face and chest, and the nightmares started recurring. Worst of all, I had changed emotionally – how, I don't know – but when I came back, all I wanted was to be by myself. Suddenly I didn't want to be married any more. I didn't want to be with Jan, or even to see Sarah.

I began behaving impossibly. Jan was destroyed; she couldn't make out what she had done wrong – and of course I couldn't explain, because she hadn't done anything. The trouble lay in me. All I could say was, 'I don't know what the matter is. I just don't want you around.'

Things became so bad that she decided she'd take Sarah to live with her parents in Ireland. I mortgaged our house as far as I could afford, to give her some money, and we agreed to try a separation. So she planned to move across, and I faced the prospect of living on my own.

Even as I was walking out, on the day she was leaving, I said, 'You know, this is probably a mistake.' We went through with it for the time being; but, almost as soon as she'd gone, I seemed to realise what I was throwing away. Three or four months later I rang her up and said, 'Listen, I'm off to the jungle for six weeks, but when I'm home again, will you come back?' Her response was guarded: she said she'd come across, because she wanted to talk, but she didn't commit herself.

While I was away she moved back in, so that I found her and Sarah in the house when I returned. Things remained up and down for a while, but then, I'm glad to say, we got back to the level we'd been on at the beginning.

At the time I just didn't know why I behaved as I did. Now I see that the trouble must have been post-traumatic stress, coming out months after the event. When I returned from the Gulf, I didn't feel any different from normal, but a few of the guys noticed that I wasn't myself, and it seems to have been the pressure of life in Africa that brought the problem to a head.

On the family front, my mother was pleased that, of her three sons, I was the one who had had that unnerving experience. 'I knew that if *anyone* would come back, you would,' she said.

My Dad had always maintained he would never forgive my cousin Billy for getting me involved with the SAS in the first place, and my reply had always been, 'Well – look at the good side. If I hadn't joined up, I'd never have met Jan, or had Sarah.' Now he wasn't going to change his tune, and he said very little about my long walk. But I think that he was secretly proud of me. Oddly enough, in the past few years he'd gone right back to where he had started in terms of shooting; having given it up, and frowned on me for wanting to kill birds and animals, he was once again as keen as ever.

As for our visit to Buckingham Palace: it was all very splendid going to London, and an honour to meet the Queen, but I would have much preferred to receive the Military Medal in front of the whole Regiment. My ideal would have been to have all the guys on parade, and for every man who had been decorated to be brought out of the ranks and get his award with all the rest watching. I knew that the medal-winners included some of the bravest soldiers in the world. In the SAS, no award is given away, and every one had been fully earned. When I came home, I pinned the medal on Sarah, and she wore it as a badge.

Lying in bed four years later, I still see incidents from the patrol, and hear the sounds, as clear as day. I see rounds flying between us during the first contact. I see Stan walking off down the wadi with the goatherd. I see the two hooded Arabs waiting for me on top of the mound. I try to put the images from my mind, but they creep back in. More and more I realise how lucky I was not to be shot, not to be captured, not to be caught up in the barbed wire on the border. Sometimes I feel that I must have used up all my luck.

All in all, my experience taught me a good deal about myself. Most people, I think, don't know what they're capable of until they're put to the test. Before the Gulf War, if somebody had told me I could walk nearly 300 kilometres through enemy territory in seven nights, with no food and practically no water, with inadequate clothes, no proper sleep and no shelter, I wouldn't have believed him. When I had to, I did it. Whether I could do it a second time is another matter.

In 1991 I was at a peak of physical fitness, and armed with the skills, the endurance, the competitive instinct and the motivation which SAS training had instilled in me. In any event, I devoutly hope I'll never again be faced by such a challenge. With an ordeal of those dimensions, once in a lifetime is enough.

Glossary

AWACS Airborne warning and control system aircraft
Basha Sleeping shelter
BCR Battle casualty replacement
Bergen Haversack
BG Bodyguard (noun or verb)
Casevac Casualty evacuation
CO Commanding Officer of the regiment
Comms Communications
DF Direction finding (equipment)
Director, The Officer commanding Special Forces, generally a brigadier
DPM Disruptive pattern material camouflage clothes
E & E Escape and evasion
ERV Emergency rendezvous
FMB Forward mounting base
FOB Forward operating base
GPS Global positioning system (navigation aid)
GPMG General-purpose machine gun (Gympi)
Head-Shed Headquarters
Int Intelligence
Loadie Crewman on RAF military flight
LUP Lying-up position
Magellan Brand name of GPS
MSR Main supply route
NBC Nuclear, biological and chemical
OC Officer commanding the squadron
OP Observation post
PNG Passive night goggles
PSI Permanent staff instructor

REME Royal Electrical Mechanical Engineers
Rupert Officer
RTU Return to unit
RV Rendezvous
SAM Surface-to-air missile
Sangar Fortified enclosure
Satcom Telephone using satellite transmission
Shamag Shawl Arabs use as a head-dress
Shreddies Army-issue underpants
SOP Standard operating procedure
SP Team Special Projects or counter-terrorist team
SQMS Squadron Quartermaster Sergeant
SSM Squadron Sergeant Major
Stag Sentry duty
TACBE Tactical rescue beacon
TEL Transporter-erector-launcher vehicle
U/S Unserviceable
VCP Vehicle control point

Weapons

203 Combination of 5.56 calibre automatic rifle (top barrel) and 40mm. grenade launcher below
.50 Heavy machine gun
66 Disposable rocket-launcher
GPMG 7.62 medium-calibre general purpose machine gun
Minimi 5.56 calibre machine gun
M19 Rapid-fire grenade launcher

Acknowledgements

I wish to thank the following:

Duff Hart-Davis for all his encouragement, patience and valuable time that he spent on this project.
All my family and friends for the patience and understanding they showed me throughout this whole adventure.
My editor Mark Booth and his team at Random House for their help and hard work.
Jeff Pope and Paul Greengrass at LWT for the initial debrief.
Last but not least Barbara Levy my agent for pointing me in the right direction.

War Dogs

To Judith
For whom every day is a battle . . .

Chapter One

... and for the price of a plane ticket you find
yourself in some hostile country; where even your
'friends' treat you with suspicion and you know,
only too well, that you are expendable!

No way was this decrepit old Trislander, with its misfiring
engines producing puffs of smoke, oil and occasional flames,
going to be able to land intact on that short piece of corrugated
earth beneath us.

I knew it, the men around me knew it, but the pilot – a veteran
crop duster from Indiana, USA – simply didn't seem to understand the problem as the plane just kept going down, lower and
lower; clipping branches with its spinning wheels as he aimed
through a minimal gap in the tangled trees.

The ground was coming up fast now and the pilot sweated
hard; peering as if hypnotised through the filthy, bug-splattered
windscreen. His gum-chewing jaws had ceased their rhythm
whilst he held his breath; juggling levers with the precise abandon
of a true professional. Suddenly he exhaled and leaned back in his
sheepskin-covered seat as his feet did a little tap dance on the foot
pedals. We were going in.

The impact was violent as he dropped the crate vertically from
about ten feet, braking immediately and causing the plane to
snake frantically and for a moment uncontrollably over the rough
ground. No room for any mistake; the forest was straight ahead
and getting closer, fast. We weren't going to make it, and I'd left
my rosary at home!

The stench of burning rubber from the locked tyres filled the
aircraft, and in a gut-wrenching moment it skidded in a tight arc
and shuddered to a gasping halt. We'd arrived ... Just another
day in the life of a mercenary on his way to work.

Silence and more silence. No one spoke, no one moved, not
even a sigh of relief. It was a time for patience. The action would,
no doubt, come later.

The soft drone of a distant vehicle started the darting eyes.

1

Everyone looked at everyone else, questioning with no voice. Friend? Enemy? How would we know until it was too late?

A battered Range Rover pulled into the clearing, followed by an open lorry filled with tough-looking men who dispersed before the vehicles had stopped, surrounding the aircraft with grim expressions, cocked weapons and itchy fingers. We looked out of the windows, searching for a familiar or friendly face; seeing nothing to calm our churning stomachs.

Kit chuckled. 'It's OK, lads, they're friendly. Just a welcoming committee.'

The tension evaporated like steam from a kettle as we clambered out to back-slapping, handshakes and bear hugs.

This was the Republic of Albania, whose ethnic groups claimed descent from the ancient Illyrians, Greeks and Romanians. In 1967 the country closed all mosques and churches, banned organised religion and declared itself to be the 'first atheist state', but the fact remains that 70 per cent of the population are active Muslims, sympathetic to the plight of those being persecuted in neighbouring Yugoslavia and willing to assist anyone prepared to fight for their cause.

Albania is a land of erratic mountain ranges, gnarled, twisted ravines and thick, impenetrable forests, an almost ideal spot for the start of a covert recce into war-torn Yugoslavia by the small group of mercenaries – assisted in these early stages by our Albanian Muslim 'friends'. I had just come along for the ride, to take a few pictures, write a few words – and was rapidly beginning to wish that I hadn't!

We stood and watched as the old aeroplane coughed and restarted its engines to begin a futile attempt at ungluing itself from the bumpy ground. It roared and whined, rattled and revved, starting its staggering run-up to take-off. After what seemed only about a hundred metres it was away; climbing steeply, almost vertically, clear of the threatening trees. The pilot looked back over his shoulder in triumph. His shining-teeth smile said it all.

We all climbed into the already overladen truck, our destination unknown, to begin the bumpy, dusty, scary trip. Through villages, over skinny mountain trails, across bridgeless swollen rivers until finally, and not a moment too soon, civilisation appeared in the guise of a group of military-type huts in a clearing. The convoy slowed and we knew that this was home for a while.

We clambered down from the lorry, throats parched, eyes filled with prickly dust, hair matted, coughing and spluttering – glad to be anywhere as long as the ground wasn't moving. The group that had met us moved off without a word, and we were left alone to contemplate; but not for long. A tall, grey-haired man with an upright military bearing emerged from one of the huts with two companions, his hand outstretched in welcome. A brief hand-shake and Kit, our group leader, was led back to the hut, leaving the rest of us once again in silent contemplation.

Studiously avoiding eye contact, I casually gazed around at my resting 'comrades', none of whom – with the exception of Kit – I had met before. They were a mixed bag – a 'wild bunch', more like raggedy-assed outlaws of the American West than soldiers. The style of dress was varied and interesting, if a little weird, with personal preferences obviously much more important than any resemblance to military convention. Camouflage prevailed from a wide range of countries: US tiger stripe from the Vietnam era and British NATO DPM dominated, with a little Italian, German and Russian thrown in for cosmopolitan effect. One member was dressed dramatically in black from head to foot. 'Looks intimidating, dunnit?' he commented, adjusting his rather fetching over-the-shoulder shotgun belt. Berets with SAS, Para and Foreign Legion badges, and of course the inevitable bandannas, adorned shaven heads. Bodies bristled with grenades, and numerous pouches carried whatever the owner felt was necessary for his comfort and survival. It was easy to imagine we were on a film set, waiting for the director to cry, 'Roll 'em!'

Pete was lazing against a wooden crate, pale, taut and muscular. He obviously kept himself very fit but was tense and not inclined to small talk. He must have been about forty-five years old, but it was difficult to be sure. He moved young but his eyes were stagnant pools of decay.

Jim was the talker, chattering on endlessly to bored faces showing no sign of interest. 'Well I says to him, sod off, I'm not paying that. So he says, what will you pay? I says, twenty bucks and he says, OK. So I bought this Rolex. It's the real thing ... Look!' Nobody was taking any notice of him, but off he went again without taking a breath. 'How much bloody longer do we have to wait?' He was very twitchy as, still yakking, he passed cigarettes around.

Steve declined with a curt 'Enough ways to die without those things.' He was a strong, proud man, composed and together. No doubt very capable in an emergency. His sand-coloured beret bore the insignia of the SAS – not that that proved anything, of course.

Kit was unflappable. He smiled a lot and never stopped moving. For a big man he was light on his feet and could easily keep up with the whippets of the group. Originally from Newcastle, he'd been around the block a few times, learning about war the hard way, with a warm gun and little else. Kit had become a friend in the past few months, and was trusted and relied upon by all. He'd been in this dodgy 'volunteer' business for a long time and was respected by the men under his command. An essential ingredient for a mercenary leader: stripes and pips didn't mean a damn thing with this lot . . . believe me.

Then there was the kid – they called him 'Sprog'. Everyone liked him; perhaps because he didn't play the tough-guy role like most of them. The kid came from Warrington and was about eighteen years old. This was going to be his first taste of action and he was trying hard, but seemed totally confused about everything; especially why he was here.

Mick was standing apart from the rest of the group. Full of manic self-pity and explosive language, he was bitter about something, anything – everything. It was difficult to warm to him, so nobody bothered to try. 'Life's too short to dance with ugly women' was Steve's reason for ignoring him.

Nigel wandered back from the tree line where he'd been relieving himself. He was the odd one out, well educated and from a wealthy background. Apparently a month ago he had been caught reading the *Times* by one of the group, but was converted now and took the *Sun* – because the paper was softer. He used to be an officer in the Guards until something went wrong and he left in a hurry. Now he was a mercenary . . . nobody knew why.

There was an older guy who for obvious reasons was known as 'Pop'. He was a little mature for a mercenary, late fifties, maybe early sixties. Pop had seen it all and just didn't care any more. He waited, sipping dark rum from a GI water bottle, eyes flitting around the forest perimeter, just in case . . .

Four of the team kept to themselves. No names were given.

4

They were Australian Croats and had returned to the mother country 'just to help out'. An exception to the rule that only money can buy loyalty.

It was an odd feeling to be simply a 'spare part', with no practical function, and although the 'professionals' were amiable enough, there was always a degree of suspicion and doubt in their eyes. Some were open in their conversation, others guarded and hostile.

It was not a comfortable wait, and I was grateful when Kit returned with our Muslim contact. It appeared that the function of our team was to undertake a recce of Mostar airfield. The objective was simply to check out the movement of military aircraft and personnel. Engagement was to be avoided, if possible. It was a 'sneaky beaky' recon operation, loved by all, judging by the smiles and nudges.

Happy days were here again. My companions were now electrically charged by the news, travel weariness and boredom long gone. Apocalyptic events were about to take place and the group was metamorphosed – action and excitement were the very life blood of the mercenary soldier. That was what it was all about ... and the money, of course.

Weapons were selected from the back of a covered jeep. Maps were pored over, with great emphasis being placed upon the trig points which clearly indicated mountainous terrain. Escape and evasion techniques were discussed and argued about. Money in the correct currency was allocated, together with maps, radios and compasses. Everyone was apprised of the purpose of the mission. Kit made it clear that the whole exercise was covert. The Bosnians and Croatians were allies at this time, both fighting the Serbs, but they were unaware of our objective and would therefore be just as big a threat to its success as the JNA. 'So be careful, lads,' was his pointed recommendation.

As most of the journey would be taking place after dark, one man in four was assigned passive night-vision equipment, 'Big one' and 'Big two', products of the famous German optical company, Leica. This type of equipment uses a single image intensifier tube to amplify naturally occurring residual light from the moon and stars, and because the goggles can be strapped to the user's head, the hands are free at all times for more important things. Infrared systems are for use inside a building and are

5

rarely employed in external situations where their location can very easily be detected and tracked, with unpleasant results.

The meeting was now coming to its natural close. The intense focus of the men had begun to wander and serious questions were being replaced by the usual banter of men anxious to get on with it.

Kit sighed in a resigned manner and looked around the group. 'You're just a bunch of fuckin' assholes. If you mess this up, I'll shoot you myself.' He said it with a smile, but you could never be sure with Kit.

The forest was dense, dark, forbidding; thick with sounds and then, in an instant, silence. Leaves dripped with perspiration in the struggle to breathe clean air; smells invaded the nostrils like musty unwashed clothes. The dazzling flicker of laser-like shafts of daylight soundlessly blasted holes through the canopy of rotting vegetation, temporarily blinding anyone foolish enough to look upward.

If I concentrated, listened carefully, I could feel the invisible life surrounding us, hear the trees growing and the pulsating hearts pumping blood through the veins of thousands of insects, reptiles and animals. Tree trunks, vines and horrible twisted, sticky growths grabbed at us with threatening gestures as we sliced a trail with our swinging machetes.

'You've got to look through the foliage,' I was told, 'not at it.' I never learned how, but my more experienced colleagues had trained and finally mastered this essential woodland fighter's art.

All this – and a human enemy too.

Twenty-six boots mulched a trail through the droppings of a million animals as we tramped single file for about two hours, until dusk turned rapidly into inky darkness and spooky sounds. A suitable clearing was located and we bivvied down for an uncomfortable night. With adrenaline now used up, weariness took over, and within minutes the camp was silent as we slept with apparent disregard for the enormous snakes, spiders and bats which I was convinced were waiting to devour us.

We were awakened in the damp, chilly morning by the comforting sound of the Rolling Stones' 'Jumping Jack Flash' all tangled up with machinery noises. It took a while for us to figure out that the music wasn't coming from our camp. Even though we were brain dead, logic prevailed. 'Don't move,' someone hissed. Nobody moved. Kit and Steve, by some unspoken signal, slid away towards the sound and disappeared into the undergrowth. Within minutes they returned, grinning from ear to ear. 'It's all right, children, our transport has arrived.'

No more than 150 yards from where we had slept was a narrow road, cut through the forest and invisible from the air. The music was coming from the radio of what can only be described as a vintage farm lorry, being driven by a young boy hardly big enough to see over the steering wheel. He looked about eight years old and by his broad smile we could tell it was all a bit of a joke to him. The radio continued to blast out its message of joy as he beckoned us into the back, which was full of pig shit, chicken feathers and other disgusting things which we all tried hard to ignore. The smell was unbelievable. After a while, Pete located its source.

'Oh Christ,' he moaned wearily, I'm sitting on a dead sheep, and the bloody thing is crawling with maggots!'

As there was no room for him to move, the rest of the journey was spent trying to stop them crawling all over him. To help pass the time everyone joined in the hunt. They move fast, those little white wriggling buggers.

It was an easy trip to Pulaj. Our rendezvous point on the Albanian–Yugoslav border was close to a convenient estuary where, according to Kit, Muslim contacts would be waiting for us. I did wonder why we had taken such a tortuous route to the coast, but when I asked, Kit told me to mind my own business; in a friendly way, I hasten to add.

Our new mode of transport was lying there waiting for us in all its World War II glory: a battered old ex-Royal Marine 'rigid raider' – a steel-bottomed inflatable boat – with a pitifully small, rusty outboard motor which looked destined to cause trouble. The craft, measuring some sixteen feet by six, was hardly big enough for the group, but otherwise ideal for the task.

Kit had calculated that it would take about three days for the coastal trip, then a fast 'tab' to reach our destination at Dugi Rat, about fifteen kilometres east of Split. The whole boat trip would take place only at night; during the day we would come inland and rest up. It would be fatal to travel in the craft by daylight. We would make an excellent target, with little opportunity of evading attack from the shore or the sea, and if hit carrying all of the spare fuel required, we would stand a nil chance of survival.

It was still very early in the morning, and the world was poised and expectant as we tried to make small talk over coffee with the three Albanian contacts. They told us how grateful they were that we would be fighting for them against the hated Serbs, voices rising in hysteria as they glared at one another, then finally running out of conversation and mumbling to themselves. The mercs, most of them experienced in this type of thing, showed little emotion. The simple fact was that they didn't really give a damn. Muslims today, Africans tomorrow ... whoever paid the best.

Our biggest problem at the moment, and one that needed immediate attention, was Pete: he stank! With the odd maggot still dropping from the folds of his clothing, and bits of flesh and skin welded to his new Para jacket, he was a mess and something of a liability. If we could smell him, so could anyone, therefore it became necessary for him to be the first to have a dip in the Adriatic. This and a thorough soaping made him just bearable to be around, although for the next week, even with your eyes closed, it was possible to tell when he was within ten feet.

We had a lot of time to kill before nightfall. Ever since the plane had landed east of Shkodra, we had all been subjected to a series of stops and starts, and here was another one. Small irritations could become big ones under such circumstances, if not dealt with or avoided. So we played cards, drank gallons of tea and listened to lunatic conversation. The planned helicopter flight from Split to Mostar became the main target for the banter, especially as this appeared to be something of a Mickey Mouse operation – judging by the logistics so far. Volunteers to kick-start it were selected by the size of their boots, or by who had experience with radio controls, and comments about the probable mental or visual limitations of the pilot were endlessly thrown around until everyone fell silent, realising that the best course of action was sleep; who knew when the next opportunity might come?

Chapter Two

They do not solicit sympathy or expect gratitude.
Nor do they seek respect, honour or fame. Life is
simple for the mercenary ... Full payment for
services rendered – on time! And you can forget the
flags, medals and trophies.

Kit woke us at dusk as a slight sea mist offering excellent cover began to engulf the shore. It was time to 'cam up'. Some did it themselves, others let a partner cover the areas of the face that would shine in the moonlight. No one spoke. We were finally on our way. The raider was slid into the sea and we all clambered in as it settled in the water, a little low for safety. Someone murmured, 'I hope the bloody sea ain't rough,' voicing everyone's thoughts at that moment.

The coast of Yugoslavia, between our departure point and our destination, has about six lighthouses to protect its shipping. These were an obvious hazard to us, and great care would have to be taken when we came within range of the powerful beams. Kit selected Molunat as our first lying-up point. This meant passing lighthouses at Ulcinj and Budva, and two at the estuary of Boka Kotorska. All went well on our first night at sea. The engine behaved itself, and the first day was spent on a shale beach surrounded by steep cliffs, with no chance of a surprise attack from the land. For which we were all extremely grateful.

By now we were well into Yugoslav waters, which presented another problem. Serb patrol boats made continuous passes over this area, and moved quickly. At the speed our overladen craft could travel we would stand no chance of outrunning or outshooting them, so avoidance was the only weapon we had, a sobering thought as we tried to make ourselves comfortable on the gravel and pebble beach.

We all awoke at different times throughout the day, and for different reasons; by mid-afternoon everyone was up. Unnecessary moving around was frowned upon, so murmured conversation seemed the only way to pass the time. Kit, however, had other ideas.

9

'Don't just sit there playing with yourselves. Strip your fucking weapons and don't forget the copper slip.' He glared at Mick, Pete and Sprog.

'Copper slip?' Sprog mouthed silently in Pete's direction.

Pete threw a plastic bottle of lubricating solution to him without a word, and started checking his own AK-47 magazine to make sure that it contained only twenty-nine rounds instead of its full capacity of thirty – leaving an empty space at the bottom for dirt and general debris to collect.

'After you've done that, check your water bottles and see that the fucking radio batteries are fully charged. Then make sure your FFDs – first field dressings – are kept in the same place on all of you. I don't want to be hunting around for them if you get hit.'

After an hour of feverish activity, Kit still wasn't satisfied. 'Let's see your morphine and syringes; check your boot laces for wear and replace them with paracord if they're iffy.' Then, turning to Sprog, 'Get rid of that bloody chiming wristwatch.'

Sprog took the watch off and started to tie it around his neck with paracord, like the other men.

'No. When I said get rid of it, I meant ditch the bloody thing. If it starts chiming at the wrong time we're all in trouble.'

Sprog looked at him in dismay, but thought better of starting an argument, burying the watch in the shingle without saying a word.

Kit drew us together for further advice on the rest of the trip, pointing out that the next phase was likely to be the most hazardous. We would soon be entering the stretch of water known as 'bomb alley', on our way past Dubrovnik, an area of constant bombardment from the offshore Serb fleet and retaliation from inland Bosnian artillery. Muffled booms of heavy artillery opened up in the distance as he finished the lecture with a smart-ass 'I told you so' expression on his chops.

The rest of the day drifted past with only a small rockfall to break the monotony. Just for a moment there, we thought that we had been sussed from above: weapons were cocked and hearts started pumping as we craned our necks to look up the vertical cliff face, expecting the worst. We had nowhere to run on that small shale beach, not even a boulder to protect us. We froze: nothing happened. Jim started to giggle with relief; Steve told him to shut up, then everyone started to laugh as a large bird flew out from a ledge about halfway up the cliff face.

Daylight merged into dusk, and as night-time approached we started to organise ourselves for the second phase. Kit was very quiet, gazing out to sea, checking the sky and looking at his watch. We were all ready to go, but there was a problem. It may have been an ideal night for lovers, with a full moon and twinkling stars, but for a group of mercenaries on a 'sneaky' mission in enemy territory, it was most certainly a no-no.

Bomb alley was no place to be on a night with such visibility, and Kit wisely – we all agreed – decided to stay put. We did what all good soldiers do on such occasions: we got our heads down.

The early-morning rain awoke us this time. Some of the men had had the common sense to bring Gore-Tex waterproofs; those less organised had to make do with bashas to keep out the downpour.

It was a miserable way to spend the day, which seemed to go on endlessly. Manic Mick had obviously decided that Sprog was going to be his entertainment for the day, and kept throwing pebbles in his direction and needling him mercilessly until we'd all had enough.

'For fuck's sake, leave the kid alone,' Pete spat at him.

'Mind yer own fuckin' business.'

Sprog moved away from Mick and crouched by Pete for support.

'Gutless little bastard. If you want to be a soldier, you've got to be a man first.'

'What, like you?' Sprog muttered.

'What was that?'

Sprog turned to face him defiantly. 'I said, *like you!*'

'Yeah, that's right, virgin. Like me.'

'What have you ever done that's made you a man, apart from killing unarmed people in Africa?' Sprog knew he'd gone too far, but he couldn't back down now.

Mick leapt to his feet, his face contorted in fury. 'You cheeky little git, I'll have you for that.'

'Sit down, Mick, and shut up! You asked for it, now leave him alone or we'll break your fucking legs and leave you here to rot.' Steve had slowly edged between them, towering over Mick and staring at him menacingly. The combined force of everyone's malevolent glare finally did the trick, and Mick sank into a moody, face-twitching silence for the rest of the day.

As darkness fell, the downpour continued unabated. The

11

temperature dropped dramatically and the very real possibility of hypothermia became a serious threat to our soaking-wet bodies. Sprog and Pop had already started to show signs; shivering uncontrollably, with vacant expressions and difficulty in concentrating on the most simple tasks.

'Exercise is what you need; a bit of paddling will do the trick,' Kit said as he rubbed his stiffening hands together before joining us to drag the raider over the slippery pebbled surface into the cold, unwelcoming waves. The conditions were ideal for concealment, and would no doubt reduce any serious activity at sea from the Serb frigates and the inshore artillery.

The little engine did its best to get us out from the shore, aided by some furious paddling. It spluttered for a few heart-stopping moments, but with a few friendly words of encouragement – most of them with four letters – it manfully beat in time to our fluttering pulses as we hugged the coast to Cavta, looped away from Dubrovnik and chugged back inshore to Lopud, the first of many small islands. We had survived bomb alley unscathed and could watch with detached awe the sky being illuminated by the spasmodic bombardment.

The next and final lying-up point was going to be one of the small islands between Dubrovnik and Split. We had an almost infinite choice of temporary resting places, although some care was required. Many of the 'landlords' would be Serbs and would not take too kindly to having us as guests. Everyone was pleased to set foot on shore once again; sailors we weren't. We were cold. We were wet. We were tired. The raider was dragged ashore, which wasn't easy, as by now it was full of water. Nobody cared any more. It was nearly daylight and time for some desperately needed shuteye. Most of the group slept through the entire day, waking only to the smell of cooking. Not the smartest thing to do under the circumstances, but hot food can make all the difference to morale, and on some occasions the risk is justified. We stuffed ourselves with sausage and beans, anxious to be on our way, and still chewing dragged the boat into the sea. We were now only a bob and a weave away from Dugi Rat as we slipped around the eastern side of Hvar island. The lighthouse at Sucuraj, a potential hazard, was non-operational. Perhaps a casualty of the offshore bombardment – a bit of luck at last.

We followed the coastline tightly, passing what had once been holiday beaches at Tucepi and Baska Voda. Even in the darkness it was possible to see the deep craters in the sand and odd bits of suspicious metal lying about, where only a year ago children had laughed and played whilst their parents lay soaking up the sun.

The raider chugged around the final bit of coastline, entering the cove at Omis. Kit whispered, 'Cut the engine, we'll paddle the last few kilometres. No talking.' The prearranged truck was waiting for us and we were greeted without warmth by four heavily armed, shemagh-adorned Muslim soldiers, complaining in an agitated manner that we were a day late.

We tried a quick burst of '*Kaka ste?*' – How are you? – but only got stony silence in return before the little guy with the scar over his left eye started rattling on and gesturing at his watch. Nobody was in the mood for criticism and it all got a bit heated as we dragged our tired, stiff bodies over the rough ground to the truck and slumped into the back. As we were covered by a tarpaulin, we could hear them muttering at us in the now familiar phrase, '*Ye benti peca matarina*' – roughly translated as 'Piss off, mother-fuckers.' The vehicle lurched away, its crunching gears only adding to their irritation.

The trip was about twenty kilometres, just about bearable under a tarp with twelve men who hadn't washed for a week. Even after three days at sea, Pete's relationship with the decomposed sheep was still apparent, and revolting in such close proximity.

Our arrival at Split airfield was met with great excitement. We were ushered into a small hut on the perimeter and offered meat and beans mixed together in a large encrusted pot, with great hunks of bread to soak it up and a vicious rocket-fuel drink of rakia to help wash it all down. The Muslim people are unable to keep anything secret, and within moments, heads were popping through the doorway of the hut to look us over.

The rakia, combined with weariness, started to take its toll, and we would have loved to have been able to get our heads down, but it was not to be. The pilot had arrived and was anxious to show us his new toy, which, much to our delight, wasn't the relic we'd feared. A Soviet Mil Mi-8 HIP helicopter stood on the runway, fully armed with eight pods of 57mm rockets. The only flaw in its immaculate bodywork was an exquisite line of ventilation holes, running from the pilot's cockpit side window along the cabin, stopping just before the external fuel tanks at the rear. Another few inches and the helicopter would have been just a flaming ball in the sky. We clambered in, spreading ourselves loosely around the twenty-eight-seat chopper as Zlatco, our pilot – renamed 'Zippo' by Jim, because, like the lighter, he seemed very reliable – gunned the massive five-bladed rotors.

The helicopter had been pre-warmed, and as soon as the blades dropped into their 'whump whump whump' rhythm he quickly climbed away, savagely veering east to our intended landing point somewhere in the Valley of Imotski. His enthusiasm for the task of flying us over this treacherous territory knew no bounds as the HIP dipped and climbed over the mountains and forests below, hugging the tree line in an attempt to avoid detection from the radar at Mostar. We drew a little small-arms fire over the front line of Imotski which sounded like someone hammering on the outside of the chopper – in all probability from Croats, unaware that they possessed a helicopter. Zippo told us in his fractured English that only three days ago they had used SAM missiles to knock out two of their own MiGs, captured from the Serbs a few weeks before at some cost to life. Zippo was very philosophical about it, muttering, 'Ah, the fortunes of war,' before tailing off into silence once again.

The trip was mercifully short. Fifteen minutes of roller-coaster ride after a meal and the rakia could have been something of a problem for our already sensitive stomachs. But before anyone could embarrass themselves, we had dropped into a small clearing, hovering a foot above the ground. Zippo was gesturing wildly for us to disembark through the already open doors – he wasn't going to hang around and risk damage to his new toy.

The Valley of Imotski – no man's land. The heavy rain would help us by covering the sound of our arrival, but it was still wise to get clear as fast as possible. The area was technically unoccupied, but groups of Chetniks were known to roam here, doing just about what they damn well liked. 'Evil people,' was Kit's comment. 'Big hairy bastards, like mountain men. Really evil.' The Chetniks – or White Eagles, as they were called by the locals – were responsible for most of the massacres taking place, and were feared and hated by just about everyone in the country.

Without further discussion we gathered our gear together and legged it for about seven kilometres, following the contour of the hills to avoid detection, finally locating a suitable lying-up point for a breather and to check our position on the map. It was decided that we should 'basha' out at this point for the day and get some much-needed rest. We were about thirty-five kilometres from Mostar airfield, and it was going to be busy from now on, with no time to relax until the recce was completed.

The following night we moved about twenty-three kilometres, dropping Jim, Nigel, Mick and Pop at the first lying-up point, each with a radio and spare batteries.

'Check the radios first and let me see you do it before we go. Communication is vital and don't forget it.' Kit was insistent.

Mick, still not over his recent humiliation, growled a reply. 'We all know what to bloody do, Kit.'

Pop banged the radio on the heel of his palm. 'Bloody light's flickering.'

'Give it here,' said Nigel. 'It's probably a dodgy connection.'

He examined the battery, scraping the connections with the blade of his Swiss army knife, and tossed it back to Pop. 'It's OK now. Seems like some sea water got in, so keep your eye on it.'

Kit gave them a sweeping glance before grabbing his bergan. 'OK then, if everything's checked, we'll move out.'

We'd all cammed up ready and moved stealthily forward a further eight kilometres to discuss the overall plan, making this the RV – rendezvous-point. It was agreed that the E&E – escape and evasion – plan, if necessary, would be a bluff attempt at convincing our captors that we were the UN and had lost our bearings. We had all been allocated 'liberated' UN armbands, and Kit had made sure that the team was now carrying European FN rifles, instead of the preferred AKs, to substantiate the story. The major flaw in this plan was that we would also be carrying explosives, grenades, timers and claymores, not exactly what you would expect a peacekeeping force to have in its possession. Ah well, no plan is perfect. Ask General Custer . . .

Three of the four Australian Croats and Sprog were left at the RV. Instructions to protect the area with claymores were given, and a code of two radio clicks for incoming, and a reply of three if safe to do so, was agreed.

The close observation of Mostar airport would be undertaken by Kit, Pete, Steve and Ivan – the fourth Australian Croat, who, like his comrades, was a deserter from the Australian artillery.

Mostar airfield, used as a civil and military base, was situated south-west of the town and just off main route seventeen, leading to the coast. We were approaching it from the west side and had heavy woodland to contend with, plus the distinct possibility of mines and perhaps roaming Serb patrols. The night was cold and progress agonisingly slow. Everyone wanted to get to our destination as quickly as possible. Get it over with and get out. Sounds – any sounds – made us flinch, pausing until the source was located. We would move forward on our toes like military-booted ballet dancers, tense, looking down for trip wires, up and back for the enemy, occasionally getting slapped in the face by branches springing back, wanting to strike out in frustration. We must have had about two kilometres to go to the end of the tree line when Ivan froze, wobbling on one leg, the other poised in the air.

'Kiiit!' he breathed in a drawn-out gasp. 'I can see some string.'

There it was sure enough, the dew lying white upon its surface, a length of cord far too thick to be invisible, leading to an unsophisticated but effective booby trap. A wooden spike had been driven into the ground with about three inches protruding above the earth, and the charge, rather like a larger version of the old pineapple grenade, was attached to it. The thickness of the trip wire had saved us this time.

From here on in, we would have to be ultra-cautious. Kit chose not to disarm the booby trap, marking it with a small piece of white tape instead. Should patrols be checking their traps, to find them disarmed would give away our presence. We found only one other, and this was dealt with in the same manner.

We approached the tree line with some relief and were met by the unexpected smell of cooking. Steve moved ahead to check the source, whilst the rest of us kept well back. He returned within minutes with the glad tidings that there was a Serb post dug in outside the perimeter, fortunately some way from our position and no immediate threat. Kit and Ivan left us at the tree line, taking passive night-vision equipment, grenades and their FNs, crawling out into the exposed ground between the woods and the perimeter fence. Thankfully the immediate area was long grass, making their initial foray difficult to detect.

As they disappeared into the night, we settled down to wait. It was nearly three a.m. when they returned; two hours had passed surprisingly quickly. Kit was excited, we could tell. He said nothing at that point, merely beckoned us back into the woods, covering the same route as before to enable us to remove the white tape from the trip wires and cover our tracks. When we arrived at our RV he couldn't stand it any longer.

'Would you fucking believe it, there's three bleedin' gorgeous MiG-21s on the runway, all tooled up. We've got to give it a go.'

'I thought this was only supposed to be a close OP recce, Kit?' Pete reminded him. 'We're not getting paid for taking out MiGs, are we?'

'Yeah, I know, but it's so easy. Although there's a load of mines around the place and probably some roaming patrols in the woods, the actual perimeter fence is unguarded.'

'What happens if it all goes wrong?' Pete said flatly.

'It won't fucking go wrong, you miserable sod. The MiG-21s are only about fifty metres inside the perimeter fence, fully armed and ready to go, with loaded twin-barrel GSh-23 cannon and bloody vicious-looking AA-2 Atoll air-to-air missiles. It's a fucking gift, man!'

It was decided that it would be worth our while to take a pop at them. The pompous military terminology for this objective would be 'a target of opportunity'. Kit just thought that it was a bloody great idea.

But there was a problem. Due to an oversight on the part of our beloved leader, or a sodding great cock-up, depending upon your viewpoint, it was discovered that the lads at the lying-up point, some twelve kilometres back, still had the timers. There was talk of lynching, but it was decided that Kit was more use to us alive than dead . . . though only just.

'So who's going back for the gear then?' Kit looked around at three men suddenly afflicted with deafness.

'It's a fucking long way, Kit. Through all of those mines and the Serb patrols. What's it worth?' Pete was on the hook.

'Booze, bonus, or no stag for a month. Take your pick.'

'How much bonus?'

'A ton.'

'Nah, it's too risky for a ton.'

'OK, my final offer. No stag for a fortnight and a ton.'

'You're on!' Steve jumped to his feet.

'Hang on a minute, I'm doing the negotiating,' Pete pointed out irritably.

'I think you'd both better go, just in case of aggro. Split the cash deal, with the pair of you off stag for two weeks. OK?'

By now, the darkness was evaporating. Speed was vital, and without any further delay Steve and Pete slipped away into the forest gloom, leaving the rest of us to plan the attack for the following night.

They arrived back knackered with the equipment, which had been modified by a friend back in Britain from video recorder timers, with a booster enabling a twelve-volt charge to be transmitted. The units were made waterproof by encasing them in Tupperware containers, and sealing the wire entry holes with Plasticine. Very hi-tech.

Kit had explained the plan of action to us in their absence. The timers would be buried or stashed at the rear end of the jets and set for a one hour forty-five minute delay, allowing us plenty of time to make our escape before all hell broke loose. Thirty kilos of plastic explosives would be used, adequate for the job, he said – without conviction.

Admitting his lack of knowledge of aircraft construction, Kit reasoned that the weakest part of the aircraft was probably the belly. This was where the main charge was to be set, with additional small charges beneath the fuel tanks. The plastic explosive would be held fast by masking tape, which would overcome any tendency for it to fall off in a change of temperature. The charges would be linked by detonator cord to each aircraft. With just one detonator, all of the aircraft should go up at the same moment. Kit was no explosives expert and admitted that it was 'a guessing job'.

It was daylight by now and we all fell into a fitful sleep, waking to the heavenly sound of rain. Nice noisy rain to deaden and cover our tracks.

The final brief was given. Two men stayed at the RV and six went out this time. Four remained at the perimeter to provide back-up if necessary – with limited resources, essentially the twenty-round-magazine FNs and grenades. Kit and Ivan would cut through the perimeter wire, enter the compound and lay the explosives. Everyone cammed up, checked equipment and moved out, faces set in grim determination.

It was an almost ideal set of circumstances as Kit cut through the wire fencing: pitch dark, pissing down with rain and the enemy loath to expose itself to such unpleasant conditions. The MiGs, sleeping menacingly in the torrential downpour, waited to be destroyed. It was a laborious process, taking longer than anticipated. The masking tape would not stick easily when wet, the plastic explosive kept slipping from their hands and it was difficult to find things when they were dropped. There was a moment of panic when one of the hut doors opened and a shaft of light cut through the black compound, momentarily exposing Ivan in its glare.

'Jeezus, that's fucked it,' Pete breathed through clenched teeth, easing his safety catch off in readiness.

We literally held our breath, willing the gods to intervene.

Both men froze as a Serb soldier scuttled across the runway and into another hut, causing yet another blast of unwanted illumination. With both doors open at the same time it would only take a glance in their direction and the game would be over.

The second door slammed as he sprinted back with his head down, carrying a bottle of something. A burst of laughter greeted him as he entered the first hut, closing the door behind him. Darkness again, soft, friendly, safe blackness. We could complete the task and set the timers.

Kit and Ivan slipped out through the fence, tying the previously cut slit with paracord, and joined us back at the tree line, nodding to indicate that all was well. We were in a hurry now; the job was completed and everyone just wanted to get out as fast as possible.

Steve went ahead, slowly picking his way through the undergrowth, the last man removing the white tape from the trip wires. We made no sound as a Serb patrol suddenly appeared to our right. I think we all saw them at the same time, stopping dead in our tracks as they moved past us talking in hushed whispers. We waited. How far would they go? Would they come back? As soon as they were out of earshot, Kit held a brief discussion on whether we should compromise our position by killing them.

'This is a bit fucking dodgy. They're gonna slow down our retreat if we've got to worry about avoiding them, but if we kill them, there's no way we're gonna be able to get away with the UN scam if we're stopped trying to get back through Croatian lines.'

Ivan shook his head. 'It doesn't feel right to kill them. The noise may attract attention anyway.'

'You're right. Let's sit it out for a bit and see what happens.' Kit had dropped back into his military training mode: if in doubt, do nothing.

We waited impatiently for twenty minutes, at which point the patrol returned, passing us in a line on its way back to base. We had made a wise choice.

The RV was approached with the two click, three click code.

Little conversation was necessary as we bundled the gear into our bergans and headed in the direction of high ground some distance away to watch the effects of our work. We had almost thirty minutes to spare as we nestled down low in excited anticipation. Kit checked his watch continuously as we all stared in the direction of Mostar; licking our lips, drumming our fingers, waiting ... waiting. First there was a dull thud, followed by another in quick succession. A pause drifted into a muffled roar, and then it happened.

The explosion was like a hundred separate orchestrated sounds, exquisite to hear, wondrous to behold. Three fully armed jets with full fuel tanks don't go quietly. They light up the night and just keep on blasting. I swear the ground shook as huge balls of flame erupted into the low sky. Oily smoke swirled and mingled with already ominous clouds as the overheated ammunition – sounding like giant firecrackers – cut through the dense forest air. The sheer power of the destruction held us spellbound in frightened awe. It would continue until the jets were simply piles of twisted and charred metal. And all this devastation from a plastic Tupperware box. You'd better be careful next time your wife goes to one of those parties!

I looked across at Kit. He was sweating, the beads of perspiration running down his face and mingling with a look of angelic contentment. The Australians said nothing, simply shaking hands and nodding. Pete muttered a hissing 'yesss!' as Steve gave a mock salute to the dead and dying, inevitable in the midst of that carnage.

We broke radio silence for the first time, contacting our lying-up point with the brief message that we were on our way back.

The tab back to the Croatian lines was uneventful, although great care had to be taken as we got closer. It would have been an annoyance if anyone had been killed by our allies at this late stage of the game.

Now amongst a friendly force, with the past days of tension behind us, Kit suggested that rest and recuperation were called for, and a ride to Split was arranged in a military police lorry. With the help of the Croatian-speaking Australian, Ivan, and a little bit of wheeling and dealing.

We arrived at the prestigious Split hotel where the manager, who seemed to be expecting us, handed Kit a bulky envelope containing thirty thousand Deutschmarks – roughly ten thousand pounds – which were furtively counted in the corner of the reception before being distributed to eager hands. After a quick drink at the shiny, chrome-plated bar, the thirteen of us, raggedy-assed, in filthy clothes, faces covered in cam, moved into six sumptuously decorated rooms on the second floor overlooking the bay, with smartly uniformed UN personnel as fellow guests in the four floors above us.

We stripped off our gear, leaving it where it lay, and padded into the showers, emerging squeaky clean and feeling a whole lot better for the effort. Then one by one we slumped on our beds for a decent kip, with the sound of exploding MiGs still ringing in our ears.

On our second day at the Split hotel we were approached by a wealthy-looking man with an Australian accent, who told us he was from Posusje. He bought us a few drinks and said that some of his friends were very impressed with our latest job and would like to offer us more work if we were interested. It seemed that news travelled fast. But as I said before, the Muslims never can keep a secret . . .

For the next few weeks we all enjoyed life: no guns, mud or sleeping rough in the forest. The UN had a party every Friday night – to which we were not invited. No matter; with a shave and a smart suit we got away with it for a while before we were found out and barred by the 'Rodneys', who expressed their dislike of the riff-raff element invading their festivities by pointing out that we were nothing but opportunists and military effluent, ignoring us in the corridors and moving away from us in the restaurant.

Shortly after, our group began to break up. Mick went first, and was later arrested for killing someone in a bar-room brawl in Tuzla. Three of the Croat Australians had their own battles to fight and left for the front line a few days after him. We were sorry to see them go, but the simple fact was that we were fighting the war for different reasons.

The wealthy Australian came back to see us again, and now Kit was ready to talk to his new friends. The freelance warrior has to look at all options.

He was taken to meet the governor of the town of Posusje, a man in his mid-fifties, of medium height, grey-haired, with an athletic build and a very dominant personality. His name was Drago. Kit listened to what was said through an interpreter. 'He offered me money to go to his town. His exact words were: "For every task you perform, there is money for you." He told me that funding for weapons and equipment was *nema problema*.'

Kit said that he would think about it and came back to the Split hotel to talk it over with the remaining members of the group and some other British and French volunteers who had joined us briefly in their hunt for the most lucrative employment. Everyone was by now getting a little bored and dispirited by their confinement and lack of income.

A few more days passed in idle contemplation and occasional piss-ups in the hotel bar or one of the many pick-up joints in town. The men lounged around, talking in comfortingly regional accents, from Manchester, London, Wales and Cornwall – but what they said and the manner in which it was voiced caused any thoughts of home and normality to be quickly dispelled.

'How do you know which is the enemy?' I asked; both sides wore the same uniform of the former Yugoslav army. They told me that the regulars wore a full uniform, with distinguishing patches, so that wasn't so bad. The worst were the men wearing tracksuits, who were totally unpredictable and either to be avoided or shot without question. In between were the militia-men, who tended to wear part uniform, but were without any command structure or obvious objective. Most of the time no one seemed to know who was shooting at whom or why!

'It's a bloody mess,' Alex from Manchester muttered softly. 'I've been here six months and I still don't know the difference between Serbs, Muslims, Croats or Bosnians, or what any of them are trying to achieve.'

Silent until now, Mark, from the Cornish holiday town of Mevagissey, spoke. 'I've only been here for five weeks. I couldn't get a job at home and always fancied being a merc, so I bought a plane ticket to Split and then hitched a ride to Zagreb. I asked around the place and a taxi driver directed me to the army headquarters at 25 Ilica. I told them that I had no military experience, but that didn't seem to matter. They gave me an old uniform, a rifle, a thousand rounds and six grenades; then I was taken to the front line.'

His voice tailed off and I waited for him to continue, but he didn't. So I asked what had happened at the front.

'I couldn't understand a bloody word that was being said,

22

nobody spoke English, and on my first recce things went wrong . . .' Mark stopped in mid-flow and looked at the others.

Alex shrugged his shoulders. 'It's OK, tell him,' he said.

'Well, I was sent out with another Brit "volunteer". He was from London, a bit of a cockney clown. We were in single file going through the woods and he was in front, walking along without a care in the world, not with caution, not with care, fooling about with a boogie shuffle walk, waving his AK-47 in the air to imaginary rock 'n' roll music. The track curved and he disappeared for a moment . . . then I heard a "whump" sound, it was sort of muffled and he started to fall. I thought, silly sod, he's tripped over, but he was flying through the air like an enormous doll all covered in red stuff. I couldn't believe it. I yelled out, calling his name, screaming his name, but he didn't answer, he just lay there jerking and spitting and gurgling soft pink milk-shake bubbles. I was terrified. He just stared at me as if I was to blame, but it wasn't my fault he'd stepped on a mine. I stood there, I wouldn't go close, couldn't go close, his legs were gone, his arms were gone. I stopped screaming, he stopped gurgling. It was all quiet. But his eyes still stared at me through his blackened, charred face, his hair and clothes still smouldering. Stupid bastard, my brain told me as I turned around and slowly walked back. I didn't look over my shoulder, not once . . .'

Mark started to sob softly and turned away. Nineteen years old, and the memory will stay in his subconscious forever. He had relived his nightmare as the rest of the men had no doubt relived theirs.

Later, we talked of the atrocities that some of the newcomers had witnessed, this time without the machismo that is an integral part of mercenaries' personal armour, but instead with anger, horror and fear. Even these professionals did not understand the reason for the mutilated bodies with hearts and ribs wrenched out, arms and legs hacked off, eyes gouged with red-hot pokers. It was the way that children had been treated that got to them most.

'Can you fucking believe these crazy bastards? I saw a kid of about six. The same age as my daughter. They'd shoved a grenade in her mouth and pulled the pin. Her pregnant mother was dead by her side with her stomach sliced open and her unborn baby lying by her side in the dirt,' Alex spat.

'Why do they kill the old people? I can't understand why they kill the old people,' Billy, another recent arrival, said. 'I saw one two days ago who'd been garrotted and thrown in a pit. She looked like my granny. The bastards had even taken her false teeth out.'

'Who are they?' I asked. 'Serbs, Chetniks?'

'They're all the bloody same,' Kit replied distantly. 'It's just that some are worse than others.'

Death and injury they accepted, but this! They talked of men who had had their testicles hacked off and pushed into their mouths.

'Why do they do that?' Billy broke in again.

'It's because Muslim men are circumcised and Serb men aren't. So the simplest way to find out if a man's your enemy is to make him drop his pants and have a look at his dick. If it's been skinned, then . . .' Kit tailed off, further explanation unnecessary.

Before or after death? No one wanted to know the answer to this question.

For the mercenaries, every day was different, every week and every month brought tension, boredom, panic, madness. But it was like a drug, the catchword was 'buzz'. If you asked any of them why they did it, they would tell you that 'half the time we don't get friggin' paid'. They admitted that they didn't make good civilians, so what was left? Just the buzz, it seemed, a day's work doing what they liked doing best.

A decision had to be made, but it wasn't easy. Pete, Jim, Steve and Nigel wanted to take the offer. Pop and Sprog weren't so keen. Meanwhile Kit was approached by yet another anonymous character in a grey business suit. This time the deal was a short-term job leading a team in the northern town of Osijek, some three hundred kilometres away from the luxury of the Split hotel. This temporary 'gig' was accepted as a means of earning some fast money whilst mulling over Drago's long-term offer.

Chapter Three

... And few are immune to the 'Genghis Khan'
image of themselves as the invader. Conqueror and
slayer.

Sprog and Pop had decided to stay behind in Split for a while, joining us later in Osijek. Their intention was to bum a ride in a UN chopper out of Split airport – easy to do; most UN pilots were easily bribed with a CZ 9mm handgun.

Their decision was based upon utter laziness. This breach of etiquette was discussed in their absence, and in a heated exchange it was agreed that the matter was serious enough to be considered 'desertion in the face of the enemy' – a grave war crime, and, in accordance with the rules of warfare (mercenary version), punishable by a fate worse than death.

Kit had decided that it would do them good, and be a test of their skill under fire, for the management to discover that the rest of us had departed without paying the bill. It would be interesting to find out when we saw them next how they had dealt with the problem. Anyway, they should have come with us, shouldn't they?

So, as the seven of us stole out of the hotel in the early hours of the morning, Pop and Sprog were left snoring in their cots to await the wrath of the management.

Creeping along the corridor in single file to exit through the rear window of the hotel like naughty schoolboys, we had difficulty stifling giggles at the ridiculous spectacle we must have presented: grown men, clad in camouflage gear and big boots, mincing along on our toes. Getting through the small window was in itself a test of military ingenuity, as we silently passed weapons, ammo and bergans to Nigel, who dropped them to a waiting Ivan. It all went beautifully, and why not? They were, after all, professionals at getting out of dodgy situations – referred to in the textbooks as escape and evasion.

We had to do it this way; the bar bill alone would have taken all of the money earned on our last job!

We tiptoed across the crunchy gravel of the hotel drive and threw our stuff into the 'pinkie' carefully parked on a slope the previous evening in anticipation of the plan. Still giggling, we clambered aboard. 'Everybody in?' Kit whispered urgently. We looked around. Nigel was missing.

'No Nigel,' Steve replied.

'Where the fuck is he? Somebody go and find the useless bastard!'

Steve and Jim slowly uncoiled themselves from their cramped positions on the mound of equipment in the rear and started back towards the hotel just as a shadowy figure appeared carrying a large square object under his arm.

'Where the hell have you been?' Steve hissed at him. 'And what the fuck is that?'

'Nothing,' Nigel replied as he pulled himself into the vehicle. 'Sorry to keep you waiting, lads.' He turned to a smouldering Kit waiting at the wheel and with a supercilious smile, available only to ex-Guards officers, said in his cultured tone, 'You may drive away now, cabby.'

The steering wheel started to buckle under suppressed homicidal inclinations. 'Later,' Kit said, 'we'll have a chat about this later, you stupid prick!'

This was no time for a showdown, so with a gentle push from Jim the Land Rover was rolling and we were away. Leaving Sprog and Pop very much in the shit . . . we all hoped.

Our destination was Osijek, some three hundred kilometres north-east of Split – as the crow flies. But there was a problem. Isn't there always? Just about every kind of enemy imaginable lay in the area of central Bosnia and the chances of us all surviving the trip were slim. So Kit had concluded that the scenic route was best.

We would head west along the coastal road, with the sea on our left and the rolling fields on our right. The downside of this detour would be an extra three hundred and fifty kilometres. With seven men and their gear jammed into the Land Rover, it wasn't funny any more.

The air was heavy with a smouldering ground fog – a consistent feature in Croatia – as we trundled out of town and picked up the main Adriatic road, settling down to a boring, uncomfortable drive to the next town, Sibenik, approximately sixty klicks away. It was still too dark to see anything, so we all simply sat, staring blankly into the solid mass of mist, while Kit, his face tight up to the windscreen, attempted to keep us on the road.

Shhhhiiit! Flump, flump, flump. We all heard the rhythmic sound of flapping rubber and felt the lurch of the Land Rover as its front end slewed drunkenly to the centre of the road. Just thirty kilometres west of Split on the coastal road to Sibenik; a flat tyre and no bloody spare. Not a word was spoken. The resigned expressions said it all . . . it was a bit of a bastard.

Cigarettes were shoved despondently between pinched lips in anticipation of divine intervention. We waited, but nothing happened. The pinkie just sat there lopsided. Collective deep sighs broke the silence as it became evident that someone in this group of lazy sods would have to get up off his ass and do some work. The question was, who?

The ciggy butts were flicked away, curving tracer arcs in the sky, as Kit stared with dull eyes around the desolate countryside. 'Anyone in the AA?' The humour was strained; nobody responded.

We slowly clambered out and looked at the guilty wheel with absolute hate. The tyre was shredded, impossible to repair. Pete passed the information on to an agitated Kit, still gazing at the expansive countryside with little interest in the view. We could tell that his brain was refusing to take it in.

The cause of the blow-out was not obvious; no glass or uneven surfaces were apparent and as we had not been travelling fast at the time, why the hell had the tyre shredded? The answer came quickly as the red-clay roadside started to spit angrily upward. It took a while before the team had logged the reason for its agitation . . . but it was simple once you knew.

We were being attacked by someone, somewhere. Out there in the hills some unfriendly bastards were shooting at us, and we hadn't done a thing to irritate them . . . yet.

There wasn't much cover. In fact there wasn't any bloody cover, so we dived back in the Land Rover as Kit forced it to hobble erratically down the road. Swerving to avoid a hit wasn't a problem; the car had developed its own evasion tactics as it swayed and hopped away from the ever-advancing spray of bullets, its now buckled wheel gouging a deep trough in the dirt.

It's an odd fact that missiles have a different sound when they are after you; ask any soldier and he will tell you the same thing.

27

They sound vengeful and persistent. Just like a swarm of wasps that have decided that you are the one with the jam tart and they are going to have some. We all felt like that at this moment; exposed and vulnerable. The enemy was invisible but he had decided that he wanted us . . .

The windscreen splintered, and there was a dull thud as a round dug deep into the door pillar. Another one followed, spraying glass everywhere. They had our range now and the small-arms fire might well be followed by mortars. A mortar hit would wipe us out in a second; there was only one thing to do: ditch the Land Rover and run for it. 'Hold on!' Kit screamed as he swung the wheel and rolled the car off the road and through a hedge into an adjoining ploughed field, bringing the Land Rover to an abrupt halt as we scrambled out.

Never one to forget his early training, even in the heat of battle, Kit then uttered the immortal word used in so many famous military manoeuvres: '*RUN!*' Steve pointed to a copse about five hundred metres to the left, which seemed like a good idea. So with heads down we staggered towards it, carrying our weapons and extra ammo across the undulating ploughed field as the purple-red tracers peppered around us, getting closer by the second. Thank God nobody was hit; with all that slipping and sliding over the rough ground we must have made lousy targets, anyway.

Time for a collective nervous breakdown. We were trapped. And they, whoever they were, could now do whatever they wanted until we got ourselves sorted out.

'Follow the tracer.' Our bloodshot eyes watched the graceful curve of the incoming shit until we had sorted the position of our attackers. 'Look! To the left of the farm. In the depression. Can you see it?' Yes, the mist had cleared enough. We could all see it . . . Now what?

'Right, lads. We'll go and do them, shall we?' Kit was smiling. He does that kind of thing.

'Pete, Jim, you two man the AKM. Give us cover. Straight down the line. And lay it on heavy.' Looking at me he said, 'Stay still, keep your head down and shut up!' I could handle that.

'Ivan, you go with Steve to the right. Nigel you're with me. OK, Pete, lie flat on your back and feed . . . Now do it!'

The AKM was set up on its tripod and blasting in bursts of three at the source of the incoming. Boom-boom-boom . . . pause.

Boom-boom-boom . . . pause. Kit and Ivan grabbed some grenades and a couple of 66 rocket launchers, crawling out to go their separate ways in the general direction of the source of trouble.

The onslaught became sporadic as the enemy kept his head low. The men zigzagged across the open ground. Three hundred metres is a long, long way to run – especially with a hangover!

I just had to look up . . . carefully. In time to see Nigel trip and fall to the ground. Within seconds he was up again, hopping and scuttling like a demented rabbit across the uneven earth. He arrived at Kit's side as they both took cover behind a mound of earth. Kit looked over at Ivan and Steve, also safe behind cover. A quick wave and they were off again, darting, diving and rolling in the ploughed field as our AKM kept up its staccato bursts of covering fire.

Sudden silence. A nervous wonder-what's-going-to-happen-next stillness. We should have known. Whump! Whump! Fucking mortars. That's what's going to happen next. Christ! I hate bloody mortars, they just come out of the sky at you and blow bits off your soft, warm body.

Their aim was off. Thank God. Obviously the AKM fire was making them keep their heads low and it was all guesswork, but they could still get lucky.

I looked up again. There was dense smoke coming from the depression. A phosphorous grenade had been lobbed in by Kit or Nigel. That was the signal to stop firing. Kit and the rest of the lads were going in for the kill and didn't want to be hit by our covering fire. The clattering burst of an AK-47 on full auto drifted back to us, followed by a shrill scream that went on and on and on, echoing across the murky countryside as it slowly trailed away.

Pete continued to reload the AKM magazines as we waited blindly for the outcome. Brother, were we in trouble if the lads had blown it!

'Come on, you Geordie git, stand up.' Jim was getting anxious. 'What the fuck are they doing over there?' We could see nothing. The rolling mist had returned like a blanket, muffling all sound and reducing vision to a little over a hundred metres. We strained our ears and three pairs of eyes tried to bore holes into the nothingness. We were getting more than a little concerned when a slight movement to the left caused us to dive for cover.

The figure was unmistakable. Emerging from the spooky grey mist loomed four ghost-like characters from a Wagner opera, led

29

by one Christopher Freeman. They arrived back at the copse looking totally knackered. It was a full five minutes before any of them could give us the story.

There had been three of them. Young, inexperienced and now very dead. They'd been members of the extremist Croatian militia the HOS. 'Cowboys and wankers,' Kit commented. 'They deserved to get it.'

There had been no reason to attack us. We were not their enemy. Kit had tried to explain this to the remaining live member of the group. But he had become offensive and had tried to grab a weapon in retaliation. So he'd had to die with his comrades. 'They won't listen, these kids. All they want to do is dress up in black jumpsuits covered in bloody stupid badges and kill people.' He showed us a British army commando knife and a knuckle duster, taken from one of the bodies. 'Look. Kids' stuff. Straight out of fantasy land.'

We wearily gathered our gear together and headed back to the Land Rover. Nigel was moaning as he limped along, dragging his right foot. Apparently he had been hit in the heel, and although the bullet had passed cleanly through the skin it had ruined his recently purchased American Danner boots. 'They cost me one hundred and fifty quid, guaranteed waterproof. Now they're crap . . . The bastards!'

'Serves you bloody right. If we hadn't been delayed by you at the hotel the whole thing wouldn't have happened.' Kit's logic prevailed and Nigel fell silent.

The Land Rover looked kind of forlorn with its front end buried in the field. It was no use to us now and its demise gave us yet another problem to contend with. Transport for seven men, six weapons, ammunition, seven bergans, claymores and ancillary equipment, and it was still only five a.m.

Somebody had to say it. 'What are we going to do, Kit?' It had to be Jim. He never knew when to keep his mouth shut. Kit didn't answer.

'Kit, I said, what are we going to do?' You could feel the heat.

'I'll tell you what *you're* going to do, my son. You're going to get us some transport.' Jim looked along the straight road in both directions. Nothing. Not a movement, not even a bicycle.

'How?' he asked in a small voice.

'Well, my son, you'll just have to walk back to Split and hire something from Hertz, won't you?'

'You must be joking. There is no bloody way I'm walking back to Split. It's Nigel's fault, you said so yourself. Make him go back!'

Kit shook his head. 'Don't be a dipshit. Can you see Hertz letting you have a car looking like that? Now shut up and let me think.' He sat down and let out a sigh. Things were not going too well and the sky was getting lighter. Soon the main coastal road would be busy with all sorts of people – some might even be friendly.

'Somebody make a brew.' Ivan foraged in the back for the cooking gear and dragged out a square cloth-covered bundle; the cloth slipped to the ground, revealing an elaborately framed painting.

'What the hell is this?' The question was directed at Nigel. It was the parcel he had carried out of the hotel.

'That, dear boy, is a painting.'

'I know it's a bloody painting, you sherbert. What I really meant was, what is this bloody painting doing in the back?'

'It's mine.'

'You mean you stole it from the hotel.'

'Well . . . I liberated it. They obviously didn't know what it was. Otherwise they wouldn't have hung it in the corridor.'

'OK, smartass. What is it then?'

'It's a Renoir. An original, worth thousands of pounds.'

'Bollocks! Who the fuck is Renoir?'

'A French impressionist painter.'

'You mean you jeopardised the whole trip for this piece of rubbish?' Kit got to his feet and walked over to Ivan, looking at the picture with some interest. 'Look, we haven't got time for this now. Chuck it in the back. If he's right we split the money. If he's wrong . . .' The threat was left hanging in the air as the sound of a vehicle approaching took precedence over the proceedings.

It was a BOV-M, an armoured patrol vehicle, available to the federal army, the Yugoslav militia or anyone else who could steal one. This one might have been sent out to check on our recent firefight, or perhaps was just on early-morning patrol. Whatever the reason, it seemed wiser to keep our heads down and hope that the crew didn't notice the hole in the hedge. The APC lumbered past without so much as glance from the observer and sped on its way in the direction of Split.

Our brew was ready and the business of the painting was forgotten for the time being – it's all a matter of priorities. At this

31

moment the most pressing consideration was transportation. We still had a long way to go and hitch-hiking was most definitely not an option.

Steve looked at his watch for the tenth time. We had been waiting for over an hour. A few small cars had passed, Renaults, Fiats and the inevitable VW Golfs. None was large enough for our requirements.

'How about another brew?' It was Nigel this time, no doubt feeling bad about his role in placing us in this predicament.

'Oh, go on then,' Kit replied in a resigned voice. 'Only one sugar, I'm slimming.'

Everyone was thoroughly pissed off by now and it showed in the pile of dog-ends littering the field, and in our twitchy behaviour. It wouldn't take much for someone to start a punch-up. Thank God Mick wasn't with us any more. He'd been a surly bastard at the best of times and would have been unstoppable by now.

Kit drained the last drop of his tea and climbed to his feet.

'Look, we're going to have to leave the Land Rover, so sort out the gear and leave anything we don't need. Pete, you come with me. I'm sick of waiting around like a vulture. Let's go and get something.'

Pete grabbed his AK. 'Forget the gat. We'll stand out if we carry guns. Let's go. If we're not back in an hour . . . wait. Forever if necessary.'

They slipped through the hole in the hedge as the rest of us started to sort through the gear. Less than a minute later they were back, smiling. 'There's a non-military lorry coming from the direction of Sibenik. It's ours. I don't care how you do it, but get that bleedin' lorry.'

It was easy. Six men in DPM, faces covered in camo cream and brandishing automatic weapons, will tend to focus anyone's attention, even in Croatia. The lorry driver stopped. Steve waved a gun in his direction, indicating our wish for him to exit the vehicle. He did so, very quickly, and knelt in the road expecting the worst. I guess this sort of thing happened all the time. They dragged the frightened old guy into the field and threatened him with the internationally understood finger-slicing-the-throat sign. He nodded his head, and was still nodding it as Pete tied his arms and legs with paracord whilst we threw our gear, including the painting, in the back and drove away in his rusty old lorry. We were on our way once again.

There was a cold wind blowing from the sea and it soon became pretty uncomfortable in the open back as we tried to cover ourselves with the bergans and some sheets of plastic. Kit, Steve and Pete kept looking back through the cab window with self-satisfied smirks on their ugly faces as we lopped off the klicks on the final stretch of the road into town. We were all bloody hungry by now. Nobody had eaten, washed or shaved since last night, and a proper break in a civilised place was very appealing.

That was before we saw two bloody great rock-filled trucks blocking the road. It was the ZNG – paramilitary national guard – well tooled up. They would no doubt be very interested in an old lorry overflowing with weapons, ammunition and six foreign soldiers of no fixed abode.

Kit pulled to the side of the road. We needed to get a story going, and fast. Kit got out, and under the pretext of checking the load started telling us what to do – apart from panic, that is.

'Look, lads, we've got to stop, there's no choice. We'd never batter our way through those lorries, and even if we did they've got MG-42s. They'd cut us to pieces. I'm going to bluff it out. If it goes wrong, you're on your own, OK?' He got back in the cab before any of us could reply. It didn't matter. What could we have said?

The last few hundred metres were the worst. Click, click, click. We could hear the safety catches coming off as we approached the checkpoint. The lorry hissed to a halt and Kit, together with the Croat-speaking Ivan, climbed out of the cab, their faces wreathed in warm, friendly smiles.

'*Dobro jutro*, gentlemen. *Da li govorite engleski?*' Kit was formally polite as he tried out his limited Serbo-Croat, withdrawing his ID card and a letter from the governors of Zagreb which explained our role as 'volunteers'.

The ZNG guys didn't seem in the slightest bit interested in the paperwork as they climbed over the truck, examining the bergans and equipment. 'Down!' The order was barked by the one with the most badges. We obliged, and huddled in the road. Our furtive eyes locked on to the menacing machine guns. 'Where are you going?' The question was addressed generally. Nigel started to answer but was cut up by Ivan, who replied in Croatian. The officer smiled – a good sign?

'*Da!* The women, eh!' The smile disappeared. Sod it! I'd thought things were looking up.

'Why have you so much equipment and so many weapons if you were only in Split for the women?'

Ivan didn't pause for a second as he rambled away, laughing and gesturing at the rest of us standing there without a clue about the direction or the content of the conversation. We smiled back at the officer.

The two soldiers had completed their examination and returned to the captain. They went into a huddle. The atmosphere had suddenly become tense. Kit looked around at us all, his expression clearly saying, 'Cool it.'

As the captain returned to our group it became apparent that his manner had changed, yet again. He stood in front of Steve and looked him up and down, focusing on the pistol in his belt.

'Ah! A Skorpion. Nice pistol. It is new, is it not?' Steve looked at the officer and then at the rest of us, a resigned expression on his face. He handed the gun to the officer without a word. It was wheeling and dealing time.

Two of the soldiers worked their way around us like professional pickpockets at an outdoor market, pointing at wrists and hands with murmured demands concealed as comments. 'Nice watch . . . good ring . . . pretty chain.' All were handed over with ill-concealed contempt. It was over in ten minutes. We had been picked as clean as oven-ready chickens.

We all felt like shit as we climbed back on the truck. Losing the stuff didn't really matter. None of us would carry anything of value in a battle zone anyway. It was just the knowledge that we had been treated with disrespect that rankled.

The incident was not mentioned again. Everyone seemed embarrassed about the whole episode, and there was little conversation as we arrived in Sibenik without any further problems.

The newer part of Sibenik suffers a little from ugly high-rise apartments and an air and sea-polluting aluminium smelting plant. But it's a quiet town . . . at this time of the morning anyway. And that was all that mattered just then.

A big breakfast of eggs, sausage and some kind of ham at the Restaurant Mornar on Ulica Vlade Perana, and a wash and shave made us all feel a hell of a lot better. Not difficult in our current state of low morale. We ate and cleaned up fast, anxious to be on our way to the next town, Zadar, about sixty kilometres west.

Zadar was, according to Kit, 'like the OK Corral'. A comforting thought, and one that we could have done without.

'All aboard for the magical mystery tour.' Jim was cheerful as we walked back to the lorry, parked out of the way at the rear of the empty vegetable market. We obviously didn't want to draw any more attention to ourselves than was necessary.

The tired old engine finally started with a moan of anxiety, anticipating the long drive ahead to our ultimate objective, Osijek. A few gear crunches from Pete and we were off again, heading out of town on the Ulica Borisa Kidrika and feeling a whole lot more human.

Soon we were outside the town and on the open road once again. 'Keep a sharp lookout. Scan the hills and the road ahead. We don't want any more surprises.' Kit didn't need to give us this advice. Nobody wanted another working-over like the last one.

The wind had now dropped and the last of the ground mist was evaporating rapidly, leaving us with a bright, crisp morning. The clear air had exposed the sparkling sea and the clean, open countryside. Large roadside signs still displayed messages to overseas visitors: 'Welcome to paradise', 'Enjoy our beaches', 'Come back again'. The sun shone on the beaches of Murter, Drage and Biograd, which lay to our left bordering the peaceful Adriatic Sea. Not so long ago the now shrapnel-scarred motel at Pirovac had been full of happy tourists and happier Croats. Would they ever return?

Who could forget this genocidal war? The tourists might. But when your local postman runs around with a blazing Kalashnikov, killing women and children, and the dentist organises nighttime raids on the homes of the old and infirm, how can things ever return to normal? Yugoslavia is dead and so are most of its people. Just look into their eyes!

As Zadar appeared on the horizon we congratulated ourselves on an uneventful trip. There had been sounds of sporadic firing on occasion, but always in the distance; nothing had occurred to threaten our current good humour.

We knew it couldn't last. On the approach to the outskirts of the town two ominous-looking Ladas were parked across the road. A smoking Simca lay in a ditch with its engine still running. We could just make out some tracksuits lounging against the cars, cigarettes hanging from their arrogant lips. This was trouble for sure, and Kit, who was in the back with us this time, clicked off his safety catch and told the rest of us to do the same. It was too late. As we approached, six more tracksuits appeared from the roadside ditch to our left and right. This was an ambush, and we were in it.

The lorry slowed to a halt at the checkpoint and we could now see that the driver of the Simca was still in his car. He was alive, just, and covered in blood from dozens of bullet holes. It was all over for him as he waited for the end to come.

The tracksuit boys were jumpy. 'Papers!' Kit did his friendly smile act once again and handed them the ID and documents. 'Out!' We all gathered by the roadside in a group.

This time it was different. They were agitated, in a hurry. We were obviously professional soldiers, a problem to be disposed of, fast.

The leader was about twenty-two years old and spoke English with an educated accent. Conning this guy wasn't going to be easy.

'What is your business here? *Gdje idete?*' Where are you going?'

'We are from the UN,' Kit replied.

They sniggered and told us to turn out our pockets. 'Hurry, hurry!' They were strung out, probably on something.

'You have few possessions for members of the United Nations,' the leader commented sarcastically. 'Are you poor people? No jewellery. Cigarette lighters. Watches.'

His sneering manner was beginning to piss Kit off as the abuse continued and he started to jab him in the chest. Nigel and Steve were edging slowly back to the lorry when we were all told to kneel down. This was getting silly. The lorry was full of weapons. They knew it, and we knew that they knew it. They also knew that if push came to shove we would go down fighting. These men don't like fighting – just killing. There's a big difference.

'Catholic or Muslim?' The leader was off again, cocking his AK-47 as he waited for an answer to the irrelevant question.

'Fuckin' atheist.' Steve had had enough. The point of no return had been reached. The tracksuits looked to their leader for guidance. The next move was his.

None of us actually heard the trumpets as the cavalry arrived in the guise of a German TV van, closely followed by a car full of American journalists. Within the space of a few seconds the road was full of cameramen and guys scribbling in notebooks. We were suddenly forgotten in this photo-opportunity. The tracksuited militiamen preened themselves, looking suitably tough for the camera. They became expansive when asked what they considered their role to be in this war. They were eager to impress the world with their importance. We were simply grateful and slipped away with our tails between our legs once again.

Kit was right. Zadar wasn't a town you would want to stay in for a bit of peace and quiet. Splintered glass and bullet casings littered the road, as staccato bursts from automatic weapons, crackling like a Chinese dragon dance, echoed endlessly in the narrow alleys. We could see shadowy figures, armed to the teeth, crouching behind burned-out cars as our lorry lumbered through the side streets on the way into the centre of town.

From our position in the exposed back of the truck, we were aware of rooftop snipers watching our progress with weapons cocked, waiting for a steady target. We covered them as best we could, any moment expecting a grenade to land in our laps. 'Sod this,' Steve growled in my ear as the steady beat of a GPMG opened up from a building to our right.

Kit hammered on the window, gesturing to Pete. 'Get the fuck out!' he yelled, as Pete did his best to make the old lorry do wheelies down the narrow stone streets.

Avoiding the overturned and burned-out cars was an impossible task. Ramming them out of the way was easier but not very comfortable for those in the back, as we were thrown from side to side, making it impossible to track any would-be snipers on the roofs. The whole thing was unreal, like one of those dream sequences you see in out-of-focus existential French films. Our lorry was being ignored as wild-looking people appeared suddenly, as if from nowhere, legs apart, AK-47s firing wildly from the hip at empty shop doorways. Seconds later, others would leap out and fire back, hosing the area indiscriminately as yet another window exploded, spraying glass upward like silver confetti. Nobody wore uniforms or identification of any kind. How did they know who they were firing at? This was Dodge City, and these bloody Croats were gun-crazy.

The lorry lurched twice and headed for the front of the Archaeological Museum. I just caught the sign saying 'Closed on Mondays' as Pete wrestled us back into a straight line again. We looked behind and saw the cause of the bump; two crushed bodies lay in the road.

My attention was distracted by three men thirty-five metres directly ahead in the town square. They were kneeling in the road, pointing a long tube at us and trying desperately to aim it at the bucking lorry. Kit and Steve saw them at the same time and scrambled to a standing position on the swaying floor, opening up with their AK-47s as we thundered towards the square. The whole thing happened very quickly. A sudden whoosh and the air was sucked away as a rocket screamed over our heads. Seconds later, an explosion came from behind us and debris filled the air from a gaping hole in the town's library. Our lorry struck the three men responsible, throwing them like dolls into the gutter.

'Foot down. *Go, go, go!*' Kit screamed wildly as Pete started to slow. 'Turn right and just keep going.'

It seemed that the east side of town was the battleground for today. We hurtled through the winding side streets and out of the town gate, past the archaeological ruins and the mosque. On the outskirts, things became quieter and it was possible to slow down and drive at a less frantic pace as we approached Murvica. Even the buildings weren't as badly damaged as those we had recently passed. But there were no people . . . anywhere.

We were back on the main E65 now, heading north-east for a while through the slightly damaged towns of Policnik and Posedarje until we reached a fork in the road. If we turned right at this point, the road would take us to Karlovac, a mere forty kilometres from the Croatian capital of Zagreb and all the comforts of home with Kit's friend, Tony Abranovich, a colonel in the Croatian army. It was not to be. We turned left. The coastal road was still the safer route. Avoiding confrontations was our objective.

The old lorry was starting to cough a bit, steam coming from its nostrils in short, sharp bursts. Soon we were going to have to ditch it and borrow something else.

Steve was driving now, and as the weather had become warm and pleasant the rest of us were in the back, soaking up some winter sun. The coastal road was fairly straight at this point and it was possible to see many miles ahead, making another surprise ambush or road block unlikely.

We had passed the flat, elongated island of Pag and were

staring out to sea at the rocky outline of Rab island when, with a gigantic hiss of displeasure, the lorry shuddered to a halt, steam pouring from the engine compartment. We were all very relaxed about the whole thing as we climbed down and watched Nigel lift the bonnet and cautiously remove the filler cap. There was little we could do until the engine had cooled.

'Nigel, you and Pete stay with the truck,' Kit ordered. 'You lot, come with me.' He walked the few metres to the beach and took off his boots and socks, rolling up his trousers. 'I'm going paddling. Come on, race you to the sea.'

With that, he was off and running. The rest of us, caught up in the silliness of it all, followed him, chortling, into the waves. We splashed around like kids for about twenty minutes, feeling the anxiety of the past hours lift. It was bloody cold but it didn't seem to matter.

We returned to a muttering Nigel and Pete, who were obviously a little put out at being excluded from this brief moment of pleasure.

The engine had cooled enough for them to examine it in our absence and they had detected a burst hose, repairing it as best they could with the military version of the all-in-one tool kit: wide black 'gaffer' tape. The radiator was filled with water from our canteens as Kit climbed in, eyes lifted skyward in prayer. He turned the key . . . The engine started, running a little unevenly . . . but running.

We moved off slowly, knowing that the repair was only temporary. A new set of more suitable wheels would be needed, and very soon.

The scrubby, desolate but heavily industrialised island of Krk to our left marked the last twenty-five kilometres before we would arrive in the busy and potentially hazardous seaport town of Rijeka. Kit decided that we would skirt the town on this occasion and turn eastward, getting back as quickly as possible on the main E65 leading us into Zagreb. It wasn't quite as simple as it appeared. An autoroute link was under construction, creating havoc with our map-reading. Many of the smaller roads no longer existed. The whole area was a mass of huts, thick, oozy mud, and abandoned earth-moving equipment. None of the vehicles was suitable for our needs – a great pity.

We finally joined the main road at the village of Gornje, about a hundred and thirty kilometres from Zagreb. Between us and our first major stop was Karlovac, the scene of some vicious fighting in the past months. There was no way to avoid it!

It had been a long day. We were hungry, dirty and worn out by the unpredictable events of the past nine hours. The mental picture of Pop and Sprog still living the life of gentlemen in the Split hotel was unbearable. With a bit of luck they had been thrown out or arrested. Even this thought was no consolation as the lorry trundled on.

We were about three kilometres away from the village of Lokve when Ivan drew our attention to a weathered sign off to the left saying 'Autocamp' – holiday camping site. Empty now and a little overgrown, but still looking attractive to our tired eyes, it was set amongst the trees with an adjacent lake and a few log cabins. Close by were the restaurant and grocery store, now fallen into disrepair.

We looked at Kit like puppy dogs begging for a bone. It was pathetic, but it worked. 'OK, let's bivvy down for the night and start early in the morning. We may need our wits about us in Karlovac.' Then he added: 'Check it out first. Every cabin. Every hut. Every bloody thing, mind you!'

Pete, Nigel, Jim and Steve went to work, approaching the buildings stealthily, peering through windows first and then entering with AKs on auto. You can't be too careful. Mercenaries are anyone's target in most war zones, and especially in Croatia. Kit, Ivan and I waited, keeping our eyes and ears tuned for the slightest sound or movement as dusk settled in.

The men returned to the lorry looking very laid-back about it all. 'It's OK, the place is clean.'

Kit decided, however, not to make use of the buildings. He reasoned, against some opposition, that it was wiser to sleep outdoors, amongst the trees, in our bivvy bags. Just in case someone came back after dark. The necessary gear was unloaded from the lorry and we all relaxed, wandering over to the lake to watch the fish swirl and jump as they came up for their evening snack of flies.

'Anyone fancy some fresh fish?' Kit was staring at the silver back of what looked like a trout.

'How the hell are we going to catch enough fish for seven of us? It could take hours,' Nigel commented.

'No . . . minutes. If you don't mind getting wet.'

'Oh yeah. What are you going to do? Tickle them out?'

40

Kit took a grenade from his webbing, pulled the pin, and with a graceful overhead lob threw it into the centre of the lake. A distant muffled road preceded an enormous cascade of water. Within seconds tranquillity returned as the smooth surface was restored.

'Fuckin' hell!' Jim, who had been lighting a fire, stood with his mouth open in wonder. 'That's what I call direct action; and to think I used to sit for hours by the canal at home.'

About three dozen fish floated to the top, awaiting collection by an equally impressed Nigel, already removing his smock for a swim.

Watching Nigel sweep the area, grabbing at the slippery fish, gave the lads some much-needed entertainment. Cries of 'Round 'em up, cowboy!' and 'Plonker' filled the air as he was directed to each fish, plucking them out of the water and dropping them into his knotted string vest.

He arrived at the bank triumphant and deposited his catch at our feet. Some had only been stunned by the blast and were now wriggling in a desperate attempt to escape. These were dealt with and carried to the smouldering fire.

Nigel peeled off his clothes and spread them by the fire as Pete and Ivan set about making a feast of the trout.

'How would you like them cooked, sir?'

'Would you care for a starter?'

'Perhaps sir would like a house vino or a glass of *pivo*.'

The banter continued throughout the meal, the past three hundred kilometres of terror and frustration temporarily forgotten in the pleasure of the moment.

We all helped clear away any signs of our presence and settled down for the night in our bivvies, spread out over a wide area. A guard had been selected by the 'short straw' method of democracy. Steve had lost this time and would do the first four hours. Pete would follow. We were all on our chinstraps by now. Sleep came quickly and was undisturbed.

A thick layer of the dreaded Croatian ground mist shrouded everything when we awoke. From our prone positions it was impossible to see anything. Even Jim, sleeping only about three feet away from me, was invisible, though easy to locate by his gentle snoring.

Movement to my left made me instinctively sit bolt upright. Stupid move. Kit and Ivan were already up and boiling water for coffee. They looked odd, with the bottom part of their bodies lost in the mist. Slowly the rest of the lads woke and crawled out of their bags to a welcome warm drink served up by a serious-looking leader.

'Now listen, lads. The next major town is Karlovac. It's only a few kilometres from the Serbian lines . . .' His voice tailed off until we could barely hear it. 'It's going to be rough, but there's no way we can avoid it. Check your weapons and ammo and keep your wits about you. We'll have to play it by ear. Now load up and let's move out.'

The old lorry didn't like the cold, wet mist. The engine groaned as it tried to turn over, and our hearts sank into our stomachs. On the fourth attempt it coughed and sprang into life, burbling and missing a beat from time to time as we pulled on to the main road. It was still only five a.m., and roadblocks – manned mostly by part-time soldiers who liked their kip – were unlikely to cause any problems for a few hours. Which was just as well, since the mist would make them impossible to see anyway.

The early-morning cold sliced through us all as we sat huddled in the open back. Foot-stamping and hand-rubbing had little effect as we all gradually turned white and then blue.

'Let's get the sleeping bags out.' Jim, at last, was using his head. We unrolled and snuggled into them.

'Course, you're in dead trouble if you've got to get out fast.'

'Shut up, Nigel. Just sit there and freeze your balls off if you don't like it,' said Pete from the depths of his Buffalo bag.

'I was merely pointing out that tactically it's an unwise procedure.'

'You can be a right pompous git sometimes, Nigel.'

Nigel fell silent. A few minutes later he crawled sheepishly into his bag. He was right, of course, but at this moment we didn't want even to consider the possibility of another roadblock.

Kit must have sensed our discomfort as he leaned out of the cab window, turning his head back in our direction. 'We'll get a decent motor in Karlovac, with a heater. Trust me. There's bound to be something lying around.'

It was eighty kilometres to Karlovac, through vast areas of exposed countryside, along endless stretches of straight road offering the sniper a clear line of fire. There would be dangerous bends with unknown conclusions, and the Serbian artillery on our right. We needed something to take our minds off the bitter cold and the feeling that we all looked like rats in a barrel. We really needed a lesson in Serbo-Croat from Ivan . . . didn't we?

It was straight out of *The Sound of Music.* 'Now repeat after me,' he said in a singsong voice.

We looked at him dumbly. 'Oh, sod that, Ivan. Not now, for Chrissakes!' Pete was not amused.

'You will be grateful. It is good to know another language.'

'French, German, Italian, maybe. But not Serbo-Croat.'

'The knowledge could save your life, my friend.'

Jim turned to the irritated Pete. 'He's right. None of us knew what the bloody hell was being said at the checkpoints. Did we?'

Our silence was taken to be acceptance of the impending lesson, and we continued the trip reciting conversational Croatian in unison.

We had driven through the towns of Kupjak and Skrad, with their familiar streets of burned-out and looted houses. Old women shrouded from head to foot in black, like spectres of death, spat and screamed hysterically at us as we passed, collapsing in anguish and frustration as the stones they threw had no effect upon our progress. Because we wore a strange uniform, we were the enemy. In Croatia, everyone is the enemy.

As we approached Bosanci, the stillness of the countryside was being methodically replaced by noise, muffled at first, but becoming distinctively aggressive. Karlovac was now a mere twenty kilometres away.

Sounds of heavy artillery fire register in the stomach and the bowels before the brain.

With Ivan's short language course we were now slightly bilingual, but had mixed feelings about the benefit this might bestow upon our chances of survival as the distinctive howl of a low-flying MiG fighter/bomber heading for Karlovac reverberated in our ears, making us cower in the back of the lorry like beaten dogs.

We were heading into a proper war zone this time. That was what we'd come for . . . wasn't it?

Chapter Four

The men live in a twilight mercenary reality whilst
away from home. A world defined by myth and
splintered militarism. Ideological motivation is not a
prerequisite for the job . . .

A smouldering yellow-grey haze hovered menacingly over the city of Karlovac as our clapped-out lorry crept cautiously along the rubble-strewn streets. The incoming Serbian cocktail of heavy artillery, T-55 tanks and a rocket onslaught from MiG fighter/ bombers had gutted the front-line buildings on the east side of the town. An acrid stench of cordite burned our throats as chaos stared back at us, our tired minds refusing to take it all in.

Waxen-faced bodies lay everywhere. Many had obviously been there for days, judging by the degree of decomposition and the interest shown by packs of starving dogs. A pile of thirty to forty tattered and bloody corpses was stacked untidily against the fractured wall of a restaurant. Vibration from the next bombardment would bring it crashing down, burying the bodies . . . yet again.

The first line of that old Animals song, 'We gotta get outta this place', jammed itself firmly in my mind and ran round and round. I tried to avoid thinking of the second line, 'If it's the last thing we ever do'.

The lorry stopped. Kit and Steve clambered out. The rest of us climbed down, stiff and awkward, to join them by the roadside. Ragged people walked past, glancing at us with blank, zombie-like stares as they carried their few possessions – to God knows where – in prams and wheelbarrows.

A British Warrior patrol car slunk alongside. Its observer gave us a casual once-over and then sped away, uninterested.

'We don't need this. It's not our problem. If we detour around the west side of town and park somewhere we'll miss most of the crap.'

Kit wasn't interested in any discussion on the matter. He, like the rest of us, just wanted to get out. So without another word we all climbed back into the truck and continued weaving through the narrow, debris-littered streets. After about twenty minutes of dodging rubble we pulled up and Kit got out again. 'Steve, you come with me. The rest of you, stay put. Don't get out of the truck.'

They moved quickly away, disappearing into an alley in the direction of the front line, taking their pistols but leaving their AK-47s behind.

The intermittent crackle of small-arms fire somewhere close by caused us to scrabble for our weapons. An instinctive reaction born of suppressed panic. The noise ended abruptly and we returned thankfully to the waiting game.

'Fancy a drink? There's a bar over there.' Nigel pointed to a slightly damaged pizzeria just as a man staggered out and began to weave his way in our direction, collapsing almost immediately before shaking convulsively and lying still in the gutter.

'Two sheets to the wind,' Jim said.

'It's three sheets to the wind actually,' Nigel corrected him.

'Whatever . . . He's pissed out of his skull anyway.'

'So would you be if you had to live in this fucking place,' Pete added.

We lapsed into silence, closing our eyes for a semi-snooze while we waited for Kit and Steve to return.

'Look . . . look!' Pete nudged me awake, nodding his head toward the man's body and pointing to a group of about a dozen rats now slowly approaching the inert figure. They snuffled around him for a few minutes, then two of the larger ones started to crawl over his body, while another moved around to his head and began to lick his mouth. Sucking the alcohol-based saliva, no doubt.

They were nosy little sods, scrambling in and out of his pockets and up his trousers. Some were already nibbling away at his grotty old boots. The rat at his mouth was a big bastard, black and shiny, about the size of a cat. He appeared to be in charge of the operation; the rest just seemed to follow him, keeping a little way behind at all times.

Blacky soon got tired of sucking at the man's mouth and moved on to his nose, nibbling at the nostrils with a lot more enthusiasm. We could see blood and bits of flesh being torn away.

'Christ! They're eating him . . .' Jim choked back his excitement.

The whole thing was getting a bit sick now and we knew that we should stop it, but nobody did.

As we watched, the rest of the rats started to crawl over the

45

body, and in minutes the man's nose and the right side of his face were eaten away. The creatures seemed suddenly to get bored, moving to his hand and starting again. Within seconds the bloody face had attracted large blue flies, unperturbed by the rats – I suppose there was plenty for everyone.

The rats were slowing down. The feverish activity had ceased and they began to wander away with fat little bellies to sleep it off.

As we watched, a dog appeared from an alley nearby and sniffed at the body. For a moment our interest was renewed. The dog cocked its leg up on the fly-blown face, and the hot liquid steamed into the gaping wound that was once a cheek. Then the man moved.

We looked at one another, guilt etched upon our faces, as Kit and Steve, driving a new-looking Land Rover with Karlovac Brigade stickers, pulled up, blocking our view of the body.

No time to think . . . thank God.

They both leapt out of the vehicle. 'Shift the gear over, fast.'

We stood in a line, passing equipment from one to another. Within a few minutes the lorry was empty, Nigel ensuring that his genuine Renoir was stowed away safely.

'Everyone in? Lets go.'

With another Serbian bombardment ringing in our ears we headed north-west. Away from the town. Away from the battle. Away from the sight of that body, quivering and jerking into consciousness.

'Anything happen while we were away?' Steve asked.

We stared at one another with hooded eyes. Pete spoke. 'Nah, bloody boring.' He quickly changed the subject. 'You took your fuckin' time getting some wheels.'

The memory would linger. Best not to prolong it by discussion.

'Where did you get the motor?' Ivan asked a beaming Kit, who had switched on the radio – an added bonus.

'We had to wander about a bit. It's a right mess at the front. Fucking M-84 tanks everywhere, most of them blown to hell. Some silly sod had left this motor with the engine running. It was a gift. Is he gonna be pissed off when he gets back.'

Kit chortled merrily and started singing along with the gypsy music on the radio. He was flying at the moment, high on adrenaline. We all felt relieved to be able to move fast and in some comfort at last.

The 'blitzkrieg' of Karlovac continued as the MiGs swooped

low, cluster-bombing the town. Shells whistled their fluttering chorus overhead, always followed by the dull thumps which precede an explosion. Mortar fire and artillery retaliated, but seemed ineffective in slowing down the incoming barrage.

Groups of soldiers – many volunteers – manned heavy weapons hidden from the air in graveyards and bushes. Some waved at us as we passed. Many would die this day, a long way from home.

'We've got to avoid the main highway now,' said Kit. 'It's about fifty kilometres to Zagreb and a bit of peace and quiet. We'll go through the back roads and head for Plesivica.'

We were soon on the secondary road to Ozalj, after which we turned north-east through twisty but relatively safe lanes. All was calm again, although the battle at Karlovac continued at a muffled distance.

'I'm spitting feathers.' Pete reminded us that we hadn't eaten or had a drink for hours. 'What about a brew, Kit?'

'Yeah, sure. Why not? I think we're out of the shit by now anyway.'

We had just passed Krasic and were approaching some ruins of apparent archaeological interest – judging by the entrance cost. It seemed like a nice tourist-like place to stop and enjoy a cup of tea, amongst the silent pine forests and fast-running streams. Under different circumstances it might well have been.

Folk music was playing softly from the radio as we slumped around the Land Rover, letting our minds wander over the events of the past twenty-four hours. It seemed crazy in retrospect: the changes of fortune; the tension and torment; even the occasional high points – mostly from simple relief at surviving.

How did these men who lived their lives in the murky world of mercenary soldiering manage to retain their sanity? Did the things they saw and did affect them in the lonely hours? Did dark doors open in their minds?

I had asked Kit about this some weeks ago. He had denied having any regrets or hauntings. Later, he admitted to nightmares – on occasions. He also admitted to almost always pissing himself in firefights. 'You canna help it,' he had told me without embarrassment. 'You don't know you've done it until after-wards.'

We washed the mugs and filled our canteens from a nearby

stream of clear spring water, then made ourselves comfortable again in the comparative luxury of the Land Rover.

'Hang on a minute, Kit. Don't you think we should remove the Karlovac Brigade stickers?' Nigel was on the ball. We'd forgotten them.

'Whoops!' Kit grinned. 'Yeah, you're right. Rip 'em off, will you? It could make things awkward with the police in Zagreb.'

The stickers came off easily and within minutes we were away on the final thirty-five-kilometre run into the capital city of Croatia.

The last bit of the trip was over some difficult off-road terrain. The four-wheel-drive Land Rover was a godsend. Many of the smaller lanes and cart tracks were not shown on our maps and we had to resort to the compass on several occasions, often cutting through fields and farmyards. Much to the dismay of the farmers, who probably thought that they were being invaded.

Our first sight of Zagreb was the Sava river, as the ornate shopfronts and Viennese-style buildings of the town began to appear around us. The city had a time-warp feeling about it – lost somewhere in the 1920s, with Mount Medvednica dominating the northern skyline. It was easy to feel that we were arriving at our holiday destination; until Kit broke the spell.

'Right, lads. You can cut out the sightseeing. Our first port of call is the army headquarters at 25 Ilica. We've got to see my friend Tony Abranovich. He's a colonel in the army. You'll like him. He's a little dumpy fella with a ginger beard – looks a bit like Bob Hoskins.'

The military headquarters were in a large grey building only a short distance from the Trg Republike – Republican Square. The building was austere on the outside but with a spacious and impressive interior, where we were quickly approached by two armed military policemen who insisted upon searching us and removing all weapons before asking our business.

The tall, aggressive one spoke first. 'You ... are ... *engliski*?'

Ivan was outside, guarding the Land Rover, so it was down to Kit.

'*Da. Ja sam engleski. Zao mi je. Ne razumijem Croat.*' Yes. I am English. I am sorry. I don't understand Croat.

Kit was trying his best, as Jim whispered the immortal words, 'Didn't he do well!' in his best Bruce Forsyth voice.

The shorter guard smiled and in perfect English replied,

'Trying to speak our language is important, even if you get the odd word wrong. Now, what can we do for you?'

'My name is Freeman and these are my men. Is it possible to see Colonel Abranovich, please?'

'For what purpose do you wish to see the Colonel?'

'He is a friend. We have come a long way to meet him.'

The guards walked a few yards away and went into a huddle. The short one returned as the other walked briskly to the bottom of the grand stairway.

'My colleague will see if the Colonel is available. Please wait here.' He guided us into an adjoining room.

In less than two minutes a small man wearing an American bomber pilot's jacket, with a Browning pistol at his hip, bounced into the room. A huge smile spread across his face as he saw Kit waiting for him.

'Ah, Kit my friend. It is good to see you again. Come, we shall take coffee.'

He ushered us out into the hall and we followed him down a flight of stairs leading to the canteen. Coffee was ordered as Kit and the Colonel swapped stories, Tony Abranovich bursting into high-pitched laughter from time to time.

The good-old-boy stuff continued for about an hour, while the rest of us amused ourselves playing with the pinball machines until we became aware that the conversation had taken a serious turn, now being conducted in conspiratorial whispers. We slowly drifted back to the table. Too late. The deal had been completed.

Colonel Abranovich stood up. 'I will arrange rooms for you in a local hotel.' To the rest of us he said, 'I shall, no doubt, meet you again before you leave. Meanwhile, I wish you a pleasant stay in my city.' He turned back to Kit and with a meaningful smile said, 'No trouble, mind you. I do not control the police, and they are very strict.'

We were left to drink more strong, black, stomach-churning coffee and stare at the ornate ceiling for some time, before a sergeant returned and in poor English tried desperately to explain to a confused Kit the whereabouts in the western part of the city of our hotel.

The high-rise Panorama Hotel in Trg Sportova was an ideal 'crash' for a bunch of unwashed, unshaven slobs. Not too particular, and not far from the centre of town and the night life –

still active in spite of occasional attacks from Serb jets and the odd terrorist bombing.

The sergeant had warned us about sniping. Apparently old women of Serbian descent were often seen crouching in the windows of their flats taking pot shots at passers-by in the street, regardless of their nationality. He also pointed out, glancing at our DPM clothing, that they had a preference for those in military uniform.

All of this was as nothing compared with the horrors of the past few days. We checked the windows facing the army headquarters as we left, though. You can't be too careful.

The feeling of being on a Continental holiday continued as we merrily unloaded equipment and weapons, carrying them a little self-consciously through the lobby and into the lift.

Although it was still only late afternoon, weariness descended on us quickly. Pete and Ivan couldn't stop yawning, and any decisions that had to be made were best left until later. We democratically tossed a coin for bedrooms – two with a view and two without – and lay down on our beds, dirty boots and all. The gentle cursing from Jim in the next room became a lullaby as sleep took over.

'Wake up, you lazy sods!' The bedroom door crashed open. The morning light filtered through our window and with it the sounds of early-morning city traffic, a comforting noise that meant civilisation. It was seven o'clock. We had slept for thirteen hours.

We were up, washed and dressed in our clean camos within ten minutes as an agitated Kit ran round checking on things. God knows what he was checking, but his early military training made it a compulsion.

'Are you all ready for breakfast?' he yelled across the hall. Stupid question. We trooped down to the restaurant, famished.

Ivan asked us what we wanted and ordered in Croatian from a hovering waiter. The normal Yugoslavian breakfast of coffee and rolls with butter and jam or honey was not what we had in mind, and our insistence on *slaninu sa jajima* – bacon and eggs – caused something of a problem to the young waiter, who disappeared for well over twenty minutes while another kept us going with strong coffee.

The greasy bacon and runny eggs arrived, piled high on a large plate. We dived in, ignoring the white blobs of congealed fat. It was worse than Kit's cooking – impossible but true.

Back in our rooms, feeling slightly sick, we were summoned to a keffudle in Kit's room and told of the arrangement with Abranovich.

The man who had contacted Kit in Split had done so at the request of the governors of Osijek, on the recommendation of Colonel Abranovich. We were to have three days' R&R in Zagreb. Then we would meet an American contact, who would take us to the town of Osijek and introduce us to the commander, a Spanish ex-journalist named Eduardo Florez who was responsible for the defence of the town. Wages had been agreed at a converted rate of one hundred pounds a month – plus the odd bonus. Kit looked at the men. 'Is that OK?'

They looked at one another and Pete spoke. 'Not much choice, have we?'

'Yeah, you've got a choice. Don't accept it and go home.'

Kit was not happy with the deal either but there was little he could do about it. No doubt he had tried his best to up the ante, but there were a lot of mercs coming to Yugoslavia and it was a buyer's market at the moment.

'It's only for a short time, lads. Then we're off to Posusje; maybe I can get a better deal for you there. Let's have a show of hands.'

Ivan's hand was the first up. He wasn't here for the money: this was a debt he felt he owed his mother land. Slowly the rest of the men raised theirs. Although they would not easily admit it, money was a secondary consideration to excitement, comradeship and just simply being in a battle zone. As Jim at his poetic best put it: 'It makes you feel alive. Much better than nine to five.'

'Agreed, then?' Kit looked round.

'Yeah,' they all replied in quiet unison.

'Right. The next three days are yours. Relax. Take in the sights and don't get into any punch-ups. I'm going shopping. Anyone want to come?'

Few of us had been to Zagreb before, so we opted to accompany Kit on this first trip into town, keeping a sharp lookout for old women in windows.

Areas of the city were pockmarked with shell fire from marauding MiGs, but the inhabitants seemed oblivious to the damage as they walked the leafy squares and narrow cobbled passageways about their daily chores with a relaxed, unconcerned manner.

We dived in and out of bars, sampling local beers and wines,

51

which did little to settle our stomachs after that breakfast. Ivan caught a passing tram and went off on his own to look up a relative living in the upper town of Gorji Grad, and Pete, feeling more nauseous than the rest of us, decided to sleep it off on a park bench and join us later.

As it was Friday, the Dolac market was in full swing, and Jim decided that he would go and nick something. We asked him what he wanted. He replied, 'Anything,' as he walked away standing out like a sore thumb in his DPM gear.

The remaining four of us wandered around Nama – a large department store – for a while, before deciding that it was time to try some food at further risk to our digestive systems. We looked at menus in the windows of restaurants, finding that food was expensive in most of the better-class places, and finally opting for the Kaptolska Klet in the northern part of town.

The menu was in Croat and the waiters busy with local customers, so we looked for familiar phrases, not wishing to make any mistakes with this our first main meal. Heading the list of food was something Kit recognised, *zagorska krumpirska juha* – hearty potato soup. It seemed safe enough. We ordered it.

An enormous bowl turned up at our table. It smelt good, and though it looked a little dodgy, we attacked it with vigour, leaving little but breadcrumbs on the red checked tablecloth.

Although it was cold when we left the restaurant, the sky had become a clear, unclouded blue, and it was possible to see the mountains in the north without difficulty. Even in these few short hours it was easy to forget why we were here, as we basked in the winter sun in yet another spacious, flower-filled garden on our way back to the hotel.

'Fancy some exercise?' The hotel was set amongst tennis courts, swimming pools and other sports facilities. Kit liked to keep fit.

Steve was keen. Nigel wasn't. I was of non-combatant status; it means lazy. With this lack of support the exercise fanatics decided not to bother at the moment either, so we went back to the hotel for a doze and to await the return of Ivan, Jim and Pete.

Pete was in his room when we arrived, looking rough. His skin was yellow and he was doubled up in pain, sweating heavily as he lay moaning on the bed. The breakfast, or something, had really upset him. It wasn't like Pete to exaggerate a condition. If anything he would play it down.

Kit looked at him anxiously. 'You gonna be all right?'

Pete opened his eyes. 'Yeah. Sure. It's just that bloody breakfast. Never could take greasy food.' He leapt up and ran to the bathroom, retching horribly.

'Shiiit! That's all we need right now.' Kit picked up the phone. '*Da li u hotelu ima doktor?*' Is there a doctor in the hotel?

He turned to us. 'There is a doctor here. He's coming up now. Go and get Pete into bed.'

Pete looked ashen as he hobbled back to bed and collapsed.

'The doctor's on his way, my son. You'll soon be right as rain.'

A sharp knock on the door and the doctor walked in briskly, heading straight for the bed. '*Na sta se zalite?*' What's the trouble?

Kit spoke. '*Govorite il engliski?*' Do you speak English?

The doctor nodded and started to examine Pete, taking his temperature and pressing his abdomen as Kit explained the symptoms.

'It is not serious,' he said finally to a relieved Kit. 'No food or drink for twenty-four hours. Give him this.' He handed Kit a bottle of liquid, waving away an offer of payment. 'Colonel Abranovich will settle my bill. Phone me again if his condition deteriorates. He should be well by the morning. Good day.'

Ivan and Jim arrived almost together and came into the room looking anxiously at the bedridden Pete.

'Has he been shot?' asked Jim.

'No, he hasn't been shot, you prick! It's just a bad stomach upset.' Kit was feeling a little tense after what could have been a minor disaster.

We left Pete to sleep and went downstairs to the lounge for a chat and to learn of Jim's futile attempts at stealing from the market.

'The bastards wouldn't take their eyes off me,' he whined. 'I stood no chance. Anyway, it was a bloody food market. Nothing worth nicking.'

We decided to spend the rest of the day rubbernecking around the city by tram car. We bought twenty-four-hour passes, which gave us unlimited travel for thirty dinars. There were a lot of laughs, and the occasional odd glance at my uniformed colleagues, who were acting like demented kids, hollering at passing girls, jumping on and off trams and other such irresponsible acts resulting from a temporary freedom from anxiety.

As dusk approached, the lights of the city began to change the appearance of the pink and grey buildings. Steve reminded us that we had a sick colleague back at the hotel who might need some help, so we changed trams once again, leaping off almost outside the Panorama.

Pete was sitting up in bed, looking a lot better. The medicine seemed to have worked. The pains had decreased and he was no longer being sick. In fact, he was a little pissed off at missing the day. 'Where are we going tonight, Kit?' He tried to smile.

'You aren't going anywhere, sunshine. You're ill. Maybe tomorrow, we'll see.'

Pete didn't argue. It was all a bluff anyway. He was where he wanted to be, for the moment.

Ivan turned on the radio and tuned it to VHF 90.5, Radio Zagreb. English-speaking programmes were broadcast on this station every day except Saturday. We settled down to hear the news and in a moment were brought swiftly back to harsh reality, with reports of Serbian attacks on towns and villages to the south and further Chetnik atrocities on helpless women and children.

Looking out of the balcony window at this fairy-tale town, it was, once again, impossible to believe that this beautiful country was being torn apart from inside.

Jim, ever sensitive to the plight of others, broke the spell. 'Are we going out on a piss-up tonight, lads?'

'Dunno. Who wants to go out?' Kit didn't seem too keen. He looked around for a response. Nobody seemed eager to leave Pete alone again, so we agreed that tomorrow night we would paint the town. Tonight we would stay in, play cards, watch TV . . . and tell a few lies to one another.

Our evening of domesticity passed pleasantly enough. At midnight we turned in, sleeping soundly as the city grew quiet around us.

The unmistakable sound of a low-flying MiG woke us as it screamed into a fast climb. An explosion followed, then another, and the hotel shuddered. The war was back. It had followed us into our dreams.

Steve and I ran to the balcony overlooking the city, watching early-morning workers dive for cover as another jet came in on a tight curve, hurling its silver-canistered cluster bombs as it blasted away with its cannon; kicking up the asphalt in neat little lines along the main street in pursuit of scurrying citizens.

The rest of the guys joined us, struggling into their clothes as incoming rockets whistled overhead. Crumph! A building was hit less than two hundred metres away. A muffled explosion followed as windows blew outwards and crimson flames stretched upwards, immediately blackening the once crystalline-white stonework.

As we watched, the whole side of the structure collapsed. People with arms waving in panic – as if trying to fly – followed the debris downward as it piled up on the pavement below. There was no movement from the bodies as they lay silent and hideously contorted. No fear or pain on their slackened faces gave any indication of their thoughts in those last few moments of terror.

The attack had only lasted for a few destructive minutes, and now the jets had gone, leaving clean white trails of smoke in the sky and an eerie silence hanging over the city. A lonely bell began to ring from a local church as the people came slowly from their homes and shelters to pick up the pieces once again.

Zagreb had few defences in the early days of the war and was a soft target for Serbian air assaults aimed primarily at the radio station on the mountain peak of Sljeme, with the odd diversion intended to weaken resolve and create fear within the community.

'What shall we do?' Pete had struggled out of his bed and was staring over our shoulders.

Kit shrugged. 'It's not our war, I keep telling you that! We are here to do specific things for sums of money. We do them right and we get paid. We do them wrong and we get killed. The fuckin' Croats don't care about us. It's their problem, not ours.'

Ivan spoke. 'I've got to help them, Kit.'

'Sure, I understand that, Ivan. You're different, these are your people. Go and give them a hand if you want to.'

'Do you mind if I go and help?' Jim was already putting on his boots.

Kit turned to him. 'You're joking? You've never helped anyone in your bleedin' life!' His voice rose as he stared at Jim incredulously.

'I just want to go. That's all. Is it OK?'

Kit shook his head resignedly. 'Yeah, sure. Anyone else for the Florence Nightingale detail?'

'We'll go,' Nigel and Pete volunteered. Steve nodded his head affirmatively.

As Kit looked at them one by one, his face creased into a grin.

'The magnificent fuckin' seven. We're all a bunch of prats. Come on, then.'

The next four hours were spent loading dead and injured bodies into lorries and ambulances and clearing roads of brick and stonework. We were harassed by the plague of cameramen and journalists drawn like flies to areas of devastation, but the Croat people were warm and friendly to us; obviously grateful that foreigners were prepared to be so generous with help in an emergency. No one seemed shocked at the attack on the town, and the whole thing was treated with a strange detachment. They all knew that much worse was happening elsewhere in their country.

The final count was fifteen dead and twenty-three wounded. Two buildings badly damaged and about twelve slightly. It could have been worse. Tomorrow it could well be.

An old lady of about eighty came up to us and touched my arm. As I looked down at her watering eyes she spoke in a soft, wavering voice.

'Ja se sovem Katya. Milo mi je da sam vas upoznao. Hvala vam na pomoci.'

I turned to Ivan for a translation. He put his arm around her frail shoulders and told me that she had said, 'My name is Katya. I'm very pleased to meet you. Thanks for your help.' It was enough.

'Come on, lads. We've done our share. You'll ruin our image if we keep this up. Fuckin' mercenaries, my ass. You're a bunch of pansies.'

Kit had finished his coffee, supplied by a team of firemen, and was anxious not to hang around and become more of a target for the journalists and cameramen. Questions required answers. He was already on the run from the police at home and didn't want his picture spread all over the British daily papers.

We got to our feet as Colonel Abranovich approached. 'Thank you for your help, gentlemen.' He turned to Kit. 'I would like to see you at our headquarters later, if you can spare the time. Your contact has arrived and we must make arrangements.'

Kit agreed to meet him later in the day, after a long soak in a bath. We waved goodbye to the few remaining members of the rescue teams and returned to our hotel for a well-earned breakfast.

We all perched on the edge of Pete's bed. He had recovered

quickly, but the thought of another meal of greasy bacon and eggs had reminded him of the need to eat.

'I just can't face it,' he said in a mournful whisper.

'Try something else then,' Steve suggested.

'Like what?'

'Scrambled eggs. They can't mess those up. Can they?'

We all decided to play it safe, ordering *kajganu* and *vocni sok*, with *preprzen hieb* and *marmaladu* – scrambled eggs, fruit juice, toast and marmalade. It arrived fast and properly cooked. I guess they were prepared for us this time.

For the rest of the day we loafed around the hotel, having a risky lunch brought to our rooms. Ivan and Nigel went off for a swim in the local pool. Kit went to meet Abranovich on his own.

The occasional wail of an ambulance punctuated the normal sounds of the city as time drifted lazily by. Radio Zagreb reported the earlier incident in a bored, monotonous tone, pointing out that citizens should remain alert for further attacks. Clever, these media people.

Kit returned after about three hours and seemed a little preoccupied for a while. When asked if there was anything wrong he assured us that there wasn't. He said he was just mulling things over in his head, but none of us was convinced.

We were to meet an American guy called John Fontain at a jazz club run by Bosko Petrovic – a local vibes player – at nine o'clock that evening. Arrangements were to be made with him for our trip to Osijek.

'Let's clean up and go and have a few beers first. See the nightlife. Then meet the Yank.'

We sprang into action, shaving and covering ourselves with some disgusting aftershave purchased from the Nama department store on our trip around town yesterday.

'Take your pistols.' It was almost an afterthought. Kit was sliding his 9mm CZ inside his shirt.

'What do we need guns for? It's not a war zone, Kit,' Nigel started to whinge.

'Don't argue. Regardless of what you may think, for us it is a war zone. So do as you're told and take your fuckin' pistol. Hide it, mind you. But take it.'

Nigel muttered something inaudible as he grabbed his Browning, stuffing it in the rear of his waistband. The rest followed suit, staring at Kit's back as if he'd lost his mind.

Polished and sparkling, we left the hotel and headed, high on anticipation, for the centre of town and a night of sublime pleasure at anyone's expense. Lock up your daughters, the boys are back in town.

Calo, our hotel waiter, had told us that the best area for a good night out was Tkalciceva. Feeling lazy, we waved down a passing taxi – pointless really, it was only a few blocks away.

We piled out of the Mercedes cab into neon-painted darkness and the welcoming glow of nightclubs offering escape from reality. Hordes of animated people jostled one another as they prowled the streets, laughing, joking and having a good time. Amongst the noise and gaiety of overflowing discos, bars and knocking shops it was easy to forget that the hoarding covering shop-fronts and offices was concealing the unsightly scars of cluster-bomb damage.

First stop was a bar opposite the cathedral – Gostionica Badanj. It was crowded and noisy, just the sort of dive for us to relax in. No pretence. No dress rules. No aggro. That was, until an English-speaking student type wandered over from his group of loud-mouthed friends to accuse Jim of being a hired killer with no interest in his country apart from earning blood money at their expense.

'You English?'

'Yeah, that's right, pal.'

'Not the UN though.' His eyes narrowed as he waited for an answer.

'Well, sort of . . .'

'How do you mean, sort of?'

'Well, we're here to keep the peace for you lot.'

'You are mercenaries, yes?'

'Volunteers!' Jim tightened.

'It is the same thing. Predators, jackals, feeding on the grief of my people.'

Jim had heard it all before. If you earned your living as a mercenary, this kind of needling was par for the course and, like politics or religion, impossible to debate amicably – especially in a noisy bar. On this occasion Jim tried to avoid trouble, wandering away from the source of aggravation and instead trying to engage an attractive girl in conversation. The mouthy student followed him with two others, obviously intending to use Jim's attempt at social intercourse as justifiable reason to continue the altercation.

The whole thing was starting to look nasty, as voices were raised and one of the bigger men pushed Jim against a table, sending bottles and glasses crashing to the floor. Jim clambered to his feet, his hand diving to his boot. In the dim light we saw the glint of a blade, held rapier-fashion in his clenched hand. Jim always carried a Gerber boot-knife and would not hesitate to use it if provoked. With three men having a go at him, that was enough provocation for anyone!

Kit, Nigel and Ivan were standing by the bar, laughing and joking with the locals; they had so far been unaware of the incident. The loud music and overcrowding had masked the raised voices until the crash of the table drew our attention. They looked over and saw Jim climb back to his feet. He was staring across the room with an expression on his face that we had all seen many times before . . .

'Oooh, Christ . . .' I couldn't hear but could lip-read Kit's words as he strode across the room, his massive twenty-stone frame creating a wake of bruised bodies. Nigel and Ivan followed him, with the rest of us close behind.

'*Proverite, molim vas, gume?*' Kit thundered at the student.

The Croat looked at him in astonishment, then stared at his friends.

Ivan whispered urgently in his ear, 'Kit, you've got that wrong. You have just asked him if he would like his tyres checked!'

A second went by as Kit tried to find the right words, not knowing that the man spoke English better than he did. When language failed him, he hit the Croat low, causing him to let out a blast of air and fall to his knees in agony. The room became quiet, apart from the sound of Michael Jackson on the juke box.

One of the other men hesitated for a moment, then swung at Kit and missed, sprawling on the floor with his friend as the other held up his hands in a gesture of capitulation.

'If you get up we'll hammer you,' Kit yelled at the two men, before turning back to the bar to finish his drink. They stayed down until we left . . . ten minutes later.

It would soon be time to meet the American at Bosko Petrovic's jazz club. We walked on this occasion, to clear our minds and laugh at the fracas in the bar. It was a mild event by normal standards of bar-room punch-ups. But if Jim had used that knife, everything would have gone down the toilet.

The cool sounds of jazz filtered through the night as we

approached the club, and a nice relaxed atmosphere greeted us as we entered. The doorman let us in free, no doubt as a result of the military uniform.

A quick scan around the place soon revealed our contact, unmistakable in his badge-covered USAF flying jacket and 'Strike Force' baseball cap. He was in his early forties, very fit-looking, with a Hollywood-craggy face, cropped grey hair and a cigar. He was even chewing gum!

'Hi. You must be Freeman.' A Californian drawl, no less.

Kit looked him over and took a sharp intake of breath.

'Oh aye, canny lad,' he replied in his best Geordie, reserved for those he is about to take the piss out of. 'An' you must be Fontain.'

'Colonel Fontain, actually. But we're all friends here. Call me Johnny, or "Groundhog" if you prefer. I was a jet-jockey in 'Nam. They called me that 'cos of my low-flying tactics.'

Steve moaned softly as Groundhog climbed to his feet, vigorously shaking hands with us whilst asking our names.

'Just so's there's no misunderstandin', the US Government is neutral at the moment. Officially uninvolved. I'm an adviser to the Croatians. Independent. You understand what I'm saying?'

We nodded seriously; it seemed the only thing to do.

'OK, guys. Now here's the game plan. We leave Zagreb at 0600 hours. Day after tomorrow. The sixteenth. OK so far?'

'You mean Monday?' Kit was playing it dumb.

Johnny didn't answer. Nothing could stop him now.

'You follow me on the back roads and I'll take you through the Serb lines without any problems. Then when we get to Osijek, I'll introduce you to the commander of the military installation. OK?'

We nodded dumbly, fascinated by this asshole cartoon character.

'Any questions, guys?'

Questions! This jerk was on full automatic. He didn't want questions, just the opportunity to talk.

'Get some beers inside you, guys. This is gonna be a long night.'

He was right! We got the whole bit: stories of the USAF's 8th Tactical Fighter Wing in Vietnam; the Tet offensive; low-flying air strikes over the Mekong Delta. We were in a time warp of nostalgia as our minds numbed in defence. He went on and on as the soft, cool music percolated through his thick cigar smoke until all we could see was his mouth moving hypnotically.

At midnight the band stopped playing and the bar closed.

Johnny invited us back to his hotel to continue our one-sided chat. There was no way we could take any more, so we made our apologies and trooped back to our rooms – brain dead.

Sunday morning passed in a sleepy haze. We missed breakfast, which at least saved us the trouble of making further decisions on the delights of Croat cooking. At two p.m. a sergeant from the military headquarters appeared, asking Kit if he would go to see Abranovich about some weapons. Three of us tagged along and were once again welcomed with great courtesy by the Colonel, who enquired about our meeting with John Fontain.

We didn't want to talk about John Fontain . . . ever.

Kit spent some time with the Croatian soldiers, demonstrating some recently obtained weapons of which they had no practical knowledge. He was surprisingly patient when some of them were unable to grasp the intricacies of assembly, lovingly separating the components, explaining their function yet again.

We returned to our hotel a little later than anticipated after detouring around the town for the last time. The few days' R&R had passed quickly, but I suspected that Kit wanted to be on the move again.

The evening was spent packing, and it was only ten thirty when we hit the sack. Tomorrow at six we would be back in Vietnam again with Colonel Groundhog. We needed our sleep.

It was a familiar feeling, stealing out of the hotel in the morning darkness. This time, however, our bill was paid, so it wasn't nearly as much fun.

The Land Rover was loaded quickly and Kit returned to our rooms for one last check under the beds where the armaments had been stashed. Check, check, check and check again. The soldier's motto.

At six a.m. precisely a matt-black Cherokee four-by-four pulled up and a wide-awake and grinning Colonel Fontain hit the streets running.

'Hi there, guys. Ready? OK, let's move out.' Then, as an afterthought, 'You look kinda crowded in there. Anybody wanna ride with me?'

Hell would freeze over first. Kit came to the rescue.

'That's good of you, Johnny, but for insurance reasons the men have to travel together with me. It's in the policy.'

Bless his lying little soul.

We crept out of Zagreb by the back door, with one last glance at a city lost somewhere between yesterday, today and an uncertain tomorrow. It was peaceful at the moment in dawn's early light, but the scars remained, hidden from sight. Until the next wave of shiny silver canisters fell from the sky.

Chapter Five

We're not all killers ... Some of us really care ...
Especially if the money is right.

The huge brake lights of the black Cherokee blinked at us through our mud-splattered windscreen as the Colonel confidently weaved through the damp and solitary streets, often darting into dark alleyways barely wide enough for the vehicles to pass through undamaged.

Within thirty minutes we were clear of the town and entering the open suburbs. He turned and waved, indicating that we could speed up a little as we neared the main road, soon to pass over the Zelina river. He had kept up a steady pace, about thirty metres ahead of us, occasionally checking in his mirror to see that all was well.

Nigel, who was in the back with us, located our position on the map and told us that the first major township was Bjelovar. He pointed out that we would travel through about eight villages before we reached it, each one a potential hazard from marauding bands of Chetniks or the unpredictable militia. Even the local police could cause trouble.

A convoy of white-painted UN vehicles – the safest colour in Bosnia – passed us, heading into Zagreb with supplies and assistance. In preparation for the next attack, perhaps?

We had been travelling for about an hour and had gone through five villages. Each one had been visited at one time or another by people with a tendency to destroy anything in their path. The reversed 'C' sprayed on the walls of the looted, burned-out houses left us in no doubt. The Chetniks had deposited their calling card.

Johnny waved out of his window, pulling off the road and stopping in a cloud of red dust. He gave the terrain a professional once-over before walking the few metres back to our vehicle, a cigar clenched firmly between his teeth.

'OK. So far, so good,' he mumbled through a cloud of smoke.

'We're gonna stay on this road until we reach Bjelovar. Then we're gonna head north for a while and pick up the main road heading east. After that it's gonna get hairy. Especially when we reach Nasice, about forty kilometres east of Osijek.'

He stared at us as if to detect any sign of concern. He was unlucky. The men had been there, done it. I had learned to hide any visual signs of trepidation.

'Any questions?' He pulled a nice-looking nickel-finished Colt 38 super-automatic from his shoulder holster and checked the nine-round magazine, slipping it in and out with a practised movement. 'Keep your eyes peeled, guys. Soon it'll be party time.'

'Any chance of a brew?' Jim asked in a flat, bored tone.

'I don't think that's a good idea, son. We're kinda exposed here. Maybe later.' He turned, checking the hills again, and strode back to his car.

'Fucking plonker,' Pete muttered at the receding figure.

The Cherokee pulled away at speed, its rear tyres throwing stones back at us. It was as if Johnny was showing his displeasure at the English weakness for a cup of tea.

We had to accelerate quickly to catch up with the speeding Colonel as he drove rapidly through the villages of Haganj, Zabno and Rovisce, all showing the usual signs of destruction. Many of the houses were still burning. Some, with crosses painted on them, had been left completely untouched, clear indication of ethnic cleansing by a recent raiding party of Chetniks.

No checkpoints so far, and good progress was being made as we entered the outskirts of Bjelovar. There a funeral party gathered protectively around a grieving woman, who was beating her chest hysterically as she wailed in grief for her dead husband being buried in a makeshift grave between a disused factory and an upturned tank. The men stared at the retreating scene impassively, hardened to the reality of war and the sight of other people's suffering.

As we slowed down to negotiate still smoking craters and untended bodies in our path, an old crippled woman in a wheelchair pushed herself into the middle of the road and stopped. We screeched to a halt only a metre away from her.

Pete started to laugh. 'Silly bitch, she could get herself killed doing that.' He started to get out to push her to the side of the road.

'Wait! I don't like the look of this,' Kit muttered as he clicked off his safety catch. 'It doesn't feel right.'

Within seconds of his remark the burning, hissing sound of incoming rounds peppered the road ahead, stitching neat ventilation holes along the side of our Land Rover, narrowly missing five ducking heads. The old woman, helpless and alone, had been a decoy.

We could see nothing from our confined space and had that rats-in-a-barrel feeling again as Steve gave the car some wellie, almost climbing over the slow-moving Cherokee in his haste to get the fuck out of the place.

The Colonel, seeing us about to mount him, accelerated away, leaving us a good hundred metres behind to face the snipers who were now coming out of the buildings to attack us head on, lobbing grenades at our vehicle with gay abandon. We were in no position to retaliate, apart from the odd shot from the open side window. Not very accurate and not very effective in a speeding vehicle.

'*Stop!*' Kit screamed as the rounds started to find their target. Steve braked hard and slewed into an arc, bouncing off the wall of a house. We were out and running before forward momentum had ceased, diving headlong behind anything we thought would protect us from the whining bullets.

'Anybody see them?' Kit crawled along his wall and cautiously lifted his head.

'No. Nothing.'

Silence. Except for our still-running engine.

'Well, we can't stay here. Pete, you go through the garden and around the back. I'll do a runner across the road. Give me some covering fire. Ready. *Go!*'

Kit leapt to his feet and hurtled across the unprotected road as Pete disappeared behind the house. Ivan, Jim and Nigel poked their AK-47s above the wall, spraying the area as best they could.

A dull sound of gunfire from further down the road made Ivan and Jim stop their haphazard shooting and listen.

'Sounds like a shotgun. Who the fuck uses a shotgun?' Nigel cocked his head in concentration.

'It's a semi-auto – it's got to be to sustain that rate of fire – and it's coming our way.'

Boom . . . boom . . . boom . . . boom . . . boom. Somebody was busy out there, and it wasn't Kit or Pete. They had an SA-80 and an AK-47. So who the hell was it?

The shotgun sounds continued, with occasional AK-47s replying in their familiar staccato bursts. The firefight was taking place some distance away from our position by now, and rather tentatively we lifted our heads, waiting for them to get blown off, but it didn't happen. Sheepishly, we climbed to our feet, feeling that we had been invited to a party and had arrived at the wrong house.

The five of us stood there feeling like spare pricks as the noise continued, moving closer by the second. We looked at one another and Steve took the initiative, suggesting that we should move slowly along the back of the houses in the direction of the firing. It seemed like a sensible idea, the alternative being just to wait there and wonder what the hell was going on around us.

In single file, with our heads very firmly low, we inched along the rear of the houses, tripping over the grotesque figure of a naked body with a rope around its neck and a circle with four reversed 'C's carved on its chest. I stared down at the figure in dumb horror. The man's face was contorted with pain as his sightless eyes gazed at me. His toothless mouth was filled with lumps of bloody flesh, torn from his groin.

'Keep moving,' Steve hissed. I kept moving.

A shadowy figure appeared, running at speed across our line of sight. Ivan had seen him first and had raised his weapon, letting off a few rounds as the man looked at us in momentary dismay. The Chetnik was in the wrong place at the wrong time. His punctured body hit the ground and lay still. We looked at the corpse of a man about twenty years old, wearing jeans, a Mickey Mouse T-shirt and gold earrings. Just a kid, who should have been at work in an office or factory. Not playing soldiers. Not killing people for fun. Not lying dead with five rounds of lead buried deep in his chest.

'Let's move.' Steve led us closer to the sounds of battle as an AK and an SA-80 opened in unison; we guessed that Kit and Pete were now participating in the fray. The shotgun still kept blasting regular bursts of fire. This boy sure had rhythm.

We moved more slowly now and could hear voices as we turned into an alley and were confronted by the backs of two men crouched behind a pile of mattresses. Their sixth sense must have warned them, too late, that they were in trouble. As they twisted to face us a hail of automatic fire from four weapons cut them literally to pieces and threw bits of torn flesh into the road.

'Now what?' Nigel whispered to an unsure Steve. 'Do we go on? Wait? Piss ourselves?'

'Shut up, Nigel. Move back.'

We did as we were told and cleared the alley, waiting for someone else to make the next move. It didn't take long.

First we saw the barrel of a shotgun, followed by the dapper shape of Colonel Fontain, looking furtive as he went into the unknown. Kit and Pete were close behind, tense and ready.

We breathed again and Steve called out to them. 'Fontain, it's us. You can unbuckle your gunbelt now.'

So the Colonel wasn't a complete prat after all. He had driven on for a while, parked and returned to help us out. And done a bloody good job of it. Now we would have to pay the price.

'I guessed you guys could do with some help. There were about twenty of them at first; some ran away when it started to become a shootin' war but a dozen or so stayed to fight it out. They didn't anticipate an attack from the rear though. Scared the bastards to death when I came in blasting with the Franchi SPAS.'

Yeah, yeah, yeah. Kit closed his eyes. Would we ever live this down? Listening to Groundhog repeat this story over the next few days could be a fate worse than death.

The Chetniks had, it seemed, fled into the hills, leaving Bjelovar for another day. We collected our vehicles and headed out of town, with no regrets and no thanks from the citizens.

With Colonel Fontain riding point, we headed northward through the slightly damaged villages of Kupinovac, Rakitnica and Semovci. No roadblocks appeared to ruin our day any further, and we settled in for a peaceful drive past wooded valleys and sparkling waterfalls.

A sign just before Durdevac pointing to the right directed us to Osijek. Colonel Fontain pulled off the road, indicating to us that we should follow him down a narrow bush-lined lane. He stopped and came to the side of our vehicle, looking serious.

'We're soon gonna be hitting the secondary road into Osijek. Before we get there we go through Virovitica. It's the last town and a major crossroads. So look out for troop movement at the intersection and any other kind of shit like that. Expect trouble at all times from here on in. It reminds me of when I was in 'Nam. We were on the outskirts of Khe San when . . .'

He paused, suddenly realising that this was not the time or place for reminiscing, and shook his head, smiling apologetically.

'Another time perhaps.' He turned to Kit. 'You guys can have your brew now if you like. It's safe here.'

We didn't need another word of encouragement as we all piled out of the Rover and set up the Peak stove. Soon the kettle was boiling and each of us had a hot mug of tea grasped firmly in our chubby little hands. Even the Colonel succumbed to the evil leaf and gulped back a cup of the life-restoring fluid.

When Fontain returned to his vehicle, having some difficulty turning in the tight lane, Kit drew us together. 'He's right this time. The next hundred kilometres are going to be rough. It's a fairly straight, open road. A sniper's dream. A mortar-man's dream. They'll both have all the time in the world to zero in on us, and we'll have nowhere to run or hide.' You could always rely upon Kit to restore your confidence.

The Colonel had finally managed to turn his Cherokee and waited as we did the same to the Land Rover. Then we followed him back to the road heading for Virovitica and the long, dangerous trip down the main drag.

Brake lights hastily applied made Nigel hit the anchors, bringing us to a shuddering halt in the middle of the road. The Cherokee reversed back alongside us and an excited Colonel yelled through the window, 'Police roadblock ahead!'

Kit was calm about it. 'No problem. We've got papers from Tony Abranovich, haven't we? We are a legitimate military force going about our duties. Don't panic, Johnny.'

'Yeah . . . Of course you're right, Kit. Jumpy, I guess.'

He restarted his stalled engine and drove on, and we followed cautiously towards the block. A thick chain was suspended across the road and six heavily armed men glared at us as we slowly approached. One of the policemen moved forward waving his hand in the air and mouthing the words 'Stanite ovde.' Stop here.

He bent down and peered through the windows of our vehicles, turning to his men and shouting something in an urgent voice as muzzle flashes lit their faces. They were shooting at us!

We couldn't charge the roadblock, which is common practice under such circumstances. The thick chain would have stopped us dead. Our options were limited, so we did the only thing possible: reversed at full speed and leapt out into a stinking, water-filled ditch.

Kit was hopping mad. 'The stupid bastards!' He turned to Nigel and Pete. 'You flank them. Don't worry about casualties. Shoot the fucking idiots.'

He gave them a few minutes to get clear, then leapt out of the ditch, grabbing a 'trombone' – a rifle grenade launcher – from the Land Rover. Without further discussion he stood up and sent a clear message of disapproval. The two police cars exploded in a bright orange flash, killing four of the policemen outright. Nigel and Pete finished the other two with brief bursts of fire. It was soon over.

The whole thing had been a stupid waste. The policemen had been drinking heavily and were probably pissed out of their skulls. Bottles of *votku*, *konjak* and *pivo* – vodka, brandy and beer – lay everywhere, no doubt liberated from the local bar.

'Drunk and scared. A lousy epitaph,' Steve said wearily as we dragged the bodies into the ditch. 'I guess the Chetniks will get blamed for this too.'

Johnny was surprisingly quiet as he walked back to his car and started the engine. Kit went over and asked if he was all right.

'Yeah, I'm fine. Kit. Guess I'm getting too old for this kind of thing. It gets to me sometimes. Vietnam was a long time ago. I was a young man then . . . I'll be OK. Thanks for asking.'

We could hear the Rolling Stones singing 'Paint It Black' drifting back from his cassette player as he moved away. He was trying for a morale boost from an old Vietnam favourite, we guessed, and warmed to him for admitting a weakness. Everyone's bottle ran out from time to time.

The citizens of Virovitica had heard the sounds of battle, and as we entered the town we were met by empty streets. Kit figured that it was safe to stop here due to the roadblock and flashed his lights at the Colonel, who pulled over and cut his engine. A large bearded man approached us alone from a nearby house; realising from our uniforms that we were not Serbian or Chetnik, he questioned us about the gunfire. Ivan explained in a vague manner that there had been a few snipers in the fields and the problem had been taken care of.

He seemed satisfied with this explanation, shaking Ivan by the hand and inviting us into his home for refreshments, which were gratefully accepted.

His wife fussed around us as if we were honoured guests, bringing loaves of home-baked bread, soup, huge spicy sausages and Zilavka – a dry white wine from Herzegovina. We spent a very pleasant hour with Dina and Antunovic, discussing the sadness of the war – with Ivan translating. But it was easy to work out for ourselves the meaning of the often-repeated phrases '*Sta ovo znzaci? Ja ne razumem.*' What does this mean? I don't understand. They were not alone. We didn't understand either.

All too soon it was time to go, and we bade them farewell with a chorus of '*Hvala vam mnogo*': Thank you very much. We meant it. This was the first bit of genuine hospitality we had received since arriving in Yugoslavia.

'Hope they don't get any repercussions from the police,' said Jim as we were climbing into the car.

'Nah,' Steve replied. 'Like I said, the Chetniks will get the blame.'

We pulled away as the couple waved their goodbyes, and were soon out of town and on the main road heading for Osijek.

The hum of tyres on the flat asphalt road soon produced a hypnotic effect on our weary brains. We had a little more space to stretch out and relax now, as Kit had relented and allowed Steve and Pete to travel in comfort with Johnny, who had become, temporarily at least, bearable.

The road was fairly straight and free from hot spots, so we were able to doze and listen to local music on the radio. We passed through about six villages and two roadblocks, at a cost of eight packets of cigarettes and two bottles of whisky. One of the militiamen at Mikleus had actually given us some water. Strange people, strange war. One minute they shoot at you, the next they invite you into their homes.

We sailed through Cacinci and Fericanci, but became involved in an incident in Moticina where two drunken youths had driven a stolen lorry full of explosives off the road and into a ditch. The lorry had turned over but they had managed to get out unharmed. We arrived just at the point when local people, unaware of impending disaster, were running to assist them. As the explosives detonated, spraying shrapnel into the air, and rounds of ammunition buzzed everywhere, the idiot villagers just stood and watched. Four of them were cut down by flying metal.

We pulled up just behind Johnny, who was screaming at them to move back. I guess they didn't understand the language, although his arm-waving didn't need any translation. Kit and Ivan ran toward the nearest group, dragging them away as yet another explosion blasted balls of flame high into the air. The heat finally drove the villagers back, leaving their petrol-doused friends to burn as we watched, unable to approach the bodies.

The locals stood in small groups, stunned by this stupid accident, and for a moment the cause of it was forgotten in their shock and despair.

Kit and Ivan, both with some medical experience, set about helping those injured, while Colonel Fontain, back to his usual self, took charge of the proceedings.

'OK, you goddam gooks. Make up some stretchers and get these people to a hospital. *You!* Fatso. Get something and put out the fire. Where's the goddam ambulance? Where's the doctor? Jesus, what a bunch of bums.'

Of course nobody understood a word of what he was yelling in his strong Californian accent. They stared at him as if he had gone mad.

A police car, followed closely by a lorry carrying members of the Croatian National Guard, pulled up, and assuming that there had been some form of attack, pointed their weapons at the supposed culprits. Us.

It took a few minutes of Ivan's time, and the letter from Colonel Abranovich, to convince the police that we were innocent, and they backed off, listening to the reason for the mayhem. Then they screamed off, sirens blaring, in the direction taking by the fleeing youths.

We did all we could to help the injured, covering the charred dead in bodybags found in the back of Johnny's Cherokee, and were once again treated to a meal by one of the villagers, in his home at the top of a hill overlooking the village. Meanwhile the youths had been captured by the police some way out of town, and it was discovered that they were making a living by stealing arms and selling them to the highest bidder. In all probability they would be shot for this, and who would argue?

Before leaving the village Johnny, who had returned to his role of Groundhog, gave us yet another pep talk.

'OK, you guys, now listen up.' He paused for dramatic effect.

'After we pass the next town of Nasice, it's a straight run into Osijek. No bends. No cover. No fucking nothing. As you're aware, Vukovar fell to the Serbs a little while ago, so the whole area to the north, above the river Drava, and the south-east is open to them.

We've got to get through the net and into Osijek, and it's not gonna be easy.'

We'd all got the picture way back and Kit wasn't interested in any further discussion. He took a deep breath.

'Look, Johnny. Underneath all that crap you're a nice guy. But most of us have been here longer than you, and we know all of this stuff. The bottom line is that we play it by ear, like we always do. Now jump in your car like a good colonel and let's get the fuck out of here.'

The Colonel started to speak but thought better of it, striding back to his Cherokee, gunning the engine and hurtling out of the village. Steve and Pete were left staring after him.

'Sod it,' said Steve with feeling as he turned to Kit. 'What did you want to say that for? It was a bloody sight more comfortable riding with him, and some of his Vietnam stories were interesting.'

'Yeah. You could have left it till we arrived in Osijek,' Pete added morosely.

'Bollocks! If you don't want to walk, then shut up and get in. We've got to catch the bugger up now!'

It took about twenty minutes before we caught sight of the smoking rear end of the Cherokee. Johnny was still giving it some boot. Our speedometer showed ninety-five mph, and we still couldn't catch up with him!

'This is stupid,' said Kit, as Johnny, seeing us in his mirror, started to pull away.

Kit flashed the lights. Johnny didn't slow. Kit tried again, and this time the brake lights flickered and stayed on as the Cherokee slowed and finally came to a halt.

Kit got out and walked to the car, and opened the door. We couldn't hear the conversation but it took a good ten minutes before he returned looking pleased with himself. He climbed back in with us, turning to Pete and Steve.

'If you want to ride with him it's OK now. I've sorted it all out.'

'How did you do that?' Pete asked.

'Easy. I apologised. He's a good guy, but he lives in the past and can't get it out of his system.' And then, thoughtfully, 'Maybe we'll all be like that someday . . . Anyway, go and ride with him. He needs the company and we need the space.'

Johnny waved back at us before pulling away, and we followed close behind at a fast but steady speed of about seventy, while listening to the BBC World Service on the short wave. Sarajevo was getting it today, and the city's main street had been dubbed by the media 'sniper alley'. Those guys loved to tag and glamorise everything; it made better copy.

Slowing only slightly as we passed through Nasice and Jelisavac, we were forced to stop once again at a roadblock just before entering Koska. It looked professional this time, with two APCs and about a dozen uniformed men, thankfully Croatian regulars, who warned us in no uncertain terms that the road ahead was open to continual attack from artillery, mortar fire and, especially past Bizovac, highly trained Serbian snipers. We were advised not to continue.

Kit and the Colonel went into a brief huddle and came over to the rest of us with serious expressions and words of great wisdom. We were filled with awe at their military ingenuity.

Kit spoke first. 'Right. Now here's the plan. It's pretty complex, so listen closely.' He waited until we were silent and attentive.

'We shall leap into the vehicles with great enthusiasm in front of these inexperienced Croat soldiers. Then we shall drive like bastards from hell into Osijek, without getting hit by any of the Serbian mortar or artillery fire. Then we shall stop for a cup of tea. Is that clear?'

'That sounds easy enough,' Nigel replied drily.

'What happens if we do get hit?' Jim added his bit.

Kit gave him a stony glance. 'I learned my soldiering in the British army and the Foreign Legion. Johnny was taught military tactics in Vietnam by the US army. How can you doubt our skill at formulating military decisions? Anyway, sunshine, after due consideration there is no ... other ... fucking way.' He smiled apologetically. 'Sorry, lads, just keep your heads down.'

Johnny silently nodded in agreement as Kit thanked the Croats for their advice, explaining that we had a job to do and that it was in Osijek. After gulping down a quick thick black coffee we were on our way, with sweaty palms and churning stomachs.

The vehicles swiftly gathered speed, reaching about a ton. The Cherokee ahead could have managed a little more, I guessed, but we were loaded up with equipment and slower anyway. Too soon the village of Bizovac appeared on the horizon.

'Keep your eyes peeled for shooters,' yelled Kit as he put his foot down and hit the main street, hurtling through it in a blur of smoking buildings and staring villagers. We were through, and back on the main road, in minutes.

Only fifteen lousy kilometres left when the familiar 'crump, crump' of advancing mortar shells fell around us. Kit swerved instinctively as earth was thrown against the windscreen and a shock wave smashed against the side of the car.

'We're fucked. They've got our range already,' he screamed, battling to keep the weaving vehicle on the road.

Johnny wasn't faring much better as mortars fell thick and fast around his bucking Cherokee, which looked in danger of turning over as we steadied up and shot past him. He tried braking, without success, skidding and spinning around, momentarily stalling his engine.

The mortars stopped and we could hear the flooded Cherokee engine refusing to start again.

'Shit! Shit! Shit! What'll we do, Kit?' Jim was yelling. 'We can't leave them.'

'We can't go back either. We'd be sitting ducks,' Kit replied through gritted teeth.

A black cloud of smoke from the Cherokee's exhaust solved the problem. The engine had finally started, and with a burst of speed the Colonel was soon up with us. He was revving the engine like a madman as he overtook us again in a cloud of oily smoke and sped ahead, rolling from side to side, almost out of control.

The sickening crunch of mortar shells started up again, the side windows of both vehicles splintering as we swerved to avoid the advancement as best we could at this speed. This time they were punctuated by small-arms fire from close by, ripping past us with sounds like tearing canvas. With little opportunity for evasive action on these straight roads, we just kept on going. Some of the men swore, some prayed. It served the same purpose: kept the mind occupied until we were out of range. It took forever.

The rear end of the Colonel's beautiful Cherokee had been ripped away by one of the blasts and was flapping in the breeze. We could see Pete and Steve looking stunned but unhurt in the back as they turned to look at us.

The whole attack had taken somewhere between five minutes and five hours. Whichever, we had all aged ten years and were emotionally drained. We listened to Jim sobbing quietly, whilst he cursed at his weakness. Nobody looked at him or cared. This sort of thing affected different people in different ways. No shame was attached as long as you didn't let your mates down.

We had almost reached the outskirts of Osijek when Johnny waved at us to pull over into a brush-surrounded gully. He clambered out, a little unsteadily, and came back to us. His face was white and he was trembling uncontrollably as he leaned heavily against the battered Land Rover.

He tried a smile. It didn't work.

'I gotta get outta this business.' His voice was shaking as he tried to regain control. 'Look at my goddamn Cherokee.' It was a sorry sight, peppered with small-arms fire, dented by mortar blasts, and the back end hanging by a piece of twisted metal.

He lit a cigar and blew a cloud of thick smoke which hovered below the peak of his baseball cap. A few more deep drags and he stopped shaking, his colour slowly returning to a normal Californian tan.

'If only I could call in some air support. A couple of F-100 Super Sabres or Huey Cobras. We could blow those bastards to hell.'

'Come on, Johnny, you're not in 'Nam now.' Kit said it kindly, not wishing to make matters worse for the shell-shocked Colonel.

Pete and Steve had joined us with blackened faces, both looking shaken up from the hit the Cherokee had taken.

'Hello dere, man. Gimme some skin.' Jim managed to retain a sense of humour with his reference to their darkened features, but they were too far gone to respond and slumped to the ground before their legs gave out.

We all felt fairly safe in the gully, surrounded by dense brush, and it was decided that we should take this opportunity to tidy ourselves up and check the vehicles before making our grand entrance into Osijek.

That was when Ivan got it. No one knew where it came from. Just a single, sharp crack. The bullet hit him in the back and came out of his chest. He spluttered once, fell and stood up again looking bewildered. He stared at us, his eyes slowly moving to the tops of their sockets as he let out a sigh and collapsed across the bonnet. Everyone froze. It wasn't fair. We had thought that it was all over.

'Ivan . . .' Pete's voice trailed away as he rolled the body over and felt for a pulse.

'Anyone see where it came from?' Kit asked, already knowing the answer.

'Could be anywhere, just anywhere,' Steve replied flatly, looking at the pool of blood dripping over the bonnet on to the dusty ground.

'Check out the area before we make another move,' Kit instructed. 'If there's someone still out there I want him.'

We crouched behind the vehicles and scanned the whole zone with binoculars, but not a movement was seen by any of us. Kit placed Ivan's body in the back of the Land Rover, covering him with the Croatian flag that he had always carried in his bergan. His death had shocked us more than anything that had so far taken place, and we were numb with grief as we sorted ourselves out and climbed back into the vehicles after checking the surrounding countryside one more time.

We discussed the incident many times later. There had been no cover for a sniper out there, just flat, unplanted fields for miles and miles. It would have been impossible for a man to have got away without being seen. We would never know the answer.

Colonel Fontain suggested that a possible solution was the old Vietcong trick of burying snipers in the earth, a straw enabling them to breathe until a target came into range. Maybe he was right. It seemed a reasonable assumption. Nothing else worked.

With dampened spirits we arrived in Osijek. There were no banners to greet us, no trumpets to acknowledge our arrival. We were the saviours of the city but nobody cared as we limped through the streets straight into the arms of the local police, who, deciding that we were undesirables, took Ivan's body to the mortuary and locked us in the cells for the night to await questioning in the morning. We were tired and didn't argue. It was as good a place as anywhere to sleep.

A small man with dark hair, an olive complexion and an unsmiling face woke us early, peering through the cell bars as a police sergeant unlocked the door for him to enter. Colonel Fontain strode over to the camo-clad figure and shook hands, turning to us with a grin.

'I'd like you guys to meet Eduardo Florez, Commander of the First International Company of Croatia.' It was five a.m. and a cock was crowing somewhere in the distance. This should have told us something about the man standing before us.

Florez said nothing, merely nodding his head as Fontain did some fast introductions which were received with a deadpan expression through a haze of cigarette smoke.

We were immediately released by the police without any form of apology and taken to army headquarters in a large building on the west side of the town. Boarded and sandbagged against rocket attack, it resembled a fortress, standing almost untouched alongside the badly damaged adjacent buildings.

The Colonel had completed his job, delivering us to Osijek as arranged, and we said our goodbyes with a strange tinge of sadness. As he walked wearily away from us, his hunched, beaten figure bore little resemblance to the Groundhog caricature we had met in Zagreb only a few days before. Even Johnny would admit it now, that Groundhog had evaporated in the damp Croatian mist, somewhere on the road to Osijek. Colonel Johnny Fontain was burned out and heading homeward to the good old USA.

Florez went straight into it, no messing.

'As you already know, my name is Eduardo Florez and I am a Spanish ex-journalist, not a professional soldier.' His English was good, with only a slight Spanish accent.

'I was neutral and objective when I first came here to cover the war, but the neutrality didn't last long – I lost it in the second week. I soon decided which was the good side and which the bad. It's not black and white, of course; I know that. Now I fight for the side of right. I fight for the Croatian people.'

He paused for effect, continuing in a more positive tone.

'These people are being persecuted on all sides by armies more powerful and better equipped than they. But the Croatian people have heart and they will survive with our help.'

Jim whispered, 'And so say all of us.' Florez cut him down with a lethal glare.

'I shall continue. My prime function is to collate information from behind enemy lines and pass it up through the chain of command for others to act upon. Your function is to provide me with this information and to train additional men to fight for the cause against the Serbian oppressors.'

Indicating that we should follow him to a large map of the area, he turned to Kit. 'Freeman, isn't it? I gather from Colonel Fontain that you have been commissioned in the Croatian Army as a lieutenant. Is this correct?'

Kit pulled out a photo ID card which none of us had seen before and put it on the table. It read: 'Darren Abbey. Republika Hrvatska. Vojna Iskaznica. R436467. Rank of zapovjednik voda'.

'A false name, Mr Freeman. Never mind. Your documents are

in order. You will assume the position of second-in-command and the responsibility of training the men up to your standards.' He handed the ID back to Kit.

'Now to the map. Osijek lies south of the Drava river, as you see. To the north we have our front line, which is a few metres from the woods. The Serbian front line cuts through the woods and curves through the zoo on our left.'

'The zoo?' Steve broke in. 'A proper zoo!'

'Yes. The Osijek Zoo.'

Jim had to have his say. 'Do you mean a zoo with lions and tigers and all that stuff?'

'Yes. That's what I mean.' Florez was getting impatient. 'OK for me to carry on?'

'Sorry.' Jim apologised for the interruption.

'The Serbs have many tanks and artillery pieces. In addition they have some air support . . . little, but some. We have none of these things at the moment. Just men who are prepared to die and will do so if they are not properly trained.'

He paused once again as Kit looked over the map with a practised eye.

'Mines. Have the Serbs laid mines?' Kit queried immediately.

'Yes. There are mines on the north side of the river. But we are not equipped or experienced enough to deal with them.'

'OK. That'll be one of our first jobs.' Kit was enjoying this. 'The Serb tanks. What have they got?' he continued.

'Mostly T-55s.'

'Mmmm . . . T-55s. A range of about twelve hundred metres with their 100mm guns. I guess they can hit your front line easily.'

Commander Florez didn't bother to answer this hypothetical question, walking back to his desk to light yet another cigarette as he turned to Kit and said, 'Perhaps it would be wise for you all to familiarise yourself with the town for the rest of the day. I have important things to do right now. We can continue our discussion tomorrow when you have patrolled the area and observed our defences.'

'That suits me fine, Commander Florez. One last thing. Where do we sleep?'

'Oh. Of course, forgive me. You and your men can stay in this building. We have three floors and there are many soldiers sleeping here already. Some are your countrymen. Now I must go. I shall see you tomorrow.'

The map became the centre of attention for the next half an hour as the men discussed tactics and objectives. Jim and Pete, losing interest after about ten minutes, decided to bring the gear in and sort out some living accommodation for us.

The whole building was empty. Everyone was out on patrol, training or at the front, which gave the three of us a great opportunity to look around before Kit, Steve and Nigel joined us on the first floor.

'This fuckin' place is disgusting! Look at it! It's like a pig sty.'

Kit was right. The stench alone made us feel sick. The floors were covered in clothes, beer cans, mildewed takeaway food cartons and rat droppings. Piles of ammunition were stacked up against a wall, making the place a time bomb waiting to go off.

'There's no way I'm sleeping in this shit hole. We'll take that corner over there,' Kit said, pointing at the east window area as he started kicking the clothing and rubbish into a pile away from his chosen place.

'Open the windows and get rid of the stink,' he told Pete. 'Now, you lot, get some water and clean the floor. Then we'll put our stuff down.'

Everyone set to and cleaned up, until the floor was sparkling. Then we laid our sleeping bags in a neat line and waited for the return of the original inhabitants. This could be entertaining.

An hour drifted past as we dozed on our sleeping bags before the silence was shattered by the clatter of heavy boots and boisterous voices. We looked up to see four Croat soldiers standing in front of us, staring at the pile of rubbish that was once their home.

This could be a problem. We didn't have Ivan around any longer to translate for us. We looked at Kit as he searched through his memory banks for a suitable phrase.

'*Dobar dan gospoda.*' Good afternoon, gentlemen. So far, so good.

The largest of the soldiers looked at Kit, measuring him up, then growled, '*Sta ovo znaci?*' What does this mean?

We all understood the question from our brief lesson with Ivan. Kit, however, had run out of replies, so he stood up and tried to look superior. 'It means that I am a lieutenant in your army, my sons, and you are simple privates. So if you want to talk to me get someone who can speak *engleski.*'

He thrust his ID card under their noses. They glanced at it, not obviously impressed.

'*Da*. You are *engleski* lieutenant. We understand. We speak the English . . . a little.'

'Good. Then get this fucking place cleaned up and fast. You're a bunch of bastard slobs. While I'm here we'll do things my way!'

'*Da. Zapovjednik voda!*'

They sprang into action and within ten minutes the whole area was looking clean and tidy. Kit walked around, barking orders like a British sergeant major, insisting that they fold all of their gear in neat little piles at the base of their beds.

Later in the day the rest of the men shambled in, back from perimeter patrols and work parties. They were a mixed bunch of vagabonds, deadbeats and bums, with the occasional committed soldier, distinguishable by his professional bearing and manner, standing out like a flower amongst weeds. There were about fifty of them altogether, gawking at the orderly room in open-mouthed amazement. All were treated in the same manner and ordered to clear their respective areas until they were up to the standard expected.

We spent most of the afternoon wandering around the shell-damaged town. Kit commented incredulously on the locals. 'Look at them! I don't believe it. They're all back out again as if nothing had happened.' He was right. The people of the town were stepping over rubble and twisted metal as they went about their daily routines, ignoring the chaos around them as they bought provisions and stood in groups chattering about God knows what.

We borrowed a jeep later, driving out of town over the last remaining bridge across the river Drava for a look at our front line along the south side of the woodland.

Osijek had taken a bit of a beating last night as we were locked away safe in the jail. Artillery and rocket fire had lit up the night sky for several hours. The police had told us that T-55 tanks had moved into position close to the river on the western side of town but had been driven back by RPG-7-armed Croatian soldiers. The general view was that it was not a serious advance, but merely a test of the defences. The real thing would come later.

The shelling had come to an abrupt halt as the sky lightened. Yet another ceasefire had been called and, for a brief period, maintained.

It wouldn't last, we were assured by a Croatian captain. They never did. This was about the eighth.

We returned to our now spotless home with a clearer picture of the town and the problems which faced its defence. Kit immediately surveyed the map, anxious to get on with the job.

Later in the evening Commander Florez introduced us to several English volunteers. Carl, another instructor, from Liverpool, was lean and permanently mean-looking. He was known to Kit from an earlier period in Zagreb, when they were both with the 102nd Brigade. Dave had the words 'Yorkshire Ripper' painted on his helmet, while a young, fresh-faced, likeable kid named Roy looked completely out of place with these hardened men.

They told us that there were about twenty English-speaking lads in Osijek at the moment. Some British, AWOL from the army or the Foreign Legion, a few Americans and a couple of Australian Croats. Many more were expected to join us within the next few days as the war magnetically attracted men with a desire and sometimes a need for violence and legalised killing.

This was to be the Croatian army's only English-speaking company, and Kit Freeman its chief training officer. A formidable task, but as Kit said over supper, 'I like a challenge.'

Early mornings in Croatia are invariably damp and misty. This one was no exception as we all gathered in Commander Florez's office for an informal operations briefing. The Commander arrived a little late, allowing us the opportunity of listening to the BBC World Service in his absence.

The only news of any interest was the war. The announcer told us in unemotional measured tones that 'Reports from Croatia say there has been renewed shelling of the eastern town of Osijek. At least five people were killed when the town was bombarded overnight. Reuters news agency quoted Croatian police as saying that hundreds of shells and rockets had been fired from positions occupied by the Serbian-dominated federal army and Serb irregulars. The Croatian authorities said that this was the worst ceasefire violation since the beginning of January, when the current truce came into force.'

Not totally accurate but close enough, as small-arms fire started chattering once again from across the Drava river.

'Good morning.' Commander Florez swept in looking agitated. He wore Foreign Legion para wings on the wrong side of his DPM smock.

'Your attention please, gentlemen. Under cover of last night's artillery attack, a number of Serbian tanks managed to progress to the river. They were turned back on this occasion. But we must be vigilant. This was merely an attempt at probing our defences. Further JNA raids will follow. Of this you can be sure.'

His eyes swept the room, alighting on the new man, Kit.

'Have you any ideas on how to deal with this threat?'

Carl looked up, his eyes narrowed. He was obviously not very pleased about the new chain of command structure, feeling a little put out by Kit's position as second-in-command.

'Yes, Commander Florez, I've got a lot of ideas but I need more information about the enemy before offering them to you.' Kit was cautious about making decisions at this early stage. 'I'd like to spend part of the day with a few of my men checking the area. Tomorrow at the briefing I'll give you the information you need.'

Florez pursed his lips before nodding his head in acceptance and lit his fifth cigarette in less than an hour.

'Very well, be as quick as you can. Time is of the essence.'

The briefing became a general discussion, with section leaders detailing the previous day's action with reports on casualties and collateral damage. The Commander looked serious as he gathered his papers and headed for the door, intending to report to his superiors.

Kit caught him as he was leaving and an animated discussion took place out of earshot. Much Latin hand-waving from Florez indicated that he had given in to Kit's wishes. Whatever they were.

'What are you after?' Pete asked as Kit came back, glowing with success.

'I've got us a house,' he replied. 'I can't stand the noise of all that fuckin' snoring and moaning. So I told Florez that I couldn't operate under those conditions and he said that we could take any of the empty houses we liked. As long as it was down by the front line.'

This was great news and we were elated, gathering up our gear in readiness for a change of address as the rest of the volunteers looked on with a mixture of envy and pleasure: without Kit ordering them around they could slip back into their piggish existence.

Carl, Dave and Roy, together with a few other chosen ones, had decided to join us at our out-of-town residence. Now the foreign contingent would have their own centre of operations.

A desirable building was soon located and communications established by linking in the telephone system and liberating two television sets and a video player. Soon the house had all of the conventional reassurances of a home from home, if we over-looked the gaping holes in the roof from the last Serbian artillery bombardment. The original owner was himself a Serbian who had recently been killed by angry Croats, his family fleeing to escape the same fate.

Our small group had expanded considerably and now totalled thirty-two men of mixed nationalities, leaving just enough room in the house for Sprog and Pop, who we assumed still intended to join us at some point; although we had heard nothing from them since leaving them in Split a thousand years ago.

The BBC had moved into our lives a few days earlier, adding some glamour to a boring and uneventful existence. The crew, led by producer Stephen Lambert and co-producer Roger Courtiour, were shooting a documentary for the BBC TV series *Inside Story* – subsequently titled *Dogs of War*. They followed us day and night, sticking cameras and microphones into our faces at all the wrong times, exposing every little human flaw and weakness to the world. Kit Freeman was centre of attention in most of the footage, telling his life story and giving his views on the war in Croatia and the mercenaries' part in it. Carl, Dave and a man named Frenchie were featured artists, with Commander Florez and a few others in supporting roles. The interviewer seemed to enjoy talking to Dave, asking him about his obsession with the Yorkshire Ripper and the Black Panther. Dave, his gold front tooth flashing in the lights, was happy to oblige and with no hesitation told of his wish to emulate these psychotic murderers and kill people, legally, for the buzz.

As we left to recce the immediate area, Kit and Carl had a little 'splat' at one another over the question of which way to aim M-18 claymore anti-personnel mines. A stupid argument developed, even more ridiculous because the mines say quite clearly on the side, 'Front toward enemy'. Carl wasn't having it, insisting that the instruction was wrong. Nothing that Kit could say would convince him, and in the end, exasperated, he cut one in half, showing Carl the position of the 700 steel balls and the explosive charge. This settled the argument once and for all, but created more friction between the two men, which would bubble to the surface in tense moments.

We drove along the banks of the river Drava, past the hospital, and joined the front line at our side of the river, later crossing over at the last remaining bridge to have talks with the Croatians in the trenches as they curved past the edge of the woods. Their attitude to Kit's questions clearly indicated that morale was dangerously low. Many were going AWOL and the ones that had stayed were not confident of their ability to withstand a heavy assault. The simple fact was that they were waiting for something to happen. Today, tomorrow . . . sometime. The frightening knowledge that their equipment and armaments were inferior to those of the advancing enemy made their plight even more desperate.

Many of them were simple peasant farmers and children with no military or battle experience. The fear in their eyes was contagious and we were all glad to leave them in their uncertainty. We returned to our new base to have a nice cup of tea while lazing in comfortable armchairs as we drifted into normality: watching football on our liberated televisions as the intrepid Michael Eley, the BBC cameraman, continued to run around the place, merrily sticking his long black lens up everyone's nose.

Chapter Six

> ... It's for the money. All this freedom fighter stuff is
> crap! We're here for the 'dosh'. Not so a few people
> can have their independence. I don't give a damn, as
> long as the money is there. At the end of the day, a
> war is a war ...

The shrill yelp of the telephone jarred the tranquillity of our six a.m. breakfast. Carl grabbed at it, too late. Kit got there first, still chewing a faceful of scrambled egg. He listened attentively, with visibly mounting tension, his only verbal response a curt 'Yeah. Yeah. Understood. No problem.' The phone went down hard as he turned to the men, poised in anticipation, and in a matter-of-fact voice gave them the news they had all been waiting for. 'OK, we're in business.'

A red alert had been called as yet another squadron of T-55 tanks was detected approaching the river at a position south-west of the zoo. No one knew if this was the beginning of the big push or just another probe, as renewed artillery fire whistled overhead, creating more casualties somewhere in the centre of town.

Shelling continued steadily as the men dived into their battle gear, hurriedly slapping camo cream on unwashed and unshaven faces in an atmosphere of crackling anticipation. Weapons were feverishly loaded and checked for smooth operation until Kit told them to relax and do the job properly.

'My fucking bolt's jammed!'

'I can't find my ammo!'

'Our Father, which art in heaven ...'

For some, this was their first action, and many faces were filled with blank apprehension as they joked with one another, smiling with tight lips and rapidly moving Adam's apples which threatened to choke them.

'Has anyone seen my fucking grenades?' Jim wandered around with a little boy lost look.

'There's loads in the truck,' someone told him. He slouched out into the freezing dawn, still in his underpants.

'Shut the bloody door!' Steve yelled after him, as our centrally heated room became immediately cold.

'Yes, Mum.' The door slammed, shutting out the forever damp morning gloom.

The men who were ready silently lined up outside the house. Carl reminded them that this was a real emergency, ordering the guards to return and take up their posts inside the building. Those who remained loaded the waiting lorry with explosives and weapons.

'Now don't drop anything!' he warned, as inexperienced hands fumbled with the heavy gear. 'You! Stay behind. We don't want to lose the fucking cook.'

The phone rang again in short, urgent bursts. Kit grabbed it in his huge paw and jammed it to his ear. 'Understood. OK, out.' He replaced the phone, slapping it with frustration, and stood up, shaking his head.

'Fucking good. Just hold back, he said. There's nothing really kicking off at the moment. No one is allowed on the roads. The police are stopping everyone.'

Commander Florez had informed him that the tanks had turned back . . . another false alarm. The men were instructed by a disappointed Kit to stand down and await further developments.

There was an almost audible sound of deflation as the frenzy of activity ceased abruptly. The men muttered amongst themselves, finally sitting on their beds, looking like boxers who had had their chance of a title fight taken from them by a crooked manager.

'Shit! I was just getting geared up,' spat Dave – the 'Yorkshire Ripper' – as he threw down his AK-47, which bounced on the bed before hitting the floor with a loud clatter.

'You prat!' yelled Kit. 'The fucking safety's off.'

Jim returned from the truck, shivering, his arms full of grenades.

'Ten quid a dozen. Roll up, roll up. Nice and fresh.'

Greeted by a wall of silence, he stared at his comrades with questioning eyes.

'Whassamatter?'

When Nigel told him, he dropped the grenades in disgust.

'Commander Florez is coming here at seven-thirty. So finish your food and then we'll spend half an hour outside, training.' Kit started to hustle them before terminal lethargy took hold. 'Now move it, you bunch of dipshits!'

The attack on the town had ceased, but the dull 'crumph' of mortar fire continued from the front line as the lads shambled out of the house and prepared themselves for the torture that is known as exercise. They ran in groups of three up and down the lane outside, dropping to undertake sit-ups on command with less than total enthusiasm. Kit didn't care about their commitment as long as they did it. He knew from personal experience that the fit fighting man is the efficient fighting man. The lads were surprised that someone of his size could keep up with them, but then Kit was full of surprises.

The final fifteen minutes of the exercise period was taken up by the aptly named 'murder ball', a game with few rules and a lot of physical contact. You just grabbed the ball and ran with it, touching a tin can to score. The opposition's task was simply to stop you. The few rules excluded the use of automatic weapons and hand grenades. Apart from these, almost anything else was legitimate.

A distant siren sounded the all-clear as Florez swept in, his arms full of papers and maps. The men were told to clean up and rest, and the section leaders were summoned to the first briefing of the day.

Kit was told to forget any plans he had made for infiltration behind enemy lines and concentrate upon training the team, as many of the lads would be a liability in their present state of inexperience. He agreed without argument that training should take precedence over a further recce and called the leaders together for instruction.

Carl, whose speciality was explosives, took a small group into the local woods to give them the benefit of his knowledge on detonation techniques, with special attention on the use of claymore mines and how to ensure that they were pointing the correct way! We could hear his curt Liverpudlian voice for a short while as we walked past.

'Now. This stuff is called detonation cord. Right. It's packed with PTM explosive. The average speed of that is seventeen kilometres a second . . .'

As we moved out of earshot Kit repeated his last remark with a smile. 'Seventeen kilometres a second? Wow!'

We sauntered along leafy woodland paths, as if out for a Sunday stroll, while discussing the function and application of facial camouflage; the importance of staying still, not smoking or talking and the different types of hand signals used for communication in the dense woodlands. The inexperienced amongst us were instructed on ambush techniques: how to escape from them, and more important, how to avoid them in the first instance.

Kit made a special point of addressing the Croat members of the group when he said, 'A lot of Croatian soldiers have died unnecessarily in this war because they spend too much time watching Rambo films. War isn't like that. You don't get up and walk away as the credits roll. Forget the bandannas, the ammo belts around your neck and the bloody stupid knives. Learn to be a proper soldier and you may live to tell your family that you fought for your country.'

He turned to the rest of us as they discussed his comments amongst themselves. 'The poor bastards. They're a Mickey Mouse army at the moment, but they've got heart, and that counts for a lot.'

Loud explosions and occasional howls of pain from the nearby wood indicated that Carl was getting enthusiastically stuck in to his favourite occupation of blowing things to hell. A young Croat private stumbled past us, white as a sheet, holding his hands to deafened ears. Kit stopped him to ask if he was all right.

'*Na sta se zalite?*' What's the trouble?

The soldier stared back, looking stunned, pointing to his ear. '*Zlo mi je. Vrti mi se u glavi.*' I feel sick and I feel dizzy.

He was told to return to the house and await medical help, and he muttered his thanks as he lurched away.

As the explosions continued, making it obvious that we were in an area of potential danger, it seemed wiser to move to a safer part of the wood for the survival exercise game of hare and hounds.

'OK, two of you cam up. We'll give you three minutes to disappear. Then we're coming to get you. If we find you before you can get back here, you're in for a good kicking, all right!'

Kit pointed at Frenchie, a Welsh ex-Foreign Legionnaire – so he claimed. 'You and Roy can be the hares. Now go!'

They were off like a shot, soon becoming invisible as the dense wood swallowed them up. Kit counted quickly and the hounds followed, eagerly prodding bushes with their rifle butts and climbing trees for an overview of the terrain. The hares lasted less than five minutes and were told in no uncertain terms what dismal failures they were.

'You're a pair of bloody fairies and wankers! What are you?'

'We're a pair of fairies and wankers,' Roy and Frenchie repeated in solemn unison before being given a severe 'beasting' by their joyous captors.

Carl and his team joined us later, having completed their basic explosives training, and we all embarked upon the next phase of survival education: the dreaded E&E – escape and evasion. This lively interlude, which involved many kickings for those unfortunate enough to be caught, was followed by CTR – close target recce, also a disaster for the inexperienced soldiers. Finally the hard routine of combat operation in the field was drilled into the men – weapons at hand, belt kit on, all equipment packed away. No smoke, flame or noise. Some basic theory of compass work, map-reading, and night-vision aids was touched but not dwelt upon; most of the men were knackered by now and incapable of absorbing any further information anyway.

It had started to drizzle, making everyone look and feel miserable as we slumped on the wet grass, smoking and waiting for the next cruel joke to be played on us by the instructors. Carl pointed to the lake and Kit nodded his head. Now what?

'OK lads. Now you've rested up a bit, it's time for some boat practice.'

Kit led the men down to the lake where two rubber dinghies were moored. 'Six of you in there and six in the other one,' he ordered, just as Commander Florez appeared through the now heavy downpour, protected by a hooded DPM poncho.

'When I say "Ready", I want you to paddle like hell for the other bank. The winners can get out and the losers continue against another team.'

Kit gave the order and they were off, paddling like madmen for the opposite bank and the chance of a break while some other poor sods went through it.

They were about ten metres from us when Florez asked Kit for something and was given two hand grenades. He pulled the pins rapidly, and with an overarm motion lobbed them high into the air. They landed with dull plops just behind the slower dinghy, exploding almost immediately and creating cascades of water which rocked and nearly swamped the boat. He stood for a moment before walking back to the instructors, where they all doubled up with laughter.

'Oh, he is a card,' Steve murmured without humour. 'Perhaps he'd like a row in the lake and we could chuck grenades.'

Everyone was cold and soaking wet by now so the race was aborted and we returned to the house for some warming soup. Florez stayed chatting with Kit and Carl for a while before disappearing into the woods again on his way back to headquarters, leaving the men from the targeted dinghy to discuss how incredibly amused they were by the grenade-throwing incident, how much fun it had been, and what a joker Florez had turned out to be. Various forms of retribution were discussed; most would have got them shot.

Darkness comes early on rainy nights and after a hard day's work is often welcomed for its comforting release from the fatigue of the day. Men who ply their trade as mercenaries are no different; they also like to veg out after a day at the factory.

The bombardment of the early morning had not been repeated and even the mortar fire had stopped in the afternoon. Now the whole place was silent except for the English-language video of *Commando* that someone had nicked from a damaged shop in town.

With thirty-two men of various dispositions inhabiting the house there were bound to be arguments, some heated, but oddly few physical. In general, everyone got on just fine, making allowances for the odd eccentricities, of which there were many.

If you listened to them talking around the fire in the evenings, never before in the history of military warfare had so many men from élite fighting groups been in one place at the same time. SAS, Foreign Legion, Paras, Delta Force, Selous Scouts, Green Berets . . . we had them all here, with badges and stories to prove it!

Then there was Dave, of course. His needs were simple. All he wanted to do was kill – like the Yorkshire Ripper or the Black Panther – for that buzz. His glazed eyes hypnotised you as he spoke in a steady whisper: 'They had no feeling, no compassion. It's higher than any drug can get you – I think. Having that feeling of taking people out . . .'

The following morning, while the section leaders continued with basic training, Kit and other officers were told to attend army headquarters for a meeting with Colonel Florez. Discussion centred on a proposed covert operation behind enemy lines, to test enemy defences and obtain information on dug-in artillery positions and tank deployment. The meeting went well and Kit was enthusiastic, until Florez made the tactical error of informing him that he wanted his own men to lead the patrol, with Kit and his group merely observers. You could have heard a grenade drop as he made it clear that the new boys would be led by a group of thirty ex-woodsmen named – wait for it – 'Yellow Submarines'. We never did find out why!

In retrospect I think that this marked the beginning of serious friction between Kit and Eduardo Florez. There had been a few occasions in the past days when Kit had bitten his tongue when Florez had suggested something which he knew to be idiotic. But as a soldier, and a good one, he was used to taking orders and did so even if he felt the decision was wrong. On this matter Kit was adamant.

'Don't you think it would be wise to infiltrate with a smaller force?' he suggested.

'No, I do not.' Florez was equally intransigent.

Kit gazed around the room, desperate for eloquence.

'Look, Commander Florez, I have had a great deal of experience in sneaky patrols. Fewer men cause less disruption, are easier to control and are no less likely to succeed.'

Florez was quiet for a moment. It made sense, and he knew it, but he wasn't about to have his authority undermined. Finally he spoke.

'We shall do it my way.' His tone was sharp as he turned back to his papers, indicating that there was to be no further discussion on the matter. Kit had lost the first round.

The rest of the day went by in preparation for the night patrol. Check . . . check . . . check . . . Weapons, night-vision equipment, grenades. Black tape over shiny bits and make sure that nothing rattled. Velcro pouch fasteners were taped over – they may be fast but they're bloody noisy.

We were ready as darkness crept across the river. A silver half-moon occasionally peeped from a cloudy sky as Kit, Steve, Nigel, Pete and I joined the team of thirty ex-woodsmen and climbed aboard the trucks. The BBC crew wanted to come with us, but Kit waved them away with a 'Not this time, lads' as we pulled away heading for the river Drava and enemy lines.

The Croats were a noisy bunch, laughing, joking and gesturing at the British mercs, who sat quietly pissed off and muttering at the rear.

'Buncha fuckin' morons,' was Pete's only comment.

'Maybe he's right. Up to a point,' mused Kit, still smarting from the meeting with Florez. 'People who live in an area can often sense if there's trouble ahead. We may just stumble into it like fucking tourists.'

He fell silent for a moment. 'But he is definitely wrong about the amount of guys he's sending and who's in charge of the operation.'

We reached our front line and disembarked, making final adjustments to our facial camo. The moon kept popping out to look at us from time to time, making Kit even more nervous about the chances of a large group of men advancing through enemy lines undetected.

The leader of the Croats was a small, cocky man with a whippet face and a large moustache, obviously well immersed in his role as partisan fighter. He drew his men around him and began softly to sing their anthem of freedom, or something. Nobody asked us to join in, so we just waited impatiently until they had finished.

At Nigel's suggestion we were tempted to break into the old Beatles song, actually giving tongue to the line, 'We all live in a . . .' but it seemed childish and not in keeping with our image as professional soldiers.

The Croat captain's command of English was poor, and we struggled to discuss our objective in any detail. He was inclined to be pig-headed and arrogant, ignoring any advice offered by a willing Kit as he strode away, instructing his men to separate into groups of ten and search the surrounding countryside for ammunition dumps, tank depots and artillery pieces. If found, they were to be indicated on maps. That was it! Off they scurried, like boy scouts on a badge-gaining expedition.

'I don't believe it!' Kit stood there watching them climb over the defensive mound of earth marking the front line and walk into the pitch black no man's land ahead.

'Come on, let's follow the last lot. At least we can save them from being slaughtered.'

We could hear crunching feet and the crack of breaking branches ahead as we rapidly caught up the final group, whose section leader was a little more co-operative than the captain had been. He listened to Kit's advice, slowing his men down and spreading them out a little as we approached the heavily mined northern zoo area.

Kit had brought with him his most advanced detection device – a can of party string.

'Spray it out in front of you and watch it settle. It makes trip wires easily visible,' he told us.

It worked perfectly, and although not MOD-recognised was bloody effective.

'Step over. Don't cut the wires. With a bit of luck the Serbs will never know we've been here,' he told us. With this herd of buffalo blundering about . . . some chance!

Our ears were strained as we moved stealthily towards the cages. Florez had been telling the truth; it was a proper zoo. Lions and tigers roamed about aggressively, the silver moon reflected in their staring opalescent eyes. We weren't welcome and it was obvious that we had disturbed their slumber as they paced back and forth, hissing and swinging their angry tails at us.

'Hope they don't bark,' Pete whispered.

'Shut up!' Kit breathed. 'Since when have cats barked?'

The ten men around us were doing their best to move inconspicuously, but they just weren't good enough. They stumbled and fell, talked constantly in stage whispers. One lit a cigarette, keeping it hidden in his cupped hand until Kit struck him a glancing blow on his arm. Soon we would be nearing the enemy lines, with little chance that our presence would go undetected. Something had to be done to avoid what looked like the makings of a massacre. The gig should have been easy but it wasn't. God knows what the rest of the plonkers were doing.

We had reached the northern part of the zoo when somebody must have pulled a trip wire. All hell broke loose; an explosion to our right blasted earth high into the air, rapidly followed by concealed muzzle flashes a few metres away. Rounds zipped over our heads like ballistic bees and were followed by rifle grenades flattening the overgrown bushes around us. Then it was daylight as a flare burst and twinkled overhead, illuminating prostrate bodies. The noise was deafening as it rebounded off the concrete walls of outbuildings. An elephant trumpeted. Somebody screamed. Somebody cursed. Somebody hurtled past, his clothes on fire. It wasn't a sneaky operation any more, more like a badly organised firework display. It was time to get out.

'Kit! Where's Kit?' screamed Pete. Our beloved leader was nowhere to be seen.

'Perhaps he's been hit.'

A young Croat of no more than sixteen grabbed Nigel by the

arm, blood pouring from a gaping wound in his side. '*Treba mi doktor.*' I need a doctor.

Nigel did not understand. '*Govorite li engleski?*'

'*Da.* A doctor . . . It hurts.'

'It's supposed to fucking hurt!' He grabbed the boy and slung him on his back, ignoring his cries of pain. 'Shut up or I'll leave you for the Serbs,' he said.

The game was up. Twenty crashing figures came pounding through the wood to join us in our retreat as yet another flare burst high above, followed by the chatter of machine-gun fire cutting a path through the undergrowth, too far to the left to be a threat.

'Just as well the Serbs are crap,' Kit muttered breathlessly as he suddenly appeared from the wood, catching up with the fleeing mob.

We made it back to the south of the zoo and out of range, only to be met by shrieking monkeys leaping frantically from tree to tree in their enclosures as they tried desperately to get away from this man-made hell . . . just like the rest of us.

Nigel dropped the kid for Kit to look at.

'Tut, tut, tut, and what have we got here?' Kit cleaned off the blood, exposing a deep trough where a bullet had passed cleanly through the skin. 'It's nothing to worry about,' he told the grateful boy as he applied a field dressing to the wound.

Commander Florez wasn't happy with the result of the infiltration attempt and, slightly chastened, agreed that a smaller group should try again the following evening. He didn't notice Kit's little smile of satisfaction as he was leaving, and nobody ever found out who was responsible for pulling that trip wire . . .

The British mercenaries slept late the next day, waking to a bright morning for a change. They sipped coffee and lounged in comfortable armchairs while the birds sang sweetly outside in the battle-scarred countryside, having adapted to the all-pervading smell of cordite and the intermittent sounds of mortars and gunfire. Last night's failure was discussed and they laughed at the memory of the Croat captain as he ran petrified in front of his men all the way back to our line. It was amazing that not one person had been killed with all that shit flying around out there.

Tonight it would be different. It would have to be. Reputations were at stake; a fact that Kit pointed out to the art class who were amusing themselves between patrols by painting symbols on their helmets – Vietnam style. It was a great pity that Johnny Fontain had gone; he would have loved this. Dave naturally went for 'Yorkshire Ripper', neatly printed with a fibre-tip pen. Other popular themes were 'Hired Gun', 'Hell Sucks' and 'Terminator'. It was all kids' stuff, and the older, more experienced guys wanted no part of it.

Steve sat against the side of the house, lazily stirring a can of vegetable soup with a dirty plastic spoon, watching sudden raindrops plop into the food with disgust. The waiting was almost over. Soon it would be time to start work. The kids with their logoed helmets and their talk of killing had depressed him, and he had felt the need to escape for a while.

'You OK?' Nigel joined him, also bored.

Steve looked up, irritated by the intrusion. 'Yeah. I'll be glad when it's over. I hate covert patrols.'

'Me too. All this sneaky beaky stuff gives me the creeps.'

'Yeah, I know. Maybe I'm getting too old for this stuff.'

'Maybe we both are.'

They fell silent, aware that there was nothing further to be said.

'Kit wants us inside to discuss the op. He asked me to come and get you.'

Steve slowly poured the rain-diluted soup away and stood up, following Nigel into the house.

Kit was waiting for them as they entered, maps everywhere. 'OK. You can all listen.' He stared at the rest of the men. 'But don't interrupt! The patrol will consist of five men. Steve, Jim, our friend Marko, because he is a Croat-speaking Australian, and finally Malaria. You all know he is an ex-Spanish Legionnaire.' He counted on his fingers. 'That's only four,' he said smiling. 'Oh, and then there's me, and of course the groupie over there,' pointing in my direction.

He pinned one of the maps to the wall, indicating to the chosen men that they should join him at it.

'We are moving out at one a.m., so it's a good idea if you get some shuteye after the briefing. It's gonna be a long night.'

The chosen men did as they were told and tried to get some sleep amidst the constant chatter and bantering that went on day and night throughout the house. Kit, however, continued to dive in and out of the place, checking, checking, checking, like an old mother hen.

The camouflage-sprayed Lada estate was loaded and waiting

as the men, rubbing sleep from their eyes, jammed themselves in and Kit slipped behind the wheel. 'The magical mystery tour is coming to take you away . . .' he murmured as he released the clutch and the overloaded car pulled away toward the Drava bridge.

This time we avoided the zoo and cut through our lines about two kilometres to the east, once again using the party string technique to mark trip wires. Our passage went undetected and we arrived at the far edge of the wood without disturbing so much as a sleeping insect.

'A piece of piss,' breathed a satisfied Kit as we crawled into the open fields. Black clouds now masked the moon as we headed for a clump of trees to our right and a last minute kefuddle.

'Now you all know why we're here,' Kit whispered as he looked at his map, illuminated by the dim glow of a Betalight. 'It's in and out. No enemy engagement. Just information. Right?'

We followed him as he crawled to the edge of the tree cover, where he stopped and listened, waving to indicate that all was well. We moved out into the open country, getting that prickly feeling at the back of our necks as the cold sweat began to condense on the surface of our skin.

The field was like a swamp after the continuous rain, and the slurping suction of the mud made our movements less coordinated than we would have liked. Very soon we were covered from head to foot in the stuff, making the facial camo cream applied earlier superfluous.

At Kit's signal we split into two groups and, still crawling, moved in different directions, each man carrying his chosen weapon plus L2 grenades and a 66mm disposable rocket, just in case it all went wrong.

We slithered around like crocodiles, manoeuvring over ridges and sliding into gullies. In the total blackness only the whites of our eyes were visible. Kit held up his hand. We stopped and listened. Somewhere close by and to the right he had heard the sound of a man coughing. He indicated a turn to the left and we crawled with difficulty to the top of a large mound of sandy earth, to be confronted by rows of tanks. They were everywhere – T-55s, T-72s. There must have been twenty of the hulking brutes, their huge guns glinting as the quarter-moon slid from behind the clouds for a few seconds.

'Shiitt!' somebody whispered as we dropped low and waited for darkness to return.

'Stay here. I'm going for a closer look.' Kit slid down the mound and disappeared almost immediately. In less than two minutes he was back, breathing heavily – a huge lump of moving mud.

Flashing teeth in his encrusted face showed us that something good had happened out there, but we would have to wait for the details. He looked at his watch and beckoned us away for our rendezvous with the other group.

We had to wait for them in the open. The few minutes seemed like eternity until we heard the prearranged finger-snapping signal. They arrived by our side looking depressed. 'Nothing,' said a disenchanted Steve. Kit looked at him, making a tut, tut sound. 'OK, we go again. This time in one group.' He slid away and the five of us followed in line as it started to rain once again.

We slithered eastward, in the general direction of the zoo, as heavy rain started up again, deadening the sounds of our sluggish progress through the boggy earth. Like so many times before, I was wishing that I had given this one a miss. Not only was it dangerous, it was bloody uncomfortable. They didn't seem to care much, these mud rats, as they moved their hips in unison like synchro swimmers.

All at once Kit stopped, holding up his hand. He had seen something . . . We followed the direction of his pointed finger and sure enough it was possible to make out the rough shape of a building surrounded by stacks of steel barrels. We lay in total silence, listening until the sound of faint voices could be heard, filtering through the beating rain.

As we tried to locate the source, someone struck a match, its orange flame momentarily illuminating a small group of Serbian soldiers sitting on the drums, trying to keep dry under a poncho. They were about thirty metres away with their backs to us, oblivious in their discomfort.

Marko nudged Kit and pointed at himself and at the building, moving his fingers in a walking motion. Kit looked sceptically at him for a moment. Marko smiled and nodded his head, putting his hands together in prayer. Kit stared at him, and with an expression of resignation raised a thumb, indicating his cautious consent. Marko was gone like a snake, without a second glance.

He was good at this, his thin body gliding over the mud without making a sound as he reached the side of the building away from the Serbs and stood up, waving at us. We could just make him out as he peered through the windows and checked the barrels before dropping to his belly and sliding back to our position. He pushed his mouth tightly up to Kit's ear and we were just able to make out the words, 'Ammunition. Fuel.'

'Fucking great. Now we can go home!' The last words came from Jim.

In the pouring rain Kit marked on his map the positions of the tanks, ammunition and fuel dumps. The job was done and we turned to make our retreat with Malaria in the lead position as we headed gratefully towards the wood line. We had covered about two hundred metres and were just standing up from our crawling position when a movement caught my eye, dead ahead. By the time I had given it some thought it was all over. A two-man Serb position, directly in front of us, had been missed on our way in but we had stumbled upon it on our way out. Thank God Malaria was awake!

A Serb soldier, hearing the sounds of movement, had looked up to receive a faceful of AK-47 rounds which literally blew his head off, leaving a smouldering stump where his neck used to be. The other soldier fearfully jumped to his feet with his hands raised in surrender, as Kit, from simple reactive fright, shot him dead with five rounds in the chest. 'Leg it!' Kit yelled as he grabbed their weapons and took off, slipping and sliding on the slippery surface like a pissed ice skater.

We ran like hell towards the inviting trees, expecting a machine-gun burst from the Serb lines to cut us down at any moment, but it didn't happen. What did happen was worse. The earth in front of our running feet suddenly erupted and a dozen angry Serbs appeared from a bracken-covered trench – we had missed these coming in as well!

'Spread out!' someone screamed as the whole area was sprayed with automatic fire. Chaos, total and unrelenting. We all ran around one another like Keystone Cops, trying to avoid being hit by the barrage, making it into the wood to regroup without any casualties. Jim had a rifle grenade with him, and intending to slow down any pursuers he chucked it in their direction – or at least he meant to. In the heat and panic of the moment he must have had a relapse. Forgetting his early training, he used a live round in the chamber to propel the missile, which, finding itself blocked by the grenade, exploded, badly injuring him in the neck and chest. He went down writhing in shock and agony as the rest of us looked on in horror.

For some reason the Serbs did not chase us into the wood. Perhaps they suspected that we might lead them into an ambush. Whatever the explanation, we were able to make it to our own lines without further hassle, carrying a bleeding and very sick Jim on a lashed-together stretcher through our lines and to the waiting car, as the early sun came up like a bright red balloon. It had been a long night.

Jim was worse than we had suspected and was rushed to Osijek Hospital, where there was talk of sending him back to the UK for extensive treatment. Marko had also been hurt in the blast, not realising it until we were back home and he found his shirt covered in blood. It was not serious, needing only a good clean-up and some stitches.

Most of the details regarding the engagement were kept from Florez. Kit didn't want to burden him with trivia. Jim's injury was explained away as a simple blowback caused by an excess of mud in his weapon, and the whole exercise was deemed a complete success, thereby proving a point about small group infiltration. Kit had won round two.

As we showered and cleaned the thick mud from our bodies Nigel asked Kit about his recce on the tanks.

He smiled. 'How many tanks did you see?'

Nigel replied, 'About twenty, maybe twenty-five. Why?'

Kit's smile turned into a grin. 'There were twelve, some of them broken. The rest of what you saw were nothing more than full-sized wooden models.'

'Cheating bastards!'

'Come on, let's get our heads down.'

Commander Florez returned in the late afternoon. Fortunately we were awake by then, in time for him to hit us with yet another idea. His superiors had ordered an attack on Velika Pumpa, using the knowledge gained on last night's recce.

He explained that the pumping station and depot situated at the northern point of the zoo was a strategic target which, according to intelligence sources, was being used as the central ammunition and supplies point for the JNA. Self-propelled guns and tanks were hidden there. He also pointed out that the target was heavily defended by experienced soldiers.

He continued, 'This information would account for the extensively mined northern area of the zoo and the Serbians' aggressive retaliation on your abortive recce with the Yellow Submarines.' He gave Kit and the rest of the men a meaningful look.

'Before we consider a frontal assault, we must gain more information on the terrain and available armament. I suggest another recce. This time we bring back a prisoner for questioning. That is all, for the time being. We shall discuss it in detail later.'

Kit was the first to speak after Florez had left.

'It's no good looking at those fucking maps. They're crap! Let's go and have a poke around and see if there's something there. If there is, let's do it. We've got night optical gear and there's gonna be the lowest moon in six days. Just do your rain dance.'

Kit and Carl sat drinking at the kitchen table, discussing the probability of success should the attack take place. Carl, who disliked and distrusted Florez even more than Kit did, was unhappy about the whole thing. He stared morosely into space, concerned by the scale of the attack and the probable casualties.

'You've gotta watch him. He doesn't know what he's doing.'

Kit wasn't listening and turned to Carl. 'Who?'

'*El bandido* over there. Pancho Villa.' Carl continued, 'One thing we mustn't do. I'm not dragging any kids into it. I'm not having that on my conscience just so he can make himself famous.'

Kit nodded in agreement but said nothing. There had been a silent vote of no confidence in Florez from day one, when it was discovered that he'd had no military experience before being handed the position of commander on a plate. Further discussion with some of the original section leaders had led to the conclusion that it was his media connections that appealed to higher authorities, and with them the opportunity for excellent worldwide propaganda for the Croatian cause. His track record before our arrival had been abysmal, with many casualties being taken on unsuccessful missions.

A general depression deadened the atmosphere in the room as the men fidgeted and snapped at one another, staring vacantly at burning cigarette ends and empty cups. Waiting around for something to happen was no one's idea of fun.

'When's it likely to happen?' said Roy, looking nervously at Kit.

'I dunno. Florez didn't say when. He just said sometime soon.'

The gloom was broken by a request for interviews from the BBC producer. Roy, looking dispirited, followed the crew outside together with Dave, Andy and a few others, and when asked what he was doing in Croatia, replied, 'I don't really know. My mum thinks that I'm working at Euro-Disney.' He turned to the camera and waved, his chirpy young face grinning through thick camouflage paint. 'Hello, Mum.'

Andy told the BBC that he was AWOL from the British army, and said unconvincingly that he would probably choose to stay in Croatia permanently because he was having such a great time. A voice added quietly, 'In a body bag,' to dark laughter from the rest of the men.

Dave offered his philosophy with a smile. 'It's like Vietnam here. You get everything you want. You're the law and nobody messes with you!'

Kit and some of the others had joined us in an attempt to lift their spirits when the field telephone burbled in his pouch. The transmission was brief. 'That was a badly broken-up message from the patrol, sounds as if they're in a bit of trouble. So we're going out as a back-up.' The interview was called to a halt as the men ran back to the house, grabbed their weapons and jumped on the moving lorry, with the BBC crew included on this occasion.

When we arrived on the hilltop adjacent to the wood line, Kit tried to make contact again. 'Foxtrot. Foxtrot. This is the bear, over.' All he got was a crackle of frying bacon. 'These radios are shit. It's doing my head in . . .' He tried again. This time another broken message informed him that it had just been a little skirmish and our help was no longer needed. He stood up as artillery fire could be heard in the distance. 'So this is what they call a ceasefire. The bastards.'

No operations were called for that night, so we lazed around and let the sweat dry on our camo-tinted skin. The distant gunfire was temporarily forgotten as our heartbeats returned to normal. The radio played softly and cards were dealt, more by habit than with enthusiasm. Less than an hour passed before boredom set in and the lads dropped out of the game one by one. By now the air was thick with cigarette smoke and a lull fell over the banter as the men yawned, stretched and scratched their unwashed bodies.

'What about that time you were in Surinam, Carl?'

'Yeah, tell us about that!'

It was beer and bullshit time again – art forms at which all

101

mercenaries excel. Topics ranged from heroic exploits with women and wars to football teams and pop music; lies were told with such conviction and so often that the storyteller now believes them, even if nobody else does. Who cares? It's all part of the game. Amongst the banter and the beer cans being crushed, someone will always ask the universal question, 'What's your favourite weapon?' This comes almost always from a young, inexperienced kid with a bandanna around his forehead and tattoos on his arms. The older merc will look at him with an expression bordering on contempt, replying cryptically, 'Whatever I've got in my hand, son.' But it doesn't end there. Someone else always picks up the question. It's what most of them want to talk about anyway, waiting for the opportunity, waiting for an opening . . . waiting.

Guns hold the greatest fascination. Even experienced soldiers worship their weapons. They clean them, oil them, polish them, cradle and caress them, talking to them in hushed whispers that no one else can hear.

After the inevitable debate on merit has reached its climax and all the alternatives have been torn to shreds, the Kalashnikov AK-47 remains supreme with the mercenaries. With its formidable fire power of thirty rounds of 7.62mm cartridges, each with a penetrating core of steel, the weapon will spit out a hundred rounds in less than a minute, travelling at 1,600 miles per hour – at close range literally cutting a man in half! Awesome, available, reliable, cheap and beautifully balanced . . . Poetry in motion.

You can bury them, dig them up and fire them. Neglect them, abuse them but still rely on them. African warriors sing freedom songs dedicated to the Kalashnikov. US troops in Vietnam often ditched their issued M-16s in favour of captured AK-47s. From the snowy wastes of Russia, through forests, deserts, towns and jungles, the 'Klash Klack' may well be the last sound you ever hear.

Jason waxed lyrical about automatic weapons. 'I love them. The bright orange flame a yard long spitting from the barrel. The noise and the feeling that goes all through your body. It's a high . . . fantastic.'

Another young guy piped up. 'You gotta look mean! It doesn't matter how you do it, but you gotta look like you ain't gonna take no crap from nobody. Me, I always wear my ammo belts crossed over my shoulders like a Mexican bandit I saw in the films. It's bloody heavy, mind you, but with four or five days of stubble on my face and loads of grenades hanging on my belt, I look really hard. I never smile . . . well, not often, anyway . . .'

He dried up when he realised that his mouth was running away with him as Kit and the rest of the pros shook their heads in disbelief, sighing deeply.

'Shut up, you prat. Didn't you piss yourself when we went out last night?'

The kid died a little under the scorn of his superiors, knowing that he should have kept his outburst for the younger lads. Slowly he moved from his exposed position to join his peers in the corner of the room where they were reverently displaying their fighting knives to one another.

Their voices were hushed, not wishing to draw attention to themselves. 'Look at this one, it's a Buck, US army issue. Fucking great, innit? Feel that blade . . .'

The men showed little interest in these toys; their knives were battered and tortured old friends, used for opening cans, digging holes, cutting wood for fires – if necessary for killing the enemy, but only as a last resort.

'They don't understand,' whispered Kit, overhearing the muffled conversation. 'It takes a lot of bottle to kill a man with a knife. It's messy and they never die straight away. They cough and struggle and you've got to pull it out and try again somewhere else. Sometimes the knife gets stuck and won't come out – then you're in trouble.'

Men who live and die by the gun have a love affair with the tools of the trade, and the subject is inexhaustible. They continued to swap opinions until the early hours as one by one they dropped off into a fitful sleep, dreaming of the ultimate weapon . . .

Carl was absent from breakfast the next morning. This had happened before after one of his drinking bouts. As the day progressed, Kit's concern at Carl's absence escalated. He wandered about asking, without success, if anyone had seen him. It was suggested that Carl and two other instructors had decided to leave, but as their bergans were still by their beds the theory was discounted. Several hours and many questions later the truth was revealed. Apparently Carl – pissed out of his skull with Terry and Richie – had publicly mocked Commander Eduardo Florez, threatening to leave in the morning. Instead, Florez had ordered that they should be arrested in their beds by the military police and thrown into jail.

Kit thought that this might be a test to see if he would attempt to get them out. But he was resigned to their fate, saying in a matter-of-fact tone, 'Army regulations are army regulations. I can follow that. I know where I am. It's the civilian law I have trouble with. Anyway, they had too much knowledge of our activities over the next two weeks, so they had to be put somewhere out of the way.' He paused for a moment, finally saying, 'We're just guests in this country, a lot of people forget that!'

Florez was none too happy about the whole thing, making his feelings clear to the BBC interviewer later in the morning. 'I hate more and more the so-called professional soldier. Some of them are animals. They do not have any respect for the human person. They simply come here because they want to kill. This is not my way.'

Florez would no longer accept Carl in his group after the public embarrassment, and upon his release from jail he was forced to return to the UK.

The morning briefing, from a tight-lipped Florez, once again dwelt upon the proposed raid on Velika Pumpa. Croat intelligence had concluded from its information from our recce groups and other ground forces that the build-up of the JNA was for the specific purpose of an intended major offensive upon Osijek in the very near future, in a stroke gaining yet more territory. The UN were proposing to visit Eastern Croatia shortly and would have no choice but to accept Osijek as a Serbian-held sector when proclaiming borders. A previous infiltration by our recce team had shown that a frontal assault by Croat forces would be impossible, due to large earth deposits designed originally to stop water rising from the river when in flood. An alternative method of attack was needed and Kit had been given the task of finding it.

However, Velika Pumpa was not the immediate problem. The current ceasefire – yet another – was enabling the Serbs to continue their build-up without harassment. This was not acceptable to the concerned powers at military headquarters who, desperate for a solution, thought up a devious and illegal plan of action and offered it to Commander Florez.

When the good people of Osijek were fast asleep in their beds, four of the lads drove into town intent upon an errand of utmost secrecy, their mission – should they choose to accept it – being to kick-start the war again as quickly as possible. Kit, who had worked out the details of the strategy, led them to playing fields, churches, schools and already shelled houses, where they dug shallow holes and laid anti-tank mines, placed upside down and covered with sacks of sand. These were detonated with one-minute fuses, exploding all over the city, much to the merriment of the 'terrorist' force. The UN observers who were monitoring the Serbian ceasefire, assuming the explosions to be artillery or mortar shells coming in from the JNA, blamed them once again for breaking the agreement and gave permission for the Croatian army to retaliate against this act of aggression. We were back in business. The news broadcast of the following morning confirmed the official view: 'There was yet another ceasefire violation last night when the eastern town of Osijek came under heavy shell fire . . .'

The whole thing was supposed to be hush-hush and would probably have remained so had the *Inside Story* team not reported our involvement in it when *Dogs of War* was transmitted in the UK some months and ten ceasefire violations later. Like the volunteer badges said, 'Freedom Fighters for Croatia'. What the hell, we were only doing our jobs . . .

Our two main tasks for the foreseeable future were clear: to harass the enemy; and to check out his defences and deployment. We were going to be busy, busy, busy over the next few weeks, planning and popping across the Drava for a look-see.

A familiar sight met us as we returned from one occasional visit to the underground bar at the Osijek Hotel. Lying sprawled out on the settee in spotlessly clean camos were the welcome figures of Pop and Sprog. At last they had made it.

'About fucking time,' Kit said gruffly. 'Where the fuck have you been?'

'Missed us, did you? You Geordie sod. Leaving us behind to pay the hotel bill.' Pop looked at him, eyes twinkling.

Nigel came in, seeming pleased to see them, and shook Pop's hand. 'It's great to see you again, you old bastard.'

'Well, what have you been doing here while we've been living it up in Split? Where's Ivan, Jim and Pete?'

Kit told them how we had lost Ivan on the trip, and how Jim had been injured in the grenade blowback. He filled them in too on the Osijek gig, explaining quickly the impending attack from the JNA.

'Looks like we came at the wrong time,' Sprog muttered. 'More fucking aggro.'

'What happened at the hotel after we left?' Kit smiled in anticipation.

'You bastards! We had to do some fast talking at the nick when they arrested us, but in the end we convinced them that we were just employees of yours and not responsible for your actions, so they let us go. The big problem was that some prat nicked a painting from the hallway. Worth a bit it was, too! But as we didn't have it on us they couldn't prove anything. Which one of you took the bloody thing?'

We looked at Nigel. 'I told you it was valuable,' he said defensively, turning to Pop. 'It's a Renoir, you know.'

'No it fucking isn't! The bloody thing is just a copy by a local artist who is doing two years in the slammer for fraud. It's only worth a bit since he got caught and put away. Apparently he's sold Picassos and Van Goghs all over the world and become famous for his forgeries.'

Nigel sighed. 'Ah well, life's a bitch.'

'Then you die,' Pop added flatly.

We hung around for a while waiting for Steve to return from patrol and go through the same procedure of hand-shaking and insults. It was good to have Pop and Sprog back with us; none of the new lads here was quite 'family' in the same way.

A tour of the town seemed appropriate, so we climbed into the Lada and took off for a drive, first taking them over the bridge to see the front line and chat to some of the English-speaking Croat soldiers. Time had become an important commodity since the last briefing, and we didn't hang around for too long, dodging here and there as we explained the layout of the city and its defences, finishing up at a local bar to celebrate their arrival. As they were not yet established as members of the Croatian force in Osijek or under any commitment, we left them to wander around for a while, alone, whilst we returned to headquarters and the job in hand. We had started to drive out of town on our way back when Kit skidded to a halt, staring at a British-plated Range Rover parked outside a restaurant.

'Either that's the SAS or it's somebody trying to flog something,' he said with a knowing look.

We pulled over, parked, and Kit disappeared through the

restaurant doors and down the stairs. He was gone for about a half an hour, reappearing with a face lit up like a Christmas tree.

'It's Mike Stanton munching away in there! He's come over to flog some gear. I've told him he can stay with us and save some money on hotel bills.' Mike was an old buddy of Kit's from way back, now involved in the enterprising world of arms and equipment supply to whoever had the crinkly green stuff. Mike had told Kit that Dave Tomkins, another much-admired old friend and colleague, was intending to make the trip to Bosnia in the near future, selling amongst other things a new American Armbrust anti-tank weapon; lacking backblast, these are ideal for urban combat in the confined space of buildings or vehicles. Dave, a well-known and respected character in the mercenary world for the past twenty years, was a civilian entrepreneur without formal military training, but none the less competent and courageous under fire; proven by some hair-raising exploits in Angola and Colombia over the past few years. Kit was delighted at the news, bubbling over with enthusiasm as he described him in great detail as lean, tanned and elegantly dressed, with a tendency to wear expensive jewellery. He continued rambling on with stories of past adventures as we drove back to base. There an impatient Florez was waiting with the news that forty or more volunteers were expected within the next few days. Kit took this opportunity of telling him about Pop and Sprog, and he asked to meet them as soon as they returned from town.

The influx, although welcome, would cause problems with billeting the men all in one place. Kit put forward the idea of moving out of the already cramped house into something larger and more suitable. Various alternatives were discussed and abandoned; it was essential that we were away from the town and close to the front line. Finally, the now disused school was suggested. It would give us all the space required, plus outbuildings which could be used for storage and a playground outside for much-needed drill instruction.

Life was upbeat for a while as the lads divided into two groups: the 'locusts', whose job it was to obtain new gear; and the 'vultures', who toured the area appropriating reusable equipment. Both parties descended on the town and outlying areas in the dead of night, borrowing, stealing and liberating essential items of bedding, cutlery and cooking utensils. Lorries went missing from neighbouring farms as the transportation of equipment took precedence over everything. A dozen microwave ovens appeared one morning, donated by a kindly shop owner – or so we were told by a furtive-looking Nigel. Florez never asked how the transformation of the school had taken place but he seemed happy that for a while, at least, the men were behaving like a military unit with a common cause.

Chapter Seven

These, in the day when heaven was falling, The hour
when earth's foundations fled, Followed their mercenary calling And took their wages and are dead . . .

Epitaph on an Army of Mercenaries: A. E. Housman

Beli Manastir is a cute little place, a place where you could spend a
nice quiet holiday away from it all. It least it was, before the JNA
turned it into a garrison town and armament stronghold. About
twenty kilometres north of Isijek, and close to the Hungarian
border, it was an ideal stop-off point for transporting weapons
from outside the country.

Convoys of lorries heading towards Beli Manastir from somewhere inside Hungary had been detected for many weeks,
convincing our intelligence that their final destination was the
Serbian front line just across the river from us. The big push was
coming and something had to be done to slow it down, fast. A
serious attack on the arms movement was not feasible at this time,
due to our distinct lack of suitable equipment and trained men,
but hit-and-run tactics were.

'Love it, love it, love it.' Kit Freeman was in his element,
surrounded by friends, old and new, and with sneaky beaky
operations coming out of his ears.

The relocation from the domestic bliss of the house into the
school was now complete. Windows had been sandbagged
against flying glass, bunks appropriated from various sources
and the gymnasium at the far end of the building turned into a
very efficient armoury, with its roof and walls sandbagged
against shelling and mortar attack. The whole process had been
undertaken with lively enthusiasm by the lads as the building
took on an appearance of military efficiency. They even had their
flag flying over the parade ground – a red and white chequered
shield, crossed with a lightning bolt and sword, bearing the
legends '3FC HV' and 'Freedom Fighters for Croatia'. A lot of the
men actually began to smarten themselves up; some even washed
and shaved!

109

Covert operations, now called *'keeni-meeni'* by the ex-SAS men in the group – a Swahili term for the movement of a snake in the grass – were almost a continuous activity, being undertaken throughout the day and night as information on enemy movements was collated and returned to army headquarters in Osijek for assessment. Kit, in a moment of madness, did a skinny-dip night-time swim across the Drava, returning with a detailed layout of the Serbian-placed mines. Although we all knew they existed, their number and exact positions on the far bank were unknown and had been a constant worry since our arrival in Osijek. Kit couldn't rest until he had checked them out and indicated them on our maps. Later, though, he regretted his expedition, as he tried in vain to remove the camo cream from his huge body.

Most of the new consignment of men had now arrived; from France, America, Spain, Germany and the UK and of course various parts of Yugoslavia. Many, far too many, were inexperienced. Some were simply adventurers out for a fast but risky buck. A few were useless, condemned forever to the kitchen and a long way from anything that went bang or fired a projectile.

The BBC crew continued to float about the place, finally deciding after about a month that there was enough in the can. The finished product – shown on television in 1992 – was an ambiguous overview of a bunch of vagabonds, outlaws and Walter Mittys . . . frighteningly close to the truth.

Payment for performing in this epic was by way of a candlelit dinner for fifteen men in Osijek, names being drawn democratically from a helmet. It was a pleasant evening, only slightly marred by the whistle of Serbian artillery shells passing overhead as we reached the second course of *lignji* (squid) or *govedina* (beef). Most of the lads were sorry to see the BBC go. The crew and directors had done their job well and should be congratulated for their unobtrusive handling of the occasional tense moment, and their subtle conclusion.

The lads were more relaxed after the BBC had gone. Conversation and action with cameras and microphones around the place is never natural. Most of the time they were talking for the crew while pretending that a cameraman wasn't lying on the floor as they put their boots on. It had become almost a ritual, giving the Beeb what they wanted, acting out the role of 'dogs of war'.

Florez wanted a prisoner for questioning. 'Now. Tonight!' he said. It was already ten p.m. A 'snatch' group volunteered and four men grabbed their weapons and jammed themselves into the recently liberated and now camo-resprayed VW Golf GTi. The little overladen car hurtled away, its back wheels spitting mud and stones as it screamed off into the falling snow.

'This sneaky stuff is OK if you're out there doing it, but waiting around ain't my idea of fun,' said a jumpy Pete to no one in particular.

An hour passed. The dull thump of mortars continued, together with occasional small-arms fire; the sounds had become so much a part of life that you really had to concentrate to even hear them.

'Something's going on over there.' Roy was starting to pace up and down.

'Something's always going on over there. Sit down. You're making me nervous now.'

Someone switched the television on, and Pete jumped up and turned the sound down. 'Can't hear anything with that noise,' he said, glaring at the culprit.

'It's getting cold in here since it started to snow, innit?'

'Roy, why don't you shut up?' said Pop. 'The lads are out there in the middle of it and all you can do is rabbit on about the fucking weather.'

The room fell into an expectant silence, remaining so for the next twenty minutes until the sound of the returning car made us all jump up from our chairs and rush outside to meet it. The recce group, all in one piece, fell out of the car with a very frightened and bleeding prisoner – who had 'slipped on the stairs, your honour', judging from the fast-appearing bruises on his face. The man wasn't wearing a regular JNA army uniform, just bits and pieces of uncoordinated camouflage, leather pouches and a necklace of dried and blackened ears. He was a big, mean-looking bastard with manic staring eyes which flashed briefly as he was pushed unceremoniously into the building; suddenly he lost his cool and cowered as he blubbered away in Serbo-Croat, saliva running down his chin.

'Radio Florez and tell him we've got him a present,' Kit told Steve, as he dragged the man to his feet and sat him in an upright chair.

They stared at one another, eyeball to eyeball, for a full minute, as if attempting to psych one another out and gain the mental upper hand. The captor and the captured. The big Chetnik

111

sneered, contempt spreading across his scarred face. He was making his second mistake; the first had been getting caught.

Kit walked away, trying to get a grip on his rising anger, then turned and yelled, '*Da li govorite engleski?*' as the recce team clicked off their safety catches, pointing their weapons into the mouth of the now shivering prisoner.

The man didn't reply and clutched at his throat as if choking.

'OK. One more time. *Da li govorite* fucking *engleski?*'

The man looked up. '*Da* fucking?' he questioned.

'So you understand "fucking", do you, my son, but do you understand English?'

'*Mogu li dobiti . . . vodu?*' Can I have water?

'No, you can't have any water, you Chetnik bastard!' Steve replied impatiently, kicking the chair away and watching the prisoner curl up protectively on the floor.

'Hang on a minute, Steve. Put him back in the chair,' Kit said. 'Let's abide by the Geneva Convention. Get me a flannel and a bucket of water,' he instructed Roy, who did as he was told, returning with the question, 'What's the Geneva Convention, Kit?'

'I'll tell you later. Give it to me!'

Kit dipped the flannel deep into the water, holding it as it dripped on the Chetnik's face. The man's tongue darted through his cracked lips, searching for the moisture as it ran past his open mouth. The big ugly bastard didn't look so tough now, as his eyes rolled and his body sagged to the floor. He looked up at Kit, suspecting that all was not well, and curled in a ball, sobbing with terror.

'Haul him up on the chair again,' Kit told Steve and Pop. Then to the Chetnik, 'Last time, sunshine. Do you speak English?'

The man cringed away but said nothing. Kit waited for a full minute, then rammed the soaking-wet flannel over the man's mouth and nose, holding it until he struggled free. He waited and repeated the process, this time not allowing the Serb to move his head away until he started to splutter and choke.

'If you don't talk to me, I will drown you. Understand?' Kit was getting pissy now.

The prisoner gurgled as once again Kit thrust the wet flannel over his face, holding it tightly and making it impossible for the Serb to breathe. He counted slowly out loud . . . eighty-five . . .

112

eighty-six . . . The man fell limply to the floor, his chest heaving, just as Florez entered the room, looking anxiously at Kit.

'Is he all right? You haven't killed him, have you?'

'He's fine. We were just having a little chat when he came over all faint, so I got him a cold flannel for his forehead.'

'OK. I take him now. You have other things to do. I have planned an ambush for tomorrow night and I shall be coming with you. Don't make any other arrangements.' Florez started to leave with two military policemen holding the prisoner upright. Reaching the door he stared back, accusation written across his face as he said quietly, 'I don't know if you men are the solution . . . or the problem!'

The room was silent as we looked at one another, digesting his words of condemnation. Everyone knew in their heart of hearts that there was some truth in what he had said, although no one would admit it. These men were the warriors of the storm and could not afford the luxury of guilt, shame or regret.

'I'd like to see how he makes out without us, the plonker,' Pete said tetchily.

'What's the Geneva Convention, Kit?' Roy wasn't going to give up easily.

Kit took a deep breath. 'Well, in a nutshell, the Geneva Convention is a set of rules which govern the way prisoners are treated.'

'Oh . . . so you were joking about drowning him, then.'

'Roy, my son. These bastard Chetniks are the scum of the earth. They rape, torture and destroy . . . just for the fun of it. When you've been here for a while you'll see what I mean. If they ever capture you, which God forbid, they'll burn your eyes out then cut your fucking head off and stick it on a pole, just to show people that they've caught a mercenary. Nobody is going to stop me from giving the fuckers a hard time . . Nobody!'

The whole group nodded their heads in total agreement. Many of them had witnessed, first hand, the results of Chetnik savagery and none felt any sympathy for the prisoner as we all trotted off to bed.

Early-morning drill had become an integral part of the day at our new headquarters. Up at six and out on the parade ground for an hour's square-bashing. Lots of 'get your hair cut, you 'orrible little man' stuff – all taken with humour and a pinch of salt. A military sergeant major would have had a fit with this squad of oddballs wearing low-slung six-shooters, cowboy hats, long hair and earrings. It wasn't easy for the group leaders to knock these mongrels into shape – most of them had left the army because they didn't like, or couldn't take, enforced discipline, and had no inclination to continue it with the volunteer force. After parade we went to the firing range for some much-needed weapons practice – cutting up targets with a warm AK-47 is much more fun!

Then came SOPG – standard operating procedure, grenades. We started with a lecture on theory, with dry runs for those without any experience of the beasts. Kit laid a few stories of grenade fumbling on the new men, just to frighten them into taking care. Tales of a 'green' squaddie who had dropped a grenade after removing the pin and releasing the lever, injuring twenty men around him and mercifully killing himslf – who would have forgiven him? Grenade pins being pulled out by foliage in woods and jungles, short detonation times, duds and liberated grenades, doctored by the enemy. A tricky business is grenade warfare, it seems.

A short period of hand-to-hand combat came next, with a few bloody noses substituting for battle scars, followed by a fast run around the playground. So ended the morning training period for another day. An hour lounging in front of the television set rounded off an active morning.

The daily patrols had received their orders from Kit and left to infiltrate the enemy lines once again, while Florez filled Kit in on the details of the proposed ambush. For some time now, snipers had been picking off men on the Croatian front line. Although the number of deaths and injuries was low, the soldiers had become nervous at being subjected to indiscriminate attack, and morale was suffering as a result. The snipers always seemed to strike as the light was fading in the afternoon and the ambush planned to hit them as they were moving into position.

Kit's old friend Mike Stanton had arrived to take up the offer of accommodation, and we were introduced to this fresh-faced, moustached man of forty or so, wearing jeans, checked shirt and desert boots. He stayed for the briefing, becoming more interested as the story unfolded, finally asking if he could take part. At first Florez was sceptical, but with assurances from Kit on Mike's competence, he finally agreed.

'We have less than an hour to prepare and cross into Serb lines,'

Florez pointed out as he applied camo cream and checked his AKMS and bipod. 'You had better borrow some gear from one of the men,' he said to Mike. 'We cannot wait for you if you're not ready.'

Kit helped him scrounge the necessary, saying, 'You've got an itchy finger, haven't you, Mike?' Mike just giggled away like a kid going to the seaside.

'Ready?' Florez stood by the door, anxious to get away.

'Yo!' Mike replied, now fully kitted out with other people's gear and ready to go.

'He's a fucking nutter, mind you, so watch out,' Kit whispered as we climbed into the truck.

For a tactical infiltration, the whole thing was a disaster. Kit and Mike just couldn't take it seriously. They pissed about, laughing and joking all the way to our lines, becoming silent for only a few moments as we ventured into the woods. Florez installed the ambush across the path, suspected to be the route taken by the snipers, and he and Kit set up their AKMS on bipods, ready. The others were positioned by Florez in such a way that had the enemy approached, our men would have been cut down by their fire. He wouldn't listen when Kit tried to explain the positional error, insisting that his was the correct decision.

We waited . . . and waited. Three hours passed . . . four hours passed in silence before a buzzing sound captured our attention. Nobody moved as we tried to locate the source. It was close, very close. Florez was looking around nervously. It was getting louder, rising and falling in waves. As the sound reached a climax, it suddenly dawned: some bastard had fallen asleep and was snoring!

I looked up cautiously, only to see Kit and Mike pissing themselves with laughter as they threw stones in the direction of the noise in an unsuccessful attempt to waken the guilty party from his slumber.

As darkness filtered through the dense trees it became obvious that the Serb snipers had taken the day off, and stiff as boards from the long wait, the ambush was aborted. There was nothing left but to pack our gear and move out, making our way back to the friendly lines after phoning ahead to ensure a friendly welcome from the Croatian front-line troops.

Things were tense between Kit and the Commander after the ambush incident. It wasn't anyone's fault that it hadn't come off as planned. Perhaps it was just as well. Had there been an attack, wiping our own men out with his haphazard deployment could well had ended Florez's career.

Over the next few days, the snipers returned with a vengeance, killing eight men and injuring twelve others. Not only were they popping away at the front-line soldiers, but our patrols were being ambushed as they went about their routine business. Some of the Serb marksmen were deadly. Some, you never saw, never heard, never sensed. A whip-like crack and a body was lying at your feet with a look of surprise on its face and a neat bloodless hole terminating its existence. Then silence as the birds stopped singing and your neck hairs prickled with sweat, waiting for the bullet that you would never hear.

It couldn't go on. The woods were fast becoming a no man's land as men developed mild illnesses, preventing them from going on patrols into enemy-held territory.

'Something's got to be done about these bloody snipers,' Kit said to no one in particular. 'They're doing my head in.'

Pop, Steve, Nigel, Roy and a dozen others nodded blankly.

'Well,' said Kit. 'I'm open to suggestions.'

'What about . . . No, it wouldn't work.'

'What if . . .'

'How about mining the place?' Roy offered.

'How can we mine a place with them shooting at us?' Steve replied with more than a trace of sarcasm.

'Got it!' Kit jumped up and peered at the map. 'The zoo, that's the answer. We'll create a diversion, that'll fuck 'em up.'

'The zoo,' said Nigel flatly. 'What are we going to do? Let the animals out?'

'Yeah! You've got it in one. Gather round, children, and make yourselves comfortable. Uncle Kit's gonna tell you a story. This is going to be a bit of a laugh if we can pull it off.'

The map was taken from its place on the wall and spread on the table for all to see. Beer cans were zipped open, cigarettes were lit. It was down to business. The Bear had a plan.

'We've got to draw attention away from the zoo. That's the first priority. The Serbs know we're after something, that's why they're bringing in the snipers, so we've got to create a diversion for a few nights and make them think we've lost interest.' Kit looked around at the men, who were attentive and excited.

'We'll change our tactics. Tonight, six of us will head towards

Beli Manastir and bivvy down through the following day. Tomorrow we'll hit anything that moves – or doesn't, for that matter. Now, the guys that come have got to be good and willing, so let's see some volunteers.'

Twenty hands shot up.

'Can't take you all. Only five. Pop. You sure you wanna come?' Kit looked at his old friend. 'It could be fucking dodgy.'

'Perhaps you're right, Kit. The old legs ain't what they used to be. I might slow you down.' He withdrew his hand with a sigh of regret.

'OK, I'll make the decision. Steve, Pete, Nigel, Roy ... no ... Damiar. We'll need someone who speaks Serbian.' He looked around the room at eager faces and pointing in my direction – the only non-eager one – 'And you as a spare. You're definitely a spare something.'

He pursed his lips at the crestfallen looks from the lads. 'Don't worry. Some of you can come on the zoo breakout when we get back. Anyway, this is gonna be a shitty one.'

Over the bridge again. This time keeping well to the east of the zoo, we clambered through our muddy trenches, smiling and saying, '*Dovidjenja*' – see you later – to the tired and scared Croatian soldiers, who gave us that look which clearly said 'madmen' or 'prats' – it's difficult to interpret Croatian looks. We were loaded like packhorses with L2 grenades, AK-47s, FNs, 66mm M72s, claymores and of course our secret weapon, canisters of brightly coloured party string.

It was going to be a long haul through this enemy-infested twenty kilometres of countryside. We were all afflicted with the condition known as fighter-pilot twitch, our heads twisting and turning at the slightest sound. We managed to skirt the Kopacki Rit swamp without losing anything or anybody in its oozing mire, and headed due north, finding every little bit of cover mother nature had provided. A Serbian helicopter worked the tree line, dipping and hovering as its spotter/gunner peered through his dirty plexiglass door-screen. For a heart-stopping moment we thought he had seen us as he suddenly veered in our direction, swooping low over the swamp before climbing with a roar and heading back northwards.

We slogged on through the desolate open country for the rest of the day – most of which was spent face down in the mud. The odd Serb patrol passed, often a little too close for our well-being. The main road connecting Osijek with Mohacs, to the north of Beli Manastir, created a wall of uncertainty as we lay on our bellies counting passing military vehicles carrying clean and efficient-looking soldiers and supplies southwards from Hungary. An ambush was tempting but foolish. Compromising our position at this stage would jeopardise the entire operation; this was a job for our return trip.

Steve was sent up the road for a few hundred metres and Pete down, giving us a signal. As the road became clear we scuttled across like rabbits and dropped into the brush, just in time, as another APC blasted past. The bloody thing looked brand new. Where did they get them?

We skirted Bilje, the only village on the route, and headed out into the hilly area and a little more cover. With Steve upfront as scout we made better time, and within an hour were over halfway to our destination.

'We'll find somewhere safe and bivvy soon,' Kit said. 'We've got to flank Beli Manastir in the darkness, so it's only going to be a short kip.'

A small hollow was found and we settled down to some cold grub – C rations and water; we couldn't afford the luxury of drawing attention to ourselves with smoke or smells from food cooking. The lying-up point was well concealed and its position so easy to protect that only one man was needed for stag. The short straw was duly elected, changing every hour. By the time you had managed to shut off and get to sleep it was time to get up again!

With brains only half in gear – due to lack of sleep – we started out again, rubbing our eyes, with dense expressions on our sagging faces.

'How long is it gonna take, Kit?' Pete sounded knackered.

'Depends,' was his disgruntled reply.

'Bollocks then!'

We ambled sleepily onward, through the damp morning darkness, tripping over stones and quietly cursing. Soon lighted buildings began to appear to our left.

'Beli Manastir,' whispered Kit.

The place was larger than I had imagined, with gentle traditional buildings and cobbled streets now illuminated by arc lights, enabling maintenance work on vehicles to continue throughout the night. Through the darkness, and outside the town, it was just possible to make out the monastery itself – after which the town had been named – now shared by Serbian soldiers and monks in an uncomfortable alliance.

We had been lucky so far. The twenty-kilometre trip had taken less than five hours, right through the centre of enemy lines with no real confrontation.

Kit held his arm up and we dropped like puppets with our strings cut. Singing . . . we could hear singing, right behind us as we melted into the ground. Three soldiers appeared, arm in arm, swaying as they staggered in the direction of town. There was no way they were going to miss us. We were lying across their path. 'Damiar, do something,' Kit breathed. 'Now!'

Damiar looked over at Kit, shrugging his shoulders with a 'like what?' gesture. Kit replied with an 'anything' expression. It was like watching a silent movie, only not so funny. One of the Serbs stumbled over Nigel's prone body. '*Izvinite*' – Excuse me – he slurred, not even looking down.

Damiar climbed to his feet, dropping his helmet in the grass, as inspiration spread across his cherubic face. He swayed forward, taking a bottle from the Serb's hand, pouring the liquid down his throat in one deft movement. '*Specijalno pivo, da?*' Strong beer, yes? The Serb looked at him with unfocused eyes and held his hand out for the now empty bottle.

Damiar fumbled in his smock, withdrawing his cigarettes and offering them in return.

'*Izvolite cigaretu?*'

The soldier continued trying to focus as he answered, '*Ne pusim . . . Prestao sam da pusim.*' I don't smoke . . . I've given it up.

We could all hear and understand the dialogue so far and it wasn't going too well. This sort of thing always worked in the movies, but we had to get a soldier who had quit smoking!

Damiar was beginning to panic as he offered his cigarettes to the others. Both refused. The four of them stood there swaying and looking blankly at one another.

Finally Damiar spoke. '*Da li bih vam mogao doneti neko pice?*' Can I get you a drink?

He had struck the right chord. They turned to one another and smiled, clasping Damiar around the shoulders as they all staggered back the way they had come.

'Fuck it. Now what?' Kit climbed to his feet as the three Serbs and Damiar disappeared into the darkness to sounds of tuneless singing.

This was a problem of major proportions. In the darkness the drunken Serbs had been unable to distinguish Damiar's different uniform and shoulder patch, but in the light of a bar he was going to be in dead trouble, and so were we.

'We can't hang around,' Kit whispered. 'It'll start getting light in a few hours and we've gotta be long gone by then.'

'We can't leave him. Shall I follow and do them?' Steve suggested.

'No, you can't do that. Someone will know they're missing at roll call in the morning.' Kit scratched his shaven head and stared at the stars in desperation. 'Shit, this could be funny if it wasn't so tragic. Let me think.'

We sat there on the cold ground as our brains went into overdrive, watching Kit fiddle with his radio.

'It's no good, we've got to move out. If we wait, the delay will jeopardise the whole caper.'

We gathered our gear together, this time having to cope with Damiar's as well, and loaded ourselves up, ready for the off. We looked back in the forlorn hope that Damiar would appear, but no such luck.

'OK, let's go,' Kit said in a resigned tone, leading us on our anti-clockwise loop around the town. We tried to keep our failing wits about us. There was a lot of noise coming from the square as lorries were loaded for a pre-dawn run southwards, reminding us that we were here to stop this sort of thing.

For some reason Pete had finished up getting lumbered with most of Damiar's gear, and his progress was suffering as a consequence. He stumbled and muttered curses, dragging behind us as we tried to make up some lost time. It wasn't going to work. His extra load was simply too much, so we stopped and waited for him to catch us up for a redistribution of his pack.

'I'm knackered, Kit. Can't we stop for a bit?' His face was white with effort as he panted up to us.

'Five minutes only. No talking.'

We took some of the gear from Pete, who visibly straightened before our eyes before lying back for a blissful few minutes' break. A sharp crack of breaking twigs and the rustle of bushes put a stop to that. Kit and Nigel grabbed their AKs and rolled to the side of the clearing, safety catches coming off as they went. Steve, Pete and I froze. Only our eyes moved. Something was out there. Kit and Nigel slid away to flank the intruders, leaving the three of us to play targets, pretending to hear nothing as we busied ourselves with the gear.

Crack! In the darkness it sounded like a pistol shot, and we instinctively ducked. 'Sod this!' Pete grabbed for his weapon and clicked off the safety, aiming directly at the sound of the noise.

'It's me . . . It's me . . . Damiar. Don't shoot . . .'

By that time Kit and Nigel were behind him as he walked out of the brush, hands in the air.

'You were fucking lucky there, my son,' Pete said. 'I was just about to let one go.'

'Yeah, it's been a lucky night all round,' Damiar replied. 'Two of the bloody Serbs passed out before we got to the bar and I left the other one with them. I'm supposed to be going back to sign them all in, but I don't think I'll bother.'

'Great to see you back,' Kit said hurriedly. 'Now let's move!'

Daybreak was cutting through the dense clouds as we skirted the sleeping village of Popovac, keeping far to the west out of harm's way. Our attempt at silent approach was almost ruined by a dog barking at us from the nearby farmhouse as we stole some eggs, causing some consternation but stopping before any damage was done. We scurried away like poachers in the night, heading for our first target, the main E73, the route through the Hungarian border taken by supply trucks into Beli Manastir.

It was time to find a suitable spot for a lying-up point. We all needed a good rest and daylight made travelling a hazardous occupation this far into Serbian-held territory.

'This'll do.' Kit threw down his pack. We had come upon a small copse a long way from any buildings, with a clear view on all sides. It was a good spot in which to kip unseen, unless we had to defend it. In which case it was bloody terrible.

Without any further discussion we all got our heads down, leaving Nigel on first stag with Pete to follow two hours later. We slept like babies, until woken by the 'cook' shoving fresh free-range eggs at us. We munched away slowly as Kit gave us a quick recap on the mission and its objectives.

'Now you all know why we're here?'

We nodded in unison.

'Just in case you've forgotten, I'll remind you.' This time we shook our heads, but he carried on regardless. 'We are here to harass the enemy and draw his attention away from our main target, which is the zoo. We are not here for a full-scale battle. We are not here for a face-to-face punch-up. We are not here for a fight of any kind . . . understand?'

'Yes, Kit,' we choroused.

'It's shoot and scoot. Blow and go. OK?'

'What are we going to blow first?' Steve asked.

'I'm glad you asked that, Steve, it shows initiative. I dunno.'

He had all day to think about it as we listened to trucks passing no more than a hundred metres away from us as they trundled their way south. In the late afternoon Pete covered himself with branches and crawled slowly to the edge of the road, reporting back that two tank transporters had gone past with T-72s on board. Pity we missed that one.

Typically, it had started to drizzle. A fine mist filled the air and darkened the sky, uncomfortable to work in but useful cover for our purpose. The question was, should we attack a convoy with RPG-7 rocket launchers or blow the road with anti-tank mines? One way we were sure of a worthwhile target, but with problems getting out. The other was hit and miss but we could be miles away before the big bang. A show of hands was called for. Democracy rules, OK?

'What if we attack and another convoy is following close behind? I don't fancy being caught out this far from home. We'd never get away with legging it.' Nigel voiced everyone's thoughts.

'That's no problem. One of us could go up the road and another down, signalling when there was nothing in view.' Pete added his opinion.

Kit was silent for a moment. 'If we had more time we could work out the schedule. These Serbs are methodical bastards. I'll bet the convoys run like clockwork.'

'Yeah, but we haven't got more time,' Pete replied, unnecessarily.

'We'll blow the road.' Kit's voice was matter of fact. 'If we set it up at night we can get back to Beli Manastir and cause some havoc there before making our way back to Osijek.'

Decision made, we sorted through our claymores, trip wire, timers and plastic-bodied Yugoslavian TMA-2 anti-tank mines.

'Are we gonna use timers, "clackers" or trips?' Damiar asked.

122

'It's gotta be trips. We don't know when a convoy is coming and we don't want to be around when it does. Do we?'

The gear was now sorted, laid out and checked. At last light we were ready to go, as the Serb chopper droned over our heads, following the road south toward Osijek – searching for terrorists, maybe?

In the gloom of drizzling rain we crawled across the open ground and up to the road. Nothing had passed for an hour or more, signalling, we hoped, the end of transportation for the day.

We dug like beavers for well over an hour, burrowing under the road as far as possible with our limited digging equipment. Trip wires were attached and positioned across the road, right side only. We weren't interested in empty trucks going back northwards. Claymores came next: some positioned each side of the road and facing inwards on a time delay to get men running from lorries, others facing outwards to pepper them as they ran away. The claymore anti-personnel mine is a vicious beast, spreading an arc of steel balls over sixty degrees wide and two metres high – like a static shotgun.

We completed the task before nightfall, returning quickly to collect our gear before beating a hasty retreat. Just in case we'd got it wrong and other traffic used the road before the daybreak convoy run.

'Check and clear everything. Everything! Bag up your shit and stow it in your bergans. We don't want anyone to know we were here. If it all goes wrong they could follow our tracks and ambush us further down the line.'

Kit did the final check, as always, before we moved out of our hole and retraced our entry route back towards Beli Manastir.

With the lightened packs we were able to maintain a good pace over the smooth ground, arriving at the town ahead of schedule. Men were moving around loading and unloading as we found a hollow and crawled into it for a kefuddle.

'Two of us will go in,' Kit said before we'd even had a chance to settle. 'The rest of you keep a good lookout. I don't want any surprises. Steve, you come with me.'

They kitted themselves out with grenades and explosives, checking their pistol and AK-47 magazines before reapplying camo cream to their faces and hands.

'You ready?' Kit said.

Steve nodded.

'Let's do it!'

They moved slowly towards the back of a storehouse until they were hidden from the street ahead, then, jumping to their feet, they ran like whippets, pressing themselves against the wall before inching forward to look around the corner of the building. All clear. They looked back at us, waved, and were gone.

There was a lot of noise coming from the town centre. Guttural engine clatter and exhaust fumes filled the air and drifted in our direction.

'That's a fucking tank,' Pete said in an authoritative tone.

'Reckon?' Damiar whispered.

'Too bloody right,' Pete confirmed.

'We'll soon know, when the lads come back.'

All I ever seemed to do was wait. I remembered the quote, but not the source: 'They also serve who only stand and wait . . .' Still, it was a whole lot better than running around getting shot at for a living, like these guys.

Nigel looked at his watch for the fourth time. 'They've been gone for half an hour,' he said. 'It's getting cold sat here.'

'Go and have a look if you're bored,' Pete told him with a smile. 'I'm sure they could do with some help.'

'Bollocks!' was Nigel's traditional response.

The engine noise died down and was replaced by loud, urgent voices.

'What are they saying, Damiar?'

'Can't hear . . . Something about a crane . . . lifting . . . dunno.'

A clanking, grinding sound took over, drowning out the raised voices. It was driving us mad. Like when the screen goes blank on a television and they continue in sound only, and you sit there trying to imagine what the characters are doing.

'Go and have a peep,' said Pete. 'I won't tell.'

'You go, if you're so curious.'

Pete shut up and sat picking mud off his smock, flicking it in the air.

'Look! They're coming back.'

The shadowy but unmistakable figure of Kit could be seen lurking by the corner of the outbuilding as he waited for Steve to join him. He gave a thumbs-up; everything was OK.

They dropped to their bellies and snaked across to our position in the hollow, arriving breathless but high on adrenaline.

'Did you get on all right?' asked Damiar quickly.

124

'Did we get on all right? You'd better believe it. Let's get the fuck outta here. This is no place to be right now.'

'Are we going straight back?' Damiar panted as we tried to put as much space as possible between us and the town.

'No,' replied Kit. 'We've got to make sure all of the roads into Osijek are fucked up. Hang on, let's have a quick shufty.'

He rummaged in his smock and withdrew a crumpled De rouck cartography map of Yugoslavia, bought in a Zagreb bookshop. Not very tactical, but easy to read, with all the trig points clearly indicated.

'Look, there's Osijek. We've still gotta do the 17-1, before or after that little village . . . Lug, isn't it?' A crease on the map made the name difficult to read. He continued, 'We've set the timers in Beli Manastir for one hour. That means,' he looked at his watch, 'we've got forty-five minutes before it blows. Bags of time.'

Off we went again, circling east towards our third objective. All at once Kit held up his hand, stopping us dead in our tracks.

'This is stupid. We don't need six of us to blow a poxy little road.' He pointed at Nigel. 'You can handle that, can't you? Take Pete and Damiar, some timers, mines and a few claymores. Don't bother about trips – just blow a few fucking great holes in the road.' He added a warning: 'And be careful about patrols. We've been lucky so far but they're out here. Move a little, stop, wait and listen. If everything's quiet, move on. You know the drill.'

He looked at Nigel, who was busily sorting through the gear, and added quietly, 'And look after yourself. We'll meet you back here in thirty minutes.'

They scuttled off, leaving us to embark upon our final mission; the railway linking Osijek with the north. Time was foremost in our minds as we headed westwards to pick up our final objective. This one should be easy; we could blow the rails at almost any point we chose. There was no tactical advantage in selecting a specific position – with the exception of a bend in the tracks, perhaps.

'There it is!' The dull moonlight etched the burnished curves of the track a few hundred metres before us. 'It's bloody exposed,' Steve murmured.

Kit was scanning the open area with his night-vision binos. He pursed his lips in doubt.

'Yeah, let's move up a bit. We can crawl down that depression over there.' He pointed to our right, where there was some marshy ground and a slight dip leading to it. 'Come on, we're behind schedule.'

The point at which we arrived at the track had been levelled with gravel chippings, making the planting of explosives and timers a simple task. The whole process took less than ten minutes of feverish activity. We were sweating like pigs as we slithered up the depression and, crouching low, ran back to our bergans, strapping them on as we made our way back to the rendezvous position.

Nigel and the lads were already there, faces beaming with satisfaction. 'All done, boss,' he said. 'Ready to go when you are.'

'No trouble with patrols?' Kit asked him.

'Nothing. It was a doddle. We did a line along the centre of the road. It's going to make a hell of a mess when it blows.'

'*If* it blows,' Pete whispered.

Kit checked the time, staring in the direction of Beli Manastir in the failing light. 'I'd love to be around when it all goes up. Oh, and I forgot to mention . . . Those tank transporters we saw on the road are there. Two lovely T-72s aren't going to be much use to the Serbs after all the stuff we shoved in them detonates.'

He looked again at the town and with a final disappointed shrug waved us on.

It didn't sound like an explosion at first – more like distant rolling thunder. In the dense night air, filled with rain and damp mist, the noise had become distorted and muffled. We stopped and turned, seeing the night sky take on an orange glow as repeated blasts melted into one gigantic roar, subsiding briefly before starting again on a lesser scale, much closer and to our left.

'That's the railway,' said Kit, as another series of explosions to our right joined in. 'Two, three, four . . . five.'

'And that's the road,' Nigel added. 'They all worked!' He was elated at his first solo success in demolition, insisting upon explaining in detail to a bored Steve how and where he had placed the mines.

Apart from the glow in the sky there was little else to see. We made our way back to Osijek and through the jubilant lines of soldiers, who had also seen and heard the results of our night's work.

By the time we arrived at the school, Florez was waiting by the entrance, having driven out from headquarters to meet us with the news that intelligence reports had confirmed all of the missions as successful. A convoy travelling down the main E73 from Hungary had lost four trucks carrying men and machinery. The arms and ammunition buildings at Beli Manastir had been partially destroyed, with two tanks reduced to scrap metal, and the railway and road had been badly damaged but with no casualties. Repairs to both could be completed within a week, we were told. It didn't matter; we had achieved our objective, and the diversional breathing space required, without loss or injury. Florez was a very happy man – which pleased Kit not a bit.

'That bastard's going to take all the credit for this and it had nothing to do with him,' he fumed as he angrily scrubbed camo cream from his face. 'But what can you do?' He shrugged. 'That's the army.'

We wearily dropped our gear where we stood as some of the lads came over to congratulate us, shaking our hands and pouring much-appreciated drinks for our parched throats. Nigel went straight into his demolition story, explaining in great detail how he had worked out the correct positioning of the mines. The kids listened. The vets didn't. Nigel enjoyed reliving it, though, and it was harmless fun for a change. All was well in our camp of vagabonds and gypsies, for the time being at least. The next heavy op was going to be the zoo. But not before a warm bath and a long, long kip.

The following day drifted past in a blur of semi-consciousness as we tossed and turned, trying to avoid fragments of conversation from the lads as they went about their patrols and other duties. The occasional loud voice filtering through a dense wall of sleep and the odd shriek from a passing shell interrupted our slumber. Nothing mattered much. The whole operation had been outrageous, and we deserved the rest.

'Jumping Jack Flash' finally did the job. Waking with a start, we were faced with a grinning Pop – who took his collection of Stones tapes everywhere.

'Great operation, Kit, bloody magic! Now get up, you lazy sod, there's trouble at mill.'

Kit sat bolt upright, staring straight ahead, his hand moving rapidly toward the AK-47 propped by the side of his bed. 'Whassamatter. Oh . . . Pop. What did you say?'

'We got a problem. Dave's knifed a German journalist in a brawl.'

Kit was fully awake now. 'There's nothing I can do about it, Pop. Has he been arrested yet?'

'Yeah. They came and got him straight away.'

'Well. That's the end of it then.' Kit sighed. 'Something like this was always on the cards for Dave anyway. You only had to listen to him to see that he'd go off the rails and do somebody one day.'

The room was full of chatter. The incident had caused quite a stir in the town last night, but no one knew any details, apart from the fact that a fight had started in a bar and a journalist had been stabbed. No doubt Florez would enjoy filling us in later with a lecture on the unacceptable behaviour of the mercenaries under his command.

We had slept the day away and felt better for it. As evening set in, Steve, Pete, Nigel and Sprog were playing cards, loudly arguing when Sprog kept winning. Kit and I were going over my notes, and the rest of the lads were sprawling around the place, doing nothing but with a lot of style.

What sounded like a heavy table being dragged across the floor in the next room grabbed our attention. Then the noise changed into the distinct clatter of continuous fire from a weapon on full auto.

'Fucking hell, we're under attack,' Pete screamed as he dived for the floor, followed by most of the others.

The noise stopped abruptly, at about the same time as we realised that we had taken no hits. But before we could move from our prone positions the door to the next room opened and a blood-covered Australian stumbled in, collapsing on the floor. Kit and Steve were the first ones up, dashing into the room to find an equally bloody Damiar and another guy holding his punctured arm.

'What the hell's going on?' was the immediate question. Unnecessary; the picture was clear. Damiar, looking white and sheepish, held a Zaggi in his limp hand, its magazine now empty and on the floor by his side. The walls around him were peppered with a neat row of holes from floor to ceiling.

'The fucking thing just went off,' he said mournfully. 'There was nothing I could do to stop it.' The gun dropped from his hand as he passed out.

The 9mm Zaggi is a very bad Croatian copy of the SMG, its major fault being a continuous discharge of the magazine as the trigger is pulled, with no way to halt it. Damiar had been cleaning the gun, tripped the trigger by accident and sprayed the room, shooting himself and two others as he tried, unsuccessfully, to withdraw the magazine. It must have been a terrible experience for those men, trapped in that room with an uncontrolled automatic weapon spitting at them, and with nowhere to run or hide. Everyone's nightmare.

Fortunately, although the men required hospitalisation, none of the injuries was fatal; thanks to Kit, who injected morphine into Damiar and saved his life with an insane, horn-blaring drive to Osijek Hospital where the doctors took over, pumping blood into his leaking body. He smiled up at us as we started to leave, murmuring 'Sorry ... so sorry,' as he drifted in and out of consciousness. There was nothing more we could do for him, so we collected the two walking wounded from the casualty wing and returned to base, just a little depressed at the stupidity of the whole thing.

'Let's get the show on the road.' Last night's episode forgotten, Kit was planning the zoo caper. 'This time we'll take a team of ten. We need to be in and out fast. Once we've opened the cages we'll have more than the Serbs to contend with.'

A large-scale map of the zoo had been acquired, by kind permission of somebody who knew somebody who used to work there. We were all staring at it, trying to get our bearings.

'Everybody got it sorted then?' Kit started drawing impressive-looking lines on the map. 'This is the perimeter fence and here are the Serbian lines, through the north of the zoo. First of all we'll cut the perimeter wire in twenty places, just to make it easy for the animals to find exits. Make sure you've all got wire-cutters.'

'When are we going?' asked Roy.

'Tonight,' replied Kit.

'Tonight?' repeated Roy, his voice rising an octave.

'Tonight.' Kit smiled. Roy's face was a picture of dismay at the immediacy of the mission. 'Are you sure you wanna come, Roy?' he enquired.

'Oh yeah, 'course I do. Just asking, that's all.'

We were leaving at dusk, this time travelling light, with just wire-cutters and personal weapons, plus a few grenades, maybe a claymore or two ... You never can tell how it's going to turn out. Can you?

Chapter Eight

Those who kill for pleasure are sadists, Those who kill for money are professionals, Those who kill for both are MERCENARIES. . . . that's what it said on the T-shirt.

Operation Zoo Quest was finally adopted as a suitable title for our mission of liberation after many silly alternatives were tossed around and rejected. The name, chosen by a nostalgic Nigel who recalled watching the programme on television as a kid, was appropriate for the task, or so he assured us as we plotted and planned throughout the entire day, trying to predict the problems that would arise from releasing dozens of wild animals into the open countryside. Would they run? Would they attack us? Would they stay put? We decided that the probable answer was all three. It didn't help.

'We'll operate in three groups, each with a radio and call sign. I'll stick with the Bear. You, Steve, can lead one of the other teams. What call sign do you want?' Kit was cooking with excitement.

Steve thought for a moment. 'I think Snake would be an appropriate name for us . . . we'll be slithering in and out.'

'Fine, you plonker. Take Sprog and . . .' He looked around the eager faces, his gaze settling on a new American volunteer, an ex-CIA guy – or so he told everyone. 'Do you wanna go, Spooky?'

'Uh . . . Uh . . . yeah. But I ain't killing no animals, mind you.'

'Nobody's killing any animals, Spooky. That's not the objective. Will you fucking listen?'

He turned to Steve. 'OK. That's you, Sprog and Spooky in group two. Now, how about you, Pop? Do you want to lead a group? You've been a lazy old sod since you got here.'

'Yeah, OK, I'll give it a go.'

'Right. What about a call sign?'

'How about Hippopotamus?'

'Are you taking the piss? You can't have that!'

'Why not?'

'It's too fucking long to start with! Think of something shorter like . . . Frog or Pig. Something like that.'

130

'Sod off! Why should I have a crappy call sign when you're having the poncey ones. We'll have Hippo, OK?'

'Yeah, OK. You take Roy and Tommy in group three and I'll have Pete and Franz.' The latter was a German ex-GSG-9 lad, hard as nails, twice as ugly and known to all as Kraut.

I was given the option of accompanying the group of my choice, so I went for Kit's. Better the devil you know, as my old grandpappy used to tell me.

Kit called a halt to our planning brief as he went to the telephone. *'Gde ima doktor koji govori engleski?'* Where's there a doctor who speaks English? His Serbo-Croat wasn't perfect, but the hospital receptionist got the message, leaving Kit to wait, drumming his fingers impatiently, staring at the ceiling.

'Doctor? The patient brought in last night. Damiar . . . I don't know his other name. How is he?'

After a few minutes of one-sided conversation he returned to the table and our questioning eyes.

'He's had a bad night but is showing some improvement. The doctor said that an early diagnosis indicates that he could lose the use of his left arm where it was hit at the elbow. They won't know for sure until later in the week.' He sighed. 'Gutsy little bastard he was, too.'

There was a short silence as we all tried to think of something to say. Nothing came, and a cup of coffee seemed as good a solution as any to break the spell of descending gloom.

'He'll be all right,' said Pete. 'He uses his right arm anyway.'

'What for?' Roy asked.

We all looked at one another, smiling, then laughing at his naivety. The melancholy mood lifted and we returned to work on our 'Save the Animals' mission of mercy.

'Better check the radios,' Kit suggested. 'The bloody things are crap. What we don't need is to lose contact with one another out there.'

We checked, finding that only four out of a possible twelve actually worked – and those squawked and burped at us. Batteries were flat, water had shorted connections out, others were fit only for the knacker's yard. In fact, most of the gear supplied to us by the Croats was old, battered and in many cases bloody dangerous, requiring an almost constant programme of maintenance. Many of the weapons in use by the Croatian army were of World War II vintage, rusty and worthless, due to the arms embargo inflicted on them by the more powerful countries of America, Britain and others. We could never fully understand why the Serbians weren't penalised in the same way. 'Fucking politics,' was Pop's profound explanation.

Commander Florez suddenly appeared at the door without warning and Kit took the opportunity of asking him if any information had been obtained from the recently captured Chetnik. Florez was evasive and kept changing the subject, getting snappy as Kit prodded for an answer. His whole attitude made us suspicious. We even wondered if the man had escaped whilst in his custody and he was trying to hush the whole thing up.

'How are your plans coming along?' Florez asked, looking over our shoulders at the map of the zoo. 'Do you want some of my Yellow Submarines to help you?'

Kit struggled for a while before answering. 'Everything's coming along fine, sir, but thanks for the offer. We've got it sorted now. Anyway, I expect there are more important things for your men to do than mess around letting animals out.'

'Yes, you're right.' Florez nodded gravely, completely missing the irony in Kit's comment. 'When are you going?'

'Tonight. At dusk.'

'Good luck. Report to me when you get back.' Florez turned abruptly and left, bad vibes hanging in the air like the smell of dog shit.

We spent another two hours going through the motions of planning and trying to make some sense of the old zoo map, with its creases and tea stains obliterating much of the important detail. We discussed escape and evasion tactics should the whole thing go belly up, and made final adjustments to our gear and equipment. Now there was nothing left to do, apart from getting our heads down for a few hours before the sun set and it was time to do the business.

Clattering noises from the kitchen woke us one at a time. Pop, always the first one up, was making some scrambled eggs for us. We rose slowly, stumbling bleary-eyed to join him at the table, and ate in silence as the daylight slowly faded.

'It's time to go, lads.' Kit's voice had a finality about it that was disturbing.

We picked up our meagre equipment, trooping slowly out to the now open-top DAF truck. It had been modified a few days

132

earlier by Kit, who complained that the low roof 'does my head in'. His alteration, though extreme, did allow us a clear view of the sky, and we registered immediately that the weather was far from ideal for a trip of this nature. It was a clear evening, with a full moon lingering behind dark clouds, constantly threatening us with its silvery light. It was a moon for werewolves to howl at, lovers to gaze at, astronomers to contemplate through telescopes. What it wasn't was a moon for wandering around enemy-infested countryside. We all knew it, felt it deep in our gut, but nobody said a damn thing as we turned left and started to drive over the Drava bridge for what felt like the hundredth occasion. Only this time it was different.

Franz saw it first, pointing down into the thick, mud-coloured water as it swirled through the weeds below the bridge. We stared, but could see nothing. 'There. Over there!' He moved his arm as the current swept piles of debris downriver. 'Look! On the opposite bank.' It was difficult to make out the shape for a while until our eyes had become accustomed to the gloom. 'Can you see?' Kit stopped the truck as the moon broke from behind a cloud, illuminating the surface in its eerie light. Yes, we could see. A body. No, two . . . three bodies; floating face down in the river, their white, bloated flesh shining in the moonlight. We watched as two broke away from the bank and drifted under the bridge. The third, a naked woman, was caught in the reeds by her tangled, shoulder-length hair which gently waved in the heavy swell. She was young, maybe only sixteen. We could see her face now as the movement of the water turned her body in our direction. She had been pretty, before her eyes had been burned out with hot pokers.

'What shall we do?' Sprog broke the silence.

Kit looked at his watch, suddenly making a decision. 'We can't leave them floating downriver like that. We'll get them on the bank and radio back for help. Come on, otherwise the current will drag them too far down.'

The first two bodies had now drifted under the bridge, coming to rest on our side of the river. The torrent – caused by heavy and continual rain – buffeted, lifted and sucked them back as we tried to grip their slippery flesh.

'For Christ's sake, get a grip on them!' Kit swore at the sky.

We grabbed at ankles, arms, anything, in an attempt to speed the process up, bile rising in our throats as we saw that one body, that of an old woman, had been slashed at the chest and its heart torn out through smashed ribs.

'Fucking Chetniks!' Pop spat, turning to Sprog who was now vomiting in the bushes. 'Bastards . . . bastards . . . bastards!'

None of us were feeling good, swallowing back the nausea, feeling our stomachs churn as we lifted her out of the river, watching water drip like a curtain on to the muddy bank at our feet.

The other body, an old man, was easier to lift. His arms and legs had been hacked off. All that was left was a torso. His toothless mouth was still open, showing blackened gums from wrenched-out teeth.

We gave the bodies one last glance before covering them with a poncho. A prayer seemed appropriate but nobody knew the words.

'What about the girl?' Steve asked.

'It ain't gonna be easy,' Kit replied. 'The far side of the bank is mined.'

'Yeah, I know. But we can't leave her.'

We crossed the bridge on foot and stood on the bank looking down. She was caught firmly by her tangled hair as the reeds wrapped themselves around her naked body like protective serpents.

'Get me a torch, rope and some party string,' Kit ordered Tommy. 'And tell Sprog to stop bringing his boots up and radio in and get someone out here to collect the bodies.'

Pete drove the lorry over the bridge, turning it to face the river and switched on the headlamps. The oblique beam picked out the silver lines of tripwires, criss-crossing the bank.

'Good idea, Pete. That'll help a lot. I won't need the party string now.'

Kit, Steve and Franz slid down the steep bank, stopping short of the first line of wires as Kit moved forward to cut them, indicating the position of the mines as he did so. Progress was slow and dangerous, taking a good twenty minutes before they reached the river edge. They looked at one another but didn't speak.

'Gimme the rope. I'll go in,' Franz said quickly, wading out chest high into the reeds and unsteadily tying it around the floating corpse. He paused as the lapping water twisted her body, pushing it against him. Her tortured face was next to his for a moment before he turned to the bank, the beam from the lorry headlamps etching deep lines around his tightened mouth as his Adam's apple jerked convulsively.

'Pull . . .' He guided her in gently, until she was at the bank side, her hair still caught in the reeds.

'Steve, give me a knife,' Kit asked quietly.

'You're not gonna cut her hair are you?' Franz pleaded. 'She wouldn't want it cut.' His voice was unsteady.

Kit ignored him and chopped away at the reeds until the body was floating freely. Then he threw the rope up to the rest of us on the bank above.

'We'll guide. You pull.'

We looked at the mud covered body, slim, youthful. In her early teens, as we had guessed. There was nothing to say as we carried her to rest with the other two bodies – her parents in all probability.

We wondered in which riverside village they had lived. Were they farmers? Perhaps in Nard, only a few kilometres away, or Belisce maybe . . . We would never know. There was some slight consolation, however, slender but worth hanging on to. One day the men responsible for this act could be the men in our sights. Revenge is sweet, sometimes more so than financial gain. Right now there wasn't a mercenary here who wouldn't have hunted them down for the sheer pleasure of seeing them die in agony.

We climbed aboard the truck as some medics arrived to collect the bodies, waving at them as we pulled away. The delay had lopped an hour off our schedule and dusk had turned into darkness before we crawled over the trench line, once again into no man's land.

'Shine on, shine on, harvest moon, up in the sky . . . Fuck this for a game of soldiers. When I was in 'Nam,' Spooky started, but never finished.

'Jesus! Don't you give us that Vietnam crap. We heard it from bleedin' Fontain all the way from Zagreb.' Kit glared at him. 'Now forget it, or we'll all start on our war stories.'

'Just tryin' to be friendly, brother. Don't mean no harm.'

He was really just trying to get the picture of those bodies out of his mind in the only way he knew how. Soldiers have a habit of using humour to disguise their fears and frustrations.

We kept in single file, nervous and twitchy. This was sniper country and we made beautiful targets in the moonlight. Kit held up his hand and we froze, then he waved us forward into a huddled group.

'The perimeter's ahead. We'll all go through at one spot, then split up. Steve, you can do the difficult bit and go through Serb lines into the northern enclosure. You can do the east side, Pop, and make sure you cut at least twenty gaps in the fence. Big ones, mind you. We'll do the west side. Our entry will be the RV. Got it?'

He looked to see if there were any questions. There weren't.

'If any group runs into trouble from man or beast then get out. The rest will have to take care of themselves. Finally, if you've got to blow any cage doors, do it last, with thirty-minute timers. See you back here in one hour.'

Osijek Zoo was built in the traditional style, with narrow overgrown hedges lining the visitor walkways. The wilder species were caged in rows and the less dangerous kept in walled compounds. Parts of the zoo had been fenced off in an attempt to provide certain animals with the opportunity of roaming freely in something close to their natural habitat. Bears were kept in deep pits; monkeys, chimpanzees and gorillas in large wire-mesh buildings. The whole place had a run-down look about it – and why not? It was right in the middle of a war zone.

We could hear the methodical 'snip, snip' of Pop's team cutting way at the perimeter fence as we crept away, heading into the centre of the zoo. To our left we could make out the tigers and panthers as they stalked us, thankfully on their side of the bars. 'Soon, my darlings,' said Franz, as he stopped and looked at a beautiful lioness. 'You can go out on the tiles soon.'

There was a bit of a commotion coming from the monkey house to our right, and we assumed this to be the arrival of Steve's team on their way through to the Serb lines in the north. The screaming and chattering could attract the attention of guards and cause a problem for Steve, but we consoled ourselves with the thought that the Serbs would probably attach little importance to the noise, being used to it by now.

Kit pointed at the reptile house but walked on. Nobody felt like having snakes or alligators crawling around the place.

We arrived at the far western point of the zoo and stopped to check the map just as the moon disappeared behind a nice large, dense cloud. It was time to start springing the animals.

'Where do we start?' Franz whispered.

'I don't fucking know!' Kit replied. 'The more I think about it,

136

the more I realise what a stupid idea it was.' He had a ponder. 'We'll cut through the fences of the open area first; that'll free the wild deer, zebra, water buffalo and whatever else they've got in there. Then we'll move back the way we came, levering the padlocks off the rhino and hippopotamus enclosures. After that we'll do the cats, then we'll get the fuck out.'

The first part was easy, snipping away at the fencing until our hands were raw and the cutters refused to bite. The next bit wasn't too bad either. It was the third that was difficult. Every time we approached the doors of the lion or tiger cages the creatures wandered over and looked at us, standing there with their eyes flickering in the moonlight, a look of curiosity on their faces as they swung their tails and licked their lips. We all took it in turns. As one of us walked away from the door the animal did the same, settling itself down for a sleep at the back of the cage. We would wait for a while and try again. Each time the cat would uncurl itself, get up and nonchalantly pad back to stare at us.

'Let's give up, Kit. This could go on all night.'

'No! There's got to be a way. Let's find some food.'

Kit took off in the direction of a large building at the back of the cages, returning with a huge sack of raw meat.

'Go and get some more. There's loads of it.'

Four trips later we had bags of bones and meat piled at regular intervals outside the cat houses.

'We've gotta do this quick. Get the food as far back as you can keep chucking it in faster than they can eat it. As soon as they're gobbling, break the padlock but leave the door shut. It'll take them a while before they realise they can get out. By then we'll be long gone.'

The idea worked. The animals leapt on the food, tearing it to pieces and ignoring us completely as we set upon the padlocks with our bolt-cutters. The only one to give us trouble was the lioness Franz had spoken to on the way in – I think she had taken a fancy to him and wanted to be taken for a walk. She succumbed in the end though, growling and purring at the same time as she tore the food to shreds.

'Let's go!' Kit was already on his toes and heading for the RV when the sound of automatic fire broke the enforced silence.

'Double fuck!' Franz yelled. 'That'll make the animals panic. They'll be out of those doors in seconds and after us. Don't forget we're covered in blood from the food we slung in.'

The auto fire increased, followed by mortars. Somebody had been rumbled. We reached the perimeter at the same time as Pop and his lads, and scrambled through breathlessly. Obviously Steve's group were attracting the attention of the Serbian gunfire.

'We'd better go and support them,' Kit said, climbing back through the fence and into the compound.

We all followed him as he legged it in the direction of the gunfire, cutting back out of the zoo and into the woods to flank any attackers from the right. Suddenly it was bedlam, with mortars landing around us and kicking up the soft mud in our faces. We could hear running feet, and Steve appeared, followed by Roy a few metres behind.

'Where's Tommy?' Kit screamed above the roar of mortars.

Steve pointed back into the woods.

'Is he hit?' Kit asked.

Steve shook his head. 'No, I don't think so.'

'Let's go and get him then.'

We were getting mortars, auto fire and rifle grenades now as we picked our way through the mined woodland. This was not the way it was supposed to happen. It should have been a laugh, and for a while it was. But not any longer.

The shape of a charging figure appeared ahead, arms flailing as he tried to keep his balance, hurtling through the dark, wooded night, bumping into trees, branches tearing at his face and hands, everything a blur of green. The stuff was catching him up . . . passing him . . . coming back. Wood chips splintered from tree trunks as the impact of bullets sent them flying through the air like needles, puncturing his skin. He tripped, staggered for a second and fell, rolling into a ball as he smashed into a tree and lay still.

We stared at the inert body for a second as the firing continued, getting closer and closer and accompanied by the sound of thudding boots. Steve ran forward before Kit could stop him.

'You'll never make it!' he shouted after the running figure.

Tommy had fallen about three hundred metres away. The Serbs were almost on him now, intent on catching the intruders. Their bullets zipped through the foliage above our prone bodies.

Steve reached Tommy as he started to rise, shaking his head, finally clambering to his feet. They both took a deep breath and started their dash back to safety as we stood, giving them covering fire above their heads.

Steve stumbled and lost his balance, and Tommy tripped over

him, still running. He should have stopped, but didn't. He'd regret it later, but now was all that mattered. Run, Tommy run . . .

We could hear the Serbs crashing through the undergrowth. Steve rolled behind a tree. He knew he wasn't going to make it. You can't outrun a bullet travelling at sixteen hundred miles an hour.

Tommy had reached us by this time, trembling uncontrollably as he jabbered away with his excuses for not waiting for Steve, but nobody wanted to listen.

'I wish we'd brought mortars,' said Kit as he directed Pop, Roy and Franz to the left of the oncoming Serbs, who we could hear but still not see. 'Flank them,' he ordered, as the rest moved to the right. 'Chop them up and let's get out of here.'

The firefight was brief. A dozen M-26 grenades lobbed into the undergrowth with rapid bursts of AK fire did the trick. The Serbs – suddenly aware that they were facing stiffer opposition than anticipated – skidded to a halt as they saw us crouched in a gully, then turned to run back the way they had come with a hail of bullets surrounding their fleeing figures and cutting the foliage to ribbons.

Steve walked slowly from behind his tree, looking suddenly old and tired, his face white with a mixture of fear and fury. He tried the nonchalant technique for effect.

'This has turned into a right pantomime, Kit. Anyone got a fag?' Pete passed him one and lit it with shaky hands.

Tommy walked over to him, about to speak. 'Don't say a word, you gutless bastard,' Steve snarled. His tone made the unspoken threat as he turned away, paused, then faced him again. His eyes narrowed as he looked into the face of the man who had left him to die.

'Take care of it later, Steve, we've got to get back. The fucking animals will be on the loose after all that noise. Come on, leave it for now.' Pop picked up Steve's gun and handed it to him. 'It'll keep until we get back.'

Pop was right. There were a lot of strange noises coming from the compound now. We could sense rather than see movement as we picked our way, more carefully this time, out of the wood into the open country, gratefully reaching the mound of earth which preceded our lines.

It was a tense ride back, with few words spoken by anyone. Tommy sat in sullen, gloomy silence, his eyes avoiding contact

139

with his comrades as he stared at the floor of the truck. It was going to be difficult, if not impossible, to live this one down – and he knew it.

Even crossing the bridge had lost its coming-home-safe feeling. Our eyes were drawn to the swirling water as once again we pictured those lifeless, bloated bodies.

The post-op brief with Florez was cut short by news from intelligence sources that our Zoo Quest liberation effort was causing the kind of disruption we had dreamed of. Most of the animals had managed to find their way out of confinement through our holes in the perimeter fence and into the woods. Although the information was sparse at this early juncture, reports had been received that a rhino had charged a group of Serbians engaged on a pursuit patrol after our engagement, killing one and injuring two others. Monkeys swinging through trees were causing chaos among itchy-fingered guards, and best of all, a lion had burst through the tent of the JNA field commander, attacking his aide and destroying operational maps and paperwork in the process. By mutual agreement the whole thing had been a good crack, if tainted by the Tommy and Steve incident.

The following days were filled with rumour. Croatians on the front line reported many incidents of deer and antelope grazing in the fields opposite. Hippos were seen blowing water spouts as they wallowed in the river, and one report swore that a chimpanzee was spotted dragging a grenade launcher through the woods. A sad occurrence was the death of a water buffalo, killed stepping on a mine as it made its way down the river bank. The stories went on and on, each providing fuel for the next person with a fertile imagination. One fact beyond dispute was the story of a Croatian corporal who took a baby monkey home for his kids to have as a pet!

Three days after the event Florez arrived clutching a communication from headquarters and handed it to Kit with a half-smile. 'Read this,' he instructed, and turned away, looking through the window to hide his amusement.

Kit scanned the document quickly before bursting into laughter. He turned to us. 'You have all been bad boys. This is a copy of a letter from Greenpeace, who have written to the UN complaining of your actions in letting wild animals loose to fend for themselves in the countryside. They say that it was an irresponsible act and one that should be punished. They also condemn the wilful destruction of trees and shrubbery.'

He turned to Florez. 'Are they serious?' he questioned.

'I'm afraid so,' Florez replied.

'You can't fucking win, can you?'

There was a lot of shit flying around the place over the next week as teams of investigators sought to trace the persons responsible for the release of the animals. Florez wisely kept his head down, denying any involvement and suggesting that the JNA were probably responsible. Without proof the matter gradually diminished in importance as many of the animals were recaptured and returned uninjured to the zoo. Some, however, made their escape from the area and remain free to this day, presumably still roaming the battle-scarred countryside of Croatia, wondering what the hell all the noise is about.

The battle at Velika Pumpa was looming, getting closer by the hour, minute, second . . . Many of the lads were nervous at the thought of a full-scale attack on a well-equipped and trained enemy. They muttered in dark corners, shaking their heads. Fragments of conversation were overheard, punctuated with the odd word: 'money . . . not getting enough . . . our weapons are crap . . .'

Bunks were often empty in the morning as their occupants disappeared in the night, heading for a less dangerous part of the country. Kit was philosophical about the whole thing, pointing out that as volunteers they were free to stay or go as they pleased. That was what he said anyway.

One last recce was called for, this time to determine finally the extent of heavy weapons available to the JNA at Velika Pumpa – not that the result would make any difference. The Croats had no choice but to attack, unless they were prepared to surrender or pack their bags and walk away.

Members of the recce team were selected by the democratic short-straw method. Kit would lead a team of three men, chosen by fate: Billy, a Canadian of Croat descent; John, a Scouser; and Jezz, from deep in the Welsh valleys. The CTR – close target recce – was planned for last light, taking in a fast observation of Beli Manastir on an anti-clockwise loop back to Velika Pumpa and home. They were going to travel light this time; belt order, weapons and a few grenades. Speed was of the essence.

The little Golf GTi was used for this recce, speeding off in a cloud of exhaust with the lads waving through the mud-spattered windows with apprehensive smiles. Nobody likes going on the last trip, the last patrol, the last anything, especially if you're combat superstitious – and everybody is. Just check out the St Christophers, crosses, medallions and lucky pieces worn or carried by the lads. Listen to the tales of bullets ricocheting off Zippo lighters, belt buckles, even wristwatches. They figure that it can't do any harm, and you never know for sure . . . do you?

We knew something had gone wrong when Steve woke us at four a.m., having got up for a piss to find the lads had not returned. Their beds were empty and the car wasn't parked outside. The operation should have taken no more than five hours, six at the most. They should have been back by three at the latest. Steve looked out of the window at the sky now streaked with cold, orange light as the morning sun cut through the dense clouds. Without turning he murmured, 'They've been snaffled. I can feel it.'

'No way!' Pete replied. 'Maybe they're back and just chatting to the guys at the front.'

We made some coffee, sipping it moodily amongst cigarette smoke and nervous chatter as another hour passed.

'They'll be all right. It's no big deal. Just a little hike,' Pop tried to console us. 'The whole thing is a piece of piss for Kit.'

'We can't just sit here. Let's take the lorry down to the front and find out.' Steve was already heading for the door.

'OK. But you'll see. They'll be down there having a cup of tea and a good laugh when we arrive.' Pop didn't sound convinced as he threw his coat on and joined us at the lorry.

For the next hour we drove up and down the line asking if anyone had seen the men return. A sergeant at the western point had been on duty when they left and pointed out the Golf, still parked a few hundred metres away, confirming our worst fears.

'Let's go in and find them,' Pete suggested without enthusiasm.

'Where do we look?' Steve replied.

'We'll head towards Velika Pumpa and circle around to Beli Manastir. They may be trapped and need back-up.'

Steve asked the sergeant if he had heard any sounds of small-arms fire in the night. He thought for a moment and spoke to one of his men, returning with the information that sporadic gunfire had been heard from the direction of the pumping station at about

1200 hours. The sounds had lasted for less than five minutes, after which all was quiet.

It was going from bad to worse. We sat, bleary-eyed, looking over the lines into the woods without the slightest idea of our next move.

'We'd better report this to Florez and let him make the decision. That's what he's paid for,' said Nigel, suddenly coming awake and taking control. 'Come on!' He climbed into the driving seat and started the engine, while the rest of us wearily stepped up into the back.

A loud yell from the wood line stopped us in our tracks. The Croats trained their weapons on movement from the trees. We looked in the direction of the sound, straining our eyes in the early-morning gloom. The yelling continued, and another voice joined in ... then another. The words were indistinct, barely audible above the chatter of gunfire in the distance. Then the bushes parted slowly, revealing four white figures with their hands high in the air, shouting at the top of their lungs: *'PRIJATELJA! PRIJATELJA!'* Friend! Friend! We were too far away to be sure of their identities but knew instinctively who they were, and ran to the trenches to watch the disgusting sight of an almost bollock-naked Kit, Billy, John and Jezz hobbling barefooted into focus; hopping the last few metres to safety pursued by a dozen Serbs, who did a quick about-turn and disappeared back into the wood, away from the line of highly amused Croat soldiers.

They arrived shivering at our side, bruised, bloodstained and filthy. 'Good morning,' said Nigel. 'This jogging will be the death of you, Kit.'

'Get me some clothes. I'm fucking freezing.' His teeth were chattering as he jumped up and down to keep warm.

'We haven't got any spare clothes. Get in the car and I'll drive you back.' Steve climbed into the driving seat of the Golf and waited for them.

Ten minutes later we were back at base. Spooky took photographs of the four pathetic figures for his collection of memorabilia, as an angrily embarrassed Kit covered himself with a blanket. 'Get some coffee, somebody,' he demanded gruffly, still shivering in the warm room.

As they gulped at their warm drinks we waited patiently for an explanation, until we could stand it no longer.

'So what happened?' Roy asked, with the courage and stupidity of youth.

'Give us a minute!' John replied tersely. 'We're escaped prisoners of war, you know. We need time to readjust.'

'Yeah,' Jezz broke in. 'I might write a book on it when I get back home: *My Six Hours of Captivity and Terror at the Hands of the Serbian Army*. It could make me a fortune like those Gulf War blokes.'

'The title's a bit long and the porridge a bit short, don't you think?' Nigel said cynically.

It was obvious we would get no sense from them until they had settled in. The hysterical humour resulted from relief at their escape, and who could blame them? Being a prisoner of an unpredictable enemy is every soldier's worst nightmare.

Kit finally broke the silence on his third cup of coffee.

'Let's get this over with,' he said in a resigned tone. 'We'd done the recce on Beli Manastir and everything was going great. Then on the way back through the woods we lay up for a bit because there were a lot of patrols about – it was like Piccadilly Circus out there. We were in a hollow, curled up like babies, when a twelve-man section of JNA soldiers literally stumbled over us. They froze as we pretended to be invisible, but they weren't having any and stuck their guns up in a aggressive manner. With all that fire power pointing in our direction there was nothing else to do but put our hands up. They herded us together and I let Billy do the talking because they might have shot us if we spoke in English . . .'

Billy broke in. 'They just asked me who we were and what we were doing. So I told them that I couldn't say and gave them the big four – name, rank, serial number and date of birth – but they weren't very interested.'

Kit continued. 'The section leader seemed to be a new boy and didn't really know what to do with us, so they all had a little chat before prodding us in the direction we were going anyway. When they got us to the pumping station they slung us in an outbuilding and left us for about ten minutes before coming back and making us strip off. Then they did us over with their fists.' He pointed at the bruises on their bodies. 'I think they did it just for a bit of fun. None of them asked any questions, just battered away as we did our "ouch, ooh, agh" routine for about five minutes, then they got bored and left us alone.

'We had a chat about what to do and figured that tomorrow

could be a bad day for us if we stayed. The Serbs would have to do something, and we reckoned it was either a trip into Beli Manastir for interrogation, which was a no-no, or they would top us, which was an even bigger no-no. We all agreed on that . . . even Billy. We had a look around the building and found a few rotted wooden slats at the back covered by piles of sacks. Jezz took a cautious peep through the slit window at the front and told us the soldiers were about twenty metres away having some grub and making a bit of noise in the process. So we pulled away a few more strips of wood and with nothing to lose, moved the sacks and had it away on our toes.'

He pointed at their torn and bloody feet. 'Fucking painful running through the woods it was too. Look! I've broken my toenail.'

They all looked a hell of a lot more damaged than they were. Most of the cuts were superficial, caused by bumping into trees and branches as they ran through the darkness. Even the bruises were mild; they would have been a lot worse had the Serbs used gun butts instead of fists. They did look a sorry sight though, almost naked but for the blankets covering their scratched, slimy, mud-and-dried-blood-covered bodies; with Kit nursing a swollen left testicle which he refused to reveal for inspection.

Were we sympathetic? Were we commiserating? We were not. Getting caught . . . the plonkers!

Although the recce hadn't quite turned out as intended, the group had managed to check out some areas of Velika Pumpa as they were being herded away into the shed, enabling them to confirm the presence of self-propelling guns and rather more tanks than Florez had led us to suppose.

The result of the recce was phoned through to army headquarters and a briefing – which included all of the remaining volunteers – was called for 1800 hours that evening. Its objective was to devise and finalise attack plans for proposed implementation within the next few days.

Florez arrived early, loaded down with maps, compasses and weather reports as if preparing for a re-enactment of the D-Day landings. He scurried about the place like Action Man, with deep furrows creasing his brow but not quite managing to conceal indecisive eyes or the nervous tic that seemed to have developed over the past few weeks.

When unsure of himself, he had the habit of pressing his tongue against the inside of his cheek, creating a large lump which moved up and down as he studiously avoided eye contact. All the signs of a last stand were mirrored in his face as he called Kit over with the rest of the section leaders and poured himself a drink, lighting a cigarette from his previous one. It was obvious to us that this man didn't know his ass from his elbow, or, more relevantly, his butt from his barrel. Regrettable as it was, he was in charge of the operation. The men weren't too happy about going along with the game, hoping that Kit and the rest of the experienced officers would be able to convince him to follow their line of reason.

Fear hung like sweat in the air as the lads trooped into the briefing room. You could smell it on their breath, see it in their eyes, even feel the vibrations in their speech as they chattered inanely, voices rising and falling as the hubbub increased to deafening proportions. Battles are different from firefights, patrols and recces. Battles are places where people get killed in bulk – like discount warehouses. Piled high and sold cheap!

Commander Florez called for silence and blew a stream of smoke through his nose which briefly hid his face from the group. 'Your attention, please. Attention!' It wasn't going to work. They were here to talk, not listen.

Kit stood up, bellowing, 'Will you lot shut the fuck up for a minute?'

The roar of voices slowly subsided to a mumbling drone as most of the men looked in the direction of the officers and saw the impatient figure of Kit Freeman glowering at them. They shuffled their feet as they sat down in preparation for the bad news.

'You all know why we're here.' Florez spoke quietly.

Somebody belched loudly, causing a ripple of amusement to create once again a barrier between the officers and the men.

'I will repeat . . . as you did.' He looked at the offender, and a smile flitted across his face at the joke. 'You know why we're here.'

He pointed to a map behind him and turned to Kit, whispering something inaudible. Kit stood and moved to the map.

'Right, I'll make it brief. Most of you are aware that the JNA are poised to take Osijek. The build-up has been going on for quite some time now, and many of you have been on recces for the specific purpose of collating information on their supplies and weapons. Those that haven't can talk to those that have. The latest reports from Croatian intelligence have confirmed the intention of the JNA to attack and capture the town within the next few days. I'll say it again . . . within the next few days. So, lads, we gotta do it to them before they do it to us.'

The room was now silent as Florez poked his tongue in his cheek again, looking around the room with hooded eyes. He rose to his feet, attempting to take control, clearing his throat loudly.

'I'm sure that I can rely upon you to do your duty and drive the Serbs back . . . and demolish their armament . . . and soldiers.' He floundered, his voice wavering as the well-prepared pep talk ground to a halt under the suspicious gaze of the men lounging expectantly before him.

There were isolated catcalls from the back of the room.

'You gonna lead us in, Florez?' an anonymous voice enquired.

'From the rear!' Hysterical laughter greeted the one-liner, rolling around the room and coming to an abrupt halt as Kit jumped to his feet in an attempt to save the situation.

For a few moments he stood, saying nothing, and the room became silent under his accusing stare.

'OK. That's enough! Shut up and listen. What you hear may save your life . . . or mine.'

Florez tried again, but his mojo wasn't working. The delivery was mechanical, without passion or fervour – both essential ingredients for any speech inciting men to violent action. He'd picked the wrong bunch at the wrong time. Dying for a cause wasn't in the contract; they'd checked the small print.

A chair scraped and crashed to the ground as three men climbed noisily to their feet, walking out without comment – apart from a single finger in the air. The door slammed with a finality that cut like a knife through the remaining men. The whole thing was turning into a fiasco.

Kit stood his ground. 'Any of the rest of you wanna leave?'

They shuffled and mumbled, but remained seated, feeling vulnerable under his cold stare.

'What did you come here for? You're soldiers . . . mercenaries. You're paid to fight other people's battles. That's what you do!' His voice was rising with emotion. 'Christ Almighty, we're not talking about a major offensive here. The Serbs are crap, you've all said it. So what's the problem?'

He'd grabbed them by the short and curlies and now waited patiently for a reaction.

A lone voice piped up. 'He's right. A bloody good punch-up

will do us all good. We've been getting lethargic with all this fucking patrol crap.'

That voice in the wilderness did the trick. In a moment the room buzzed, as opinions flew thick and fast and everyone took on the vacant role of commander of operations, offering tactical advice over the babble.

Kit allowed them to continue, knowing that the battle of hearts and minds was won, for the time being at least.

'Let's get it in perspective.' Kit raised his voice over the fading roar. 'Let's understand the objective clearly. We're not taking on the JNA. We're not out for a confrontational battle. What we're going to do is simple. We are going to destroy their armaments, their fuel and supplies, their ability to strike at this town. In other words we're gonna cut off their balls.'

'How we gonna do that then, Batman?' The tone was more sarcastic than questioning.

Florez had been sitting quietly, listening to the wave of revolt subside, his tongue tracing the inside of his cheek. He climbed to his feet and moved hesitantly to the map.

'The sole purpose of the operation is strategic. To blow ammunition and fuel dumps, destroy tanks and remove the threat of invasion. We want to make the JNA move on to another town and leave this one alone until the UN arrive and accept it as part of Croatian territory. That's the objective. I'll leave the tactics to those more qualified.' He finished abruptly and returned to his seat, duty completed.

'Time is of the essence, lads, we've only got hours now and there's a lot of organising to be completed. The group leaders will tell you what to do. So get stuck in and let's do the work we're being paid for.'

Those last words should have stuck in Kit's throat. These volunteer soldiers were being paid a pitiful basic wage plus an occasional bonus – often late and without guarantee. They had every justification for walking out. Only Kit and a few other officers were receiving salaries commensurate with the risk; sums in the region of two thousand Deutschmarks per week, plus a further ten thousand DM bonus for the Velica Pumpa offensive.

Florez looked relieved as the room emptied, leaving the officers to undertake the task of organising the offensive. He stayed for only a short while before making his excuses and returning to headquarters in the town.

The battle planning continued: crayons drew brisk lines across maps, notes were shoved into the hands of runners to deliver to respective group leaders. Nobody noticed the day fade and darkness take over. By tomorrow's light we would be ready . . . there was little choice.

Kit glanced at his watch for the first time. 'Bloody hell, it's twelve o'clock. I'm knackered. Let's get our heads down,' and as an afterthought, 'It's done anyway.'

I looked at the pile of mugs, cigarette ends, bottles and cans. The table looked like a battle zone with a great many casualties waiting to be dumped in a suitable container and dispatched to God knows where.

Although tired, we couldn't sleep, tossing and turning as yet another shadowy figure crept across the room on his way to the kitchen for coffee, hushed conversation or to check his weapon for the hundredth time. Even Kit was unable to settle, grunting and twisting in a mild nightmare. Come the morning some of the men would have gone, their courage failing in the lonely small hours when no one was watching.

'The most recent ceasefire seems to be holding as the eastern town of Osijek returns to normal after many weeks of bombardment from Serbian artillery,' the BBC World Service announcer droned in an authoritative tone as we sat eating breakfast. 'But not for long,' Spooky added absently, buttering his fourth piece of toast before stealing a sausage from Roy's unprotected plate. 'This one will give them something to talk about,' he continued, still muttering to himself.

There was a lot of it about this morning, a strange isolation from reality, as if they were all pretending that this was just another day instead of the one they had dreaded for the past few weeks.

Kit leaned over, grabbing Roy's remaining sausage. 'You don't want that, do you?' An irrelevant question; he'd eaten it before Roy could answer.

'After you've finished breakfast, report to your section leaders for work detail. Final briefing at midday. Don't be late.' He looked around the room meaningfully before leaving for another meeting with the brass at brigade headquarters in Osijek.

A huge photograph of Velika Pumpa dominated the entire east wall of the briefing room, an impressive panoramic view, accomplished by taking dozens of colour stills from the top of the thirty-storey Osijek Hotel and joining them together to form a massive mural of infinite detail. This was more like it.

For this final briefing, Kit was alone, pacing to and fro, obviously anxious to start the proceedings. He moved to the blackboard before the lads were seated.

'Right! Let's get on with it,' he said impatiently. 'Malaria, you're in charge of the sixty-mil mortar to be sited a kilometre behind us.' He pointed first to a position on the map and then to the photograph. 'Your team is here. To the right will be a four-man group protecting your flank, with claymores about a hundred and fifty metres to your left.'

The positions of the mortar team, flank protection, and claymores were indicated on the blackboard. 'You got that?' Nodding confirmed understanding – just as well because Kit wasn't hanging around for slow responses.

'My group will move forward, placing claymores to defend our left flank, with four men to our right. The flanking guard will be equipped with night vision to enable them to follow the operation and identify the attack team on its return.'

Kit paused for a moment to let the information sink in as he pointed to the positions. 'Has everyone got that?'

'What about communication?' Steve enquired.

'I was coming to that,' Kit replied gruffly. 'No talking . . . none. All signals will be by way of radio clicks until after the operation has been completed. The only one you need to be concerned about is three clicks. That's when I initiate the attack with a RPG-7, which, with a bit of luck, will take out the ammo dump. I'll be backed up by two lads with 66s who will open up immediately as I reload before sending in two more rockets.'

He called to Malaria, who was busy doodling on his pad: 'Are you listening?'

Malaria looked up and nodded, his thumb extended in the universal signal of agreement.

'Your first round will be smoke; this will enable me to direct all further mortars on target. You will then expend all ammunition, doing as much damage as possible. Remember, you'll be firing over our heads, so make sure you get it right first time!'

'What's the weather forecast?' Nigel asked.

'Wet! Drizzle with a westerly light wind,' Kit replied.

He continued drawing on the blackboard before turning to the lads once again. 'After the briefing I want all of the leaders to come up and familiarise themselves with the terrain shown on the photographs. It's gonna be dark and the area after the track is mined, so you had better be sure of every blade of grass, in case we've got to go in . . . which is unlikely.'

'What sort of opposition are we likely to meet?' asked Pop, always the cautious one.

'I'm glad you asked me that, Pop, 'cause I don't know,' Kit replied calmly. 'Florez has told me that there are about two hundred Serbs in Velika Pumpa at the moment but not all of them are combat-trained soldiers. Some are simply civilian workers employed to do menial tasks. Trouble is, they'll be wearing uniforms as well, so we don't know who is or who ain't. Don't worry, though, we can kill 'em all and let someone else sort 'em out later.'

'Jesus Christ, Kit! There's less than thirty of us. Fucking outnumbered or what!' Pete exploded.

'We've got the tactical element of surprise. Anyway, you've already been told that we're not there to fight them. Just kick shite out of the place, not engage in a fucking firefight!' He gave Pete a withering stare.

'Yeah, let's kick some ass,' Spooky added enthusiastically, jumping to his feet.

'Bollocks!' Nigel spat. 'You fucking Americans and your gung-ho crap.'

'Right. If there are no more questions, be ready for the off at 0400 hours. We'll be travelling down to the bridge by coach so don't forget your bucket and spade.' Kit finalised the proceedings and started to pack away his maps, while the team leaders gathered around him for that last-minute answer to that last-minute doubt.

The rest of the lads dispersed rapidly, heading back to their rooms; to write letters, talk to their weapons or just get their heads down for a few hours of fitful sleep. As the day drew to a close, none would rest as adrenaline pumped and anxious stomachs churned, making it impossible to relax as they watched the big hands of the school clock march incessantly towards dawn.

Chapter Nine

We don't make good civilians. It's a well known fact.
So what's left? Just the 'buzz' it seems. Doing what
they do best.

Bleary-eyed and sleepy, they stood in wavering, ragged columns, staring straight ahead with ashen faces, limp and vacant. Headaches, backaches, colds, and other mysterious pains had plagued them this damp morning, refusing to go away. Had this been a conventional army they would all have been on sick parade, carrying notes back to irritable sergeants requesting to be excused duty.

It was not to be. Mercenary forces rarely, if ever, have qualified medics on the payroll. If you can't shoot, you can't earn.

The weather was lousy, an unremitting, drizzling rain that ran down your neck and gnawed into your bones, making them feel like lead. Last night's met report hadn't mentioned the bitter cold. Like grasping fingers it clawed at minds and extremities as they stood in shivering lines, wishing that they were anywhere but here.

'Morning lads,' a chirpy Kit Freeman greeted them. 'First we'll all jump up and down – one at a time. I want to hear if you rattle.'

He moved in front of each man as one by one they jumped in the air, and pointed to pouches or weapons creating sounds that would betray their presence to the enemy. The MG-42s – German World War II machine guns – were causing the biggest problem. With sheet steel construction and badly fitting feed plates, they rattled and clanked at the slightest movement. 'Tie that down. Tape that up,' was the curt order.

A small rattletrap coach with 'Yugo Excursions' emblazoned in bright orange along its side had arrived a few minutes earlier, causing chuckles of mirthless amusement.

'Going on a sightseeing tour are we, Kit?' Big John, one of the new recruits from Bolton, asked with dry sarcasm in his deep, husky voice.

'Told you to bring your bucket and spade, didn't I?' Kit replied, passing radios with ear pieces to section leaders and confirming their call signs for the umpteenth time.

He shouldered his RPG-7, grabbing six rockets in a single, practised movement.

'The coach is only taking us over the bridge this time, lads; we're walking through the cornfield from there. We want to avoid Serb observers detecting anything that might be construed as an offensive. So we'll split up after we disembark and regroup at the RV.'

Moodily we climbed into the brightly decorated coach, its interior adorned with coloured pictures of inviting mountains, villages and seascapes. 'Osijek, the garden city, gateway to Hungary,' they proclaimed without conviction.

'Gateway to hell,' Steve muttered, as he curled up for a ten-minute doze before we hit the white-painted, graffiti-covered Drava bridge and showtime.

Squelchy mud sucked at our boots as we stepped wearily from the coach into thick, ground-hugging mist. We watched it roll across the chopped cornfield in waves of ethereal surf, right up to the river bank and beyond. Gloomy and dank-smelling, it muffled all sounds as we moved in silent, preoccupied groups towards the mound separating us from enemy territory. One by one we slipped through a previously made tunnel in the earth – avoiding a skyline silhouette – to make our solo twenty-five-metre dash across the open area of no man's land and into the safety of the woods.

'It's like those old war films you see on the telly, ain't it? Like when they're escaping from Stalag something,' whispered Sprog, counting the men arriving breathlessly by our side.

Kit turned up last, looking exhausted and a bit pissed off. 'Who dug that fucking tunnel?' He glared at Pete and Steve, who apparently hadn't made allowances for the size of the Bear in their calculations and would pay dearly in the bar on our return.

The mist had crawled its way across the fields, over the dyke mound, settling eerily throughout the wood. Bushes became figures as the swirling white smoke twisted around the under-growth, hiding our boots, hiding our comrades, hiding the enemy. We plodded on, ears tuned to the slightest sound, trigger fingers poised in readiness for a solid figure to rise from the cotton-wool earth and fill the air with the crackle of gunfire.

Nigel – at the sharp end – stopped abruptly, beckoning Kit

forward as he pointed to a telltale wire glistening in the dew. We watched as he traced it gingerly with his finger across our intended path and into the undergrowth; knowing that if the wood was mined we were in the shit, with this enveloping mist hiding everything at ground level.

We stood immobilised with fear as Kit disappeared to do his thing. Nobody moved, breathed, blinked . . . just in case.

Thirty-five seconds later – exactly – he returned, grinning broadly, with the news that it was merely a disconnected wire, left from a previous sweep a few nights before.

'The whole area should be clear. Me and Spooky did it on Tuesday night when you were all kipping,' he offered by way of consolation. 'But you can never be too careful,' he added whimsically.

Bent double like burdened animals, we continued our nervous trek through the wood, our darting eyes never still for a second until we arrived at Malaria's designated mortar position without further incident. The chilly, drizzling rain, combined with slow progress, had taken its toll. Without body heat to combat the cold, our fingers were rigid and our clothes and bergans soaking wet and cumbersome.

Kit put his hand in the air, rotating a single finger to signal stop. With gratitude for his kindness flooding through us, we rapidly unloaded thirty HE mortar bombs, red smoke phosphorus bombs, ammunition and claymores in readiness for the lads to set up in their respective positions. Malaria and his mortar team immediately darted about, trying to locate suitable firm ground on which to site their L-16A2 on its K-mount base plate, as the flanking team equipped with a MG-42 moved to their position on the right.

With no time for idle chitchat, and a further kilometre to travel, Kit beckoned the rest of us onward over the first track, slowly through the long grass and up to the second. We had a nasty moment as Pete waved us down, pointing to a figure on the dyke mound. We froze – which was easy in this temperature – and clicked off safety catches before he signalled us forward again. It had been a sack or something. Definitely non-hostile. 'Useless sod,' Nigel breathed as we staggered on.

By the time we arrived at our attack position some three hundred metres from the target, our throats were dry and swallowing required some effort. We unloaded grenades, rockets, launchers and spare magazines for the AK-47s, handing them out to the lads as Kit peered through the long yellow grass at Velika Pumpa, vaporising between the ground mist and the slowly lifting darkness. He checked his watch again, muttered something about being late and ordered the six men in Spooky's flanking team, armed with two German MG-42s, to move to our right for support and protection. Pete and Nigel went off to set up claymores on our left. In less than five minutes they were back, preparing their 66s and grenade launchers in readiness for the imminent onslaught.

Kit slowly eased the radio from his pouch and with a deep sigh pressed the signal button three times before bringing his RPG-7 slowly to his right shoulder, nestling it lovingly into the base of his neck. 'Here we go, here we go, here we go,' he sang softly, aiming through the leaf sights at the unfenced ammo dump. His index finger curled gently around the trigger.

There was a pregnant pause as he took a deep breath, exhaling slightly before the final pressure. Steady . . . steady . . . we willed him as his finger tightened.

The release of the missile startled us for a moment. We watched it spit from the end of the tube with a thunderous hiss, flattening the long grass in its wake as the warhead sped towards the target in a graceful arc. For a moment it faltered in its path as a brisk wind tore at the tail fins, threatening to blow it off course. We held our breath as Kit – never one to wait and see – stuffed another up the tube in readiness. We shouldn't have worried. The rocket curved slightly, but as the wind dropped, resumed its course and buried itself dead centre in the ammunition hut.

There was a millisecond's pause before the sky erupted with bright orange flame, spitting overheated rounds in the air and making us duck as they zipped across the open field. A second explosion followed as Steve, John and Nigel opened up with their 66s, hitting ammunition cases piled up by a waiting lorry.

Kit was on the radio, yelling into the mouthpiece above the roar of outgoing 66s, 'Smoke, you bastard . . . smoke!' Malaria must have got the message, a 'whumph,' followed by billowing red clouds, landed thirty metres to the right of the operations hut, making the occupants run in terror straight into the next barrage. Pete and Nigel whooped like gleeful children as they opened up

155

with grenade launchers at the Serbs, who were now running around like headless chickens.

Kit grabbed the radio again, cradling it in his shoulder while he tried, with difficulty, to reload the RPG-7. 'Left thirty, over . . .' His conversation was aborted as we heard the rhythmic beat of the MG-42 from our right. There were no signs of earth being kicked up in the Serb compound, meaning only one thing. Our flanking team was under attack.

'Shit! I didn't expect them to counter so soon,' Kit yelled, sending another rocket into a group of three dug-in T-55 tanks. He missed them by inches. Roy came running back from the flanking team with the bad news that a dozen JNA were attacking them from the woods.

'Sorry, Roy, I'm a bit busy at the moment. Can you pop back later?' Kit screamed sarcastically over the noise.

Roy looked at him as if he had lost his mind. 'The fucking flank is under attack, Kit!' His eyes were wide with fear. 'Do something about it.'

'You've got the MG-42s. You do something about it!'

With that, he loaded his RPG again, then turned back to the frightened lad, calmly saying, 'Tell Spooky he's got to take care of the problem. We're gonna storm the place any time now. He's got to hold them. Remember . . . got to!'

Christ! Doesn't time fly when you're having fun? I looked at my watch. So far we were only four minutes into the assault. Just enough time to boil an egg.

Roy took one more pitiful glance at Kit's preoccupied figure before turning and sprinting back to the flank team, soon disappearing in the slowly evaporating mist.

Kit's radio burbled, the earpiece no longer required. 'Keep it coming for two minutes exactly. Then cease fire,' he told Malaria. 'We'll be going in then.'

The ammo dump was now history, blazing away vigorously, spurting out clouds of acrid smoke which blew occasionally in our direction with the ever-changing wind. There was still a lot more to accomplish before we had achieved our objective, as Kit pointed out, aiming at one of the T-55s he had missed earlier.

'How did they do that?' he spluttered, as the tank's bow machine gun opened up and the 100mm turret gun sluggishly tracked in our direction.

'Down!' he yelled. The whistling shell tore over our heads,

156

sucking the air from above us and exploding harmlessly into the dyke.

'Did you see anyone get into the tank?' he asked helplessly.

We hadn't. Not that it mattered. This was no time for debate. The gun dropped slightly, then re-elevated for another salvo, the 7.62 machine gun maintaining its rhythm, ensuring that we kept our heads low.

'I'm gonna have to get it this time or we're in real trouble.' Kit lay on his back, cradling the RPG. 'Lay down some grenades to give me cover,' he instructed Pete. 'I've got to stand up to use this thing and there's no way that fucking machine gun won't get me first.'

The biting hiss of bullets continued in sporadic bursts as Pete loaded his trombone – grenade launcher – and pulled himself up into a kneeling position. A tight smile tugged at his face as he peered through the grass, rounds zipping past his head. He squeezed and dived to the ground as the charge whipped through air. There was a dull explosion. He'd missed.

'Prat!' Kit hollered, his face contorted with fury. The big gun had stopped moving and was now aiming straight at our position. What were they waiting for?

'Oooh ... fuck ... it!' The drawn-out oath preceded Kit's movement by seconds. He leapt to his feet, levelling the RPG and pulling the trigger in one movement. The warhead covered the distance to the tank before he had time to dive for cover, exploding in a flash of brilliant white light as it impacted on the supplementary fuel tanks. The machine gun was silent. We poked our heads cautiously above the grass and saw a burning mass of twisted metal lying on its side in the ditch, a single scorched body lying a few metres away.

'Fucking brilliant!' John pounded Kit's back. 'What a star.'

'It's not over yet. We've still gotta get the fuel dump. Malaria can't seem to hit it, so it's down to us.' Kit still wasn't pleased with progress so far, it seemed. The whole thing was taking far too long, giving the Serbs time to reorganise. Any time now we were due for a counterattack.

Machine-gun fire from our right reminded us that Spooky was going through a hard time as well. The burst of MG-42 mixed with AKM, RPK and grenades indicated that far more than a dozen Serbs were now attacking our flank. If they got past Spooky and the lads the game was over.

With the only active tank disabled and the others hopefully unmanned, it was time for a final offensive on the remaining targets before the JNA got their act together and retaliated in force. Seven T-55s and one T-72 had been reported by Croat intelligence, plus static and mobile artillery. Trouble was, we couldn't see the bloody things through the smoke.

'We're gonna have to go down there and look,' Kit suggested with as little enthusiasm as the rest. 'Otherwise the job's gonna be unfinished and the Serbs can still do Osijek.'

'We can't just walk around looking for bleedin' artillery, Kit. The JNA will see us. There's nowhere to hide. The area's too open,' Pete pleaded.

After a thirty-second communication with his grey cells, Kit agreed. 'Tell you what. We'll take out the fuel dump first. Then we'll move to a different position away from the smoke and see if we can locate the rest of the equipment. OK?'

'Yeah. Anything you say, Kit, as long as we don't do it right now.'

The fuel dump was sited at the extreme left of the camp, well away from the tents and what was left of the operations hut. Kit loaded the RPG with his penultimate rocket, planting a loving kiss on its nose as the others levelled their 66s. They knelt in line, sighting through the haze, and fired as one. The rocket led the way, twisting and buffeting through the dense rain. The rifle grenades brought up the rear, but they weren't needed. The hollow-charge warhead did its job without assistance, splitting the air with a scream of pleasure as it slid gracefully into the fuel dump and exploded in a fury of ignited gas. The air reverberated as a muffled howl rapidly changed into a roar. Debris hurtled skywards like fragments of shrapnel – and almost as deadly.

'What the hell did they have in there?' Pete yelled wildly.

'God knows. But it ain't there now,' replied Kit laconically.

Impenetrable oily smoke spiralled upwards in waves, corkscrewing to thirty metres or more before bursting wildly into clouds of black, flaming tar, falling like napalm on the panic-filled Serbs who ran screaming from this nightmare. Their clothes, skin and hair were burning wildly, and the viscous substance clung like glue, refusing to extinguish as they rolled on the ground, beating one another feverishly.

We gazed in awe at the impact of our rocket attack. The whole area was ablaze; the heat-dried long grass surrounding Velika

158

Pumpa became a brush fire, a brisk wind fanning the flames and sweeping them across the field in jagged lines toward the JNA perimeter trenches some eighty metres away.

'Bet that'll piss them off,' Steve muttered absently, slinging his AK-47 over his shoulder.

How right he was. A dull thud, a puff of smoke and flying earth made us aware that somebody had decided enough was enough. It was payback time.

'Christ, they're accurate,' Steve said, as another mortar burst less than five metres away from the group on our right.

'They've got range cards out. Look!' Kit was right. Small white rectangles were scattered about the edge of the field, enabling the Serb mortarmen to zero in with almost absolute accuracy on any position.

'Let's move. Now!' It seemed one of Kit's better ideas as another mortar landed, its blast causing Pop to stagger and fall backwards in a heap.

'Are you all right?' Steve dragged him to his feet, shaken but unharmed.

'Course I'm all right! It's not the first time I've been knocked over by a mortar blast.' Ever conscious of his age, Pop pulled himself erect, away from Steve's grip, and snatched up his fallen gear roughly.

'Let's go, comrades.'

The monotonous drum of the MG-42 had started up again. We headed away from its throbbing beat across the track between us and Velika Pumpa, into a wilderness of sound and fury. It seemed the whole world was in flames.

'Jeeesuuus! Look at that! Will you look at that?' Pete had stopped for a moment to adjust his bergan straps, his normally pale face glowing in excitement at the sight before him. The reflection of the flames flickered in his bloodshot eyes as he licked his dry lips like an animal savouring his prey.

Kit snarled at him. 'Move, you dozy bastard. We haven't got time to admire the fucking view.'

Bent low, we shook ourselves into a line and followed the edge of the dyke for another hundred metres towards the Serb camp, firing sporadic bursts at a wall of shimmering heat. There was no one there – we knew it. But it felt better than just walking blindly into nothingness. A hedgerow twenty metres behind us shook as

159

if struck by a heavy wind, flying apart as another mortar missed us by too small a margin.

'Good, aren't they?' Admiration from the normally silent Benny.

'Too fucking good,' replied Steve, opening up into the void with another worthless burst of AK fire.

'Cease fire. You're just wasting ammo,' Kit told him impatiently. 'You may need it later.'

A clear area ahead made us drop to our bellies, sliding through charred, acrid-smelling grass. The stubble tore at our hands and we gagged, wiping tears from our running eyes. A thin film of oil impregnated the earth and caused the irritation and a strong desire to cough was suppressed in anticipation of attracting interest from the enemy.

With heads and stomachs pressed tightly to the earth, we could see clearly under the hovering blanket of smoke as we inched forward in a straggling line. Kit paused, looking over his shoulder towards us, as a vague shape loomed fifteen metres to our right, and we followed his boots as they changed direction towards it. Bingo! Kit made no sound, but his lips formed the words. Straight ahead were a matching pair of SPGs - self-propelled guns. Behind them, and about five metres further on, we could just make out the distinct shape of a T-72 tank turret, with three dug-in T55s close by. Not quite a full house but their destruction would certainly complete our mission to everyone's satisfaction.

For a moment we stared in the direction of the tanks, absorbed in thought and forgetting our exposed position in the middle of an open field, surrounded by a rapidly reorganising Serbian army intent upon punishing the perpetrators of this carnage.

Still on our bellies, we could see their legs beneath the mist and smoke. The sound of voices heading in our direction jolted us back to reality. The Serbs were hunting in packs, systematically prowling the field but as yet unable to see us beneath the obscuring cloud which threatened to expose us within minutes – seconds if the wind picked up again.

Kit cursed under his breath. Our options were limited. We could put our hands up and rely upon their kind hearts to send us home after a good telling-off, or leap to our feet and be cut down in a hail of bullets. The final, and most appealing, choice was to crawl as quickly as possible towards the tanks and hide until someone thought of something better.

Telepathy is a wondrous form of communication. When practised in tight situations, it rarely fails. With a nod from Kit we wriggled in unison towards the tanks, any second expecting a shout to be followed by a stream of bullets pumping into our rear ends. But we made it – just – the cloud of smoky mist finally thinning out and drifting upwards as a breeze blew across the open space. We were safe for a moment in the tank ditch, until daylight arrived in time to bring more trouble.

'Innit time for a cuppa?' Pete muttered as he dived in on top of us.

'Yeah, I was just thinking that myself. Where's the canteen?' Pop replied, his voice muffled under a pile of bodies trying to sort themselves out.

'You've just blown the fucking thing up.' Kit quietened them down before it got out of hand.

We untangled ourselves, finally working out which boot belonged to which foot, and lay gasping for breath against the side of the T-55 after the exertion of the belly sprint.

'What have we got left?' Kit looked around at the sparse armoury, seeing one RPG rocket, three 66s, a few grenades and some plastic explosives. He nodded. 'That's enough to make a decent stew, I reckon.'

He rummaged in his bergan, bringing out a length of detonation cord and several detonators. 'Remember Mostar?' he whispered. Those present at that attack nodded; the others guessed.

'What's the date?' Kit asked unexpectedly, looking at Pop as he unpacked the explosives.

'I dunno. Uuh . . . March the . . . I can't remember.'

'It's March the twenty-first,' Nigel responded. 'Why?'

'It's my thirtieth birthday tomorrow,' replied Kit thoughtfully. 'Wonder if I'll make it.'

There wasn't time to speculate; a Serb rifleman poked his head over the edge of the ditch, his mouth open in a scream that would never come.

Steve saw him first and yanked him forward on to the bayonet he was using to cut the detonation cord. It sank in his soft flesh up to the hilt, and we watched him quiver and twitch, his eyes widening as the knife twisted into his stomach, withdrew and slit his throat. Blood pumped from the pulsating arterial wound, spraying Sprog's face and chest. He jumped to his feet, frantically wiping at the warm liquid as it ran into his eyes, down his cheeks

161

and into his open mouth. Repulsed by his first sight of and proximity to violent death, he shuddered and sank to his knees, his face the colour of putty, blood soaking into his para smock.

The waxen face stared up at him accusingly, head askew, eyes gazing vacantly at the unseen sky.

'Don't you dare vomit,' Kit told Sprog sternly.

'Don't worry, I won't.' He gulped, looking at the body of a very young man lying dead before him. 'He's just a kid,' he sighed. 'Christ, he's younger than me.'

We could easily work out what was going through his mind as he stared at the corpse.

Kit dragged everyone back to the present problem. 'Shove him over there. We'd better get on with it. Someone's gonna come looking for him soon and we don't want to be around when they do.' The kid was dragged away and stuffed out of sight under the tracks of a tank.

We no longer knew what was going on above the surface of our hole in the ground. The mortars had fallen silent as visibility returned and the Serbs found no target to fire at. We were sure, however, that their hunt for us was continuing.

'Pop, you and Steve cover the rim but keep your heads down until I tell you. I'll set up some timed charges on the tanks. Then we'll do the clever bit.' Kit moved quickly to the bow of the nearest T-55.

'What's the clever bit?' John enquired.

Kit hesitated. 'Getting out before the fucking things blow.'

'How the hell are we going to do that? It's at least a hundred-metre run before we hit the perimeter. I'll never make it,' Pop pointed out.

'You'll make it, Pop. A spoonful of fear and a couple of bullets make a wonderful stimulant. Better than any of those vitamins you take.'

Kit and Nigel ignored his moaning and set about attaching explosives to the tanks. Sprog was still in shock but no longer pale as he moved to help them, his trembling hands holding the plastic in position as Nigel taped it to the most vulnerable parts of the armour plating and pushed in detonators, Kit bringing up the rear with detonation cord and timers.

'That's it! I've set them for fifteen minutes. That'll give us plenty of time to get out.' He tugged at Pop's arm. 'Stick your head up and see if it's clear.'

Pop looked at him as if he had gone mad. 'You stick your bloody head up!'

'Quiet!' Kit spat, pulling Pop down.

The sound of advancing boots and muffled voices came closer, stopping momentarily above the rim. We held our breath, looking at the timer as it ticked its way backwards to zero. The voices drifted away, finally silent as they moved out of earshot.

'That's two minutes gone. Now for fuck's sake look over the top!' Kit ordered.

Pop didn't argue on this occasion, realising that time was running out, and with the support of our hands moved gingerly to the rim of the ditch. 'It's clear to the right,' he reported, 'but they're still poking around for us. Most of them are in a huddle and the others are trying to put out the flames around the ammo dump and operations room.' With that he slid back down.

'OK. That's it then. Up and over. Run like hell to the right. Steve, you and me will bring up the rear. When we get past their trench positions we'll send in our last rockets on the SPGs. Before we go I'll just give Malaria a quick buzz and get him to send in some mortars to distract them and give us cover.'

He grabbed the radio, looking at the ticking timer as he hit the call button. There was no response. He hit it again. It crackled and Malaria's too-loud voice came over the hissing air waves. Kit gave his call sign, immediately instructing him to expend ammunition at a point twenty metres right of his original smoke position. Button off.

'Just hope he remembers it,' were his last words before the sizzling sound of incoming shells burst in exactly the right position.

'Let's go! And don't forget it's my birthday tomorrow.'

Kit was first over, rolling then twisting as he leapt to his feet, the rest of us so close behind that we kept tripping on his flying legs.

Bent double with our faces downward, all we could see was smouldering ash and charred tree trunks as we hurtled towards the safety of the wood, now only fifty metres away. We could hear the dull 'crump, crump' of mortars landing somewhere to our rear. Malaria was doing a grand job distracting the Serbs; so far none had fired at us. The whole escape was going well.

The empty Serb trenches and sanctuary were now only a matter of a few metres in front of us when the chatter of auto fire sounded off to the left and the ground started sprouting around our feet as bullets walked toward us, cutting a line across our path. We spread out instinctively as they were joined by the sound of incoming mortar fire whooping over our heads. In less than a moment we had turned from joyous victors into frightened rabbits. The noise was deafening and the terror absolute as bullets snapped around us, trying to damage our fleeing boots. Pete went down, a groan of agony escaping from his lips as he rolled into a ball. Kit grabbed him, dragging his limp body into the trench ahead. We were lost in a delirium of violence as we tumbled in behind, grateful to be alive if only for a moment.

Malaria had exhausted his supply of ammo and stopped firing. We were on our own.

'Nigel, look after Pete,' Kit instructed, loading the RPG with his final rocket. 'Pop and Steve, grab the 66s. We've got one last shot, so make it count. Target the SPGs, I'll go for the T-72.'

By now the isolated Serb mortar attack from our left had been joined by another from a sandbagged position close to the western perimeter, turning the sporadic bombardment into a continuous barrage. Like sharks smelling blood, they were determined that we would not get out alive and were pounding our position with more enthusiasm than accuracy. The trees behind us were being flattened as we crouched low, just waiting for our final rocket attack before we could get the hell out of here.

'Pete's all right,' Nigel said. 'It's just a flesh wound.'

'Can he use a gun?' Kit responded automatically, then looked at his watch and muttered, 'Shit, we've been here twenty minutes, the whole thing's taking too long.'

'Yeah, I can use a gun,' Pete replied before Kit had finished grumbling. He hoisted his AK from his shoulder sling.

'Good,' Kit replied in a flat, calm voice. 'If you look over there by the mound of earth you'll see four Serbs with autos coming at us. Take them out!'

Four JNA soldiers with little regard for personal safety were charging through their own mortar fire in our direction, bobbing, weaving and screaming like madmen, a continuous spray of bullets from their blazing Kalashnikovs preceding them.

Pete and John looked at one another, nodded and stood upright, spewing rounds in the direction of the advancing Serbs, who, taken aback by this display of stupidity, broke ranks and released their triggers for a split second. That was all the lads needed. The first man hit the ground as ten rounds slammed into him, dropping to his knees for a second before crumpling in a heap on the still smouldering grass only about three metres from where Pete stood. Another stumbled, falling on a spot milliseconds before it erupted as a mortar shell landed, blowing him into the air like a rag doll. The other two, gathering their wits, opened up again, only to be cut down by Pete's fireburst as they charged forward, almost reaching our position.

Meanwhile, Kit had screwed the rocket propellant cylinder into the warhead and loaded it into the muzzle of his RPG-7. He pulled the safety pin, nodding to Pop and Steve to take aim at the SPGs with their 66mm M-72s, and lay against the wall of the trench with his back to the target. 'Ready . . . fire!' He turned quickly, sighting at the tank some ninety metres away through the falling mortars, and squeezed the trigger savagely as Pop and Steve did likewise. The rocket ejected with a whoosh of escaping propellant, the backblast flattening the bushes behind as it screamed away at 120 metres a second. It remained true to its course, never wavering a centimetre as it homed in on the T-72 low in its bunker. A metallic crack followed as it dived through the open turret door and exploded inside the tank, igniting diesel fuel auxiliary containers in the process. Much to our disappointment, little visible damage seemed to have occurred – even with this direct hit – the advanced armour-plating absorbing the PG-7 HEAT warhead. We knew, however, that the inside of the tank had been totalled and was now inoperable.

The 66s arrived on target milliseconds later, pounding into the self-propelled guns with enthusiastic zeal, blowing their tracks high into the air as they teetered for a moment, failed to regain balance and rolled over on to their sides.

'Bit fucking lucky with that shot, weren't you, Kit?' Pop jibed.

'Lucky! What do you mean, lucky! I was aiming for the turret opening.'

'Balls!'

The bantering was temporarily aborted as the explosives attached to the three T-55s detonated in unison, leaving a junk heap of twisted, smoking metal. The air was once again filled with the dense odour of cordite, oil and flame.

'The job's finished,' Kit commented in a matter-of-fact tone. 'Let's get out!'

It was easier said than done. With renewed vigour the JNA were increasing their mortar attack, focusing a deliberate and continuous barrage on our vulnerable position on the eastern perimeter. Machine-gun fire kicked into gear on our right flank, supporting a fast-moving twenty-strong infantry platoon coming at us with vengeful expressions on their blackened faces.

'I don't like the look of this. We're pinned down here,' Peter murmured ominously.

'Oh really?' Nigel replied in his best Guards officer put-down voice. 'That's a very astute observation, old boy. Have you anything constructive to add?'

'Yeah. Let's get the fuck out of here!'

'Stop nattering, you two, and lay down some covering fire. We'll make a run for it into the trees and cover you.'

With no further discussion, Pop lobbed two M-18 smoke grenades in the direction of the advancing Serb platoon and scrambled out of the trench, leaving us momentarily stunned at his immediate reaction to Kit's order. With a quick adrenaline burst the rest of us followed close behind, as clustered mortars dropped like hailstones, bursting around our darting figures.

'They're trying to fucking kill us!' Steve yelled. He sprinted past, his long legs blurred as he leapt over mortar holes appearing from puffs of smoke everywhere we looked.

Benny suddenly took off, flying through the air with his arms waving like a demented swan, before hitting John in mid-flight, bringing him crashing to the ground in front of Sprog, who tripped over them both. They landed in a heap, lying dazed for a moment before continuing their dash to the safety of the wood, now only a few metres away.

'Everybody here?' Kit enquired, gasping for breath. 'Everybody OK?'

Benny didn't look too good. He had taken some shrapnel in his side and the gaping wound had opened up with his final sprint. He was sweating and gritting his teeth with pain. Kit looked at the injury, peeling back his smock for a closer inspection. Benny started to gasp. It was a nasty one. Not life-threatening under normal circumstances, but these weren't normal circumstances.

'Stand still and let me have a look!' Kit prodded the bleeding cavity. 'Mmmmm. Yes,' he murmured in a practised medical tone before fumbling in his first-aid pouch and sticking a morphine needle into Benny's exposed shoulder. 'That'll make you feel better.'

The renewed chatter of small-arms fire focused our attention back to the trench, where Pete and Nigel were doing their best to slow down the advancing Serbs, without much success. Heavy machine-gun fire from a foxhole on the far side of the camp was now elevated above their heads, aiming for the tree line and our position just inside it, cutting large chunks of bark from the trees and spraying them around us like jagged pointed arrows. Mortars continued to fall in waves, unseen until they were caught by branches in their orbit and exploded over our heads. Fragments of shrapnel fell like burning metallic leaves, scorching our clothes and singeing our hair.

John had started to panic, and Kit dragged him back from the edge with a brusque order to cover the lads in the trench. After a feverish hunt through his bergan for grenades, he knelt to support Pop as he opened up with automatic fire, cutting through the first line of Serbs about to overrun a desperate Pete and Nigel. A second line stepped over their comrades without a backward look, firing in staccato bursts at the tree line and the trench. The onslaught had reached the peak of its fury, every training manual forgotten as the air was filled with the most frightening sounds and smells imaginable: screams, shrieks, roars, deafening blasts. Almost continuous explosions converged with rapidly concentrated focus on seven men – all scared shitless.

'We've got to get them out. Now!' yelled Kit, as Pete looked pitifully back at us for a second before lobbing a grenade high in the air, more in hope than accuracy.

Four AK-47s burned their barrels red in a five-second blast of consolidated fire power as Nigel and Pete – knowing that this was their last chance – leapt over the edge of the trench and came tearing towards us, weaving and bobbing, jumping and crouching. The Serbs, momentarily surprised by the audacious move, kept firing at the trench. By the time they had worked it out, the lads were safe.

The AKs kept up a steady rhythm, spent shells flicking through the air and piling up around our feet. The situation was getting desperate. Our ammunition was dangerously low and we had a casualty to carry out. But as often happens in such circumstances, fate took a hand. The infantry attack slowed as casualties increased, finally petering out before pulling back in disarray. The mortars and machine guns ceased firing as if a tap had been turned off.

The silence felt so sweet you could roll it around your mouth and taste it. For the first time we were able to assess through the mantle of smoke, crimson flame and intermittently exploding ammunition the considerable damage we had caused.

'Let's go,' Kit said quietly, looking at the childlike bundle of Benny lying on the charred bracken. 'Carry the poor sod,' he sighed, tucking his RPG away for another day.

We straggled aimlessly back through the woodland, battle sounds still echoing in our deafened ears. Splintered tree stumps smouldered with wispy, bitter-smelling smoke that burned our nostrils before curling upwards through skeletal branches. The lifeless, mangled bodies of small furry creatures lay burning at our feet as we trudged wearily towards the flanking position, held – we hoped – by Spooky and the lads.

The MG-42 had long since ceased its distinctive drumming, and we speculated on what we might find, fearing the worst. There was no sound from the clearing as we approached, circling cautiously, weapons cocked and ready for almost anything. Steve, at 'point', waved us on and we reached the clearing with some trepidation.

Dozens of dead and dying Serbian soldiers lay around the perimeter line. Spent shell cases littered the ground. Spooky, leaning against the machine gun, looked beaten. The others were spead unevenly around the clearing in exhausted piles.

'You OK, Spook?' Kit mumbled wearily, walking over to the slumped American.

'The Alamo or what?' Spooky replied, looking at the bodies strewn around the field.

'Oh. So you're Jim Bowie now, are you?'

'No, Kit. He got killed.'

'Many casualties?'

'Some. Four injured. Not serious. None of our lot killed.'

'That's something.'

'You?' he asked Kit.

'About the same.'

Kit collapsed at his side on the grass. 'I could do with a fag,' he sighed.

'You don't smoke,' Spooky pointed out.

'I know. But it's times like this I wish I did.'

'Yeah. I know what you mean.'

I think they would have stayed there all day if it were possible, uttering the odd word from time to time between slow swigs of ice-cold beer – if we'd had any.

'Shall I check the bodies?' Pop asked.

'Yeah. You look at the Serbs and tell Nigel to patch up our guys. We'd better not hang around,' Kit answered, slowly rising to his feet.

Pop wandered around the inert bodies with Sprog in tow, still looking as if he were in shock from the incident in the tank ditch. They poked the bodies, turning them over, removing anything of interest. The Serbs' weapons were piled up for disposal or liberation, depending upon condition or value.

'Nice knife.' Pop, holding a Russian bayonet in his hand, turned to Sprog. 'Want it?'

The kid looked at him in disbelief, walking away without a word as Pop stuck it in his belt to sell or swap at a later date.

He continued checking alone as Sprog sat against a tree, staring into space at a hazy picture still haunting his mind.

'What we gonna do with the injured Serbs?' Steve asked cautiously.

'How many are there?' Kit enquired.

'Three. All badly hurt.'

Kit thought for a moment as Steve looked at him with an 'I'm not doing it' expression.

'What do you think, Spooky? Kill them or leave them?'

'Dunno, Kit. It's your decision. But if you . . .'

The quivering whistle of an incoming mortar brought the conversation to an abrupt halt. We all looked at one another in astonished disbelief.

'The bastards. Don't they know we've had enough for one day?' Spooky groaned, leaping to his feet, weariness forgotten.

The first mortar shell was followed closely by another, only seconds behind, shattering trees a good twenty metres ahead. Fortunately the Serb calculation was a little overcompensated – they assumed we had been moving faster and had covered a greater distance. The inspiring chat between Kit and Spooky had delayed our departure and might well have saved lives.

In seconds the pile of listless forms sprang into agitated life, clutching weapons in preparation for whatever came next. Apprehensive faces turned skywards, watching the barrage increase in ferocity as further mortars were brought into action, their shells spiralling overhead from a mauled but not yet defeated JNA force impatient for blood.

If that wasn't enough, the distinct sound of pounding boots grabbed our diverted attention and focused it towards the wood. A small group of bandanna-wearing Serbian irregulars burst crazily through the undergrowth, furiously spraying the clearing as they ran towards us, screaming at the top of their Chetnik lungs and taking us completely by surprise. Not for one moment had we expected this spirited retaliation after giving them such a severe pounding only minutes before at Velika Pumpa.

Bewildered and in disarray, we had little time to organise ourselves, managing more by luck than judgement to return fire with equal ferocity, piling rounds into the enemy as we hastily withdrew into the battered woodland and straight into the ceaseless incoming mortar barrage.

A sheer wall of almost continuous fire from Spooky and his flanking team forced the Serb attack to falter, while a few hand-thrown grenades from Steve drove them back for cover beyond the clearing, where they sniped away in isolated bursts at our retreating figures backing up to the tree line with mortars coming in behind us. Now with a hidden Serb patrol ahead, mortars landing behind us and five injured men, we were in a spot of bother.

Kit yelled over to John a few metres away and still running, 'Sort them out. Send in some grenades!'

John nodded to confirm the instruction and courageously knelt in the open to take aim. It was then that he repeated Jim's earlier almost fatal error. His adapted Yugoslavian Zastava required the recycling of gas in its chamber to provide propulsion for the grenade. In the chaos surrounding him he forgot this simple rule, recocking the weapon and putting a live round in the chamber. When he pulled the trigger the round, finding its exit blocked, blew the weapon apart in his hands.

For some of us it was *déjà vu* of the worst kind. Small pieces of razor-sharp metal zipped through the air, cutting everything in their path. For the briefest of moments, time froze. Then Kit rushed back into the open and grabbed John by the arm, dragging him into the trees. John's face was a bloody mess of hanging flesh and exposed bone. Metal had penetrated his shoulder, eye and mouth. Teeth were hanging from his torn gums, swinging loosely as Kit dumped him on the ground in whimpering shock.

'You four . . . get them back.' He pointed at the flanking team, who hurriedly lifted Benny and John to their unsteady feet.

'Wait!' Kit looked at John's mouth and with a quick tug removed three teeth from his gums. 'He might swallow them. Now go!'

'Orhin, orhin . . .' John tried to mumble through uncontrollable lips.

'No morphine,' Kit replied. 'Sorry, John, you aren't going to be able to run if you're spaced out. You'll have to put up with it until they get you back.' With that they were off, veering to the right and away from the incoming mortar fire, dragging both the injured men limply between them.

'Right, lads, we need to do something about those Serbs. This mortar fire and them shooting at us is doing my head in. Pop, Nigel, you flank them clockwise. Steve, Sprog, you go the other way. We'll count to twenty and open up to grab their attention as you circle around. Don't be long. I wanna get out of here.'

'. . . eighteen, nineteen, twenty. Fire!' The bursts were short. It was pointless wasting ammunition on a target we couldn't see. Seconds later AK fire opened up from our right. Steve and Sprog were doing the business, with Pop and Nigel joining in moments later.

They returned, panting breathlessly. 'We got two of the bleeders. Didn't want to waste time chasing the others so we came back.' Pop was holding his chest, breathing hard in hesitant gasps. 'Is that all right?'

'Yeah, that's fine,' Kit replied. Fatigue was flattening his voice to an almost inaudible whisper. 'Now it's our turn to go home.'

He looked at the sullen morning sky, now streaked with orange daybreak. His lips moved silently; he was calculating the spaces between mortar shells and relying upon his sixth sense to judge the period between barrages. For a full three minutes he counted as they fell, exploding around us in bursts of bone-destroying smoke. Finally he uttered an urgent, 'Ready? The next break and we're off!' before kneeling in a sprint position. We followed his example, poised for a signal and a crouching, zigzag dash for deliverance from this misery.

A shell burst behind us, followed by another – closer this time. The Serbs had re-elevated, their aim now getting dangerously focused.

171

Kit tensed, his face a mask of concentration as he leapt to his feet like a pursued antelope, starting to lean into a turn.

The shell burst came as a shock to us all. Without warning, it exploded less than a metre behind his poised, unbalanced body, its discharge throwing him forward head first into a tree trunk before twisting him around with its uncontained force and lifting his body off the ground, dumping him in a heap. He tried his best to rise, staggering momentarily, grabbing at air before looking at us through helpless, this-is-it-I'm-dying eyes. then he slumped to the ground.

We couldn't believe, wouldn't believe it! Kit killed by a rogue mortar – never! Steve dived across to the prone figure, shaking him wildly, but he didn't stir.

'Try his pulse!' yelled Pop, running forward to help. 'Kick him. Do something . . . anything. But get him up!' Steve felt his pulse. It was slow but steady, his breathing shallow.

'Lazy bastard. Get up!' Sprog screamed. 'Kit, Kit . . .' His voice trailed away, tears in his child's eyes.

Oblivious to the continuing attack, we crowded around the unconscious figure, suggestions coming from all directions. Mouth-to-mouth, face-slapping, body-shaking . . . everything was tried unsuccessfully before we resorted to the advanced cold-water technique. It did the trick. As liquid from four canteens spread over Kit's face he opened his eyes as if trying to work out where he was and struggled to his feet, leaning groggily against a tree, looking as if he were returning from a good night out.

'You all right, Kit?' No response. 'Kit, can you hear me?' His eyes flickered, stayed open and he dropped like a stone.

The Serbian irregulars had returned with JNA replacements, sniping across the clearing at us, more irritating than accurate. Ricocheting rounds spun through the undergrowth, adding yet another dimension to our increasing panic.

'Kit . . . Kit . . . can you hear me?' Nigel had joined Steve to help prop Kit up. No reaction. His eyes moved skywards, his head slumped. He was out again.

'We gotta go. With or without him.' Spooky interrupted our paramedic demonstration with an urgent reality.

'Yeah, you're right,' replied Steve, taking charge of the situation without consultation and ordering two of the biggest lads to drag the bulky Kit, as once again we prepared to evacuate the position, fighting a rearguard action against the Serb platoon now gaining confidence at our lack of retaliation.

'Around to the right,' screamed Steve, his nerve ends displayed for all to see. 'Follow the line taken by Benny and John . . . Now!'

With a last blast of covering fire from Spooky raking the Serb position, we jumped to our feet. As if possessed by demons we dived headlong into the bushes, waiting for the next mortar blast to take at least one of us out in a puff of smoke.

We ran blindly, stupidly, frantically along tracks that could be mined, leaping over smouldering tree trunks and pushing aside branches that barred our way. We laughed hysterically at frightened animals crossing our path and threw jokes into the faces of panting comrades as our panic subsided with the knowledge that we were safe out of mortar range.

Malaria's position appeared a few metres ahead, now empty apart from his booby-trapped mortar and piles of cigarette butts. We didn't pause, veering to the right and struggling through the long yellow grass. Kit kept coming and going as we ran, occasionally muttering rubbish about his thirtieth birthday, which event seemed to be playing on his concussed mind.

The dyke embankment welcomed us like a castle fortification as we jostled for position and dived head first through the inviting gap, cursing Pete and Steve for not making the hole larger as we struggled through the narrow tunnel and safety.

Steve slipped the radio from Kit's pouch, punching buttons in a haphazard fashion before getting a receive signal. His message was brief. 'This is the Bear. This is the Bear.' He used Kit's call sign to avoid confusion. 'Request ambulance and medics at the bridge for injured men. Over.' The line crackled and a voice replied, '*Da. Koliko?*' – Yes, how many? Steve scratched his head before answering, '*Tri*!' a smug smile of satisfaction breaking out on his face at the correct translation.

Benny and John, with Spooky's team, were crumpled in a heap some two hundred metres ahead, anxiously waiting for our arrival. We dragged ourselves on, crawling most of the way to join them as soldiers from the Croatian line ran to help us.

Both John and Benny were in a hell of a state, barely conscious; hunched up and moaning in agony as we approached. Benny's gaping wound, now covered in pulsating blood, oozing encrusted mud.

'Christ . . .' Sprog turned away. 'Will he be alright?'

Pop shrugged, but said loudly for Benny to hear, 'Course he'll be alright. A few days in hospital and he'll be back on the job.'

John's facial injury had also turned nasty. His eye was a pulpy mess of flesh, his battered mouth a yawning cavity of congealed blood. The mad scramble through tearing branches had added to both their injuries.

With help from the Croatian soldiers we hoisted the casualties into a covered truck, driving slowly to the bridge and waiting medics who immediately injected John and Benny with a blissful sleep called morphine. Kit woke for the briefest of moments, but unable to register any interest in the proceedings, slumped back again. We lifted the three of them on stretchers into the ambulance, which sped off on a siren-wailing trip to Osijek hospital.

Chapter Ten

'Listen,' said Spooky. 'We're not here for the killing or
the money. It's the comradeship and excitement that
most of us want. If there's a price to pay, so be it . . .'

It was a subdued bunch of twenty-five men who slumped by the
Drava bridge, gazing blankly into the muddy river as it swirled
beneath them. A few threw stones, watching them plop in the
water as they waited patiently for transport back to base.
Memories flickered like death's-head moths trapped in a jar.

One of the guys in Spooky's team kept dry-firing his shotgun,
click, click, click, beginning to get on everyone's nerves. Steve
grabbed the Remington from his hand, hurling it spinning
through the air. The owner stared at him for an instant, shrugged
his shoulders and lit a cigarette, too bushed to care. Pop started to
hum a tune which sounded familiar. Something that might have
been classical but wasn't . . . just the theme from M A S H.

I waited for a medevac chopper to swoop over the skyline and
whisk us away. It didn't. The mind wanders when exhausted.

Nigel took some folded sheets of paper from his wallet,
scanning the first page before tearing them into pieces and
throwing them away. The top section, caught by corn stubble,
read: 'Dear Mum and Dad, I don't want to alarm you but things
are getting a bit nasty here now, and I don't know if I'll be coming
back from the next job. Give my love to Jean . . .'

The pages blew lightly across the field. He should have kept the
letter, saving himself the trouble of rewriting it another time.

Steve jabbed absent-mindedly at the earth with his bayonet –
that bayonet. Sprog watched him clean the dried blood of the
Serbian boy soldier from the blade.

Pete nursed his arm, complaining that he should have gone to
hospital with the others.

'Do you think they'll be all right? Kit looked real bad,' Sprog
said distantly, still staring at the bayonet and looking like a lost
kid a long way from home, but no longer scared.

'Sure they'll be all right,' Pop and Steve replied in unison.

'John's injury looked nasty,' Spooky added unnecessarily, to nods from some of the others.

'What about my fucking injury!' Pete winced in apparent pain as he moved position to face the others.

'Bollocks! It's a flesh wound. If you were in Spooky's army you'd get a purple heart and be sent on R&R to Saigon or somewhere.' Nigel shut him up with a contemptuous glance.

'Stupid of John forgetting he had a round up the spout, wasn't it?' Pete threw in quickly, before realising he had overstepped the mark and dropping into brooding silence.

There was a long pause as we listened to the distant sound of gunfire coming from the Croatian line. 'I'm going home,' Sprog whispered, more to himself than anyone in particular.

'We're all going home as soon as the bloody coach comes,' snapped Steve.

'No. I mean *home*! Back to England. I'm gonna get a proper job. I'm pissed off with people I don't know trying to kill me.'

They all fell silent, considering his remark and realising that at this moment few would remain if given an opportunity to do otherwise.

'You'll feel different tomorrow,' Nigel said softly. 'Especially when we get our bonus for this job.'

'No. Not this time. I'm too young to die in some crappy foreign country.' He turned to his mates, adding with a smile, 'Specially with a bunch of psychos like you lot.'

Pop chucked a grenade at him and he caught it high in the air.

'You forgot to take the pin out, Pop.'

'Sod it! Throw it back and I'll try again.'

'Here's the coach,' murmured Steve, not moving from his spot as the vehicle slowly turned on to the bridge, pulling up in a cloud of smoke a few metres away.

'Look at it! "Yugo Excursions". It's the last time I'll book with them. Fucking sightseeing tour, my ass.' Spooky climbed to his feet, throwing his bergan on the coach before him. 'Still, the job proved one thing. You don't have to live a long life to feel old!'

We climbed aboard without a further word being spoken and settled into contemplative silence. The coach shuddered, crunching its gears before taking us across the bridge for what was to be the very last time.

Commander Florez was waiting, impatient and apprehensive. He had heard of the injuries by radio and was especially concerned by the fact that Kit would not be available to provide a detailed account of the operation for his superiors at brigade headquarters.

'How is he? Can he talk?' were his first words as we tumbled out of the coach.

'We don't know how he is,' replied Pop. 'Anyway, when we left him twenty minutes ago he was unconscious . . . like Benny and John.' Pop was reminding Florez that not only Kit had been injured.

'Oh, yes, of course.' Florez realised his apparent lack of concern for the others. 'And how are they?'

'Fucking awful!' Steve growled impatiently. 'How would you feel with lumps of shrapnel in your face and body?'

Florez could tell he wasn't getting anywhere and tried a different approach.

'I'm sending out a scouting party of Yellow Submarines, although I've been told by soldiers on the front that the whole operation was a great success.'

'Yeah. We can see the smoke,' Steve said flatly, turning to look at the distant skyline and the black clouds still hovering over Velika Pumpa.

'I'll leave you to sort yourselves out and come back later.' Florez edged away, unsure of how to continue his debriefing, and disappeared into an outbuilding.

We straggled across the compound through schoolhouse corridors to our rooms, dropping bergans, weapons and ammunition pouches in our wake. Nothing on earth had such appeal as sleep, long, blissful, free-from-noise-and-smoke sleep. The last thing I remembered was Nigel's voice muttering 'Bollocks!' as the world turned a soft grey, then black.

Without Kit to wake us, we slept the rest of the day and the following night, waking at about eight a.m. to the sound of Pop at the stove cooking an immense pile of scrambled eggs. We hadn't eaten for more than thirty hours. 'Yugo Excursions' didn't provide food and we'd missed breakfast at Café Velika Pumpa.

'You know what day it is, don't you?' Sprog mumbled through a mouthful of yellow mush.

'Yeah, it's Sunday,' replied Nigel.

'Not just any Sunday. It's March the twenty-second.'

'So?' Nigel queried.

177

'It's Kit's birthday, for fuck's sake. Don't tell me you forgot, after he kept reminding us all the way back?'

'No, course I didn't forget!'

We continued chomping like cows in a field, intent upon clearing the grass back to its roots.

'Better phone the hospital,' Steve said suddenly, climbing to his feet and moving to the phone. 'See how the old bastard is.'

'Sod the phone! Let's jump in the Lada and go down there. Pete ought to have his arm looked at anyway, and the other lads could do with some professional treatment.' Spooky kicked his chair back and still chewing, gulped a mouthful of coffee before heading for the door. 'Anyone coming?' We trooped behind him, standing outside for a moment as we discussed the improbability of getting twelve people into a five-seater car, and opting instead for the chopped-roof DAF truck.

The countryside this bright morning was strangely quiet without the occasional shell passing overhead or the dull crunch of mortars. The sky was clear with a hint of blue, and it felt good to be alive. Birds chirped and twittered, and it wasn't raining – for a change.

Benny was in the operating theatre when we arrived. His condition was unknown by the receptionist, and all other staff members quoted the same mechanical stuff about him being 'as well as can be expected' without knowing the cause or extent of his injuries.

John was lying flat in bed, his head, neck and shoulders completely covered in bandages, with only a small hole where his nose should have been. A sign in Serbo-Croat, English and French stated, 'Nil by mouth.' Unnecessary; he didn't have one.

Kit lay in the next bed, white and bloodless, looking like Frankenstein's monster in its late stages of development. Multi-coloured tubes ran from just about every orifice, with wires attached to his chest leading to a machine with a limited musical range. He shifted his eyes as we entered, without moving his head – just in case it came off.

What do you say to a monster with a huge hairy chest? Nothing; you just wait until he's finished filling the bottle by the side of his bed and pretend you haven't noticed. Then you say something original like 'How do you feel?' and hope that he doesn't tear your throat out.

A doctor and two nurses probably saved us by appearing at his side, examining with great interest the chart at his feet. Steve waited for a moment as they rambled away in Croatian before asking about his condition in very bad Serbo-Croat. The doctor smiled at his attempt, instructing a nurse to take Kit's temperature before replying in perfect English, 'He is an extremely lucky fellow. Had he not been a large man he would have been killed by the blast. He is concussed. Three ribs are broken and he has suffered hyperextension-hyperflexion injury to his neck.' Our blank looks drew another smile. 'Sorry. The sudden thrusting forward and snapping back of his unsupported head has caused severe whiplash. Oh . . . and we found this embedded in his shin bone.' The doctor handed Steve a 7.69 round. 'It must have been a ricochet, otherwise the velocity of the bullet would have shattered the bone. Like I said, he's a very lucky man.'

Steve tried again. '*Hvala vam na pomoci, Doktor.*' Thanks for your help, Doctor. He'd got it dead right; we were impressed. The doctor ackowledged the gratitude, sweeping away with his entourage in tow.

Four of us stayed with Kit, listening to the steady 'beep, beep' of his cardiac machine and feeding him information about Florez, as Pete and the others with minor wounds joined a small queue in the out-patients' department, soon returning with bandages, antibiotics and tales of primitive torture.

It wasn't much fun trying to communicate with coloured tubes, beeping machines, voodoo eyes and an immobile neck. So with a chorus of farewells we were starting to leave when Spooky reminded us about Kit's birthday. Can you sing 'Happy Birthday' to someone in that state? It doesn't seem right somehow, but we tried. To be honest I think even Kit had lost interest in the celebration of his birth. Another time maybe. At least he had lived to see it.

The Mayor of Osijek greeted our return to the school; a nice man full of praise for our efforts in saving his town from the invaders. Commander Florez fussed around, beaming with pleasure at the lavish praise showering from on high. He explained in infinite detail his attack strategy and execution plan. Hands were shaken and minor injuries discussed. We were invited to the Mayor's home for a meal . . . one day soon.

'We should live so long,' muttered Pop through immobile lips, smiling graciously at the invitation.

Photographs were taken for the local newspaper, with Florez

shaking hands for the camera as the mercenaries all looked on with suitably grim 'Soldier of Fortune' expressions. It was soon over and we drifted inside to lick our wounds, both mental and physical.

There was little for us to do now that the threat of invasion had ceased. Patrols were no longer required but training continued as further mercenaries arrived seeking work in the region. On Tuesday morning Sprog did not appear at breakfast. We checked his bunk and locker to find that all of his belongings had disappeared. Further investigation solved the mystery. He had taken the early train south with two other mercs to a small town called Vinkovci. Out of the frying pan . . .

The next few days were spent in idle loafing, hospital visits being the high point. Kit continued to improve rapidly, his powerful body responding to treatment and enforced rest. Within days he was up, hobbling around on crutches, his damaged neck held firmly by a metal brace. Benny was also fortunate, the injury to his side showing remarkable recovery after surgery to remove several large lumps of shrapnel. John, however, wasn't doing quite so well. Fragments of metal, always the most difficult to locate and remove, were embedded in his eye, and the hospitals in Osijek and Zagreb didn't possess the essential equipment to remove them. His sight was in danger of being lost if specialist surgery wasn't available, and this problem gave Kit something to think about as he lay in the adjoining bed, watching nurses inject needles into John's eye, asking him if it hurt.

Florez did not visit. He even sent Slavko – the leader of the Yellow Submarines – to fill us in on the results of their Velika Pumpa verification patrol. Normally he appeared two or three times a day, giving orders, suggesting incursions.

'They are gone.' A man of few words, was Slavko.

'Could you perhaps elaborate?' Nigel enquired in his most pompous voice.

'*Da!* The JNA have left.'

'Oh. That's so much better,' said Nigel sarcastically. 'Any chance of some detailed info?'

Slavko looked at him perplexed. 'Info?'

'Information,' Steve cut in. '*Do you have any detailed information?*'

'*Da*, I have information.'

We waited impatiently as Slavko worked through his book of

two thousand useful English phrases. He smiled. A big, gap-toothed grin of accomplishment. 'The JNA have left Velika Pumpa with all equipment.' He flipped through a few more pages. 'They have pulled back to Beli Manastir and are moving out of the area.'

'You mean that they have withdrawn?'

'*Da.*' He delivered another enormous smile before giving Steve, the nearest body to him, a rib-crushing bear hug.

'*Hvala vam mnogo* . . . Sorry I forget. Thank you very much.'

'*Molim,*' replied Steve modestly. That's all right. He shook Slavko earnestly by the hand with the air of a conquering hero.

'We fucking did it then! Scared the bastards off. That'll please Kit and the lads.' Malaria punched Steve on the arm, dancing round the room in exhilarated relief at not having to repeat the process.

Complications had set in with Benny, slowing his recovery, and his reaction to the news of our success didn't induce the kind of enthusiasm expected. He tried, but you could see in his eyes that the pain was acute, taking precedence over just about everything. John showed some signs of pleasure by lifting his thumb upward. Kit, however, was ecstatic at the result, even moving his head slightly, if cautiously. He had been told that they were letting him out tomorrow – another cause for celebration.

He turned up late in the morning of the following day, hobbling on alloy crutches covered in camouflage tape – just to make him feel at home. He seemed to have developed a Florez fixation while in hospital. 'Do you know that bastard never came to see me. Not once,' were almost his first words.

When Kit and Florez finally came face to face they circled one another like suspicious dogs, both unsure of how to proceed. Many stories had circulated over the past few days suggesting that Florez had told his commanders that he should take credit for the raid. Like Chinese whispers, they grew and grew; in the end even those present began to doubt their memories. Kit bottled up his anger until it smouldered, burning anyone stupid enough to discuss Florez and Velika Pumpa in his presence. They stalked one another moodily, avoiding contact wherever possible. It wasn't going to work any longer, we could tell. The time had come to move on, leaving Florez to sort out his own salvation without the benefit of professionals to take care of the sticky bits. But not until Kit was fit and well again.

181

A sleek, heavily laden Range Rover pulled up by the school-house entrance, and its two occupants piled out, stretching arms and yelling loudly for Freeman. One was immediately recognised as Kit's old friend Mike Stanton; the other was a stranger. Dave Tomkins was in town on a mission of mercy – to sell arms to the Croatian army. He looked completely out of place in this world of cropped hair and unwashed camo clothing, being tall, sophisti-cated and casually dressed. His long grey hair framed an expensively tanned, just-back-from-the-Riviera face. Kit wel-comed the pair with a look of absolute joy. It was party time and everyone was invited.

I couldn't keep up with the animated chatter, and left them to their own devices for a few hours. Raucous bursts of laughter echoed throughout the building as they lied and bragged to one another, laughing at past experiences and those to come, before getting down to the serious business of moving the merchandise – in this instance weapons, ammunition and military clothing.

Kit phoned HQ at Dave's request and asked to speak to Commander Florez. The conversation was short and without any pleasantries. An appointment was made for Dave to present his samples to the brass for inspection the following day. That night Osijek was hit again, this time by three old comrades hell bent on recapturing the good old days.

Kit's only visible reminder of the battle was his inability to walk unaided; crutches not being part of the image a mercenary wishes to portray to his critical public. He was offered a parrot from Osijek Zoo to accompany him on his shoulder as he hobbled about the place, but he declined with threats so malevolent that the subject became taboo – to his face at least.

Unable to take part in training programmes, he kept himself busy trying to organise medical assistance for John, in the process learning about bureaucracy, Balkan style. They have a magic word in this country which is repeated by all, regardless of allegiance or ethnic group. The word, which solves all problems, is spoken sometimes with a smile, sometimes a frown. Either way the message is the same. *Sutra* – tomorrow, always tomorrow. never *danas* – today. After numerous telephone calls and *sutras* coming out of his ears, Kit was able to get John transferred to Osijek eye hospital where with equally limited resources the doctors tried their best, without success, to remove the metal fragments.

Running out of ideas by now, the next move came in a flash of inspiration. Kit had developed an affinity with Roger Courtiour, associate producer of the BBC *Inside Story* documentary, and had been given his home telephone number. He rang, explaining the problem in short, gasping sentences and requesting assistance from the BBC to bring John home to the UK. It was a long shot, born of desperation, but Roger Courtiour agreed after consultation with his colleagues. Arrangements were immediately made for John to be taken by train to meet a Yugoslavian lady representative of the BBC in Zagreb. Kit was jubilant, vowing never to watch ITV again, and leaving within hours to make the journey with a bandaged John by his side, on his way home at last to Britain and specialist NHS eye care.

Roger Courtiour made these comments to me when discussing the incident some time later:

'I recall that there was a distinct possibility that John might lose the sight in one eye, and obtaining suitable treatment for a British mercenary in Croatia at that time was a long way down in the pecking order of things. To some degree this was understandable. The Croatians had inadequate medical facilities for their own injured people, let alone a foreign mercenary. Kit contacted me, requesting assistance which we were only too pleased to provide – proving that BBC film-makers do have hearts.

'This was a side of Kit that I actually respected. He looked after the people under his assumed command and accepted responsibility for their welfare in times of misfortune – a quite genuine side to his nature.

'He knew about soldiering and tried to look after his men. It did seem entirely appropriate to help when he came through and said that they wouldn't give him any money to get John out, and would I please do something for him.'

With that problem solved, Kit returned to the barracks, only to find that Dave's sales pitch to the brass at brigade headquarters hadn't met with the desired enthusiasm. The Croatians argued that the asking price was far too high, and no amount of haggling made any difference. It was a bummer, Mike and Dave's dangerous trip a waste of time. Still, they were here now and there must be some kind of deal available for enterprising businessmen in a war zone.

'What about the armoury?' Kit suggested without explanation.

'What about the armoury?' Mike replied.

'I've got a friend in Zagreb who's interested in some weapons. I met him by chance when we were waiting for the BBC bird yesterday.'

'What's his name?' Dave pricked up his ears.

'Ivan Urirch – he's the chief of police.'

'The chief of police?' Dave repeated, curiosity making him lean forward in anticipation.

'Yeah. He wants some arms to send down to his police friends in Bosnia. The armoury here is full of gear . . . and I've got the key.'

In Kit's own words: 'I went and sucked up to Florez and said that as I couldn't do much at the moment, was it all right if I had a couple of days off in Zagreb.' Florez agreed – no doubt glad to be rid of him for a while. With the first part of the scheme resolved, final planning took place. Kit and his friends sneaked out in the dead of night, creeping through the shadows, and looted the armoury; Kalashnikovs, ammunition, Zolyas, grenades and side arms were taken and stowed away in the Range Rover. Mike paused as the tailgate was closed.

'What happens if we get stopped?'

'Don't worry,' Kit reassured him. 'I've got my ID card. It won't be a problem.'

The first part of the trip went without mishap but as darkness lifted an ominous shape appeared in the road before them, in the shape of two enormous sandbags, behind which were the unmistakable barrels of automatic weapons – an official check-point manned by the police.

Dave Tomkins turned to Kit. 'You'd better know what you're fucking doing!' he said. 'I'm trying to get used to five-star hotels. There's no way I'm spending another night in jail.'

The car slid to a halt, Kit and his ID clambering out from the back seat. 'Morning, Officer. Looks like a nice day. Can I help you?'

The policeman, gun cocked, indicated that he wanted to look inside the vehicle. Kit, playing for time, continued speaking in English, while the others simply sweated. The policeman was joined by another getting anxious at the delay. '*Nemojte se pokretati!*' – Don't move – he barked, thrusting the barrel of his gun in Kit's ribs and pushing him away as the first officer opened the rear door. There was a metallic clank as a Zolya rocket launcher rolled to the edge, dropping on to the road at his feet. That did it; with the threat of terrorism rife in the area these men were taking no chances, especially with a bunch of suspicious-looking foreigners. Kit waved his identification card, pointing at himself and the others as the police surrounded them. There was the sound of safety catches being released. 'Commandos! Commandos! Osijek . . . We are from Osijek,' Kit yelled, as the officer in charge looked at the ID card, examining the occupants of the vehicle suspiciously before walking back to his car and making a phone call.

'Who do you think he's phoning?' whispered Dave.

'I dunno. Hope it isn't Osijek brigade headquarters,' replied Kit through clamped teeth. 'We're in the shit if he does.'

'We're in the shit if he doesn't.'

The officer returned, still looking perplexed, but with little choice, allowed them to proceed through the checkpoint, taking note of the vehicle number as they passed with triumphant smiles.

'Fucking close that, wasn't it?' Mike muttered, exhausted by the tension. 'I thought they were gonna shoot us for a second.'

'*Nema problema*,' replied Kit, almost wetting himself with relieved laughter.

The weapons were received by a grateful police chief without question, and the sum of 3,000 Deutschmarks was paid for the haul – plenty enough for a gigantic piss-up in Zagreb, with a little bit left over for a rainy day.

Kit left his friends, who had further business in the area, and hitched a lift with an American mercenary, returning apprehensively to Osijek the next day. He need not have worried; so far the loss of the equipment had gone unnoticed, and as the days passed the likelihood faded that the mysterious disappearance of all that hardware would be attributed to him.

Kit finally ditched the crutches after about ten days and was left temporarily with a slight limp, his freedom from reliance upon them making him aware that the time had come to hit the road again. Florez no longer made any attempt to co-exist with the volunteers, making his feelings of contempt for them evident at every opportunity. But the simple fact was that Kit and the team had accomplished their task and were no longer required. They had trained an effective fighting unit, organised infiltration patrols and destroyed the JNA offensive which had threatened Osijek with Serbian domination – not a bad epitaph for a bunch of vagabonds and psychopaths!

It was time for pastures new. Posusje beckoned and a telephone call to Governor Drago confirmed that the offer made some months ago in Split still remained open for negotiation.

'How the fuck are we going to get there?' Pete groaned, memories of perpetual road blocks engulfing his mind. 'Posusje's right down by the coast, innit? Just past Split.'

'Stop whining, you miserable sod. There's a ceasefire on at the moment, so we shouldn't have problems like the last time,' Kit replied in his Don't-give-me-no-aggro tone.

'But, Kit . . .'

'Do you wanna come or not?' Flat, final, no room for discussion. Pete shut up and nursed his arm, a habit he had dropped into when feeling aggrieved.

'Right. Who wants to come then? Let's see a show of hands.'

Nigel, Pop, Steve and a hesitant Pete raised their arms. Spooky resisted for a moment before joining them. 'Is that it then?' Kit enquired. 'What about the rest of you?' Shrugging shoulders indicated indecision. Some would stay for a while, others would go home; wherever that might be.

'OK, so we've got six, including me.' Then, looking in my direction, 'Oh, mustn't forget him . . . seven.'

Transport; the perennial problem. Nick a lorry or a Land Rover and be arrested by police *en route*. Florez would love that. He'd be on the phone like a shot if any vehicles disappeared. Kit rang the Panorama Hotel in Zagreb, hoping to catch Mike Stanton.

'Mike, it's Kit.'

'Yeah. What are you after?' A nasty, suspicious mind has Mike.

'A lift to Posusje.' Kit was nice and casual. Get the fish on the hook before reeling him in.

'OK. Dave's finished his deal and gone home, so I can go that way. When do you wanna leave?'

'We'd like to go tomorrow, if possible.' That's it, sneak in the 'we' gently, so he doesn't notice.

'We . . ?' He does . . . sod it. Keep talking fast.

'Yeah, me and a few of the lads. We've been offered a little job by the Governor.' Play it pitiful. Appeal to Mike's better nature.

'OK, see you tomorrow. Halves on the petrol mind you. Bye.' Gotcha!

We ate breakfast, and without bothering to wash our plates loaded the bergans to capacity with anything that wasn't nailed down. Kit rang Benny, still in Osijek Hospital, and told him about

John going home, wishing him a speedy recovery and offering him the opportunity of joining us in Posusje when fit again. Benny didn't even think about it before replying, 'Thanks, but no thanks.' Who could blame him?

Malaria drove slowly through the shell-battered town, allowing us our last look at its clanking trams, boarded-up shop windows and blank-faced inhabitants; none of whom gave a damn for the truckload of men passing by. We arrived at Osijek station feeling just a little bit unappreciated and bade farewell to a misty-eyed Malaria, who insisted on hugging us one by one before letting us go – just in time to watch the 0900 train to Zagreb pull out without us.

With an hour or more to kill before the next train, we were at a loose end, with little to do but guard our belongings and drink the bitter mud they call *kafu* – coffee. Pete started again about the journey. 'Why can't we fly down? Look at the map, there's an airfield at Pleso.'

Kit answered him in exasperated tone, as if talking to a child. 'There's a war on, dummy. If there are planes flying out of Pleso they'll be military, and if I'm wrong, the civilian ones won't be going south anyway. They'd get blown out of the sky by Serbian artillery. Now forget it. None of us wants to travel by road if there's a choice, but there isn't.'

Pete made a face and nursed his arm, wincing for effect rather than sympathy. He'd realised long ago that pity for his injury was in short supply.

Kit, never one to sit still for long, wandered off and engaged a pretty-looking girl in conversation, returning after ten minutes with her telephone number scribbled on a matchbox.

'Lot of good that's gonna do you,' Pop told him.

'You never know,' Kit replied. 'I might be back here one day on holiday when the war's over.'

A scuffle from the station entrance brought the ribbing to an abrupt halt. A station guard was wrestling with a young Croatian soldier who, holding a handgun aloft, was shouting drunkenly at the top of his voice. Kit tried his best to interpret. 'He's saying something about going home ... can't understand it all.' The official was losing the battle. 'Suppose we'd better help,' muttered Kit, striding across to the fracas, with Steve close behind.

'*Zovite policiju!*' gasped the guard, holding on to the man's arm like grim death.

187

'We don't need the police,' Kit answered in English. 'Just let go of his arm and leave it to me.' The guard released the soldier's arm and sprang back out of the way. 'Naughty, naughty!' Kit waved his finger at the young man then hit him low, watching him double up before wrenching the pistol from his grasp. He quickly released the magazine and cocked the pistol; a round popped out. The Croat had been waving the gun with a round up the spout, just waiting for a gentle squeeze. This made matters worse. The arrogant stupidity of it offended Kit's military senses, and without pausing he hit him again, standing back as the young man gasped for breath on the platform.

'I've been fighting in the war,' the Croatian choked in perfect English, 'I'm going home.'

'You're walking around the place pissed out of your skull, with a loaded gun just waiting to go off. You could kill somebody just because you're incompetent. Now fuck off before I report you.' The soldier picked up his gun and slunk away, to disdainful looks from his countrymen.

'It's all good fun, isn't it?' Kit said, shaking hands with a grateful guard, who didn't understand a word that had been spoken.

Our tired old train finally puffed and clanked its way into the station, and we climbed aboard with our heavy bergans, thankful that our long journey was underway at last. After settling down, we plunged into silent contemplation, looking through dirty carriage windows at the once pretty villages of Koska and Jelisavac before the railway line crossed over the main road heading north-west towards Varazdin; the last stop before the southward run into Zagreb.

Steve broke the brooding silence, thinking aloud more than trying to start a conversation.

'Poor old Ivan, getting killed like that,' he whispered to himself. 'Damiar, Jim, Benny, John. They'll never be the same again. Remember old Johnny the Groundhog? Wonder where he is now. Back home in the good old US of A, I guess. Fucking glad that Tommy left; I'd have killed the bastard if he'd stayed on. Still, we had some good times, didn't we?'

He looked around for a response but Kit wasn't listening, lost in his own memories out there in the Yugoslavian countryside. Nigel nodded, saying nothing. Steve didn't pursue the question, sinking inside himself for the rest of the journey until with a shuddering halt we arrived in Zagreb, where Mike was waiting for us.

'You're late,' were his first words. Kit had phoned him with our arrival time. His second words were, 'How the fuck am I gonna get all these blokes and bergans in my Range Rover?'

'Don't worry, we'll manage,' replied Kit. 'Two in front, three in the rear seats and three in back. The bergans can go on top.'

'OK! Let's load up and get on the road then. Oh, I've got some good news,' Mike added.

'What's that?' Kit asked quickly, suspecting a problem.

'The ferry has started operating again since the ceasefire came into force. So we've only got to get to Rijeka and it's a boat ride around the coast and straight into Split.'

Pete could have kissed him, his smile of gratitude lighting up the whole of Zagreb station.

It was straight down the E65 this time. Fifty kilometres of almost perfect road taken at speed. One road block interrupted our progress, but the police looked at Kit's almost worn-out ID, accepted two bottles of booze and waved us on – right into Karlovac and a lot of bad memories about rats and dead bodies. Steve, still in nostalgia mode, narrated the story to Mike, Pop and Spooky, who didn't seem to be that interested; you had to be there. The place had changed a bit since our last visit, and not for the better. Buildings which had stood undamaged before were now piles of rubble, people still wandered with vacant expressions, stray dogs continued to plunder suspicious bundles. But the shelling had been suspended . . . for a while at least. We didn't stop for a burger or a piss. With over a hundred klicks to travel and an absolute certainty that the ceasefire was just a temporary blip – enabling all sides to catch their breath – speed was of the essence, and we tore through the town a little higher than the designated speed limit.

The last twenty kilometres were the worst. Not because of military intervention or militiamen causing aggro . . . No, it was Spooky. You can't keep an American ex-something quiet. They've always got a tale to tell. Like when I was in . . . 'Shut up, Spooky, or I'll rip your tongue out,' said Kit.

Rijeka is a crappy town, a yellowish industrial haze full of bad vibes. Rows of dirty, rust-encrusted cranes littered the skyline, with sea-stained tankers jostling each other for position in the cluttered port. Transit city Balkan style. And the place stank of

189

sulphur! We passed the National Museum, heading for the Jadrolinija Ferry Wharf, only to find the ticket booth closed. Panic . . . until we saw a scribbled sign, *'Otvoreno podne'* – Open noon. Further panic; it was now four o'clock!

Kit read the timetable with a bit of help.

'Christ, the ferry to Split only runs at night!'

'What time's night?' enquired Pete, still sitting in the car.

'Six o'clock!' Kit replied in a voice of doom.

'How long does it take?' Pete asked, leaning through the open window and coughing from the sulphur fumes.

'I don't bloody know. It's about three hundred kilometres or so to Split . . . Forever, if the rest of the boats are anything to go by.'

An old man shuffled up to the door, opening it with a cup of coffee balanced in his other hand. He turned to us with an apologetic smile, saying, *'Dobar dan. Otvoreno sada.'* Good afternoon. Open now.

' 'Bout fucking time,' growled Spooky. 'This ain't no way to run a railroad.'

'Railroad?' the old man queried. 'Not railroad. Station that way,' he said, pointing to the left. 'This is ferry.'

'Yeah, yeah, yeah,' replied Spooky, shaking his head. 'I know. It's just an old American saying.'

Kit took out a suspicious wad of money from his back pocket, handing the old man a pile. 'When does the ferry get in?' he asked as he pocketed the change without looking at it – always a sign of a wealthy man.

'Uskoro' – soon – replied the old man, before adding, *'mozda'* – maybe.

'What does he mean, maybe?' Pete started to tense.

'Don't fret. They always say maybe. It's like *sutra* – part of the culture,' Nigel said soothingly.

With less than two hours to wait – maybe – there was little we could do but hang around the harbour and pour scorn upon sailors leaning over the rails of their ships, flicking cigarette butts into the filthy, oil-slicked water. It seemed like another world. No sounds of battle, just the scream of seagulls and Kit and the lads yelling obscenities at marooned seamen, who were happy to shout back in languages none of us understood, although the gestures were universal.

The blast of a horn focused our interest seaward, just in time to see a scruffy old ferryboat rounding the inner harbour, reversing its screws dramatically as it slid into berthing position alongside the wharf. Luxury it wasn't, and I could see Nigel's face drop at the thought of spending the next seventeen hours aboard the tub without the facility of a cocktail bar.

'You gotta look on the bright side,' Kit told him. 'At least nobody is gonna be shooting at you. Unless the ceasefire is broken again.' He paused for a moment before adding thoughtfully, 'course if it is, we're really in the shit. Serb gunboats patrol these waters and we'll be sitting ducks with these uniforms on.' If looks could kill . . .

Mike edged his Range Rover cautiously on board with no help from the crew, who were busy chatting to one another as they watched, no doubt hoping he would blow it and end up in the drink. Other vehicles followed equally carefully, and within half an hour we and dozens of refugees were heading out to sea and past the island of Krk. We couldn't see it in the darkness of course, but we knew it was there – Pete told us so.

The monotonous chug of the engine combined with a bone-juddering vibration soon lulled us into a stuporous desire for sleep. We were easily seduced, crawling into uncomfortable positions on deck before engaging neutral brain activity and getting our heads down, like all good soldiers on active duty.

Most of us were awakened throughout the night by directional shifts, engine fluctuations and plain discomfort, grunting at one another like old drunks on bomb sites before slipping back into fitful sleep. The lullaby from Spooky's orbital sander simulation didn't help, until silenced by a flying size twelve.

Zadar came and went, the brief stop allowing more passengers to embark upon this voyage of discovery. Chains clanked, floodlights glared in our eyes and a group of soldiers noisily booted their way past us. One stopped, looking down at Steve before poking him in the ribs with his AK.

'Wassamatter?' Steve rubbed his eyes sleepily, squinting up at the man angrily.

'You Steve Brown?' he asked curtly.

'Yeah. Do I owe you some money or what?' Steve climbed to his feet, not wanting to be in a prone position if aggravation loomed.

'Nah. I'm Bill Willis. We was together in the mob at Goose Green. Don't you remember me?'

Steve looked closely at the man, clad in black from head to foot with a giant cross at his neck.

He shook his head. 'Sorry, mate.'

'Come on, you gotta remember me. They called me Preacher.'

Steve kept shaking his head, but trying to appear friendly asked, 'What are you doing here?'

'With Dobroslav Paraga's lot. The HOS. Still savin' souls. The bastard Chetniks'll keep me busy for a while yet.'

Steve smiled and shook the man's hand. 'Nice to see you again, Bill. Perhaps it'll all come back when I'm properly awake.'

'Yeah. Catch you later.' He handed Steve a playing card before walking away to join his comrades now disappearing towards the bow.

'Do you know him?' asked a curious Pete.

'Yeah, I know him all right. He's a fucking religious maniac. Sees himself as an angel of death or something, bringing destruction on the devil's disciples. First it was the Argies. Then Colombian drug-dealers. Now it's the Chetniks. He leaves a cross on the bodies of men he kills. They ought to have binned the guy at Aldershot. He's a nut!'

'Who's Dobroslav Paraga?' Pete turned to Kit for an answer.

'He runs the paramilitary wing of the Hrvatska Stranka Prava – HOS. They're against almost everything in this country; extremist bastards, best left well alone.'

Steve flicked the playing card in his fingers absent-mindedly before catching sight of the inscription. 'Look at this!' In the dim bulkhead light a black ace of spades surrounding a smiling death's-head skull stared at us; behind it was a blood-dripping scythe and the words 'WE KILL FOR PEACE'.

'Lemme see that.' Spooky snatched it away. 'These are like the cards they used in 'Nam. The guys left them on bodies after an attack to frighten the gooks.'

'Like I said, the man's a nut.' Steve sighed. 'I'm off this boat before he comes back. That's for sure.'

It was getting light now as the ferry manoeuvred its way past the larger scattered islands of Kaprije, Zmajan and Zlarin, lost somewhere in the inevitable cold morning mist. Sibenik was hidden completely from view, if not memory. 'Remember that bloody road block before Sibenik?' Nigel reminded us with ill-concealed venom.

It all came back in a flash of humiliation – thanks, Nigel, we needed that – the frisking fingers of ZNG scumbags diving into our pockets, bad breath making us gag as they looted our few possessions, their smiles of pleasure at our impotence as they waved goodbye. Some things you don't want to remember; feeling like shit is one of them.

We rounded the coastline, kicking in tightly to Ciovo island before bearing left for a first welcome sight of Split harbour. Civilised, modern and above all peaceful. Not a tank or artillery piece could be seen anywhere; even the roads were unmined! We grabbed our gear feeling like holiday-makers and trundled to the ship's rail, leaving Mike the task of driving his Range Rover ashore.

'Breakfast! Anybody for breakfast?' Kit headed towards the Bastion self-service restaurant, leaving Mike to find somewhere to park the car. Back in minutes with a 'sod em' look on his face, he told us he had left it in a space reserved for officials with a note stuck on the windscreen saying '*Doktor*'.

'Doctor! A British-plated Range Rover, full of olive bergans, webbing and military equipment?' Pop questioned.

'Could be an army doctor,' Mike reasoned with a shrug.

Through mouthfuls of breakfast we discussed our next move, deciding against spending time looking around Split in favour of a direct drive to Imotski, then Posusje. The journey, of around fifty kilometres, should take about an hour. But ominous news coming from the café radio indicated that Croatian intelligence had detected Serbian troop movement in the area, meaning only one thing: as far as the JNA were concerned, the ceasefire had run its natural course.

'Look, lads.' Kit turned in his seat to face us. 'I don't know what to expect on this trip, so keep your weapons at the ready and be prepared for anything. It should be easy, but if the war kicks off again, no one knows where it'll start and it's just our luck that it'll be right here on the road to Posusje.'

We decided to chance our luck with the main northern route out of town, turning right to eventually pick up the Cista Prova road and reaching Imotski without difficulty. Posusje was only ten kilometres away and we were optimistic about reaching it before trouble started. We should have known better.

A distant thud, muffled but distinct, dragged our listless minds back to reality. Mike turned the radio off as we listened, hoping we'd been mistaken. We looked at one another with challenging eyes. 'Nah,' said Peter hopefully. 'It was thunder.' Mike pulled over and switched off the engine; in silence we waited for confirmation. Long minutes ticked silently past before another dull sound gently shook the earth, soon followed by others, until they merged into one. Heavy artillery fire to the north, in the direction of Duvno. No doubt about it this time – the spell had been broken.

'Let's go,' Kit said quietly. 'Another ten minutes and we'll be in Posusje.'

We crossed the border from Croatia into Bosnia-Herzegovina with a leaden feeling in the pits of our stomachs. What were we letting ourselves in for this time?

A narrow lane, bushes on both sides, no clear view. Around the corner a group of burly, fierce-looking armed men. Hay bales across the road. 'Fuck it.' Steve breathed, clicking off his safety. The others followed suit.

'Relax,' Kit soothed. 'It's bound to be Drago's men this close to town.'

Logical. Nobody had thought of that. As Kit opened the door they looked at him with undisguised suspicion, old hunting rifles at the ready and not a Kalashnikov in sight.

'Looks like trouble,' whispered Steve, wiping revealing beads of sweat from his eyes.

'*Da li govorite engleski?*' Kit held his hands high, just in case.

'*Da.*' A giant walked from the rear of the group, dressed in bandoliers of shotgun cartridges and an old side-by-side twelve-gauge.

'We have come to meet Governor Drago,' Kit told him.

'He is expecting you?' The man's lips didn't move.

'Yes, we are here at his request to train your men to fight the Serbs.'

The giant moved back, instructing a young woman to return to the village and check out the story. She reappeared after what seemed an awfully long time, and whispered sweet nothings into his beard. He nodded, then they all went into a huddle before turning with smiles of welcome.

'You are Freeman, yes?' the woman asked coyly, fluttering her eyes, farm-girl style. 'The Governor said he is looking forward to meeting you again. Please follow us to the village for refreshment where he will join you shortly.'

Kit nodded and began to climb back in the car, pausing for a moment as the sound of artillery fire started up again in the distance. It was closer this time, with nearby high-pitched auto fire providing a rhythm accompaniment. Somebody was getting a thorough going-over out there in the hills, and it sounded like the action was heading our way.

Chapter Eleven

Don't worry about it. Just learn from the rest of us
and remember that each day is different. Some days
you can be courageous and some days you can't.
Some days you can kill and others . . .

The part-time soldiers of Posusje clambered on to the Range
Rover, gleefully straddling bonnet, roof and running boards as
the bearded pied piper led us through increasingly narrow lanes,
finally reaching the outskirts of the scarred village. Deep craters
and a cottage with its roof demolished by shellfire proved – if
proof were needed – that enemy action had taken its toll, even in
this unstrategic place. The lane curved gently to the left, bringing
us alongside the damaged building where we could see a sobbing
middle-aged woman hunched against crumbling walls, grief
racking her body in juddering spasms. A child of six or seven
foraged through the rubble for a doll, a game, a ball . . . any kind of
toy to bring comfort.

We'd seen it many times before in villages all over the country.
But like the sight of your own blood, you never really get used to
it.

'Are we gonna stop and help?' Pete asked.

'What good would it do?' We can't rebuild her house for her,
can we? We can't bring back her possessions. What's the point?'
Kit wasn't being cruel, just practical. 'Forget it, Pete, there's worse
to come.'

We drove on, wondering who was right, until we reached
Posusje, which looked a little like an old town from the American
West, spread out loosely, with empty streets, and small cafes and
bars substituting for saloons.

'Easy pickings for the JNA, innit?' Steve muttered.

The beard pointed us to a small house with '*Otvoreno*' painted
on a board above the door. No sign saying 'Bar', 'Café' or 'Lil's'
Place'; just 'Open'. In we went, getting hit by a solid wall of lung-
destroying smoke from a million Turkish cigarettes.

'Drago come soon,' the big guy grunted. 'You wait, have rest.

196

Drink *kafu, pivo* – coffee, beer. Goodbye.' He was gone, back to the farm and his cows and pigs, his soldiering over for the day.

We waited for an hour, feeling sick on endless cups of battery-acid coffee and nicotine air. The locals, not bothering to hide their curiosity, stared at us as if we were aliens from some distant planet.

'Take me to your leader.' Spooky tried to communicate with two wizened turban-wearing faces; blank stares showed no sign of humour.

Drago arrived, looking tough and capable, two henchmen backing him up. Curt but charismatic, he shook hands with everyone before getting down to business.

'This is the deal,' he said brusquely. 'I want a unit trained and equipped for the defence of my town. Funding is readily available for these things.' Kit listened attentively, the word 'funding' being especially attractive.

He continued, 'In addition to training the men of Posusje, I want you to operate a special operations force contracted out to any village or township unable to afford their own defence and requiring your brand of military expertise. The work will involve blowing bridges, attacking convoys, driving back JNA and Chetnik offensives. You will travel around the country firefighting and return to base for your weekly wage and bonus. Do you understand?' Well rehearsed, without taking a breath.

Kit nodded, his lips pursed in concentration, as Drago lowered his voice to a whisper.

'You will be paid two thousand Deutschmarks per week, plus a bonus for every task you perform successfully. These men with you will receive a lesser but still generous sum which we will discuss later. Is this acceptable?'

Kit looked around the table at hopeful expressions, nodding his head.

'Come with me now. I have a farmhouse about fourteen kilometres outside of town for you to live and train in.'

We trailed him like lemmings from the bar and clambered into the Range Rover, following his Toyota Land Cruiser through lifeless streets, past occasional empty shops and out into the barren countryside.

So this was private enterprise Bosnian style. Shades of The Magnificent Seven ... Drago's hired guns. All this and a farmhouse to live in; a mercenary's wildest dreams come true.

197

Drago's Cruiser did a fast right, bumping over hardened mud tracks before lurching to a halt. We stayed put for a few moments, taking it all in. The farm sprawled its way over a peaceful valley surrounded by acres of mixed countryside – ideal training land. Snow-tipped mountains overlooked us, the bright winter sun glinting off jutting peaks. 'I can do with some of this,' Pete sighed, his head somewhere in the Swiss Alps.

We off-loaded the gear as Kit joined Drago, discussing the business arrangement in greater detail, we presumed. Lots of arm-waving, pointing and animated conversation ensued; some laughter and a manly hug. Drago passed Kit a wad of money and slapped him on the back. All was well.

The Cruiser reversed out into the road, and Drago gave us a brief wave before accelerating back in the direction of town. Kit headed straight for Mike.

'Here's some money. I've told him you're the logistics expert and he wants gear for about twenty men.'

'What does he want and how much did he give you?' Mike asked anxiously.

'Boots, DPM clobber, webbing. He gave me a hundred and sixty thousand Deutschmarks. Is that enough?'

Mike nodded. 'I'll have to go back to the UK for most of it, though. There's nothing in this country.'

'I told him that and he said OK. How long do you think it'll take you to get back?'

Mike grimaced, 'Depends on how long it takes to get to Split airport. Depends on available flights. Depends . . .'

'Cut the crap, Mike. How long?'

'There's a fucking war going on here, Kit, and a lot of ifs, buts and maybes.' He paused. 'Say two to three weeks.'

'OK. You'd better get a few hours' kip before you leave.'

Finding somewhere to bed down was easy in this rambling old building; the large rooms afforded space, comfort and a relaxed atmosphere – apart from a strange *Marie Celeste* feeling about the place which we couldn't quite put our finger on.

Cold soup stood in pots on a dead fire, cut bread and rancid butter on plates, covered in grime, mildew and mouse droppings. Coarse woollen clothing hung in cupboards and a ginger cat examined us suspiciously from its window perch. Something strange had happened here, you could sense it with the short hairs at the back of your neck. We checked outside, searching through outhouses for signs of an attack, a struggle, bodies; anything to give us a clue about the previous inhabitants. Nothing, not a sign of violence anywhere.

As Spooky said, 'It looks like they just upped and went.'

We slept like logs, snored like pigs and woke to the familiar sound of the greater cropped Geordie warbling its daybreak melody.

'Let's get the fucking show on the road!' Kit coaxed us into life after our first good night's sleep for quite a while. 'Come on, you idle bastards. The FNGs – fucking new guys – are gonna be here soon and we want to show them what hot shots we are. Don't we?' He shook Spooky's bed, yelling, 'Hustle, hustle, hustle,' deep into his vibrating right ear.

'Sergeant Bilko or what!' Spooky groaned, rolling over in agony, his eyes blinking rapidly in the morning light.

'I fucking hate it when you're like this, Kit,' moaned Steve, stretching as he looked out of the window at the backdrop of mountains.

Breakfast wasn't the normal blow-out. Supplies had been forgotten and the mouse droppings on what remained in the larder didn't make cheese and scraps of meat appealing. So it was coffee, coffee and then more coffee, before a brisk warm-up jog around the farm buildings.

At eight o'clock the first group of trainees arrived by horse and cart, followed in quick succession by others in lorries and beat-up old cars and on foot. Ages ranged from sixteen to sixty: Mountain men with gnarled faces and toughened bodies, kids with bum-fluff beards. All carrying proudly their obsolete but well-cared-for weapons: battered long-barrelled hunting rifles, one shot and reload, deadly accurate at long range but useless against the metallic vomit of an AK-47; shotguns, elaborately etched, beautifully maintained, at short range devastating, but who wants to get that close?; knives, large-bladed, rusty and pitted. Kit was going to have his work cut out. Discipline? Forget it!

'OK, you bunch of deadbeats, get in line!' Kit yelled at the top of his voice. Ranko, an ex-London waiter, translated. They shuffled, giggling, into a column.

'Shut the fuck up!' Kit was in a hurry. These men had a long way to go and only two weeks to get there.

The day flew past in a blur of running bodies. Up and down hills, through dense woodland. Hare and hounds, push-ups, sit-ups. The whole para bit. At the end of the day the poor bastards were totally knackered and Kit was hoarse from screaming orders.

For the next ten days it was train, train, train. Instil agression. Preach tactics. Inspire loyalty. Run, jump, scream, KILL! They had bottle, these men, none dropping out from injury or fatigue. Their eyes gave out a clear message, alive with hope, burning with fever: they were the saviours of their town – it was written in the wind.

Mike returned with the consignment of British DPM clothing, boots and webbing – most of which had been obtained from the Survival Shop in Bristol. He stayed just long enough to say hello-goodbye, as other pressing business matters demanded his attention; especially since the war was hotting up again after its fourteenth ceasefire.

A further week of arms familiarisation and drill followed, the farmers adjusting to their new automatic weapons, grenades and Zolyas like schoolkids with computers. Now fully kitted out and dressed like soldiers, they were beginning to behave like soldiers too – even saluting!

Kit Freeman, in less than a month, had transformed these unprogressive country folk into a small but effective army with the most important attribute available to any general – balls!

Drago was more than impressed as he watched the squad perform in fields around the farm, blasting trees and cardboard cut-outs, screaming as they attacked piles of inanimate hay bales and blowing huts to matchwood. All great fun. He shook Kit by the hand, demonstrating his pleasure by passing over wads of paper in large denominations to a smiling training officer.

Serbian MiG fighter/bombers attempting low-level strikes on Imotski had caused problems over the past few days. Mountainous peaks virtually surrounding the town made the run-in difficult, and getting out without slamming into the rock face was even more hazardous for inexperienced pilots. Posusje, some ten kilometres to the east, was getting the jettisoned cluster bombs and rockets instead, and the unpredictability of raids, combined with the odd hit, made for a nervous existence in the town. Without suitable weapons, there was little Kit and his team could do about the air strikes until a word in the ear of someone high up provoked positive reaction, and SAMs – surface-to-air missiles – were deployed high up on the hills, soon starting to discourage the attacks, which we assumed were designed to soften up defences before a ground assault by JNA forces.

With training complete and the Posusje commando force raring to go, Drago and Kit spent many late nights poring over maps, making telephone calls and generally trying to drum up some business – not difficult with a unique product.

Duvno, twenty kilometres north, was worried about a marauding Chetnik band attacking villages west of the town, and offered 100,000 Deutschmarks for the group to sweep the area clean. Horror stories made the gig even more interesting and Kit accepted it without question.

'Bastards. I'm gonna just love giving them a good kicking,' he told us after his meeting with Drago.

Twenty men in three Rovers, loaded to the springs with nice new gear and just itching to see action. Up at dawn and on the road, passing Ostrac, Mesihovina and Cebara, before going in-country to the left of Duvno, where Kit sent out a scout car to survey the land before proceeding north. We waited for its return, chewing grass and thinking great thoughts.

Steve returned with an all-clear wave from three hundred metres ahead. We rapidly caught up with him before passing the Busko Jezero lake, reminding us of our earlier grenade fishing episode. Pete looked at Kit with a how-about-it expression.

'Nah, can't mess around on our first op, can we? Maybe on the way back. A fish supper would go down nicely.'

A brief stop at Prisoje for a B&B – brew and briefing. The map was laid out and the current village causing concern indicated with a red grease pen.

'We'll drive in to this point, park up and go the rest of the way on foot. This village was hit last night according to reports, so with a bit of luck they'll still be in the vicinity.' Kit pointed to a small hamlet of maybe forty houses. 'No Chetnik prisoners, mind you. Kill them all!'

Tobacco-chewing Ranko, the leader of the Bosnian volunteers, spat a stream of evil brown fluid, adjusted his eye patch and translated in machine-gun Serbo Croat. Smiles widened and the men exchanged vengeful glances, adopting aggressive postures copied from film posters.

Pete felt compelled to take the piss. He handed an eager-looking kid his scrim scarf to wear as a bandanna, saying, 'Rambo.

201

You look like Rambo.' The youngster understood only one word, but it was enough.

Another five kilometres and we parked the Rovers, stuffing them into a copse and covering them with bracken. Vladimir, the pock-marked slob of the group, and bespectacled Milenko were left on guard, much to their annoyance, until Kit explained just how important their role was. We moved off slowly, unsure of the terrain or the accuracy of our map, heading towards the trig point with little idea of the strength of our quarry but with a strong, almost obsessive desire to make contact.

Keeping close to the edge of the field, with bushes helping to conceal our movement, we loped towards a nearby woodland, crawled under a barbed-wire fence and formed two groups, spreading out in the direction of the village a few kilometres beyond the northern edge. Spooky, leading 'B' group, stopped almost immediately, spinning around and dropping to his knees, then crawling back a few metres as he waved us to him.

'There's a woodsman's hut down there,' he whispered. 'It looks like they're using it as a base.'

Kit moved forward on his belly, fumbling for his binoculars as he went. Back he came after only a few moments, face flushed with excitement. 'Looks like you're right, Spook. I could only see two of them. The others could be inside the hut or out pillaging. We'd better move back a bit and wait until nightfall.'

Steve dropped back to the vehicles to prepare Vladimir and Milenko for hostile proximity and probable conflict. Their exclusion from an impending confrontation with Chetniks pissed them off even more!

With each man taking a turn at watch, we lolled and snoozed in the rough bracken as the hours ticked away. Like the man said, it's ninety per cent boredom and ten per cent panic – this was the boredom bit.

'What happened to the people who lived in our farm?' Pete, never one to beat around the bush, asked Ranko.

'Ne razumem.' I don't understand. He looked perplexed at the question.

'Bollocks! You can speak and understand English better than I can.'

Ranko stared at Pete for a moment, gradually moving his gaze to the rest of us waiting for an answer. 'They went away,' he shrugged, lifting his palms upwards in an expression of unconcern.

'They went away. Just like that?' Kit repeated suspiciously.

'They were Serbian pigs.'

He had answered the question, and no further discussion was necessary or forthcoming. No doubt their bodies were buried somewhere on the hundred-acre farm, never to be seen again.

Nigel slid back. 'There's movement from over there.' He pointed to the edge of the wood, where crashing sounds and laughter could now be heard.

Slithering forward, we inched to the edge of the brush-covered rim and peered through dense foliage at a group of twelve men carrying radios, clothes and various household appliances. They were back-slapping one another, jostling and bellowing with laughter. It must have been a hell of a joke; some could barely stand as they rolled drunkenly against one another.

'They have raided the village,' Ranko translated unnecessarily. 'What shall we do?'

'Wait until they are inside the hut,' Kit replied. 'Then we'll go and do the bastards.'

The Chetniks, dressed typically in their heavily armed mixture of military and civilian guerrilla-fighter apparel, played around in the clearing as their two comrades came out of the hut to join them, grabbing oddments from bulging pockets and pouring wine and beer down open gullets. I could feel Ranko, Toni and Obrad tighten beside me as they watched. Kit, realising that they were poised to go off with a bang, said quickly, 'Cool it . . . wait. You'll get your chance soon.'

The horseplay continued as the Chetniks became more intoxicated throwing bottles in the air for haphazard shooting practice before finally staggering into the hut. 'Sloppy gits!' murmured Steve, turning to Kit for the go sign.

There was little need for sophisticated military strategy under the circumstances. Kit stood and the rest followed. Crouching low, they headed for the hut, paused, looked at one another. Kit nodded his head, and with a technique reminiscent of Chicago's St Valentine's Day massacre they simply blasted the hut to smithereens. Shell casings buzzed through the air and thirty-round magazines were exchanged without pause. Long after the mercs quit, the Bosnians continued blasting away, anger, frustration and pain freezing their trigger fingers on hold. The AK-47 has a cyclical rate of 600rpm; a rough calculation indicated that well over one thousand rounds went into that hut in the space of a minute. It's difficult to believe that anyone could have survived the onslaught, but a low moan disproved that theory.

'Fuck it, someone's still alive,' Steve groaned. 'Who's gonna go in and find him?'

Kit snatched a grenade from his webbing, thumbed the men back and lobbed it into the pile of shattered wood, the explosion buffeting the leaves around him as he walked away. 'That solves the problem. 'Course, we could have used grenades in the first place, but it wouldn't have been so much fun.' With the deafening sounds of gunfire still ringing in our ears we trailed behind him as he headed for the village, knowing in our gut that killing the Chetniks was the easy bit.

Stepping from the gloomy wood into bright blue sky and crisp autumn light we passed through a field of corn stubble overlooking a valley. Below lay a village, frost-covered red-tiled roofs glittering in the brittle sunshine. Cobbled streets intertwined, winding their way past brightly painted bow-fronted shops. Recollections of storybook tales, castles in the air and fairy-tale princesses . . . we were in a time warp. Approaching the outskirts we had every reason to expect a grateful king to grant our every wish.

There's a clear visual distinction between ethnic cleansing and attacks which involve mortar or shellfire – easy to detect from almost any distance. In the former there are no holes blasted in the earth, walls or roofs. No signs of major explosions. It's difficult to describe, but we knew that this was a village of the living dead as we patrolled slowly down the empty cobbled street, staring at once neat front gardens now littered with household possessions, discarded as looters lost interest in their quest for something better. Shattered windows showed strips of charred curtain. Walls were blown outward from dynamite, roof tiles scattered everywhere. The reversed 'C' was sprayed on white walls, often covered in dried execution blood.

Nobody spoke. We wandered tense and expectant from one side of the road to the other, looking up and down with jerky head movements. Checking for snipers, maybe. No. Just blocking the mind. Keep moving . . . stay on the ball. Whatever you do, *don't think!*

We heard a cracking sound, and dived in a heap behind the

cover of a garden wall, feeling stupid as a charred roof beam fell behind us, followed by part of a ceiling crashing into the room below.

'Getting jumpy, lads, aren't we?' Kit clambered out first, just to prove a point.

We were getting closer to the village centre, waving AK's at the sky, looking good, feeling sharp. An old man appeared from nowhere, carrying a tray full of something that looked oddly familiar.

'Oh Christ,' whimpered Nigel, white as a virgin's wedding dress.

The old guy just stood there silently, his gaze disappearing into infinity as he held the tray for our inspection.

'What is it?' Pete called, moving closer. 'Breakfast?'

He wished he hadn't said it, blanching at the sight of about thirty men's testicles, settling in congealed blood.

'Fuckin' hell!' he managed to choke, before repeatedly vomiting over his boots. 'Fucking bloody hell.' What else could he say?

The old man beckoned, shuffling silently through narrow lanes until we arrived at a large grey-stone building in a side street on the far side of the village. Ranko translated the sign above the door so quietly that he just mouthed the word: 'Abattoir.' The old man pushed the door open, standing aside for us to pass.

More than fifty naked corpses lay on the grey slate floor, thick with blood in various stages of coagulation. Men and boys with arms tied behind their backs, scrotums ripped from their bodies, gaping black holes where their manhood once lay. Blood and stomach contents oozed thickly through open, toothless mouths with bloated lips.

The body postures were grotesque – impossible unless all major bones had been broken before death. Cigarette burns were livid on waxen, pockmarked skin, eyes gouged from sockets, fingers smashed to a bloody pulp. They had been left bleeding to death with their faces reflecting an incomprehensible agony. Lifeless, they begged with hands like claws, clutching at lost hope. *No more, please God, no more!*

I suppose in moments of extreme shock senses operate in sequence, allowing the brain to determine which function dominates. In this instance our eyes recorded the scene, ensuring that the picture would forever stay in our subconscious. The shutter clicked on motor drive, taking it all in – later we would flick through the photographs in the privacy of our minds.

The smell came next, a cloying stench of death. Sweet, sickly, gaseous, it clung to the skin, burned the eyes, tearing at the throat. We could taste it deep down in our bowels.

'Let's get out of here, lads,' Kit choked, slipping as he turned on the smooth, blood-washed floor.

The old man whimpered from the doorway like an animal in pain unable to express its emotion. He was still holding the tray of testicles, unable or unwilling to put them down.

'*Zasto?*' he sobbed. Why? '*Zasto, Zasto, Zasto?*'

We didn't know why, but we did know who. And they wouldn't be doing it again.

Breathing deeply in the clean air, we followed the old guy back into the village. Ranko tried to talk to him, without success. Conversation seemed inappropriate anyway, so we trailed behind in silence, often catching sight of bundles of clothing in the streets which turned out to be crumpled bodies, wondering what came next. . . with not long to wait.

The schoolhouse was our next stop; this time the old man just pointed, leaving us to walk up to the entrance alone.

They had tried to barricade themselves in. Trestle tables, chairs and bookcases littered the floor, blown away by dynamite. Women and girls lay in untidy heaps, some still alive . . . just. We lit cigarettes for comfort, moving gently around the bodies, unsure of how to behave with young girls of eleven or so who had been raped and buggered before merciful death, their naked bodies slashed with a cross and the Chetnik reversed 'C'.

Many of the older women had been blown apart internally, a charge inserted into the vagina and detonated. Broken glass was found in the bowels of numerous bodies, breasts were sliced off, pregnant women bayonetted in the stomach. We did the best we could for the thirty battered, blood-soaked and traumatised living and left them to mourn their friends, lurching into the open air to suck more fresh oxygen deep into our lungs. I don't recall more than ten words being spoken by any of us in the hour we were there.

The old man had disappeared and we were left to continue our search of the village alone, choosing houses at random. The first was empty and untouched – another sign of selective ethnic cleansing. The second had been ransacked and burned. Two children, no more than nine months old, were found decapitated in a corner with their arms and legs hacked off. They had been set on fire and looked like charred black statues. Kit picked one up, later saying, 'I wasn't wearing gloves and my fingers went straight through the body with a crisp, crackling sound. I felt sick and threw it away in disgust . . .'

Apart from the old man and the few survivors in the school, we saw no other form of life in the village as we methodically searched each house, just recurring scenes of despair and inhumanity. Most of us wished that the Chetniks had not died so easily in the wood, other forms of death seeming much more appropriate.

There was little else we could do to help the injured, and nothing for the dead – apart from burying them, an impossible task with so many bodies. Kit organised a work detail and an abandoned truck was located and the bodies collected and taken to the edge of the village, where they were piled unceremoniously into a tarpaulin-lined pit, doused in petrol and set alight. We walked away, the Bosnian soldiers moving their lips in silent prayer, not wishing to see the searing flames engulf the remains of nearly one hundred and fifty defenceless people.

Emotions were exchanged without speech as we skirted the wood on our return to the RV point, gaunt expressions clearly indicating those mental processes working inside the skull. The men stumbled across the cornfield, tired and haggard, with hate blazing in their faces, substituted in an instant by pain, vengeance, horror and finally helplessness. They kept shaking their heads as if being bothered by flies.

Wispy smoke greeted us as we approached our hidden vehicles. After a few seconds of anxiety we were greeted by Milenko with steaming mugs of coffee.

'Put that fire out, you wanker,' Kit snarled. 'Haven't I taught you? No smoke on patrols!'

It didn't need translating. Milenko got the message loud and clear as Kit snatched his coffee from him, downing it in one gulp.

The Bosnians narrated the story to their countrymen as we removed the bracken from the Land Rover, tears forming in many eyes as the final chapter was related. All the way back to Posusje they sang deep, mournful folk songs, swaying in grief as they gazed into the middle distance with their arms intertwined.

Drago took the news of the atrocities with grim acceptance,

immediately contacting his client in Dunvo. He took Kit aside, and after emotional appreciation told us of another band of Chetniks operating in a commando group in the Zenica area, about ninety kilometres north-east of Posusje. They were moving fast and had terrorised seven villages in one night; killing, burning and looting. The problem was guessing their next target. A quick look at the map, marking villages already hit, seemed to indicate a pattern, and it was agreed that they were moving south-west in our general direction.

'Which village are we gonna go for, then?' Pop asked.

'Dunno, it's dificult to judge. Other reports have been coming in of Chetnik attacks further south, around Bukovica and Kresevo.' Kit shrugged. 'Your guess is as good as mine.'

Further map-poring, notes and telephone conversations with English-speaking Bosnians led Kit to finally make a decision. 'We'll head for Matorac, it's about fifty kilometres north-east. Maybe we'll get some clearer indication there.'

An early night, plagued with dreams. We were awakened by MiGs on another dawn raid over Imotski. 'Sod them! I thought you told me the SAMs had stopped it,' moaned Pete, lying frog-eyed in his big farmhouse bed.

'Sorry about that, Pete. I'll make sure it doesn't happen again,' Kit replied sarcastically. 'Now you're awake you can get break-fast!'

We gobbled fast, carrying cups of coffee out to the waiting Rovers, loading RPGs, 88s, claymores, AKMs and 47s in readiness for whatever. 'Sling in the bivvy bags. We'll be out all night. Maybe more,' Kit pointed out. 'And don't forget your teddy bear, Pete.'

This was mountainous country, with winding lanes overlooked by grey scrubland. Here we were, exposed again. Still, there were nearly thirty of us this time, an army no less. Ready to be wiped out in seconds by a few well-placed mortars.

We bypassed Mostar and its memories of exploding MiGs, heading north on the main route before cutting off with nervous tension to less hazardous roads. Kit's calculation of distance was based upon a direct route to Matorac; this wasn't direct, adding about fifty kilometres to the trip.

We arrived at a small hamlet near Kresevo in two hours, familiar signs of looting everywhere. The villagers, gathered in groups, didn't want to talk about it. 'Chetniks?' they queried, fearing reprisals. 'Not Chetniks ... bandits!' They shook their heads and smiled, saying, 'They have gone now, all is well.'

'Miserable, lying, gutless bastards!' Pop spat. 'How the fuck can anyone help them if they won't tell the truth?'

'It is not for you to judge,' replied Ranko. 'These people have to live here tomorrow ... many tomorrows. Long after you have gone home to your peaceful English country.'

Pop calmed down instantly, knowing that Ranko had spoken the truth and realising at the same instant that Chetnik raiders could live in this village or the next. Someone's cousin, uncle, brother, husband ... anyone!

We stopped at other chattering groups, who paused in their animated conversation to stare at us suspiciously and give the same vacant response. The shutters had come down. We were wasting our time here.

Dusina was the same, so we drove on, questioning anyone prepared to talk to us, stopping in bars and cafés *en route*, not for refreshment, just information. Many people hurried away as our camouflaged vehicles pulled up beside them, not wanting to get involved, not wanting to be seen talking to foreign soldiers.

'This is a waste of time,' Kit said impatiently after our twelfth attempt. 'Nobody's gonna tell us fuck all.'

Matorac was little better, although some children, eager to show how adult they were, told us of lorries coming in the night and dragging men off to be shot. One, whose grandfather had been taken away, pointed north, saying, 'That way. They went that way.' At last we had a lead, however tenuous.

After five hours' road dust and a million one-sided conversations, and well pissed off at mute Bosnians, we stopped for a well-earned brew. No milk. 'Shit!' You could hear Steve's anguished tone echo through the valley.

'Not worry. I'll get some from over there.' Ranko spoke to Nikola, no more than a kid, who took off at a trot in the direction of a nearby farm.

It wasn't a good place to stop, surrounded as we were by mountainous country. But then the whole place was the same, so there was little choice. Steve and Nigel unloaded the 'hexy' stoves, filling billy cans with water in readiness. Cold beans spooned from cans and dry rolls munched with little enthusiasm, we waited.

A yell from the farm made us jump to our feet. Nikola was

running back, waving wildly, '*Dodjite ovamo!*' he screamed. Come here! He was babbling away so rapidly that only his countrymen could understand.

Ranko listened, turning to Kit, his face grim. 'The farm has been looted and burned. Nikola says the family are dead inside. Come.'

Without waiting for approval, he and the other Bosnians raced back to the building. Kit ordered Pete, Nigel and Pop to stay with the vehicles, and the rest of us followed, chickens flying everywhere as we thundered through the cobbled yard, not knowing what we would find.

'White Eagles,' Ranko choked before entering.

'How can you tell?' Steve asked. 'There are no symbols this time.'

'I just know,' replied Ranko, becoming agitated at the questioning. 'It's either White Eagles or Arkanoci.'

Through the low doorway we could just make out the shape of an inverted figure, strung by its ankles from a roof beam. The dim light made it impossible to judge age or sex. We followed Kit as he led the way cautiously into the house, seeing the body of a man, stripped naked, with his stomach ripped open. Grey intestinal matter flowed freely from the gaping wound and slid down his body into a pool on the stone floor. The stench of open drains filled the room, making us gag in uncontrollable spasms. Nikola coughed once, cleared his throat and ran outside, retching as he hit the air.

Rapidly averting our gaze, we caught sight of another body. A young woman in her early twenties lay sprawled against the ledge of an open window as if trying to escape, her face contorted and a strange grey mist covering blank, protruding eyes. Her head had been smashed to a pulverised mash, an iron bar still lying by her side; she had one ear missing.

The house had been looted, soft furniture set on fire. Charred and still smoking it gave off the pungent smell of an incinerator.

'I'm getting pissed off with this, it's doing my head in,' Kit muttered to himself. Moving towards the stairs, he instructed the rest to check the outbuildings.

He headed upstairs, banging and clattering around the bedrooms before suddenly stopping. The creak of sliding furniture gave way to a yell.

'Up here. Now!' he barked.

We leapt up the stairs in time to see him lift the limp body of a uniformed young man, a pitchfork jammed firmly in his chest, blood bubbling from his mouth as he pleaded with Kit for mercy. Ranko stared at the boy, spitting in his face. 'Chetnik scum!' The kid babbled, his eyes mesmerised with fear as Ranko tore a pink ear from a thong around his neck.

Kit dropped the shaking figure to the floor and walked out, beckoning us to follow, leaving the Bosnian alone to interrogate the boy.

We waited in the open for the inevitable single shot. Ranko joined us moments later.

'They killed the woman first, thinking she was alone,' he whispered as we walked slowly back to the vehicles. 'Her husband was working outside and hurled the pitchfork through the window before they overpowered him. I asked him where his friends had gone and why they had left him, but he wouldn't tell me . . . so I shot him.'

Ranko looked at Kit as we pushed the farm gate open, searching his face for answers, but there were none. Kit had long forgotten the question.

A dog barked behind us, and a flash of black and brown sent the chickens scurrying once again as a large Alsatian ran at us, growling displeasure at our intrusion on its territory. Too late; we were beyond the gate and safe from its snarling teeth. Another hound to join the ever-increasing packs of hungry domestic pets seen scavenging in most small towns and villages these days.

Kit stopped us for a moment and in a confused tone explained his predicament. 'I don't know what to do now. We can't keep driving around the country in the blind hope we'll find them, and nobody's telling us nothing.'

Ranko nodded his head in silent agreement as we reached the cars.

'Where's the fucking milk then?' Pete roared. 'We're bloody gasping here.'

Kit looked at him for a full thirty seconds, his mouth beginning to twitch into a smile. Pop giggled, and both collapsed in a heap, their bodies convulsing with a laughter so infectious that we found ourselves joining in. Tears ran down their faces in waves as they rolled hysterically on the ground, holding their sides in gleeful agony. Difficult to understand? Ask any combat soldier for the answer.

We finally managed to get them aboard, still chuckling, and

headed north for a final attempt at tracking down the raiding party. The whole thing was developing into a futile operation. Morale, especially among the vengeful Bosnians, had reached an all-time low.

'I've had enough,' Kit moaned from the passenger seat. 'We'll loop around Merdzanici and head back. There's no point in wasting any more time on this. Drago's got loads more jobs for us to do.'

For the next two hours we kept stopping, kept asking, kept getting blanks. The people were frightened, refusing to be involved. 'Fuck 'em,' commented Steve after another failure to communicate.

Out on the open road he put his foot down, swaying round corners with the other two Rovers doing their best to keep up. A puff of smoke from a green pine-studded hillside opposite made him slam on the brakes, skidding to a halt. The other cars slid sideways behind us, one rolling into a water-filled ditch. The first puff was followed by another; this time a mortar shell hit the gully, sending a plume of stagnant liquid high in the air. We were out like rabbits, diving headlong into the bushes beyond. Small-arms fire kicked into action almost immediately, stitching the grass five metres to the right, getting closer. Another mortar hit the gully, seconds before a rifle grenade slammed into the ditched Rover, blasting it to scrap metal before our eyes. It went quiet suddenly, before the fuel tank exploded, sending metallic fragments high into the air.

'Who the fuck's that?' Steve groaned. 'Can't be the JNA, they're not in this area yet.'

Kit checked for injury amongst the men; they were OK, none hit by gunfire or flying metal.

We were pinned down, any movement drawing fire from a very accurate sniper.

'Betcha it's the fucking Chetnik patrol,' growled Nigel. 'We found them at last.'

'They found us,' Kit added quietly. 'And now we're in the shit.'

Another mortar shell landed way off course, followed once again by sustained bursts of small-arms fire, splashing into the ditch and ricocheting off our vehicles. A prolonged burst, seemingly from a single source, tailed off and silence fell. Twenty minutes passed slowly. Kit edged his head above the bush . . . no sniper fire.

'We can't stay here all day. Spooky, you come with me. We'll flank them and see what's going on.'

Crawling along the bush line, they made a dash across the road and into the opposite field, clambering exposed up the hill before reaching the pine wood with not a single shot being fired at them. Less than five minutes later they were waving from the top. The attackers were gone, leaving piles of spent ammo cases as souvenirs.

'Just hit and run. Seems familiar,' Kit mused on their return. 'Gimme the map.'

He and Ranko pored over it for ten minutes, discussing alternatives and possibilities before arriving at a decision.

'Here!' Kit pointed. 'The Chetniks are heading for this village.'

'You sure?' Nigel asked doubtfully.

'Definitely. Absolutely.' His tone was positive before pausing. 'Mmmm . . . Maybe. They'd better be, because that's where we're going.'

With almost an hour's delay, there was no way we could follow on foot, choosing instead the tortuous route through tricky, winding lanes.

Now down to two cars, overcrowding and lack of manoeuvrability caused a few problems, especially on tight corners, so we ditched the vehicles and struck out across the fields as fast as our legs could carry us. We reached the hilltop overlooking Kit's trig point . . . too late. Smoke was pouring from a barn, uniformed men running in our direction.

'Down!' Kit ordered. We hit the earth hard, grunting in pain.

Steve eased himself up, peering through the scrub. 'They look pissed. They're staggering all over the place.'

'Are they still heading our way?' Kit asked, keeping his head low.

'Yeah, in fact they're climbing the hill now.' Steve ducked down to meaningful glances. Safety catches were released in readiness.

It was all over in seconds as thunderous gunfire echoed across the open valley and bodies rolled untidily back down the slope, looted property falling from lifeless hands. Drunk and incapable, the Chetniks had made a final and stupid mistake. They should have wiped us out at the ambush or at least legged it; instead greed drove them on to more killing and looting.

'Ranko, you and your lads go down and check the place out.

I've seen enough to keep me going for a long, long time,' Kit said wearily, sinking to his knees.

'Amen to that,' was the silent but universal response.

Vladimir returned first, with the news that Ranko wanted to bury the victims, asking if we minded waiting. Eight this time, hurriedly shot and decapitated. Sick as it was, we all smiled when Spooky suggested that this particular band of Chetniks were on piecework – payment on body count.

The Bosnian peasant-soldiers dragged themselves up the hill towards us with blackened, tear-stained faces. Sullen and uncommunicative, they told us nothing of what horrors they'd found in the hamlet, and we didn't ask. Who needs more pictures in an already overcrowded scrapbook? Once again they hummed mournful tunes on the long trip back to Posusje.

Two days' rest turned into three, permitting some serious loafing to be practised in the many small taverns dotted about the place. We took this opportunity to check out the town and meet the inhabitants, who knew nothing about our reason for being there, and couldn't understand why this group of unshaven wild men kept touring the streets each day, often with painted faces. Muttering groups of men and women stared with undisguised suspicion at our every move, often scurrying indoors as our Range Rovers pulled into the main street.

'Makes you feel like a Hell's Angel, dunnit? The way they disappear like that, dragging their daughters behind them.' Pete clambered out of the Rover, dropping into his outlaw swagger.

On our third day, Kit, with two other lads, took a trip into Split for some well-earned irresponsibility. They were gone all day, returning with bad news learned from an old friend Kit had met wandering in the Varos district. Sprog – seventeen-year-old Paul Eugene Thomas from Warrington – having left Osijek for Vinkovci, had decided upon a final bit of action in Sarajevo before returning home to a life of normality. As the sun set on his first day there, a journalist from the Reuter's agency found his body curled up in an alley, a neat hole drilled dead centre in his forehead. Still clutching his beloved folding-stock AK–47, his cherubic face registered confusion. The brief article and photograph, torn from a magazine Kit had been given, dampened our spirits as we recalled Sprog's speech by the Drava bridge a few short weeks before: 'I'm pissed off with people I don't know trying to kill me . . . I'm going home.'

214

Another day, another Deutschmark. Trig point 1916, close to Jablanica. A radio station passing information on troop movements back to the JNA. 'Needs silencing,' said Kit. Only half the team went this time, leaving most of the Bosnians behind to guard the village. White Eagles still roamed unabated. Atrocity stories were coming in daily. It was only a matter of time before they got around to Posusje.

It took a day to reach the place and another hour to find a suitable stop to stash the Rover. That done satisfactorily, we climbed the steep hill, found a hollow to hide away in and played poker with an old, greasy forty-two-card deck, waiting for dusk and a last-light attack to ease our escape in the subsequent darkness. Cold food, little movement, no conversation. The long afternoon dragged into a bitter, damp evening.

Five men climbed the final three hundred metres, finding the exterior of the building unguarded. Inside, men could be seen drinking, reading and lounging. Careless. . . it would be the death of them.

Kit and Steve went in first, crashing through the door, yelling like banshees from hell, with Nigel following and Spooky bringing up the rear. The Serbs stood no chance. They froze, gaping at the wild-eyed intruders for a millisecond before dying for their cause without a movement in defence. An overkill of thirty kilos of explosive finished the job and the lads were back at our sides in less than fifteen minutes.

'Textbook operation, that was. Easy money for a change.' Kit whistled a tuneless melody most of the way back.

Chapter Twelve

It's like . . . it's like . . . a sledgehammer. You hold it
low, at your hip, and create a wall of devastation in
front of you. Squeeze, bam! Everyone's scared of a
shotgun. You can't miss and they know it.

Serbian MiGs screamed low over Mostar airfield, landing gear
locked in readiness for a touchdown kiss. In the grey dawn light
the orange glow from roaring afterburners sent luminous threads
shimmering through the damp morning sky. On the ground all
was confusion; noise, dirt and the familiar terrain of burnt-out
houses and burnt-out people, living for what remained of their
lives in Shit Street, ex-Yugoslavia.

One by one the MiGs bounced on the tarmac, smoke belching
from tortured tyres, slowly taxiing to a comforting breakfast and a
few embellished stories. Kit fidgeted as he watched, itching for his
beloved RPG-7 and a hundred HEAT warheads, no doubt
remembering the last time we were here in the dead of night,
leaving just before the place erupted in a blaze of writhing metal.

We'd pulled over on our way back from Jablanica just to stare at
them thundering over our heads like fiery ·birds of prey.
Gruesomely beautiful killers, never to see the face of their enemy
in death. It was a risky stop, but in relative darkness well worth
the gamble.

'Bleedin' wankers! Look at them strutting about the place.'
Pete's petulant voice grated on our ears as he stared jealously at
the pilots, climbing down to jokes from their crews.

'I bet they've been bombing Imotski again,' he added. 'Don't
know how they can kill innocent people.'

'Not like us then,' Nigel muttered sarcastically, crunching the
Rover into gear and slamming his foot on the accelerator. Thirty-
five kilometres and we'd be home. The rest of the guys were
snoring by the time we hit Knespolje.

Posusje slept as we cruised through the main street, odd
windows showing light from early-morning risers. A lone dog
barked, starting others. Within minutes howls echoed around the
village, and by the time we turned left towards our farm, anxious

faces were appearing at half-open doorways in anticipation of invasion.

Nigel flipped the wheel like a professional parking attendant, showering red dust as we skidded to a halt. Engine off, chirping crickets . . . silence. 'We're home,' to a whispered chorus of 'Thank God.' Milenko nodded from his lonely guard position on the roof, but seeing weary faces he said nothing. We left the gear on board, going straight to bed in our filthy clothes. Dirty boots dropped noisily on the floor, and we were out of it in seconds.

The squeal of brakes and loud voices dragged us back through a haze of sleep. Drago's Land Cruiser stood in the yard, polished and shiny.

'*Dobro jutro,*' he greeted us, face beaming, grey hair combed, a picture of health and vitality. Why the hell couldn't he speak English at this time of the morning?

'*Dobro jutro,*' we chorused back, like children being greeted by a schoolteacher.

'I'd like you to meet someone.' He stood back to reveal the shapely figure of a member of the other sex; known in polite society as a woman.

We rubbed our eyes sleepily. A gift perhaps, as thanks for services rendered? Take her away for now, we're too tired. Later, maybe.

'This is Freda Valk,' he continued, smiling at Pop's attempt to finger-comb his thinning hair. 'She's a journalist from Holland and wants to get through the blockade into Sarajevo. Can you do it?'

In late 1992 there were only two ways to get into Sarajevo – still are, for that matter: one with a United Nations relief flight – hairy and unpredictable; the other even less certain – overland, with or without the kind permission of the less than inviting Bosnian Serbs surrounding the place with large-scale shooters.

Drago had asked a complicated question simply, and waited for the answer. Kit sighed deeply, his breath coming in a drawn-out gasp.

'How much?' He looked at the girl.

She shrugged her shoulders, gesturing helplessly. 'I will pay what it costs. Can you get me there?'

'Of course,' he replied, confidence oozing from every pore. 'When do you want to go?'

217

'Right now!' she answered, brittle-voiced, trying the butch war correspondent bit. Kate Adie eat your heart out.

'No. Not now. I'll need some time to sort out the route. Come back later.'

'I'm in a hurry.' Her voice rose in petulant frustration at Kit's apparent lack of interest.

She had a look about her. *Haute couture* in the face of flying bullets, never a hair out of place. You could bet even money that she wouldn't get creased on the trip.

'I've told you. Come back later or not at all. I'm not attempting it unless I can get some information on the opposition in the area.'

She fell silent, shuffling from foot to foot. The hard-nose act hadn't worked. Should she try the soft approach?

'I'd be really grateful.' Eyelashes fluttered, mournful, little girl conning daddy.

Kit turned dismissively, reaching for his telephone as Steve scrabbled around for maps.

'We gonna take her, ole buddy?' Spooky asked, watching them through the window as they drove away.

Kit was phoning contacts, checking odds, throwing dice. 'Yeah, we'll take her if the money's right.'

Twenty minutes of phone calls followed, with long gaps in the conversation. Lots of 'yeah, yeah' and 'bollocks!'. Friends in the UN offered advice. Trig points and likely problem areas were checked out. Kit left to give her the good news – returning with the bad.

'Sarajevo's under heavy siege. The Serbs have knocked out a Hercules supply plane on its way out and they're moving in more heavy artillery.' He handed us a tattered British newspaper, heavily into the phrase 'Strangulation of Sarajevo' – repeating it three times in as many paragraphs. 'They're holding Mount Igman and Mount Bjelasnica, bombarding the town day and night. It's gonna be a right bastard to get in and an even bigger bastard to get out.' As he rambled on, we just knew that the price was going up for poor old Freda.

Sarajevo was about one hundred and ten kilometres from Posusje – as the crow flies. But as I've said before, crows we weren't.

Maps had begun to mean very little over the past months. Towns and villages indicated often no longer existed. And if they did, they were often given different names by their new land-lords. Over the past week Duvno had been renamed Tomislav-grad by dominant Bosnian-Serb forces. The whole thing was getting very confusing for lads brought up on rigid British army chart discipline, and was made even worse by the fact that few people knew which town was held by which force. With about eight to choose from, it was a hazardous guessing game.

After due consultation, and with the Mostar road now closed by police, Kit chose the main UN supply route from Tomislavgrad to Vitez, through Kiseljak then eastwards into Sarajevo. This way we would get some support if necessary from passing UN convoys . . . maybe!

Freda was packed and ready as we pulled up at her digs. Toshiba laptop, khaki holdall and crisp olive battledress . . . straight out of *Cosmopolitan*. She looked like a pro all right, mirror Ray-Bans coolly reflecting our image as she waited for Pete to load her gear while taking pictures with a shiny, motor-driven Nikon.

'Ready?' Kit slid in beside her, smiling back at us like a Cheshire cat. We just knew the trip was going to be – well, interesting.

With only a trace of an accent she asked about the mercenary role in the country, nodding as the odd note was inscribed in her alligator-skin-covered Filofax. We learned that this was her first overseas assignment and she meant to do well, regardless of the risk to herself. 'Commendable,' Nigel pompously agreed in his best Oxford accent. 'I'm sure you will do excellently in all your endeavours . . . especially with all that posh gear.' The sarcasm went unnoticed and she continued with her mechanical question-ing for the next hour until we pulled into Vitez for some refreshment and a piss – us, not her. She'd never do that sort of thing.

Blue-helmeted UN everywhere and a camera in overdrive, Freda snapped their every move. God knows why; they weren't doing anything vaguely interesting. But with smart, unused uniforms they had a lot of style.

Fifteen minutes later we were back on the road, heading east before the loop into Kiseljak. All was well in the world, no road blocks, no unpleasant sounds and the smell of Chanel No. 5 up our snouts. It seemed that the Serbs were, at least temporarily, keeping their word and allowing aid to pass unhindered into Sarajevo.

Kiseljac looked a bit iffy. With houses still burning, roads with deep craters and little movement from the inhabitants, an atmosphere of brooding anticipation hovered about the place. Like they used to say in the old Western films, 'It's quiet. Too damned quiet.'

'I don't like the look of this,' Kit murmured, right on cue.

Slowing down to negotiate the potholes, he glanced at Freda, whose lipstick was beginning to smear from repeatedly nervous licking as she wriggled in her seat, a damp patch of sweat showing beneath her armpits.

A group of young men lounged against the wall of a café, unarmed but tense. One ambled across and seeing the woman called to his friends, who broke into macho laughter. He sidled up to the car and stuck his head through her window, leering at her. '*Da li ste slobodni veceras?*' Are you free this evening? Freda didn't understand the words or the implication. Kit, who had tried it himself in the past, did.

'Fuck off!' He glared at the kid, who understood the method of delivery, if not the expression.

We were so intently focused on the interaction between them that for a moment other matters were forgotten. Serious miscalculation! A flurry of peripheral movement in the café entrance attracted our attention; hooded figures with Kalashnikovs raised were running in our direction. Sharp staccato bursts from their gun barrels made it clear that this was exit time.

Kit hit the pedal and with a vigorous roar the diesel-engine Land Rover hesitated before a sick cough sent it into spasm, jerking twenty metres before expiring with a hiss.

'SHIT!' Spooky was out, spraying the road before the last splutter, Kit feverishly turning the key. The engine snorted, died, coughed like an early-morning smoker and started again, lurching away as Spooky threw his final burst, which downed two and frightened the rest into confused retreat. Pete joined him on the final chorus with short bursts of farewell.

'What on earth were they after?' the incredulous newshound breathed, in a fair imitation of Marilyn Monroe.

'Your Gucci watch. Jewellery. Your body . . . Whatever.'

'Were they Chetniks?' She was excited now that we were away and safe.

'Nah, just kids on the make. The country's full of them.'

Her face glowing with delight, she stopped chattering, instead making feverish, exaggerated notes.

I'd just love to see the article on this event: 'Ambush! Journalist close to death. Our intrepid reporter in Bosnia lives to tell the tale.' Like the man said: 'Never let the truth ruin a good story' – or something like that.

The town of Brnjaci had been tormented a bit, although nothing to speak of. The inhabitants peered through windows, fearing the worst and pleased to see a single vehicle speed on its way without stopping. We waved enthusiastically at the apprehensive faces, trying to transmit hope, receiving a vacant response. A crying child at the roadside induced Kit to pull over. He handed her a bar of chocolate which she snatched from his hand, soundlessly shuffling away without a smile or a backward glance. Traumatised by executions, bombs and unspeakable horrors, the kid had the hollow look of a twisted tree once struck by lightning.

Rakovica came next, and with it the decision to slip off the main route on to smaller, less obvious roads for the final leg of our trip. With less than twenty kilometres to travel, the sounds of incoming shells had become commonplace, dust from their explosive impact rising above the town, high-pitched whistling drowning odd attempts at jittery conversation. Freda hadn't said a word for the past half-hour, but her lipstick was immaculate again.

First stop Sarajevo airfield. Serbs at one end, Bosnians the other. One group defending aircraft, the other attacking them – steady employment for all. Freda had a brief chat with Sky TV journalists at the Bosnian section, swapping stories, telling jokes, doing their thing. We waited in the Rover like unwanted chauffeurs until she'd sucked her information sources dry and exhausted her welcome.

Climbing back in and settling herself down, she told us to head for the centre of town and find Vojvode Punika 6a – the Sarajevo Holiday Inn. Once the home of journalists covering the 1984 Winter Olympics, it was now satellite city and meeting place for the world's top media vultures.

The western side of the city was no mans land, patrolled by gun-toting Serbs who stomped about the place as if they owned it, peering into slow-moving cars, just itching for a reason to open up on the occupants. Freda waved her press card to insolent comments from subnormal gun freaks. They glanced in our direction, focusing on the blonde, ignoring her companions.

Driving slowly away, we looked back; three were arguing and pointing angrily in our direction. They should have checked us out, but it was too late. We were out of range and speeding into the film set of *Demolition Man*.

The town was in absolute and total chaos. An acrid stench of burning filled the streets, sweetened by the sickly odour of death. Shattered glass crunched underfoot as people ran singly and in groups across open spaces, waiting for a sound they would never hear. Graffiti-scrawled walls proclaiming 'HELP BOSNIA NOW' and 'STOP GENOCIDE . . . ARM BOSNIA' gave out a message to the world's TV cameras, who cared more about ratings than restitution. Roy had been right when he'd told his mum that he was going to work in Disneyland; for this was indeed the land of wicked fairy tales.

On our left a queue had formed at one of the few water collection points. Ragged people bent warily to fill their plastic cans and bottles, ears tuned to the slightest sound. Groups such as these, waiting for bread, meat or medical supplies, had been wiped out many times before when lined up like targets for bored snipers or indiscriminate shellfire.

You can imagine the conversation in towering office blocks as marksmen scan the streets below for a random target: 'I bet you a hundred dinar I can hit that woman in the red dress,' one might mutter to his equally apathetic spotter. An abrupt crack, a blue puff of smoke from his barrel and she falls lifeless. He smiles contentedly, pocketing the money. Later in the morning he misses and hands it back. This goes on all day. Some you win . . .

Masonry, already loose from a recent bombardment, fell crashing to the ground, shattering in the road before us. Kit swerved, cursing in pure Geordie at its impertinence. We couldn't understand a word he said so Freda was not offended by the outburst.

'Left. Turn left!' Kit had driven past the hotel, hurling the Rover into a curve down Bulevar Borisa Kidrica. Now he reversed out in gear-crunching irritation.

Freda sat for a moment as Kit kept the motor running. 'Aren't you coming in for a drink?' she almost begged, eyelashes flapping like butterfly wings.

'No thanks, we've done our job and delivered the package,' he replied a little too abruptly.

'Fine ... Well, uh ... thanks for getting me here safely.' She handed him a package which he pocketed without checking. 'I'll see you around, maybe?'

'Doubt it. We'll only be here for one night, then we head back to Posusje.'

Suddenly changing his mind, he offered to take her gear in. We tagged behind, curious to see media-land for ourselves. Polished chrome, tinted glass – piles of it splintered on the floor – and sounds of frenetic activity. Crazy people with foreign voices yelled into satellite phones, fingers jammed into ears to stop incoming abuse from impatient colleagues waiting their turn.

'Goddamn it! My battery's gone dead. Send me a new one ... no, make it two. Wait ... wait ... more disks,' the CNN guy screamed, puce-faced. Next to him an ITN journalist spoke in a rapid but unemotional tone about thirty people killed by mortar fire while standing in a bread line. 'Yes, of course we have pictures,' he answered icily, eyes raised skywards. 'These copy people ...'

We followed Freda to the third floor – BBC territory – where she had been told to make contact with another Dutch journalist. He wasn't there and hadn't been seen all day. Whirling figures threw options at her, none appealing to her sense of adventure. So we went to the bar, always the hub for newspaper hacks.

She ordered vodka after checking with calculating eyes for the 'in' drink as she posed on the only vacant stool. We went for beer and brandy.

The drone of conversation diminished slightly at our arrival. Curious eyes penetrated dense cigarette smoke, then were averted as we stared back. They were no smiles of welcome, no warmth in their eyes. We were mercenaries; lepers with no cause, no country and no place to hide. Hyenas in a fresh-meat factory called Bosnia. Shunned even by other predators.

Although it was bright daylight the bar was dull. Lights flickered from occasional power failures and the room had an uncomfortable, oppressive atmosphere. Most of the window openings were covered in plastic sheeting – the glass having been blown away – making it impossible to see out of the building. Whispered conversation from an adjoining table informed us that a major offensive was expected very soon. Freda looked uncomfortable at the thought.

'Thanks for the drink. We'd better be off.' Kit shook her hand. 'Best of luck.'

'Oh, you're going now?' It was a question and an appeal. She didn't want to be left alone . . . not yet.

'Yeah, we want to have a look around before we go back.'

Nigel lagged behind, kissing her hand. Always the gentleman, was Nigel.

We pulled away from the hotel, counting windows. Out of ninety on one side of the building only five glazed ones remained; plastic sheeting flapped in the wind but there were no direct hits. Lucky so far, but it was only a matter of time.

We drove in silence past the Miljacka river, strewn with floating debris, and headed towards the centre of Sarajevo. They called it Sniper Alley, this direct route to the airfield, and it was easy to see why. High buildings with unobstructed views would make the job a doddle for anyone with a steady hand and a telescopic sight. Ex-Corporal Freeman, second at Bisley 1979, would just love the job if the money was right.

'Wonder where Sprog got it.' Nigel was thinking aloud.

'Dunno,' Kit replied in a distant voice. 'Does it matter?'

'No, I guess not. Just curious, that's all.'

'Did they send his body home?' Spooky asked.

'Dunno that either.' Kit wasn't interested in continuing the conversation, lapsing into thoughtful silence.

As we reached the National Theatre building a shell roared in from the direction of Mount Igman, sounding more like a train than a warhead. The noise they make is different in the confined space of a town – more thunderous than whistling. It crashed into an already derelict office block and became the straw that broke the camel's back, bringing the entire building down in a slow-motion collapse of dust, glass and masonry.

We stared as Kit slowed. No casualties, apart from a small boy pushing his bicycle across the road. He'd been blown off his feet by the blast and sat gazing at the twisted frame with a mixture of horror and disbelief etched across his puckered face.

'Wanna go for a wander?' Kit asked, turning off the main drag and into a side street by the Young Bosnia Museum.

'Yeah, why not?' we chorused with more bravado than enthusiasm.

224

With a strange shiver running between our shoulder blades we stepped out of the false security of the Rover, feeling stupid and vulnerable as we picked our way past shattered shop fronts and piles of rubble. Only last year my neighbour came here with his family on holiday, returning with tales of visits to exotic mosques and exciting cable car rides to Mount Trebevic. They'd just got out in time as the rumble of civil war began in earnest after many years of uncertainty.

Soon tiring of target twitch, we ambled into the covered market, stopping long enough to have a welcome coffee. Grey-faced people scurried past with shopping bags on bikes or prams, peering at us questioningly as they headed home with provisions for the next siege.

'Let's go back. I've had enough of this goddamned place.' Spooky didn't like the exposed feeling. He, like Kit, needed a gun in his hand to feel comfortable when under threat.

'Never did like FIBUA,' muttered Kit as we reached the car. 'Prefer the jungle any day.'

Monotonous mortar fire was shaking up the south side and the express-train roar of incoming artillery shells vibrated buildings around us like an earthquake about to happen. It seemed that the predicted offensive had begun. Kit started the engine and reversed into an alleyway, turning until we faced the river and mountains. In the failing light, purple tracers drifted in graceful arcs towards the town, popping with an incandescent glow as they found a target. People ran past us in huddled groups, pushing and shoving their way home. This was no place for us; we were just a taxi service and the meter was running.

With the help of a friendly French UN observer, pissed off with his role as submissive voyeur, we found ourselves suitable shelter for the night – a cellar crawling with rats beneath a burned-out shop. Deciding that shared accommodation was better than none, we discussed territorial boundaries with the original tenants, reaching agreement after long negotiation and a few squashed bodies. Their cannibalistic nibbling and occasional resentful squeaks kept us awake for a while, but our policy of non-involvement finally allowed us to slip into fitful sleep as the siege continued above us.

Choking dust woke us early, filling the entire cellar from floor to ceiling and settling in our open mouths and nostrils. We coughed our lungs up, spluttering for five full minutes before we were able to rise. Desperate to breath fresh air. Desperate to get out of town.

The Serbian artillery had – more by luck than judgement – managed some serious devastation throughout the night-time onslaught. And in the fragile gloom, buildings tottered, waiting for a brisk gust of wind to bring them crashing down. Two bodies lay spreadeagled in the road not twenty metres from our parked motor, battered by the impact of falling stonework. A man ran as we approached, arms filled with spoils taken from their lifeless hands. Survival was more important than any other human emotion.

'Bastard!' yelled Nigel after the fleeing figure of a youth with greased-back hair and a pony tail, who turned with a universal 'up yours' gesture, laughing at Nigel's impotent rage. 'Cheeky sod!' Nigel started after him, picking up speed quickly for a man just awake. The kid turned, surprised at the reaction, and made a dash for an alley. He had almost reached it when a whiplike crack from above split the air, spinning him round before dropping him face down in the road, where he twitched for a moment before lying still. Another shot followed, kicking up cement at Nigel's feet as he lurched to a halt and dived behind a parked car. We could see his face as he crouched, wondering.

'They're up early this morning,' Kit said calmly, not being in the line of fire.

We watched as Nigel took a deep breath and with a bound threw himself back in our direction, weaving as he ran panting to our side. 'Lot of fucking help you were,' he snarled.

'You shouldn't have chased him,' Spooky pointed out. 'What's the point? They're gonna kill one another regardless of our intervention, so let them get on with it.' He was obviously in one of his more philosophical moods.

We now had the hazardous business of getting into the Land Rover in full view of a sniper intent on scoring a hit.

Feeling a little irritable from his lack of a bacon and egg breakfast, Kit was in no mood for messing about with tactical discussion and headed towards the corner of the building, weapon poised and safety off. Crack. Crack. We ducked instinctively. No need. The sniper had targeted a passing cyclist, missing once again. It was easy to imagine him up there cursing as he tried to resight on the target, fumbling with a spare clip as the rounds from Kit's gun found him unprepared. We watched the guy fall forward, clutching at the window frame, before tumbling fifteen floors to the ground with a dull, satisfying thud, just ten metres away from the body of the thief.

'The sooner we're out of this place the better.' Kit turned the key and we headed out of town with no regrets, waving at the Holiday Inn as we passed. Just in case Freda was watching.

Minutes later, moving at top speed, we had passed the trenches and the Bosnian checkpoint and were heading for no man's land once again. This time was different. Without Freda to protect, we weren't stopping for any asshole with a cannon and if necessary would shoot our way out. They must have been telepathic; not one Serb made any attempt to halt us as we whooped our way joyously out of Sarajevo city with its quadraphonic sounds of destruction and its odour of impending doom.

With the open road ahead, our immediate problem was food and a wash and brush-up. Rat droppings in Pete's pants made him and the rest of us wonder where the little bastards had been as we slept. Crotch itch only added to the worry, gathering momentum as our imagination ran riot with visions of infested pubic areas, gnawed dicks and subsequent bodily infestation. The uneasiness plagued us as we scratched our way through Kiseljak, stopping by a UN lorry pulled into a lay-by as two men changed a tyre.

After a quick brew and a splash of water down our trousers, we were on our way again, still convinced that by the time we reached Posusje we would all be speaking in high-pitched voices.

The decision to try the shorter route, turning left after Kiseljak, was made simply to speed our return. Still a UN supply route, it was less used but more prone to haphazard road blocks from just about anyone feeling adventurous. 'Bollocks to 'em,' was Kit's answer to Spooky's doubts. 'I wanna get back and have a bath.' He wound the Rover up, bouncing over rocks and hollows, scratching as if demented and becoming more desperate by the minute.

The countryside was getting mountainous again, with deep folds of earth and sprawling pine forests. 'Great bandit country,' Spooky informed us unnecessarily.

'You're right, Spooky, so keep your bleedin' peepers open. The trouble is, by the time you see something it's always too bloody late to do anything about it!' Kit replied.

The sign said Gornji Vakuf, one of the few British bases in this area and unfortunately also the scene of recent outbreaks of Muslim-Croat fighting. Times they were a-changing. When we had arrived in Yugoslavia it had been a two-way battle. Now it was developing into a three-way fight between Muslims, Croats and Serbs – plus splinter groups in it for themselves. A country that had been dangerous was now becoming DANGEROUS! And it was no longer possible to trust anyone – civilian or military.

Each village we passed through showed some sign of armed conflict: graffiti-covered walls peppered with small-arms fire; windows smashed; odd buildings collapsed or burned – always some left untouched; bodies in neat piles at the cemetery gates awaiting quick burial before they began to decompose. It was as if an epidemic was spreading through the country. A sickness. A plague of ethnic insanity. No one seemed immune.

We had learned to drive through such places, alert but uninvolved. The inhabitants, lost in their own despair, continued the ritual of shopping, gossiping and tidying their homes as if programmed robots. Kids played in bombed-out houses using sticks for guns.

'You be a Serb and I'll be Croatian. Bang, bang, bang. You're dead. Now it's my turn.' They played the same game for hours, changing sides and arguing over who was the winner. 'It wasn't real. Daddy didn't get dragged from our garden last week, he'll be back later on. Mummy told me so.' They have large observant eyes that see all, but their child minds allow for selective comprehension. It's all in there somewhere, though.

The very last house was untouched. White walls with green-painted louvred windows. The family tending their garden waved as we passed, smiling as they no doubt did at coaches crammed with holiday-makers. Less than twenty metres away another home had been levelled by explosives. We waved back, smiling like idiots. As they say here, 'What can we do? This is a war.'

There's a lake about five kilometres south of Makljen, and a rock jetty by the big gorse bush. If you're ever there, the size nine Danner boots left by the side of it belong to Nigel; you'll recognise them because of the bullet hole in the left heel. He'd appreciate their return, but will understand if your need is greater than his.

Kit had become irresponsible yet again – he does that from time to time – a quick dip in the crystal water suddenly becoming essential for his continued well-being. Without a word of explanation, the Rover drifted off the road, plunged slowly down the embankment and halted. Kit was out in seconds, throwing clothes and caution to the winds. We stared at him splashing in the water like a carefree two-year-old, refusing for about five minutes to follow his example. Spooky lost his marbles next, rapidly followed by Nigel and Pete. They played around for fifteen minutes, leaving Nigel sunning himself on a rock as another brew was made and we played picnics with chocolate bars and dried biscuits, joking about the hell-hole called Sarajevo, and about poor Freda, who would no doubt be wishing by now that she was anywhere but in the Holiday Inn.

The tractor sound grew louder, more guttural, heaving itself up a steep gradient and breaking into our snooze.

'Whassat?' Pete groaned, sitting up sleepily.

'Just a farmer. Shut up and go back to sleep,' Spooky chided.

The noise increased, changing tone as gears were engaged.

'That's a fucking tank!' Kit logged it first and was up and into the Rover only seconds before the rest of us. Nigel hurriedly grabbed his clothes and dived head first into the open back. We were on the road and motoring before a T-55 snout appeared over the hill, and it was ten kilometres before Nigel realised he'd left his boots behind. Nobody was going back for them.

A few inevitable police checkpoints and random road blocks hampered our progress after Runboci, but only one had the makings of trouble. Busy listening to Nigel going on about his Danners and laughing at his anguished moans, we rounded a tight right-hander, skidding to a halt as a pile of hay bales barred our path. Seconds later a lout appeared, alone at first, then waving a brand new Czech Skorpion in our direction as his six mates moved to search the car, bad breath and body odour everywhere. Kit wasn't having it this time and told him so in mixed, expletive-punctuated, Croat-English. For a moment it looked nasty. The guns hovered menacingly in our direction before the leader eyeballed Kit's much-abused ID card. He snatched it from Kit's hand and examined it, checking the photograph thoughtfully, then lowered his gun and in a tone of reverent submission waved his men back and bade us goodbye. As we drove away, we could hear him hurling abuse at his companions.

'Why did he do that?' Pete asked as we gathered speed.

'God knows. Perhaps he didn't understand. Maybe he can't

read and thought it was some form of official document,' Kit replied, grateful whatever the reason.

For a while the roads were straight, open-spaced and free of threat. The wheels hummed on the dry asphalt and the sun shone warmly through the windows. We dozed, thinking of home, beer, football matches and sometimes wives – our own and other people's.

'Look at that!' Pete woke us from a stupor, pointing to a commotion in a village side street. 'What the fuck's going on?'

An old lorry was moving toward us in sporadic bursts, slowing then accelerating again. Bursts of raucous laughter came from about a dozen men surrounding it. We stared as it came alongside, the driver waving as he poured beer down his throat with the hand that should have been on the steering wheel.

'Christ! They've got someone tied to a rope from the back. They're dragging the poor bastard behind along the road.'

A man of about fifty, arms and legs tied, was being hauled by his ankles, bouncing and twisting as the lorry gathered speed. His screams of pain were muffled as blood gushed from his smashed gums. Old women stood by their doorways throwing stones as he passed, nudging one another as the rocks struck his body.

Kit slammed the Rover into reverse, pulling ahead of the lorry and causing the driver to brake hurriedly. The laughter stopped as the tight-lipped torturers stared in disbelief at this intrusion into their game. Kit climbed from the car, glaring back at them, moving to help the victim. The group moved forward threateningly as he knelt by the man's side.

'What the fuck's going on?' Kit rose after a brief examination. There was no response to his question.

'I said, what the fuck's going on?'

A young man in his early twenties moved closer, holding his palms upwards. 'It is none of your business, English. Now go before we do the same to you.'

Kit ignored the threat. 'Just tell me what is going on! Then we'll go.'

The reply took some time as the Bosnian thought it over. 'The man is a Serb. They are responsible for all of these outrages against my people.'

'You mean you're doing this just because he's a Serb? Has he done anything against anyone?'

'No.' The reply was curt, inviting no further discussion.

Kit beckoned to Pete and Nigel. 'Pick him up and put him in the motor.' He turned to the young man. 'You're all as bad as one another. Now piss off, the lot of you, before I get nasty.'

The victim was conscious now and lay moaning as Kit started the engine, allowing it to idle for a moment as he instructed Spooky to cover the threatening crowd with his weapon.

'This country is gonna be the biggest fucking graveyard in the world if you don't all learn to live with one another,' he yelled out of the window, angry for all sorts of reasons; some he didn't fully understand himself.

Slowly he let in the clutch, watching the fist-waving throng advance towards us. 'Give 'em a quick blast, Spooky.'

They drew back as the unexpected volley burst above their heads, cowering in understandable terror as we drove away.

Ten kilometres out of town, Kit pulled to the side of the road. The man had suffered roadburns, cuts, bruising and a bad dose of absolute terror. Field dressing took care of the first three problems, twelve slugs of brandy the last. Now it was time for him to fend for himself. He thanked us with tears streaming down his face and we left him walking back to the only life he had known since childhood, in the village in which he had been born.

'Won't he get more of the same?' Pete asked as we watched him disappear through the trees in the direction of his home.

'Probably,' Spooky replied. 'But where else does he have to go?'

We drove on in silence, passing through a strangely normal Lipa, and turned on to the Tomislavgrad-Posusje road, which was crowded with fleeing refugees, oddly travelling in both directions. The usual haggard faces ignored us as they headed, brain dead, towards another sound of gunfire. Another gutted village. More of the same, as Pete had commented earlier.

Our Bosnian semi-pro warriors welcomed us with partisan fighter hugs and exaggerated cheers of joy, appearing from their covert positions in the wood as we approached Posusje through the narrow, twisting lanes. Ranko came forward, his face a mask of sadness.

'They have been here again,' he said sorrowfully.

'Who's been here?' Kit asked, his eyes narrowing.

'The planes,' Ranko replied. 'Come, I will show you.'

MiG bombers from Mostar had visited once again, showering the town indiscriminately with cluster bombs, killing two children and a lone villager and his horse as they toiled in the fields.

231

Silver canisters could be seen scattered about the earth, 'Made in Britain' prominently stencilled on their sides. This wasn't the first time we'd seen evidence of British weaponry in use by the Serbian army, but it always came as a shock to think that you could be killed by something made in a Midlands factory by your next-door neighbour's brother-in-law or whoever. What made it even worse was the thought that he was safely at home in front of the TV as they exploded around you.

'When did they come?' Spooky asked.

'Early . . . very early this morning.'

'I fucking told you!' Pete screamed. 'It was those bastards we watched landing at Mostar.'

'Yeah well. What can you do? This is a war.' Kit turned to Ranko. 'Anything else happened?'

'Pop has gone.'

'What do you mean, Pop's gone?'

'You'd better ask Steve. That's all I know.'

We left Ranko at the field and drove hurriedly back to the farm, just in time to catch Steve as he was leaving to give the Bosnians mortar instruction. Kit called to him as we pulled into the yard.

'What's happened to Pop?'

'Don't really know. Just after you left he went into a bit of a downer. Didn't hardly talk for most of the day. Then he suddenly appeared with his gear packed and said he was going home.'

'Why?' More an accusation than a question.

'He left you a note,' Steve replied flatly, walking towards the farmhouse.

Kit picked up the small piece of crumpled paper from the table. Only a few lines were scrawled, as if Pop had been in a hurry.

'Sorry about this, Kit, but I've had it here. I should have waited until you got back and told you to your face but I couldn't, so that's it. I think my bottle's gone and I'm going home to sit in a pub and bore people to death for a change. All the best, Rodney.'

'I never knew his name was Rodney.'

'Shut up, Pete!' Kit snapped, reading the note again. 'Sod it. I'm gonna miss the old sod. Now there's only four of us left.'

'How old was he?' Nigel asked, turning to Kit.

'Don't really know. He was always touchy about his age. Late fifties, maybe older.'

'That's that then!' Upbeat Spooky finalised the gloom. 'Better get the gear in, guys.'

232

With little to stow away we were finished in minutes, slumping by the window and watching Steve put the part-timers through their paces in the distance. Most of these country boys seemed able to pick up the intricacies of professional warfare with ease, enthusiastically blasting hell out of a hut assembled for that specific purpose with loud cheers following each successful hit. A noisy hour passed until the hut was demolished, targets destroyed and there was nothing left to aim at. They marched in formation back to the yard where Steve dismissed them in the time-honoured fashion, waving goodbye as they trudged back to their families for the night.

'They're coming along. You've done well,' Kit praised.

'Yeah. They're still a bit wild,' Steve replied. 'But we're getting there.'

'Who the fuck's that?' Nigel looked out of the window at the sound of an over-revving car engine.

The Land Cruiser had swept in through the gate, its headlights blazing in the evening gloom. Moments later the Governor bounced in, flak jacket open to display a sparkling Zastava Z9 tucked into a black shoulder holster. He held out his hand in welcome, grinning broadly.

'You did well.' Drago handed out their bonus for a successful operation. Steve looked on, a bit pissed off that he'd missed out on what appeared to be a doddle job.

'I know you must be tired, so I will leave and return on Thursday. There is something serious I wish to discuss which will involve you all.'

With a parting pat on the back for Kit he strode towards the door; only then did we notice his new combat boots as they squeaked his exit.

'Oh, what the fuck is he up to now?' Spooky moaned, drinking his first cup of real American coffee for a fortnight. 'Don't you just hate it when he does that mysterious stuff?'

Kit looked at Steve. 'Do you know what's been going on?'

'No, not really. We heard whispers about Kupres while you were away, and a guy turned up in uniform yesterday. He was a colonel I think, maybe a general. I'm never sure of rank with these Yugo outfits. He hung around the place with Drago, making notes and watching the Bosnian soldiers train. That's about it.' Steve paused as Kit pondered, then added, 'I think there's a punch-up brewing, and a big 'un.'

With Velika Pumpa still fresh in our minds, the last thing anyone wanted was another full-scale battle, and Kit, impatient as always, couldn't wait two days for the answer. 'I'm going to see him tomorrow after we've had some shuteye,' he said, heading for his bedroom and some peace and quiet.

We slept badly, kept awake by Kit's recurring nightmare – which he wouldn't discuss – and Steve's snoring. Add to this the thought of another full-scale frontal assault and you've got the recipe for insomnia.

Kit was up early the next morning, disappearing in a cloud of dust before we had time to rub the sleep from our eyes. The sky was grey and humid; lightning flashed once, twice. Then the rain came in a deluge, sweeping across the open fields and battering against the dirty windows. A miserable way to start the day, made even worse by a sad breakfast without Pop's chatter and the overloud rhythm of the Stones in full cry.

Pete grunted, Nigel grunted, Steve grunted. Only Spooky seemed unperturbed by Pop's absence. The morning drifted past as the torrent continued, turning mountain trickles into streams, and finally floods, until the field was a swamp. Steve stopped grunting and cursed; soon it would be training time and he didn't fancy getting wet.

We drank coffee, smoked endless cigarettes and listened to the World Service telling us that the war was escalating. The same old regurgitated stuff on an endless loop tape: 'General Prylac, Commander-in-Chief of all Croatian forces in Bosnia, said . . . Radovan Karadzic, the Bosnian Serb leader, replied to UN threats, "Drop one bomb and forget about peace" . . . Atrocities . . . Serb strangulation of Sarajevo . . . Ethnic cleansing . . .' The voice droned on like a verbal parasite, savouring every adjective.

'I'm pissed off with listening to this.' Steve uncurled himself and looked out of the window at a break in the clouds. 'Think I'll do some weapons practice when they all turn up.' He went outside as the rain finally stopped, sloshing through deep puddles in the yard, and headed for the armoury.

Kit turned up late in the afternoon, looking pleased with himself and avoiding direct questions. He hadn't been to see Drago, choosing instead to do a little business in Split. A neatly typed list of weapons left lying around confirmed our suspicions that he was getting itchy feet, and for the next hour he shuffled paper and made endless phone calls with monosyllabic acknowl-edgements – giving little away. Pete couldn't stand it, hovering around with his ears flapping like a bored neighbour.

'What's going on, Kit?'

'None of your business.'

'Bollocks then.'

Drago rang, complaining that the phone had been engaged. He wanted to come over now instead of Thursday and was bringing someone to meet us.

Tall and gaunt-looking, Kobacevic was every inch a soldier. He strode into the room, followed by the short, dumpy Drago, introducing himself immediately with a brief résumé of his past experience with the French Foreign Legion and other élite groups. Now an officer in the Croatian army, he led an outfit named the Green Berets – what else? The conversation jumped around for a while as he and Kit swapped reminiscences about harsh training techniques and patrols in French Guiana. His manner was cold and abrupt. This friendly routine was all icing before he handed us a slice of the cake.

'I have spoken to Governor Drago at some length and he has agreed to allow you to assist me in the defence of Kupres. My men need reinforcement for what I believe to be a major offensive by the JNA.' He paused, his face taking on a grave expression. 'I must warn you that the Serbian army want Kupres badly for strategic reasons and have every intention of taking it. Therefore, in my opinion they will, no doubt, send professionals like yourselves, and not conscripts.'

'What type of attack do you anticipate?' Kit asked knowingly.

'Tanks and infantry.'

'How many?'

'Impossible to judge. An educated guess would be a dozen tanks at the most. Probably T-55s, with foot soldiers in support, of course.'

'What's your strength in Kupres?'

'I have two hundred men.' Kobacevic's voice had developed an irritated edge; he was not inclined to accept cross-questioning from subordinate officers.

Kit nodded, taking it all in. Drago hadn't said a word and seemed uncomfortable with Kobacevic controlling the action.

'OK, seems feasible. When do you want us?'

'I'm sorry it is such short notice, but I think the attack is imminent so we cannot afford delay. It must be tomorrow.'

'We'll leave soon after dawn.' Kit stood and shook his head, watching the pair leave with a sigh of here-we-go-again.

'Do you suppose Pop knew this was coming?' Steve asked. 'It's a bloody good time to pull out, innit?'

Kit didn't reply, already instructing the excited Bosnian soldiers to sort out equipment and load the Land Rovers ready for an early off.

Dawn was four a.m. Thunder once again rolled across the mountains from a moody sky, rattling us into life as it shook the windows. Heavy rain following in short torrential bursts only added to the gloom. Kit was edgy. Pete silent for a change. Nigel, Steve and Spooky moved like men possessed by Valium. We drove through the village in convoy, while sleepy villagers stood by their doors in hushed approval, waving farewell.

Chapter Thirteen

Retire? I'll never retire. Even when I'm sixty I'll
wanna keep my hand in somewhere. To me a soldier
doesn't mature until he's about forty anyway, and
that's when you start to earn your big bucks . . .

Kit Freeman, 16 February 1994

The Land Rover bucked, wheezed and rattled. Trees shook and
howling rain flowed down the windows in liquid curtains. Zero
visibility for Kit, crouched at the wheel singing about long and
winding roads until, bored by the repetition of the first lines,
lapsing into brooding silence. Dark houses passed silently. The
occasional cock crowed. Butterflies flapped in our stomachs. I
watched the second Rover slide around tight bends, hanging on to
our tail with Ranko grappling with the wheel as he tried
desperately to keep up.

Pete started to snore. A low, mournful sound from deep down
in his chest, with odd whimpers from his throat, dreaming like a
fireside dog in a winter's evening.

'Shut him up!' snarled Spooky, curled up in the rear cargo
space.

'Let him sleep,' Kit snapped.

Spooky mumbled something threatening, then turned over and
covered his head with a poncho. Silence, except for tyre hiss and
diesel drone.

Tomislavgrad came and went in the first flash of fork lightning,
illuminating the stark outline of destroyed buildings and reminding us of our last visit, when it was called Duvno.

Pete woke with a start, muttering, 'Incoming?' Steve told him it
was only lightning.

'Ours or theirs?'

'Ours.'

'You sure? It seemed bloody close.'

'Go back to sleep, you prick.'

'Road block ahead . . . I think.' Kit pressed his face to the
windscreen, clearing the misted surface with his nose. Sure

enough, two cars were barring our way as we slowed to a halt, nervous and expectant; at this time in the morning it was unlikely to be an official checkpoint.

'Don't get out!' Kit screamed as Steve started to open the door. 'Wait, and keep you eyes peeled.'

Expecting the worst, we waited. Nothing happened. No hooded figure. No hyped-up psycho with a Skorpion. No gun-chewing freak with attitude. We were starting to feel silly, like when you're waiting for roadwork lights to change and they don't. Kit finally inched the Rover forward and pushed the vehicles from our path, waiting for gunfire to open up from the bushes.

'That was strange,' murmured Pete as we accelerated through the gap, followed by a confused Ranko with his front bumper up our ass.

Suica was yawning itself awake as we slowed to enter the main street, stopping for a quick one in the local café and shaking the morning cramp from our bodies. People did their usual furtive appraisals, smiling tight-lipped at our *dobro jutro*s, moving quickly on as Steve tried to expand his knowledge of the language with conversation. 'Miserable sods,' he muttered as they left him mid-flow.

Twenty minutes and we were on our way again, passing a sign saying 'Kupres 30 km'. The final leg of a journey, like the last steps at the dentist, is invariably the worst: in this instance none of us wanted to arrive.

We met Kobacevic on the southern plateau, surveying the landscape with huge naval binoculars. His skeletal face, now hooded in the driving rain, was set in granite as he turned to meet us with awake-all-night slits where his eyes should have been. A curt nod, a barely perceptible facial twitch, a brief handshake. It was easy to understand his preoccupation. Vast open areas spread around us with few trees to offer infantry cover. This was fast-track country – tanks rule OK!

Visibility was tight in the dense, rolling mist, making the Commander's bino-scan more prophetic than practical; but he looked good, silhouetted against the skyline, watching his men flounder in the thick mud as they attempted the impossible task of trench excavation with folding shovels.

Kit ran his experienced eyeballs across the scene, shaking his head as he walked towards a group of struggling soldiers for a quick natter. He returned still shaking his head; now grim-fraced and muttering beneath his breath.

'Line up over there!' he suddenly barked at the lads, pointing to a position several metres away. 'Now listen. This may be the only chance I get to talk to you alone and you ought to know that I think we're in trouble here. These guys don't know what the fuck's going on, and what's worse, they've got no artillery or training in tank warfare.' He paused and looked across at the lonely figure of Kobacevic, nodding in his direction. 'He isn't much better than his men although he pretends to be. Keep close to me at all times, and when the shit hits, follow my lead. Understand what I'm saying?'

They nodded, hesitant and agitated at Kit's concerned tone.

'Gather round.' He spread a map out on the grass, jabbing his finger at grease-pencilled crosses to the south-west of Kupres. 'If it all goes belly up, these are the RV points, so commit them to memory.'

We scribbled hurried notes on fag packets, returning to our lines for a vigorously bellowed 'Fall out!' just to impress the natives.

Kobacevic climbed on to the roof of a supply wagon, tottering precariously for a few moments, lifting his magic binos for a sweep of the misty horizon beyond the town.

His lips moved. '*Da . . . ima tanks.*' Yes . . . there are tanks.

'*Koliko?*' asked his sergeant. How many?

Kobacevic shook his head. '*Ka daleko.*' Too far. He shrugged, his voice trailing away into silence as he continued his watch over the roofs of the town, focusing on several bright lights coming from the north some twenty metres behind a tree line. Something was moving but the mist obscured vision, and only shadowy figures and the muffled roar of throaty engines gave any clue to what was going on in the distance.

'What do you want us to do?' Kit asked. 'Apart from wave a magic wand.'

The dubious mixture of sarcasm and humour made no impact on the statue. Kit huffed a bit, repeating the request.

'Dig in and wait. That's all we can do,' Kobacevic muttered absently.

'No it isn't.' Kit's voice took on a cutting edge; waiting wasn't his style. Preparation, now that was something else.

'What if we dig some berms or lay out some mines on the road into town?'

'Berms?' Kobacevic enquired lazily, as if the word had momentarily slipped his mind.

'Yeah berms. So the tanks have to climb them, exposing their bellies as they come over the top. They make an easy target and the underside has less protection ... as I'm sure you know, Commander.' Tact was never one of Kit's strong points, and his voice was beginning to quiver with frustration.

'No, we haven't the manpower or the time to do either.'

It was like talking to a sponge. Kit gave up with a shrug and led the lads down the hill, instructing them to dig vertical tube foxholes in the positions he indicated.

'Narrow as possible, mind, with just enough room to snuggle into. The tanks will just roll right over your heads without crushing you. Then you're behind them and it's a piece of piss.'

Nigel and Steve led one team, Pete and Ranko the other, digging away furiously as the revving sounds in the distance increased in volume.

Kit left them working and returned to Kobacevic. 'Have you got forward listening posts ... Commander?' He was still asking questions and still trying to get some constructive answers.

'No. We do not need them.'

'How you gonna tell how many tanks are approaching, for Chrissakes?'

Kobacevic ignored the challenge, without warning jumping down from the truck and walking away to his second-in-command, who was running from trench to trench, gesticulating wildly.

Lorries were bringing in supplies from town, with the odd villager to boost numbers and help with the laborious digging. Most were old and weary; the young were already slaving away in the mire. An air of despondency hovered over the field, gnawing at any slight optimism that may have once existed in the troops. No one laughed, cursed or moaned. Only the sound of distant engines broke the silence. Shovels slurped as they sank into the wet earth.

'Will they come today?' Pete asked quietly.

'There's a lot of activity over there, but with this driving rain and the mist, visibility is shit for both armies ...' Kit's voice tailed off with an 'I dunno' shrug.

Flares were starting to pop, showering an eerie orange-white light over the town. The clunk of heavy machinery and rattling

240

chains drifted through the soggy air, building in a crescendo before dying abruptly into a deathly hush. Everyone stopped work, staring into the distance. Watching faces asked the question. Were they leaving? Had they aborted the attack? Can we go home now . . . please? Bumph, bumph, more flares; closer this time. We could just make out running figures as they burst at their peak, drifting lazily downwards and sizzling on the wet earth.

Kobacevic ordered his men back to work as he continued his medieval king routine of scrutinising the landscape at a safe distance. Kit joined him briefly for what seemed a heated exchange of views on how to tackle the impending attack. The Commander wasn't going to listen.

An hour passed in almost perfect silence, as the lull continued with only distant sounds of clicking from the JNA encampment. Rain water was collecting in the trenches and men were feverishly bailing with their helmets. We waited hungrily at the mess tent for something wet, warm and comforting.

'Bloody Kobacevic, he just won't listen . . .' Kit's voice tailed away as he turned towards the town.

At first it was just a dull rumble from a single point to our left; then it spread across the horizon in waves and built in intensity until the earth quite literally trembled, becoming a sound so overpowering that we were at the same time paralysed with fear and ready to run, hide, dig a hole and bury ourselves; anything to stop that noise. The Croats dived into their water-filled trenches in panic, crouching low and doubtless cringing with understandable fear. We stayed on the hill, watching as huge monsters surrounded by heavily armed infantry crawled through the mist, puffs of grey smoke pouring from their vertical exhaust pipes.

They moved slowly at first, coming straight through the town centre, hesitating as they climbed the slope, then deploying in a line before us. A second and third wave appeared in the classic pincer movement from the right and left sides of the houses, easing into an unhurried staggered line. Engines idled, guns creaked into position, as well-tooled infantry soldiers leapt from their APCs and took position behind them.

The roar diminished to an ominous drone, steady, hypnotic, awesome. Twenty-five tanks idled, each with a platoon crouched at its rear – seven hundred men against two hundred ill-equipped country boys and a handful of vagabond mercenaries.

'Sod this for a game of soldiers! Innit time for a sharp exit, Kit?' Pete stared goggle-eyed as we waited with churning stomachs and dry lips for the referee to blow the whistle and start the game. Philipivich had put his binoculars away and stood beside us, already beaten.

First came the clunk of engaging gears; then engines revved as the tanks inched forward on some invisible command, stopping to re-elevate with clanking chains and hissing exhausts. Without warning the whoop of shells turned into an earsplitting blast as they crunched into the earth, blowing shattered bodies from shallow trenches to slide on the muddy surface like fallen skaters.

The lads looked at Kit for guidance. He grabbed his AK, muttered something to himself, and waved them down into the field below, where he drew them into a group. They fired at shadows as they ran blindly into the battle area, yelling to psych themselves and deaden their hearing to the clank of tracks and the roar of V-12 engines.

The first row of tanks were T-72s, firing HEAT-FRAG. Behind came the older T-55s, losing ground a little as the faster leaders wound themselves up to full speed, grinding the first line of shallowly entrenched soldiers into the mud.

Using flares to confuse thermal detection devices, Kit, six British mercs and the toughened men from Posusje did their best to halt the rolling terror, dashing around like madmen with the Bosnian soldiers, who fought bravely with the little armament they had at their disposal. It was a battle without any chance of victory. Men ran from their trenches in terror, falling under the tracks of advancing machinery. Screams echoed across the battlefield, lost in the roar of explosions and the chatter of Serbian machine-gun fire.

The JNA took Kupres that night. It was a massacre, as the untrained men ran around the battlefield, confused and disorientated. Philipivich lost over fifty men and the Serbs gained another small piece of real estate to add to their mounting territorial expansion.

We legged it . . . simple as that. 'He that fights and runs away may live to fight another day.' *Musarum Deliciae* said it first, but Kit repeated it – almost accurately – as we stumbled, gasping, over a ridge three kilometres away from the evaporating sound of conflict.

'Everybody here?' Kit counted twenty-two. 'Who's missing?'

Ranko did a double check. 'Nikola, Milan and Milenko.'

'Shit!' They know the RV, don't they?'

Ranko nodded slowly, with doubt flickering in his dark eyes.

'It's stupid travelling in the dark, so we'll wait until dawn. If they're not here by then we'll have to go on without them.' Kit's tone was irritated and final.

Five a.m. No sign of the missing men. Kit was getting fidgety, peering anxiously over the gully edge in all directions and glancing at his watch as each minute ticked by. A helicopter chopped its way overhead, swooping low as we crouched in the hollow. They were obviously searching for something, turning in a steep climb to clear the hedges by inches and hovering as the spotter leaned out and searched the ground around us with a scoped M76 sniper rifle. We could feel the down draught from the rotor blades as Kit lined his weapon on the man only two hundred metres away, rolling back with a sigh of relief as the pilot climbed vertically and disappeared over the pine trees in a puff of blue exhaust smoke.

'Looks like an old Bell UH-1H.' Spooky stared over the ridge at the receding helicopter.

'Bell fucking what?' Steve queried.

'A Huey . . . American chopper used in 'Nam. Look, you can just make out the oversprayed markings on the tail.'

'Wonder where the Serbs got that from?'

'That's the business to be in,' Kit muttered from his map search.

'What business?' Steve looked at him blankly.

'Arms dealing. That's where the money is. Not lying here in this crappy hole waiting to be shot at.' He looked at his watch. 'Fifteen minutes and we're off. Somebody go out and look for them. Maybe they've got lost.'

Nigel and Pete crawled over the ridge in the direction of Kupres with a warning not to go far, leaving Kit plotting a course through mountains to the nearest town, Livno, about thirty kilometres south-west.

With just two minutes before the allotted time, all five men returned, Milan looking sheepish as he explained to an irritated Ranko that they had gone to the wrong RV point and had been waiting a kilometre to the east. Ranko translated for Kit, who gave them both a shrivelling look of disbelief before returning to his route planning.

It took three days and two nights to reach Livno, scavenging food from houses, farms and waste bins, sleeping in barns and hedges, ducking and diving at the slightest sound. A welcome light moment was seeing Nigel run across a farmyard pursued by an angry old lady waving a brush at him as he tried, unsuccessfully, to carry two plates of cakes stolen from her kitchen. She actually caught up with him as he clambered over a gate, hammering him into submission with witch-like screams and curses.

Serbian patrols hampered our progress, appearing at the most unlikely places and causing moments of alarm. We dived for cover, holding our breath, as they passed, sometimes only a metre away. Mountains often formed impossible barriers, making tortuous detours necessary, forcing us to backtrack for hours over rugged terrain until we were dirty, hungry and exhausted.

Nikola sprained an ankle after a fall that could have injured him severely. He tumbled twenty metres as the rocky path gave beneath his feet and plunged headfirst into a river, staying under until Kit, in a moment of *Baywatch* heroism, dived in and rescued him. He wished he hadn't bothered. In the bitter cold they both shivered, fearing hypothermia, until blankets were liberated from a clothes line and a risky fire warmed them back to normal temperature.

Day three, with less than five kilometres to travel. A GPMG rattled as we crossed a road, dirt kicking at our feet. A copse on the hill was providing cover, smoke filtering from the trees. We couldn't run with Nikola hobbling on lashed-together crutches; anyway we were all too bloody knackered.

'Who's gonna go and do 'em?' Kit asked wearily from yet another water-filled ditch.

Ranko volunteered, taking Milenko and Milan as punishment for their crime of misdirection. We watched them flank the emplacement, flagging slightly as they reached the top, then crawling around the rear of the copse. One detonation blast and a few seconds of auto fire, then Ranko appeared, fist waving in triumph.

We tried singing to boost morale, joining in choruses of Bosnian folk songs. Then we attempted to remember our own, learned at school and since forgotten. We gave up after a few short verses of 'Hi Lily Hi Low', feeling stupid and not sure if it was a traditional folk song or not.

Kit held up his arm, still covered in the blanket. Through the trees we could see a town; people stood talking casually and wandered aimlessly across the square. The whole scene was one of relaxed informality.

'It looks clear, but go and check it out first,' Kit instructed Steve and Ranko.

Watching through binoculars, we could see them skirt the nearest houses before slipping through a gap and disappearing from sight behind a warehouse. Twenty agonising minutes passed before they reappeared, smiling, with a group of Bosnian soldiers in tow. Lots of greetings, hugs and even kisses, then a hearty meal of some kind of stew, ladled down our welcoming throats with large spoons that nearly choked us in our enthusiasm to fill our bellies.

We were in no hurry to return in defeat to Posusje, and spent the day in relaxed contentment, telling porkies to the Bosnian soldiers and listening politely to their stories in return. Jungle drums had passed the Kupres fiasco down the line, complete with tales of rape, torture and pillaging. One of the soldiers lived there; his family remained. The bullshitting stopped as tears ran down his cheeks and he left to cry alone.

That evening, dirty and stinking, we were invited to a party at the town hall. Cries of '*Zivela!*' – Cheers! – greeted us, and the night blurred with generous helpings of *viski, votku* and the local drink of *vinjak* – work it out! At three a.m. we'd had it, staggering back to the army camp in no fit state for nothin'.

'Come on . . . wakey wakey.' Kit was up before us, face clean-shaven and sparkling. Don't you just hate it when you feel like shit and there's this guy looking fresh and energetic with a clean uniform and creases in his trousers?

'Where did you get that gear, you old bastard?' asked Pete, lying in a pool of vomit.

Kit touched the side of his nose with his forefinger. 'Never you mind, my son. Better get up and wash, I've got us a lift back to Posusje and it's leaving in ten minutes.'

Half an hour later, after chewing endless cups of the treacle they called coffee, we clambered on to a military truck bound for Split, but detouring for our benefit. The ride was bumpy but the fresh air useful to our rebelling stomachs. Many stops were required as nausea and a bad case of the Indian curries made regular bush trips necessary. Glad we were to see our village, and gladder still to arrive at the farm.

245

Drago took it well, listening to our tales of woe with sympathy and understanding, the loss of his Land Rovers seeming more important than the fall of Kupres. Then he and Kit had a heated exchange out of earshot, which Kit refused to discuss when he returned, but his manner was overcast, remaining that way for the next two days as we recovered from our ordeal.

The Kupres episode cast a veil of gloom over everyone which refused to lift as the days passed in further patrols and training periods for new volunteers. The few remaining members of the original group had been in Yugoslavia for over a year now and were becoming weary of the catch-as-catch-can existence, the constant insecurity and the life of perpetual motion. At one time Bosnians and Croatians were allies in a common cause; now things had changed. Friends and neighbours were torturing and killing one another, murdering the children they'd once played with. Agreement couldn't be reached on the matter of territorial rights and government leaders bickered constantly; the country was at war with itself.

Pop sent us a postcard from Blackpool, signed with a flourish and the immortal words 'Wish you were here', to which he'd added, 'Don't you?' He was right; we'd have done almost anything for a ride on a roller-coaster and a pint on the seafront. We pinned the card to the kitchen wall, gazing at the picture of relaxed, sunlit beaches. It just made things worse.

Reports of small skirmishes in neighbouring villages had introduced a new daily routine: clock on, grab your gun, jump in the Rover, off for a brief firefight and back home for tea; remembering to clock off again. 'It's like working in a bleedin' factory,' moaned Pete after the seventh trip in three days.

Kit was spending most of his free time on the telephone these days, or off on business trips in Split; always returning with lists which necessitated yet more phone calls. Mysterious boxes with indecipherable labels appeared in the stores, and Mike returned, staying for a few nights of animated and secretive conversation. Money changed hands and Kit chuckled himself to sleep.

On Wednesday morning, Drago came in with another 'job sheet'. This time we were off on a trip to a now nonexistent village near Mamici where the governors felt they were under threat from a marauding band of irregulars.

Intermittent attacks over the past few nights had led them to conclude that an invasion was imminent, and they wanted it crushed. We arrived as dusk was settling in. Mortar explosions had flattened six houses on the perimeter and sporadic small-arms fire rattled the still air, as people huddled in shop doorways in what had become the universal condition of fear. It was too late in the day to start patrolling the hills and we were given an empty house as a control centre, unloading our gear for an early start.

By dawn the mortar and small-arms fire had stilled to a blissful peace, as we lay on our beds wondering what had woken us from our dream-filled sleep. 'That's a baby crying!' Steve whispered. 'Sounds like it's just been born.'

In a house still blackened by recent hits, a child was born to eighteen-year-old Zenca Erchak. Her husband, a part-time soldier away in the hills somewhere, had become a father for the first time. He was never to share in her joy, never to hold his crying baby or see his wife's contented smile. For at 8.48 that morning the first Serbian shell of the day landed on the house, killing them both. The second landed on our command building, causing little damage and no casualties.

Steve, big tough Steve, cried that day as he helped clear away the debris, finding little Zenca still clutching her child, a look of disbelief on her pale, lifeless face. Steve was a hard man; some would say cruel, even callous. He was after all a mercenary.

Carrying her body into a neighbour's house, he cursed the world and all the bastards in it, pacing up and down as he clicked his AK safety catch on and off in impotent rage. He was going to kill the bastards one by one . . . he swore it.

Kit tried to reason with him, taking the practical view that this sort of thing happened all the time. But for some reason, years of simmering frustration finally erupted and Steve was unable to accept the pointless death of one unknown young girl. Perhaps in his mind she represented all the helpless deaths he had witnessed in countries all over the world.

Steve kept his word. Over the next few days he and Kit led endless patrols, finally locating the mortar position responsible for the attacks on the village. A brief firefight ensued and the men stormed the position without casualties. Nigel and Pete dragged Steve off two Serbian prisoners as they sobbed in terror at his brutal beating, but they were unable to stop him kneeling them down and emptying a magazine into their bodies.

The next day we were due to return to Posusje. We woke in the morning to find Steve's bed empty and his gear missing. He'd disappeared in the early hours without even leaving a note of explanation. Kit did some checking when we got back, coming up with zilch. Rumours of aid work in Rwanda filtered back through the network but were never confirmed. Steve had simply vanished from the circuit and has never been seen or heard of again.

Morale went from bad to worse. The Kupres cock-up and now Steve leaving; Kit was pissed off with the whole thing. Enough was enough. You could see it in his eyes and the way he moved around the place, dispirited and preoccupied.

On Saturday he said he was going into town for a quick pint and a natter with some of his old mates from Mostar. He stayed away for three full days without any form of communication, sliding back through the farm gates in a civilian Range Rover with British plates.

'I'm out of here!' were his first words, before explaining to a crestfallen Nigel and Pete his new role as an arms and equipment dealer. We helped him load the mysterious boxes into his car and watched him hurriedly stuff his belongings into a black holdall: 'Forget the bergan, that's for squaddies.' A quick handshake with the Bosnian soldiers and a manly hug for Pete, Nigel and Spooky.

'See you around, lads,' and he was off into the wild blue yonder and a new life of wheeling and dealing with the big boys.

'Ethnic cleansing' was the buzz phrase these days, making the Muslims a worthy cause and media underdogs in just about every magazine and television report. Persecution, genocide, subjugation: great copy for the newspaper parasites. Kit was to become a saviour to the oppressed, for once able to take the moral high ground, and it felt good for a change.

Zagreb was his first port of call; tricky with a car full of bent gear and no mates to back you up at police checkpoints. Bribes worked better than bullets in most cases and the trip was uneventful if nervous. First stop, police headquarters and a lengthy meeting with old friend Inspector Urirch. A deal involving transportation and storage of military equipment was top of the agenda. Kit needed someone he could trust while he was on whistle-stop tours or out of the country, and Urirch was happy to oblige with offers of a safe house on the outskirts of town. A police inspector's salary needs the occasional transfusion.

Next call was Colonel Tony Abranovich. As always, he was

pleased to see Kit, especially scrubbed and in civvies. This was the new model Christopher Freeman, fast-talking and hyperactive. An entrepreneur/mercenary, a different breed of cat. No longer did his life depend upon the AK-47. For the warrior turned businessman the ultimate weapon had become the HR8A-BK continuous-paper-roll-fed, non-jamming, full-auto-memory, F-5.4-cut Casio calculator, complete with universal currency compensator as an optional extra and usually worn in its fast-draw position in the left armpit inside pocket, cocked and ready at all times, day or night. When in combat mode the calculator went into its familiar chuga, chuga, chuga rhythm, laying down some heavy bright-green stencil numbers across a black display panel as the paper jerked from its mouth in an endless stream. Deutschmarks, dollars, sterling, and of course the Swiss franc – bam! bam! the machine barked its answer. 'When? Where? OK, fifty per cent up front, trust me!' Abranovich was impressed and the meeting was enlightening, profitable and cordial for both. After a slap-up meal in a four-star, Kit left Zagreb to travel south and set up shop at a deserted farm near Suica; filling the outhouses with MG-42 GPMGs, M-53 GPMGs, AKMs, 47s, ARMSCOR MGL grenade launchers and a variety of Soviet pistols, many still in waxed paper wrappers. In a small copse adjacent to the farm he stashed his major investment, a heavily camouflaged fifty-two-year-old Soviet T-55 tank, just waiting for the highest bidder.

Building up this stock had been a long-term project, starting months before Kit had made the final decision to pull out of the shooting war.

'What set me off on the trail were my visits to Bosnia. I started collecting gear and selling it as a job lot. This went on for a few months, with me getting better and better at it and making a few bob without getting shot at. Then one day I was having a drink in Split and a group of Muslims approached me – word gets around – asking for certain items of equipment, which I agreed to supply. Some of it was difficult, but I managed with a little help from my friends. The black market is very active here and it's not breaking any arms embargo because the stuff's already in the country . . . and if it isn't, it soon will be. You can buy an RPG-7 from a barman in Split – no problem!'

The procurement of weapons has never been a problem for those with specialist knowledge, contacts and cash . . . lots of cash.

Kit Freeman was now in possession of these three essential ingredients for success in his new role. Plus the fortunate set of circumstances that had made his turf Yugoslavia, which along with Spain, Portugal and Czechoslovakia was one of the easiest countries in the world in which to buy and transport arms. End-user certificates are considered to be something of a burden to the businessman dealing in military hardware.

'They're all at it in Yugoslavia; it's become a bloody red-hot business these days. Selling pistols and small arms and smuggling them back to Britain to flog to squaddies in Aldershot pubs for about two hundred Deutschmarks . . . Makarovs, CZs, Berettas, Tokarevs, the lot. Not only is the gear coming out, it's also going in. British pilots are flying stuff into the Croatian island of Krk. Iranian 747s are bringing weapons into Zagreb airport under the very nose of the United Nations Protection Force and nothing can be done about it. Croatia is free to import arms but not pass them on to Bosnia . . . Disgusting it is!'

Trips back home to the UK became necessary as business expanded. And after a two-week break in the Lake District to finally cleanse his pores of camouflage cream and his ears of the shriek of battle, he drove south to set up deals with the Muslim parliament in London. Using his code names Mustapha (Christopher) and Yahaha (John), he made covert arrangements in the luxury of top hotels where advice was given on the most suitable weaponry, its availability and, most significantly, its price. Promises were made and broken, deals teetering on the edge of completion collapsed. But he continued ducking and diving until a million pounds changed hands; bringing it back to his home in Wales in a cheap nylon rucksack costing £4.75 from the Army and Navy store.

There are a lot of expenses in the supplies business. Bribes, overland delivery and storage eat up a great chunk of the money, and associates in Bosnia expect part payment upfront, with the balance on delivery. They are at the sharp end, where things can, and often do, go desperately wrong.

You can question the morality of Kit's chosen profession – many do. But is the man who pulls the trigger any different from the man who supplies the weapon, or the politicians who plan the war?

Chapter Fourteen

I've shot blokes right in front of me . . . Not just once
or twice but many times – but that's work.

You can't help but like him, this amiable bear of a man. Shaven
head, enormous grin and snappy Geordie dialogue peppered
with expletives. It's difficult to believe that he's a killer, difficult to
believe he has seen and done those things. Almost impossible to
picture him prowling through the jungle on a recce or crouched in
a tree, cradling a sniper rifle.

It all changes, however, when he tiger-stripes his face and
hands with black/olive/brown camouflage paint and dons his
well used DPM para smock with the subdued Foreign Legion
wings on his right breast. His eyes change to smouldering slits as
the jaw line sets in concrete, and he becomes everyone's
nightmare . . . right before your eyes.

I first met Kit through a mutual associate, also a mercenary, and
we talked of the old days well into the night: of 'Mad Mike' Hoare
and his exploits in the Seychelles; 'Colonel' Callan in Angola; John
Banks and his own brand of SAS – Security Advisory Service; and
of course his own exploits with the DEA in Colombia, before his
more recent and final gig in Bosnia/Croatia. Two weeks later I
met him again, this time to suggest a book on his life as a Soldier of
Fortune, a Dog of War . . . whatever the media call freelance
soldiers these days. Kit was keen on the idea, saying that he'd
thought of trying to write one himself, one day.

The initial chats were the easy part. Getting him pinned down
to a specific time and date for an in-depth interview was
something else, a bit like trying to catch a fly with chopsticks;
difficult and requiring some patience and skill. Numerous
arrangements were made and broken, although courtesy phone
calls were received from colleagues using ambiguous phrases
such as 'Kit is unavailable at the moment but will contact you in a
few days'. Sometimes he just didn't turn up; then the phone
would ring and his cheery voice would apologise yet again and a

further meeting would be arranged. I finally got him, nailing his feet to the floor and beating him into submission with the butt of an AK-47. This is Kit's story . . .

From the tender age of seven Kit knew that he was bound for a military career. His father had served with the British army for much of his adult life and his grandfather before him. Kit would continue the family tradition; of that there was little doubt.

'Me dad was a right friggin' hard case, he was. I remember when I came home on leave for the first time, thinking I was bit of a Jack the lad. I was a bit pissed and said some things which were bang out of order. He waited until I'd finished ranting, and said, "I suppose you think you're a man now – outside!" Then he battered seven pillars of shit of me . . . Good old boy. I miss him dearly.'

Kit's memory of his father was very clear, and it was obvious from his tone and moistening eyes that his death at fifty-four still affected him in those quiet moments.

Christopher Freeman is an enigma: loyal to his friends, benevolent with his time and money, loving, caring, warm and friendly; he is also callous, cruel, dangerous and of course a cold-blooded contract killer! That's his job and the reason that many governments, including our own, pay him and people like him large sums of money to help them. Especially when things could go embarrassingly wrong.

Why does he do it? The simple fact is that he just loves his work and is very competent at what he does, taking great pride in doing a job well for itself alone. Monetary reward doesn't seem to be a factor in his desire to excel, although it is the prime motivator in his involvement with any overseas conflict. He readily admits to having little regard for territorial rights, political leanings or moral viewpoints, and would, if necessary, work for any government offering a bigger pay cheque.

'It's a simple economic fact. Where there's a war there's a pile of loot just waiting. Sod the cause, that's for somebody else to worry about. We're in it for the dosh!'

Kit and his colleagues have their own morals, and the unpredictable governments of the world offer business and large amounts of money to those prepared to die for them in some distant land. At the moment Bosnia is the marketplace, but when this income source dries up it could be any of the twenty or so countries that have internal conflicts and need experienced military advisers unhampered by rules and regulations.

Security consultants are always in demand on those little islands controlled by dictators with little or no military skills. Weapons are – due to the fall of Eastern Bloc countries – easy and cheap to obtain. It's a growth industry, it seems, and Kit is shrewd enough to take advantage of this fact and exploit it for his own ends, unlike many mercenary soldiers who are happy with a gun and a fistful of dollars.

Kit's military career has now spanned a period of twenty years, starting at the tender age of thirteen when he joined the Royal Fusiliers as a cadet. Later he entered the junior Parachute Regiment and found that he possessed a natural talent with SLR, producing one-inch groupings with a high degree of consistency. This intuitive skill led to his selection for the shooting team, and after six months of dedicated practice on the Aldershot firing range he achieved a second at the junior Bisley, giving him a taste of success when interviewed and photographed for the military magazine, *Pegasus*.

But he was not a happy man.

'The prospect of battalion life stuck at Ash Rangers, with each day spent on the rifle range shooting at targets, really did my fucking head in! What I wanted was a trade.'

With several options open to him, he transferred to the Royal Artillery 29th Commando Regiment, RA, in Plymouth, undertaking the medic's course before being posted to the Citadel Medical Centre at 29 CDO. Still not settled, he moved yet again, this time to 148 Battery (Para Commando, forward observation battery for the RN) where he undertook and passed the OP course/Signals. Within a very short period he had a personality clash with one of the second lieutenants and did twenty-eight days for striking an officer, leading to a further transfer to the 4th Field Airborne Artillery at North Camp, Aldershot.

A change of direction seemed worthy of consideration at this career juncture, and Kit chose the SAS selection route, but failed and got RTU (return to unit). No reason was given, apart from 'Too immature' scrawled on the bottom of his application form. It was suggested by the commanding officer that he might like to try again in eighteen months.

'Failed. I couldn't believe it.' Kit uttered the words in a flat, unemotional voice, intentionally creating a barrier against further questioning on the subject. He could still hear judgement being passed by the selection board officer, his cold public school accent echoing around the large unfurnished room, shattering the very essence of his military ambition. Until now he had never truly realised how desperately he had wanted to emulate his father in becoming a member of this most élite corps of fighting men. But he knew in that instant he would never try again.

Back to 4th Field Airborne Artillery – totally gutted, pissed off and dispirited. He was thankfully posted to Belize, where he spent a period training and developing further skills in the art of jungle warfare, which he thoroughly enjoyed. Possessing a natural aptitude for stealth and an affinity for the hot, sticky climate, Kit found that jungle fighting gave him the excitement lacking in his previous role as a sniper, and it was with regret that he was only able to spend six months there before returning to the UK and routine military tasks.

It was this period of enforced inactivity that led him into an incident that would change his life . . .

'What I thought was a dressing-down for the theft of petrol was in fact rather more serious. I'd been having an affair for six months with a woman who was married to an army captain. I swear I didn't know she was married, but nobody believed me. There was nothing to indicate that there was a man living in that house . . . nothing. It was bare of any masculine furnishing of any kind. There were no military photos, men's clothing or objects of any kind. They had me by the balls and that was me finished. The bastards gave me "Services no longer required" and I was out of the army. Discharged due to an error of judgement!'

So that was that! An ignominious conclusion to an interesting career in Her Majesty's forces: an uninspiring meander through various training establishments, a few trips overseas, some experience of action in the jungle and a little urban conflict. The zigzag course through the minefield of army training was over – it was the end of everything. Childhood memories lingered; tales of battles and heroes, death and glory. Tell me some more, Dad, it's over, it's over, it's over!

Back home, in civilian life, the months drifted by aimlessly. Odd jobs, a bit of this and a bit of that. No career, no direction, no sergeant barking orders. Nothing quite filled the gap; how could it? Thoughts of other forms of military service began to invade his mind, popping in and out, taunting and teasing, until one stayed and flourished. The French Foreign Legion; they would surely take him on with his experience. This was the answer to his predicament. In November 1984, after five months in the wilderness, Kit made his decision.

'It was easy. I simply went to Paris by coach, got on the Métro and then walked to the top of the hill where I just knew the fort was. I didn't have a map but I knew instinctively that it was there. I knocked on the huge door and a distant little voice answered in French, and like a prat, I said, I've come to join the Legion. The door opened and the voice told me to come in. He was an American guy, nice and friendly. He searched me first and then fed me loads of food and drink – then I had to do all the dishes!'

Without realising it, Christopher 'Kit' Freeman was about to embark upon his first step into the world of mercenary soldiering. The Legion constitutes perhaps the most élite form of mercenary, certainly the most glamorous and professional, undeniably the most formidable.

The first week in this grey, utilitarian building was spent on endless interviews, tests and medical examinations. It's tough to get into the Foreign Legion these days; only about one third of the applicants are selected. But the chance of starting life anew remains one of the principal objectives of the new recruit . . . exactly the reason that Kit was there. Morale is high on the list of essential requirements, a quality often absent from the erratic character of many entrants. Unsuitable people are not an asset to a unit with an international reputation for military efficiency; gone are the days when drop-outs, vagrants and misfits gravitated to the Legion. Interpol computers are used extensively to screen out undesirables and those with proven criminal records. If a man is wanted anywhere in the world for a major crime he is immediately arrested and detained until the relevant authority can claim him.

With the initial selection procedure complete, the fortunate few are dispatched overnight to L'étranger at Aubagne, a suburb of Marseilles, which serves as the Legion's main induction and administration centre. The document of allegiance is signed, but only after further medicals, tests and checks into criminal activity have been performed by the Legion's military police. The 'chosen ones' are then taken to Castelnaudary in southern France, home of the training regiment 4e étranger.

'We didn't stay at the barracks for long, shipping out the next day in our respective companies. I belonged to 1st Company (Premier) and we were sent to a farm in the hills to do four weeks' basic to earn our kepi. After the initial training period, the final test was the ninety-kilometre kepi march, which was not a lot of fun. All failures were back-squadded to the oncoming group, repeating the whole vicious process. Success meant a further six weeks at Castelnaudary barracks.'

A large part of this final training period included learning all of the Legion's marching songs – in French! Le bleux, to instil esprit de corps, raise morale and bind men from differing nationalities.

The top three trainees at Castelnaudary barracks normally stay behind and attend the NCO course, finally becoming instructors themselves. Kit managed a distinguished second place, 'but they couldn't wait to get rid of me! I was out on the piss at every opportunity and they didn't want me to stay behind as an NCO.' The failure to respond to Legion discipline meant that he and three others were selected for parachute training – and he won his para wings, yet again!

Posted to the 1st Company of the Regiment Etranger Parachutiste (commando and anti-tank), Kit started to make some real progress at last and was elevated to Premier Class (lance-corporal), prior to being dispatched overseas to the traditional Foreign Legion hunting grounds in Chad, Djibouti and French Guiana. He undertook and successfully completed his French commando course and was now fully trained at killing people – in two languages!

Kit spent nearly four years with the Foreign Legion, a great deal of which was in many ways similar to his life in the British army. Repetition and rigid discipline, however, started to eat away at him until terminal boredom set in and a way out was sought. Not easy, especially when you consider the stories of brutality and death served upon deserters. But it was time for a change, and with a fellow malcontent named Simon he boarded a bus from Marseilles to Paris, hopped on a ferry to London – all without passports – and sold his Legion gear to a little shop in Victoria. Thus ended another phase in his military career.

London . . . broke and on the run from the Foreign Legion! Not an enviable position to be in, even for the ever-resourceful Kit Freeman. A well-paid job seemed an appropriate goal and he easily obtained one as a bouncer, living in the twilight world of late-night revellers and potential physical abuse. It was a living, but fate and the way of the warrior beckoned him yet again. This time it was the classic man-in-a-pub situation and an opportunity to return to the thing he does best.

'Mozambique. That's where the action is,' the man explained, telling Kit what to do when he arrived, who to contact and what would be expected of him. It all seemed a hell of a lot more interesting and profitable than his job as a bouncer – what could he lose? His first five-week contract brought him £4,500 working with the guerrilla forces; he didn't kill anyone, didn't have to put up with military crap, and he came home jubilant and moderately wealthy. He was given a second contract, returning to Mozambique for nine weeks. On this trip he met and became firm friends with a leading figure in the mercenary world who would later become his guru, learning from him everything about survival in this dangerous and often treacherous game.

Now that Kit was 'on the circuit', offers of work were readily available to him, and he spent much of his time in the area of Islington known as the Angel, where rooms are taken for short periods to set up mercenary contracts. Here he picked up a nice little earner in Colombia, working for the American DEA – Drug Enforcement Administration – where his specialist jungle training came in handy on search-and-destroy missions. He was enjoying this freedom lacking in discipline with high financial reward. He was at last truly a 'freeman', and that suited him just fine . . . until Khadija came along.

The romance turned quickly into marriage, temporarily changing his life into one with softer edges, less frantic, more deliberate. Kit quit the roving life and became a bodyguard to the rich and famous, only occasionally leaving her for work overseas in Colombia. They made plans for their future together – only there wasn't one.

Within two years Khadija had died of encephalitis, a disease of the brain for which there is no cure. Kit was devastated. She had touched him and found the vulnerable boy beneath the tough northern soldier, made him want something more than artillery fire and the sound of marching feet; but she had gone, and part of him and his dream had gone with her.

'Madness overtook me, I'd had enough. Nothing mattered any more and I became a nasty piece of work, battering people at the slightest provocation.' Trouble with the law inevitably ensued,

257

with drunken pub brawls and the theft of a police car leading to brief periods in Bedford and Durham jails on remand for theft, fraud, and a charge of armed robbery, which was finally not proven.

Kit knew he could not continue with this destructive lifestyle, and with the help of close friends gradually hauled himself back from the edge.

Then a war called to caress his wounds, to dry his eyes and salve his tortured soul. The war was Yugoslavia, then in 1991 broken and fragmented into Bosnia/Herzegovina, Montenegro, Macedonia, Slovenia, Croatia and Serbia. Not a Geneva Convention war. A killing, torturing, dirty war – just the kind of war a man like Kit needed right now. What could they do to him? He was already dead.

This time he went without contacts or thought of financial gain. Overland to Zagreb, then to Gospich, easily finding allies to help him in his cause. A taxi driver who fought part-time with the Croatian Tiger Brigade against the dominant Serbians introduced him to the action. In his first conflict he was injured by a detonation blast while retaking Gospich; but he had performed well, ducking, diving, killing and maiming with a total disregard for his own safety. They were impressed by this crazy Englishman, but they didn't know the reason for this outward display of courage and daring . . . not that they would have cared.

The events at Gospich had raised Kit's standing with his new-found friends to such an extent that he was offered the rank of *zapovjednik voda* (lieutenant) and given an official Croatian soldier's ID under the assumed name of Darren Abbey. His salary was 47,000 dinar per month (£250). Now he was legit!

For a while Yugoslavia became his stamping ground, where he could rebuild his shattered life and utilise the skills kindly taught by the British army and the French Foreign Legion. He came home on the odd occasion, returning at the request of an associate for a recce on Mostar airfield which led to his final year as an active mercenary.

Kit returned triumphant to the Welsh town that had become his home for a well-earned period of rest and recuperation, only occasionally interrupted by visits from Special Branch concerned about his intentions and future objectives now he was back in the UK. They needn't have worried; the gypsy life had temporarily lost its appeal. Time passed pleasantly, as the camo-tinted pores cleansed themselves of olive dye and memories were locked away.

Haunted still by the death of his wife, and romance the last thing on his mind, fate did a strange thing. At a Swansea discothèque he met a pretty Welsh girl named Rose – strange because the word 'rose' is the English translation of the Arabic word *khadija*. Kit still finds this eerie. 'It made the hairs on me neck prickle.' The chance meeting developed into courtship; long drives into the Welsh hills, dinners in darkened restaurants and an interesting trip to Brighton ...

'When I returned to Britain I was using my Darren Abbey alias because of police problems before I left for Yugoslavia. I didn't need any aggro at the time, deciding to turn myself in at a later date. It was Rose's birthday and we went away for the weekend, booking into the Oakwood Hotel in Brighton. Without my knowledge the place was very close to where they were holding the Conservative Party Conference that year. Big mistake! I was signing the forms at the reception desk and noticed that one of the police on security duty was clocking me a bit funny. About fifteen minutes later, as we were unpacking, somebody started battering on the door. I went to see who it was, only to find a police team kitted out with Heckler and Kochs waiting outside. Fucking crazy; they were crouched against the walls, bulletproof vests ... the lot! I told them they could put all that stuff away because Rose wasn't used to that sort of thing and she was doing her nut.

'They had me on the floor, did the body-search routine and stuck cuffs on, before arresting me as a suspected terrorist. I ask you. Me a bleedin' terrorist! Then I was taken to the Brighton nick and kept waiting for someone from the intelligence service. A guy finally turned up and told me that they knew who I was; the copper in reception had recognised me from the TV programme *Dogs of War*. The intelligence bloke went on a bit, threatening all sorts of things before saying that they thought I was here to do some damage to the party conference for the IRA ... Me motor, left in the NCP car park, was torn apart as they searched, without any luck, for something incriminating. I was finally taken to Brixton Prison and kept for a week until visited by some Special Branch guys and some other people who brought maps with them. For two days we had these meetings about Osijek. They wanted to know where the Serbian mines were placed so British Royal Engineers could deal with them. Later I was up before the judge for past crimes and fined £4,000 and given a two-year probation.'

Rose wasn't going to put up with any of this mercenary stuff and made it clear that for Kit it was time to settle down and get a proper job.

Using his ill-gotten gains he started a legitimate business venture which briefly prospered, then exploded, leaving him broke and for a while dejected. This was not an acceptable position for a warrior. His military training, coupled with his positive mental attitude, rapidly locked on to automatic fire, seeking a way out – fast.

'I didn't know what to do for a while. I owed money with nothing coming in and it was desperate times. First I thought of going back to the front line in Bosnia but Rose put her foot down, so that was that. Then I decided to contact the Muslim parliament in London again; so I rang with the old Mustapha routine and they were very pleased to hear from me. At the time the whole war was going down the tubes because they didn't have enough gear for their troops. So I jumped in the car and headed for Gotham City and was back in the supplies business.

'When a meeting was being arranged, a coded destination was given – "I'll meet you outside Buckingham Palace at 10.30" would mean something totally different, a location prearranged at an earlier discussion. The Muslim buyer would say, "I have x amount to spend", and I would provide equipment to this sum – making allowance for my commission, of course!'

Ivan Urirch remained the contact in Bosnia, arranging storage in sheds and outbuildings in the Zagreb area. It had to be this way; Kit wasn't going back against Rose's wishes. He was in love and his new family came first.

For such an outwardly gregarious man, he was lonely, desperately needing the new family who had backed and supported him. He wasn't about to let them down.

Kit spent ten weeks in and around London, meeting new people and arranging for delivery of goods by Australian mercs in Bosnia; once again coming home with enough money to repay his debts and start another business venture.

'Fighting's a risk I don't want to take any more. I've been shot before, but next time it might be for real and I could be dead . . . I've got something now that I've never had before and I want to keep it.'

So . . . Christopher Freeman had emerged, relatively unscathed, from the traumas of his mercenary and military past, and his path right now is clearly, if not irrevocably, directed at the business end of the game.

He has recently moved away from South Wales and is now living in a quiet suburb somewhere in the north of England. He's still a young man in his early thirties, but a lot of blood has passed under the bridge in the past few years. It's going to be difficult to settle into a conventional existence, with a wife, dog and 2.4 children . . . Hell! It's going to be impossible.

Glossary

66 lightweight and disposable anti-tank rocket launcher

AK-47 Kalashnikov assault rifle (see **Klash**)

APC armoured personnel carrier

Arkanoci Arkan's men (Serb nationalist militia commander)

Armbrust portable anti-tank system with no backblast

basha single square sheet of material used for sleeping shelter

beasting military slang term for a beating

bergan military term for rucksack

berm tank entrenchment

big four minimum information given to the enemy (name, rank, serial number and birth date)

bivvy waterproof sleeping bag cover or term for settling down for the night (to bivvy down)

blow and go detonate explosives and depart in haste

brew-up hot drink

BSA Bosnian-Serb army

camo camouflage face paint or combat clothing

cam up to apply face paint

Chetnik Serbian irregulars (general term)

chinstrap army term for state of exhaustion

chopper helicopter (general term)

claymore mine area protection anti-personnel mine

COP covert operations vest

CP checkpoint

Danner brand name for expensive and very desirable military boots

DEA US Drug Enforcement Administration

DPM disrupted pattern material (camouflage)

E&E escape and evasion

ethnic cleansing racial or religiously motivated killing

FFD first field dressing

FIBUA fighting in built-up areas

flak jacket upper-body armour

FRAG fragmenting

gat weapon (American underworld use; from Gatling gun)

gig a contract or mission

GPMG general purpose machine gun

GSG-9 German special forces

HEAT high-explosive anti-tank (explosive detonates at critical distance before impact and penetrates armour plating)

HEP high-explosive plastic

HESH high-explosive squash-head (explosive spreads on target surface before detonating)

Hind Soviet attack helicopter/gunship

HOS extremist Croatian militia

Huey US helicopter used extensively in Vietnam

HVO Bosnian-Croatian militia

ID identity document or card

JNA Yugoslavian national army

keffudle soldier-speak for a conference

Klash Kalashnikov assault rifle (see **AK-47**)

klicks kilometres

LUP lying-up point

mag weapons magazine containing ammunition

Makarov Soviet pistol

merc mercenary soldier

MG-42 pre-1945 German 7.92 machine gun

MiG Soviet fighter/bomber

MoD Ministry of Defence

Mortar Light, portable infantry support weapon

NVA night-vision equipment

OP observation post

PE plastic explosive

phos phosphorus grenade

pinkie long-wheelbase Land Rover

porridge period of confinement or capture

RPG-7 hand-held rocket launcher

RPK AK-47 with larger and longer barrel

Rupert/Rodneys term used by the lower ranks for an officer

RV rendezvous point

SA-80 automatic weapon in current use by British army

SAM surface-to-air missile

Serbo-Croat language in general use in former Yugoslavia

shemagh shawl used by people in Middle East

shoot and scoot attack and get out fast

Skorpion Czech 7.62mm. machine pistol

sneaky beaky slang term for covert operation

SOP standard operating procedure

SPG self-propelled gun

squaddie soldier

stag sentry duty

stripes and pips visible indication of commission/authority

T-55 Soviet tank; entered production in 1944

T-72 Soviet tank; entered production in 1972

tab fast march over a long distance; often with a full pack

tiger stripe method of applying camouflage paint to skin

TMA-2 Yugoslavian-manufactured plastic-bodied mine

Trislander light aircraft requiring minimal take-off/landing area

UN United Nations

UNPROFOR United Nations protection force

White Eagles Chetnik group of irregulars known for their brutality

Zolya rocket launcher